Recorded Solo
Concert Spirituals, 1916–2022

Recorded Solo Concert Spirituals, 1916–2022

Compiled by
RANDYE JONES

McFarland & Company, Inc., Publishers
Jefferson, North Carolina

Library of Congress Cataloguing-in-Publication Data

Names: Jones, Randye, compiler.
Title: Recorded solo concert spirituals, 1916–2022 / compiled by Randye Jones.
Description: Jefferson, North Carolina : McFarland & Company, Inc., Publishers, 2023. |
Includes bibliographical references and index.
Identifiers: LCCN 2022059837 | ISBN 9781476684710 (paperback : acid free paper) ∞
ISBN 9781476648453 (ebook)
Subjects: LCSH: Spirituals (Songs)—Discography.
Classification: LCC ML156.4.B56 J65 2023 | DDC 016.78225/3—dc23/eng/20221213
LC record available at https://lccn.loc.gov/2022059837

British Library cataloguing data are available

ISBN (print) 978-1-4766-8471-0
ISBN (ebook) 978-1-4766-4845-3

Front cover image: © 9dream studio/Shutterstock;
record of "Go Down Moses" (Library of Congress)

Printed in the United States of America

*McFarland & Company, Inc., Publishers
Box 611, Jefferson, North Carolina 28640
www.mcfarlandpub.com*

To my eldest sister, Debra Jones Flowers,
for always being there.
Whether I was selling Girl Scout cookies
or newly published books,
I have always known that her love and support come
without me asking and without obligation. Love ya!

She taught him truth that liberates the soul
From bonds more galling than the slaver's chain—
That manly nurtures, lily-wise, unfold
Amid the mire of hatred void of stain;
Thus in his manhood, clean, superbly strong,
To him was born the priceless gift of song.

   —from "The Singer," by Eva Jessye (1895–1992)

Table of Contents

Acknowledgments

A multitude of people played roles in the development of this guide. However, two teachers—no, mentors—directly sparked the elements in me that were necessary to make the project happen. First, Judith Womble Pinnix Howle, a voice teacher at North Carolina A&T State University in Greensboro, introduced me to the solo concert spiritual in the late 1980s in addition to the work we did together to prep me for graduate school auditions. She had grown up in an environment that exposed her to the folk spiritual and studied concert spirituals as a student at the Eastman School of Music. She believed that every voice student must be introduced to the spiritual, so she made sure to include them in my studies. I am so thankful for the introduction she gave me because most of the voice teachers who followed her had no experience teaching that music. The foundation she gave me was enough upon which to build the range of knowledge of concert spirituals I have acquired over the years, and she has become a friend with whom I have maintained contact.

The second mentor was musicologist Dominique-René de Lerma. He was the scholar-in-residence at the Florida State University (Tallahassee) during the first semester of my graduate studies. During his very short time there, he nourished my intense interest in African American music research—an interest I turned towards Negro spirituals once my required subject work was completed. I was fortunate to have become part of what I've heard called "his crew," due to the many hours we both spent in the School of Music library taking advantage of the extensive collections of scores, monographs, and recordings.

I must credit the libraries where I have worked over the last 30-plus years, especially Grinnell College, for their enthusiastic assistance in accessing print, sound, and online resources and for allowing me the time and mentoring I needed during this project. I also acknowledge the "collective wisdom" of the Music Library Association, which assisted me in finding the resources that were useful in my research. This especially includes Kathleen Abromeit of the Oberlin Conservatory Library for her invaluable insights into the identification of songs for inclusion in this guide and willingness to provide a fresh perspective in its writing.

As always, I want to acknowledge the continuous support of family and friends who didn't exactly understand my interest in Classical music but encouraged my studies, performance, and research activities, nonetheless.

Finally, I extend prayers of thanks to a gracious Lord for seeing me "On Ma Journey."

Introduction

As interest in the study and performance of musical works by persons of color has grown, musicians who had previously never been exposed to this music are joining those of us for whom this music has been a years-long source of solace and fulfillment. One of the styles that have seen a resurgence of interest is the Negro spiritual as composed for concert performance.

The folk music that became known as the Negro spiritual has been presented as concert music since it was performed by the Fisk Jubilee Singers in the 1870s. Composer and baritone Harry T. Burleigh (1866–1949) wrote his setting of the spiritual "Deep River" for publication in 1916 and launched what has become a century-long fascination with the solo vocal concert performance of Negro spirituals.

Yet, all too often, the singer who wants to study and perform concert spirituals discovers that their vocal teacher has little or no knowledge of the technical or interpretative considerations unique to performing concert spirituals. Thus, they find themselves looking to other sources for self-study. Conversely, voice teachers who want to introduce concert spirituals to their students face the challenges of locating resources to assist them in reinforcing vocal techniques and developing opportunities to study the cultural dynamics that can be drawn from these songs.

Commercial recordings of classically trained singers performing concert spirituals can serve as an excellent resource for studying those songs; however, developing knowledge of the recordings that present exemplars of established performance practice can involve years of hit-and-miss exposure.

This guide gathers into one resource information about commercially produced recordings of Negro spirituals composed for solo concert vocalists. The thousands of tracks listed here cover more than a century of recordings on compact discs, long-playing albums, 78 rpm records, 45 rpm discs, digital streaming files, audio cassettes, and demonstration recordings from musical score collections.

My goal is to provide a means for singers, vocal instructors, accompanists, musicologists, and others seeking recordings of concert spirituals to enhance their study of the performance practice. These recordings are useful in song preparation for the vocal studio, concert hall, worship service, or competition settings. They are suitable for study by the first-time explorer of the songs to the devotee with decades of experience singing and/or coaching spirituals.

Entries to the guide were limited to commercially produced recordings. In some cases, there are hundreds of recordings of a single spiritual, and in others, only one or two. It is the same for composers and vocalists. There are some musicians whose body of work is extensive and easily obtainable, and others represented on recordings so rare as to be nearly impossible to find.

This guide lists recordings in a variety of formats that present the user with a range of options for listening depending on the user's level of access. It also classifies the performers by the standard voice types commonly designated within the world of Classical music—soprano, mezzo-soprano, contralto, countertenor, tenor, baritone, bass-baritone, bass—using vocalist if the performer's voice type could not be determined—to assist those who are looking for recordings performed by a specific voice type.

The user can explore the recordings referenced here to delve into the changes in performance practice over the decades in which the concert spiritual has developed as well as the musical styles, from Blues to Gospel, that composers and performers brought to their work.

Track entries for 29 of the most frequently recorded spirituals—representing approximately 58 percent of the tracks listed in the guide—begin with introductory notes, including biblical references, song texts, and codes connected to a list of art song collections that contain that specific concert spiritual (the complete list of codes and their corresponding collections follows this introduction). In the cases where the codes are not listed with a spiritual, the setting was likely only available as sheet music. Also, several of these notes include comments about performance practice, compositional approach, textual significance, or relevant historical information. The spirituals that received this additional treatment are listed in the general index.

When information is available, the track entries include a variety of vocal and/or instrumental accompanying forces—such as chorus, piano, orchestra, guitar, flute, violin, etc.; however, those forces are always secondary to the role of the vocal soloist in the listed performance.

Since the contents referenced in this guide are commercially produced sound recordings, the contents are structurally organized in the manner of a discography. However, this guide is intended to encourage the use of the recordings themselves, rather than solely to provide historical data.

A typical entry is organized in the following manner:

· · · · · · ·

Uniform Title[a]

1111

Track Title[c]
Composer/s[d]
Vocalist/s Name/s (Voice Type/s)[e]
Album Title[f]
Publisher; Publisher Number; Release Year; Format[g]
Accompanied by[h]
Dialect[i]

[a] **Uniform Title** (in boldface type): Because track titles of the spirituals are often affected by composer/performer/publisher decisions—including whether the track title uses dialect, the tracks have been organized under an assigned uniform title.

[b] Track Entry Number: Number assigned to identify entry for the general, song title, and name indexes.

[c] Track Title: Title of concert spiritual as indicated on the recording or via a reliable secondary resource.

[d] Composer/s: Composer(s) of concert spiritual as indicated on the recording or via a reliable secondary resource. If the composer is determined by my assessment, the name is enclosed [in brackets]. If I was unable to do an adequate assessment, "No composer identified" is indicated.

[e] Vocalist/s Name/s (Voice Type/s): Name(s) of vocal soloist(s) and voice type(s). If none was listed or was unable to be determined from a secondary resource, "Vocalist" was assigned.

[f] *Album Title*: Title of the album cover or of tracks indicated on labels when no unifying album title was assigned.

[g] Publisher; Publisher Number; Release Year; Format: Publishing or distributing company followed by its assigned number for physical formats. Release Year: Year the recording was released or re-issued, which may be different from the year of recording or earlier issues. If unknown/uncertain, the approximate date is enclosed in brackets. Format: Track's physical format or digital streaming

h Accompanied by: Vocal and/or instrumental forces accompanying singer

i Dialect: My assessment of whether the singer used:

- No dialect discerned;
- Light dialect (relying almost exclusively on softening final consonants);
- Moderate dialect (modifying some sounds, such as "th" in "the" to "de" or "ah" instead of "I");
- Heavy dialect (most of the text has been modified from standard English based on the score and/or the performer's interpretation).

If I was unable to do an adequate assessment, no level is indicated.

The guide includes a bibliography of books and other relevant resources. In addition to a general index, including indexing of album titles, music store listings, and biblical references, there is an index by track title and a name index of composers and vocalists.

The Conundrum of Paul Robeson

Throughout this guide, where I can identify that a track has been reissued on a different recording, that connection has been noted. However, if I was unable to find a reliable source (usually the reissued recording itself) that identifies a track as a reissue, I have chosen to err on the side that the track is not a reissue.

The artist whose recordings forced this decision was bass-baritone Paul Robeson (1898–1976). The approximately 800 track entries by Robeson are the largest grouping in this guide. To give an example of the challenge addressing his tracks presented, the second edition (published in 2000) of *Paul Robeson: Artist and Activist on Records, Radio and Television*, by Allan L. Thompson, identified seven different recording dates by Robeson of "Balm in Gilead"

between 1942 and 1960. I have identified over 20 recordings of the spiritual by Robeson. While some albums indicated reissue information, most do not. Therefore, entries in this guide may be reissued but are not identified as such.

About the Tracks and Their Contents

For those who enjoy seeing statistics, here are the top ten entries based on the track information gathered for this guide:

Spirituals most frequently recorded:

Deep River	281
Sometimes I Feel Like a Motherless Child	258
Swing Low, Sweet Chariot	190
Were You There	186
Nobody Knows the Trouble I've Seen	180
Go Down Moses	169
Every Time I Feel the Spirit	164
He's Got the Whole World in His Hands	132
Joshua Fit the Battle of Jericho	126
Ride On, King Jesus	125

Performers most frequently listed:

Robeson, Paul	800
Anderson, Marian	721
Hayes, Roland	265
Price, Leontyne	179
Norman, Jessye	135
Hendricks, Barbara	132
Moses, Oral	96
Battle, Kathleen	82
West, Lucretia	76
Estes, Simon	74

Composers most frequently listed:

Composer	
Composer not identified	953
Burleigh, Harry T.	692 [314]
Johnson, Hall	559 [76]
Brown, Lawrence	370 [320]
Hayes, Roland	365 [69]
Boatner, Edward	158 [68]
Traditional	139
Bonds, Margaret	98 [12]
Hogan, Moses	91 [4]
Dett, Robert Nathaniel	58 [8]

I want to clarify the last category. Over the years, an unfortunately large number of recordings and resources that referenced concert spirituals did not list the composer's name. Instead, they either list nothing at all or use the term "Traditional."

One of the focuses of this guide has been to address this lapse where feasible so that users have more opportunities to connect the track with the composer of that setting.

If I found a recording of sufficient length to evaluate, I listened to the recording. If I was able to recognize the setting or compare what I heard against music scores by various composers, I added that determination to the track information. That composer's name appears in the guide inside brackets. In the statistics above, the numbers listed beside the composer's name that are enclosed inside brackets represent the tracks credited due to my evaluation. So based on my assessments, Burleigh's credited production should be at least 45 percent higher than the 692 tracks indicated, and Lawrence Brown's credited recordings should be at least 86 percent higher.

If I was unable to find a recording or what I found was insufficient to allow me to analyze it adequately, I used the designation "Composer not identified." I also took a different approach to the use of the term "Traditional." The tracks listed as "Traditional"

in this guide represent recordings performed a cappella by the singer where no composer was indicated for the track.

Songs Selected for Guide

It did not take me long in researching spirituals to understand that what constitutes a spiritual is not as straightforward a decision as it might seem. Musicologist Eileen Southern (1920–2002) provided a very concise explanation of the spiritual:

With regard to genre, the spiritual falls into the category of folk music; that is, it existed for a long period of time in oral tradition before being written down in musical notation. Generally, the name of the original author of a folksong has been forgotten. In any event, the people have taken over the song and re-shaped it to such an extent over the years, that the song bears little resemblance to its pristine form, apart from the basic melodic structure and the essential message of the text. During the process of oral transmission, the song is adapted to the music taste of both performers and listeners. With regard to class, the spiritual represents religious or sacred folk music, often referred to as folk hymnody. In essence, the so-called Negro spiritual is the religious musical expression of black folk in the United States. It must be distinguished from the "gospel song" which, although religious, is the invention of a *single* personality who provides a definitive version of his song by writing it in musical notation or by making a recording of it.[1]

For more than a century, there has been a spirited debate about the history of the Negro spiritual and what makes a song a spiritual. For this guide, I have included songs historically connected to the people enslaved during the antebellum period of the United States and some of those by unknown creators that were included in collections such as the two-volume set, *A Collection of Spiritual Songs and Hymns*, compiled by Richard Allen in 1801. I also included a

---

1. Eileen Southern, "An Origin for the Negro Spiritual," *The Black Scholar* 3, no. 10, Black Music (Summer 1972), 8–9.

select number of songs written in the style of a spiritual, such as Hall Johnson's "Fi-yer" or Robert MacGimsey's "Sweet Little Jesus Boy."

What has not been included in the guide are composed hymns that have sometimes been performed using the interpretative style of a spiritual. This includes the many recordings of "Amazing Grace" that I found on albums of spirituals.

There were many occasions when I had to research a particular track to determine whether it should be included in the guide. Some of the research involved seeking reliable print and online resources, and on other occasions, I consulted with specialists who have extensive knowledge of spirituals for advice. And yet, I must acknowledge that the nature of the Negro spiritual left me with sometimes imprecise decision-making.

The albums listed in the guide have at least one song identified as a concert spiritual for solo voice. Only the album tracks that are concert spirituals are listed in the guide. The album titles are indexed with the name of the vocalist(s) and the year of release. The album publisher information (catalog number and year of release) is added to the index separately.

Vocalists and composers listed in the guide are in a separate name index with either their voice type or composer status following their names. Musicians who are both vocalists and composers will have separate entries for each role.

Dialect

An important part of developing the performance practice of concert spirituals is the use of dialect, which was derived primarily from the enslaved peoples captured and brought to the United States from the African continent. Choral director, educator, and author Felicia Barber (b. 1975) presented two theories about the origins of African American English—or what will be referred to throughout this guide simply as dialect:

> The dialect hypothesis, or dialectologist view, surmises that the African slaves after arriving in the United States acquired the English language at a slow rate, and primarily from the English spoken by British and other white immigrant groups. This argument also believes that during the African slaves' process of language acquisition, mistakes were made that were later passed down through future generations.... Conversely, the second argument for the origins of AAE is the creole hypothesis. This view believes that establishment of AAE resulted from a developed creole that blended English with a variety of West African Languages. In this view it is believed that a pidgin was created by the slaves (out of a variety of West African languages) during their passage to the New World in an attempt to speak with each other, and also their captors. Recordings listed in this guide represent the range of use of dialect—from none to extensive use. Pioneering composers like Burleigh, R. Nathaniel Dett (1882–1943), Roland Hayes (1887–1977), Florence Price (1887–1953), Hall Johnson (1888–1970), and Edward Boatner (1898–1981), to contemporary composers, chose how much of the text in their concert spirituals would reflect the manner of speech used by the original creators of folk spirituals.[2]

The user will find some help in choosing recordings using dialect, an important facet in performing concert spirituals. The tracks regularly offer my assessment of the amount of dialect I heard in the recordings. This effort was significantly aided by access to the free and paid online databases that are making more and more historical recordings available.

Let me add a couple of cautionary words of advice related to singing in dialect. First, learning to effectively use dialect in singing concert spirituals is just as important and challenging as working with any other language. Even if AAE is "native" to your culture, it is still necessary to develop

---

2. Felicia Raphael Marie Barber, *A New Perspective for the Use of Dialect in African American Spirituals: History, Context, and Linguistics* (Lanham: Lexington Books, 2021), 26–27.

the skill of singing in dialect within the vocal techniques of the classically trained singer. This includes vowel and consonant placement—which can sometimes be vastly different when the dialect is spoken than when sung. Second, there is often more than one way to enunciate a word in dialect. AAE is affected by regionalisms just as other dialects are. However, it is important to be consistent in the choices you make throughout the song unless you must adjust to accommodate the vocal line. In other words, choose the Standard English enunciation of a word each time that word appears in the spiritual or choose to sing the word in dialect throughout.

As an aid to those who want to use recordings of concert spirituals to study applications of dialect in performance, I listened to as many recordings as I could to assess the level of dialect the performer(s) used in the track. The four categories I assigned are already mentioned above. If I could not find a recording of the track, or the track was only a short excerpt that was too brief for me to review adequately, I left the dialect assessment for that track entry blank.

An Inescapable Question

One of the many questions that persist about the performance of concert spirituals is whether the vocalist must be Black to sing spirituals. As I have done in previous writings, I continue to advocate for the study and performance of concert spirituals no matter the racial background of the performer. I could spend a chapter stating my reasons, just as I did in *So You Want to Sing Spirituals* (Rowman & Littlefield, 2019), but I will merely refer you to that source if you want my more detailed explanation.

This guide does not indicate the race or national origin of the performers or composers, but there are non–Blacks and those who are not native to the United States included

in its pages. And there are superb performances by non–Black performers just as there are mediocre recordings by African Americans listed within.

Tenor Roland Hayes told a story of how a German audience began jeering him, a Black man, the instant he stepped onto the concert stage. However, he not only silenced them with the singing of German lied, but they gave him a standing ovation because of the beauty of his singing and his perfect enunciation of the German text.

Hayes reflected on his views regarding the art of singing:

> When I began my career, I realized that if I would speak to all men, I must learn the language of all men. What good could I do if I knew only my own ways and the thoughts of my own people? So I learned to sing the songs of all people. The song I sing is nothing. But what I give through the song is everything. I cannot put into words what I try to do with this instrument that is nearest to me—my voice…. With me it is a matter of faith and work, being and doing. We must be in ourselves the thing that we would do and should do; and we shouldn't talk about it; we should just do it, and do it in such way that no one is hurt but everyone is benefitted.[3]

The same applies to singing concert spirituals. It's the effectiveness of the performance, not the race of the musician, that counts.

The Spirituals Database

I launched The Spirituals Database (www.spirituals-database.com) in 2015 when I wanted to be able to share aspects of my research although the work that has resulted in this guide was still years away from completion. The free, searchable online database offers links to audio and video recordings of tracks—where available, and other information about the recordings that I did not include in the guide.

---

3. Marva Griffin Carter, "Roland Hayes: Expressor of the Soul in Song (1887–1977)," *The Black Perspective in Music* 5, no. 2 (1977): 191. https://doi.org/10.2307/1214079.

In Closing....

Musicologist Natalie Curtis Burlin described her experience as a witness to the singing of a Negro folk song.

> Seated in rows, reverent and silent, they waited for something to happen. And as they sat, patient in the early warmth of the April sun, suddenly a rhythmic tremor seemed to sway over the group as a sweep of wind stirs grasses; there arose a vibration, an almost inaudible hum—was it from the pine trees or from this mass of humanity?—and then the sound seemed to mold itself into form, rhythmic and melodic, taking shape in the air, and out from this floating embryo of music came the refrain of a song quavering by one voice, instantly caught up by another—till soon the entire gathering was rocking in time to one of the old plantation melodies! Men, women and children sang, and the whole group swung to and fro and from side to side with the rhythm of the song, while many of the older people snapped their fingers in emphasis like the sharp click of an African gourd rattle. It was spirited singing and it was devout; but the inspirational quality of the group-feeling made this music seem a lambert, living thing, a bit of "divine fire" that descended upon these black people and the gift of tongues. It was as tho the song had first hovered in the trees above their swaying forms, intangible, till one of them had reached up and seized it, and then it had spread like flame.[4]

As solo singers, we cannot expect to be able to duplicate the experience described above; however, we can see it as our job to discover and understand what it took for those songs to come into being and to make every effort to share what we discern about those songs with the audience. And with the aid of the composer who set the concert spiritual and the other musician(s) who join us in its performance, we can achieve a goal that is worthy of the effort.

Even the singer who finds themselves drawn to this music for the first time has the opportunity to tap into its deep wellspring and seek out the elements that give tribute to the old and enliven with the new.

These words by poet James Weldon Johnson (1871–1938) seem as fresh and appropriate today as they were when he wrote them decades ago:

> There are no indications that the high regard attained by the Spirituals will be followed by any marked decline in interest. The vogue of these songs is by no means a suddenly popular fad; it has been reached through long and steady development in the recognition of their worth. Three generations ago their beauty struck a few collectors who were attuned to perceive it. A little while later the Fisk Jubilee Singers made them known to the world and gave them their first popularity, but it was a popularity founded mainly on sentiment. The chief effect of this slave music upon its white hearers then was that they were touched and moved with deepest sympathy for the "poor Negro." The Spirituals passed next through a period of investigation and study and of artistic appreciation. Composers began afterwards to arrange them so that their use was extended to singers and music-lovers. And then they made their appearance on concert programs and their appeal was greatly broadened. Today, the Spirituals have a new vogue, but they produce a reaction far different from the sort produced by their first popularity; the effect now produced upon white hearers is not sympathy for the "poor Negro" but admiration for the creative genius of the race. The Spirituals have passed through and withstood many untoward conditions on the long march to the present appreciation of their value; they have come from benighted disregard through scorn, apathy, misappraisal, even the ashamedness and neglect of the race that created them, to where they are recognized as the finest distinctive artistic contribution America can offer the world.[5]

---

4. Natalie Curtis Burlin, "How Negro Folksongs Are 'Born': Natalie Curtis Burlin Records a Remarkable Example of Creative Crowd Psychology," *Current Opinion (1913–1925)* 66, no. 3 (March 1919), 165.

5. James Weldon Johnson, and J. Rosamond Johnson, *The Books of American Negro Spirituals* ([Boston]: Da Capo Press, 1977), 17–18.

Spirituals in Musical Collections
(Arranged in Code Order)

Codes assigned to art song collections containing
at least one solo concert spiritual—see title notes and general index.

Code	Collection
[AAGS]	Albritton, Andy M. *Great Spirituals: An Anthology or Program for Solo Voice and Piano for Concert and Worship.* Van Nuys, CA: Alfred, 2007. (med-high/med-low voice eds., optional accompaniment CD)
[AASP]	*American Art Songs for the Progressing Singer.* Milwaukee: Hal Leonard, 2017. (soprano, mezzo-soprano, tenor, and baritone/bass eds.)
[AB10]	Bell, A. Craig. *Ten Negro Spirituals.* Piano ed. London: Pitman, Hart, 1956.
[ASSA]	Taylor, Vivian, ed. *Art Songs and Spirituals by African-American Women Composers.* Bryn Mawr, PA: Hildegard, 1995.
[CCSo]	*Classical Contest Solos.* Milwaukee: Hal Leonard, 1997. (soprano, mezzo-soprano/alto, tenor, baritone/bass eds.)
[CLSA]	Lloyd, Charles, Jr. *The Spiritual Art Song Collection.* Van Nuys, CA: Alfred, 2000.
[CW40]	White, Clarence Cameron. *Forty Negro Spirituals.* Philadelphia: Theodore Presser, 1927.
[DRSA]	Ragland, Dave. *Spirituals & Art Songs,* v. 1. [Nashville, TN]: Dave Ragland, 2017. (high/low voice eds.)
[DSSS]	Sneed, Damien. *Spiritual Sketches.* [New York]: Lechateau Arts, 2013. (CD available separately)
[EJMS]	Jessye, Eva. *My Spirituals.* New York: Robbins-Engel, 1927.
[EM34]	Milkey, Edward T. *34 Spirituals.* New York: Mayfair Music, 1961.
[ERCC]	Clark, Edgar Rogie. *Copper Sun: A Collection of Negro Folk Songs.* Bryn Mawr, PA: Theodore Presser, 1957.
[ERCN]	Clark, Edgar Rogie. *Negro Art Songs: Album by Contemporary Composers for Voice and Piano.* New York: Edward B. Marks Music Corp., 1946.
[ESAA]	Simpson–Curenton, Evelyn. *African American Music for the Classical Singer: Spirituals and Hymns.* Alexandria, VA: E.C. Curenton, 2018.
[FH25]	Frey, Hugo. *A Collection of 25 Selected Celebrated American Negro Spirituals.* New York: Robbins Music, 1926.
[FHFN]	Frey, Hugo. *Famous Negro Spirituals: A Collection of 25 Famous Negro Spirituals.* New York: Robbins, 1900s.
[FHUN]	Hall, Frederick. *Unusual Negro Spirituals.* Winona Lake, IN: Rodeheaver, Hall-Mack, 1964.

[FP44]	Heard, Richard, ed. *44 Art Songs and Spirituals by Florence B. Price.* Fayetteville, AR: ClarNan Editions, 2015.
[FP4S]	Price, Florence. *Four Songs.* Art Songs by American Women Composers, v. 15. San Antonio: Southern Music, 2000.
[FRMA]	Rupp, Franz, ed. *Marian Anderson Album of Songs and Spirituals.* New York: Schirmer, 1948.
[HCTN]	Chambers, H.A. [Henry Alban]. *The Treasury of Negro Spirituals.* New York: Emerson Books, 1959.
[HJCO]	Johnson, Hall, Julius P. Williams, John L. Motley, Eugene Thamon Simpson, Louise Toppin, William Brown, and Joseph Joubert. *The Hall Johnson Collection: Over 50 Classic Favorites for Voice and Piano Including Two Performance CDs.* New York: Carl Fischer, 2003. (with performance CDs)
[HJTS]	Johnson, Hall. *Thirty Spirituals.* New York: G. Schirmer, 1949. (New ed. w/CD, 2007)
[HLBS]	Luedeman, H. *Best of Spirituals & Gospels.* New York: Schott, 2001.
[HT25]	Burleigh, Harry Thacker. *25 Spirituals Arranged by Harry T. Burleigh.* Milwaukee: Hal Leonard, 2012. (high/low voice eds. w/CD)
[HTBA]	Burleigh, Harry Thacker. *Album of Negro Spirituals.* Melville, NY: Belwin-Mills, [1917], 1969.
[HTBS]	Burleigh, Harry Thacker. *The Spirituals of Harry T. Burleigh.* Melville, NY: Belwin-Mills, 1984. (high/low voice eds.)
[HTC1]	Burleigh, Harry T. *The Celebrated Negro Spirituals: Arranged for Solo Voice,* Album No. 1. London: G. Ricordi, 1917.
[HTC2]	Burleigh, Harry T. *The Celebrated Negro Spirituals: Arranged for Solo Voice,* Second Album. London: G. Ricordi, 1919.
[JARS]	Althouse, Jay, comp., ed. *Ready to Sing—Spirituals: Eleven Spirituals Simply Arranged for Voice and Piano, for Solo or Unison Singing.* [Van Nuys, CA]: Alfred, 2000.
[JAS1]	Althouse, Jay, comp., ed., arr. *Spirituals for Solo Singers: 11 Spirituals Arranged for Solo Voice and Piano: for Recitals, Concerts, and Contests.* Van Nuys, CA: Alfred, 1994. (med-high/med-low voice eds., optional accompaniment CD)
[JAS2]	Althouse, Jay, comp., ed., arr. *Spirituals for Solo Singers: 10 Spirituals Arranged for Solo Voice and Piano: for Recitals, Concerts, and Contests,* v. 2. Van Nuys, CA: Alfred, 1994. (med-high/med-low voice eds., optional accompaniment CD)
[JB3a]	Boytim, Joan Frey, ed. *36 Solos for Young Singers.* Milwaukee: Hal Leonard, 2001.
[JB3b]	Boytim, Joan Frey, ed. *36 More Solos for Young Singers.* Milwaukee: Hal Leonard, 2012.
[JBBS]	Boytim, Joan Frey, ed. *The First Book of Baritone/Bass Solos.* Milwaukee: G. Schirmer, 1991–2005.
[JBES]	Boytim, Joan Frey, ed. *Easy Songs for the Beginning Baritone/Bass.* Milwaukee: G. Schirmer, 2000. (with CD)
[JBMS]	Boytim, Joan Frey, ed. *The First Book of Mezzo-Soprano/Alto Solos.* Milwaukee: G. Schirmer, 1991–2005.
[JBTS]	Boytim, Joan Frey, ed. *The First Book of Tenor Solos.* Milwaukee: G. Schirmer, 1991–2005.
[JCCA]	Carter, John Daniels. *Cantata: for Voice and Piano.* New York: Southern Music, 1964.
[JHSS]	Hairston, Jacqueline B. *Songs and Spirituals,* volume 1. Fayetteville, AR: Classical Vocal Reprints, 2019.
[JJ16]	Johnson, John Rosamond. *Sixteen New Negro Spirituals.* New York: Handy Bros. Music, 1939.

[JJAN]	Johnson, J. Rosamond. *Album of Negro Spirituals*. [New York]: Edward B. Marks Music Co., 2000.
[JJBA]	Johnson, James Weldon, John Rosamond Johnson, and Lawrence Brown. *The Books of American Negro Spirituals: Including the Book of American Negro Spirituals and the Second Book of Negro Spirituals*. New York: Viking Press, 1940. (Da Capo, 1977)
[JPNS]	Payne, John. *Negro Spirituals: For Low Voice with Piano Accompaniment*. New York: G. Schirmer, 1942.
[JSSp]	Silverman, Jerry. *Spirituals*. New York: Chelsea House, 1995.
[JW10]	Work, John W. *Ten Spirituals: For Solo Voice and Piano*. New York: Ethel Smith Music, 1952.
[LB5N]	Brown, Lawrence. *Spirituals: Five Negro Songs*. London: Schott, 1923.
[LB6N]	Brown, Lawrence. *Six Negro Folk Songs*. New York: Associated Music Publishers, 1943.
[LBNF]	Brown, Lawrence. *Negro Folk Songs*. London: Schott, 1930.
[LLS2]	Larson, Lloyd. *Spirituals for Two Voices: Medium Voice Vocal Duets*. Carol Stream, IL: Hope Publishing, 2008.
[LMSO]	McLin, Lena J. *Songs for Voice & Piano* (Med. High Voice ed.) San Diego: Kjos Music, 2003.
[MBCF]	Bonds, Margaret. [*Five Creek—Freedmen Spirituals*]. New York: Mutual Music Society, 1946.
[MBIH]	Bonds, Margaret. *In His Hand: Seven Spirituals for Voice and Piano*. [King of Prussia, PA]: Theodore Presser, 2010.
[MBRM]	Bonds, Margaret. *Rediscovering Margaret Bonds: Art Songs, Spirituals, Musical Theater and Popular Songs*. Fayetteville, AR: Classical Vocal Reprints, 2021.
[MH10]	Hayes, Mark. *10 Spirituals for Solo Voice: For Concerts, Contests, Recitals and Worship*. Van Nuys, CA: Alfred, 1998. (med-high/med-low voice eds., optional accompaniment CD)
[MHDR]	Hogan, Moses. *The Deep River Collection: Ten Spirituals Arranged for Solo Voice and Piano*. Milwaukee: Hal Leonard, 2000. (high/low voice eds.)
[MM4S]	Mills, Marvin. *Four Spirituals for Denyce Graves*. Washington, D.C.: DC Press, 1998.
[PLSY]	Liebergen, Patrick. *Spirituals for Young Singers*. Delaware Water Gap: Shawnee Press, 2013.
[PMSC]	McIntyre, Phillip. *Spirituals for Church and Concert*. [United States]: H.T. FitzSimons, 1990.
[RCSS]	Carter, Roland Marvin. *Sweetest Sound I Ever Heard: Spiritual Art Songs for High Voice and Piano*. Fayetteville, AR: Classical Vocal Reprints, 2020.
[RHMF]	Hayes, Roland. *My Favorite Spirituals: 30 Songs for Voice and Piano*. Mineola, NY: Dover, 2001.
[RNDS]	Dett, R. Nathaniel. *Spirituals*. New York: Mills Music, 1943.
[RONS]	Owens, Robert. *Negro Spirituals für Bass und Klavier* (*Negro Spirituals for Bass [Baritone] and Piano*). Salzgitter, Germany: Ostinato–Musikverlag, 2005.
[RS12]	Saar, R.W. *Twelve Negro Spirituals: for Solo Voice and Optional Harmonised or Unison Chorus*. London: W. Paxton, 1927.
[RW14]	Walters, Richard, ed. *14 Sacred Solos*. Milwaukee: Hal Leonard, 2004. (high/low voice eds. w/CD)
[RW15]	Walters, Richard, ed. *15 Easy Spiritual Arrangements for the Progressing Singer*. Milwaukee: Hal Leonard, 2005. (high/low voice eds.)
[RWBC]	Walters, Richard, ed. *The Boy's Changing Voice: 20 Vocal Solos*. Milwaukee: Hal Leonard, 2013.

[RWCC]	Walters, Richard, ed. *The Christmas Collection: 53 Songs for Classical Singers*. Milwaukee: Hal Leonard, 2002. (high/low voice eds.)
[RWSC]	Walters, Richard, ed. *The Sacred Collections*. Milwaukee: Hal Leonard, 2001. (high/low voice eds.)
[RWSS]	Walters, Richard, ed. *The Student Singer: 25 Songs in English for Classical Voice*. Milwaukee: Hal Leonard, 2005. (high/low voice eds.)
[SBFD]	Baynes, Sydney. *Francis & Day's Album of Famous Negro Spirituals….* Transcribed & Arranged by S. Barnes. London: Francis, Day & Hunter, 1932.
[SONS]	Okpebholo, Shawn E. *The Shawn E. Okpebholo Collection of Negro Spirituals*. [Wheaton, IL]: Yellow Einstein Press, 2013. (CD available separately)
[SOTS]	Boatner, Edward. *The Story of the Spirituals: 30 Spirituals and Their Origins: Voice and Piano/Guitar*. [New York]: McAfee Music, 1973.
[STON]	Boatner, Edward, assisted by Willa A. Townsend. *Spirituals Triumphant Old and New: Printed in Both Round and Shaped Notes*, rev. and enl. Nashville: Sunday School Pub. Board, 1927.
[UBOR]	Brown, Uzee, Jr. *O Redeemed!: A Set of African–American Spirituals, for Medium–High Voice and Piano*. Dayton, OH: R. Dean Publishing, 1994.
[UBTM]	Brown, Uzee, Jr. *Tryin' to Make Heaven My Home*. [Dayton, OH]: Lorenz, 2002.
[VLCH]	Labenske, Victor. *Concert Hall Spirituals: Settings for Piano and Voice*. [United States]: Woodland Music Press, 1999.
[WF10]	Fisher, William Arms. *Ten Negro Spirituals: in Song Form*. Boston: O. Ditson, 1925.
[WF70]	Fisher, William Arms. *Seventy Negro Spirituals*. Musicians Library. Boston: Oliver Ditson, 1926.
[WGST]	Still, William Grant. *Twelve Negro Spirituals: Arranged for Voice(s) and Piano*. New York: Handy Brothers Music, 2008.
[WPNN]	Patterson, Willis C., ed. *The New Negro Spiritual Collection*. Ann Arbor: Willis Patterson Publishing, 2002.
[WR5N]	Rogers, Wayland. *Five Negro Spirituals*. WR Editions, n.d.
[WRN8]	Reddick, William. *Two Negro Spirituals*. New York: Huntzinger & Dilworth, 1918.
[WRN9]	Reddick, William. *Two Negro Spirituals*. New York: Huntzinger & Dilworth, 1919.
[WWGG]	Whalum, Wendell, Betty Jackson King, Roland Carter. *God Is a God!* Hampton, VA: Mar-Vel; [Chicago]: Jacksonian Press, 1983.

THE TRACKS

Ain't Got Time to Die

1

Ain't Got Time to Die
Johnson, Hall
Albert, Donnie Ray (Baritone)
Donnie Ray Albert in Recital
Cinnabar Records CNB1402; 2003; CD
Piano
Light dialect

2

Ain't Got Time to Die
Johnson, Hall
Anderson, Marian (Contralto)
Jus' Keep on Singin'
RCA Victor LSC 2796; 1965; LP
Piano
Heavy dialect

　　　Also released with *Marian Anderson: Beyond the Music; Her Complete RCA Victor Recordings* (Sony Classical 19439836492 [2021]; CD)

3

Ain't Got Time to Die
Johnson, Hall
Anderson, Marian (Contralto)
He's Got the Whole World in His Hands: Spirituals
RCA Victor 09026-61960-2; 1994; CD
Piano
Heavy dialect

4

Ain't Got Time to Die
Johnson, Hall; Kaiser, Kurt
Battle, Kathleen (Soprano)
Pleasures of Their Company
EMI/Angel CDC-7 47196 2; 1986; CD
Guitar
Moderate dialect

　　　Also released with *Great American Spirituals* (Angel CDM 7 64669 2 [1992]; CD) and *Great American Spirituals* (Musical Heritage Society 513725Z [1994]; CD)

5

Ain't Got Time to Die
Johnson, Hall
Davis, Osceola (Soprano)
Negro Spirituals
Ondine ODE 715-2; 1988; CD
Piano
Moderate dialect

6

Ain't Got Time to Die
Johnson, Hall; Link, Peter
Davis, Osceola (Soprano)
Climbing High Mountains
Watchfire Music; 2008; CD

7

Ain't Got Time to Die
Johnson, Hall
Dever, Barbara (Mezzo-soprano)
Best of the Hall Johnson Centennial Festival Celebrating the 100th Anniversary of Hall Johnson's Birth
Hall Johnson Collection O33D2; 2002; CD
Piano

8

Ain't Got Time to Die
Johnson, Hall

Fox, David (Tenor)
Ain't Got Time to Die: Songs of the American Spirit
First Presbyterian Church in the City of New York FPC 1002; 1997; CD
Chorus

9

Ain't Got Time to Die
Composer not identified
Heard, William N. (Vocalist)
Songs from the Sanctuary: Hymns, Spirituals & Classic Gospels
Heardsong Productions; 2013; CD
Chorus

10

Ain't Got Time
Composer not identified
Hendricks, Barbara (Soprano)
No Borders
Altara ALT 1010; 2005; CD
Chorus
Moderate dialect

11

Ain't Got Time to Die
Johnson, Hall
Holmes, Eugene (Baritone)
Eugene Holmes Sings Spirituals
Avant Garde AV-115; 1968?; LP
Piano
Moderate dialect

    Also released with *Spirituals* (Schubert Records SCH-102 [1988?]; LP)

12

Ain't Got Time to Die
Johnson, Hall
Honeysucker, Robert (Baritone)
Good News
Videmus Records VIS 735; 2007; CD
Piano

13

Ain't Got Time to Die
Composer not identified
Lord, Marie-Josée (Soprano)
Amazing Grace

ATMA Classique ACD2 2686; 2014; CD
Chorus
Moderate dialect

14

Ain't Got Time to Die
Composer not identified
McFerrin, Robert (Baritone)
Negro Spirituals
Jacques Canetti 27 193; 1965; 45 RPM

15

Ain't Got Time to Die
Johnson, Hall
McFerrin, Robert (Baritone)
Deep River and Other Classic Negro Spirituals
Riverside Records RLP 12-812; 1959; LP
Piano
Heavy dialect

    Also released with *Classic Negro Spirituals* (Washington Records WLP 466; [1959] LP)

16

Ain't Got Time to Die
Johnson, Hall
Miles, John (Tenor)
The Classic Spirituals
Epiphany 83-1027; 1983; LP
Instrumental ensemble

17

Ain't Got Time to Die
Johnson, Hall
Moses, Oral (Bass-baritone)
Songs of America
Albany Records TROY1011; 2008; CD
Piano
Heavy dialect

    Also released with *Sankofa: A Spiritual Reflection* (Albany Records TROY1802 [2019]; CD)

18

Ain't Got Time to Die
Johnson, Hall
Simpson, Eugene Thamon (Bass)
Hall Johnson Spirituals and Other Folk Songs

Private Label; 2016; CD
Piano

19

Ain't Got Time to Die
Johnson, Hall
Toppin, Louise (Soprano)
*He'll Bring It to Pass: The Spirituals of Hall
    Johnson for Voice and Piano*
Albany Records TROY846; 2006; CD
Piano
Heavy dialect

20

Ain't Got No Time to Die
Johnson, Hall
Weathers, Felicia (Soprano)
Spirituals & Kodály Folk Songs
Decca SXL 6245; 1966; LP
Piano

    Also released with *Arias and Spirituals*
(Belart/Universal Classics 461 5922; 1999;
CD)

· · · · · · ·

Ain't That Good News

21

Ain't That Good News
Dawson, William L.; Russ, Patrick
Battle, Kathleen (Soprano)
Pleasures of Their Company
EMI/Angel CDC-7 47196 2; 1986; CD
Guitar
Moderate dialect

    Also released with *Great American
Spirituals* (Angel CDM 7 64669 2 [1992]; CD)
and *Great American Spirituals* (Musical Heritage Society 513725Z [1994]; CD)

22

Ain't That Good News
Dawson, William L.
Blackmon, Henry (Baritone)
Negro Spirituals
Vega 19179; 19-?; LP
Chorus, piano

23

Ain't-a That Good News
Dawson, William L.
Blackmon, Henry (Baritone)
Negro Spirituals
Mirasound Records SGLP 6047; 19--; LP
Organ

24

Ain't-a That Good News!
Brown, Uzee, Jr.
Brown, Anthony (Baritone); Jones, Arthur
    (Tenor)
Toil and Triumph
Spirituals Project; 2002; CD
Piano
Heavy dialect

25

Ain't That Good News
Clark, Joe
Cabell, Nicole (Soprano); Cambridge,
    Alyson (Soprano)
Sisters in Song
Cedille Records CDR 90000 181; 2018; CD
Orchestra
Heavy dialect

26

Ain't That Good News
Composer not identified
Clark, Clarence Carroll (Baritone)
Ain't That Good News/Were You There
Okeh 8044; 1922; 78 RPM
Orchestra

27

Ain't-a Dat Good News!
Credit, Roosevelt André
Credit, Roosevelt André (Bass-baritone)
Ol' Time Religion
CD Baby; 2007; CD, Streaming audio
Piano

28

Ain't-a That Good News
Brown, Uzee, Jr.
English-Robinson, Laura (Soprano)
Great Day!

Allgood; 2005; CD
Piano
Heavy dialect

29

Ain't a That Good News
Boatner, Edward
Forest, Michael (Tenor)
The Spirit Sings: American Spirituals
Shenandoah Conservatory SU003; 199-?;
    CD

30

Ain't a That Good News
Brown, Uzee, Jr.
Heard, Richard (Tenor)
*Ain't a That Good News: African-American
    Art Songs and Spirituals*
HM Classics HMC9602; 1998; CD
Piano
Moderate dialect

31

Ain't That Good News
Hogan, Moses
Hendricks, Barbara (Soprano)
Give Me Jesus
EMI Classics 7243 5 56788 2 9; 1998; CD
Chorus
Heavy dialect

32

Ain't a Dat Good News
Lloyd, Charles, Jr.
Jefferson, Othello (Tenor)
*Good News: African American Spirituals
    and Art Songs*
Cambria Records CD 1270; 2021; CD
Piano
Moderate dialect

33

Ain't-a That Good News
Brown, Uzee, Jr.; Fairgold, Noam
Lynch, Lester (Baritone)
On My Journey Now: Spirituals & Hymns
Pentatone Music PTC 5186 57'; 2017; CD
Chorus, piano, organ

34

Ain't That Good News
Boatner, Edward
Matthews, Benjamin (Baritone)
A Spiritual Journey
Ebony Classic Recordings ECR 0001; 2000;
    CD
Piano

35

Ain't That Good News
Boatner, Edward
Matthews, Benjamin (Baritone)
A Balm in Gilead
Ebony Classic Recordings ECR 0001; 2000; CD
Piano

36

Ain-a That Good News?
Dawson, William L.
Miller, Jeanette (Soprano)
No Man Canna Hinder Me
MiJon Record Productions MJ240; 1979; CD
Piano

37

Ain't a Dat Good News
Lloyd, Charles, Jr.
Paige-Green, Jacqueline (Soprano)
The Spiritual Art Song Collection
Warner Bros. SVBM00004; 2000; Score w/CD
Piano

38

Ain't That Good News
Composer not identified
Pickens, Jo Ann (Soprano)
*My Heritage: American Melodies/Negro
    Spirituals*
Koch Schwann 3-1447-2; 1993; CD

39

Ain't That Good News
Hogan, Moses
Ragin, Derek Lee (Countertenor)
Negro Spirituals
Virgin Classics 0946 363305 2 5; 2006; CD
Chorus
Heavy dialect

40

Ain't a That a Good News
Scharnberg, Kim
Robinson, Faye (Soprano)
Remembering Marian Anderson
d'Note Classics DND 1014; 1997; CD
Orchestra

41

Ain' a That Good News
Dawson, William L.
Thompson, Jeanette (Soprano)
Negro Spirituals
Pavane Records ADW 7267; 1992; CD
Chorus
No dialect discerned

42

Ain't-a That Good News
Brown, Uzee, Jr.
Tucker, Eric Hoy (Bass-baritone)
Southern Salute: Southern Songs & Spirituals
White Pine Music WPM218; 2012; CD
Piano
Moderate dialect

· · · · · · ·

All of My Sins Are Taken Away

43

All of My Sins Are Taken Away
Composer not identified
Thomas, Edna (Soprano)
All of My Sins Are Taken Away/Ai Suzette
Columbia 3526; 193-?; 78 RPM
Orchestra

· · · · · · ·

Amen

44

Amen!
Brown, Uzee, Jr.
Brown, Uzee, Jr. (Baritone)
Great Day!
Allgood; 2005; CD
Piano
Light dialect

45

Amen
Brown, Uzee, Jr.
Heard, Richard (Tenor)
Ain't a That Good News: African-American Art Songs and Spirituals
HM Classics HMC9602; 1998; CD
Piano
Light dialect

46

Amen
Composer not identified
Humphrey Flynn, Edwina (Soprano)
Edwina Sings at Christmas
Private Label; 1997; CD
Chorus

47

Amen!
Young, E. Edwin
Maynor, Kevin (Bass)
Songs of America from Another American
Guild GMCD 7247; 2002; CD
Piano

48

Amen
De Cormier, Robert
McCorvey, Everett (Tenor)
Ol' Time Religion
American Spiritual Ensemble ASE012; 2001; CD

49

Amen
Composer not identified
Moses, Oral (Bass-baritone)
Extreme Spirituals
Cuneiform Record Rune 241; 2006; CD
Instrumental ensemble

50

Amen
Hairston, Jester; Bailey, George
Moses, Oral (Bass-baritone)
Amen! African-American Composers of the 20th Century
Albany Records TROY459; 2001; CD

Piano
Light dialect

51

Amen
Hairston, Jester
Ragin, Derek Lee (Countertenor)
Negro Spirituals
Virgin Classics 0946 363305 2 5; 2006; CD
Chorus
Heavy dialect

52

Amen
Scharnberg, Kim
Robinson, Faye (Soprano)
Remembering Marian Anderson
d'Note Classics DND 1014; 1997; CD
Chorus, orchestra

53

Amen!
Thomas, André J.
Tucker, Eric Hoy (Bass-baritone)
Southern Salute: Southern Songs & Spirituals
White Pine Music WPM218; 2012; CD
Piano
Light dialect

· · · · · · ·

And I Cry

54

An' I Cry
[Jessye, Eva]
Ayers, Vanessa (Mezzo-soprano)
Done Crossed Every River: Freedom's Journey
Arcadia ARC 2004-2; 1995; CD

> Also released with *Opera Ebony Sings Spirituals* (Ebony Classic Recordings [2002]; CD)

55

An' I Cry
Jessye, Eva
Matthews, Benjamin (Baritone)
A Balm in Gilead
Ebony Classic Recordings ECR 0001; 2000; CD
Piano

· · · · · · ·

Angels Done Bowed Down

56

De Angels Done Bowed Down
Perry, Zenobia Powell
Rhodes, Yolanda (Soprano)
The Angels Bowed Down
Cambria Master Recordings CD-1237; 2019; CD

· · · · · · ·

At the Feet of Jesus

57

At the Feet of Jesus
Johnson, Hall
Patterson, Willis (Bass)
The New Negro Spiritual
W. C. Patterson; 2002; Score w/CD
Piano
Heavy dialect

58

At the Feet of Jesus
Johnson, Hall
Toppin, Louise (Soprano)
The Hall Johnson Collection
Carl Fischer VF5 CD1–VF5 CD2; 2003; Score w/CD
Piano
Light dialect

· · · · · · ·

Balm in Gilead

[Genesis 37:25; Jeremiah 8:22, 46:11]

"There is a balm in Gilead, To make the wounded whole; There is a balm in Gilead, To heal the sin-sick soul. Sometimes I feel discouraged, And think my work's in vain…"

[Available in DRSA, DSSS, ESAA, HCTN, HJTS, HT25, HTBN, HTBS, HTC2, JSSp, JW10, MH10, PLSY, RW14, RW15, SONS, VLCH]

This spiritual's literary structure follows a regularly used format of a refrain that states the textural theme followed by verses. The verse text is the personal outcry of a soul in distress, followed by the refrain of reassurance that there is a cure for that distress. A subsequent verse calls for the listener to be a witness of this saving balm to others.

59

There Is a Balm in Gilead
Composer not identified
Arroyo, Martina (Soprano); Baskerville, Priscilla (Vocalist)
There's a Meeting Here Tonight
Angel S-36072; 1974; LP
Chorus
Light dialect

      Also released with *Negro Spirituals* (EMI 7243 5 72790 2 4; 1998; CD)

60

There Is a Balm
Baker, Bradley
Baker, Bradley (Baritone); Anderson, Michele (Soprano)
Not a Word: Spirituals, Hymns, Songs
AYA Worldwide Records 6-09682-2; 2001; CD
Piano

61

There Is a Balm in Gilead
Smith, Hale
Battle, Kathleen (Soprano); Norman, Jessye (Soprano)
Spirituals in Concert
Deutsche Grammophon 429 790-2; 1991; CD
Orchestra
Heavy dialect

62

There Is a Balm in Gilead
Hayes, Mark; Taylor, Marie (adapted by)
Black, Randall (Tenor)
Then Sings My Soul: A Collection of Sacred Hymns and Spirituals
Private label; 2006; CD
Piano

63

There Is a Balm in Gilead
Sneed, Damien
Brownlee, Lawrence (Tenor)
Spiritual Sketches
LeChateau Earl Records 888174029597; 2013; CD
Piano
No dialect discerned

64

There Is a Balm in Gilead
Clark, Joe
Cabell, Nicole (Soprano); Cambridge, Alyson (Soprano)
Sisters in Song
Cedille Records CDR 90000 181; 2018; CD
Orchestra
No dialect discerned

65

There Is a Balm in Gilead
[Burleigh, Harry T.]
Chaiter, Yoram (Bass)
Spirituals & Other Songs
Romeo Records 7311; 2014; CD
Piano
Moderate dialect

66

Balm in Gilead
Simpson-Currenton, Evelyn
Chandler-Eteme, Janice (Soprano)
Devotions
Sligo Records; 2007; CD
Piano

67

Balm in Gilead
Burleigh, Harry T.
Davis, Ollie Watts (Soprano)
Here's One: Spiritual Songs
KJAC Publishing KJAC0123; 2003; CD
Piano
Moderate dialect

68

There Is a Balm in Gilead
Richner, T.

Davis, Osceola (Soprano)
Negro Spirituals
Ondine ODE 715-2; 1988; CD
Piano
No dialect discerned

69

There Is a Balm
Lloyd, Charles, Jr.
English-Robinson, Laura (Soprano)
Let It Shine!
ACA Digital Recording CM20020; 1994;
    CD
A cappella
Light dialect

70

There Is a Balm in Gilead
Dawson, William L.
Entriken, Ellen Goff (Soprano)
*Ain't Got Time to Die: Songs of the American
    Spirit*
First Presbyterian Church in the City of
    New York FPC 1002; 1997; CD
Chorus

71

Balm in Gilead
Ryan, Donald
Estes, Simon (Bass-baritone)
Steal Away: My Favorite Negro Spirituals
Deutsche Schallplatten DS 1041-2; 1994; CD
Piano
Light dialect

72

There Is a Balm in Gilead
Dawson, William L.
George, Roderick L. (Tenor)
*The Spirituals: Featuring the American
    Spiritual Ensemble*
LexArts; [20--]; CD
Chorus

73

Balm of Gilead
Composer not identified
Green, Elnora E. (Contralto)
15 Spirituals

Private Label J3RS 2286; 1979; LP
Piano

74

There Is a Balm in Gilead
Dawson, William L.
Gustafson, Edra (Soprano)
Favorite Sacred Songs
Echoes of Faith CAM 33-64140; [1950]; LP
Organ

75

Balm in Gilead
[Burleigh, Harry T.]
Hampton, Jonathon (Vocalist)
Negro Spirituals: Songs of Trial and Triumph
Private Label; 2017; Streaming audio
Piano
Light dialect

76

Balm in Gilead [from *Conversion* (Baptism)]
Cornelius, II, John
Heaston, Nicole (Soprano)
*Marilyn Horne Foundation Presents on
    Wings of Song. Recital No. 9*
Marilyn Horne Foundation DCD 5028;
    2001; CD
Piano

77

There Is a Balm in Gilead
Hogan, Moses
Hendricks, Barbara (Soprano)
Give Me Jesus
EMI Classics 7243 5 56788 2 9; 1998; CD
Chorus
Light dialect

    Also released with *Spirituals* (EMI
Classics 0946 346641 2 7; 2005; CD)

78

There Is a Balm in Gilead
Hayes, Mark
Hudson, Marlissa (Soprano)
Libera
AMP Records AGCD 2106; 2010; CD
Piano
No dialect discerned

79
Balm in Gilead
Okpebholo, Shawn
Jefferson, Othello (Tenor)
Good News: African American Spirituals and Art Songs
Cambria Records CD 1270; 2021; CD
Piano, flute

80
Balm in Gilead
Burleigh, Harry T.
Jones, Arthur (Tenor)
Wade in the Water
Orbis Books; 1993; Book w/cass
Piano
Heavy dialect

81
There Is a Balm in Gilead
Burleigh, Harry T.
Kennedy, Charles (Vocalist)
Heart & Soul: Songs of Harry T. Burleigh
Publisher not known; 1994; Cassette

82
Balm in Gilead
Walters, Richard (ed.)
Kruse, Tanya (Soprano)
15 Easy Spiritual Arrangements for the Progressing Singer
Hal Leonard HL00000391 (high); HL00000392 (low); 2005; Score w/CD
Piano
No dialect discerned

83
There Is a Balm in Gilead
Hayes, Mark
Lima, Philip (Baritone)
Songs of a Wayfarer
Private Label; 2017; Streaming audio
Piano
Light dialect

84
Balm in Gilead
Okpebholo, Shawn
Liverman, Will (Baritone)
Steal Away

Yellow Einstein; 2014; CD
Piano, flute
No dialect discerned

85
Balm in Gilead
Dawson, William L.
Mann, Celeste (Mezzo-soprano)
Songs in the Spirit: A Concert of Sacred Music
Private Label; [2012]; CD
Piano
Light dialect

86
There Is a Balm in Gilead
Dawson, William L.
Martin, Marvis (Soprano)
The Spirituals of William L. Dawson
St. Olaf Records E-2159; 1997; CD
Chorus

87
Balm in Gilead
Edwards, Leo
Matthews, Benjamin (Baritone)
A Balm in Gilead
Ebony Classic Recordings ECR 0001; 2000; CD
Piano

88
Balm in Gilead
Dett, Robert Nathaniel
Matthews, Inez (Mezzo-soprano)
Inez Matthews Sings Spirituals (Great New Voices of Today, v. 6)
Period SPL-580; [1950]; LP
Piano
Heavy dialect

   Also released with *Inez Matthews Sings Spirituals* (Essential Media Group; 2011; CD)

89
Balm in Gilead
Brown, Lawrence
Maynor, Kevin (Bass)
Paul Robeson Remembered

Fleur de Son Classics FDS 57929; 1998; CD
Piano
Light dialect

90

There Is a Balm in Gilead
Composer not identified
McDaniel, Yvette (Soprano)
Simply Spiritual
YM01 DIDX 046103; 1997; CD
Piano

91

There Is a Balm in Gilead
Baldwin, Dalton; Jessye Norman; Patterson,
    Willis
Norman, Jessye (Soprano)
Spirituals
Philips 416 462-2; 1990; CD
Piano
No dialect discerned

Also released with *The Jessye Norman Collection: Sacred Songs & Spirituals* (Philips B0004506-02; 2005; CD)

92

There Is a Balm in Gilead
Composer not identified
Norman, Jessye (Soprano)
Oh, Happy Day! Gospels & Spirituals: The Ultimate CD
Ultimate; 2010; CD

93

There Is a Balm in Gilead
Composer not identified
Norman, Jessye (Soprano)
Negro Spirituals
Philips 9500 580; 1979; LP
Piano

94

Balm in Gilead
Saylor, Bruce
Norman, Jessye (Soprano)
In the Spirit—Sacred Music for Christmas
Philips B0005508-02; 2005; CD
Chorus
No dialect discerned

95

There Is a Balm in Gilead
Traditional
Norman, Jessye (Soprano)
Gospels & Spirituals Gold Collection
Retro R2CD 40-26; 1995; CD
A cappella
Light dialect

Also released with *An Evening with Jessye Norman* (Opera D'Oro Recitals OPD-2011; 1999; CD)

96

There Is a Balm in Gilead
Dawson, William L.
Oglesby, Isador (Tenor)
Isador Sings Negro Spirituals
Oglesby Recordings Album 3; 1983; LP
Piano

97

Balm in Gilead
Composer not identified
Pleas III, Henry H. (Tenor)
Deep River: A Spiritual Journey
Rowe House Productions; 1999; CD

98

There Is a Balm in Gilead
Dawson, William L.
Price, Leontyne (Soprano)
The Essential Leontyne Price: Spirituals, Hymns & Sacred Songs
BMG Classics 09026-68157-2; 1996; CD
Chorus
Heavy dialect

Also released with *The Essential Leontyne Price* (BMG Classics 09026-68153-2; 1996; CD), *Complete Collection of Songs and Spiritual Albums* (RCA Red Seal 886979 40502; 2011; CD), *I Wish I Knew How It Would Feel to Be Free* (RCA Red Seal LSC 3183; 2011; CD) and *Leontyne Price Sings Spirituals* (RCA Red Seal 88691928242; 2012; CD)

99

There Is a Balm in Gilead
[Burleigh, Harry T.]

Robeson, Paul (Bass-baritone)
Andere Amerika, Das
Eterna 8 10 021; 1966; LP
Piano

100

Balm in Gilead
Burleigh, Harry T.
Robeson, Paul (Bass-baritone)
Paul Robeson Live at Carnegie Hall
Vanguard VCD-72020; 1987; CD
Piano
Moderate dialect

101

Balm in Gilead
Burleigh, Harry T.
Robeson, Paul (Bass-baritone)
The Odyssey of Paul Robeson
Omega Classics OCD 3007; 1992; CD
Piano

102

Balm in Gilead
Burleigh, Harry T.
Robeson, Paul (Bass-baritone)
The Very Best of Paul Robeson
Future Noise Music FVDD033; 2009; CD
Piano

103

Balm in Gilead
Burleigh, Harry T.
Robeson, Paul (Bass-baritone)
Spirituals
Columbia Masterworks ML 4105 ; CBS
    62483; [1948]; LP

104

Balm in Gilead
Burleigh, Harry T.
Robeson, Paul (Bass-baritone)
The Power and the Glory
Columbia/Legacy CK 47337; 1991; CD
Piano
Moderate dialect

105

Balm in Gilead
Burleigh, Harry T.

Robeson, Paul (Bass-baritone)
Songs for Free Men, 1940-45
Pearl GEMM CD 9264; 1997; CD
Piano

106

There Is a Balm in Gilead
Burleigh, Harry T.
Robeson, Paul (Bass-baritone)
Songs of Free Men: A Paul Robeson Recital
Sony Classical MHK 63223; 1997; CD
Piano
Light dialect

107

Balm in Gilead
Burleigh, Harry T.
Robeson, Paul (Bass-baritone)
Spirituals
Columbia Masterworks 17379-D; 1945; 78
    RPM
Piano
No dialect discerned

108

Balm in Gilead
Burleigh, Harry T.
Robeson, Paul (Bass-baritone)
The Essential Paul Robeson
Vanguard VSD 57/58; 1974; LP
Piano
Light dialect

109

Balm in Gilead
Burleigh, Harry T.
Robeson, Paul (Bass-baritone)
Balm in Gilead/Go Down Moses
Columbia Masterworks 17467-D; [194-]; 78
    RPM
Piano
No dialect discerned

110

Balm in Gilead
[Burleigh, Harry T.]
Robeson, Paul (Bass-baritone)
Negro Spirituals (And More)
Discmedi DM-4674-02; 2009; CD

111

There Is a Balm in Gilead
[Burleigh, Harry T.]
Robeson, Paul (Bass-baritone)
Paul Robeson Sings Negro Spirituals
Musical Masterpiece Society MMS-2162;
    [19--]; LP
Piano

112

Balm in Gilead
[Burleigh, Harry T.]
Robeson, Paul (Bass-baritone)
Scandalize My Name
Classics Record Library 30-5647; 1976; LP
Piano
Light dialect

113

Balm in Gilead
[Burleigh, Harry T.]
Robeson, Paul (Bass-baritone)
Deep River
Great Voices of the Century GVC 2004;
    1999; CD

114

Balm in Gilead
[Burleigh, Harry T.]
Robeson, Paul (Bass-baritone)
The Originals: "Spirituals"
Yoyo USA; 2006; Streaming audio

115

Balm in Gilead
[Burleigh, Harry T.]
Robeson, Paul (Bass-baritone)
Paul Robeson's Treasure Chest
Leverage; 2008; Streaming audio
Piano

116

Balm in Gilead
[Burleigh, Harry T.]
Robeson, Paul (Bass-baritone)
Five Classic Albums Plus Bonus Tracks
Real Gone Music RGMCD287; 2017; CD

117

Balm in Gilead
[Burleigh, Harry T.]
Robeson, Paul (Bass-baritone)
Five Classic Albums Plus Bonus Tracks
Real Gone Music RGMCD287; 2017; CD

118

Balm in Gilead
[Burleigh, Harry T.]
Robeson, Paul (Bass-baritone)
Drink to Me Only with Thine Eyes
MD Music; 2010; Streaming audio
Piano
No dialect discerned

119

Balm in Gilead
[Burleigh, Harry T.]
Robeson, Paul (Bass-baritone)
Spirituals
Sony Music Média SMM 5012802; 2000;
    CD

120

Balm in Gilead
[Burleigh, Harry T.]
Robeson, Paul (Bass-baritone)
Complete Recordings
Universal Digital Enterprises; 2018;
    Streaming audio

121

Balm in Gilead
[Burleigh, Harry T.]
Robeson, Paul (Bass-baritone)
Complete Recordings
Universal Digital Enterprises; 2018;
    Streaming audio

122

Balm in Gilead
[Burleigh, Harry T.]
Robeson, Paul (Bass-baritone)
Spirituals
Columbia Masterworks M-610; 1946; 78
    RPM
Piano

123

There Is a Balm in Gilead
Dawson, William L.
Ruduski, Meredith (Soprano)
Steal Away: The African American Concert Spiritual
SFM; 2015; CD
Chorus

124

Balm in Gilead
Composer not identified
Rustin, Bayard (Tenor)
Bayard Rustin Sings Spirituals, Work & Freedom Songs
Bayard Rustin Fund; 1988; Cassette
Piano
Moderate dialect

    Also released with *Bayard Rustin Sings Spirituals, Work & Freedom Songs* (Bayard Rustin Fund; 2003; CD)

125

There is a Balm in Gilead
Composer not identified
Rustin, Bayard (Tenor)
Bayard Rustin, the Singer
Bayard Rustin Fund; 1992; CD
Piano
Moderate dialect

126

There Is a Balm in Gilead
Traditional
Rustin, Bayard (Tenor)
Elizabethan Songs & Negro Spirituals
Fellowship Records 102; [1952]; 10' LP
A cappella
No dialect discerned

    Also released with *Bayard Rustin—The Singer* (Black Swan Series; Parnassus Records PACD 96083; 2022; CD)

127

There Is a Balm in Gilead
Johnson, Hall
Straughter, Maralyn (Soprano)
Negro Spirituals of Hall Johnson

Variety Recording Service Var 0753; [196–]; LP
Piano

128

There Is a Balm in Gilead
Burleigh, Harry T.
Thomas, Indra (Soprano)
Great Day: Indra Thomas Sings Spirituals
Delos DE 3427; 2012; CD
Piano
No dialect discerned

129

There Is a Balm
Dawson, William L.
Thompson, Jeanette (Soprano)
Negro Spirituals
Pavane Records ADW 7267; 1992; CD
Chorus
No dialect discerned

130

Balm in Gilead
Composer not identified
Verdejo, Awilda (Soprano)
Awilda Verdejo Sings Spirituals
Angeluz Performances; 1999; CD
Piano

131

There Is a Balm in Gilead
Composer not identified
Watts, Leonardo (Baritone)
On Ma Journey: A Memorable Collection of Negro Spirituals
Onyx Recording Associates ORA-101; 1961; LP
Chorus

132

Balm in Gilead
Composer not identified
Williams, Wayne (Tenor)
Music from My Life
Movideo Productions 02-1993; 1993; CD
Piano

· · · · · · ·

Bear the Burden in the Heat of the Day

133

Bear de Burden
White, [Walter]
Robeson, Paul (Bass-baritone)
Spirituals/Folksong/Hymns
Pearl GEMM CD 9382; 1989; CD

134

Bear the Burden
White, [Walter]
Robeson, Paul (Bass-baritone)
Green Pastures
ASV Living Era CD AJA 5047; 1987; CD

135

Bear the Burden in the Heat of the Day
[White, Walter]
Robeson, Paul (Bass-baritone)
Paul Robeson Sings (see online) *Negro Spirituals*
Musical Masterpiece Society MMS-2162; [19--]; LP
Piano

136

Bear the Burden in the Heat of the Day
[White, Walter]
Robeson, Paul (Bass-baritone)
Negro Spirituals
Concert Hall SVS 2611; [19--]; LP

137

Bear the Burden in the Heat of the Day
[White, Walter]
Robeson, Paul (Bass-baritone)
Negro Spirituals
Chant du Monde LDX 74376; 1982; LP
Piano

138

Bear the Burden in the Heat of the Day
[White, Walter]
Robeson, Paul (Bass-baritone)

American Balladeer
Collectables Records COL-CD-6502; 1990; CD

139

Bear the Burden in the Heat of the Day
[White, Walter]
Robeson, Paul (Bass-baritone)
Ol' Man River: His 56 Finest 1925–1945
Retrospective RTS 4116; 2008; CD

140

Bear de Burden
[White, Walter]
Robeson, Paul (Bass-baritone)
The Essential Collection
Primo PRMCD6233; 2018; CD

141

Bear the Burden in the Heat of the Day
[White, Walter]
Robeson, Paul (Bass-baritone)
Encore, Robeson!
Monitor MP 581; 1960; LP

· · · · · · ·

Been Down in the Valley

142

Been Down in the Valley
Oglesby, Isador
Oglesby, Isador (Tenor)
Isador Sings Negro Spirituals
Oglesby Recordings Album 3; 1983; LP
Piano

· · · · · · ·

Behold That Star

143

Behold That Star
Burleigh, Harry T.
Anderson, Marian (Contralto)
He's Got the Whole World in His Hands: Spirituals
RCA Victor 09026-6[1960]2; 1994; CD
Piano
Light dialect

Also released with *The Rich Voice of Marian Anderson* (Editions Audiovisuel Beulah; 2019; Streaming audio) and *Marian Anderson: Beyond the Music; Her Complete RCA Victor Recordings* (Sony Classical 19439836492; 2021; CD)

144

Behold the Star
Dawson, William L.
Ayers, Vanessa (Mezzo-soprano)
Black Christmas: Spirituals in the African-American Tradition
Essay Recordings CD1011; 1990; CD
Chorus

145

Behold That Star
Burleigh, Harry T.
Brown, Anthony (Baritone)
Spirituals
Brown/Smith Productions; 1995; CD
Piano
Light dialect

146

Behold the Star
Dawson, William L.
Clark, Lisa (Soprano); Wright, John Wesley (Tenor)
The Spirit of the Holidays
American Spiritual Ensemble; 2009; CD

147

Behold That Star
Composer not identified
Hagen-William, Louis (Bass-baritone)
Negro Spirituals
Quantum QM 6909; 1993; CD
Piano
Light dialect

148

Behold That Star
Dawson, William L.
Martin, Marvis (Soprano)
The Spirituals of William L. Dawson
St. Olaf Records E-2159; 1997; CD
Chorus

149

Behold That Star
Composer not identified
Norman, Jessye (Soprano)
Jessye Norman at Notre Dame: A Christmas Concert
Philips 432 731-2; 1992; CD
Orchestra

Also released with *Festkonzert aus Notre-Dame* (Philips 438 079-2; 1992; CD) and *Jessye Norman à Notre-Dame: Récital de Noël* (Philips 438 078-2; 1992; CD)

· · · · · · ·

Better Be Ready

150

Better Be Ready
Dett, Robert Nathaniel
Blackmon, Henry (Baritone)
Negro Spirituals
Vega 19179; [19--]; LP
Chorus, piano

151

Better Be Ready
Dett, Robert Nathaniel
Blackmon, Henry (Baritone)
Negro Spirituals
Mirasound Records SGLP 6047; [19--]; LP
Organ

· · · · · · ·

Blind Man Stood on the Road and Cried

152

De Blin' Man Stood on de Road an' Cried
Burleigh, Harry T.
Browning, Marcus (Vocalist)
De Blin' Man Stood on de Road an' Cried/ Deep River
Edison Bell Radio 1347; [193-]; 78 RPM
Piano

153

De Blin' Man Stood on de Way an' Cried
Composer not identified

Evans, Charlie (Vocalist)
Sing God's Plan
Private Label; 2005; CD
Piano
Light dialect

154

De Blin' Man Stood on de Road an' Cried
Composer not identified
Hagen-William, Louis (Bass-baritone)
Negro Spirituals
Quantum QM 6909; 1993; CD
Piano
Light dialect

155

The Blind Man Stood on the Road and Cried
Henderson, Skitch
Hines, Jerome (Bass)
Standin' in the Need of Prayer
RCA Victor LPM-2047; [1960]; LP

156

De Blin' Man [from *Five Spirituals for Baritone and Cello*]
Balentine, James Scott
Jones, Timothy (Baritone)
Love Comes in at the Eye
Albany TROY1734; 2018; CD
Cello
Moderate dialect

157

Blind Man Stood on the Way and Cried
Composer not identified
Kaskas, Anna (Contralto)
Sacred Songs
SESAC YTNY 5735-YTNY 5736; [19--]; LP

158

De Blin' Man Stood on de Road an' Cried
Burleigh, Harry T.
Lynch, Lester (Baritone)
On My Journey Now: Spirituals & Hymns
Pentatone Music PTC 5186 57'; 2017; CD
Piano

159

The Blin' Man Stood on the Road an' Cried
Burleigh, Harry T.

Oby, Jason (Tenor)
The Life of Christ: Collected Spirituals
Private Label TSU4749; [200-]; CD
Piano
Moderate dialect

160

De Blin' Man Stood on de Road an' Cried
Composer not identified
Pickens, Jo Ann (Soprano)
My Heritage: American Melodies/Negro Spirituals
Koch Schwann 3-1447-2; 1993; CD

161

De Blin' Man Stood on de Road an' Cried
Johnson, Hall
Toppin, Louise (Soprano)
The Hall Johnson Collection
Carl Fischer VF5 CD1–VF5 CD2; 2003; Score w/CD
Piano
Heavy dialect

162

De Blin Man Stood on de Road
Composer not identified
West, Lucretia (Mezzo-soprano)
Lucretia West Sings Spirituals
Westminster WP 6063; [1957]; LP

163

De Blin' Man Stood on de Road
Morgenstern, Sam
West, Lucretia (Mezzo-soprano)
Spirituals
Westminster WL 5338; 1954; LP
Men's voices

164

De Blin' Man Stood on de Way an' Cried
Schweizer, Rolf
Wolf, Lars (Vocalist)
Die Schwarze Stimme Europas
Cantate 666000; 1971; LP
Chorus, organ, percussion

· · · · · · ·

By and By

[Matthew 11:28-30; Mark 7:37]

"Oh, by and by, by and by, I'm going to lay down my heavy load. I know my robe's going to fit me well, I tried it on at the gates of hell...."

[Available in AB10, CW40, EM34, FH25, HCTN, HTBA, HT25, HTC1, JJBA, RWSC, SBFD, WF70]

"By an' By" was one of the dozen spirituals Burleigh chose to publish in his 1917 *Album of Negro Spirituals*. This first collection of concert spirituals for solo voice was used by recording artists of the era to introduce spirituals to the world of Classical music in a new way. These songs also inspired other composers to explore how the folk songs spawned by the enslaved of the United States could be similarly treated.

The text of this spiritual reflects the recurring theme of what the enslaved foresaw with the coming of freedom from slavery. The creator of the song knew of being tested, even to "the gates of hell," and expressed assurance that deliverance was at hand.

Tenor Roland Hayes' 1922 recording of the spiritual and the 1925 recording by Paul Robeson and Lawrence Brown demonstrate two very different approaches to the use of dialect in two early recordings. While Hayes was restrained in his use of dialect in his recording, Brown and Robeson's use of dialect was more closely in line with the score.

165

By an' By
Boatwright, McHenry
Boatwright, McHenry (Bass-baritone)
Art of McHenry Boatwright: Spirituals
Golden Crest Records RE 7024; 1968; LP
Piano
Light dialect

166

By an' By
Burleigh, Harry T.
Brown, Peggy Lee (Soprano)
Simply Peggy

Independent Records; 2003; CD
Piano
Heavy dialect

167

By an' By
Burleigh, Harry T.
Browning, Marcus (Vocalist)
By an' By/Sometimes I Feel Like a Motherless Child
Edison Bell Radio 1384; 1930; 78 RPM
Piano

168

By an' By
Burleigh, Harry T.
Clark, Clarence Carroll (Baritone)
By an' By/Oh! Didn't It Rain
Paramount 12037; 1924; 78 RPM
Piano

169

By' an' By
Burleigh, Harry T.
Cole, Steven (Tenor)
From the Southland: Songs, Piano Sketches and Spirituals of Harry T. Burleigh
Premier Recordings PRCD 1041; 1995; CD
Piano
No dialect discerned

170

By and By
Composer not identified
Delmore, Harry A. (Tenor)
By and By/My Lord What a Morning
Grey Gull 4165; [1927]; 78 RPM

171

By' an' By
Burleigh, Harry T.
Duncan, Todd (Baritone)
Negro Spirituals
Allegro ALG3022; [1952]; LP
Piano
Light dialect

Also released with *African American Spirituals* ([Apple Music]; 2008; Streaming audio)

172
By and By
Kaelin, Pierre
Evans, Allan (Bass-baritone)
Negro Spirituals
Electromusic Records EMCD 6885; 1985; CD
Chorus, other instrument(s)

173
By an' By
[Burleigh, Harry T.]
Hagen-William, Louis (Bass-baritone)
Negro Spirituals
Quantum QM 6909; 1993; CD
Piano
Light dialect

174
By an' By
[Burleigh, Harry T.]
Hall, Adelaide (Mezzo-soprano)
Spirituals
London LA 52; 1948; 78 RPM
Organ, piano

175
Bye and Bye
[Burleigh, Harry T.]
Hayes, Roland (Tenor)
*Brother, Can You Spare a Dime?: The Roots of
    American Song*
Pearl Gemm CD 9484; 1991; CD
Piano
No dialect discerned

176
By an' By
Brown, Lawrence
Hayes, Roland (Tenor)
Go Down Moses/By an' By
Vocalion 21002; 1922; 78 RPM
Piano

177
By an' By
[Burleigh, Harry T.]
Hayes, Roland (Tenor)
*Black Europe: Sounds & Images of Black
    People in Europe pre–1927*

Bear Family Productions BCD 16095; 2013; CD
Piano
Light dialect

178
Bye and Bye
[Burleigh, Harry T.]
Hayes, Roland (Tenor)
Afro-American Folksongs
Pelican Records LP 2028; 1983; LP
Piano

179
Bye and Bye
[Burleigh, Harry T.]
Hayes, Roland (Tenor)
Black Swans
Parnassus Recordings PACD 96067; 2019; CD
Piano
Light dialect

180
By an' By
Burleigh, Harry T.
Holland, Charles (Tenor)
My Lord What a Mornin'
Musical Heritage Society MHS 912250X;
    1982; LP
Piano
Light dialect

    Also released with *My Lord What a
Mornin'* (Musical Heritage Society MHS
512250K; 1988; CD)

181
Bye and Bye
Clinton, Irving
Irving, Clinton (Bass-baritone)
Clinton Irving Sings Spirituals: A Tribute
Rogers; 2001; CD

182
Bye and Bye
Burleigh, Harry T.
Jones, Fanni (Mezzo-soprano)
Negro Spirituals en Concert
Suisa; 1987; LP
Organ
Moderate dialect

183
By an' By
Composer not identified
Jones, Fanni (Mezzo-soprano)
Negro Spirituals
Evasion Disques LP613; 1974; LP

184
By and By
Burleigh, Harry T.
Little, Vera (Mezzo-soprano)
My Good Lord Done Been Here
Decca 123737; 1957; LP
Piano

185
By an' By
Burleigh, Harry T.
Lynch, Lester (Baritone)
On My Journey Now: Spirituals & Hymns
Pentatone Music PTC 5186 57'; 2017; CD
Piano

186
By and By
Composer not identified
Martin, Vivian (Soprano)
Sings Spirituals and Songs
Halo 50277; 1957; LP

187
By and By
Burleigh, Harry T.
McKinney, Jason (Bass-baritone)
Songs Inspired by Paul Robeson
United in Music; 2014; CD
Piano
Light dialect

188
By an' By
Burleigh, Harry T.
Miller, Reed (Tenor)
Go Down, Moses/By an' By
Edison Blue Amberol 3538; 1918; Cylinder
Chorus, orchestra
Moderate dialect

    Also released with *Go Down, Moses/By an' By* (Edison 80487; 1918; 78 RPM)

189
O, By and By [from *A Child of Our Time*]
Tippett, Michael
Norman, Jessye (Soprano)
Honor! A Celebration of the African American Cultural Legacy
Decca B0012660-02; 2009; CD
Chorus, orchestra

190
By and By
Burton, Ken
Philogene, Ruby (Soprano)
Steal Away
EMI Classics 7243 5 69707 2 4; 1997; CD
Chorus

    Also released with *Noël!: Voices of Christmas* (Angel Records 50999 2 42605 2 7; 2008; CD)

191
Kai Aikanaan (By and By)
Composer not identified
Putkonen, Marko (Bass)
Deep River: Negro Spirituals
Lilium LILP 101; 1991; LP

192
By an' By
[Burleigh, Harry T.]
Robeson, Paul (Bass-baritone); Brown, Lawrence (Vocalist)
Spirituals
Columbia Masterworks M-610; 1946; 78 RPM
Piano

193
Bye and Bye
Burleigh, Harry T.
Robeson, Paul (Bass-baritone)
The Complete EMI Sessions (1928–1939)
EMI Classics 50999 2 15586 2 7; 2008; CD
Heavy dialect

194
By and By
Burleigh, Harry T.
Robeson, Paul (Bass-baritone)
The Very Best of Paul Robeson

Future Noise Music FVDD033; 2009; CD
Piano

195

By an' By
Burleigh, Harry T.
Robeson, Paul (Bass-baritone)
Spirituals
Columbia Masterworks ML 4105 ; CBS
   62483; [1948]; LP

196

By an' By
Burleigh, Harry T.
Robeson, Paul (Bass-baritone); Brown,
   Lawrence (Vocalist)
The Power and the Glory
Columbia/Legacy CK 47337; 1991; CD
Piano
Heavy dialect

197

By an' By
Burleigh, Harry T.
Robeson, Paul (Bass-baritone)
Songs for Free Men, 1940-45
Pearl GEMM CD 9264; 1997; CD
Piano

198

By and By
Burleigh, Harry T.
Robeson, Paul (Bass-baritone)
Paul Robeson: Great Voices of the Century, v. 2
Memoir Classics CDMOIR 426; 1994; CD

199

By an' By
Burleigh, Harry T.
Robeson, Paul (Bass-baritone); Brown,
   Lawrence (Vocalist)
Songs of Free Men: a Paul Robeson Recital
Sony Classical MHK 63223; 1997; CD
Piano
Moderate dialect

200

Bye an' Bye
Burleigh, Harry T.

Robeson, Paul (Bass-baritone)
Paul Robeson Collection
Hallmark Recordings 390692; 1998; CD

201

By an' By
Burleigh, Harry T.
Robeson, Paul (Bass-baritone); Brown,
   Lawrence (Vocalist)
Spirituals
Columbia Masterworks 17379-D; 1945; 78
   RPM
Piano
Moderate dialect

202

By and By
Burleigh, Harry T.
Robeson, Paul (Bass-baritone)
Paul Robeson
World Record Club W9648/EMI SM 431;
   [19--]; LP
Piano

203

Bye and Bye
Burleigh, Harry T.
Robeson, Paul (Bass-baritone); Brown,
   Lawrence (Vocalist)
Songs of My People
RCA Red Seal LM-3292; 1972; LP
Piano

204

Bye and Bye (I'm Goin' to Lay Down Dis
   Weary Load)
Burleigh, Harry T.
Robeson, Paul (Bass-baritone); Brown,
   Lawrence (Vocalist)
Bye and Bye/Were You There?
His Master's Voice B 2126; 1925; 78 RPM
Piano

205

By an' By
Burleigh, Harry T.
Robeson, Paul (Bass-baritone); Brown,
   Lawrence (Vocalist)

By an' By/Joshua Fit the Battle of Jericho
Columbia DS 1785; [19--]; 78 RPM
Piano
Moderate dialect

206
By an' By
Burleigh, Harry T.
Robeson, Paul (Bass-baritone); Brown,
    Lawrence (Vocalist)
*By an' By/Sometimes I Feel Like a Motherless
    Child*
Columbia Masterworks 17468-D; 1946; 78
    RPM
Piano
Moderate dialect

207
By an' By
Burleigh, Harry T.
Robeson, Paul (Bass-baritone)
Were You There?/By an' By
His Master's Voice B.4480; [19--]; 78 RPM
Piano
Heavy dialect

208
By 'n' By
[Burleigh, Harry T.]
Robeson, Paul (Bass-baritone)
Negro Spirituals (And More)
Discmedi DM-4674-02; 2009; CD

209
By an' By
[Burleigh, Harry T.]
Robeson, Paul (Bass-baritone)
Scandalize My Name
Classics Record Library 30-5647; 1976; LP
Piano
Heavy dialect

210
By an' By
[Burleigh, Harry T.]
Robeson, Paul (Bass-baritone)
Deep River
Great Voices of the Century GVC 2004;
    1999; CD

211
Bye an' Bye
[Burleigh, Harry T.]
Robeson, Paul (Bass-baritone)
The Originals: "Spirituals"
Yoyo USA; 2006; Streaming audio

212
By and By
[Burleigh, Harry T.]
Robeson, Paul (Bass-baritone)
Sometimes I Feel Like a Motherless Child
JazzAge; 2012; Streaming audio
Piano

213
By an' By
[Burleigh, Harry T.]
Robeson, Paul (Bass-baritone); Brown,
    Lawrence (Vocalist)
Paul Robeson's Treasure Chest
Leverage; 2008; Streaming audio
Piano

214
By n' By
[Burleigh, Harry T.]
Robeson, Paul (Bass-baritone)
Five Classic Albums Plus Bonus Tracks
Real Gone Music RGMCD287; 2017; CD

215
By n' By
[Burleigh, Harry T.]
Robeson, Paul (Bass-baritone); Brown,
    Lawrence (Vocalist)
Drink to Me Only with Thine Eyes
MD Music; 2010; Streaming audio
Piano
Heavy dialect

216
Bye an' Bye
[Burleigh, Harry T.]
Robeson, Paul (Bass-baritone); Brown,
    Lawrence (Vocalist)
Ol' Man River: The Ultimate Collection
Roslin Records; 2011; Streaming audio

Piano
Light dialect

217
Bye and Bye
[Burleigh, Harry T.]
Robeson, Paul (Bass-baritone)
The Ultimate Collection
Burning Fire; 2009; Streaming audio

218
Bye and Bye
[Burleigh, Harry T.]
Robeson, Paul (Bass-baritone); Brown,
　　Lawrence (Vocalist)
*Joshua Fit de Battle ob Jericho/Bye and Bye
　　(I'm Goin' to Lay Down Dis Heavy Load)*
Victor 19743; 1925; 78 RPM
Piano
Heavy dialect

219
By and By
[Burleigh, Harry T.]
Robeson, Paul (Bass-baritone)
The Great Paul Robeson
Velvet CDVELV 101; 2001; CD
Piano
Heavy dialect

220
By 'n' By
[Burleigh, Harry T.]
Robeson, Paul (Bass-baritone)
Complete Recordings
Universal Digital Enterprises; 2018;
　　Streaming audio

221
By and By
[Burleigh, Harry T.]
Robeson, Paul (Bass-baritone)
Songs of Struggle & Love
Alto ALC 1416; 2020; CD
Piano
Heavy dialect

222
By and By
Composer not identified

Rustin, Bayard (Tenor)
*Bayard Rustin Sings Spirituals, Work &
　　Freedom Songs*
Bayard Rustin Fund; 1988; Cassette
Piano
Moderate dialect

223
By and By
Burleigh, Harry T.
Salters, Stephen (Baritone)
Spirit: Are You There, You Are There
HarmonizedDisharmony 0001; 2015; CD

224
By and By
Francis, Mark
Swan, Walter (Baritone)
He's Got the Whole World in His Hands
Walter Swan; 2004; CD
Guitar
Heavy dialect

225
By and By
[Burleigh, Harry T.]
White, Cassandra (Soprano)
Remembering the Spirituals
CBW Entertainment 837101334068; 2007; CD
Piano
Light dialect

226
By an' By
Burleigh, Harry T.
Zeppenfeld, Georg (Bass)
Dvořák und Seine Zeit
Orfeo International Music C 656 052 I; 2005;
　　CD

227
I'm Goin' to Lay Down My Heavy Load
Price, Florence
Heard, Richard (Tenor)
My Dream: Art Songs and Spirituals
Percentage Records/Sound of Art
　　Recordings CD147597; 2012; CD

Piano
Moderate dialect

. . . .
Calvary

228
Calvary
Johnson, John Rosamond
Arroyo, Martina (Soprano)
Spirituals
Centaur CRC 2060; 1991; CD
Piano
Light dialect

229
Calvary
Composer not identified
Duckworth, Zorita (Mezzo-soprano)
Forget Me Not.... Negro Spirituals
Private Label; [20--]; CD

230
Calvary
Brown, Charles
Haynes, Kimberly (Mezzo-soprano)
The New Negro Spiritual
W. C. Patterson; 2002; Score w/CD
Piano
Heavy dialect

231
Calvary
Jackson King, Betty
Honeysucker, Robert (Baritone)
*Watch and Pray: Spirituals and Art Songs
    by African-American Women Composers*
Koch International Classics 3-7247-2H1;
    1994; CD
Piano
Moderate dialect

232
Calvary
Jackson King, Betty; Davis, O.
Hynninen, Jorma (Bass-baritone); Davis,
    Osceola (Soprano)
Negro Spirituals

Ondine ODE 715-2; 1988; CD
Piano

233
Calvary
Johnson, John Rosamond
Jones, Fanni (Mezzo-soprano)
Negro Spirituals en Concert
Suisa; 1987; LP
Organ
Heavy dialect

234
Calvary
Jackson King, Betty
Jones, Randye (Soprano)
Come Down Angels
Ahhjay Records AHHJ-0001; 2003; CD
Piano
Light dialect

235
Calvary
Jackson King, Betty
Lightfoot, Peter (Baritone)
An American Tapestry
Blue Griffin Recording BGR315; 2014; CD
Piano

236
Calvary
Raphael, Michael
Maynor, Kevin (Bass)
Jazz Hymns
Guild GMCD 7224; 2001; CD
Piano
No dialect discerned

237
Calvary
Composer not identified
McDaniel, Yvette (Soprano)
Simply Spiritual
YM01 D1DX 046103; 1997; CD
Piano

238
Calvary
Traditional

Nobles, NaGuanda (Soprano)
Homage to the Journey
Selbon Records; 2014; Streaming audio
A cappella
No dialect discerned

239
Calvary
Composer not identified
Norman, Jessye (Soprano)
Spirituals: Great Day in the Morning
Philips 412 240-1; 1982; LP
Chorus, other instrument(s)

240
Calvary
Composer not identified
Norman, Jessye (Soprano)
Great Day in the Morning
Philips 6769 104; 1982; LP
Chorus

241
Calvary
Traditional
Norman, Jessye (Soprano)
Amazing Grace
Philips 432 546-2; 1990; CD
A cappella
Light dialect

242
Calvary
Johnson, Hall
Oglesby, Isador (Tenor)
Life of Jesus in Negro Spirituals
Oglesby Recordings Album 2; 1980; LP
Piano

243
Calvary
Brown, Charles
Rhodes, Yolanda (Soprano)
The Angels Bowed Down
Cambria Master Recordings CD-1237; 2019;
　　CD

244
Calvary
Jackson King, Betty

Salters, Stephen (Baritone)
Spiri4t: Are You There, You Are There
HarmonizedDisharmony 0001; 2015; CD

· · · · · · ·

Certainly Lord

245
Cer'N'Y, Lord
Johnson, Hall
Blackmon, Henry (Baritone)
Geestelijke Liederen En Negro Spirituals
Mirasound Records SGLP 6047; 1974; LP
Piano

246
Cert'n'ly, Lord
Johnson, Hall
Brown, William (Tenor)
The Hall Johnson Collection
Carl Fischer VF5 CD1–VF5 CD2; 2003; Score
　　w/CD
Piano
Light dialect

247
Certainly Lord
Johnson, Hall
Evans, Allan (Bass-baritone)
Negro Spirituals
Electromusic Records EMCD 6885; 1985; CD
Chorus, other instrument(s)

248
Certainly, Lord
Hailstork, Adolphus
Conrad, Barbara (Mezzo-soprano)
Spirituals
Naxos 8.553036; 1995; CD
Chorus, orchestra
Light dialect

249
Cert'n'ly, Lord
Johnson, Hall
Toppin, Louise (Soprano)
The Hall Johnson Collection
Carl Fischer VF5 CD1–VF5 CD2; 2003; Score
　　w/CD

Piano
Light dialect

250
Certainly Lord
Johnson, Hall
Toppin, Louise (Soprano)
*He'll Bring It to Pass: The Spirituals of Hall
Johnson for Voice and Piano*
Albany Records TROY846; 2006; CD
Piano
Heavy dialect

· · · · · · ·

Changed My Name

251
Changed Mah Name
Blair Lindsay, Tedrin
DeVaughn, Alteouise (Mezzo-soprano)
Swing Low, Sweet Chariot
American Spiritual Ensemble; 2011; CD

252
Changed My Name
Raphael, Michael
Maynor, Kevin (Bass)
The Spiritual: An Underground Railroad
Southeastern Virginia Arts Assoc.; [2000]; CD
Piano

253
Changed Mah Name
Traditional
Swan, Walter (Baritone)
He's Got the Whole World in His Hands
Walter Swan; 2004; CD
A cappella
Heavy dialect

· · · · · · ·

City Called Heaven

[Hebrews 11:13; Revelation 3:12, 21:2]

"I am a poor pilgrim of sorrow. I'm tossed in this wide world alone. No hope have I for tomorrow. I'm starting to make heaven my home...."

[Available in CLSA, CW40, SOTS]

This song is based on the hymn "The Pilgrim's Song" written by Charles A. Tindley (1851–1933), and several composers have set the song into the style of a spiritual—tracks of which are referenced below. The setting probably best known is the one sung by The Hall Johnson Choir in the theatrical production, *The Green Pastures* (1930). However, contralto Marian Anderson recorded both Johnson's setting for solo voice and that of Edward Boatner.

While the text suggests words drawn from a soul in the deepest despair, the words also express hope, if not in this life, in the life beyond.

The song is well suited to performance using a composed setting or sung a cappella. Although Boatner's score has only a couple of words of dialect, with Johnson's score laced with only a few words of dialect, recordings range from no discerned dialect used to heavy dialect without adversely affecting the pathos of the text.

254
City Called Heaven
Boatner, Edward
Anderson, Marian (Contralto)
Prima Voce
Nimbus NI 7882; 1996; CD
Piano
Light dialect

255
City Called Heaven
Johnson, Hall
Anderson, Marian (Contralto)
Spirituals
RCA Victor Red Seal 09026-63306-2; 1999;
   CD
Piano
Moderate dialect

256
City Called Heaven
Johnson, Hall
Anderson, Marian (Contralto)
Lebendige Vergangenheit

Austro Mechana Historic Recordings
    MONO 89604; 2004; CD
Piano

257
City Called Heaven
Johnson, Hall
Anderson, Marian (Contralto)
Negro Spirituals: 1924–1949
Frémeaux & Associés FA 184; 2004; CD
Orchestra

258
City Called Heaven
Johnson, Hall
Anderson, Marian (Contralto)
City Called Heaven/Lord, I Can't Stay Away/
    Heaven, Heaven
Victor Red Seal 8958; 1936; 78 RPM
Piano

259
City Called Heaven
Johnson, Hall
Anderson, Marian (Contralto)
Anderson Sings Negro Spirituals
Victor Golden Series EK-1007; [19--]; 45 RPM
Piano

260
City Called Heaven
Johnson, Hall
Anderson, Marian (Contralto)
Marian Anderson: Beyond the Music; Her
    Complete RCA Victor Recordings
Sony Classical 19439836492; 2021; CD
Piano
No dialect discerned

261
City Called Heaven
[Johnson, Hall]
Anderson, Marian (Contralto)
Marian Anderson Sings Spirituals
Flapper Past CD 7073; 1995; CD
Piano

262
City Called Heaven
[Johnson, Hall]

Anderson, Marian (Contralto)
The Very Best of Marian Anderson
Master Classics Records; 2009; CD
Piano
No dialect discerned

263
City Called Heaven
de Paur, Leonard
Arroyo, Martina (Soprano)
There's a Meeting Here Tonight
Angel S-36072; 1974; LP
Chorus
    Also released with *Negro Spirituals* (EMI
7243 5 72790 2 4; 1998; CD)

264
City Called Heaven
Johnson, Hall
Arroyo, Martina (Soprano)
Spirituals
Centaur CRC 2060; 1991; CD
Piano
No dialect discerned
    Also released with *Liederabend 1968*
(Hänssler Classic 93.719; 2012; CD)

265
City Called Heaven
Boatner, Edward
Brewer, Christine (Soprano)
Songs by Wagner, Wolf, Britten and John
    Carter
Wigmore Hall Live WHLive0022; 2008;
    CD
Piano
Light dialect

266
City Called Heaven
Brown, Angela; Cooper, Tyron
Brown, Angela (Soprano)
Mosaic: a Collection of African-American
    Spirituals with Piano, guitar
Albany Records TROY721; 2004; CD
Guitar
Light dialect

267
City Called Heaven
Johnson, Hall
Brown, Anne (Soprano)
City Called Heaven
Tono L 28035; [19--]; 78 RPM
Piano

Also released with *Anne Brown Sings Spirituals* (Mercury EP-1-5038; [195-]; LP)

268
City Called Heaven
Boatner, Edward
Brown, Anthony (Baritone)
Spirituals
Brown/Smith Productions; 1995; CD
Piano
Light dialect

Also released with *Toil and Triumph* (Spirituals Project; 2002; CD)

269
A City Called Heaven [from *Two Spirituals*]
Nelson, Robert
Brown, Débria (Mezzo-soprano)
An American Voice: Music of Robert Nelson
Albany Records TROY381; 2000; CD
Orchestra
Moderate dialect

270
City Called Heaven
Johnson, Hall
Davis, Ollie Watts (Soprano)
Here's One: Spiritual Songs
KJAC Publishing KJAC0123; 2003; CD
Piano
Heavy dialect

271
City Called Heaven
Davis, O.; Johnson, Hall
Davis, Osceola (Soprano)
Negro Spirituals
Ondine ODE 715-2; 1988; CD
Piano
No dialect discerned

272
A City Called Heaven
Composer not identified
Dobbs, Mattiwilda (Soprano)
Tva Sidor Av Mattiwilda Dobbs Och Gotthard Arner
Proprius 25 04-02-0004; [19--]; LP
Organ

273
A City Called Heaven
Traditional
Dobbs, Mattiwilda (Soprano)
Rarities
House of Opera CD96547; [20--]; CD
A cappella
Moderate dialect

274
City in Heaven
[Boatner, Edward]
Dobbs, Mattiwilda (Soprano)
M. Dobbs Sings (U.S.A.)
Soviet Gramophone Records (Melodiya) GOST 5289-56; 1960; LP
A cappella

Also released with *Mattiwilda Dobbs Sings Franz Schubert/American Negro Spirituals* (Aprelevsky 5846; [1961]; LP)

275
City Called Heaven
Johnson, Hall
Elzy, Ruby (Soprano)
Ruby Elzy in Song: Rare Recordings
Cambria Records CD-1154; 2006; CD
Piano
Moderate dialect

Also released with *The 78 RPM Collection* (Master Classics Records; 2010; CD)

276
City Called Heaven
Johnson, Hall
English-Robinson, Laura (Soprano)
Let It Shine!
ACA Digital Recording CM20020; 1994; CD
A cappella
Light dialect

277

City Called Heaven
Roberts, Howard
Estes, Simon (Bass-baritone)
Spirituals
Philips 412 631-2; 1985; CD
Orchestra
Light dialect

     Also released with *Famous Spirituals* (Philips 462 062-2; 1997; CD)

278

City Called Heaven
Ryan, Donald
Estes, Simon (Bass-baritone)
Steal Away: My Favorite Negro Spirituals
Deutsche Schallplatten DS 1041-2; 1994; CD
Piano
No dialect discerned

     Also released with *Simon Sings His Favorite Gospels & Spirituals* (Praise Productions SMG-SE; 1999; CD) and *Save the Children, Save Their Lives* (CD Baby; 2020; Streaming audio)

279

City Called Heaven
Johnson, Hall
Gibson, Caroline (Soprano)
On Ma Journey Now: Negro Spirituals in Concert
Twin Productions; 2016; CD
Piano
Moderate dialect

280

City Called Heaven
Johnson, Hall
Graves, Denyce (Mezzo-soprano)
Angels Watching Over Me
NPR Classics CD 0006; 1997; CD
Piano
Heavy dialect

281

City Called Heaven
Johnson, Hall
Hall, Myrtle (Soprano)

Myrtle Hall, Lyric Soprano
Bella Voce Records 651P-2419; 1967; LP

282

Po' Pilgrim
Hayes, Roland
Hayes, Roland (Tenor)
The Art of Roland Hayes: Six Centuries of Song
Preiser Records; 2010; CD
A cappella
Moderate dialect

283

Heard of a City Called Heaven [from *My Songs*]
Hayes, Roland
Hayes, Roland (Tenor)
Favorite Spirituals
Vanguard Classics OVC 6022; 1995; CD
Piano
Heavy dialect

     Also released with *Big Psalms, Hymns and Spirituals Box* (eOne Music/Vanguard Classics; 2015; Streaming audio)

284

City Called Heaven
Traditional
Heard, William N. (Vocalist)
Songs from the Sanctuary: Hymns, Spirituals & Classic Gospels
Heardsong Productions; 2013; CD
A cappella

285

City Called Heaven
Lloyd, Charles, Jr.
Hobson, Richard (Baritone)
The Spiritual Art Song Collection
Warner Bros. SVBM00004; 2000; Score w/CD
Piano

286

City Called Heaven
Clinton, Irving
Irving, Clinton (Bass-baritone)
Clinton Irving Sings Spirituals: A Tribute
Rogers; 2001; CD

287

City Called Heaven
Composer not identified
James, Melissa (Vocalist)
They Slice the Air
Spirituals Project; 2007; CD
Harp
Light dialect

288

City Called Heaven
Boatner, Edward
Jones, Arthur (Tenor)
Wade in the Water
Orbis Books; 1993; Book w/cass
Piano
Heavy dialect

289

City Called Heaven
Johnson, Hall
Martin, Marvis (Soprano)
Live from the Spoleto Festival, 1987
Musical Heritage Society 5169615; 2003; CD
Piano
Light dialect

290

City Called Heaven
Composer not identified
Martin, Vivian (Soprano)
Sings Spirituals and Songs
Halo 50277; 1957; LP

291

A City Called Heaven
Raphael, Michael
Maynor, Kevin (Bass)
The Spiritual: An Underground Railroad
Southeastern Virginia Arts Assoc.; [2000]; CD
Piano

292

City Called Heaven
Composer not identified
McDaniel, Yvette (Soprano)
Simply Spiritual
YM01 DIDX 046103; 1997; CD
Piano

293

A City Called Heaven
Johnson, Hall
McFerrin, Robert (Baritone)
*Deep River and Other Classic Negro
    Spirituals*
Riverside Records RLP 12-812; 1959; LP
Piano
Light dialect

    Also released with *Classic Negro Spiri-
tuals* (Washington Records WLP 466; 1959;
LP) and *Negro Spirituals* (Jacques Canetti 27
193; 1965; 45 RPM)

294

City Called Heaven
Johnson, Hall
Miles, John (Tenor)
The Classic Spirituals
Epiphany 83-1027; 1983; LP
Instrumental ensemble

295

Po' Pilgrim of Sorrow, or, A City Called
    Heaven
Traditional
Moses, Oral (Bass-baritone)
*Spirituals in Zion: A Spiritual Heritage for
    the Soul*
Albany Records TROY587; 2003; CD
A cappella
Light dialect

296

City Called Heaven
Composer not identified
Norman, Jessye (Soprano)
Spirituals: Great Day in the Morning
Philips 412 240-1; 1982; LP
Chorus, other instrument(s)

297

City Called Heaven
Traditional
Norman, Jessye (Soprano)
Amazing Grace
Philips 432 546-2; 1990; CD
A cappella
Light dialect

298

City Called Heaven
Traditional
Norman, Jessye (Soprano)
Great Day in the Morning
Philips 6769 104; 1982; LP
A cappella
Moderate dialect

299

A City Called Heaven [from *Settings for Spirituals*]
Chadabe, Joel
Oliver, Irene (Soprano)
Settings for Spirituals; Solo
Lovely Music VR-3804; 1984; LP
Electronics

300

City Called Heaven
Composer not identified
Pickens, Jo Ann (Soprano)
My Heritage: American Melodies/Negro Spirituals
Koch Schwann 3-1447-2; 1993; CD

301

City Called Heaven
Johnson, Hall
Powell, Angela (Soprano)
City Called Heaven
Private Label AP6957; 2003; CD
Piano

302

City Called Heaven
Rodriguez, Carlos
Powell, Angela (Soprano)
City Called Heaven
Private Label AP6957; 2003; CD
Piano

303

City Called Heaven
Composer not identified
Price, Eudora (Vocalist)
My Favorite Songs & Spirituals
Private Label; 2006; CD

Organ
Light dialect

304

A City Called Heaven
de Paur, Leonard
Price, Leontyne (Soprano)
Swing Low, Sweet Chariot: Fourteen Spirituals
RCA Victor LSC 2600; 1962; LP
Orchestra
Heavy dialect

Also released with *The Essential Leontyne Price: Spirituals, Hymns & Sacred Songs* (BMG Classics 09026-68157-2; 1996; CD); *The Essential Leontyne Price* (BMG Classics 09026-68153-2; 1996; CD); *Complete Collection of Songs and Spiritual Albums* (RCA Red Seal 88697940502; 2011; CD); *Leontyne Price Sings Spirituals* (RCA Red Seal 88691928242; 2012; CD); *Singers of the Century: Leontyne Price: Spiritual and Religious Songs* (Jube Classic; 2016; Streaming audio)

305

A City Called Heaven
Composer not identified
Remboldt, Avonelle (Soprano)
Rejoice Ye, My People
Chapel Records S-5165; [1960]; LP

306

City Called Heaven
Johnson, Hall
Shirley, George (Tenor)
George Shirley at 80: My Time Has Come!
Videmus Records; 2014; CD
Piano

307

City Called Heaven
Johnson, Hall
Simpson, Eugene Thamon (Bass)
Honors and Arms
Black Heritage Publications; 2005; CD
Piano

308

City Called Heaven
Johnson, Hall

Simpson, Eugene Thamon (Bass)
Hall Johnson Spirituals and Other Folk Songs
Private Label; 2016; CD
Piano

309
City Called Heaven
Johnson, Hall
Spencer, Kenneth (Bass-baritone)
4 Negro Spirituals
Columbia ESRF 1067; 1957; 45 RPM
Orchestra

310
City Called Heaven
[Johnson, Hall]
Spencer, Kenneth (Bass-baritone)
American Spirituals
Sonora MS-478; [1945]; 78 RPM
Piano
Light dialect

311
A City Called Heaven
Blanchard, Terence
Sykes, Jubilant (Baritone)
Jubilant Sykes
Sony Classical SK 63294; 1998; CD
Instrumental ensemble

312
City Called Heaven
Erb, Clayton
Sykes, Jubilant (Baritone)
Jubilant Sykes Sings Copland and Spirituals
Arioso Classics AC 00011; 2008; CD
Orchestra

313
City Called Heaven
Boatner, Edward
Thompson, Jeanette (Soprano)
Negro Spirituals
Pavane Records ADW 7267; 1992; CD
Piano
No dialect discerned

314
City Called Heaven
Johnson, Hall

Toppin, Louise (Soprano)
He'll Bring It to Pass: The Spirituals of Hall Johnson for Voice and Piano
Albany Records TROY846; 2006; CD
A cappella
Heavy dialect

315
City Called Heaven
Johnson, Hall
Toppin, Louise (Soprano)
He'll Bring It to Pass: The Spirituals of Hall Johnson for Voice and Piano
Albany Records TROY846; 2006; CD
Piano
Moderate dialect

316
City Called Heaven
Johnson, Hall
Weathers, Felicia (Soprano)
Spirituals & Kodály Folk Songs
Decca SXL 6245; 1966; LP
Piano
No dialect discerned

Also released with *Arias and Spirituals* (Belart/Universal Classics 461 5922; 1999; CD)

317
City Called Heaven
Johnson, Hall
West, Lucretia (Mezzo-soprano)
Negro Spirituals III
Club français du disque 176; 1959; LP
Piano
Moderate dialect

318
City Called Heaven
Johnson, Hall
West, Lucretia (Mezzo-soprano)
Negro Spirituals mit Lukretia West
Opera 3408; [195-]; LP
Piano

319
City Called Heaven
Johnson, Hall

Williams, Camilla (Soprano)
O' What a Beautiful City/City Called Heaven
RCA Victor 10-1425; [19--]; 78 RPM
Piano
No dialect discerned

  Also released with *Camilla Williams Sings Spirituals* (MGM Records M-G-M E-156; [195-]; LP) and *A Camilla Williams Recital* (MGM Records E-140; [1952]; LP)

320

City Called Heaven
Johnson, Hall
Wilson, Robin (Soprano)
Best of the Hall Johnson Centennial Festival Celebrating the 100th Anniversary of Hall Johnson's Birth
Hall Johnson Collection O33D2; 2002; CD
Piano

321

I Am a Poor Pilgrim of Sorrow
Coil, Pat; Wilson-Felder, Cynthia
Wilson-Felder, Cynthia (Soprano)
Spirituals: Songs from the American Experience
GBGMusik CD 1-005; 1996; CD
Instrumental ensemble

· · · · · · ·

Climbing High Mountains

322

Climbing High Mountains
Johnson, Hall; Link, Peter
Davis, Osceola (Soprano)
Climbing High Mountains
Watchfire Music; 2008; CD
Orchestra
Light dialect

323

Climbin' High Mountains
Jackson King, Betty
Matthews, Benjamin (Baritone)
Three Generations Live
Canti Records; 2000; CD

Piano
Heavy dialect

324

Climbing High Mountains
[Jackson King, Betty]
Miller-Sydney, Audrey (Soprano)
Climbing High Mountains: African American Art Songs and Spirituals
Private Label; 2004; CD
Piano
No dialect discerned

325

Climbing High Mountains
Jackson King, Betty
Taylor, Darryl (Countertenor)
How Sweet the Sound: A Charm of Spirituals
Albany TROY1244; 2011; CD
Piano

326

Climbin' High Mountains
Jackson King, Betty
Tillman, Alice (Soprano)
The New Negro Spiritual
W. C. Patterson; 2002; Score w/CD
Piano
Moderate dialect

· · · · · · ·

Come Down Angels

327

Come Down Angels
Smith Moore, Undine
Brown, Angela (Soprano)
Mosiac: A Collection of African-American Spirituals with Piano, guitar
Albany Records TROY721; 2004; CD
Piano
Light dialect

328

Come Down Angels
Smith Moore, Undine
Brown, Angela (Soprano)
The Lily of the Valley

American Spiritual Ensemble; [2003]; CD
Piano

329

Come Down Angels
Smith Moore, Undine
Fernandez, Wilhelmenia (Soprano)
Negro Spirituals
Transart 131; 2005; CD
Piano

330

Come Down Angels
Smith Moore, Undine
Honeysucker, Robert (Baritone)
Watch and Pray: Spirituals and Art Songs by African-American Women Composers
Koch International Classics 3-7247-2H1; 1994; CD
Piano
Light dialect

331

Come Down Angels
Smith Moore, Undine
Jones, Randye (Soprano)
Come Down Angels
Ahhjay Records AHHJ-0001; 2003; CD
Piano
Light dialect

332

Come Down Angels
[Smith Moore, Undine]
Miller-Sydney, Audrey (Soprano)
Climbing High Mountains: African American Art Songs and Spirituals
Private Label; 2004; CD
Piano
No dialect discerned

333

Come Down Angels and Trouble the Water
Smith Moore, Undine
Moses, Oral (Bass-baritone)
Come Down Angels and Trouble the Water: Negro Spirituals, an American National Treasure!
Albany Records TROY 1489; 2014; CD

Piano
Moderate dialect

  Also released with *Sankofa: A Spiritual Reflection* (Albany Records TROY1802; 2019; CD)

334

Come Down Angels
Smith Moore, Undine
Pleas III, Henry H. (Tenor)
Come Down Angels: A Program of Vocal Works by Women Composers
The Unveiled Voices Project; 2016; CD
Piano
Light dialect

  Also released with *Come Down Angels!* (The Unveiled Voices Project; 2017; Streaming audio)

335

Come Down Angels
Smith Moore, Undine
Rhodes, Yolanda (Soprano)
The Angels Bowed Down
Cambria Master Recordings CD-1237; 2019; CD

336

Come Down Angels
Composer not identified
Robinson, Marie Hadley (Soprano)
Come Down Angels
Meyer Media; 2011; Streaming audio
Piano
Light dialect

337

Come Down Angels
Smith Moore, Undine
Toppin, Louise (Soprano)
Ah! Love but a Day
Albany Records/ Videmus TROY 385; 2000; CD
Piano
Moderate dialect

338

Come Down Angels
Smith Moore, Undine

Toppin, Louise (Soprano)
The New Negro Spiritual
W. C. Patterson; 2002; Score w/CD
Piano
Moderate dialect

·······

Couldn't Hear Nobody Pray

339

Couldn't Hear Nobody Pray
Burleigh, Harry T.
Arroyo, Martina (Soprano)
Spirituals
Centaur CRC 2060; 1991; CD
Piano
Heavy dialect

340

I Couldn't Hear Nobody Pray
Dett, Robert Nathaniel
Arroyo, Martina (Soprano)
Negro Spirituals
EMI 7243 5 72790 2 4; 1998; CD
Chorus
Moderate dialect

341

I Couldn't Hear Nobody Pray
Dett, Robert Nathaniel
Arroyo, Martina (Soprano); Lane, Betty
(Vocalist)
There's a Meeting Here Tonight
Angel S-36072; 1974; LP
Chorus

342

Lord, I Couldn't Hear Nobody Pray
Russ, Patrick
Battle, Kathleen (Soprano)
Pleasures of Their Company
EMI/Angel CDC-7 47196 2; 1986; CD
Guitar
Moderate dialect

Also released with *Great American Spirituals* (Angel CDM 7 64669 2; 1992; CD) and *Great American Spirituals* (Musical Heritage Society 513725Z; 1994; CD)

343

I Couldn't Hear Nobody Pray
Boatwright, McHenry
Boatwright, McHenry (Bass-baritone)
Art of McHenry Boatwright: Spirituals
Golden Crest Records RE 7024; 1968; LP
Piano
Heavy dialect

344

Couldn't Hear Nobody Pray
Burleigh, Harry T.
Davis, Ollie Watts (Soprano)
Here's One: Spiritual Songs
KJAC Publishing KJAC0123; 2003; CD
Piano
Moderate dialect

345

Couldn't Hear Nobody Pray
Burleigh, Harry T.
Dove, Evelyn (Contralto)
*Ev'ry Time I Feel de Spirit/Couldn't Hear
    Nobody Pray*
ACO G-15659; [1924]; 78 RPM
Piano

Also released with *Brother, Can You Spare a Dime?: The Roots of American Song* (Pearl Gemm CD 9484; 1991; CD); *Negro Spirituals: The Concert Tradition 1909–1948* (Frémeaux & Associés FA 168; 1999; CD); *Black Europe: Sounds & Images of Black People in Europe pre–1927* (Bear Family Productions BCD 16095; 2013; CD) and *The Concerto: African American Spirituals* (Orange Amaro; 2019; Streaming audio)

346

Couldn't Hear Nobody Pray
[Burleigh, Harry T.]
Hagen-William, Louis (Bass-baritone)
Negro Spirituals
Quantum QM 6909; 1993; CD
Piano
Light dialect

347

Couldn't Hear Nobody Pray [from *Five
    Spirituals*]

Stucky, Rodney
Henderson, Mary (Mezzo-soprano)
*Come Where the Aspens Quiver.... Bring
    Your Guitar*
Fleur de Son Classics FDS 57955; 2002; CD
Guitar
No dialect discerned

348
I Couldn't Hear Nobody Pray
Hogan, Moses
Hendricks, Barbara (Soprano)
Give Me Jesus
EMI Classics 7243 5 56788 2 9; 1998; CD
Chorus
Moderate dialect

349
I Couldn't Hear Nobody Pray
Henderson, Skitch
Hines, Jerome (Bass)
Standin' in the Need of Prayer
RCA Victor LPM-2047; [1960]; LP

350
I Couldn't Hear Nobody Pray
Composer not identified
Jones, Fanni (Mezzo-soprano)
Negro Spirituals
Phonotec 815; 1977; LP
Organ

351
Couldn't Hear Nobody Pray
Composer not identified
Loiselle, Henri (Bass-baritone)
One Day at a Time
Hum Recordings HRHLCD001; 1996; CD
Piano

352
I Could'n Hear Nobody Pray
Meyer, Fredrich
London, George (Bass-baritone)
Spirituals
Deutsche Grammophon 00289 477 6193;
    2006; CD
Chorus, orchestra
Heavy dialect

353
Couldn't Hear Nobody Pray
Composer not identified
Lord, Marie-Josée (Soprano)
Amazing Grace
ATMA Classique ACD2 2686; 2014; CD
Chorus
No dialect discerned

354
I Couldn't Hear Nobody Pray
Dett, Robert Nathaniel
Maynor, Dorothy (Soprano)
Spirituals, Arias, Songs ([1940]1943)
Claremont CD GSE 78-50-59; 1994; CD
Chorus

355
I Couldn't Hear Nobody Pray
Dett, Robert Nathaniel
Maynor, Dorothy (Soprano)
Negro Spirituals
RCA Victor M879; 1942; 78 RPM
Men's voices

    Also released with *Negro Spirituals*
(Kipepeo Publishing; 2018; CD) and *Doro-
thy Maynor Sings Spirituals and Sacred Songs*
(RCA Camden CAL-344; 1957; LP)

356
Couldn't Hear Nobody Pray
Composer not identified
Moses, Oral (Bass-baritone)
Extreme Spirituals
Cuneiform Record Rune 241; 2006; CD
Instrumental ensemble

357
I Couldn't Hear Nobody Pray
Patterson. Willis
Norman, Jessye (Soprano)
Negro Spirituals
Philips 9500 580; 1979; LP
Chorus
Moderate dialect

    Also released with *The Jessye Norman
Collection* (Philips Classics 422 893-2; [1988];
CD); *Spirituals* (Philips 416 462-2; 1990; CD);

The Jessye Norman Collection: Sacred Songs & Spirituals (Philips B0004506-02; 2005; CD) and *Honor! A Celebration of the African American Cultural Legacy* (Decca B0012660-02; 2009; CD)

358

Lord, I Couldn't Hear Nobody Pray
Composer not identified
Norman, Jessye (Soprano)
Roots: My Life, My Song
Sony Classical 88697642632; 2010; CD
Instrumental ensemble
No dialect discerned

Also released with *Une Vie Pour le Chant* (Sony Classical 88883704512; 2013; CD)

359

Couldn't Hear Nobody Pray
Burleigh, Harry T.
Philogene, Ruby (Soprano)
Steal Away
EMI Classics 7243 5 69707 2 4; 1997; CD
Piano

360

I Couldn't Hear Nobody Pray
Johnson, Hall
Price, Leontyne (Soprano)
The Essential Leontyne Price
BMG Classics 09026-68153-2; 1996; CD
Chorus
Moderate dialect

Also released with *The Essential Leontyne Price: Spirituals, Hymns & Sacred Songs* (BMG Classics 09026-68157-2; 1996; CD); *The Best of Negro Spirituals* (BMG BVCM-37416; 2003; CD); *Complete Collection of Songs and Spiritual Albums* (RCA Red Seal 88697940502; 2011; CD); *I Wish I Knew How It Would Feel to Be Free* (RCA Red Seal LSC 3183; 2011; CD) and *Leontyne Price Sings Spirituals* (RCA Red Seal 88691928242; 2012; CD)

361

I Couldn't Hear Nobody Pray
Traditional
Sebron, Carolyn (Mezzo-soprano)
Resurrection, Pt. 1
Private Label; 2006; CD
A cappella
Light dialect

362

I Couldn't Hear Nobody Pray
Johnson, Hall
Straughter, Maralyn (Soprano)
Negro Spirituals of Hall Johnson
Variety Recording Service Var 0753; [196-]; LP
Piano

363

I Couldn't Hear Nobody Pray
Smith, William H.
Thompson, Jeanette (Soprano)
Negro Spirituals
Pavane Records ADW 7267; 1992; CD
Chorus
No dialect discerned

364

Couldn't Hear Nobody Pray
Composer not identified
West, Lucretia (Mezzo-soprano)
Lucretia West Sings Spirituals
Westminster WP 6063; [1957]; LP

365

Couldn't Hear Nobody Pray
Morgenstern, Sam
West, Lucretia (Mezzo-soprano)
Spirituals
Westminster WL 5338; 1954; LP
Men's voices

366

Couldn't Hear Nobody Pray
[Burleigh, Harry T.]
West, Lucretia (Mezzo-soprano)
Negro Spirituals III
Club français du disque 176; 1959; LP
Piano
Heavy dialect

367

I Couldn't Hear Nobody Pray
Composer not identified

White, Willard (Bass-baritone)
Willard White Sings: Copland; American Spirituals; Folk-Songs
Chandos Records CHAN 8960; 1991; CD
Piano
Heavy dialect

368

Couldn't Hear Nobody Pray
Composer not identified
Williams, Wayne (Tenor)
Music from My Life
Movideo Productions 02-1993; 1993; CD
Piano

369

Could Not Hear Nobody Pray
[Burleigh, Harry T.]
Winters, Lawrence (Bass-baritone)
Lawrence Winters: Recital
Hamburger Archiv fur Gesangskunst 10397; 2007; CD
Chorus, orchestra
Heavy dialect

370

Could Not Hear Nobody Pray
[Burleigh, Harry T.]
Winters, Lawrence (Bass-baritone)
Singer Portrait: Lawrence Winters
Apple Music; 2012; Streaming audio
Orchestra
Light dialect

· · · · · · ·

Crucifixion (He Never Said a-Mumblin' Word)

[Matthew 27:27-44; Mark 15:16–32; Luke 23:26-43; John 19:16-27; Acts 5:30]

"Wasn't that a pity and a shame,… They nailed Him to the tree,… They pierced Him in the side, … But he never said a mumbling word…"

[Available in FRMA, HCTN, HJCO, JBMS, JJBA, JPNS, JSSp, LLS2, MBRM, MHDR, RHMF, RONS, SOTS, WF70]

One of the most powerful sorrow songs of the spirituals, "Crucifixion" or "He Never Said a Mumbling Word" recounts the final hours of the crucifixion of Jesus Christ. Composers have tended to keep the vocal and piano parts simple, providing the requisite opportunities for interpretative freedom. Settings tend to either be written for lower voices or for higher voices who can use their chest voice extensively. The vocal line is most effective when performed with a minimal amount of embellishment.

The singer serves as a witness who is recounting the story. Maintaining a slower tempo is critical. In some of the recordings listed below, the vocalist chose to perform the song a cappella to help convey the stark beauty of the words that retell the Crucifixion story and to allow additional interpretative freedom to adjust the tempo and focus on specific words or melody.

371

Crucifixion [He Never Said a Mumblin' Word]
Payne, John C.
Anderson, Marian (Contralto)
Bach, Brahms, Schubert
RCA Victor 7911-2-RG; 1989; CD
Piano
No dialect discerned

372

Crucifixion
Payne, John C.
Anderson, Marian (Contralto)
First Time Buyer's Guide to American Negro Spirituals
Primo Collection PRMCD6038; 2006; CD
Piano
Light dialect

373

Crucifixion
Payne, John C.
Anderson, Marian (Contralto)
Negro Spirituals: The Concert Tradition 1909–1948
Frémeaux & Associés FA 168; 1999; CD
Piano
Light dialect

374

Crucifixion
Payne, John C.
Anderson, Marian (Contralto)
Spirituals
RCA Victor Red Seal 09026-63306-2; 1999;
CD
Piano
Light dialect

375

Crucifixion (He Never Said a Mumblin'
Word)
Payne, John C.
Anderson, Marian (Contralto)
*Softly Awakes My Heart: Very Best of Marian
Anderson*
Alto ALN1955; 2016; CD
Piano
Light dialect

Also released with *Marian Anderson
Sings Eleven Great Spirituals* (Kipepeo Publishing; 2017; CD)

376

Crucifixion
Payne, John C.
Anderson, Marian (Contralto)
Negro Spirituals
RCA Victor LM 2032; [1956]; LP
Piano
Light dialect

Also released with *Marian Anderson:
Beyond the Music; Her Complete RCA Victor Recordings* (Sony Classical 19439836492;
2021; CD)

377

Crucifixion
[Payne, John C.]
Anderson, Marian (Contralto)
*Marian Anderson Sings Eleven Great
Spirituals*
RCA Victor LRM 7006; 1955; LP
Piano
Light dialect

Also released with *Marian Anderson:
Beyond the Music; Her Complete RCA Victor*

Recordings (Sony Classical 19439836492;
2021; CD)

378

Crucifixion
[Payne, John C.]
Anderson, Marian (Contralto)
Alto Rhapsody; Selected Spirituals
Urania URN 22.328; 2007; CD
Piano

379

Crucifixion
[Payne, John C.]
Anderson, Marian (Contralto)
The Very Best of Marian Anderson
Master Classics Records; 2009; CD
Piano
Light dialect

380

Crucifixion
[Payne, John C.]
Anderson, Marian (Contralto)
Negro Spirituals
RCA Gold Seal RVC-1570; [19--]; LP
Piano

381

Crucifixion
[Payne, John C.]
Anderson, Marian (Contralto)
Negro Spirituals
RCA Victor 630.396 A; [19--]; LP
Piano

382

Crucifixion
[Payne, John C.]
Anderson, Marian (Contralto)
*Grandes Contraltos de la Musique Classique,
Les: Marian Anderson, Vol. 8*
Mon Patrimoine Musical Collection; 2017;
Streaming audio
Piano

383

Crucifixion
[Payne, John C.]

Anderson, Marian (Contralto)
The Concerto: African American Spirituals
Orange Amaro; 2019; Streaming audio
Piano
Light dialect

384
Crucifixion
Composer not identified
Blackmon, Henry (Baritone)
Negro-Spirituals
ARC AG 1006; [19--]; 45 RPM
Piano

385
He Never Said a Mumblin' Word
Hogan, Moses
Brown, Angela (Soprano)
*Mosiac: A Collection of African-American
    Spirituals with Piano, guitar*
Albany Records TROY721; 2004; CD
Piano

386
He Never Said a Mumballin' Word
Brown, William
Brown, William (Tenor)
Symphonic Spirituals
Columbia JC 36267; 1979; LP
A cappella
Light dialect

387
He Never Said a Mumballin' Word
Brown, William
Brown, William (Tenor)
Symphonic Spirituals
Spotify; [2019]; Streaming audio
Orchestra
Light dialect

388
He Never Said a Mumberlin' Word
Burton, Dashon
Burton, Dashon (Bass-baritone)
*Songs of Struggle & Redemption: We Shall
    Overcome*
Acis Productions APL08685; 2015; CD
A cappella
Moderate dialect

389
He Never Said a Mumberlin Word [from *The
    Life of Christ*]
Hayes, Roland
Caesar, Jackson (Tenor)
*Spirituals: Celebrating the Music, Life,
    Legacy of Roland Hayes*
CD Baby 7048606059; 2021; CD
A cappella
Light dialect

390
He Never Said a Mumblin' Word
Press, Shawnee
Carnette, Count (Vocalist)
Count Carnette Sings Favorite Negro Spirituals
Carnette Archive Recordings; 1983; LP
Piano
Light dialect

391
Crucifixion
Payne, John C.
Davis, Ollie Watts (Soprano)
Here's One: Spiritual Songs
KJAC Publishing KJAC0123; 2003; CD
Piano
Heavy dialect

392
Crucifixion
Kaelin, Pierre
Evans, Allan (Bass-baritone)
Negro Spirituals
Electromusic Records EMCD 6885; 1985; CD
Chorus, other instrument(s)

393
He Never Said a Mumballin' Word
    (Crucifixion) [from *The Life of Christ*]
Hogan, Moses
Fernandez, Wilhelmenia (Soprano)
Negro Spirituals
Transart 131; 2005; CD
Piano

394
Распятие (Raspyatiye)
Composer not identified

Filatova, Ludmila (Mezzo-soprano)
Негритянские Спиричуэлс (Negrityanskiye Spirichuzls—Negro Spirituals)
Melodiâ S10 21833 009; 1985; LP
Organ
Moderate dialect

395

Crucifixion
Robbiani, Mario
Fisher, Dorothy (Contralto)
Negro Spirituals
Edizione D'Arte Del Lions Club Milano Al Cenacolo; [19--]; LP
Instrumental ensemble

396

Crucifixion
Burleigh, Harry T.
Hayes, Roland (Tenor)
Deep River
Vocalion B3037, Vocalion R6133; 1997; CD
Chorus

397

He Never Said a Mumberlin' Word
Composer not identified
Hayes, Roland (Tenor)
Roland Hayes Sings: Negro Spirituals, Aframerican Folk Songs
Amadeo Records AVRS 6033; [19--]; LP
Piano

398

Crucifixion (He never said a Mumberlin' Word)
Fisher, William Arms
Hayes, Roland (Tenor)
Good News: Vintage Negro Spirituals
Living Era AJA 5622; 2006; CD
A cappella
Heavy dialect

399

He Never Said a Mumberlin' Word [from *The Life of Christ*]
Hayes, Roland
Hayes, Roland (Tenor)
The Art of Roland Hayes: Six Centuries of Song

Preiser Records; 2010; CD
A cappella
Light dialect

400

He Never Said a Mumberlin' Word [from *The Life of Christ*]
Hayes, Roland
Hayes, Roland (Tenor)
Roland Hayes Sings the Life of Christ: As Told Through Aframerican Folksong
Vanguard SRV 352; 1976; LP
Piano

401

He Never Said a Mumberlin' Word [from *The Life of Christ*]
Hayes, Roland
Hayes, Roland (Tenor)
Favorite Spirituals
Vanguard Classics OVC 6022; 1995; CD
A cappella
Heavy dialect

402

He Never Said a Mumberlin' Word [from *The Life of Christ*]
Hayes, Roland
Hayes, Roland (Tenor)
Charlton Heston Reads from The Life and Passion of Jesus Christ
Vanguard Classics ATM-CD-1259; 2003; CD
Piano

403

He Never Said a Mumberlin' Word [from *The Life of Christ*]
Hayes, Roland
Hayes, Roland (Tenor)
Aframerican Folksong: Telling the Story of the Life of Christ
Top Rank 39 620; [1961]; LP
Piano

404

He Never Said a Mumberlin' Word [from *The Life of Christ*]
Hayes, Roland
Hayes, Roland (Tenor)

Roland Hayes Sings the Life of Christ: As Told Through Aframerican Folksong
Vanguard VRS-462; 1954; LP
Piano

405

Crucifixion [from The Life of Christ]
[Hayes, Roland]
Hayes, Roland (Tenor)
Brother, Can You Spare a Dime?: The Roots of American Song
Pearl Gemm CD 9484; 1991; CD
A cappella
Heavy dialect

406

Crucifixion [from *The Life of Christ*]
[Hayes, Roland]
Hayes, Roland (Tenor)
A Song Recital
Columbia Masterworks M 393; 1939; 78 RPM
A cappella

407

He Never Said a Mumberlin' Word [from *The Life of Christ*]
[Hayes, Roland]
Hayes, Roland (Tenor)
Art Songs and Spirituals
Veritas VM 112; 1967; LP
A cappella
Heavy dialect

408

Crucifixion (He Never Said a Mumberlin' Word)
[Hayes, Roland]
Hayes, Roland (Tenor)
Classic Gospel Songs
Emerald/K-Tel; 2013; Streaming audio
A cappella

409

He Never Said a Mumblin' Word [from *The Life of Christ*]
[Hayes, Roland]
Hayes, Roland (Tenor)
Big Psalms, Hymns and Spirituals Box

eOne Music/Vanguard Classics; 2015; Streaming audio
Piano

410

He Never Said a Mumberlin' Word
Hayes, Roland
Hendricks, Barbara (Soprano)
Give Me Jesus
EMI Classics 7243 5 56788 2 9; 1998; CD
A cappella
Moderate dialect

411

Crucifixion
Henderson, Skitch
Hines, Jerome (Bass)
Standin' in the Need of Prayer
RCA Victor LPM-2047; [1960]; LP

412

He Never Said a Mumblin' Word [from *The Life of Christ*]
Hayes, Roland
Holland, Charles (Tenor)
My Lord What a Mornin'
Musical Heritage Society MHS 912250X; 1982; LP
Piano
Moderate dialect

    Also released with *My Lord What a Mornin'* (Musical Heritage Society MHS 512250K; 1988; CD)

413

Didn't Say One Word [from *The Life of Christ*]
[Hayes, Roland]
Jenkins, Isaiah (Tenor)
Lyric Tenor
Trans Radio TR 1010A; [195-]; LP
Piano

414

Crucifixion
Payne, John C.
Matthews, Inez (Mezzo-soprano)
Inez Matthews Sings Spirituals (Great New Voices of Today, v. 6)

Period SPL-580; [1950]; LP
Piano
Heavy dialect

     Also released with *Inez Matthews Sings Spirituals* (Essential Media Group; 2011; CD)

415

And He Never Said a Mumberlin' Word
Traditional
Moses, Oral (Bass-baritone)
Spirituals in Zion: A Spiritual Heritage for the Soul
Albany Records TROY587; 2003; CD
A cappella
Light dialect

416

And He Never Said a Mumblin' Word
Composer not identified
Newby, Marion Crowley (Contralto)
Hymns and Spirituals for Canada's Centennial
A.T.C.M.; 1967; LP

417

He Never Said a Mumberlin' Word [from *The Life of Christ*]
Hayes, Roland
Oby, Jason (Tenor)
The Life of Christ: Collected Spirituals
Private Label TSU4749; [200-]; CD
Piano
Light dialect

418

Crucifixion
Johnson, Hall
Oglesby, Isador (Tenor)
Life of Jesus in Negro Spirituals
Oglesby Recordings Album 2; 1980; LP
Piano

419

Crucifixion
[Payne, John C.]
Pankey, Aubrey (Baritone)
Negro-Spirituals
Eterna 5 30 022; [19--]; 45 RPM

Piano
Light dialect

     Also released with *Aubrey Pankey Singt Negro-Spirituals* (Eterna 7 30 005; 1959; LP); *Negro Spirituals* (Eterna 830010; 1983; LP)

420

Crucifixion
Composer not identified
Peterson, Elwood (Baritone)
Negro Spirituals
Vergara 55.1.004 C; [1963]; 45 RPM
Piano

421

Crucifixion
Traditional
Peterson, Elwood (Baritone)
Negro Spirituals
Boîte à Musique LD 073; 1961; LP
A cappella

422

Crucifixion
Composer not identified
Porter, John (Bass)
No More Crying: Negro Spirituals
Pan Verlag OV-84; [1978]; LP

423

Ei Sanaakaan (Crusifixion)
Composer not identified
Putkonen, Marko (Bass)
Deep River: Negro Spirituals
Lilium LILP 101; 1991; LP

424

The Crucifixion
Composer not identified
Ray, William (Baritone)
Negro Spirituals
Intercord; [19--]; LP

     Also released with *Sings Arias, Duets, Musical Selections and Negro Spirituals* (Intercord; [19--]; CD)

425

He Never Said a Mumblin' Word
Composer not identified

Rustin, Bayard (Tenor)
Bayard Rustin, the Singer
Bayard Rustin Fund; 1992; CD
Piano

426

He Never Said a Mumblin' Word
Traditional
Rustin, Bayard (Tenor)
*Bayard Rustin Sings Twelve Spirituals on the
    Life of Christ*
Fellowship Records E2-KL 1771; [195-]; LP
A cappella
Light dialect

      Also released with *Bayard Rustin-The Singer* (Black Swan Series; Parnassus Records PACD 96083; 2022; CD)

427

Crucifixion
Hogan, Moses
Salters, Stephen (Baritone)
Spirit: Are You There, You Are There
HarmonizedDisharmony 0001; 2015; CD

428

He Never Said a Mumberlin' Word [from
    The Life of Christ]
Hayes, Roland
Shirley, George (Tenor)
George Shirley at 80: My Time Has Come!
Videmus Records; 2014; CD
Piano

429

Crucifixion
Hogan, Moses
Simpson, Marietta (Mezzo-soprano)
Songs of Reflection
MGH Records 0800CD; 2020; CD

430

Mumberlin' Word [from *The Life of Christ*]
Hayes, Roland
Sims, Robert (Baritone)
*Robert Sims Sings the Spirituals of Roland
    Hayes*
Canti Classics 2014-01; 2015; CD

A cappella
Heavy dialect

431

He Never Said a Mumblin' Word
Traditional
Swan, Walter (Baritone)
He's Got the Whole World in His Hands
Walter Swan; 2004; CD
A cappella
Moderate dialect

432

He Never Said a Mumbalin' Word
Hogan, Moses
Taylor, Darryl (Countertenor)
How Sweet the Sound: A Charm of Spirituals
Albany TROY1244; 2011; CD
Piano

433

The Crucifixion
Owens, Robert
Taylor, Darryl (Tenor)
Fields of Wonder
Albany TROY897; 2006; CD
Piano

434

And He Never Said a Mumbalin' Word
    [from *Witness: Original Compositions in
    Spiritual Style*]
Baker, David
Toppin, Louise (Soprano)
Witness
Albany Records TROY868; 2006; CD
Orchestra
Light dialect

435

Crucifixion
Johnson, Hall
Toppin, Louise (Soprano)
The Hall Johnson Collection
Carl Fischer VF5 CD1–VF5 CD2; 2003; Score
    w/CD
Piano
Moderate dialect

436

Crucifixion [from *Son of Man*]
Johnson, Hall
Toppin, Louise (Soprano)
*He'll Bring It to Pass: The Spirituals of Hall
   Johnson for Voice and Piano*
Albany Records TROY846; 2006; CD
Piano
Light dialect

437

The Crucifixion
Traditional
Tucker, Eric Hoy (Bass-baritone)
*Southern Salute: Southern Songs &
   Spirituals*
White Pine Music WPM218; 2012; CD
A cappella
Light dialect

438

Crucifixion
Composer not identified
Tyler, Veronica (Soprano)
Sings … the Passion of Christ in Spirituals
BRC Productions; [19--]; LP
Piano

439

He Never Said a Mumblin' Word
Hogan, Moses
Walker, Alfred (Bass)
*Deep River: Featuring 10 Spirituals Arranged
   for Solo Voice.…*
MGH Records 5000; 2000; CD
Piano
Light dialect

440

He Never Said a Mumberlin' Word [from
   The Life of Christ]
Hayes, Roland
Warfield, William (Bass-baritone)
*Spirituals: 200 Years of African-American
   Spirituals*
ProArte CDD 3443; 1993; CD
A cappella
Light dialect

441

He Never Said a Mumberlin' Word [from
   The Life of Christ]
Hayes, Roland
Williams, Willie (Vocalist)
My Tribute
Discovery V42227; 1974; LP
Piano

· · · · · · ·

Death Ain't Nothing but a Robber

442

Death Ain't Nothin' But a Robber
Traditional
Rustin, Bayard (Tenor)
*Bayard Rustin Sings Spirituals, Work &
   Freedom Songs*
Bayard Rustin Fund; 1988; Cassette
A cappella
Heavy dialect

   Also released with *Bayard Rustin Sings
Spirituals, Work & Freedom Songs* (Bayard
Rustin Fund; 2003; CD)

· · · · · · ·

Death Is Going to Lay His Cold Icy Hands on Me

443

Death's Go'n'ter Lay His Col', Icy Hands on
   Me
Johnson, Hall
Brown, William (Tenor)
The Hall Johnson Collection
Carl Fischer VF5 CD1–VF5 CD2; 2003; Score
   w/CD
Piano
Heavy dialect

444

Death Is Gwinter to Lay His Cold Icy Hands
   on Me
Lloyd, Charles, Jr.
Moses, Oral (Bass-baritone)

Come Down Angels and Trouble the Water: Negro Spirituals, an American National Treasure!
Albany Records TROY 1489; 2014; CD
Piano
Moderate dialect

Also released with *Sankofa: A Spiritual Reflection* (Albany Records TROY1802; 2019; CD)

445

Death's Guanna Lay His Cold Icy Hands on
  Me
Composer not identified
Porter, John (Bass)
No More Crying: Negro Spirituals
Pan Verlag OV-84; [1978]; LP

446

Death Is Gwinter Lay His Cold Icy Hands
  on Me
Thomas, André J.
Tucker, Eric Hoy (Bass-baritone)
Southern Salute: Southern Songs & Spirituals
White Pine Music WPM218; 2012; CD
Piano
Light dialect

· · · · · · ·

Death Is Riding

447

Death Is Riding [from *Witness: Original Compositions in Spiritual Style*]
Baker, David
Toppin, Louise (Soprano)
Witness
Albany Records TROY868; 2006; CD
Orchestra
No dialect discerned

· · · · · · ·

Deep River

[Deuteronomy 3:25, 11:31; Joshua 3:1, 3:17]

"Deep river, my home is over Jordan, Deep river, Lord, I want to cross over into campground. Oh, don't you want to go to that Gospel feast, That promised land where all is peace...."

[Available in AAGS, AB10, CW40, EM34, FHFN, HCTN, HLBS, HT25, HTBA, HTBN, HTBS, HTC1, JAS2, JBBS, JJAN, JJBA, JSSp, LLS2, MH10, MHDR, RHMF, RS12, RWSC, RW14, SBFD, SONS, VLCH, WF10, WF70, WPNN]

"Deep River" was the first concert spiritual Harry T. Burleigh (1866–1949) composed for solo voice. Originally published in 1916, the third version (1917) is the setting best known and most frequently recorded.

The song is organized in an AABA form. The vocal line is deceptively simple; however, the octave leaps in each section can be challenging to reach and still maintain a soft but well-supported vocal line.

Several singers have interpreted the B section of the score by taking a faster tempo than the Lento marking Burleigh indicated. However, other than an increase in dynamics from piano to mezzo-forte, the composer did not indicate other changes.

448

Deep River
Fisher, William Arms
Alda, Frances (Soprano)
Deep River
Victrola 64687; 1917; 78 RPM
Chorus, orchestra
No dialect discerned

449

Deep River
La Forge, Frank
Alda, Frances (Soprano)
By the Waters of Minnetonka/Deep River
Victor Red Seal 1268-B; 1927; 78 RPM
Chorus, orchestra
No dialect discerned

450

Deep River
Burleigh, Harry T.
Alexander, Roberta (Soprano)
Songs My Mother Taught Me
Etcetera KTC 1208; 1999; CD

Piano
Light dialect

451
Deep River
Composer not identified
Allen, Betty (Mezzo-soprano)
On Wings of Song
RCA Custom Reader's Digest RDA43-A;
　　[1960]; LP
Chorus, orchestra
Moderate dialect

452
Deep River
Burleigh, Harry T.
Aluko, Tayo (Baritone)
*Recalling Robeson: Songs from Call Mr.
　Robeson*
Tayo Aluko and Friends TAAF CD 001;
　　2007; CD
Piano

453
Deep River
Frey, Hugo
Amaize, Odekhiren (Bass-baritone)
*For Darfur! Irin Ajo and Other Sacred Songs
　and Spirituals*
MSR Classics MS 1296; 2008; CD
Piano
No dialect discerned

454
Deep River
Burleigh, Harry T.
Anderson, Marian (Contralto)
Deep River
RCA Victor 2032; [194-]; 78 RPM
Piano
No dialect discerned

455
Deep River
Burleigh, Harry T.
Anderson, Marian (Contralto)
*First Time Buyer's Guide to American Negro
　Spirituals*
Primo Collection PRMCD6038; 2006; CD

Piano
No dialect discerned

456
Deep River
Burleigh, Harry T.
Anderson, Marian (Contralto)
The Lady
Magnum Music MCCD 017; 1996; CD
Piano

457
Deep River
Burleigh, Harry T.
Anderson, Marian (Contralto)
*The Art of Marian Anderson: Arias, Songs
　and Spirituals*
His Master's Voice EG 29001614; 1986; LP
Piano

458
Deep River
Burleigh, Harry T.
Anderson, Marian (Contralto)
Marian Anderson: Portraits in Memory
Metropolitan Opera Guild MET 220; 1993;
　　CD
Piano
Light dialect

459
Deep River
Burleigh, Harry T.
Anderson, Marian (Contralto)
Negro Spirituals
EMI 7243 5 72790 2 4; 1998; CD
Piano
No dialect discerned

460
Deep River
Burleigh, Harry T.
Anderson, Marian (Contralto)
*Negro Spirituals: The Concert Tradition
　1909–1948*
Frémeaux & Associés FA 168; 1999; CD
Piano
Light dialect

461

Deep River
Burleigh, Harry T.
Anderson, Marian (Contralto)
Prima Voce
Nimbus NI 7882; 1996; CD
Piano
No dialect discerned

462

Deep River
Burleigh, Harry T.
Anderson, Marian (Contralto)
*Softly Awakes My Heart: Arias, Songs and
    Spirituals, Original Recordings 1924–1944*
Naxos Nostalgia 8.120566; 2001; CD
Orchestra
No dialect discerned

463

Deep River
Burleigh, Harry T.
Anderson, Marian (Contralto)
Spirituals
RCA Victor Red Seal 09026-63306-2; 1999; CD
Piano
No dialect discerned

464

Deep River
Burleigh, Harry T.
Anderson, Marian (Contralto)
Tribute
Pro Arte CDD 3447; 1993; CD
Piano

465

Deep River
Burleigh, Harry T.
Anderson, Marian (Contralto)
Marian Anderson Sings Spirituals
Flapper Past CD 7073; 1995; CD
Piano

466

Deep River
Burleigh, Harry T.
Anderson, Marian (Contralto)
Great Voices of the Century

Memoir Classics CDMOIR 432; 1996; CD
Piano

467

Deep River
Burleigh, Harry T.
Anderson, Marian (Contralto)
Recital: Opera, Lieder, Oratorio
SYM1270.2; Symposium; 2005; CD
Piano

468

Deep River
Burleigh, Harry T.
Anderson, Marian (Contralto)
Rare Live Broadcast Performances
VAI VAIA 1275; 2013; CD
Orchestra
No dialect discerned

469

Deep River
Burleigh, Harry T.
Anderson, Marian (Contralto)
Lebendige Vergangenheit
Austro Mechana Historic Recordings
    MONO 89604; 2004; CD
Piano

470

Deep River
Burleigh, Harry T.
Anderson, Marian (Contralto)
Negro Spirituals: 1924–1949
Frémeaux & Associés FA 184; 2004; CD
Orchestra

471

Deep River
Burleigh, Harry T.
Anderson, Marian (Contralto)
*Love's Old Sweet Song: 25 Great Singers in
    Popular Ballads*
Academy Sound and Vision CD AJA 5130;
    1994; CD

472

Deep River
Burleigh, Harry T.

Anderson, Marian (Contralto)
Deep River
Victor 19227-A; 1923; 78 RPM
Orchestra
No dialect discerned

473

Deep River
Burleigh, Harry T.
Anderson, Marian (Contralto)
Sacred Songs and Ballads of Yesteryear
Griffin; 2011; CD
Piano

474

Deep River
Burleigh, Harry T.
Anderson, Marian (Contralto)
*Softly Awakes My Heart: Very Best of Marian
    Anderson*
Alto ALN1955; 2016; CD
Piano
Light dialect

475

Deep River
Burleigh, Harry T.
Anderson, Marian (Contralto)
Deep River/Heav'n, Heav'n
HMV B 2828; [19--]; 78 RPM
Piano

476

Deep River
Burleigh, Harry T.
Anderson, Marian (Contralto)
Negro Spirituals
La Voix de Son Maître 7 ERF 157; [19--];
    45 RPM

477

Deep River
Burleigh, Harry T.
Anderson, Marian (Contralto)
Negro Spirituals
RCA Victor LM 2032; [1956]; LP
Piano
No dialect discerned

478

Deep River
Burleigh, Harry T.
Anderson, Marian (Contralto)
Deep River/Heav'n, Heav'n (I Got a Robe)
Victor 22015; [19--]; 78 RPM
Piano
No dialect discerned

479

Deep River
Burleigh, Harry T.
Anderson, Marian (Contralto)
Deep River/I Don't Feel No Ways Tired
D.A. 1676; 1925; 78 RPM
Piano
No dialect discerned

480

Deep River
Burleigh, Harry T.
Anderson, Marian (Contralto)
Best Loved Sacred Songs
RCA RSX-15003; 1958; 45 RPM

481

Deep River
Burleigh, Harry T.
Anderson, Marian (Contralto)
Negro Spirituals, Vol. I
La Voix de Son Maître 7 ERF 17026; 1960;
    45 RPM

482

Deep River
Burleigh, Harry T.
Anderson, Marian (Contralto)
Negro Spirituals
La Voix de Son Maître 7 EJF 3; 1955; 45 RPM
Piano

483

Deep River
Burleigh, Harry T.
Anderson, Marian (Contralto)
*Marian Anderson: Beyond the Music; Her
    Complete RCA Victor Recordings*
Sony Classical 19439836492; 2021; CD

Orchestra
No dialect discerned

484
Deep River
Burleigh, Harry T.
Anderson, Marian (Contralto)
Marian Anderson: Beyond the Music; Her Complete RCA Victor Recordings
Sony Classical 19439836492; 2021; CD
Piano
Light dialect

485
Deep River
[Burleigh, Harry T.]
Anderson, Marian (Contralto)
Deep River
Audio Book & Music; [20--]; CD

486
Deep River
[Burleigh, Harry T.]
Anderson, Marian (Contralto)
Marian Anderson Sings Eleven Great Spirituals
RCA Victor LRM 7006; 1955; LP
Piano

487
Deep River
[Burleigh, Harry T.]
Anderson, Marian (Contralto)
When Marian Sang: Selected Songs from Marian Anderson's Repertoire
BMG Special Products DPC13280; 2002; CD

488
Deep River
[Burleigh, Harry T.]
Anderson, Marian (Contralto)
Softly Awakes My Heart
ASV CD AJA 5262; 1999; CD
Piano

489
Deep River
[Burleigh, Harry T.]
Anderson, Marian (Contralto)

Alto Rhapsody; Selected Spirituals
Urania URN 22.328; 2007; CD
Piano

490
Deep River
[Burleigh, Harry T.]
Anderson, Marian (Contralto)
The Very Best of Marian Anderson
Master Classics Records; 2009; CD
Piano
Light dialect

491
Deep River
[Burleigh, Harry T.]
Anderson, Marian (Contralto)
Marian Anderson, Volume 1
Pearl GEMM CD 9318; 1988; CD

492
Deep River
[Burleigh, Harry T.]
Anderson, Marian (Contralto)
Folk Song America: a 20th Century Revival. 1
Smithsonian Collection of Recordings RD 046-1; 1991; CD

493
Deep River
[Burleigh, Harry T.]
Anderson, Marian (Contralto)
Negro Spirituals
RCA Gold Seal RVC-1570; [19--]; LP
Piano

494
Deep River
[Burleigh, Harry T.]
Anderson, Marian (Contralto)
Inspirations
Emerald Echoes; 2015; Streaming audio
Piano
No dialect discerned

495
Deep River
[Burleigh, Harry T.]
Anderson, Marian (Contralto)

*Marian Anderson Sings Eleven Great
    Spirituals*
Kipepeo Publishing; 2017; CD
Piano

496

Deep River
[Burleigh, Harry T.]
Anderson, Marian (Contralto)
Spirituals
Past Classics; 2013; Streaming audio
Piano
No dialect discerned

497

Deep River
[Burleigh, Harry T.]
Anderson, Marian (Contralto)
Negro Spirituals
RCA Victor 630.396 A; [19--]; LP
Piano

498

Deep River
[Burleigh, Harry T.]
Anderson, Marian (Contralto)
*Grandes Contraltos de la Musique Classique,
    Les: Marian Anderson, Vol. 13*
Mon Patrimoine Musical Collection; 2017;
    Streaming audio
Piano

499

Deep River
[Burleigh, Harry T.]
Anderson, Marian (Contralto)
The Concerto: African American Spirituals
Orange Amaro; 2019; Streaming audio
Piano

500

Deep River
[Burleigh, Harry T.]
Anderson, Marian (Contralto)
Ave Maria: And Other Schubert Songs
43 North Broadway, LLC; 2019; Streaming
    audio
Piano
No dialect discerned

501

Deep River
Burleigh, Harry T.
Arroyo, Martina (Soprano)
Spirituals
Centaur CRC 2060; 1991; CD
Piano
Light dialect

502

Djupa vatten (Deep river)
Sköld, Yngve
Björker, Leon (Bass)
I Djupa Kallarvalvet
Artist AEP 1001; 1953; 7-in EP
Piano

503

Deep River
Burleigh, Harry T.
Blackmon, Henry (Baritone)
Negro Spirituals
Mirasound Records SGLP 6047; [19--]; LP
Organ

504

Deep River
Burleigh, Harry T.
Blackmon, Henry (Baritone)
Negro Spirituals
Vega 19179; [19--]; LP
Chorus, piano

505

Deep River
Burleigh, Harry T.; Bledsoe, Jules
Bledsoe, Jules (Baritone)
Go Down Moses/Deep River
Ultraphone AP 394; 1931; 78 RPM
Orchestra
Light dialect

    Also released with *Go Down Moses/
Deep River* (Royale 1703; [19--]; 78 RPM)

506

Deep River
[Burleigh, Harry T.]
Bledsoe, Jules (Baritone)
Wake Up Jacob/Deep River

Joe Davis 8002; 1945; 78 RPM
Orchestra
Moderate dialect

507

Deep River
Boatwright, McHenry
Boatwright, McHenry (Bass-baritone)
Art of McHenry Boatwright: Spirituals
Golden Crest Records RE 7024; 1968; LP
Piano
No dialect discerned

508

Deep River
Hogan, Moses
Brown, Angela (Soprano)
*Mosiac: A Collection of African-American
    Spirituals with Piano, guitar*
Albany Records TROY721; 2004; CD
Piano
Moderate dialect

509

Deep River
Mattson, Phil
Brown, Anthony (Baritone)
Spirituals
Brown/Smith Productions; 1995; CD
Piano
Heavy dialect

510

Deep River
Burleigh, Harry T.
Brown, Peggy Lee (Soprano)
Simply Peggy
Independent Records; 2003; CD
Piano
Light dialect

511

Deep River
Burleigh, Harry T.
Browning, Marcus (Vocalist)
*De Blin' Man Stood on de Road an' Cried/
    Deep River*
Edison Bell Radio 1347; [193-]; 78 RPM
Piano

512

Deep River
Burleigh, Harry T.
Brownlee, Lawrence (Tenor)
The Heart That Flutters
Opus Arte OA CD9015 D; 2013; CD
Piano
No dialect discerned

513

Deep River
Sneed, Damien
Brownlee, Lawrence (Tenor)
Spiritual Sketches
LeChateau Earl Records 888174029597; 2013;
    CD
Piano
No dialect discerned

514

Deep River
Burleigh, Harry T.
Bumbry, Grace (Mezzo-soprano)
Portrait, A
Gala GL 100.539; 1999; CD
Piano
Light dialect

515

Deep River
Burleigh, Harry T.
Burton, Dashon (Bass-baritone)
*Songs of Struggle & Redemption: We Shall
    Overcome*
Acis Productions APL08685; 2015; CD
Piano
Light dialect

516

Deep River
Burleigh, Harry T.
Butt, Clara (Contralto)
Dame Clara Butt: Britain's Queen of Song
Pearl GEM 0086; 2000; CD

517

Deep River
Burleigh, Harry T.
Cantril, Kenneth (Baritone)

My Lord, What a Mornin'/Deep River
London 290; [19--]; 78 RPM
Piano

      Also released with *Spirituals* (London LA 52; 1948; 78 RPM)

518

Deep River
Dørumsgaard, Arne
Carlsen, Svein (Bass)
Negro Spirituals
EuroMaster AS ECD19005; 1996; CD
Piano

519

Deep River
Burleigh, Harry T.
Carnette, Count (Vocalist)
Count Carnette Sings Favorite Negro Spirituals
Carnette Archive Recordings; 1983; LP
Piano
Light dialect

520

Deep River
Burleigh, Harry T.
Chaiter, Yoram (Bass)
Spirituals & Other Songs
Romeo Records 7311; 2014; CD
Piano
No dialect discerned

521

Deep River
Burleigh, Harry T.
Clark, Clarence Carroll (Baritone)
Deep River/I'm So Glad Trouble Don't Last Alway
Columbia 128D; 1924; 78 RPM
Piano
No dialect discerned

522

Deep River [from Crossing Jordan]
Corley, Maria Thompson
Clark, Maria (Soprano)
Soul Sanctuary: Spirituals & Hymns
Navona Records NV6406; 2022; CD

Piano, cello
Moderate dialect

523

Deep River
Burleigh, Harry T.
Conrad, Barbara (Mezzo-soprano)
Spirituals
Naxos 8.553036; 1995; CD
Piano
Moderate dialect

524

Deep River
Composer not identified
Cook, Dixon & Young (Tenor)
Triptych: A Celebration of the Negro Spiritual
CDY Records 649241879206; 2009; CD
Piano
No dialect discerned

525

Deep River
Hogan, Moses
Davis, Henrietta (Soprano)
Deep River: Featuring 10 Spirituals Arranged for Solo Voice....
MGH Records 5000; 2000; CD
Piano
Light dialect

526

Deep River
Burleigh, Harry T.
Davis, Ollie Watts (Soprano)
Here's One: Spiritual Songs
KJAC Publishing KJAC0123; 2003; CD
Piano
Light dialect

527

Deep River (after H.T. Burleigh) [from *Four Spirituals for Soprano and String Quartet*]
Taylor, Stephen Andrew
Davis, Ollie Watts (Soprano)
Rootsongs
Azica AZI 71311; 2016; CD
Instrumental ensemble
No dialect discerned

528
Deep River
[Metehen, Jacques]
Deguil, Arlette (Vocalist)
Negro Spirituals
Pathé 45 ED 1; 1953; 45 RPM
Orchestra
No dialect discerned

Also released with *Negro Spirituals* (Pathé 45-ED 1; 1953; LP)

529
Deep River
Burleigh, Harry T.
Donalda, Pauline (Soprano)
Deep River
Gramophone HO 4479 ae; 1918; 78 RPM
Piano

530
Deep River
Burleigh, Harry T.
Duncan, Todd (Baritone)
Negro Spirituals
Allegro ALG3022; [1952]; LP
Piano

Also released with *African American Spirituals* ([Apple Music]; 2008; Streaming audio)

531
Deep River
Burleigh, Harry T.
Eddy, Nelson (Baritone)
The Hills of Home/Deep River
Victor Red Seal 4371; [19--]; 78 RPM
Orchestra
Moderate dialect

Also released with *Twelve Beloved American Songs* (Victor C27; [19--]; 78 RPM)

532
Deep River
Ryan, Donald
Estes, Simon (Bass-baritone)
Steal Away: My Favorite Negro Spirituals
Deutsche Schallplatten DS 1041-2; 1994; CD
Piano
No dialect discerned

533
Deep River
Kaelin, Pierre
Evans, Allan (Bass-baritone)
Negro Spirituals
Electromusic Records EMCD 6885; 1985; CD
Chorus, other instrument(s)

534
Deep River
Fisher, William Arms
Farrell, Eileen (Soprano)
The Pause That Refreshes on the Air; [19--]; CD

535
Deep River
Sharples, Robert
Farrell, Eileen (Soprano)
Songs America Loves
London OS 25920; 1965; LP
Chorus, other instrument(s)
No dialect discerned

Also released with *Magnificent Voice of Eileen Farrell* (Jasnet Records; 2015; Streaming audio)

536
Deep River
Composer not identified
Ferguson, Margaret (Soprano)
Margaret Ferguson
Private Label; [20--]; CD
Piano

537
Deep River
[Hogan, Moses]
Fernandez, Wilhelmenia (Soprano)
The Diva Live
Transart Records TAP110; 2003; CD
Piano
No dialect discerned

Also released with *Negro Spirituals* (Transart 131; 2011; CD)

538
Река покоя (Reka pokoya)
Composer not identified

Filatova, Ludmila (Mezzo-soprano)
Негритянские Спиричуэлс (Negrityanskiye Spirichuzls—Negro Spirituals)
Melodiâ S10 21833 009; 1985; LP
Organ
Light dialect

539

Deep River
Robbiani, Mario
Fisher, Dorothy (Contralto)
Negro Spirituals
Edizione D'Arte Del Lions Club Milano Al Cenacolo; [19--]; LP
Instrumental ensemble
Moderate dialect

540

Deep River
Composer not identified
Gormley, Clare (Soprano)
Where Morning Lies: Spiritual Songs
ABC Classics 461 766-2; 2002; CD
Piano
Light dialect

541

Deep River
Burleigh, Harry T.
Graves, Denyce (Mezzo-soprano)
Angels Watching Over Me
NPR Classics CD 0006; 1997; CD
Piano
Light dialect

542

Deep River
[Burleigh, Harry T.]
Hagen-William, Louis (Bass-baritone)
Negro Spirituals
Quantum QM 6909; 1993; CD
Piano
Light dialect

543

Deep River
Composer not identified
Harris, Lloyd (Bass)
Negro Spirituals

Pléïade P45301; 1960; 45 RPM
Piano

544

Deep River
Brown, Lawrence
Hayes, Roland (Tenor)
By an' By
Vocalion B3034, Vocalion R6131; 1985; LP

545

Deep River
Burleigh, Harry T.
Hayes, Roland (Tenor)
Go Down Moses
Vocalion B3032, Vocalion R6131; 1922; 78 RPM
Piano
No dialect discerned

546

Deep River [from *My Songs*]
Hayes, Roland
Hayes, Roland (Tenor)
Roland Hayes: My Songs
Vanguard VRS-494; 1956; LP
Piano

Also released with *Great American Spirituals* (Angel CDM 7 64669 2; 1992; CD) *Favorite Spirituals* (Vanguard Classics OVC 6022; 1995; CD) and *Big Psalms, Hymns and Spirituals Box* (eOne Music/Vanguard Classics; 2015; Streaming audio)

547

Deep River [from *Five Spirituals*]
Stucky, Rodney
Henderson, Mary (Mezzo-soprano)
Come Where the Aspens Quiver.... Bring Your Guitar
Fleur de Son Classics FDS 57955; 2002; CD
Guitar
No dialect discerned

548

Deep River
Hendricks, Barbara; Alexeev, Dmitri
Hendricks, Barbara (Soprano)
Negro Spirituals

EMI CDC7470262; 1983; CD
Piano
Light dialect

Also released with *Espirituales Negros* (EMI Classics/Altaya 01636; 1983; CD); *Great American Spirituals* (Musical Heritage Society 513725Z; 1994; CD); *Spirituals* (EMI Classics 0946 346641 2 7; 2005; CD) and *The Very Best of Barbara Hendricks* (EMI Classics 7243 5 86323 2 3; 2005; CD)

549
Deep River
[Burleigh, Harry T.]
Holmes, Eugene (Baritone)
Eugene Holmes Sings Spirituals
Avant Garde AV-115; [1968]; LP
Piano
No dialect discerned

Also released with *Spirituals* (Schubert Records SCH-102; [1988]; LP)

550
Deep River
Burleigh, Harry T.
Howard, Kathleen (Contralto)
Deep River
Pathé Frères 27504; 1917; 78 RPM
Orchestra
No dialect discerned

551
Deep River
Burleigh, Harry T.
Hunt Lieberson, Lorraine (Mezzo-soprano)
Songs
Wigmore Hall Live WHLive0013; 2007; CD
Piano
No dialect discerned

Also released with *Recital at Ravinia* (Harmonia Mundi HMU 907500; 2009; CD)

552
Deep River
C., H. A.; Chambers
Hynninen, Jorma (Bass-baritone)
Negro Spirituals
Ondine ODE 715-2; 1988; CD
Piano

553
Deep River
Clinton, Irving
Irving, Clinton (Bass-baritone)
Clinton Irving Sings Spirituals: A Tribute
Rogers; 2001; CD

554
Deep River
Burleigh, Harry T.
Jimerson, Douglas (Tenor)
Stephen Foster's America
Amerimusic AM1003; 1998; CD
Piano
No dialect discerned

555
Deep River
Composer not identified
Johnson, John (Baritone)
Spirituals
Royale EP 180; [19--]; 45 RPM

556
Deep River
Burleigh, Harry T.
Jones, Fanni (Mezzo-soprano)
Fanni Jones et Oswald Russell
Audio-Visual Enterprises AVE 30701; [19--]; LP

557
Deep River
Composer not identified
Jones, Fanni (Mezzo-soprano)
Negro Spirituals
Phonotec 815; 1977; LP
Organ

558
Deep River
Burleigh, Harry T.
Jones, Randye (Soprano)
Come Down Angels
Ahhjay Records AHHJ-0001; 2003; CD
Piano
Light dialect

559

Deep River
Burleigh, Harry T.
Kennedy, Charles (Vocalist)
Heart & Soul: Songs of Harry T. Burleigh
Publisher not known; 1994; Cassette

560

Deep River
Klickman, Frank Henri
Kimbrough, Steven (Baritone)
*River Songs: From North America, Ireland, &
    Scotland*
Centaur CRC 3853; 2021; CD
Piano

561

Deep River
Burleigh, Harry T.
Leveroni, Elvira (Mezzo-soprano)
Deep River
Edison 7363-B-2-1; 1920; 78 RPM
Piano

562

Deep River
Hogan, Moses
Lewis, Cheryse McLeod (Mezzo-soprano)
Spirituals
CheryseMusic; 2012; CD
Piano

563

Deep River
Hayes, Mark
Lima, Philip (Baritone)
Songs of a Wayfarer
Private Label; 2017; Streaming audio
Piano
Light dialect

564

Deep River
Burleigh, Harry T.
Little, Vera (Mezzo-soprano)
My Good Lord Done Been Here
Decca 123737; 1957; LP
Piano

565

Deep River
Okpebholo, Shawn
Liverman, Will (Baritone)
Steal Away
Yellow Einstein; 2014; CD
Piano
No dialect discerned

566

Deep River
Composer not identified
Loiselle, Henri (Bass-baritone)
One Day at a Time
Hum Recordings HRHLCD001; 1996; CD
Piano

567

Deep River
Meyer, Fredrich
London, George (Bass-baritone)
Spirituals
Deutsche Grammophon 00289 477 6193;
    2006; CD
Chorus
Moderate dialect

568

Deep River
Burleigh, Harry T.
Lynch, Lester (Baritone)
On My Journey Now: Spirituals & Hymns
Pentatone Music PTC 5186 57'; 2017; CD
Piano

569

Deep River
Composer not identified
Madlala, Njabulo (Baritone)
Songs of Home
Champs Hill Records CHRCD071; 2013;
    CD
Piano
No dialect discerned

570

Deep River [from *Feel the Spirit*]
Rutter, John
Marshall, Melanie (Mezzo-soprano)

Feel the Spirit
Collegium Records COLCD 128; 2001; CD
Chorus, orchestra

571

Deep River
Fisher, William Arms
Martinetti, Madeleine (Contralto)
Deep River/Steamboat Song
Columbia LF 238; [19--]; 78 RPM
Piano

572

Deep River
Burleigh, Harry T.
Mayes, Doris (Mezzo-soprano)
Deep River
La voix de son maître FDLP 1080; 1959; LP
Piano

573

Deep River
Welsh, Nicky
McCue, Bill (Bass-baritone)
Bill McCue Sings the Great Spirituals
Beltona SBE 173; 1974; LP
Orchestra

574

Deep River
Burleigh, Harry T.
McFerrin, Robert (Baritone)
Classic Negro Spirituals
Washington Records WLP 466; 1959; LP
Piano
No dialect discerned

   Also released with *Deep River and Other Classic Negro Spirituals* (Riverside Records RLP 12-812; 1959; LP)

575

Deep River
Burleigh, Harry T.
McKinney, Jason (Bass-baritone)
Songs Inspired by Paul Robeson
United in Music; 2014; CD
Piano
Light dialect

576

Deep River
Composer not identified
Monzo, Oscar (Baritone)
Negro Spirituals
Dial Discos 50-2020; 1983; LP

577

Deep River
Getty, Gordon
Moore, Melody (Soprano)
An American Song Album
Pentatone PTC5186770; 2019; CD
Piano

578

Deep River
Composer not identified
Moore, Nettie (Contralto)
Deep River/Song of India
Black Swan 2045; [1921]; 78 RPM
Orchestra
No dialect discerned

   Also released with *Vocal Blues and Jazz, vol. 3: 1921–1928* (Document Records DOCD-1015; 1998; CD)

579

Deep River
Burleigh, Harry T.
Moses, Oral (Bass-baritone)
Deep River: Songs and Spirituals of Harry T. Burleigh
Northeastern NR 252-CD; 1995; CD
Piano

   Also released with *Come Down Angels and Trouble the Water: Negro Spirituals, an American National Treasure!* (Albany Records TROY 1489; 2014; CD) and *Sankofa: A Spiritual Reflection* (Albany Records TROY1802; 2019; CD)

580

Deep River
Traditional
Moses, Oral (Bass-baritone)
Spirituals in Zion: A Spiritual Heritage for the Soul

Albany Records TROY587; 2003; CD
A cappella

581

Deep River
Burleigh, Harry T.
Nash, Lorna (Contralto)
Lorna Nash, Contralto in Concert
Mark Custom Records UMC 2160; [197-];
    LP
Piano

582

Deep River
Composer not identified
Nobles, NaGuanda (Soprano)
Homage to the Journey
Selbon Records; 2014; Streaming audio
Piano
Light dialect

583

Deep River
Fisher, William Arms
Oglesby, Isador (Tenor)
*Negro Spirituals: The Musical Roots of
    American Folk Songs*
Praise PR 658; 1978; LP
Piano

584

Deep River
Ching, Michael
Overton, Kenneth (Baritone)
*Been in de Storm So Long (Songs My Fathers
    Taught Me)*
American Spiritual Ensemble; 2012; CD
Piano
Moderate dialect

585

Deep River
Burleigh, Harry T.
Pankey, Aubrey (Baritone)
*Deep River/Out in the Rain/Didn't My Lord
    Deliver Daniel*
Topic TRC 74; 1953; 78 RPM
Piano
No dialect discerned

Also released with *Aubrey Pankey Singt
Negro-Spirituals* (Eterna 7 30 005; 1959; LP)
and *Negro Spirituals* (Eterna 830010; 1983;
LP)

586

Deep River
Flynn, William
Paris, Virginia (Contralto)
Spirituals
Spotlight Classic SC 1008; 1957; LP
Orchestra

Also released with *Virginia Paris in
Australia* (Lyric Records CD 178; [2005]; CD)

587

Deep River
Burleigh, Harry T.
Pierson, Edward (Bass-baritone)
Edward Pierson Sings Hymns and Spirituals
Kemco 98-44; [19--]; LP

588

Deep River
Burleigh, Harry T.
Pinza, Ezio (Bass)
Deep River/Thunderin', Wonderin'
Columbia Masterworks 17383-D; 1945;
    10-in LP
Piano

Also released with *An Enchanted Evening* (Sanctuary Records AJA 5618; 2006; CD)

589

Deep River
Composer not identified
Pleas III, Henry H. (Tenor)
Deep River: A Spiritual Journey
Rowe House Productions; 1999; CD

590

Deep River
de Paur, Leonard
Price, Leontyne (Soprano)
*Swing Low, Sweet Chariot: Fourteen
    Spirituals*
RCA Victor LSC 2600; 1962; LP
Chorus, orchestra
Heavy dialect

Also released with *The Essential Leontyne Price: Spirituals, Hymns & Sacred Songs* (BMG Classics 09026-68157-2; 1996; CD); *The Essential Leontyne Price* ((BMG Classics 09026-68153-2; 1996; CD); *Complete Collection of Songs and Spiritual Albums* (RCA Red Seal 88697940502; 2011; CD); *Leontyne Price Sings Spirituals* ((RCA Red Seal 88691928242; 2012; CD); *Singers of the Century: Leontyne Price: Spiritual and Religious Songs* (Jube Classic; 2016; Streaming audio)

591

Deep River
Composer not identified
Price, Leontyne (Soprano)
Golden Voices Sing Golden Favorites
Reader's Digest WCD4-5781-WCD4-5784;
    1990; CD

592

Deep River
Composer not identified
Putkonen, Marko (Bass)
Deep River: Negro Spirituals
Lilium LILP 101; 1991; LP

593

Deep River
Burleigh, Harry T.
Quilico, Gino (Baritone)
Magnificat
Société Métropolitaine du Disque/Espace 21
    SMD [2001]; 2013; CD
Organ

594

Deep River
Johnson, Hall
Ragin, Derek Lee (Countertenor)
Ev'ry Time I Feel the Spirit: Spirituals
Channel Classics CCS 2991; 1991; CD
Piano
Moderate dialect

595

Deep River
Giesen, Hubert
Ray, William (Baritone)

Negro Spirituals
Intercord; [19--]; LP
Piano
    Also released with *Sings Arias, Duets, Musical Selections and Negro Spirituals* Intercord; [19--]; CD

596

Deep River
Burleigh, Harry T.
Ripley, Gladys (Contralto)
Deep River/Swing Low Sweet Chariot
HMV B.9689; [1948]; 78 RPM
Piano

597

Deep River
Brown, Lawrence
Robeson, Paul (Bass-baritone)
Classic Gospel Songs
Emerald/K-Tel; 2013; Streaming audio
Piano

598

Deep River
Burleigh, Harry T.
Robeson, Paul (Bass-baritone)
Negro Spirituals (And More)
Discmedi DM-4674-02; 2009; CD

599

Deep River
Burleigh, Harry T.
Robeson, Paul (Bass-baritone)
Spirituals: Original Recordings 1925–1936
Naxos Gospel Legends 8.120638; 2003; CD
Piano

600

Deep River
Burleigh, Harry T.
Robeson, Paul (Bass-baritone)
When I Have Sung My Songs: The American Art Song, 1900–1940
New World NW 247; 1976; LP
Piano

601

Deep River
Burleigh, Harry T.

Robeson, Paul (Bass-baritone)
The Odyssey of Paul Robeson
Omega Classics OCD 3007; 1992; CD
Piano

602

Deep River
Burleigh, Harry T.
Robeson, Paul (Bass-baritone)
Songs of My People
RCA Red Seal LM-3292; 1972; LP
Piano

603

Deep River
Burleigh, Harry T.
Robeson, Paul (Bass-baritone)
*A Lonesome Road: Paul Robeson Sings
    Spirituals and Songs*
ASV Living Era CD AJA 5027; 1984; CD
Piano
Moderate dialect

604

Deep River
Burleigh, Harry T.
Robeson, Paul (Bass-baritone)
*Sacred Roots of the Blues (When the Sun
    Goes Down Series)*
Bluebird 82876 60084 2; 2004; CD
Piano
Light dialect

605

Deep River
Burleigh, Harry T.; Irving
Robeson, Paul (Bass-baritone)
Golden Voice of Paul Robeson
EMI Music PLAY-1020; 1983; CD

606

Deep River
Burleigh, Harry T.
Robeson, Paul (Bass-baritone)
Paul Robeson: Great Voices of the Century, v. 2
Memoir Classics CDMOIR 426; 1994; CD

607

Deep River
Burleigh, Harry T.

Robeson, Paul (Bass-baritone)
*The Golden Voice of Paul Robeson: Great
    Voices of the 20th Century*
Acrobat Music AC-5160-2; 2008; CD

608

Deep River
Burleigh, Harry T.
Robeson, Paul (Bass-baritone)
Legends of the 20th Century: Paul Robeson
EMI Records 7243 520140; 1999; CD
Piano

609

Deep River
Burleigh, Harry T.
Robeson, Paul (Bass-baritone)
*Deep River/I'm Goin to Tell God All o My
    Troubles*
Victor 20793; 1927; 78 RPM
Piano

610

Deep River
Burleigh, Harry T.
Robeson, Paul (Bass-baritone)
Paul Robeson Collection
Hallmark Recordings 390692; 1998; CD

611

Deep River
Burleigh, Harry T.
Robeson, Paul (Bass-baritone)
The Great Paul Robeson
Pegasus PGN CD 811; 2000; CD

612

Deep River
Burleigh, Harry T.
Robeson, Paul (Bass-baritone)
Golden Treasury of Immortal Singers
Conifer TQ 130; 1987; CD

613

Deep River
Burleigh, Harry T.; Irving (arr.)
Robeson, Paul (Bass-baritone)
The Best of Paul Robeson
EMI NTS 181; 1979; LP

614

Deep River
Burleigh, Harry T.
Robeson, Paul (Bass-baritone)
Paul Robeson with Chorus, orchestra
Fontana BIG.417-1Y; 1958; LP

615

Deep River
Burleigh, Harry T.
Robeson, Paul (Bass-baritone)
Deep River/I'm Goin' to Tell God All o' My Troubles
His Master's Voice B 2619; 1928; 78 RPM
Piano
No dialect discerned

616

Deep River
Irving, Ernest
Robeson, Paul (Bass-baritone)
The Complete EMI Sessions (1928–1939)
EMI Classics 50999 2 15586 2 7; 2008; CD
Orchestra
No dialect discerned

617

Deep River
[Burleigh, Harry T.]
Robeson, Paul (Bass-baritone)
Ballad for Americans and Great Songs of Faith, Love and Patriotism
Vanguard VCD-117/18; 1989; CD
Piano

618

Deep River
[Burleigh, Harry T.]
Robeson, Paul (Bass-baritone)
The Best of Paul Robeson
Delta Music Group CD6252; 2008; CD

619

Deep River
[Burleigh, Harry T.]
Robeson, Paul (Bass-baritone)
The Very Best of Paul Robeson
Future Noise Music FVDD033; 2009; CD
Piano

620

Deep River
[Burleigh, Harry T.]
Robeson, Paul (Bass-baritone)
Scandalize My Name
Classics Record Library 30-5647; 1976; LP
Piano
Light dialect

621

Deep River
[Burleigh, Harry T.]
Robeson, Paul (Bass-baritone)
The Essential Paul Robeson
ASV CD AJS 244; 2000; CD

622

Deep River
Robeson, Paul (Bass-baritone)
Head Like a Rock/Lindy Lou/Deep River/I'm Goin' to Tell God All My Troubles
V Disc 51; 1943; 78 RPM

623

Deep River
[Burleigh, Harry T.]
Robeson, Paul (Bass-baritone)
Deep River
Great Voices of the Century GVC 2004; 1999; CD
Orchestra

624

Deep River
[Burleigh, Harry T.]
Robeson, Paul (Bass-baritone)
Collection
RGS Music 1404-2; 2007; CD

625

Deep River
[Burleigh, Harry T.]
Robeson, Paul (Bass-baritone)
Robeson
Vanguard VSD-2015; 1958?; LP
Chorus, orchestra

626

Deep River
[Burleigh, Harry T.]

Robeson, Paul (Bass-baritone)
Ol' Man River: His 56 Finest 1925–1945
Retrospective RTS 4116; 2008; CD

627
Deep River
[Burleigh, Harry T.]
Robeson, Paul (Bass-baritone)
Ol' Man River: The Very Best of Paul Robeson
Memory Lane; 2012; CD

628
Deep River
[Burleigh, Harry T.]
Robeson, Paul (Bass-baritone)
The Originals: "Spirituals"
Yoyo USA; 2006; Streaming audio

629
Deep River
[Burleigh, Harry T.]
Robeson, Paul (Bass-baritone)
Voice of the People
Regis RRC 1056; 2011; CD
Orchestra
No dialect discerned

630
Deep River
[Burleigh, Harry T.]
Robeson, Paul (Bass-baritone)
Ol' Man River: The Best of Paul Robeson
Emerald Echoes; 2015; Streaming audio
Piano

631
Deep River
[Burleigh, Harry T.]
Robeson, Paul (Bass-baritone)
The Historic Paul Robeson
Murray Hill Records 959062; [19--]; LP
Piano

632
Deep River
[Burleigh, Harry T.]
Robeson, Paul (Bass-baritone)
Five Classic Albums Plus Bonus Tracks
Real Gone Music RGMCD287; 2017; CD

Piano
Light dialect

633
Deep River
[Burleigh, Harry T.]
Robeson, Paul (Bass-baritone)
Ol' Man River: The Ultimate Collection
Roslin Records; 2011; Streaming audio
Piano
Heavy dialect

634
Deep River
[Burleigh, Harry T.]
Robeson, Paul (Bass-baritone)
The Essential Collection
Primo PRMCD6233; 2018; CD

635
Deep River
[Burleigh, Harry T.]
Robeson, Paul (Bass-baritone)
Paul Robeson
Forever Gold FG019; 2001; CD
Piano

636
Deep River
[Burleigh, Harry T.]
Robeson, Paul (Bass-baritone)
Best Loved Songs
His Master's Voice 7EGO 8486; 1959; 45
    RPM
Chorus

637
Deep River
[Burleigh, Harry T.]
Robeson, Paul (Bass-baritone)
Man They Couldn't Silence
Rev-Ola CR REV 208; 2007; CD

638
Deep River
[Burleigh, Harry T.]
Robeson, Paul (Bass-baritone)
The Great Paul Robeson
Velvet CDVELV 101; 2001; CD

Piano
Moderate dialect

639
Deep River
[Burleigh, Harry T.]
Robeson, Paul (Bass-baritone)
The Paul Robeson Story
Columbia 5C 052-04830; [19--]; LP

640
Deep River
[Burleigh, Harry T.]
Robeson, Paul (Bass-baritone)
The Essential Paul Robeson
Vanguard VSD 57/58; 1974; LP
Piano
Light dialect

641
Deep River
[Burleigh, Harry T.]
Robeson, Paul (Bass-baritone)
Good News: Vintage Negro Spirituals
Living Era AJA 5622; 2006; CD
Piano
Light dialect

642
Deep River
[Burleigh, Harry T.]
Robeson, Paul (Bass-baritone)
Golden Voices: Great Singers of the 20th Century
Nostalgia AZCD213; 2011; CD

643
Deep River
[Burleigh, Harry T.]
Robeson, Paul (Bass-baritone)
Recital
Supraphon SUA 10062; 1961; LP
Piano

644
Deep River
[Burleigh, Harry T.]
Robeson, Paul (Bass-baritone)

Paul Robeson
Flapper; 1993; CD

645
Deep River
[Burleigh, Harry T.]
Robeson, Paul (Bass-baritone)
Complete Recordings
Universal Digital Enterprises; 2018; Streaming audio

646
Deep River
[Burleigh, Harry T.]
Robeson, Paul (Bass-baritone)
Andere Amerika, Das
Eterna 8 10 021; 1966; LP
Piano

647
Deep River
Composer not identified
Saavedra, Waundell (Vocalist)
Stained Glass Windows: A Reflection of Sacred Arias, Hymns and Spirituals
CD Baby; 2016; CD
Piano

648
Deep River
Burleigh, Harry T.
Salters, Stephen (Baritone)
Spirit: Are You There, You Are There
HarmonizedDisharmony 0001; 2015; CD

649
Deep River
Burleigh, Harry T.
Seagle, Oscar (Baritone)
Deep River
Columbia A2165; 1916; 78 RPM
Orchestra
No dialect discerned

650
Deep River [from *Motherless Child Songs*]
Dunner, Leslie B.
Sebron, Carolyn (Mezzo-soprano)
Open Boundaries

Innova Recordings MN 108; 1989; CD
Piano, clarinet
No dialect discerned

651

Deep River
[Burleigh, Harry T.]
Spencer, Kenneth (Bass-baritone)
American Spirituals
Sonora MS-478; [1945]; 78 RPM
Piano
Moderate dialect

Also released with *Spirituals Sung by Kenneth Spencer* (E.M.I. Records Ltd. SEG 7813; [19--]; 45 RPM); *Kenneth Spencer in Memoriam* (Odeon O 83 639; 1968; LP); *Kenneth Spencer* (Laserlight Digital 16 128; 1995; CD); *Alte Lied von Alabama, Das* (Vollstaedt CDRV2337; 2010; CD); *Heimweh Nach Virginia* (Music Tales 2087269; 2015; CD)

652

Deep River
Dumont, C.
Spencer, Kenneth (Bass-baritone)
Deep River/Nobody Knows the Trouble I've Seen
Elite Special 45-A-441; [1963]; 45 RPM
Orchestra

653

Deep River
Composer not identified
St. Hill, Krister (Baritone)
Svenska Folkvisor/Negro Spirituals
Polar POLS 398; 1985; LP

654

Deep River
Baker, Steven
Stewart, Noah (Tenor)
Noah
Verve B0017012-02; 2012; CD
Instrumental ensemble
Moderate dialect

655

Deep River
Burleigh, Harry T.; Hulsberg, Alfred

Stoffel, David (Bass-baritone)
Songs with a Touch of Bass
ACA CM [2003]; 1995; CD
Piano, double bass
Light dialect

656

Deep River
Blanchard, Terence
Sykes, Jubilant (Baritone)
Jubilant Sykes
Sony Classical SK 63294; 1998; CD
Instrumental ensemble

657

Deep River
Burleigh, Harry T.
Taylor, Darryl (Countertenor)
How Sweet the Sound: A Charm of Spirituals
Albany TROY1244; 2011; CD
Piano

658

Deep River
Browne, George
Taylor, Geoffrey (Baritone)
Negro Spirituals
World Record Club MW-2005; [196-]; LP
Orchestra
Light dialect

Also released with *Negro Spirituals* (P&R; 2011; Streaming audio) and *Negro Spirituals* (Marathon Media International; 2013; Streaming audio)

659

Deep River
Kerr, Thomas H., Jr.
Taylor, Richard (Baritone)
The New Negro Spiritual
W. C. Patterson; 2002; Score w/CD
Piano
Moderate dialect

660

Deep River
Burleigh, Harry T.
Te Wiata, Inia (Bass)

A Popular Recital
Kiwi Pacific CD SLC-248; 1997; CD

    Also released with *Simple Gifts* (Deutsche Grammophon B0004772-02; 2005; CD); *A Song in My Heart* (Deutsche Grammophon 477 6686; 2007; CD) and *Homeward Bound* (Deutsche Grammophon B0018931-02; 2013; CD)

661

Deep River
Burleigh, Harry T.
Thomas, Indra (Soprano)
Great Day: Indra Thomas Sings Spirituals
Delos DE 3427; 2012; CD
Piano
No dialect discerned

662

Deep River
Composer not identified
Thompson, Derrick (Baritone)
Spirituals
Private Label; 2014; CD
Piano
No dialect discerned

663

Deep River
[Burleigh, Harry T.]
Tibbett, Lawrence (Baritone)
Lawrence Tibbett Sings
Hudson 224; 1960; LP
Piano

664

Deep River
[Burleigh, Harry T.]
Tibbett, Lawrence (Baritone)
The Best of Lawrence Tibbett
Pearl GEMM CD 9307; 1988; CD
Piano

665

Deep River
Burleigh, Harry T.
Traubel, Helen (Soprano)
Negro Spirituals: Helen Traubel in Popular Ballads

Columbia ML 4221; 1949; LP
Piano

    Also released with *Opera Stars on Radio, Vol. 1: Unpublished Broadcasts from the Fourties* (S.I.A.E. RY 11; 1995; CD)

666

Deep River
[Burleigh, Harry T.]
Turner, Claramae (Contralto)
My Heart at Thy Sweet Voice/Deep River
Silvertone Record Club S-11; 1950; 78 RPM
Orchestra
No dialect discerned

    Also released with *Lebendige Vergangenheit—Claramae Turner* (Preiser Records; 2008; CD)

667

Deep River
Composer not identified
Ventriglia, Franco (Baritone)
Franco Ventriglia Sings Negro Spirituals
Vedette Records VRMS 316; [19--]; LP
Piano, organ
Moderate dialect

    Also released with *Franco Ventriglia Sings Negro Spirituals* (Vedette Records; 2007; Streaming audio)

668

Deep River
Burleigh, Harry T.
Warfield, William (Bass-baritone)
Spirituals: 200 Years of African-American Spirituals
ProArte CDD 3443; 1993; CD
Piano
Moderate dialect

669

Deep River
Burleigh, Harry T.
Warfield, William (Bass-baritone)
Magnificent Voice of William Warfield
Music from the Past FBCD0353; [19--]; CD

670

Deep River
Composer not identified

Warfield, William (Bass-baritone)
Deep River
Columbia AAL 32; 1953; 10-in LP
Orchestra
Light dialect

671

Deep River
Composer not identified
Warfield, William (Bass-baritone)
God of Our Fathers
Capitol Records P 8578; 196?; LP
Organ

672

Deep River
Composer not identified
Warfield, William (Bass-baritone)
God of Our Fathers
Capitol P 8578; [196-]; LP
Organ

673

Deep River
Burleigh, Harry T.
West, Lucretia (Mezzo-soprano)
Negro Spirituals III
Club français du disque 176; 1959; LP
Piano
Moderate dialect
     Also released with *Negro Spirituals mit Lukretia West* (Opera 3408; [195-]; LP)

674

Deep River
Marshall, Melanie
White, Willard (Bass-baritone)
Willard White Sings: Copland; American Spirituals; Folk-Songs
Chandos Records CHAN 8960; 1991; CD
Piano
Moderate dialect
     Also released with *Willard White in Concert* (Regis RRC 1179; 2004; CD)

675

Deep River
Composer not identified
Williams, Wayne (Tenor)

Music from My Life
Movideo Productions 02-1993; 1993; CD
Piano

676

Deep River
Burleigh, Harry T.
Winter, Georg (Vocalist)
Eine Kleine Hausmusik
Teldec 66.22670; 1981; LP
Piano

677

Deep River
[Burleigh, Harry T.]
Winters, Lawrence (Bass-baritone)
Lawrence Winters: Recital
Hamburger Archiv fur Gesangskunst 10397; 2007; CD
Chorus, orchestra
Light dialect
     Also released with *Singer Portrait: Lawrence Winters* (Apple Music; 2012; Streaming audio)

678

Deep River
Burleigh, Harry T.
Woodley, Arthur (Bass)
From the Southland: Songs, Piano Sketches and Spirituals of Harry T. Burleigh
Premier Recordings PRCD 1041; 1995; CD
Piano
No dialect discerned

679

Deep River
Hogan, Moses
Yovanovich, Amy (Mezzo-soprano)
Great Day!
Prince Productions 9808P; 2007; CD
Piano
No dialect discerned

680

Deep River
Burleigh, Harry T.
Zeppenfeld, Georg (Bass)

Dvořák und Seine Zeit
Orfeo International Music C 656 052 I; 2005;
  CD

681

Deep River
Wertsch, Nancy
Zilinyi, Cheryl (Mezzo-soprano)
*Ain't Got Time to Die: Songs of the American
  Spirit*
First Presbyterian Church in the City of
  New York FPC 1002; 1997; CD
Chorus

· · · · · · ·

Did You Hear
When Jesus Rose

682

Did You Hear When Jesus Rose? [from *The
  Life of Christ*]
Hayes, Roland
Caesar, Jackson (Tenor)
*Spirituals: Celebrating the Music, Life,
  Legacy of Roland Hayes*
CD Baby 7048606059; 2021; CD
Piano, percussion
Light dialect

683

Did You Hear When Jesus Rose? [from *The
  Life of Christ*]
Hayes, Roland
Caesar, Jackson (Tenor)
*Spirituals: Celebrating the Music, Life,
  Legacy of Roland Hayes*
CD Baby 7048606059; 2021; CD
Piano
Light dialect

684

Did You Hear When Jesus Rose? [from *The
  Life of Christ*]
Hayes, Roland
Hayes, Roland (Tenor)
*Roland Hayes Sings the Life of Christ: As Told
  Through Aframerican Folksong*
Vanguard VRS-462; 1954; LP
Piano

Also released with *Aframerican Folk-
song: Telling the Story of the Life of Christ*
(Top Rank 39 620; [1961]; LP); *Roland Hayes
Sings the Life of Christ: As Told Through
Aframerican Folksong* (Vanguard SRV 352;
1976; LP); *Favorite Spirituals* (Vanguard
Classics OVC 6022; 1995; CD); *Charlton Hes-
ton Reads from The Life and Passion of Jesus
Christ* (Vanguard Classics ATM-CD-1259;
2003; CD); *Big Psalms, Hymns and Spirituals
Box* (eOne Music/Vanguard Classics; 2015;
Streaming audio)

685

Did You Hear When Jesus Rose? [from *The
  Life of Christ*]
Hayes, Roland
Holland, Charles (Tenor)
My Lord What a Mornin'
Musical Heritage Society MHS 912250X;
  1982; LP
Piano
Light dialect

Also released with *My Lord What a
Mornin'* (Musical Heritage Society MHS
512250K; 1988; CD)

686

Sister Did You Hear When Jesus Rose? [from
  The Life of Christ]
Simpson, Elmur
Matthews, Benjamin (Baritone)
Bon Voyage Recital @ McCormick Place
S.P.S. SS-8993-018; 1966; LP
Piano

687

Did You Hear When Jesus Rose [from *The
  Life of Christ*]
Hayes, Roland
Moses, Oral (Bass-baritone)
Songs of America
Albany Records TROY1011; 2008; CD
Piano
Moderate dialect

688

Did You Hear When Jesus Rose? [from *The
  Life of Christ*]

Hayes, Roland
Oby, Jason (Tenor)
The Life of Christ: Collected Spirituals
Private Label TSU4749; [200-]; CD
Piano
Light dialect

689

Did You Hear When Jesus Rose? [from *The Life of Christ*]
Composer not identified
Pleas III, Henry H. (Tenor)
Deep River: A Spiritual Journey
Rowe House Productions; 1999; CD

690

Did You Hear When Jesus Rose? [from *The Life of Christ*]
Hayes, Roland
Shirley, George (Tenor)
George Shirley at 80: My Time Has Come!
Videmus Records; 2014; CD
Piano

691

Did You Hear When Jesus Rose [from *The Life of Christ*]
Hayes, Roland
Sims, Robert (Baritone)
Robert Sims Sings the Spirituals of Roland Hayes
Canti Classics 2014-01; 2015; CD
Piano
Heavy dialect

692

Children Did You Hear When Jesus Rose? [from *The Life of Christ*]
Hayes, Roland
Sims, Robert (Baritone)
In the Spirit: Spirituals and American Songs with Orchestra and Chorus
Canti Classics; 2009; CD
Orchestra
Heavy dialect

693

Did You Hear When Jesus Rose? [from *The Life of Christ*]

Hayes, Roland
Warfield, William (Bass-baritone)
Spirituals: 200 Years of African-American Spirituals
ProArte CDD 3443; 1993; CD
Piano
Heavy dialect

694

Did You Hear When Jesus Rose [from *The Life of Christ*]
Hayes, Roland; Hairston, Jacqueline
Warfield, William (Bass-baritone); Matthews, Benjamin Sims, Robert (Baritone)
Three Generations Live
Canti Records; 2000; CD
Orchestra
Heavy dialect

695

Did You Hear When Jesus Rose? [from *The Life of Christ*]
Hayes, Roland
Williams, Willie (Vocalist)
My Tribute
Discovery V42227; 1974; LP
Piano

· · · · · · ·

Didn't It Rain

696

Didn't It Rain?
Burleigh, Harry T.
Alexander, Roberta (Soprano)
Songs My Mother Taught Me
Etcetera KTC 1208; 1999; CD
Piano
Moderate dialect

697

Oh, Didn't It Rain
Burleigh, Harry T.
Anderson, Marian (Contralto)
He's Got the Whole World in His Hands: Spirituals
RCA Victor 09026-61960-2; 1994; CD
Piano
Heavy dialect

698

Oh, Didn't It Rain
Burleigh, Harry T.
Anderson, Marian (Contralto)
*Marian Anderson: Beyond the Music; Her
    Complete RCA Victor Recordings*
Sony Classical 19439836492; 2021; CD
Piano
Heavy dialect

699

Oh, Didn't It Rain
[Burleigh, Harry T.]
Anderson, Marian (Contralto)
The Rich Voice of Marian Anderson
Editions Audiovisuel Beulah; 2019;
    Streaming audio
Piano

700

Oh, Didn't It Rain
Burleigh, Harry T.
Arroyo, Martina (Soprano)
Spirituals
Centaur CRC 2060; 1991; CD
Piano
Heavy dialect

701

Didn't It Rain
Bonds, Margaret
Brown, Anthony (Baritone)
Toil and Triumph
Spirituals Project; 2002; CD
Piano
Light dialect

702

Oh, Didn't It Rain
Burleigh, Harry T.
Bruce, Boyce (Baritone)
Run, Mary, Run/Oh, Didn't It Rain
Ultraphone AP 1567; [193-]; 78 RPM
Piano
Heavy dialect

703

Oh, Didn't It Rain
Composer not identified

Carey, Thomas (Baritone)
Go Down Moses
Da Camera Song SM 95028; 1970; LP
Piano

704

Oh, Didn't It Rain
Burleigh, Harry T.
Carlsen, Svein (Bass)
Negro Spirituals
EuroMaster AS ECD19005; 1996; CD
Piano

705

Oh! Didn't It Rain
Burleigh, Harry T.
Clark, Clarence Carroll (Baritone)
By an' By/Oh! Didn't It Rain
Paramount 12037; 1924; 78 RPM
Piano

706

Oh, Didn't It Rain
Burleigh, Harry T.
Cole, Steven (Tenor)
*From the Southland: Songs, Piano Sketches
    and Spirituals of Harry T. Burleigh*
Premier Recordings PRCD 1041; 1995; CD
Piano
No dialect discerned

707

Oh, Didn't It Rain
[Burleigh, Harry T.]
Cole, Vinson (Tenor)
Strauss, Duparc, Puccini, Nin
Connoisseur Society CD4184; 1991; CD
Piano
Heavy dialect

708

Oh, Didn't It Rain
Composer not identified
Elzy, Ruby (Soprano)
Ruby Elzy in Song: Rare Recordings
Cambria Records CD-1154; 2006; CD
Piano
Heavy dialect

Also released with *The 78 RPM Collection* (Master Classics Records; 2010; CD)

709

Oh, Didn't It Rain
Composer not identified
Hall, Nell (Soprano)
Nell Hall in a Recital of Arias, Ballads,
    Spirituals, Folk Songs
Colonial COL LP-211; [19--]; LP
Piano

Also released with *Spirituals* (Schubert Records SCH-102; [1988]; LP)

710

Oh, Didn't It Rain
[Burleigh, Harry T.]
Holmes, Eugene (Baritone)
Eugene Holmes Sings Spirituals
Avant Garde AV-115; [1968]; LP
Piano
Moderate dialect

711

Oh, Didn't It Rain
Meyer, Fredrich
London, George (Bass-baritone)
Spirituals
Deutsche Grammophon 00289 477 6193;
    2006; CD
Orchestra
Heavy dialect

712

Didn't It Rain
Burleigh, Harry T.
Maynor, Kevin (Bass)
The Spiritual: An Underground Railroad
Southeastern Virginia Arts Assoc.; [2000];
    CD
Piano

713

Didn't It Rain
Burleigh, Harry T.
Oglesby, Isador (Tenor)
Isador Sings Negro Spirituals
Oglesby Recordings Album 3; 1983; LP
Piano

714

Oh, Didn't It Rain
Burleigh, Harry T.
Parks, Karen (Soprano)
Nobody Knows
Ottimavoce 52736; 2007; CD
Piano
Light dialect

715

Didn't It Rain?
Burleigh, Harry T.
Pierson, Edward (Bass-baritone)
Edward Pierson Sings Hymns and Spirituals
Kemco 98-44; [19--]; LP

716

Oh, Didn't It Rain
Composer not identified
Reese, Ruth (Contralto)
Motherless Child
OPS 1006/79; 1979; LP

717

Oh, Didn't It Rain
Brown, Lawrence
Robeson, Paul (Bass-baritone)
The Complete EMI Sessions (1928–1939)
EMI Classics 50999 2 15586 2 7; 2008; CD
Piano
Heavy dialect

718

Oh! Didn't It Rain
Burleigh, Harry T.
Robeson, Paul (Bass-baritone)
A Lonesome Road: Paul Robeson Sings
    Spirituals and Songs
ASV Living Era CD AJA 5027; 1984; CD
Piano
Heavy dialect

719

Oh! Didn't It Rain
Burleigh, Harry T.
Robeson, Paul (Bass-baritone)
Golden Treasury of Immortal Singers
Conifer TQ 130; 1987; CD

720

Oh! Didn't It Rain
Burleigh, Harry T.
Robeson, Paul (Bass-baritone)
*Git on Board, Lil' Chillun; Dere's No Hidin'
Place/Oh! Rock Me, Julie; Oh! Didn't It
Rain*
His Master's Voice B 3033; 1929; 78 RPM
Piano
Heavy dialect

721

Didn't It Rain
Bonds, Margaret
Salters, Stephen (Baritone)
Stephen Salters/Shiela Kibbe
Musica Numeris CYP 9602; 2005; CD

722

Didn't It Rain
Burleigh, Harry T.
Spencer, Kenneth (Bass-baritone)
Volkslieder & Spirituals
Discoton 75546; [197-]; LP
Piano
Heavy dialect

723

Didn't It Rain?
Burleigh, Harry T.
Te Wiata, Inia (Bass)
A Popular Recital
Kiwi Pacific CD SLC-248; 1997; CD
Piano

724

Didn't It Rain
Kerr, Thomas H., Jr.
Tillman, Alice (Soprano)
The New Negro Spiritual
W. C. Patterson; 2002; Score w/CD
Piano
Heavy dialect

725

Didn't It Rain!
Bonds, Margaret
Tucker, Eric Hoy (Bass-baritone)
Southern Salute: Southern Songs & Spirituals

White Pine Music WPM218; 2012; CD
Piano
Light dialect

726

Didn't It Rain?
Composer not identified
Verdejo, Awilda (Soprano)
Awilda Verdejo Sings Spirituals
Angeluz Performances; 1999; CD
Piano

727

Didn't It Rain
Bonds, Margaret
Warfield, William (Bass-baritone)
*Spirituals: 200 Years of African-American
Spirituals*
ProArte CDD 3443; 1993; CD
Piano
Heavy dialect

728

Oh Didn't It Rain
Composer not identified
Williams, Wayne (Tenor)
Music from My Life
Movideo Productions 02-1993; 1993; CD
Piano

729

Oh, Didn't It Rain
Composer not identified
Wright, John Wesley (Tenor)
*Wade in the Water: Songs of the River, the
Lake, and the Sea*
Donald L. Robinson & Associates DLR-001;
2004; CD
Piano

. . . .

Didn't My Lord Deliver Daniel

[Daniel 6:1-24; Jonah 1:15-2:10; Ezekiel
32:7; Joel 2:31; Matthew 24:29; Acts 2:20; Revelation 6:12]

"Didn't my Lord deliver Daniel, Deliver
Daniel, deliver Daniel, And why not every

man? He delivered Daniel from the lion's den, Jonah from the belly of the whale...."

[Available in CCSo, EM34, FHFN, HCTN, HLBS, HT25, HTBS, HTC2, JB3a, JJAN, JJBA, JSSp, LBNF, PLSY, RHMF, RW15, RWSC, SBFD, SOTS, WGST]

730

Didn't My Lord Deliver Daniel?
Hayes, Roland
Caesar, Jackson (Tenor)
Spirituals: Celebrating the Music, Life, Legacy of Roland Hayes
CD Baby 7048606059; 2021; CD
Piano, percussion
Light dialect

731

Didn't My Lord Deliver Daniel?
Hayes, Roland
Caesar, Jackson (Tenor)
Spirituals: Celebrating the Music, Life, Legacy of Roland Hayes
CD Baby 7048606059; 2021; CD
Piano
Light dialect

732

Didn't My Lord Deliver Daniel?
Composer not identified
Carey, Thomas (Baritone)
Sechs Amerikanische Volkslieder/Sechs Negro Spirituals
Colosseum SM 3003; 1970; LP
Orchestra

733

Daniel
Composer not identified
Charles, Lee (Tenor)
Swing Low Sweet Chariot: And Other Spirituals
Riverside RLP 12-651; 1957; LP
Piano, guitar

734

Didn't My Lord Deliver Daniel?
Brown, Lawrence
Duncan, Todd (Baritone)

Negro Spirituals
Allegro ALG3022; [1952]; LP
Piano

Also released with *African American Spirituals* ([Apple Music]; 2008; Streaming audio)

735

Didn't My Lord Deliver Daniel?
Boatner, Edward
Forest, Michael (Tenor)
The Spirit Sings: American Spirituals
Shenandoah Conservatory SU003; [199-]; CD

736

Didn't My Lord Deliver Daniel?
Hayes, Roland
Hayes, Roland (Tenor)
Roland Hayes: My Songs
Vanguard VRS-494; 1956; LP
Piano

Also released with *Favorite Spirituals* (Vanguard Classics OVC 6022; 1995; CD) and *Big Psalms, Hymns and Spirituals Box* (eOne Music/Vanguard Classics; 2015; Streaming audio)

737

Didn't My Lord Deliver Daniel [from *Conversion* (Sermon)]
Cornelius, II, John
Heaston, Nicole (Soprano)
Marilyn Horne Foundation Presents on Wings of Song. Recital No. 9
Marilyn Horne Foundation DCD 5028; 2001; CD
Piano

738

Didn't My Lord Deliver Daniel
Hogan, Moses
Hendricks, Barbara (Soprano)
Give Me Jesus
EMI Classics 7243 5 56788 2 9; 1998; CD
Chorus
Light dialect

739

Didn't Ma Lord Deliver Daniel
Still, William Grant; Taylor, Vivian
Honeysucker, Robert (Baritone)
More Still: Music by William Grant Still
Cambria Master Recordings CD-1112; 1999;
    CD
Piano
Moderate dialect

740

Didn't My Lord Deliver Daniel
Burleigh, Harry T.
Jefferson, Othello (Tenor)
*Good News: African American Spirituals and
    Art Songs*
Cambria Records CD 1270; 2021; CD
Piano
No dialect discerned

741

Didn't My Lord Deliver Daniel?
Boatner, Edward
Jones, Arthur (Tenor)
Wade in the Water
Orbis Books; 1993; Book w/cass
Piano
Heavy dialect

742

Didn't My Lord Deliver Daniel
[Burleigh, Harry T.]
Jones, Fanni (Mezzo-soprano)
Negro Spirituals
Evasion Disques LP613; 1974; LP

    Also released with *Negro Spirituals en
Concert* (Suisa; 1987; LP)

743

Didn't My Lord Deliver Daniel?
Burleigh, Harry T.
Kennedy, Charles (Vocalist)
Heart & Soul: Songs of Harry T. Burleigh
Publisher not known; 1994; Cassette

744

Didn't My Lord Deliver Daniel?
Walters, Richard (ed.)
Kruse, Tanya (Soprano)

*15 Easy Spiritual Arrangements for the
    Progressing Singer*
Hal Leonard HL00000391 (high) ;
    HL00000392 (low); 2005; Score w/CD
Piano
Light dialect

745

Didn't My Lord Deliver Daniel
Burleigh, Harry T.; Lynch, Lester & Noam
    Fairgold
Lynch, Lester (Baritone)
On My Journey Now: Spirituals & Hymns
Pentatone Music PTC 5186 57'; 2017; CD
Chorus, piano, organ

746

Didn't My Lord Deliver Daniel?
Burleigh, Harry T.
Moses, Oral (Bass-baritone)
*Deep River: Songs and Spirituals of Harry T.
    Burleigh*
Northeastern NR 252-CD; 1995; CD
Piano

    Also released with *Sankofa: A Spiritual
Reflection* (Albany Records TROY1802; 2019;
CD)

747

Didn't My Lord Deliver Daniel
Brown, Lawrence
Pankey, Aubrey (Baritone)
*Deep River/Out in the Rain/Didn't My Lord
    Deliver Daniel*
Topic TRC 74; 1953; 78 RPM

748

Didn't My Lord Deliver Daniel
Brown, Lawrence
Patton. John (Tenor)
Black Spirituals and Art Songs
Narthex Recording 827N-4581; 1970; LP
Piano
Moderate dialect

749

Didn't My Lord Deliver Daniel?
Brown, Lawrence
Peterson, Elwood (Baritone)

Negro Spirituals
Boîte à Musique LD 073; 1961; LP
Piano

750

Didn't My Lord Deliver Danieli
Composer not identified
Peterson, Elwood (Baritone)
Negro Spirituals
Vergara 55.1.004 C; [1963]; 45 RPM
Piano

751

Didn't My Lord Deliver Daniel?
Boatner, Edward
Pierson, Edward (Bass-baritone)
Edward Pierson Sings Hymns and Spirituals
Kemco 98-44; [19--]; LP

752

Didn't My Lord Deliver Daniel
Brown, Lawrence
Robeson, Paul (Bass-baritone)
The Collector's Paul Robeson
Monitor MCD-61580; 1989; CD
Piano
Light dialect

753

Didn't My Lord Deliver Daniel
Brown, Lawrence
Robeson, Paul (Bass-baritone)
Paul Robeson Live at Carnegie Hall
Vanguard VCD-72020; 1987; CD
Piano
Light dialect

754

Didn't My Lord Deliver Daniel
Brown, Lawrence
Robeson, Paul (Bass-baritone)
The Essential Paul Robeson
Vanguard VSD 57/58; 1974; LP
Piano
Light dialect

755

Didn't My Lord Deliver Daniel
Brown, Lawrence

Robeson, Paul (Bass-baritone)
Encore, Robeson!
Monitor MP 581; 1960; LP

756

Didn't My Lord Deliver Daniel?
[Brown, Lawrence]
Robeson, Paul (Bass-baritone)
The Complete EMI Sessions (1928–1939)
EMI Classics 50999 2 15586 2 7; 2008; CD
Piano
Light dialect

757

Didn't My Lord Deliver Daniel
[Brown, Lawrence]
Robeson, Paul (Bass-baritone)
Negro Spirituals (And More)
Discmedi DM-4674-02; 2009; CD

758

Didn't My Lord Deliver Daniel?
[Brown, Lawrence]
Robeson, Paul (Bass-baritone)
*On My Journey: Paul Robeson's Independent
    Recordings*
Smithsonian Folkways Recordings SFW CD
    40178; 2007; CD

759

Didn't My Lord Deliver Daniel?
[Brown, Lawrence]
Robeson, Paul (Bass-baritone)
Paul Robeson Singt Negro Spirituals
Musical Masterpiece Society MMS-2162;
    [19--]; LP
Piano

760

Didn't My Lord Deliver Daniel
[Brown, Lawrence]
Robeson, Paul (Bass-baritone)
Negro Spirituals
Concert Hall SVS 2611; [19--]; LP

761

Didn't My Lord Deliver Daniel
[Brown, Lawrence]
Robeson, Paul (Bass-baritone)

Scandalize My Name
Classics Record Library 30-5647; 1976; LP
Piano
Light dialect

762
Didn't My Lord Deliver Daniel?
[Brown, Lawrence]
Robeson, Paul (Bass-baritone)
Spirituals/Folksongs/Hymns
Pearl GEMM CD 9382; 1989; CD

763
Didn't My Lord Deliver Daniel
[Brown, Lawrence]
Robeson, Paul (Bass-baritone)
The Peace Arch Concerts
Folk Era Records FE1442CD; 1998; CD
Piano
Light dialect

764
Didn't My Lord Deliver Daniel
[Brown, Lawrence]
Robeson, Paul (Bass-baritone)
Gospels & Spirituals Gold Collection
Retro R2CD 40-26; 1995; CD
Piano
Light dialect

765
Didn't My Lord Deliver Daniel
[Brown, Lawrence]
Robeson, Paul (Bass-baritone)
Negro Spirituals
Chant du Monde LDX 74376; 1982; LP
Piano

766
Didn't My Lord Deliver Daniel?
[Brown, Lawrence]
Robeson, Paul (Bass-baritone)
American Balladeer
Collectables Records COL-CD-6502; 1990; CD
Piano
Light dialect

767
Didn't My Lord Deliver Daniel
[Brown, Lawrence]

Robeson, Paul (Bass-baritone)
The Very Best of Gospel
Disconforme CDX7720; 2007; CD

768
Didn't My Lord Deliver Daniel
[Brown, Lawrence]
Robeson, Paul (Bass-baritone)
*Oh, Happy Day! Gospels & Spirituals: The
   Ultimate CD*
Ultimate; 2010; CD

769
Didn't My Lord Deliver Daniel?
[Brown, Lawrence]
Robeson, Paul (Bass-baritone)
The Historic Paul Robeson
Murray Hill Records 959062; [19--]; LP
Piano

770
Didn't My Lord Deliver Daniel
[Brown, Lawrence]
Robeson, Paul (Bass-baritone)
Five Classic Albums Plus Bonus Tracks
Real Gone Music RGMCD287; 2017; CD

771
Didn't My Lord Deliver Daniel
[Brown, Lawrence]
Robeson, Paul (Bass-baritone)
The Essential History of Gospels & Spirituals
Deja Vu; 1990; CD

772
Didn't My Lord Deliver Daniel?
[Brown, Lawrence]
Robeson, Paul (Bass-baritone)
The Ultimate Collection
Burning Fire; 2009; Streaming audio
Piano
Moderate dialect

773
Didn't My Lord Deliver Daniel
[Brown, Lawrence]
Robeson, Paul (Bass-baritone)
Negro Spirituals par Paul Robeson
Chant du Monde LD-45 3008; 1958; 45 RPM

774

Didn't My Lord Deliver Daniel
[Brown, Lawrence]
Robeson, Paul (Bass-baritone)
Negro Spirituals and Blues
Concert Hall M-2340; [19--]; LP
Piano

775

Didn't My Lord Deliver Daniel
[Brown, Lawrence]
Robeson, Paul (Bass-baritone)
Récital Paul Robeson
Chant du Monde, Le LD-M-8132; 1955; LP
Piano

776

Didn't My Lord Deliver Daniel
[Brown, Lawrence]
Robeson, Paul (Bass-baritone)
Complete Recordings
Universal Digital Enterprises; 2018;
　　Streaming audio

777

Didn't My Lord Deliver Daniel
Robeson, Paul (Bass-baritone)
Songs of Struggle & Love
Alto ALC 1416; 2020; CD
Piano
Heavy dialect

778

Didn't My Lord Deliver Daniel
Composer not identified
Saavedra, Waundell (Vocalist)
*Stained Glass Windows: A Reflection of
　Sacred Arias, Hymns and Spirituals*
CD Baby; 2016; CD
Piano

779

Didn't My Lord Deliver Daniel?
Composer not identified
Stuart, Avon (Baritone)
Avon Stuart Recital
Edition Rhodos ERS 1218; 1975; LP
Piano

780

Didn't My Lord Deliver Daniel
Boatner, Edward
Thompson, Jeanette (Soprano)
Negro Spirituals
Pavane Records ADW 7267; 1992; CD
Piano
No dialect discerned

781

Didn't My Lord Deliver Daniel?
Bohmler, Craig
Thomson, Jeannette (Soprano)
Christmas Around the World
ARTS Music ARTS49008-2; 2000; CD
Orchestra
No dialect discerned

782

Didn't My Lord Deliver Daniel [from *Witness:
　Original Compositions in Spiritual Style*]
Baker, David
Toppin, Louise (Soprano)
Witness
Albany Records TROY868; 2006; CD
Orchestra
Moderate dialect

783

Didn't My Lord Deliver Daniel
Davis, Carl
White, Willard (Bass-baritone)
Willard White in Concert
Regis RRC 1179; 2004; CD
Orchestra

　　Also released with *The Paul Robeson
Legacy* (Linn AKD 190; 2015; CD)

784

Didn't My Lord Deliver Daniel
Composer not identified
Williams, Wayne (Tenor)
Music from My Life
Movideo Productions 02-1993; 1993; CD
Piano

785

Didn't My Lord Deliver Daniel
Burleigh, Harry T.

Winter, Georg (Vocalist)
Eine Kleine Hausmusik
Teldec 66.22670; 1981; LP
Piano

786

Didn't My Lord Deliver Daniel
Schweizer, Rolf
Wolf, Lars (Vocalist)
Die Schwarze Stimme Europas
Cantate 666000; 1971; LP
Chorus, organ, percussion

· · · · · · ·

Do Don't Touch-a My Garment

787

Do Don't Touch-a My Garment
Lloyd, Charles, Jr.
Hobson, Richard (Baritone)
The Spiritual Art Song Collection
Warner Bros. SVBM00004; 2000; Score w/
    CD
Piano

788

Do Don't Touch-a My Garment
Lloyd, Charles, Jr.
Moses, Oral (Bass-baritone)
*Come Down Angels and Trouble the Water:
    Negro Spirituals, an American National
    Treasure!*
Albany Records TROY 1489; 2014; CD
Piano
Heavy dialect

· · · · · · ·

Do Lawd Oh Do Lawd

789

Do Lawd, Oh Do Lawd
Patterson. Willis
Norman, Jessye (Soprano)
Negro Spirituals
Philips 9500 580; 1979; LP
Chorus
Moderate dialect

Also released with *The Jessye Norman
Collection* (Philips Classics 422 893-2; [1988];
CD); *Spirituals* (Philips 416 462-2; 1990; CD)
and *The Jessye Norman Collection: Sacred
Songs & Spirituals* (Philips B0004506-02;
2005; CD)

790

Do Lawd, Oh Do Lawd
Scharnberg, Kim
Robinson, Faye (Soprano)
Remembering Marian Anderson
d'Note Classics DND 1014; 1997; CD
Chorus, piano
Light dialect

· · · · · · ·

Done Found My Lost Sheep

791

Done Foun' My Los' Sheep
Johnson, John Rosamond
Anderson, Marian (Contralto)
Farewell Recital
RCA Victor LSC 2781; 1964; LP
Piano

Also released with *Marian Anderson:
Beyond the Music; Her Complete RCA Victor Recordings* (Sony Classical 19439836492;
2021; CD)

792

Done Foun' My Los' Sheep
Johnson, John Rosamond
Anderson, Marian (Contralto)
*He's Got the Whole World in His Hands:
    Spirituals*
RCA Victor 09026-6[1960]2; 1994; CD
Piano
Moderate dialect

Also released with *Marian Anderson:
Beyond the Music; Her Complete RCA Victor Recordings* (Sony Classical 19439836492;
2021; CD)

793

Done Foun' My Los' Sheep
Johnson, John Rosamond
Anderson, Marian (Contralto)

Let Freedom Ring!
JSP Records 683; 2016; CD
Piano
Light dialect

794
Done Foun' My Los' Sheep
[Johnson, John Rosamond]
Anderson, Marian (Contralto)
The Rich Voice of Marian Anderson
Editions Audiovisuel Beulah; 2019;
     Streaming audio
Piano

795
Done Found My Lost Sheep
Johnson, John Rosamond
Buggs Jacobs, Claritha (Mezzo-soprano)
The Lily of the Valley
American Spiritual Ensemble; [2003]; CD
Piano

796
Done Foun' My Los' Sheep
Johnson, John Rosamond
Mims, A. Grace Lee (Soprano)
Spirituals
H & GM Records HGM 8101; 1981; LP
Piano
Heavy dialect

797
Done Foun' My Los' Sheep
[Johnson, John Rosamond]
Ventriglia, Franco (Baritone)
Franco Ventriglia Sings Negro Spirituals
Vedette Records VRMS 316; [19--]; LP
Piano, organ
Heavy dialect

     Also released with *Franco Ventriglia Sings Negro Spirituals* (Vedette Records; 2007; Streaming audio)

· · · · · · ·

Done Made My Vow

798
Done Made My Vow to de Lord
Brown, Uzee, Jr.

Brown, Uzee, Jr. (Baritone)
Great Day!
Allgood; 2005; CD
Piano
Heavy dialect

799
Done Made My Vow
Clinton, Irving
Irving, Clinton (Bass-baritone)
Clinton Irving Sings Spirituals: A Tribute
Rogers; 2001; CD

800
Done Made My Vow
Boatner, Edward
Jones, Randye (Soprano)
Come Down Angels
Ahhjay Records AHHJ-0001; 2003; CD
Piano
Light dialect

801
Done Made My Vow
Alston, Lettie Beckon
Kirkland, Glenda (Soprano)
The New Negro Spiritual
W. C. Patterson; 2002; Score w/CD
Piano
Light dialect

802
Done Made My Vow
Boatner, Edward
Thompson, Jeanette (Soprano)
Negro Spirituals
Pavane Records ADW 7267; 1992; CD
Piano
No dialect discerned

· · · · · · ·

Don't Be Weary Traveler

803
Don't Be Weary Traveler
Burleigh, Harry T.
Brown, Anthony (Baritone)

Toil and Triumph
Spirituals Project; 2002; CD
Chorus, piano
Light dialect

804

Weary Traveler
Price, Florence
Heard, Richard (Tenor)
My Dream: Art Songs and Spirituals
Percentage Records/Sound of Art
    Recordings CD147597; 2012; CD
Piano
No dialect discerned

· · · · · · ·

Don't You Let
Nobody Turn You 'Round

805

Doncher Let Nobody Turn You Roun'
Johnson, Hall
Brown, William (Tenor)
The Hall Johnson Collection
Carl Fischer VF5 CD1–VF5 CD2; 2003; Score
    w/CD
Piano
Moderate dialect

806

Don't You Let Nobody Turn You 'Round
McLin, Lena
Rucker, Mark (Baritone)
*Mark Rucker Sings Lena McLin: Songs for
    Voice & Piano*
Kjos Music Press KCD8; 2002; CD
Piano
Light dialect

807

Don't Ya Let Nobody Turn You 'Round
McLin, Lena
Sims, Robert (Baritone)
*Soul of a Singer: Robert Sims Sings African-
    American Folk Songs*
Canti Classics 9801; 2013; CD
Piano
Heavy dialect

· · · · · · ·

Don't You Weep When
I Am Gone

808

Don't You Weep When I Am Gone
Composer not identified
Elzy, Ruby (Soprano)
Ruby Elzy in Song: Rare Recordings
Cambria Records CD-1154; 2006; CD
Piano

        Also released with *The 78 RPM Collec-
tion* (Master Classics Records; 2010; CD)

809

Don't You Weep When I Am Gone
Burleigh, Harry T.
Lynch, Lester (Baritone)
On My Journey Now: Spirituals & Hymns
Pentatone Music PTC 5186 57'; 2017; CD
Piano

810

Don't You Weep When I'm Gone
Composer not identified
Williams, Wayne (Tenor)
Music from My Life
Movideo Productions 02-1993; 1993; CD
Piano

· · · · · · ·

Down by the Riverside

811

Ain't Gonna Study War No More
Composer not identified
Davis, Frank (Bass-baritone)
16 Spirituals My Father Taught Me
DeWitt Records 601; 1960; LP

812

Study War No More
Hogan, Moses
Hendricks, Barbara (Soprano)
Give Me Jesus
EMI Classics 7243 5 56788 2 9; 1998; CD
Chorus
Heavy dialect

Also released with *Les 100 Plus Beaux Airs de Barbara Hendricks* (EMI Classics 50999 085683 2 8; 2012; CD)

813

Down by the Riverside
Composer not identified
Nobles, NaGuanda (Soprano)
Homage to the Journey
Selbon Records; 2014; Streaming audio
Instrumental ensemble
Heavy dialect

814

Down by the Riverside
Composer not identified
Porter, John (Bass)
No More Crying: Negro Spirituals
Pan Verlag OV-84; [1978]; LP

815

Down by the Riverside
White, Dolores
Rhodes, Yolanda (Soprano)
The Angels Bowed Down
Cambria Master Recordings CD-1237; 2019;
    CD

· · · · · · ·

Down to the River

816

Down to de Rivah
Composer not identified
Thomas, John Charles (Baritone)
Good News: Vintage Negro Spirituals
Living Era AJA 5622; 2006; CD
Piano
Moderate dialect

Also released with *Classic Gospel Songs* (Emerald/K-Tel; 2013; Streaming audio)

817

Down to de Rivah
MacGimsey, Robert
Thomas, John Charles (Baritone)
Down to de Rivah/Steal Away
Victor 1687; 1934; 78 RPM
Piano

818

Down to de River
MacGimsey, Robert
West, Lucretia (Mezzo-soprano)
Negro Spirituals III
Club français du disque 176; 1959; LP
Piano
Heavy dialect

· · · · · · ·

Dry Bones

819

Dry Bones
Hayes, Roland
Caesar, Jackson (Tenor)
*Spirituals: Celebrating the Music, Life,
    Legacy of Roland Hayes*
CD Baby 7048606059; 2021; CD
Piano, percussion
Light dialect

820

Dry Bones
Hayes, Roland
Caesar, Jackson (Tenor)
*Spirituals: Celebrating the Music, Life,
    Legacy of Roland Hayes*
CD Baby 7048606059; 2021; CD
Piano
Light dialect

821

Dry Bones [from *Five Creek-Freedmen
    Spirituals*]
Bonds, Margaret
Hamilton, Ruth (Contralto)
*Watch and Pray: Spirituals and Art Songs by
    African-American Women Composers*
Koch International Classics 3-7247-2H1;
    1994; CD
Piano
Heavy dialect

822

Dry Bones [from *My Songs: Dream of
    Heaven*]
Hayes, Roland
Hayes, Roland (Tenor)

Roland Hayes: My Songs
Vanguard VRS-494; 1956; LP
Piano

Also released with *Afro-American Folk-songs* (Pelican Records LP 2028; 1983; LP); *Favorite Spirituals* (Vanguard Classics OVC 6022; 1995; CD) and *Big Psalms, Hymns and Spirituals Box* (eOne Music/Vanguard Classics; 2015; Streaming audio)

823

Dry Bones
Burleigh, Harry T.
Moses, Oral (Bass-baritone)
Deep River: Songs and Spirituals of Harry T. Burleigh
Northeastern NR 252-CD; 1995; CD
Piano

824

Dry Bones
Composer not identified
Putkonen, Marko (Bass)
Deep River: Negro Spirituals
Lilium LILP 101; 1991; LP

825

Dry Bones [from *Five Creek-Freedmen Spirituals*]
[Bonds, Margaret]
Robinson, Marie Hadley (Soprano)
Come Down Angels
Meyer Media; 2011; Streaming audio
Piano
Moderate dialect

826

Dem Dry Bones
Composer not identified
Spencer, Kenneth (Bass-baritone)
Negro Spirituals
Life Records C 1108; [19--]; LP

827

Dry Bones
Composer not identified
Verdejo, Awilda (Soprano)
Awilda Verdejo Sings Spirituals

Angeluz Performances; 1999; CD
Piano

828

Dry Bones [from *Five Creek-Freedmen Spirituals*]
Bonds, Margaret
Warfield, William (Bass-baritone)
Spirituals: 200 Years of African-American Spirituals
ProArte CDD 3443; 1993; CD
Piano
Heavy dialect

. . . .

End of My Journey

829

The End of My Journey
Composer not identified
Robeson, Paul (Bass-baritone)
Paul Robeson Singt Negro Spirituals
Musical Masterpiece Society MMS-2162; [19--]; LP
Piano

. . . .

Every Time I Feel the Spirit

[Isaiah 11:2; Matthew 3:6; Luke 4:1; Acts 1:8, 2:38; Romans 8:26-27; 1 Corinthians 2:13, 6:19, 14:15]

"Every time I feel the spirit moving in my heart, I will pray; Every time I feel the spirit moving in my heart, I will pray. Upon the mountain, my Lord spoke, Out of His mouth came fire and smoke; In the valley, on my knees, Ask my Lord have mercy please…. Jordan River, chilly and cold, Chill the body, but not the soul…."

[Available in AAGS, CLSA, CW40, EM34, FHFN, HCTN, HJTS, HLBS, HTBA, HTBS, HTC2, JJAN, JJBA, JSSp, LB5N, LLS2, MM4S, PLSY, RW15, SONS, WF10, WF70]

The lyrics here express spiritual renewal and the vital connections of the enslaved to the Holy Spirit. These connections often took on physical (fire, Jordan River) or ceremonial manifestations (Baptism) as the enslaved gathered to worship, pray and sing.

Prominent among the composer settings are those by Lawrence Brown and H.T. Burleigh. Burleigh used a much higher percentage of dialect in his score text; however, performers captured in the range of recordings below tended to use more dialect whether prescribed by the published scores or not.

830

Ev'ry Time I Feel de Spirit
Brown, Lawrence
Anderson, Marian (Contralto)
Deep River
RCA Victor 2032; [194-]; 78 RPM
Piano
Light dialect

831

Ev'ry Time I Feel de Spirit
Brown, Lawrence
Anderson, Marian (Contralto)
Ev'Ry Time I Feel the Spirit (1930–1947)
Naxos Nostalgia 8.120779; 2004; CD
Piano

832

Ev'ry Time I Feel de Spirit
Brown, Lawrence
Anderson, Marian (Contralto)
Good News: Vintage Negro Spirituals
Living Era AJA 5622; 2006; CD
Piano
Moderate dialect

833

Ev'ry Time I Feel de Spirit
Brown, Lawrence
Anderson, Marian (Contralto)
The Art of Marian Anderson: Arias, Songs and Spirituals
His Master's Voice EG 29001614; 1986; LP
Piano

834

Ev'ry Time I Feel de Spirit
Brown, Lawrence

Anderson, Marian (Contralto)
Marian Anderson: Portraits in Memory
Metropolitan Opera Guild MET 220; 1993; CD
Piano
Moderate dialect

835

Ev'ry Time I Feel de Spirit
Brown, Lawrence
Anderson, Marian (Contralto)
Negro Spirituals
EMI 7243 5 72790 2 4; 1998; CD
Piano
Moderate dialect

836

Every Time I Feel the Spirit
Brown, Lawrence
Anderson, Marian (Contralto)
Rarities: Broadcast Performances 1943–1952
Video Artists International VAIA 1200; 1998; CD
Orchestra

837

Every Time I Feel de Spirit
Brown, Lawrence
Anderson, Marian (Contralto)
Spirituals
RCA Victor Red Seal 09026-63306-2; 1999; CD
Piano
Light dialect

838

Ev'ry Time I Feel de Spirit
Brown, Lawrence
Anderson, Marian (Contralto)
Tribute
Pro Arte CDD 3447; 1993; CD
Piano

839

Ev'ry Time I Feel de Spirit
Brown, Lawrence
Anderson, Marian (Contralto)
Lebendige Vergangenheit
Austro Mechana Historic Recordings MONO 89604; 2004; CD
Piano

840

Everytime I Feel the Spirit
Brown, Lawrence
Anderson, Marian (Contralto)
Marian Anderson in Concert 1943–1952
Eklipse Records EKR CD19; 1993; CD
Orchestra

841

Ev'ry Time I Feel de Spirit
Brown, Lawrence
Anderson, Marian (Contralto)
Negro Spirituals
La Voix de Son Maître 7EJF2; 1955; 45 RPM
Orchestra

842

Everytime I Feel de Spirit
Brown, Lawrence
Anderson, Marian (Contralto)
*Softly Awakes My Heart: Very Best of Marian
 Anderson*
Alto ALN1955; 2016; CD
Piano
Moderate dialect

843

Every Time I Feel de Spirit
Brown, Lawrence
Anderson, Marian (Contralto)
Negro Spirituals
RCA Victor LM 2032; [1956]; LP
Piano

844

Ev'ry Time I Feel de Spirit
Brown, Lawrence
Anderson, Marian (Contralto)
Negro Spirituals, vol. II
La Voix de Son Maître 7 ERF 17025; 1962;
 EP 45 RPM
Orchestra

845

Everytime I Feel de Spirit
[Brown, Lawrence]
Anderson, Marian (Contralto)
*Marian Anderson Sings Eleven Great
 Spirituals*

RCA Victor LRM 7006; 1955; LP
Piano
Light dialect

     Also released with *Marian Anderson:
Beyond the Music; Her Complete RCA Victor Recordings* (Sony Classical 19439836492;
2021; CD)

846

Ev'ry Time I Feel de Spirit
[Brown, Lawrence]
Anderson, Marian (Contralto)
Softly Awakes My Heart
ASV CD AJA 5262; 1999; CD
Piano

847

Everytime I Feel de Spirit
[Brown, Lawrence]
Anderson, Marian (Contralto)
Alto Rhapsody; Selected Spirituals
Urania URN 22.328; 2007; CD
Piano

848

Every Time I Feel de Spirit
[Brown, Lawrence]
Anderson, Marian (Contralto)
The Very Best of Marian Anderson
Master Classics Records; 2009; CD
Piano
Light dialect

849

Every Time I Feel the Spirit
[Brown, Lawrence]
Anderson, Marian (Contralto)
Inspirations
Emerald Echoes; 2015; Streaming audio
Piano
Light dialect

850

Ev'ry Time I Feel the Spirit
Anderson, Marian (Contralto)
Classic Gospel Songs
Emerald/K-Tel; 2013; Streaming audio
Piano

851
Everytime I Feel de Spirit
[Brown, Lawrence]
Anderson, Marian (Contralto)
Marian Anderson Sings Eleven Great Spirituals
Kipepeo Publishing; 2017; CD
Piano

852
Everytime I Feel de Spirit
[Brown, Lawrence]
Anderson, Marian (Contralto)
Negro Spirituals
RCA Victor 630.396 A; [19--]; LP
Piano

853
Everytime I Feel the Spirit
[Brown, Lawrence]
Anderson, Marian (Contralto)
*Grandes Contraltos de la Musique Classique,
   Les: Marian Anderson, Vol. 4*
Mon Patrimoine Musical Collection; 2017;
   Streaming audio
Piano

854
Every Time I Feel the Spirit
[Brown, Lawrence]
Anderson, Marian (Contralto)
Black Swans: At Mid-Century
Parnassus PACD 96078/9; 2021; CD
Instrumental ensemble
Heavy dialect

855
Ev'ry Time I Feel the Spirit
Composer not identified
Arroyo, Martina (Soprano); Lawrence, T.
   Ray (Vocalist)
There's a Meeting Here Tonight
Angel S-36072; 1974; LP
Chorus

    Also released with *Negro Spirituals*
(EMI 7243 5 72790 2 4; 1998; CD)

856
Ev'ry Time I Feel the Spirit
Dawson, William L.

Blackmon, Henry (Baritone)
Negro Spirituals
Mirasound Records SGLP 6047; [19--]; LP
Organ

857
Ev'ry Time I Feel the Spirit
Dawson, William L.
Blackmon, Henry (Baritone)
Negro Spirituals
Vega 19179; [19--]; LP
Chorus, piano

858
Ev'ry Time I Feel de Spirit
Burleigh, Harry T.
Blanchard, Gerald (Baritone)
With a Song in My Heart
Blue Griffin Recording BGR117; 2004; CD
Piano
Heavy dialect

859
Everytime I Feel the Spirit
Boatwright, McHenry
Boatwright, McHenry (Bass-baritone)
Art of McHenry Boatwright: Spirituals
Golden Crest Records RE 7024; 1968; LP
Piano
No dialect discerned

860
Ev'ry Time I Feel the Spirit
Hogan, Moses; Brown, Angela; Cooper, Tyron
Brown, Angela (Soprano)
*Mosiac: A Collection of African-American
   Spirituals with Piano, guitar*
Albany Records TROY721; 2004; CD
Guitar
Moderate dialect

861
Every Time I Feel the Spirit
Dawson, William L.
Brown, Anthony (Baritone)
Toil and Triumph
Spirituals Project; 2002; CD
Chorus
Light dialect

862

Everytime I Feel the Spirit
Sneed, Damien
Brownlee, Lawrence (Tenor)
Spiritual Sketches
LeChateau Earl Records 888174029597; 2013;
　CD
Piano
No dialect discerned

863

Ev'ry Time I Feel de Spirit
Walker, George
Buchanan, Alison (Soprano)
Great American Concert Music
Albany Records TROY1370; 2012; CD
Piano
Moderate dialect

864

Ev'ry Time I Feel de Spirit
Burleigh, Harry T.
Carlsen, Svein (Bass)
Negro Spirituals
EuroMaster AS ECD19005; 1996; CD
Piano

865

Ev'ry Time I Feel de Spirit
Burleigh, Harry T.
Carnette, Count (Vocalist)
*Count Carnette Sings Favorite Negro
　Spirituals*
Carnette Archive Recordings; 1983; LP
Piano
Heavy dialect

866

Ev'ry Time I Feel de Spirit
[Burleigh, Harry T.]
Chaiter, Yoram (Bass)
Spirituals & Other Songs
Romeo Records 7311; 2014; CD
Piano
Moderate dialect

867

Every Time I Feel the Spirit
Composer not identified

Charles, Lee (Tenor)
*Swing Low Sweet Chariot: And Other
　Spirituals*
Riverside RLP 12-651; 1957; LP
Piano, guitar

868

Every Time I Feel the Spirit
Composer not identified
Cunningham-Fleming, Jeryl (Soprano)
*Stand the Storm: Anthems, Hymns, and
　Spirituals of Faith and Hope*
Private Label; 2016; CD
Piano

869

Ev'ry Time I Feel de Spirit
Burleigh, Harry T.
Davis, Ollie Watts (Soprano)
Here's One: Spiritual Songs
KJAC Publishing KJAC0123; 2003; CD
Piano
Heavy dialect

870

Ev'ry Time I Feel de Spirit
Burleigh, Harry T.
Davis, Osceola (Soprano)
Negro Spirituals
Ondine ODE 715-2; 1988; CD
Piano
No dialect discerned

871

Ev'ry Time I Feel de Spirit
[Brown, Lawrence]
Dove, Evelyn (Contralto)
*Brother, Can You Spare a Dime?: The Roots of
　American Song*
Pearl Gemm CD 9484; 1991; CD
Piano
Light dialect

872

Ev'ry Time I Feel de Spirit
Brown, Lawrence
Dove, Evelyn (Contralto)
*Ev'ry Time I Feel de Spirit/Couldn't Hear
　Nobody Pray*

ACO G-15659; [1924]; 78 RPM
Harp

873

Every Time I Feel the Spirit
[Brown, Lawrence]
Dove, Evelyn (Contralto)
*Black Europe: Sounds & Images of Black
    People in Europe pre–1927*
Bear Family Productions BCD 16095; 2013; CD
Piano
Moderate dialect

874

Ev'ry Time I Feel the Spirit
Brown, Lawrence
Duncan, Todd (Baritone)
Negro Spirituals
Allegro ALG3022; [1952]; LP
Piano

875

Ev'ry Time I Feel de Spirit
Brown, Lawrence
Duncan, Todd (Baritone)
Ol' Man River/Ev'ryTime I Feel de Spirit
Parlophone R. 3061; [19--]; 78 RPM
Piano

876

Everytime I Feel the Spirit
Brown, Lawrence
Duncan, Todd (Baritone)
African American Spirituals
[Apple Music]; 2008; Streaming audio
Piano
Light dialect

877

Everytime I Feel the Spirit
[Brown, Lawrence]
Duncan, Todd (Baritone)
Todd Duncan Recital
Musicraft 82; [194-]; 78 RPM
Piano

878

Juba: Ev'ry Time I Feel the Spirit
Morris, Robert

English-Robinson, Laura (Soprano)
Let It Shine!
ACA Digital Recording CM20020; 1994; CD
Piano
Light dialect

879

Every Time I Feel the Spirit
Roberts, Howard
Estes, Simon (Bass-baritone)
Spirituals
Philips 412 631-2; 1985; CD
Chorus
Light dialect

    Also released with *Famous Spirituals*
(Philips 462 062-2; 1997; CD)

880

Ev'ry Time I Feel the Spirit
Ryan, Donald
Estes, Simon (Bass-baritone)
Steal Away: My Favorite Negro Spirituals
Deutsche Schallplatten DS 1041-2; 1994; CD
Piano
Light dialect

    Also released with *Simon Sings His
Favorite Gospels & Spirituals* (Praise Productions SMG-SE; 1999; CD) and *Save the Children, Save Their Lives* (CD Baby; 2010; CD)

881

Ev'ry Time I Feel the Spirit
Dawson, William L.
Evans, Charles (Baritone)
*Steal Away: The African American Concert
    Spiritual*
SFM; 2015; CD
Chorus
Heavy dialect

882

Ev'ry Time I Feel de Spirit
Burleigh, Harry T.
Evans, Charlie (Vocalist)
Sing God's Plan
Private Label; 2005; CD
Piano
Heavy dialect

883

Ev'ry Time I Feel the Spirit
Darden, George
Fernandez, Wilhelmenia (Soprano)
Spirituals
Tioch Digital Records TD 1009; 1982; LP
Piano
Heavy dialect

Also released with *Negro Spirituals*
(Milan A 192; 1982; LP); *Sings Favorite Spirituals* (Phoenix PHCD 134; 1997; CD) and
Negro Spirituals (Transart 131; 2005; CD)

884

Если в сердце бьется радость (Yesli v
serdtse b'yetsya radost')
Composer not identified
Filatova, Ludmila (Mezzo-soprano)
*Негритянские Спиричуэлс (Negrityanskiye
Spirichuzls—Negro Spirituals)*
Melodiâ S10 21833 009; 1985; LP
Organ
Light dialect

885

Ev'ry Time I Feel de Spirit
Burleigh, Harry T.
Forest, Michael (Tenor)
The Spirit Sings: American Spirituals
Shenandoah Conservatory SU003; [199-];
CD

886

Every Time I Feel the Spirit
Mills, Marvin
Graves, Denyce (Mezzo-soprano)
Angels Watching Over Me
NPR Classics CD 0006; 1997; CD
Piano
Light dialect

887

Every Time I Feel de Spirit
Composer not identified
Green, Elnora E. (Contralto)
15 Spirituals
Private Label J3RS 2286; 1979; LP
Piano

888

Ev'ry Time I Feel de Spirit
Composer not identified
Hagen-William, Louis (Bass-baritone)
Negro Spirituals
Quantum QM 6909; 1993; CD
Piano
Moderate dialect

889

Ev'ry Time I Feel de Spirit
Burleigh, Harry T.; Taylor, Vivian
Hamilton, Ruth (Contralto); Honeysucker,
Robert (Baritone)
Good News
Videmus Records VIS735; 2007; CD
Piano
Heavy dialect

890

Ev'ry Time I Feel the Spirit
[Burleigh, Harry T.]
Hampton, Jonathon (Vocalist)
Negro Spirituals: Songs of Trial and Triumph
Private Label; 2017; Streaming audio
Piano
Heavy dialect

891

Ev'ry Time I Feel de Spirit
Burleigh, Harry T.
Harris, Hilda (Mezzo-soprano)
*From the Southland: Songs, Piano Sketches
and Spirituals of Harry T. Burleigh*
Premier Recordings PRCD 1041; 1995; CD
Piano
Moderate dialect

892

Ev'ry Time I Feel the Spirit
Composer not identified
Harris, Lloyd (Bass)
Negro Spirituals
Pléïade P45301; 1960; 45 RPM
Piano

893

Every Time I Feel the Spirit
Brown, Lawrence

Hayes, Roland (Tenor)
The Art of Roland Hayes: Six Centuries of Song
Preiser Records; 2010; CD
Piano
Heavy dialect

894

Every Time I Feel the Spirit
[Brown, Lawrence]
Hayes, Roland (Tenor)
Roland Hayes Sings: Negro Spirituals,
   Aframerican Folk Songs
Amadeo Records AVRS 6033; [19--]; LP
Piano

895

Ev'ry Time I Feel de Spirit
Hendricks, Barbara; Alexeev, Dmitri
Hendricks, Barbara (Soprano)
Negro Spirituals
EMI CDC7470262; 1983; CD
Piano
Light dialect

    Also released on *Espirituales Negros*
(EMI Classics/Altaya 01636; 1983; CD) and
Spirituals (EMI Classics 0946 346641 2 7;
2005; CD)

896

Ev'ry Time I Feel de Spirit
Lloyd, Charles, Jr.
Hobson, Richard (Baritone)
The Spiritual Art Song Collection
Warner Bros. SVBM00004; 2000; Score w/CD
Piano

897

Every Time I Feel the Spirit
Taylor, Vivian
Honeysucker, Robert (Baritone); Dry,
   Marion (Contralto)
Let's Have a Union
Brave Records BRAV-0923; 2009; CD
Piano
Light dialect

898

Ev'ry Time I Feel the Spirit
Clinton, Irving

Irving, Clinton (Bass-baritone)
89Clinton Irving Sings Spirituals: A Tribute
Rogers; 2001; CD

899

Everytime I Feel the Spirit
Composer not identified
Johnson, John (Baritone)
Spirituals
Royale EP 180; [19--]; 45 RPM

900

Everytime I Feel the Spirit
Composer not identified
Johnson, Yolanda F (Soprano)
Feel the Spirit!
Jublianti Artists; 2011; Streaming audio
Piano
Moderate dialect

901

Everytime I Feel the Spirit
Burleigh, Harry T.
Jones, Fanni (Mezzo-soprano)
Fanni Jones et Oswald Russell
Audio-Visual Enterprises AVE 30701; [19--]; LP

902

Ev'ry Time I Feel de Spirit
Composer not identified
Jones, Fanni (Mezzo-soprano)
Negro Spirituals
Phonotec 815; 1977; LP
Organ

903

Everytime I Feel the Spirit
[Burleigh, Harry T.]
Jones, Fanni (Mezzo-soprano)
Negro Spirituals
Evasion Disques LP613; 1974; LP

904

Every Time I Feel the Spirit
Blozan, Benjamin
Lewis, Cheryse McLeod (Mezzo-soprano)
Spirituals
CheryseMusic; 2012; CD
Piano

905
Ev'ry Time I Feel the Spirit
Okpebholo, Shawn
Liverman, Will (Baritone)
Steal Away
Yellow Einstein; 2014; CD
Piano, viola
Light dialect

906
Ev'ry Time I Feel de Spirit
[Burleigh, Harry T.]
Loiselle, Henri (Bass-baritone)
One Day at a Time
Hum Recordings HRHLCD001; 1996; CD
Piano
Light dialect

　　　Also released with *Encore* (Hum Recordings HRHLCD004; 2008; CD)

907
Every Time I Feel the Spirit
Burleigh, Harry T.; Simonson, Victor
Lynch, Lester (Baritone)
On My Journey Now: Spirituals & Hymns
Pentatone Music PTC 5186 57'; 2017; CD
Piano

908
Ev'ry Time I Feel the Spirit [from *Feel the Spirit*]
Rutter, John
Marshall, Melanie (Mezzo-soprano)
Feel the Spirit
Collegium Records COLCD 128; 2001; CD
Chorus, orchestra

909
Ev'ry Time I Feel the Spirit
Dett, Robert Nathaniel
Maynor, Dorothy (Soprano)
Dorothy Maynor in Concert at Library of Congress
Library of Congress, Music Division LCM 2141; 2007; CD
Piano
Moderate dialect

　　　Also released with *Dorothy Maynor, Soprano* (Bridge Records 9233; 2007; CD)

910
Ev'ry Time I Feel de Spirit
Walker, George
Maynor, Kevin (Bass)
The Spiritual: An Underground Railroad
Southeastern Virginia Arts Assoc.; [2000]; CD
Piano

911
Ev'ry Time I Feel de Spirit
Johnson, Hall
McFerrin, Robert (Baritone)
Deep River and Other Classic Negro Spirituals
Riverside Records RLP 12-812; 1959; LP
Piano
Moderate dialect

　　　Also released with *Classic Negro Spirituals* (Washington Records WLP 466; 1959; LP)

912
Ev'ry Time I Hear the Spirit
Johnson, Hall
McGregor, Roberta (Soprano)
Your Eyes Smile Peace
Roberta McGregor MCG01; 2000; CD
Piano

913
Every Time I Feel de Spirit
Burleigh, Harry T.
McKinney, Jason (Bass-baritone)
Songs Inspired by Paul Robeson
United in Music; 2014; CD
Piano
Light dialect

914
Everytime I Feel the Spirit
Composer not identified
Miles, John (Tenor)
The Classic Spirituals
Epiphany 83-1027; 1983; LP
Instrumental ensemble

915
Ev'ry Time
Composer not identified
Monzo, Oscar (Baritone)

Negro Spirituals
Dial Discos 50-2020; 1983; LP

916

Ev'ry Time I Feel de Spirit
Johnson, Hall
Moses, Oral (Bass-baritone)
*Come Down Angels and Trouble the Water:
   Negro Spirituals, an American National
   Treasure!*
Albany Records TROY 1489; 2014; CD
Piano
Heavy dialect

Also released with *Sankofa: A Spiritual
Reflection* (Albany Records TROY1802; 2019;
CD)

917

Ev'ry Time I Feel the Spirit
Traditional
Moses, Oral (Bass-baritone)
*Spirituals in Zion: A Spiritual Heritage for
   the Soul*
Albany Records TROY587; 2003; CD
A cappella
Light dialect

918

Ev'ryTime I Feel the Spirit
Composer not identified
Nobles, NaGuanda (Soprano)
Homage to the Journey
Selbon Records; 2014; Streaming audio
Piano, organ
No dialect discerned

919

Every Time I Feel the Spirit
[Johnson, Hall]
Norman, Jessye (Soprano)
An Evening with Jessye Norman
Opera D'Oro Recitals OPD-2011; 1999; CD
Piano
Heavy dialect

920

Ev'ry Time I Feel de Spirit
Baldwin, Dalton; Jessye Norman; Patterson,
   Willis

Norman, Jessye (Soprano)
Negro Spirituals
Philips 9500 580; 1979; LP
Piano
Light dialect

Also released with *Spirituals* (Philips
416 462-2; 1990; CD)

921

Ev'ry Time I Feel de Spirit
Composer not identified
Norman, Jessye (Soprano)
*The Jessye Norman Collection: Sacred Songs
   & Spirituals*
Philips B0004506-02; 2005; CD
Piano
Heavy dialect

922

Every Time I Feel the Spirit
[Johnson, Hall]
Norman, Jessye (Soprano)
Gospels & Spirituals Gold Collection
Retro R2CD 40-26; 1995; CD
Piano
Heavy dialect

Also released with *Oh, Happy Day!
Gospels & Spirituals: The Ultimate CD* (Ultimate; 2010; CD)

923

Everytime I Feel the Spirit
Brown, Lawrence
Pankey, Aubrey (Baritone)
Aubrey Pankey Singt Negro-Spirituals
Eterna 7 30 005; 1959; LP
Piano
No dialect discerned

Also released with *Negro Spirituals*
(Eterna 830010; 1983; LP)

924

Every Time I Feel the Spirit
Brown, Lawrence
Payne, John C. (Baritone)
*It's Me, O Lord/Nobody Knows the Trouble
   I've Seen; Every Time I Feel de Spirit*
Columbia 3662; 1925; 78 RPM
Piano

925

Ev'ry Time I Feel de Spirit
Composer not identified
Pickens, Jo Ann (Soprano)
*My Heritage: American Melodies/Negro
   Spirituals*
Koch Schwann 3-1447-2; 1993; CD

926

Ev'ry Time I Feel the Spirit
Burleigh, Harry T.; de Paur, Leonard
Price, Leontyne (Soprano)
*Swing Low, Sweet Chariot: Fourteen
   Spirituals*
RCA Victor LSC 2600; 1962; LP
Chorus, orchestra
Heavy dialect

    Also released with *The Essential Leontyne Price: Spirituals, Hymns & Sacred Songs* (BMG Classics 09026-68157-2; 1996; CD); *The Essential Leontyne Price* (BMG Classics 09026-68153-2; 1996; CD); *Leontyne Price Sings Spirituals* (RCA Red Seal 88691928242; 2012; CD) and *Singers of the Century: Leontyne Price: Spiritual and Religious Songs* (Jube Classic; 2016; Streaming audio)

927

Ev'ry Time I Feel the Spirit
Burleigh, Harry T.; de Paur, Leonard
Price, Leontyne (Soprano)
*Complete Collection of Songs and Spiritual
   Albums*
RCA Red Seal 88697940502; 2011; CD
Orchestra

928

Ev'ry Time I Feel the Spirit
Dawson, William L.
Price, Leontyne (Soprano)
Leontyne Price Sings Spirituals
RCA Red Seal 88691928242; 2012; CD
Chorus
Heavy dialect

    Also released with *Complete Collection of Songs and Spiritual Albums* (RCA Red Seal 88697940502; 2011; CD) and *I Wish I Knew How It Would Feel to Be Free* (RCA Red Seal LSC 3183; 2011; CD)

929

Ev'ry Time I Feel the Spirit
Dawson, William L.
Price, Leontyne (Soprano)
The Essential Leontyne Price
BMG Classics 09026-68153-2; 1996; CD
Chorus, orchestra

930

Every Time I Feel the Spirit
Composer not identified
Putkonen, Marko (Bass)
Deep River: Negro Spirituals
Lilium LILP 101; 1991; LP

931

Ev'ry Time I Feel the Spirit
Hogan, Moses
Ragin, Derek Lee (Countertenor)
Ev'ry Time I Feel the Spirit: Spirituals
Channel Classics CCS 2991; 1991; CD
Chorus
Heavy dialect

932

Every Time I Feel de Spirit
Brown, Lawrence
Robeson, Paul (Bass-baritone); Brown,
   Lawrence (Vocalist)
The Complete EMI Sessions (1928–1939)
EMI Classics 50999 2 15586 2 7; 2008; CD
Piano
Heavy dialect

933

Every Time I Feel the Spirit
Brown, Lawrence
Robeson, Paul (Bass-baritone)
Paul Robeson Live at Carnegie Hall
Vanguard VCD-72020; 1987; CD
Piano
Heavy dialect

934

Every Time I Feel the Spirit
Brown, Lawrence
Robeson, Paul (Bass-baritone); Brown,
   Lawrence (Vocalist)

Paul Robeson in Live Performance
Columbia M 30424; 1971; LP
Piano
Moderate dialect

935

Ev'ry Time I Feel de Spirit
Brown, Lawrence
Robeson, Paul (Bass-baritone)
Paul Robeson Sings Negro Spirituals
Philips GBL 5584; [19--]; LP
Piano

936

Ev'ry Time I Feel de Spirit
Brown, Lawrence
Robeson, Paul (Bass-baritone); Brown,
    Lawrence (Vocalist)
Swing Low, Sweet Chariot
Columbia Masterworks MM-819; 1949; 78
    RPM
Piano
Heavy dialect

937

Every Time I Feel the Spirit
Brown, Lawrence
Robeson, Paul (Bass-baritone)
The Essential Paul Robeson
Vanguard VSD 57/58; 1974; LP
Piano
Light dialect

938

Ev'ry Time I Feel de Spirit
Brown, Lawrence
Robeson, Paul (Bass-baritone); Brown,
    Lawrence (Vocalist)
Paul Robeson Chante … f16 Spirituals
Philips G 05.639 R; 1959; LP
Piano

939

Ev'ry Time I Feel de Spirit
[Brown, Lawrence]
Robeson, Paul (Bass-baritone)
Negro Spirituals, v. 2
Philips NBE11102; 1956; 7" Vinyl

940

Every Time I Feel the Spirit
[Brown, Lawrence]
Robeson, Paul (Bass-baritone)
The Odyssey of Paul Robeson
Omega Classics OCD 3007; 1992; CD
Piano

941

Every Time I Feel the Spirit
[Brown, Lawrence]
Robeson, Paul (Bass-baritone); Brown,
    Lawrence (Vocalist)
Scandalize My Name
Classics Record Library 30-5647; 1976; LP
Piano
Moderate dialect

942

Ev'ry Time I Feel de Spirit
[Brown, Lawrence]
Robeson, Paul (Bass-baritone)
Swing Low, Sweet Chariot
Columbia Masterworks ML 2038; [195-]; LP
Piano

943

Every Time I Feel the Spirit
[Brown, Lawrence]
Robeson, Paul (Bass-baritone); Brown,
    Lawrence (Vocalist)
The Peace Arch Concerts
Folk Era Records FE1442CD; 1998; CD
Piano
Heavy dialect

944

Every Time I Feel the Spirit
[Brown, Lawrence]
Robeson, Paul (Bass-baritone)
Five Classic Albums Plus Bonus Tracks
Real Gone Music RGMCD287; 2017; CD

945

Every Time I Feel the Spirit
[Brown, Lawrence]
Robeson, Paul (Bass-baritone)
The Essential History of Gospels & Spirituals
Deja Vu; 1990; CD

946

Every Time I Feel de Spirit
[Brown, Lawrence]
Robeson, Paul (Bass-baritone); Brown,
    Lawrence (Vocalist)
The Ultimate Collection
Burning Fire; 2009; Streaming audio
Piano
Moderate dialect

947

Every Time I Feel the Spirit
[Brown, Lawrence]
Robeson, Paul (Bass-baritone)
Complete Recordings
Universal Digital Enterprises; 2018;
    Streaming audio

948

Every Time I Feel the Spirit
Brown, Lawrence
Schlamme, Martha (Soprano)
Martha Schlamme at Town Hall
Vanguard VRS-9070; 1960; LP
Instrumental ensemble

949

Ev'ry Time I Feel the Spirit
Burleigh, Harry T.
Shanks, Donald (Bass)
Songs of Inspiration
ABC Classics Eloquence 426 803-2; 1989; CD
Organ
Heavy dialect

950

Ev'ry Time I Feel the Spirit
Dawson, William L.
Shelhart, John (Bass-baritone)
*Ain't Got Time to Die: Songs of the American
    Spirit*
First Presbyterian Church in the City of
    New York FPC 1002; 1997; CD
Chorus

951

Every Time I Feel the Spirit
Walters, Richard (ed.)
Stolen, Steven (Tenor)

*15 Easy Spiritual Arrangements for the
    Progressing Singer*
Hal Leonard HL00000391 (high);
    HL00000392 (low); 2005; Score w/CD
Piano
Heavy dialect

952

Av'ry Time I Feel de Spirit
Johnson, Hall
Straughter, Maralyn (Soprano)
Negro Spirituals of Hall Johnson
Variety Recording Service Var 0753; [196-];
    LP
Piano

953

Ev'ry Time I Feel de Spirit
Composer not identified
Thomas, John Charles (Baritone)
*Swing Low, Sweet Chariot/Ev'ry Time I Feel
    de Spirit*
Victor His Master's Voice 2168; 1941; 78 RPM
Orchestra

     Also released with *John Charles Thomas:
an American Classic* (Nimbus Records NI
7838; 1992; CD)

954

Every Time I Feel the Spirit
Thompson, J[eanette]
Thompson, Jeanette (Soprano)
Negro Spirituals
Pavane Records ADW 7267; 1992; CD
Chorus
No dialect discerned

955

Every Time I Feel the Spirit
Johnson, Hall
Thompson, Kevin (Bass)
*The Spirituals: Featuring the American
    Spiritual Ensemble*
LexArts; [20--]; CD

956

Ev'rytime I Feel de Spirit
Johnson, Hall
Toppin, Louise (Soprano)

He'll Bring It to Pass: The Spirituals of Hall Johnson for Voice and Piano
Albany Records TROY846; 2006; CD
Piano
Moderate dialect

957

Ev'ry Time I Feel the Spirit (Juba) [from Lyric Suite]
Morris, Robert L.
Toppin, Louise (Soprano)
Heart on the Wall: African American Art Songs for Orchestra
Albany Records TROY1314; 2011; CD
Orchestra
Heavy dialect

958

Ev'rytimes I feel the Spirit
Composer not identified
Tynes, Margaret (Mezzo-soprano)
Margaret E. Tynes Sings Negro Spirituals
Qualiton EP 1578; 1962; 45 RPM
Orchestra

959

Every Time I Feel the Spirit
Composer not identified
Warfield, William (Bass-baritone)
Something Within Me
Delmark Records DE-772; 2000; CD
Instrumental ensemble

960

Ev'ry Time I Feel de Spirit
Composer not identified
Watts, Leonardo (Baritone)
On Ma Journey: A Memorable Collection of Negro Spirituals
Onyx Recording Associates ORA-101; 1961; LP
Chorus

961

Every Time I Feel the Spirit
Composer not identified
Webb, George (Tenor)
Famous Negro Spirituals and Songs of

Elizabethan England, Ireland & the Caribbean
[Unknown] WLP7804; 1978; LP

962

Every Time I Feel de Spirit
Brown, Lawrence
West, Lucretia (Mezzo-soprano)
Negro Spirituals III
Club français du disque 176; 1959; LP
Piano
Heavy dialect

963

Everytime
Burleigh, Harry T.
West, Lucretia (Mezzo-soprano)
Negro Spirituals mit Lukretia West
Opera 3408; [195-]; LP
Piano

964

Every Time
Burleigh, Harry T.
West, Lucretia (Mezzo-soprano)
Negro Spirituals
Club français du disque 215; [196-]; 7-in EP
Piano

965

Ev'ry Time I Feel de Spirit
Composer not identified
West, Lucretia (Mezzo-soprano)
Spirituals
Westminster WL 5338; 1954; LP
Piano

966

Every Time I Feel the Spirit
[Burleigh, Harry T.]
West, Lucretia (Mezzo-soprano)
Lucretia West Sings Spirituals
Westminster WP 6063; [1957]; LP

967

Ev'ry Time I Feel the Spirit
Johnson, Hall
White, Willard (Bass-baritone)

*Willard White Sings: Copland; American
    Spirituals; Folk-Songs*
Chandos Records CHAN 8960; 1991; CD
Piano
Heavy dialect

968

Ev'ry Time I Feel de Spirit
Burleigh, Harry T.
Winter, Georg (Vocalist)
Eine Kleine Hausmusik
Teldec 66.22670; 1981; LP
Piano

· · · · · · ·

Everybody Got to Die

969

Jokainen Joutuu Oikeuden Eteen
    (Everybody Got to Die)
Composer not identified
Putkonen, Marko (Bass)
Deep River: Negro Spirituals
Lilium LILP 101; 1991; LP

· · · · · · ·

Ezekiel Saw the Wheel

970

Ezekiel Saw de Wheel
Hayes, Roland
Brown, William (Tenor)
Fi-Yer!: a Century of African American Song
Albany Records TROY 329; 1999; CD
Piano
Light dialect

971

Ezek'el Saw the Wheel
Composer not identified
Carey, Thomas (Baritone)
Go Down Moses
Da Camera Song SM 95028; 1970; LP
Piano

972

Zekiel Saw de Wheel
Chenault, Raymond

English-Robinson, Laura (Soprano)
Let It Shine!
ACA Digital Recording CM20020; 1994; CD
Piano
No dialect discerned

973

Ezekiel Saw the Wheel
Roberts, Howard
Estes, Simon (Bass-baritone)
Spirituals
Philips 412 631-2; 1985; CD
Chorus
Light dialect

    Also released with *Famous Spirituals*
(Philips 462 062-2; 1997; CD)

974

Ezechiel Saw the Wheel
Wheatley, Andres
Haniotis, Mario (Bass)
Negro Spirituals
Pastorale et Musique PM 17.047; [196-]; 45
    RPM
Piano
No dialect discerned

975

Ezekiel Saw de Wheel
Composer not identified
Hayes, Roland (Tenor)
*Roland Hayes Sings: Negro Spirituals,
    Aframerican Folk Songs*
Amadeo Records AVRS 6033; [19--]; LP
Piano

976

Ezekiel Saw the Wheel
Composer not identified
Hayes, Roland (Tenor)
Afro-American Folksongs
Pelican Records LP 2028; 1983; LP
Piano

977

Ezekiel Saw de Wheel
Hayes, Roland
Hayes, Roland (Tenor)
The Art of Roland Hayes

Smithsonian Collection RD 041; 1990; CD
Piano
Heavy dialect

Also released with *The Art of Roland Hayes: Six Centuries of Song* (Preiser Records; 2010; CD)

978

Ezekiel Saw the Wheel
Composer not identified
Heard, William N. (Vocalist)
Songs from the Sanctuary: Hymns, Spirituals & Classic Gospels, Volume III
Heardsong Productions; 2012; CD
Chorus

979

Ezekiel Saw de Wheel
Composer not identified
Hines, Jerome (Bass)
Black & White Spirituals
Supreme S 3005; 1974; LP

980

Ezechiel Saw de Wheel
Milkey, Edward T.
Jones, Fanni (Mezzo-soprano)
Negro Spirituals en Concert
Suisa; 1987; LP
Organ
Heavy dialect

981

Ezekiel Saw the Wheel
Bonds, Margaret
Matthews, Benjamin (Baritone)
A Balm in Gilead
Ebony Classic Recordings ECR 0001; 2000; CD
Piano

982

Ezekiel Saw the Wheel
Johnson, Hall
Maynor, Kevin (Bass)
The Spiritual: An Underground Railroad
Southeastern Virginia Arts Assoc.; [2000]; CD
Piano

983

Ezekiel Saw the Wheel
Bonds, Margaret
Pierson, Edward (Bass-baritone)
Edward Pierson Sings Hymns and Spirituals
Kemco 98-44; [19--]; LP

984

Ezekiel Saw de Wheel
Brown, Lawrence
Robeson, Paul (Bass-baritone); Brown, Lawrence (Vocalist)
The Complete EMI Sessions (1928–1939)
EMI Classics 50999 2 15586 2 7; 2008; CD
Piano
Heavy dialect

985

Ezekiel Saw de Wheel
Brown, Lawrence
Robeson, Paul (Bass-baritone)
Spirituals: Original Recordings 1925–1936
Naxos Gospel Legends 8.120638; 2003; CD
Piano

986

Ezekiel Saw the Wheel
Brown, Lawrence
Robeson, Paul (Bass-baritone); Brown, Lawrence (Vocalist)
Paul Robeson in Live Performance
Columbia M 30424; 1971; LP
Piano
Moderate dialect

987

Ezekiel Saw de Wheel
Brown, Lawrence
Robeson, Paul (Bass-baritone); Brown, Lawrence (Vocalist)
Songs of My People
RCA Red Seal LM-3292; 1972; LP
Piano

988

Ezekiel Saw the Wheel
Brown, Lawrence
Robeson, Paul (Bass-baritone); Brown, Lawrence (Vocalist)

*A Lonesome Road: Paul Robeson Sings
    Spirituals and Songs*
ASV Living Era CD AJA 5027; 1984; CD
Piano
Heavy dialect

989

Ezekiel Saw de Wheel
Brown, Lawrence
Robeson, Paul (Bass-baritone)
Paul Robeson Sings Negro Spirituals
Philips GBL 5584; [19--]; LP
Piano

990

Ezekiel Saw de Wheel
Brown, Lawrence
Robeson, Paul (Bass-baritone); Brown,
    Lawrence (Vocalist)
Spirituals/Folksongs/Hymns
Pearl GEMM CD 9382; 1989; CD

991

Ezekiel Saw the Wheel
Brown, Lawrence
Robeson, Paul (Bass-baritone)
Paul Robeson: Great Voices of the Century, v. 2
Memoir Classics CDMOIR 426; 1994; CD

992

Ezekiel Saw the Wheel
Brown, Lawrence
Robeson, Paul (Bass-baritone)
Paul Robeson Collection
Hallmark Recordings 390692; 1998; CD

993

Ezekiel Saw de Wheel
Brown, Lawrence
Robeson, Paul (Bass-baritone); Brown,
    Lawrence (Vocalist)
Hear, De Lam's A-Cryin'/Ezekiel Saw de Wheel
Victor 20604; 1927; 78 RPM
Piano
Light dialect

994

Ezekiel Saw de Wheel
Brown, Lawrence

Robeson, Paul (Bass-baritone)
Swing Low, Sweet Chariot
Columbia Masterworks MM-819; 1949; 78
    RPM
Piano

995

Ezekiel Saw de Wheel
Brown, Lawrence
Robeson, Paul (Bass-baritone); Brown,
    Lawrence (Vocalist)
*Hear, De Lam's A-Cryin'/Ezekiel Saw de
    Wheel*
His Master's Voice B 2838; 1928; 78 RPM
Piano

996

Ezechial Saw de Wheel
Brown, Lawrence
Robeson, Paul (Bass-baritone); Brown,
    Lawrence (Vocalist)
Paul Robeson Chante ... f16 Spirituals
Philips G 05.639 R; 1959; LP
Piano

997

Ezekial Saw de Wheel
[Brown, Lawrence]
Robeson, Paul (Bass-baritone)
Swing Low, Sweet Chariot
Columbia Masterworks ML 2038; [195-]; LP
Piano

998

Ezekiel Saw the Wheel
[Brown, Lawrence]
Robeson, Paul (Bass-baritone); Brown,
    Lawrence (Vocalist)
Ol' Man River: The Ultimate Collection
Roslin Records; 2011; Streaming audio
Piano
Heavy dialect

999

Ezekiel Saw de Wheel
[Brown, Lawrence]
Robeson, Paul (Bass-baritone); Brown,
    Lawrence (Vocalist)
The Ultimate Collection

Burning Fire; 2009; Streaming audio
Piano
Heavy dialect

1000

Ezekiel Saw the Wheel
Composer not identified
Rustin, Bayard (Tenor)
*Bayard Rustin Sings Spirituals, Work &
    Freedom Songs*
Bayard Rustin Fund; 1988; Cassette
Piano
Heavy dialect

Also released with *Bayard Rustin, the Singer* (Bayard Rustin Fund; 1992; CD) and *Bayard Rustin Sings Spirituals, Work & Freedom Songs* (Bayard Rustin Fund; 2003; CD)

1001

Ezekiel Saw a Wheel
Traditional
Rustin, Bayard (Tenor)
Elizabethan Songs & Negro Spirituals
Fellowship Records 102; [1952]; 10 ' LP
A cappella

Also released with *Bayard Rustin-The Singer* (Black Swan Series; Parnassus Records PACD 96083; 2022; CD)

1002

Ezekiel Saw the Wheel
Hayes, Roland
Sims, Robert (Baritone)
*Robert Sims Sings the Spirituals of Roland
    Hayes*
Canti Classics 2014-01; 2015; CD
Piano
Heavy dialect

1003

Ezekiel Saw a Wheel
Composer not identified
Spencer, Kenneth (Bass-baritone)
Negro Spirituals
Life Records C 1108; [19--]; LP

1004

Ezekiel Saw a Wheel
Nagel, [Otto]

Spencer, Kenneth (Bass-baritone)
Volkslieder & Spirituals
Discoton 75546; [197-]; LP
Chorus
Heavy dialect

1005

Ezekiel Saw the Wheel
Bonds, Margaret
Taylor, Darryl (Countertenor)
How Sweet the Sound: A Charm of Spirituals
Albany TROY1244; 2011; CD
Piano

1006

Ezekiel Saw de Wheel
Composer not identified
Watts, Leonardo (Baritone)
*On Ma Journey: A Memorable Collection of
    Negro Spirituals*
Onyx Recording Associates ORA-101; 1961; LP
Chorus

1007

Ezekiel Saw the Wheel
Composer not identified
White, Willard (Bass-baritone)
The Paul Robeson Legacy
Linn AKD 190; 2015; CD
Instrumental ensemble

· · · · · · ·

Feel the Spirit

1008

Feel the Spirit
Hayes, Mark
Thomas, Indra (Soprano)
Great Day: Indra Thomas Sings Spirituals
Delos DE 3427; 2012; CD
Piano
Heavy dialect

· · · · · · ·

Feet o' Jesus

1009

Feet o' Jesus
Price, Florence

Heard, Richard (Tenor)
My Dream: Art Songs and Spirituals
Percentage Records/Sound of Art
   Recordings CD147597; 2012; CD
Piano
Light dialect

1010

Feet o' Jesus
Price, Florence
Yovanovich, Amy (Mezzo-soprano)
Great Day!
Prince Productions 9808P; 2007; CD
Piano
Light dialect

· · · · · · ·

Fix Me Jesus

1011

Fix Me Jesus
[Johnson, Hall]
Anderson, Marian (Contralto)
*Marian Anderson and Dorothy Maynor in
   Concert*
Eklipse Records EKR 49; 1995; CD
Piano

1012

Fix Me, Jesus
[Johnson, Hall]
Anderson, Marian (Contralto)
Inspiration in Song
Demand Performance DPC-521; 1987;
   Cassette

1013

Fix Me, Jesus
Traditional
Battle, Kathleen (Soprano)
Classic Kathleen Battle: a Portrait
Sony Classical SK 89464; 2002; CD
A cappella
No dialect discerned

   Also released with *The Complete Sony
Recordings* (Sony Classical 88985381362;
2016; CD)

1014

Fix Me, Jesus
Johnson, Hall
Blackmon, Henry (Baritone)
Negro Spirituals
Jubilate JB 1716; 1961; 45 RPM
Organ

1015

Oh, Fix Me
Composer not identified
Carey, Thomas (Baritone)
Go Down Moses
Da Camera Song SM 95028; 1970; LP
Piano

1016

Fix Me Jesus
Cooke, Barbara Logan
Cooke, Barbara (Vocalist)
*Sometimes I Feel: A Collection of Negro
   Spirituals for Voice and Instruments*
Private Label KDISC420; 2002; CD
Instrumental ensemble

1017

Fix Me, Jesus
Credit, Roosevelt André
Credit, Roosevelt André (Bass-baritone)
Ol' Time Religion
CD Baby; 2007; CD, Streaming audio
Piano

1018

Fix Me Jesus
Brown, Uzee, Jr.
English-Robinson, Laura (Soprano)
Great Day!
Allgood; 2005; CD
Piano
No dialect discerned

1019

Fix Me, Jesus
Brown, Uzee, Jr.
Fernandez, Wilhelmenia (Soprano)
Negro Spirituals
Transart 131; 2005; CD
A cappella

1020

Oh Fix Me
Johnson, Hall
Foreman, Blanche (Contralto)
*Best of the Hall Johnson Centennial Festival
    Celebrating the 100th Anniversary of Hall
    Johnson's Birth*
Hall Johnson Collection O33D2; 2002; CD
Piano

1021

Fix Me, Jesus
Ching
Gormley, Clare (Soprano)
Where Morning Lies: Spiritual Songs
ABC Classics 461 766-2; 2002; CD
Piano
No dialect discerned

1022

Fix Me, Jesus
Composer not identified
Hendricks, Barbara (Soprano)
Negro Spirituals
EMI CDC7470262; 1983; CD
Piano
Light dialect

    Also released with E*spirituales Negros*
(EMI Classics/Altaya 01636; 1983; CD); *Great
American Spirituals* (Angel CDM 7 64669 2;
1992; CD); *Great American Spirituals* (Musical
Heritage Society 513725Z; 1994; CD) and *Spiri-
tuals* (EMI Classics 0946 346641 2 7; 2005; CD)

1023

Fix Me, Jesus
Hicks, Lori
Hicks, Lori (Soprano)
Music of My Voice
Celestial Song Productions; 2015; CD
Chorus

1024

Fix Me, Jesus
Johnson, Hall
Hornung, Lisa (Contralto); Little, Ricky
    (Baritone)
The Lily of the Valley
American Spiritual Ensemble; [2003]; CD

1025

Fix Me, Jesus
Johnson, Hall
Kirkham, Robert (Baritone)
Song Recital by Robert Kirkham
Epworth EP 8521; [197-]; LP
Piano

1026

Fix Me, Jesus
Johnson, Hall
Kirkman, Robert (Baritone)
Song Recital by Robert Kirkham
Epworth EP 8521; [197-]; LP

1027

Fix Me, Jesus
Johnson, Hall
Matthews, Inez (Mezzo-soprano)
*Inez Matthews Sings Spirituals (Great New
    Voices of Today, v. 6)*
Period SPL-580; [1950]; LP
Piano
Heavy dialect

    Also released with *Inez Matthews Sings
Spirituals* (Essential Media Group; 2011;
CD)

1028

Fix, Me, Jesus
Composer not identified
McDaniel, Yvette (Soprano)
Simply Spiritual
YM01 DIDX 046103; 1997; CD
Piano

1029

Fix Me, Jesus
Johnson, Hall
McFerrin, Robert (Baritone)
*Deep River and Other Classic Negro
    Spirituals*
Riverside Records RLP 12-812; 1959; LP
Piano
Light dialect

    Also released with *Classic Negro Spiri-
tuals* (Washington Records WLP 466; 1959;
LP)

1030

Fix Me, Jesus
Johnson, Hall
Salters, Stephen (Baritone)
Spirit: Are You There, You Are There
HarmonizedDisharmony 0001; 2015; CD

1031

Fix Me Jesus
Johnson, Hall
Simpson, Eugene Thamon (Bass)
Thanks Be to Thee
Black Heritage Publications; 2005; CD
Piano

  Also released with *Hall Johnson Spirituals and Other Folk Songs* (Private Label; 2016; CD)

1032

Fix Me, Jesus
Blanchard, Terence
Sykes, Jubilant (Baritone)
Jubilant Sykes
Sony Classical SK 63294; 1998; CD
Instrumental ensemble

1033

Fix Me Jesus
Johnson, Hall
Toppin, Louise (Soprano)
He'll Bring It to Pass: The Spirituals of Hall Johnson for Voice and Piano
Albany Records TROY846; 2006; CD
Piano
Light dialect

1034

Fix Me, Jesus
[Johnson, Hall]
West, Lucretia (Mezzo-soprano)
Negro Spirituals III
Club français du disque 176; 1959; LP
Piano
Light dialect

    • • • • • • •

Fi-yer

1035

Fi-yer!
Johnson, Hall

Brown, William (Tenor)
Fi-Yer!: a century of African American song
Albany Records TROY 329; 1999; CD
Piano
Heavy dialect

1036

Fi-yer
Johnson, Hall
Holland, Charles (Tenor)
My Lord What a Mornin'
Musical Heritage Society MHS 912250X;
  1982; LP
Piano
Heavy dialect

  Also released with *My Lord What a Mornin'* (Musical Heritage Society MHS 512250K; 1988; CD)

1037

Fi-yer
Johnson, Hall
Morrison, John (Tenor)
Best of the Hall Johnson Centennial Festival Celebrating the 100th Anniversary of Hall Johnson's Birth
Hall Johnson Collection O33D2; 2002; CD
Piano

1038

Fi-yer
Johnson, Hall
Patton. John (Tenor)
Black Spirituals and Art Songs
Narthex Recording 827N-4581; 1970; LP
Piano
Heavy dialect

1039

Fi-yer
Johnson, Hall
Toppin, Louise (Soprano)
The Hall Johnson Collection
Carl Fischer VF5 CD1–VF5 CD2; 2003;
  Score w/CD
Piano
Moderate dialect

· · · · · · ·

Follow Me

1040

Follow Me
Dett, Robert Nathaniel
Taylor, Richard (Baritone)
The New Negro Spiritual
W. C. Patterson; 2002; Score w/CD
Piano
Moderate dialect

· · · · · · ·

Four and Twenty Elders

1041

Four and Twenty Elders
Composer not identified
White, Portia (Contralto)
First You Dream
C. White PW 001-2; 1990s; CD
Piano

1042

Four and Twenty Elders
Composer not identified
White, Portia (Contralto)
Think on Me
White House Records WH-6901; 1968; LP
Piano

· · · · · · ·

Free at Last

1043

Free at Last
Perry, Julia
Honeysucker, Robert (Baritone)
*Watch and Pray: Spirituals and Art Songs by
    African-American Women Composers*
Koch International Classics 3-7247-2H1;
    1994; CD
Piano
Light dialect

1044

Free at Last
Perry, Julia

Jones, Randye (Soprano)
Come Down Angels
Ahhjay Records AHHJ-0001; 2003; CD
Piano
Light dialect

· · · · · · ·

Give Away Jordan

1045

Give-away Jordan [from *My Songs: Dream of
    Heaven*]
Hayes, Roland
Hayes, Roland (Tenor)
Roland Hayes: My Songs
Vanguard VRS-494; 1956; LP
Piano
Moderate dialect

Also released with *Favorite Spiritu-
als* (Vanguard Classics OVC 6022; 1995;
CD) and *Big Psalms, Hymns and Spirituals
Box* (eOne Music/Vanguard Classics; 2015;
Streaming audio)

· · · · · · ·

Give Me Jesus

[Matthew 27:17]

"Oh, when I come to die, Oh, when I
come to die, Oh, when I come to die, Give me
Jesus. Give me Jesus, You may have all this
world; Give me Jesus. In the morning when
I rise...."

[Available in AAGS, FH25, HCTN,
HJCO, HTBS, JHSS, JW10, LLS2, MH10,
MHDR, MM4S, SOTS, VLCH, WF70]

1046

Give Me Jesus
Johnson, Hall
Alexander, Roberta (Soprano)
Songs My Mother Taught Me
Etcetera KTC 1208; 1999; CD
Piano
Moderate dialect

1047

Give Me Jesus
Traditional

Anderson, Charmaine (Vocalist)
They Slice the Air
Spirituals Project; 2007; CD
A cappella
Light dialect

1048

Give Me Jesus
Kennedy, Fred
Arroyo, Martina (Soprano)
Spirituals
Centaur CRC 2060; 1991; CD
Piano
Light dialect

1049

Give Me Jesus
Hogan, Moses
Blanchard, Gerald (Baritone)
With a Song in My Heart
Blue Griffin Recording BGR117; 2004; CD
Piano
Light dialect

1050

Give Me Jesus
Brown, Angela; Cooper, Tyron
Brown, Angela (Soprano)
*Mosiac: A Collection of African-American
    Spirituals with Piano, guitar*
Albany Records TROY721; 2004; CD
Guitar
Light dialect

1051

Give Me Jesus
Brown, Angela; Webb, Charles
Brown, Angela (Soprano)
Soprano
Caboose Productions; 1995; CD
Piano

1052

Give Me Jesus
Hershberger, A. J.
Brown, Anthony (Baritone)
Toil and Triumph
Spirituals Project; 2002; CD

Chorus
Light dialect

1053

Give Me Jesus
Burleigh, Harry T.
Burton, Dashon (Bass-baritone)
*Songs of Struggle & Redemption: We Shall
    Overcome*
Acis Productions APL08685; 2015; CD
Piano
Moderate dialect

1054

Give Me Jesus
Traditional
Carey, Thomas (Baritone)
*Sechs Amerikanische Volkslieder/Sechs
    Negro Spirituals*
Colosseum SM 3003; 1970; LP
A cappella

1055

Give Me Jesus
[Johnson, Hall]
Clifford, Rochelle Small (Soprano)
Sacred Spaces
Private Label; 2008; CD
A cappella
No dialect discerned

1056

Give Me Jesus
[Johnson, Hall]
Cole, Vinson (Tenor)
Strauss, Duparc, Puccini, Nin
Connoisseur Society CD4184; 1991; CD
Piano
Heavy dialect

1057

Give Me Jesus
Keele, Roger; Curtis, Nancy
Curtis, Nancy (Soprano)
Nancy Curtis
Nancy Curtis Productions; 2003; CD

1058

Give Me Jesus
Johnson, Hall

Davis, Ollie Watts (Soprano)
Here's One: Spiritual Songs
KJAC Publishing KJAC0123; 2003; CD
Piano
Moderate dialect

1059

Give Me Jesus (after H. Johnson) [from *Four Spirituals for Soprano and String Quartet*]
Taylor, Stephen Andrew
Davis, Ollie Watts (Soprano)
Rootsongs
Azica AZI 71311; 2016; CD
Instrumental ensemble
Light dialect

1060

Give Me Jesus
Johnson, Hall
Davis, Osceola (Soprano)
Negro Spirituals
Ondine ODE 715-2; 1988; CD
Piano
Light dialect

1061

Give Me Jesus
Hayes, Mark
Day, Calesta (Soprano)
The Spirituals: Featuring the American Spiritual Ensemble
LexArts; [20--]; CD

1062

Give Me Jesus
Composer not identified
Duckworth, Zorita (Mezzo-soprano)
Forget Me Not.... Negro Spirituals
Private Label; [20--]; CD

1063

Give Me Jesus
Johnson, Hall
Gibson, Caroline (Soprano)
On Ma Journey Now: Negro Spirituals in Concert
Twin Productions; 2016; CD
Piano
No dialect discerned

1064

Give Me Jesus
Mills, Marvin
Graves, Denyce (Mezzo-soprano)
Angels Watching Over Me
NPR Classics CD 0006; 1997; CD
Piano
Light dialect

1065

Give Me Jesus
Composer not identified
Green, Elnora E. (Contralto)
This Is My Task
Private Label NR 18650; 1991; LP

1066

Give Me Jesus
Burleigh, Harry T.
Hayes, Roland (Tenor)
Swing Low Sweet Chariot
Vocalion B3039, Vocalion R6133; 1997; CD
Chorus

1067

Give Me Jesus
Boatner, Edward
Heard, Richard (Tenor)
Ain't a That Good News: African-American Art Songs and Spirituals
HM Classics HMC9602; 1998; CD
Piano
Light dialect

1068

Give Me Jesus
Composer not identified
Heard, William N. (Vocalist)
Songs from the Sanctuary: Hymns, Spirituals & Classic Gospels, Volume II
Heardsong Productions; 2012; CD
Piano

1069

Give Me Jesus [from *Five Spirituals*]
Stucky, Rodney
Henderson, Mary (Mezzo-soprano)
Come Where the Aspens Quiver.... Bring Your Guitar

Fleur de Son Classics FDS 57955; 2002; CD
Guitar
No dialect discerned

1070

Give Me Jesus
Hogan, Moses
Hendricks, Barbara (Soprano)
Give Me Jesus
EMI Classics 7243 5 56788 2 9; 1998; CD
Chorus
Light dialect

1071

Give Me Jesus
Johnson, Hall
Holland, Charles (Tenor)
My Lord What a Mornin'
Musical Heritage Society MHS 912250X;
    1982; LP
Piano
Moderate dialect

Also released with *My Lord What a
Mornin'* (Musical Heritage Society MHS
512250K; 1988; CD)

1072

Give Me Jesus
Burleigh, Harry T.
Honeysucker, Robert (Baritone)
Good News
Videmus Records VIS735; 2007; CD
Piano
Light dialect

1073

Give Me Jesus
Hayes, Mark
Hudson, Marlissa (Soprano)
Libera
AMP Records AGCD 2106; 2010; CD
Piano
No dialect discerned

1074

Give Me Jesus
Composer not identified
Humphrey Flynn, Edwina (Soprano)
The Lord Will Make a Way

Private Label; 2000; CD
Piano

1075

Give Me Jesus
Composer not identified
Jobson, Christine (Soprano)
By Faith: Hymns and Negro Spirituals
CD Baby; 2017; CD
Piano
Moderate dialect

1076

Give Me Jesus [from Five spirituals for
    baritone and cello]
Balentine, James Scott
Jones, Timothy (Baritone)
Love Comes in at the Eye
Albany TROY1734; 2018; CD
Cello
Moderate dialect

1077

Give Me Jesus
Hayes, Mark
Lima, Philip (Baritone)
Songs of a Wayfarer
Private Label; 2017; Streaming audio
Piano
No dialect discerned

1078

Give Me Jesus
Hayes, Mark
Lynch, Lester (Baritone)
On My Journey Now: Spirituals & Hymns
Pentatone Music PTC 5186 57'; 2017; CD
Piano

1079

Give Me Jesus
Composer not identified
McDaniel, Yvette (Soprano)
Simply Spiritual
YM01 DIDX 046103; 1997; CD
Piano

1080

Give Me Jesus
Johnson, Hall

Miles, John (Tenor)
The Classic Spirituals
Epiphany 83-1027; 1983; LP
Instrumental ensemble

1081

Give Me Jesus
Hogan, Moses
Moses, Oral (Bass-baritone)
*Come Down Angels and Trouble the Water:
    Negro Spirituals, an American National
    Treasure!*
Albany Records TROY 1489; 2014; CD
Piano
Light dialect

1082

Give Me Jesus
Composer not identified
Nobles, NaGuanda (Soprano)
Homage to the Journey
Selbon Records; 2014; Streaming audio
Piano
Light dialect

1083

Give Me Jesus
Composer not identified
Norman, Jessye (Soprano)
*The Jessye Norman Collection: Sacred Songs
    & Spirituals*
Philips B0004506-02; 2005; CD
Chorus
Moderate dialect

1084

Give Me Jesus
Patterson, Willis
Norman, Jessye (Soprano)
The Jessye Norman Collection
Philips Classics 422 893-2; [1988]; CD
Chorus
Heavy dialect

1085

Give Me Jesus
Patterson. Willis
Norman, Jessye (Soprano)
Spirituals

Philips 416 462-2; 1990; CD
Chorus
No dialect discerned

1086

Give Me Jesus
Patterson. Willis
Norman, Jessye (Soprano)
Negro Spirituals
Philips 9500 580; 1979; LP
Chorus

1087

Give Me Jesus
Sweeney, John R.
Norman, Jessye (Soprano)
Amazing Grace
Philips 432 546-2; 1990; CD
Chorus
No dialect discerned

1088

Give Me Jesus
McLin, Lena
Pierson, Edward (Bass-baritone)
Edward Pierson Sings Hymns and Spirituals
Kemco 98-44; [19--]; LP

1089

Give Me Jesus
Hayes, Mark
Powell, Angela (Soprano)
City Called Heaven
Private Label AP6957; 2003; CD
Piano

1090

Give Me Jesus
Composer not identified
Price, Eudora (Vocalist)
My Favorite Songs & Spirituals
Private Label; 2006; CD
Organ
No dialect discerned

1091

Give Me Jesus
Johnson, Hall
Quivar, Florence (Mezzo-soprano)

Negro Spirituals
EMI 7243 5 72790 2 4; 1998; CD
Piano
Moderate dialect

> Also released with *Ride On, King Jesus!*
Florence Quivar Sings Black Music of America
(EMI Classics 9 67138 2; 2010; CD)

1092

Give Me Jesus
Hogan, Moses
Ragin, Derek Lee (Countertenor)
Ev'ry Time I Feel the Spirit: Spirituals
Channel Classics CCS 2991; 1991; CD
Piano
Light dialect

1093

Give Me Jesus
Bacon, Boyd
Simpson, Icy (Soprano)
I, Too
Longhorn Music; 2012; CD
Piano

1094

Give Me Jesus
Hogan, Moses
Simpson, Marietta (Mezzo-soprano)
Songs of Reflection
MGH Records 0800CD; 2002; CD
Piano

1095

Give Me Jesus
Blanchard, Terence
Sykes, Jubilant (Baritone)
Jubilant Sykes
Sony Classical SK 63294; 1998; CD
Instrumental ensemble

1096

Give Me Jesus
Burleigh, Harry T.
Thomas, Indra (Soprano)
Great Day: Indra Thomas Sings Spirituals
Delos DE 3427; 2012; CD
Piano
Light dialect

1097

Give Me Jesus
Johnson, Hall
Toppin, Louise (Soprano)
The Hall Johnson Collection
Carl Fischer VF5 CD1–VF5 CD2; 2003; Score
  w/CD
Piano
Moderate dialect

1098

Give Me Jesus
Johnson, Hall
Toppin, Louise (Soprano)
*He'll Bring It to Pass: The Spirituals of Hall
  Johnson for Voice and Piano*
Albany Records TROY846; 2006; CD
Piano
Heavy dialect

1099

Give Me Jesus
Composer not identified
Tyler, Veronica (Soprano)
Sings ... the Passion of Christ in Spirituals
BRC Productions; [19--]; LP
Piano

1100

Give Me Jesus
Hogan, Moses
Walker, Alfred (Bass)
*Deep River: Featuring 10 Spirituals Arranged
  for Solo Voice....*
MGH Records 5000; 2000; CD
Piano
Light dialect

1101

Give Me Jesus
[Johnson, Hall]
White, Cassandra (Soprano)
Remembering the Spirituals
CBW Entertainment 837101334068; 2007;
  CD
Piano
No dialect discerned

1102
In the Mornin'
Ives, Charles
White, Willard (Bass-baritone)
*Willard White Sings: Copland; American
    Spirituals; Folk-Songs*
Chandos Records CHAN 8960; 1991; CD
Piano
Light dialect

1103
Give Me Jesus
Composer not identified
Williams, Wayne (Tenor)
Music from My Life
Movideo Productions 02-1993; 1993; CD
Piano

1104
Give Me Jesus
Johnson, Hall
Wilson, Robin (Soprano)
*Best of the Hall Johnson Centennial Festival
    Celebrating the 100th Anniversary of Hall
    Johnson's Birth*
Hall Johnson Collection O33D2; 2002; CD
Piano

. . . .

Give Me Your Hand

1105
Give Me Yo' Hand
Lloyd, Charles, Jr.
Hobson, Richard (Baritone)
The Spiritual Art Song Collection
Warner Bros. SVBM00004; 2000; Score w/
    CD
Piano

1106
Give Me Your Hand
Boatner, Edward
Ingram, Paula Dione (Soprano)
*Art. Legacy. Celebration: A Salute to Black-
    American Composers of Art Songs and
    Spirituals, v. 1*
Private Label; 2014; CD
Piano

1107
Give Me Your Hand
Boatner, Edward
Jones, Arthur (Tenor)
Wade in the Water
Orbis Books; 1993; Book w/cass
Piano
Heavy dialect

1108
Gimme Yo' Hand
Hairston, Jacqueline
Warfield, William (Bass-baritone); Matthews,
    Benjamin Sims, Robert (Baritone)
Three Generations Live
Canti Records; 2000; CD
Piano
Heavy dialect

. . . .

Glory, Glory, Hallelujah

1109
Glory, Glory, Hallelujah
McLin, Lena
Blackmon, Henry (Baritone)
Negro Spirituals
Mirasound Records SGLP 6047; [19--]; LP
Organ

1110
Glory, Glory Hallelujah
McLin, Lena
Blackmon, Henry (Baritone)
Negro Spirituals
Vega 19179; [19--]; LP
Chorus, piano

1111
Glory, Glory, Hallelujah
Corley, Maria Thompson
Clark, Maria (Soprano)
Soul Sanctuary: Spirituals & Hymns
Navona Records NV6406; 2022; CD
Piano
Moderate dialect

1112
Glory, Glory
Composer not identified

Davis, Frank (Bass-baritone)
16 Spirituals My Father Taught Me
DeWitt Records 601; 1960; LP

1113
When I Lay My Burden Down
Hendricks, Barbara; Alexeev, Dmitri
Hendricks, Barbara (Soprano)
Negro Spirituals
EMI CDC7470262; 1983; CD
Piano
Light dialect

1114
Glory, Glory, Hallelujah
McLin, Lena
Rucker, Mark (Baritone)
Mark Rucker Sings Lena McLin: Songs for Voice & Piano
Kjos Music Press KCD8; 2002; CD
Piano
No dialect discerned

1115
Glory, Glory Hallelujah
McLin, Lena
Sims, Robert (Baritone)
Three Generations Live
Canti Records; 1999; CD
Piano
Heavy dialect

1116
Glory, Hallelujah
Young, Thomas J.
Young, Thomas (Tenor)
Black Christmas: Spirituals in the African-American Tradition
Essay Recordings CD1011; 1990; CD
Piano
No dialect discerned

    Also released with *A Spiritual Christmas* (Musical Heritage Society 5167448; 2002; CD)

• • • • • • •

Glory to His Name

1117
Glory to His Name
Raphael, Michael

Maynor, Kevin (Bass)
The Spiritual: An Underground Railroad
Southeastern Virginia Arts Assoc.; [2000]; CD
Piano

• • • • • • •

Glory to the Newborn King

1118
Glory to the Newborn King
Young, Thomas J.
Ayers, Vanessa (Mezzo-soprano)
Black Christmas: Spirituals in the African-American Tradition
Essay Recordings CD1011; 1990; CD
Piano
No dialect discerned

    Also released with *A Spiritual Christmas* (Musical Heritage Society 5167448; 2002; CD)

1119
Glory to That Newborn King
Still, William Grant
Edwards, Nina (Vocalist)
Voices and piano
William Grant Still Music; 2000; CD
Piano

• • • • • • •

Go Down Death

1120
Go Down Death
Traditional
Rustin, Bayard (Tenor)
Bayard Rustin Sings Spirituals, Work & Freedom Songs
Bayard Rustin Fund; 1988; Cassette
A cappella
Heavy dialect

    Also released with *Bayard Rustin Sings Spirituals, Work & Freedom Songs* (Bayard Rustin Fund; 2003; CD)

· · · · · · ·

Go Down in the Lonesome Valley

1121

Go Down in de Lonesome Valley
[Burleigh, Harry T.]
Chaiter, Yoram (Bass)
Spirituals & Other Songs
Romeo Records 7311; 2014; CD
Piano
Light dialect

1122

Go Down in the Lonesome Valley
Clinton, Irving
Irving, Clinton (Bass-baritone)
Clinton Irving Sings Spirituals: A Tribute
Rogers; 2001; CD

1123

Go Down in the Lonesome Valley
Burleigh, Harry T.
Oby, Jason (Tenor)
The Life of Christ: Collected Spirituals
Private Label TSU4749; [200-]; CD
Piano
No dialect discerned

· · · · · · ·

Go Down Moses

[Exodus 1-4, 10:3, 13:21 ; Psalm 114:1; 1
Corinthians 10:1-13; Galatians 5:1]

"(Refrain) Go down, Moses, Way down
in Egypt land, Tell ole Pharaoh, Let my people
go. (v. 1) When Israel was in Egypt Land, Let
my people go; Oppressed so hard, they could
not stand, Let my people go. (Refrain)...."

[Available in AB10, CW40, EM34,
FHFN, FP44, FP4S, HCTN, HJCO, HLBS,
HTBS, HT25, HTC2, JBES, JJAN, JJBA, JSSp,
RHMF, RWSC, SBFD, SOTS, WF70]

Few characters of the Bible connected
with the enslaved of antebellum America as
did Moses and his role in the emancipation of
the Israelites. The story is told over 24 verses,
though most versions of the songs typically
use three to five of them. "Go Down Moses"
was an open statement of the enslaved outcry
for freedom, and abolitionist Harriett Tub-
man was known to use the song to announce
to those who wished to follow her on The
Underground Railroad that she was nearby.

The verses are organized in standard
call-and-response, with a line of text sung
by the leader followed by a repeated line, or
response, sung by the congregants.

1124

Go Down, Moses
McCoy, Tom
Adkins, Paul Spencer (Tenor)
How Can I Keep from Singing?
PSA PSA-2002; 2002; CD
Piano
Light dialect

1125

Go Down Moses
Johnson, John Rosamond
Aluko, Tayo (Baritone)
Recalling Robeson: Songs from Call Mr. Robeson
Tayo Aluko and Friends TAAF CD 001;
     2007; CD
Piano

1126

Go Down, Moses
Burleigh, Harry T.
Anderson, Marian (Contralto)
Bach, Brahms, Schubert
RCA Victor 7911-2-RG; 1989; CD
Orchestra
No dialect discerned

1127

Go Down, Moses
Burleigh, Harry T.
Anderson, Marian (Contralto)
Prima Voce
Nimbus NI 7882; 1996; CD
Piano
Light dialect

1128

Go Down, Moses
Burleigh, Harry T.

Anderson, Marian (Contralto)
Rarities: Broadcast Performances 1943–1952
Video Artists International VAIA 1200;
   1998; CD
Orchestra

1129

Go Down, Moses
Burleigh, Harry T.
Anderson, Marian (Contralto)
Spirituals
RCA Victor Red Seal 09026-63306-2; 1999; CD
Piano
Light dialect

1130

Go Down, Moses
Burleigh, Harry T.
Anderson, Marian (Contralto)
Tribute
Pro Arte CDD 3447; 1993; CD
Piano

1131

Go Down, Moses
Burleigh, Harry T.
Anderson, Marian (Contralto)
Great Voices of the Century
Memoir Classics CDMOIR 432; 1996; CD
Piano

1132

Go Down, Moses
Burleigh, Harry T.
Anderson, Marian (Contralto)
Recital: Opera, Lieder, Oratorio
SYM1270.2; Symposium; 2005; CD
Piano

1133

Go Down, Moses
Burleigh, Harry T.
Anderson, Marian (Contralto)
Marian Anderson in Concert 1943–1952
Eklipse Records EKR CD19; 1993; CD
Orchestra

1134

Go Down, Moses
Burleigh, Harry T.

Anderson, Marian (Contralto)
Negro Spirituals: 1924–1949
Frémeaux & Associés FA 184; 2004; CD
Orchestra

1135

Go Down Moses
Burleigh, Harry T.
Anderson, Marian (Contralto)
Go Down Moses
Victor 19370-A; 1924; 78 RPM
Orchestra
No dialect discerned

1136

Go Down Moses (Let My People Go)
Burleigh, Harry T.
Anderson, Marian (Contralto)
*Softly Awakes My Heart: Very Best of Marian
   Anderson*
Alto ALN1955; 2016; CD
Piano
Heavy dialect

1137

Go Down, Moses
Burleigh, Harry T.
Anderson, Marian (Contralto)
Negro Spirituals
RCA Victor LM 2032; [1956]; LP
Piano
Light dialect

    Also released with *Marian Anderson:
Beyond the Music; Her Complete RCA Victor
Recordings* (Sony Classical 19439836492; 2021;
CD)

1138

Go Down Moses
Burleigh, Harry T.
Anderson, Marian (Contralto)
*Go Down Moses (Let My People Go)/My
   Soul's Been Anchored in the Lord*
Victor 1799; 1937; 78 RPM
Piano
Moderate dialect

1139

Go Down Moses
Burleigh, Harry T.

Anderson, Marian (Contralto)
Anderson Sings Negro Spirituals
Victor Golden Series EK-1007; [19--]; 45 RPM
Piano

1140

Go Down Moses (Let My People Go)
Burleigh, Harry T.
Anderson, Marian (Contralto)
Go Down Moses/My Soul's Been Anchored in the Lord
His Master's Voice D.A. 1560; 1939; 78 RPM
Piano
No dialect discerned

1141

Go Down, Moses (Let My People Go)
Burleigh, Harry T.
Anderson, Marian (Contralto)
Marian Anderson: Beyond the Music; Her Complete RCA Victor Recordings
Sony Classical 19439836492; 2021; CD
Organ
Light dialect

1142

Go Down, Moses
[Burleigh, Harry T.]
Anderson, Marian (Contralto)
Marian Anderson Sings Eleven Great Spirituals
RCA Victor LRM 7006; 1955; LP
Piano

    Also released with *Marian Anderson: Beyond the Music; Her Complete RCA Victor Recordings* (Sony Classical 19439836492; 2021; CD)

1143

Go Down, Moses
[Burleigh, Harry T.]
Anderson, Marian (Contralto)
When Marian Sang: Selected Songs from Marian Anderson's Repertoire
BMG Special Products DPC13280; 2002; CD

1144

Go Down, Moses
[Burleigh, Harry T.]

Anderson, Marian (Contralto)
Marian Anderson Sings Spirituals
Flapper Past CD 7073; 1995; CD
Piano

1145

Go Down, Moses
[Burleigh, Harry T.]
Anderson, Marian (Contralto)
Softly Awakes My Heart
ASV CD AJA 5262; 1999; CD
Piano

1146

Go Down, Moses
[Burleigh, Harry T.]
Anderson, Marian (Contralto)
Alto Rhapsody; Selected Spirituals
Urania URN 22.328; 2007; CD
Piano

1147

Go Down, Moses
[Burleigh, Harry T.]
Anderson, Marian (Contralto)
The Very Best of Marian Anderson
Master Classics Records; 2009; CD
Piano
No dialect discerned

1148

Go Down Moses
[Burleigh, Harry T.]
Anderson, Marian (Contralto)
Global Divas: Voices from Women of the World
Rounder CD 5062/3/4; 1995; CD

1149

Go Down Moses
[Burleigh, Harry T.]
Anderson, Marian (Contralto)
60 Years of Music America Loves Best, Vol. III
RCA Victor LM 2574; 1961; LP

1150

Go Down, Moses
[Burleigh, Harry T.]

Anderson, Marian (Contralto)
Inspirations
Emerald Echoes; 2015; Streaming audio
Piano
Light dialect

1151

Go Down, Moses
[Burleigh, Harry T.]
Anderson, Marian (Contralto)
Marian Anderson Sings Eleven Great
Spirituals
Kipepeo Publishing; 2017; CD
Piano

    Also released with *Marian Anderson:*
Beyond the Music; Her Complete RCA Victor Recordings (Sony Classical 19439836492; 2021; CD)

1152

Go Down, Moses
[Burleigh, Harry T.]
Anderson, Marian (Contralto)
Negro Spirituals
RCA Victor 630.396 A; [19--]; LP
Piano

    Also released with *Marian Anderson:*
Beyond the Music; Her Complete RCA Victor Recordings (Sony Classical 19439836492; 2021; CD)

1153

Go Down Moses
[Burleigh, Harry T.]
Anderson, Marian (Contralto)
Grandes Contraltos de la Musique Classique,
Les: Marian Anderson, Vol. 9
Mon Patrimoine Musical Collection; 2017;
   Streaming audio
Piano

1154

Go Down Moses
Burleigh, Harry T.; Bledsoe, Jules
Bledsoe, Jules (Baritone)
Go Down Moses/Deep River
Ultraphone AP 394; 1931; 78 RPM
Orchestra
Moderate dialect

1155

Go Down Moses
Composer not identified
Bledsoe, Jules (Baritone)
Go Down Moses/Deep River
Royale 1703; [19--]; 78 RPM
Orchestra
Moderate dialect

1156

Go Down Moses
Composer not identified
Bledsoe, Jules (Baritone)
Poor Monah/Go Down Moses
Joe Davis 8001; [19]; 78 RPM
Orchestra
Moderate dialect

1157

Go Down Moses
Boatwright, McHenry
Boatwright, McHenry (Bass-baritone)
Art of McHenry Boatwright: Spirituals
Golden Crest Records RE 7024; 1968; LP
Piano
Light dialect

1158

Go Down Moses
Traditional
Brown, Anthony (Baritone)
Each Other's Light: Songs of Peace, Hope &
   Justice
Private label AB0906; [2017]; CD
Chorus
No dialect discerned

1159

Go Down, Moses [from *Green Pastures*]
Johnson, Hall
Brown, William (Tenor)
The Hall Johnson Collection
Carl Fischer VF5 CD1–VF5 CD2; 2003; Score
   w/CD
Piano
Heavy dialect

1160

Go Down Moses
Burleigh, Harry T.

Burleigh, Harry T. (Baritone)
Dvořák Discoveries
Music & Arts CD-926; 1996; CD
Piano
Light dialect

Also released with *Lost Sounds: Blacks and the Birth of the Recording Industry 1891–1922* (Archeophone Records ARCH 1005; 2005; CD) and *Black Swans* (Parnassus Recordings PACD 96067; 2019; CD)

1161

Go Down, Moses
Johnson, Hall
Burton, Dashon (Bass-baritone)
Songs of Struggle & Redemption: We Shall Overcome
Acis Productions APL08685; 2015; CD
Piano
Moderate dialect

1162

Go Down, Moses
Composer not identified
Carey, Thomas (Baritone)
Go Down Moses
Da Camera Song SM 95028; 1970; LP
Piano

1163

Go Down, Moses
Burleigh, Harry T.
Carlsen, Svein (Bass)
Negro Spirituals
EuroMaster AS ECD19005; 1996; CD
Piano

1164

Go Down, Moses
Johnson, Hall
Carnette, Count (Vocalist)
Count Carnette Sings Favorite Negro Spirituals
Carnette Archive Recordings; 1983; LP
Piano
Light dialect

1165

Go Down Moses
Composer not identified

Chaiter, Yoram (Bass)
Spirituals & Other Songs
Romeo Records 7311; 2014; CD
Piano
No dialect discerned

1166

Go Down, Moses
Burleigh, Harry T.
Cordon, Norman (Bass)
Water Boy/Go Down Moses
Victor 10-1114; 1942; 78 RPM
Piano
Moderate dialect

1167

Go Down Moses
Composer not identified
Deguil, Arlette (Vocalist)
Negro Spirituals
Pathé 45 ED 1; 1953; 45 RPM

Also released with *Negro Spirituals* (Pathé 45-ED 1; 1953; LP)

1168

Go Down, Moses
Roberts, Howard
Estes, Simon (Bass-baritone)
Spirituals
Philips 412 631-2; 1985; CD
Chorus, organ, orchestra
Light dialect

1169

Go Down, Moses
Roberts, Howard
Estes, Simon (Bass-baritone)
Famous Spirituals
Philips 462 062-2; 1997; CD
Chorus, orchestra
Light dialect

1170

Go Down, Moses
Ryan, Donald
Estes, Simon (Bass-baritone)
Steal Away: My Favorite Negro Spirituals
Deutsche Schallplatten DS 1041-2; 1994; CD

Piano
Light dialect

Also released with *Simon Sings His Favorite Gospels & Spirituals* (Praise Productions SMG-SE; 1999; CD) and *Save the Children, Save Their Lives* (CD Baby; 2010; CD)

1171

Go Down Moses
Kaelin, Pierre
Evans, Allan (Bass-baritone)
Negro Spirituals
Electromusic Records EMCD 6885; 1985; CD
Chorus, other instrument(s)

1172

Слышишь плач наш (Slyshish' plach nash)
Composer not identified
Filatova, Ludmila (Mezzo-soprano)
Negro Spirituals, Negritânskie Spiricuels
Melodiâ S10 21833 009; 1985; LP
Organ
Light dialect

1173

Go Down Moses
Composer not identified
Franklin, Lavinia A. (Vocalist)
Historical Interpretation of Negro Spirituals and Lift Every Voice and Sing
Recorded Publications JZB-02591; 1970; LP
Organ

1174

Go Down Moses
Composer not identified
Green, Elnora E. (Contralto)
15 Spirituals
Private Label J3RS 2286; 1979; LP
Piano

1175

Go Down Moses
[Burleigh, Harry T.]
Hagen-William, Louis (Bass-baritone)
Negro Spirituals
Quantum QM 6909; 1993; CD
Piano
Light dialect

1176

Let My People Go
Hayes, Roland
Hamilton, Ruth (Contralto)
Good News
Videmus Records VIS735; 2007; CD
Piano
Heavy dialect

1177

Go Down Moses
Composer not identified
Harris, Lloyd (Bass)
Negro Spirituals
Pléïade P45301; 1960; 45 RPM
Piano

1178

Go Down Moses
Brown, Lawrence
Hayes, Roland (Tenor)
Steal Away
Vocalion B3033, Vocalion R6132; 1985; LP

1179

Go Down, Moses
Burleigh, Harry T.
Hayes, Roland (Tenor)
When I Have Sung My Songs: The American Art Song, 1900–1940
New World NW 247; 1976; LP
Piano
Moderate dialect

Also released with *Brother, Can You Spare a Dime?: The Roots of American Song* (Pearl Gemm CD 9484; 1991; CD); *Negro Spirituals: The Concert Tradition 1909–1948* (Frémeaux & Associés FA 168; 1999; CD) and *First Time Buyer's Guide to American Negro Spirituals* (Primo Collection PRMCD6038; 2006; CD)

1180

Go Down, Moses
Burleigh, Harry T.
Hayes, Roland (Tenor)
Go Down Moses/By an' By
Vocalion 21002; 1922; 78 RPM
Piano

1181

Go Down Moses
Composer not identified
Hayes, Roland (Tenor)
The Concerto: African American Spirituals
Orange Amaro; 2019; Streaming audio
Piano

1182

Go Down, Moses
Composer not identified
Hayes, Roland (Tenor)
Sit Down
Vocalion B3038, Vocalion R6132; 1922; 78
    RPM
Piano

1183

Let My People Go! [from My Songs]
Hayes, Roland
Hayes, Roland (Tenor)
Roland Hayes: My Songs
Vanguard VRS-494; 1956; LP
Piano

    Also released with *Favorite Spirituals*
(Vanguard Classics OVC 6022; 1995; CD);
Big Psalms, Hymns and Spirituals Box (eOne
Music/Vanguard Classics; 2015; Streaming
audio)

1184

Go Down, Moses
[Burleigh, Harry T.]
Hayes, Roland (Tenor)
*Black Europe: Sounds & Images of Black
    People in Europe pre–1927*
Bear Family Productions BCD 16095; 2013; CD
Piano
Light dialect

1185

Go Down, Moses
Price, Florence
Heard, Richard (Tenor)
My Dream: Art Songs and Spirituals
Percentage Records/Sound of Art
    Recordings CD147597; 2012; CD
Piano
Light dialect

1186

Go Down Moses
Composer not identified
Hines, Jerome (Bass)
Black & White Spirituals
Supreme S 3005; 1974; LP

1187

Go Down Moses
Henderson, Skitch
Hines, Jerome (Bass)
Standin' in the Need of Prayer
RCA Victor LPM-2047; [1960]; LP

1188

Go Down Moses
C., H. A.; Chambers
Hynninen, Jorma (Bass-baritone)
Negro Spirituals
Ondine ODE 715-2; 1988; CD
Piano

1189

Go Down Moses
Clinton, Irving
Irving, Clinton (Bass-baritone)
Clinton Irving Sings Spirituals: A Tribute
Rogers; 2001; CD

1190

Go Down Moses
Burleigh, Harry T.
Jones, Arthur (Tenor)
Wade in the Water
Orbis Books; 1993; Book w/cass
Piano
Moderate dialect

1191

Go Down Moses
Burleigh, Harry T.
Jones, Fanni (Mezzo-soprano)
Negro Spirituals en Concert
Suisa; 1987; LP
Organ
Moderate dialect

    Also released with *Negro Spirituals*
(Evasion Disques LP613; 1974; LP) and *Negro
Spirituals* (Phonotec 815; 1977; LP)

1192

Go Down, Moses [from Five spirituals for baritone and cello]
Balentine, James Scott
Jones, Timothy (Baritone)
Love Comes in at the Eye
Albany TROY1734; 2018; CD
Cello
Light dialect

1193

Go Down Moses
Browne, George
Lawrence, Martin (Bass-baritone)
Negro Spirituals
World Record Club MW-2005; [196-]; LP
Orchestra
Heavy dialect

1194

Go Down Moses
Browne, George
Lawrence, Martin (Bass-baritone)
Negro Spirituals
P&R; 2011; Streaming audio
Orchestra
Heavy dialect

    Also released with *Negro Spirituals* (Marathon Media International; 2013; Streaming audio)

1195

Go Down, Moses
Meyer, Fredrich
London, George (Bass-baritone)
Spirituals
Deutsche Grammophon 00289 477 6193; 2006; CD
Chorus, orchestra
Moderate dialect

1196

Go Down Moses
Burleigh, Harry T.; Fairgold, Noam & Lester Lynch
Lynch, Lester (Baritone)
On My Journey Now: Spirituals & Hymns
Pentatone Music PTC 5186 57'; 2017; CD
Chorus, piano, organ

1197

Go Down, Moses [from *Journey Beyond Time*]
Crumb, George
Martin, Barbara Ann (Soprano)
American Songbooks II & IV
BRIDGE 9275A/B; 2008; CD
Piano, percussion

1198

Go Down, Moses
Johnson, John Rosamond
Maynor, Kevin (Bass)
The Spiritual: An Underground Railroad
Southeastern Virginia Arts Assoc.; [2000]; CD
Piano

1199

Go Down Moses
Burleigh, Harry T.
McKinney, Jason (Bass-baritone)
Songs Inspired by Paul Robeson
United in Music; 2014; CD
Piano
Light dialect

1200

Go Down Moses
Fisher, William Arms
Miller, Jeanette (Soprano)
No Man Canna Hinder Me
MiJon Record Productions MJ240; 1979; CD
Piano

1201

Go Down, Moses
Burleigh, Harry T.
Miller, Reed (Tenor)
Go Down, Moses/By an' By
Edison Blue Amberol 3538; 1918; Cylinder
Chorus, orchestra
Light dialect

    Also released with *Go Down, Moses/By an' By* (Edison 80487; 1918; 78 RPM)

1202

Go Down Moses
Composer not identified

Monzo, Oscar (Baritone)
Negro Spirituals
Dial Discos 50-2020; 1983; LP

1203

Go Down Moses
Owens, Robert
Moses, Oral (Bass-baritone)
*Amen! African-American Composers of the
    20th Century*
Albany Records TROY459; 2001; CD
Piano
Light dialect

    Also released with *Sankofa: A Spiritual
Reflection* (Albany Records TROY1802; 2019;
CD)

1204

Go Down Moses
Traditional
Moses, Oral (Bass-baritone)
*Spirituals in Zion: A Spiritual Heritage for
    the Soul*
Albany Records TROY587; 2003; CD
A cappella
Moderate dialect

1205

Go Down, Moses
Pankey, Aubrey
Pankey, Aubrey (Baritone)
Negro Spirituals
Eterna 830010; 1983; LP
Piano

1206

Go Down, Moses
Burleigh, Harry T.
Payne, John C. (Baritone)
Good News: Vintage Negro Spirituals
Living Era AJA 5622; 2006; CD
Piano
Light dialect

    Also released with *Classic Gospel Songs*
(Emerald/K-Tel; 2013; Streaming audio) and
*Black Europe: Sounds & Images of Black Peo-
ple in Europe pre–1927* (Bear Family Productions BCD 16095; 2013; CD)

1207

Let My People Go
Burton, Ken
Philogene, Ruby (Soprano)
Steal Away
EMI Classics 7243 5 69707 2 4; 1997; CD
Chorus

1208

Go Down, Moses
Composer not identified
Porter, John (Bass)
No More Crying: Negro Spirituals
Pan Verlag OV-84; [1978]; LP

1209

Go Down Moses
Composer not identified
Price, Eudora (Vocalist)
My Favorite Songs & Spirituals
Private Label; 2006; CD
Organ
No dialect discerned

1210

Go Down, Moses
Composer not identified
Putkonen, Marko (Bass)
Deep River: Negro Spirituals
Lilium LILP 101; 1991; LP

1211

Go Down, Moses
Giesen, Hubert
Ray, William (Baritone)
Negro Spirituals
Intercord; [19--]; LP
Piano

    Also released with *Selections and Negro
Spirituals* (Intercord; [19--]; CD)

1212

Go Down, Moses
White, Dolores
Rhodes, Yolanda (Soprano)
The Angels Bowed Down
Cambria Master Recordings CD-1237; 2019;
    CD

1213

Go Down, Moses
Burleigh, Harry T.
Robeson, Paul (Bass-baritone)
The Complete EMI Sessions (1928–1939)
EMI Classics 50999 2 15586 2 7; 2008; CD
Piano
Moderate dialect

1214

Go Down Moses
Burleigh, Harry T.
Robeson, Paul (Bass-baritone)
Spirituals: Original Recordings 1925–1936
Naxos Gospel Legends 8.120638; 2003; CD
Piano

1215

Go Down Moses
Burleigh, Harry T.
Robeson, Paul (Bass-baritone)
Spirituals
Columbia Masterworks ML 4105 ; CBS
    62483; [1948]; LP

1216

Go Down, Moses
Burleigh, Harry T.
Robeson, Paul (Bass-baritone)
The Power and the Glory
Columbia/Legacy CK 47337; 1991; CD
Piano
No dialect discerned

1217

Go Down Moses
Burleigh, Harry T.
Robeson, Paul (Bass-baritone)
Songs for Free Men, 1940-45
Pearl GEMM CD 9264; 1997; CD
Piano

1218

Go Down, Moses
Burleigh, Harry T.
Robeson, Paul (Bass-baritone)
The Essential Paul Robeson
ASV CD AJS 244; 2000; CD

1219

Go Down Moses
Burleigh, Harry T.
Robeson, Paul (Bass-baritone)
Spirituals
Philips 429 395 BE; [195-]; 45 RPM

1220

Go Down Moses
Burleigh, Harry T.
Robeson, Paul (Bass-baritone)
Spirituals
Columbia Masterworks 17379-D; 1945; 78
    RPM
Piano
Light dialect

1221

Go Down, Moses
Burleigh, Harry T.
Robeson, Paul (Bass-baritone)
*I Stood on de Ribber/Peter, Go Ring Dem
    Bells/Go Down, Moses*
His Master's Voice B3381; [193-]; 78 RPM
Piano
Light dialect

1222

Go Down Moses
Burleigh, Harry T.
Robeson, Paul (Bass-baritone)
Spirituals
Philips 409.115 AE; 1959; 45 RPM
Piano

1223

Go Down Moses
Burleigh, Harry T.
Robeson, Paul (Bass-baritone)
Balm in Gilead/Go Down Moses
Columbia Masterworks 17467-D; [194-]; 78
    RPM
Piano
No dialect discerned

1224

Go Down Moses
[Burleigh, Harry T.]
Robeson, Paul (Bass-baritone)

Negro Spirituals (And More)
Discmedi DM-4674-02; 2009; CD

1225

Go Down, Moses
[Burleigh, Harry T.]
Robeson, Paul (Bass-baritone)
Ballad for Americans and Great Songs of Faith, Love and Patriotism
Vanguard VCD-117/18; 1989; CD
Piano

1226

Go Down, Moses
[Burleigh, Harry T.]
Robeson, Paul (Bass-baritone)
Scandalize My Name
Classics Record Library 30-5647; 1976; LP
Piano
Light dialect

1227

Go Down Moses
[Burleigh, Harry T.]
Robeson, Paul (Bass-baritone)
The Peace Arch Concerts
Folk Era Records FE1442CD; 1998; CD
Piano
Light dialect

1228

Go Down Moses
[Burleigh, Harry T.]
Robeson, Paul (Bass-baritone)
Deep River
Great Voices of the Century GVC 2004; 1999; CD

1229

Go Down Moses
[Burleigh, Harry T.]
Robeson, Paul (Bass-baritone)
The Norton Anthology of African American Literature
Norton PN 10127; 1996; Book w/CD

1230

Go Down, Moses
[Burleigh, Harry T.]

Robeson, Paul (Bass-baritone)
Ol' Man River: His 56 Finest 1925–1945
Retrospective RTS 4116; 2008; CD

1231

Go Down, Moses
[Burleigh, Harry T.]
Robeson, Paul (Bass-baritone)
Ol' Man River: The Very Best of Paul Robeson
Memory Lane; 2012; CD

1232

Go Down Moses
[Burleigh, Harry T.]
Robeson, Paul (Bass-baritone)
The Originals: "Spirituals"
Yoyo USA; 2006; Streaming audio

1233

Go Down Moses
[Burleigh, Harry T.]
Robeson, Paul (Bass-baritone)
Paul Robeson's Treasure Chest
Leverage; 2008; Streaming audio
Piano

1234

Go Down Moses
[Burleigh, Harry T.]
Robeson, Paul (Bass-baritone)
Five Classic Albums Plus Bonus Tracks
Real Gone Music RGMCD287; 2017; CD
Piano
No dialect discerned

1235

Go Down Moses
[Burleigh, Harry T.]
Robeson, Paul (Bass-baritone)
Drink to Me Only with Thine Eyes
MD Music; 2010; Streaming audio
Piano
No dialect discerned

1236

Go Down Moses
[Burleigh, Harry T.]
Robeson, Paul (Bass-baritone)
The Ultimate Collection

Burning Fire; 2009; Streaming audio
Piano
Light dialect

1237
Go Down, Moses
[Burleigh, Harry T.]
Robeson, Paul (Bass-baritone)
The Essential Collection
Primo PRMCD6233; 2018; CD

1238
Go Down Moses
[Burleigh, Harry T.]
Robeson, Paul (Bass-baritone)
Man They Couldn't Silence
Rev-Ola CR REV 208; 2007; CD

1239
Go Down Moses
[Burleigh, Harry T.]
Robeson, Paul (Bass-baritone)
Complete Recordings
Universal Digital Enterprises; 2018;
    Streaming audio

1240
Go Down Moses
[Burleigh, Harry T.]
Robeson, Paul (Bass-baritone)
Spirituals
Columbia Masterworks M-610; 1946; 78
    RPM
Piano

1241
Go Down Moses
Sadin, Robert
Robinson, Morris (Bass)
Going Home
Decca B0008277-02; 2007; CD
Chorus, orchestra
Heavy dialect

1242
Go Down Moses
Boatner, Edward
Rolle, Gilbert-Michel (Tenor)
Musical Voyage

Centaurus Classics; 2007; CD
Instrumental ensemble
No dialect discerned

1243
Go Down Moses
Composer not identified
Rustin, Bayard (Tenor)
*Bayard Rustin Sings Spirituals, Work &
    Freedom Songs*
Bayard Rustin Fund; 2003; CD
Piano
Moderate dialect

1244
Go Down Moses
Composer not identified
Rustin, Bayard (Tenor)
*Bayard Rustin Sings Spirituals, Work &
    Freedom Songs*
Bayard Rustin Fund; 1988; Cassette
Piano
Moderate dialect

1245
Go Down Moses
Burleigh, Harry T.
Salters, Stephen (Baritone)
Spirit: Are You There, You Are There
HarmonizedDisharmony 0001; 2015; CD

1246
Go Down Moses
Hogan, Moses
Sims, Robert (Baritone)
*In the Spirit: Spirituals and American Songs
    with Orchestra and Chorus*
Canti Classics; 2009; CD
Chorus, piano
Heavy dialect

1247
Go Down, Moses
Walberg, Wladimir
Spencer, Kenneth (Bass-baritone)
*I Got a Home in-a Dat Rock /Go Down,
    Moses*
Columbia LF 274; 1957; 78 RPM
Orchestra

Also released with *4 Negro Spirituals* (Columbia ESRF 1067; 1957; 45 RPM)

1248

Go Down Moses
[Burleigh, Harry T.]
Spencer, Kenneth (Bass-baritone)
American Spirituals
Sonora MS-478; [1945]; 78 RPM
Piano
Light dialect

1249

Go Down Moses
Composer not identified
St. Hill, Krister (Baritone)
Svenska Folkvisor/Negro Spirituals
Polar POLS 398; 1985; LP

1250

Go Down, Moses
Blanchard, Terence
Sykes, Jubilant (Baritone)
Jubilant Sykes
Sony Classical SK 63294; 1998; CD
Instrumental ensemble

1251

Go Down, Moses
Composer not identified
Sykes, Jubilant (Baritone)
Spirituals
Sony Music Média SMM 5012802; 2000;
    CD

1252

Go Down, Moses
Marsh, Don
Sykes, Jubilant (Baritone)
Jubilant Sykes Sings Copland and Spirituals
Arioso Classics AC 00011; 2008; CD
Orchestra

1253

Go Down Moses
Composer not identified
Thomas, Edna (Soprano)
*Run, Mary, Run/Nobody Knows de Trouble
    I Sees*

Columbia 1606-D; 1928; 78 RPM
Piano

1254

Go Down Moses
Composer not identified
Thomas, Edna (Soprano)
Religious Music, vol. 2
Document Records; [1999]; CD

1255

Go Down Moses
Composer not identified
Thomas, Edna (Soprano)
I'se Been Buked
Suncoast Music; 2015; Streaming audio
Piano

1256

Go Down Moses
Thomas, Edna
Thomas, Edna (Soprano)
Negro Spirituals
Columbia 3361; 1924; 78 RPM
Piano
Heavy dialect

1257

Go Down, Moses
Thomas, Edna
Thomas, Edna (Soprano)
Go Down, Moses/Run, Mary, Run
Columbia 4993; [19--]; 78 RPM
Piano

1258

Go Down, Moses
[Burleigh, Harry T.]
Thompson, Derrick (Baritone)
Spirituals
Private Label; 2014; CD
Piano
No dialect discerned

1259

Go Down Moses
Composer not identified
Traubel, Helen (Soprano)
*Negro Spirituals: Helen Traubel in Popular
    Ballads*

Columbia ML 4221; 1949; LP
Piano

1260

Go Down, Moses
Composer not identified
Ventriglia, Franco (Baritone)
Franco Ventriglia Sings Negro Spirituals
Vedette Records VRMS 316; [19--]; LP
Piano, organ
Moderate dialect

Also released with *Franco Ventriglia Sings Negro Spirituals* (Vedette Records; 2007; Streaming audio)

1261

Go Down, Moses (Let My People Go)
Burleigh, Harry T.
Warfield, William (Bass-baritone)
Spirituals: 200 Years of African-American Spirituals
ProArte CDD 3443; 1993; CD
Piano
Heavy dialect

1262

Go Down Moses
Composer not identified
White, Willard (Bass-baritone)
The Paul Robeson Legacy
Linn AKD 190; 2015; CD
Instrumental ensemble

1263

Go Down Moses
Davis, Carl
White, Willard (Bass-baritone)
Willard White in Concert
Regis RRC 1179; 2004; CD
Orchestra

1264

Go Down, Moses
Marshall, Melanie
White, Willard (Bass-baritone)
Willard White Sings: Copland; American Spirituals; Folk-Songs
Chandos Records CHAN 8960; 1991; CD

Piano
Heavy dialect

1265

Go Down Moses
[Burleigh, Harry T.]
Winters, Lawrence (Bass-baritone)
Lawrence Winters: Recital
Hamburger Archiv fur Gesangskunst 10397; 2007; CD
Piano
No dialect discerned

1266

Go Down Moses
[Burleigh, Harry T.]
Winters, Lawrence (Bass-baritone)
Singer Portrait: Lawrence Winters
Apple Music; 2012; Streaming audio
Piano
No dialect discerned

1267

Go Down, Moses
Schweizer, Rolf
Wolf, Lars (Vocalist)
Die Schwarze Stimme Europas
Cantate 666000; 1971; LP
Chorus, organ, percussion

1268

Go Down Moses
Price, Florence
Yovanovich, Amy (Mezzo-soprano)
Great Day!
Prince Productions 9808P; 2007; CD
Piano
No dialect discerned

· · · · · · ·

Go On Brother

1269

Go On Brother [from *Cycle of Six Spirituals*]
Owens, Robert
Moses, Oral (Bass-baritone)
Come Down Angels and Trouble the Water: Negro Spirituals, an American National Treasure!

Albany Records TROY 1489; 2014; CD
Piano
Moderate dialect

    Also released with *Sankofa: A Spiritual Reflection* (Albany Records TROY1802; 2019; CD)

•••••••

Go Tell It on the Mountain

1270

Go Tell It on the Mountain
Composer not identified
Baker, Bradley (Baritone)
Not a Word: Spirituals, Hymns, Songs
AYA Worldwide Records 6-09682-2; 2001; CD

1271

Go Tell It on the Mountain
Work, John Wesley
Blackmon, Henry (Baritone)
Negro Spirituals
Vega 19179; [19--]; LP
Chorus, piano

1272

Go Tell It on de Mountains! (Christmas song of the plantation)
Burleigh, Harry T.
Burton, Dashon (Bass-baritone)
Songs of Struggle & Redemption: We Shall Overcome
Acis Productions APL08685; 2015; CD
Piano
Heavy dialect

1273

Go Tell It on the Mountain
Reineke, S.
Dixon, Rodrick (Tenor)
Home for the Holidays
Fanfare Cincinnati FC-001; 2012; CD
Chorus, orchestra

1274

Go, Tell It on the Mountain
Composer not identified

English-Robinson, Laura (Soprano)
Christmas Chestnuts: A Message and a Gift
Alewa ENT; 2014; CD
Piano
No dialect discerned

1275

Go Tell It on the Mountain
Auld, Robert
Estes, Simon (Bass-baritone)
Simon Estes Sings Christmas Carols
GDA Productions GDA 001; 2005; CD
Piano

1276

Go Tell It on the Mountain
Pasatieri, Thomas
Hampson, Thomas (Baritone)
Christmas with Thomas Hampson
Teldec 73135-2; 1991; CD
Orchestra
No dialect discerned

    Also released with *Christmas at Downton Abbey* (Warner Bros. Records 54625-2; 2014; CD)

1277

Go Tell It on the Mountains!
Composer not identified
Hampton, Jonathon (Vocalist)
Negro Spirituals: Songs of Trial and Triumph
Private Label; 2017; Streaming audio
Piano
Light dialect

1278

Go Tell It on the Mountain
Composer not identified
Hayes, Roland (Tenor)
Roland Hayes Sings Christmas Carols of the Nations
Vanguard VRS-7016; [1954]; LP
Piano

1279

Go Tell It on the Mountain
Composer not identified
Hendricks, Barbara (Soprano)
Shout for Joy: Spiritual Christmas (Noël sacré)

Arte Verum ARV-009; 2010; CD
Instrumental ensemble
Light dialect

1280

Go Tell It on the Mountain
Composer not identified
Hendricks, Barbara (Soprano)
Barbara Hendricks Sings Christmas
EMI Classics D 113675; 1995; CD
Chorus
No dialect discerned

1281

Go Tell It on the Mountain
Composer not identified
Humphrey Flynn, Edwina (Soprano)
Edwina Sings at Christmas
Private Label; 1997; CD
Chorus

1282

Go Tell It on the Mountain
Work, J.
Hynninen, Jorma (Bass-baritone); Davis,
    Osceola (Soprano)
Negro Spirituals
Ondine ODE 715-2; 1988; CD
Piano

1283

Go Tell It on the Mountain
Composer not identified
Johnson, Camellia (Soprano)
Christmas with Paul Plishka
Naxos 8.553506; 1995; CD
Chorus

1284

Go Tell It on the Mountain
Composer not identified
Jones, Fanni (Mezzo-soprano)
Negro Spirituals
Evasion Disques LP613; 1974; LP

1285

Go, Tell It on the Mountain
Walters, Richard (ed.)
Kruse, Tanya (Soprano)

15 Easy Spiritual Arrangements for the
    Progressing Singer
Hal Leonard HL00000391 (high);
    HL00000392 (low); 2005; Score
    w/CD
Piano
No dialect discerned

1286

Go Tell It on the Mountain! [from The
    Winds of Destiny]
Crumb, George
Martin, Barbara Ann (Soprano)
American Songbooks II & IV
BRIDGE 9275A/B; 2008; CD
Piano, percussion

1287

Go Tell It on the Mountain
Composer not identified
Maynor, Dorothy (Soprano)
Spirituals, Arias, Songs (1940–1943)
Claremont CD GSE 78-50-59; 1994; CD
Chorus

1288

Go Tell It on de Mountain
Composer not identified
Maynor, Dorothy (Soprano)
Negro Spirituals
RCA Victor M879; 1942; 78 RPM
Men's voices

    Also released with *Negro Spirituals*
(Kipepeo Publishing; 2018; CD)

1289

Go Tell It on the Mountain
Composer not identified
Maynor, Dorothy (Soprano)
Dorothy Maynor Sings Spirituals and Sacred
    Songs
RCA Camden CAL-344; 1957; LP
Chorus

1290

Go Tell It on the Mountain
Work, John Wesley

Maynor, Kevin (Bass)
Songs of America from Another American
Guild GMCD 7247; 2002; CD
Piano

1291

Go Tell It on the Mountain
Composer not identified
Norman, Jessye (Soprano)
Jessye Norman at Notre Dame: A Christmas Concert
Philips 432 731-2; 1992; CD
Orchestra

Also released with *Festkonzert aus Notre-Dame* (Philips 438 079-2; 1992; CD); and *Jessye Norman à Notre-Dame: Récital de Noël* (Philips 438 078-2; 1992; CD)

1292

Go Tell It on the Mountains
Gaul, ?
Oglesby, Isador (Tenor)
Life of Jesus in Negro Spirituals
Oglesby Recordings Album 2; 1980; LP
Piano

1293

Go Tell It on the Mountain
Composer not identified
Porter, John (Bass)
No More Crying: Negro Spirituals
Pan Verlag OV-84; [1978]; LP

1294

Go Tell It on the Mountain
Sadin, Robert
Robinson, Morris (Bass)
Going Home
Decca B0008277-02; 2007; CD
Piano
No dialect discerned

1295

Go Tell It on the Mountain
Composer not identified
Rustin, Bayard (Tenor)
Bayard Rustin, the Singer
Bayard Rustin Fund; 1992; CD
Piano

1296

Go, Tell It on the Mountain
Traditional
Rustin, Bayard (Tenor)
Bayard Rustin Sings Twelve Spirituals on the Life of Christ
Fellowship Records E2-KL 1771; [195-]; LP
A cappella
Light dialect

Also released with *Bayard Rustin-The Singer* (Black Swan Series; Parnassus Records PACD 96083; 2022; CD)

1297

Go Tell It on the Mountain
Bonds, Margaret
Taylor, Darryl (Countertenor)
How Sweet the Sound: A Charm of Spirituals
Albany TROY1244; 2011; CD
Piano

1298

Go Tell It on the Mountain
Composer not identified
Vaughn, Tichina (Mezzo-soprano)
Christmas at My Home
Bauer-Studios ACD 6085; 2005; CD
Piano

1299

Go Tell It on the Mountains
Work, John Wesley
West, Lucretia (Mezzo-soprano)
Negro Spirituals III
Club français du disque 176; 1959; LP
Piano
Heavy dialect

1300

Go Tell It on the Mountain
Work, John Wesley
West, Lucretia (Mezzo-soprano)
Negro Spirituals mit Lukretia West
Opera 3408; [195-]; LP
Piano

1301

Go Tell It on the Mountain
Work, John Wesley

West, Lucretia (Mezzo-soprano)
Negro Spirituals
Club français du disque 215; [196-]; 7-in EP
Piano

. . . .

God Is a God

1302
God Is a God
Whalum, Wendell
Brown, Anthony (Baritone)
Toil and Triumph
Spirituals Project; 2002; CD
Piano
Light dialect

1303
God Is a God
Okpebholo, Shawn
Liverman, Will (Baritone)
Lord How Come Me Here?
Navona Records NV6408; 2022; CD
Piano, narrator
Light dialect

1304
God Is God
Hairston, Jacqueline
Matthews, Benjamin (Baritone)
A Balm in Gilead
Ebony Classic Recordings ECR 0001; 2000;
    CD
Piano

1305
God Is a God
Whalum, Wendell
McKelton, Sam (Tenor)
Sence You Went Away
Albany Records TROY 387; 1998; CD
Piano
Light dialect

1306
God Is a God
Whalum, Wendell
Overton, Kenneth (Baritone)

*Been in de Storm So Long (Songs My Fathers
    Taught Me)*
American Spiritual Ensemble; 2012; CD
Piano

. . . .

Going to Set Down
and Rest Awhile

1307
Goin' to Set Down an' Rest Awhile
Suben, Joel Eric
Lennick, Jessica (Soprano)
Five Spirituals for Soprano and Orchestra
Private label; 2018; Streaming audio
Orchestra
No dialect discerned

. . . .

Going Up
to Heaven

1308
Going Up to Heaven [from *My Songs: Dream
    of Heaven*]
Hayes, Roland
Hayes, Roland (Tenor)
Favorite Spirituals
Vanguard Classics OVC 6022; 1995; CD
Piano
Moderate dialect

    Also released with *Spirituals Box* (eOne
Music/Vanguard Classics; 2015; Streaming
audio)

. . . .

Golden Crown

1309
Golden Crown
Graves, Rupert; Gantvoort, Herman
Seagle, Oscar (Baritone)
*Standin' in the Need o' Prayer/Golden
    Crown*
Columbia Record A2889; 1920; 78 RPM
Orchestra

· · · · · · ·

Gonna Lay Down My Life

1310

Gonna Lay Down My Life
Composer not identified
Thomas, Edna (Soprano)
Religious Music, vol. 2
Document Records; [1999]; CD

· · · · · · ·

Good News

1311

Good News
Sadin, Robert
Battle, Kathleen (Soprano)
Kathleen Battle at Carnegie Hall
Deutsche Grammophon 435 440-2; 1992; CD
Piano
Heavy dialect

1312

Good News! Chariot's Comin'
Hershberger, A. J.
Brown, Anthony (Baritone)
Toil and Triumph
Spirituals Project; 2002; CD
Chorus
Light dialect

1313

Good News
Composer not identified
Charles, Lee (Tenor)
*Swing Low Sweet Chariot: And Other
    Spirituals*
Riverside RLP 12-651; 1957; LP
Piano, guitar

1314

Good News
Hayes, Roland
Davis, Ellabelle (Soprano)
Ellabelle Davis Sings Negro Spirituals
London LPS 182; [1950]; LP
Piano
Heavy dialect

Also released with *Recital of Negro Spirituals by Ellabelle Davis* (Decca LM.4504; [1950]; LP) and *Great Negro Spirituals* (Replay Record; 2013; Streaming audio)

1315

Good News
Composer not identified
Gormley, Clare (Soprano)
Where Morning Lies: Spiritual Songs
ABC Classics 461 766-2; 2002; CD
Piano
Heavy dialect

1316

Good News
Hayes, Roland
Hamilton, Ruth (Contralto)
Good News
Videmus Records VIS735; 2007; CD
Piano
Heavy dialect

1317

Good News
Wheatley, Andres
Haniotis, Mario (Bass)
Negro Spirituals
Pastorale et Musique PM 17.047; [196-]; 45 RPM
Piano
No dialect discerned

1318

Good News
Composer not identified
Hayes, Roland (Tenor)
*Roland Hayes Sings: Negro Spirituals,
    Aframerican Folk Songs*
Amadeo Records AVRS 6033; [19--]; LP
Piano
Heavy dialect

Also released with *The Art of Roland Hayes: Six Centuries of Song* (Preiser Records; 2010; CD) and *Big Psalms, Hymns and Spirituals Box* (eOne Music/Vanguard Classics; 2015; Streaming audio)

1319

Good News
Hayes, Roland

Jenkins, Isaiah (Tenor)
Lyric Tenor
Trans Radio TR 1010A; [195-]; LP
Piano

1320

Good News
Brown, Uzee, Jr.
Moses, Oral (Bass-baritone)
Come Down Angels and Trouble the Water:
   Negro Spirituals, an American National
   Treasure!
Albany Records TROY 1489; 2014; CD
Piano
Heavy dialect

   Also released with *Sankofa: A Spiritual Reflection* (Albany Records TROY1802; 2019; CD)

1321

Good News
Composer not identified
Pankey, Aubrey (Baritone)
Negro-Spirituals
Eterna 5 30 022; [19--]; 45 RPM
Piano
Moderate dialect

   Also released with *Aubrey Pankey Singt Negro-Spirituals* (Eterna 7 30 005; 1959; LP) and *Negro Spirituals* (Eterna 830010; 1983; LP)

1322

Good News
Burton, Ken
Philogene, Ruby (Soprano)
Steal Away
EMI Classics 7243 5 69707 2 4; 1997; CD
Chorus

1323

Good News
Hayes, Roland
Sims, Robert (Baritone)
Robert Sims Sings the Spirituals of Roland
   Hayes
Canti Classics 2014-01; 2015; CD
Piano
Heavy dialect

1324

Good News
Composer not identified
Spencer, Kenneth (Bass-baritone)
Negro Spirituals
Life Records C 1108; [19--]; LP

1325

Good News
Composer not identified
Watts, Leonardo (Baritone)
On Ma Journey: A Memorable Collection of
   Negro Spirituals
Onyx Recording Associates ORA-101; 1961;
   LP
Chorus

·······

Gospel Train

[Galatians 4:19; Acts 15:9; Romans 10:12]

   "The gospel train is coming, I hear it just at hand; I hear the car wheels moving, And rumbling through the land. Get on board, little children, get on board Get on board, little children, There's room for many more...."

   [Available in ESAA, FHFN, HCTN, HJTS, HT25, HTBA, HTBS, HTC2, JARS, JJAN, RS12, RWSC, RWSS, RW15, SBFD, VLCH, WF70, WPNN]

1326

De Gospel Train
Burleigh, Harry T.
Anderson, Marian (Contralto)
Ev'Ry Time I Feel the Spirit (1930–1947)
Naxos Nostalgia 8.120779; 2004; CD
Piano

1327

De Gospel Train
Burleigh, Harry T.
Anderson, Marian (Contralto)
Rarities: Broadcast Performances 1943–1952
Video Artists International VAIA 1200;
   1998; CD
Orchestra

1328

De Gospel Train
Burleigh, Harry T.
Anderson, Marian (Contralto)
Spirituals
RCA Victor Red Seal 09026-63306-2; 1999; CD
Piano
Moderate dialect

1329

De Gospel Train
Burleigh, Harry T.
Anderson, Marian (Contralto)
Marian Anderson in Concert 1943–1952
Eklipse Records EKR CD19; 1993; CD
Orchestra

1330

Gospel Train
Burleigh, Harry T.
Anderson, Marian (Contralto)
Let Freedom Ring!
JSP Records 683; 2016; CD
Piano
Heavy dialect

1331

The Gospel Train
Burleigh, Harry T.
Anderson, Marian (Contralto)
Negro Spirituals
La Voix de Son Maître FBLP1039; 1953; LP
Piano

1332

De Gospel Train
Burleigh, Harry T.
Anderson, Marian (Contralto)
Marian Anderson Sings Negro Spirituals
His Master's Voice BLP 1060; [19--]; LP
Piano

1333

De Gospel Train
Burleigh, Harry T.
Anderson, Marian (Contralto)
Marian Anderson Sings Spirituals
RCA Victor Red Seal MO 1238; 1948; 78 RPM
Piano

1334

De Gospel Train
Burleigh, Harry T.
Anderson, Marian (Contralto)
Negro Spirituals
RCA Victor LM 2032; [1956]; LP
Piano

　　　Also released with *Marian Anderson: Beyond the Music; Her Complete RCA Victor Recordings* (Sony Classical 19439836492; 2021; CD)

1335

Gospel Train
[Burleigh, Harry T.]
Anderson, Marian (Contralto)
The Legendary Marian Anderson "Live"
Legendary Recordings LRCD 1031; 1990; CD
Piano

1336

De Gospel Train
[Burleigh, Harry T.]
Anderson, Marian (Contralto)
Alto Rhapsody; Selected Spirituals
Urania URN 22.328; 2007; CD
Piano

1337

De Gospel Train
[Burleigh, Harry T.]
Anderson, Marian (Contralto)
The Very Best of Marian Anderson
Master Classics Records; 2009; CD
Piano
Light dialect

1338

De Gospel Train
[Burleigh, Harry T.]
Anderson, Marian (Contralto)
Marian Anderson Sings Spirituals
RCA Victor LM 110; 1949; LP
Piano

1339

De Gospel Train
[Burleigh, Harry T.]
Anderson, Marian (Contralto)

Negro Spirituals
RCA Victor 630.396 A; [19--]; LP
Piano

1340

Da Gospel Train
[Burleigh, Harry T.]
Anderson, Marian (Contralto)
Grandes Contraltos de la Musique Classique,
   Les: Marian Anderson, Vol. 1
Mon Patrimoine Musical Collection; 2017;
   Streaming audio
Piano

1341

Gospel Train
Kaiser, Kurt; Marsh, Don; Russ, Patrick
Battle, Kathleen (Soprano); Norman, Jessye
   (Soprano)
Spirituals in Concert
Deutsche Grammophon 429 790-2; 1991; CD
Chorus, orchestra
Heavy dialect

1342

The Gospel Train
Johnson, Hall
Blackmon, Henry (Baritone)
Negro Spirituals
Stichting St. Josefkerk Discofonds
   Leidschendam JK 1006; [1964]; 45 RPM
Organ

1343

The Gospel Train
Composer not identified
Carey, Thomas (Baritone)
Go Down Moses
Da Camera Song SM 95028; 1970; LP
Piano

1344

De Gospel Train
Burleigh, Harry T.
Carnette, Count (Vocalist)
Count Carnette Sings Favorite Negro Spirituals
Carnette Archive Recordings; 1983; LP
Piano
Light dialect

1345

Git on Board [from Songs for Joy (A Suite of
   Spirituals)]
Simpson-Currenton, Evelyn
Chandler-Eteme, Janice (Soprano)
Devotions
Sligo Records; 2007; CD
Piano

1346

Git on Board, Little Children
Composer not identified
Corbett, Patricia (Soprano)
Patricia Corbett Sings…. Best Loved Songs
RCA Victor Custom GO8P-0267; [1956]; LP

1347

Get on Board Little Children
Composer not identified
Credit, Roosevelt André (Bass-baritone)
Get on Board
Private label; 2016; Streaming audio
Instrumental ensemble
Heavy dialect

1348

The Gospel Train
Kaelin, Pierre
Evans, Allan (Bass-baritone)
Negro Spirituals
Electromusic Records EMCD 6885; 1985; CD
Chorus, other instrument(s)

1349

Кто там ждет? (Kto tam zhdet?)
Composer not identified
Filatova, Ludmila (Mezzo-soprano)
Негритянские Спиричузлс (Negrityanskiye
   Spirichuzls—Negro Spirituals)
Melodiâ S10 21833 009; 1985; LP
Organ
Light dialect

1350

De Gospel Train
Burleigh, Harry T.
Forest, Michael (Tenor)
The Spirit Sings: American Spirituals
Shenandoah Conservatory SU003; [199-]; CD

1351

Get on Board
Composer not identified
Franklin, Lavinia A. (Vocalist)
*Historical Interpretation of Negro Spirituals
and Lift Every Voice and Sing*
Recorded Publications JZB-02591; 1970; LP
Organ

1352

Git on Board
Simpson-Curenton, Evelyn
Graves, Denyce (Mezzo-soprano)
Angels Watching Over Me
NPR Classics CD 0006; 1997; CD
Piano
Heavy dialect

1353

De Gospel Train
[Burleigh, Harry T.]
Hagen-William, Louis (Bass-baritone)
Negro Spirituals
Quantum QM 6909; 1993; CD
Piano
Light dialect

1354

Git on Boa'd Little Child'n
Hendricks, Barbara; Alexeev, Dmitri
Hendricks, Barbara (Soprano)
Espirituales Negros
EMI Classics/Altaya 01636; 1983; CD
Piano
Heavy dialect

    Also released with *Negro Spirituals*
(EMI CDC7470262; 1983; CD) and *Spirituals*
(EMI Classics 0946 346641 2 7; 2005; CD)

1355

De Gospel Train
Burleigh, Harry T.
Jones, Fanni (Mezzo-soprano)
Fanni Jones et Oswald Russell
Audio-Visual Enterprises AVE 30701; [19--];
    LP

1356

The Gospel Train
Composer not identified

Jones, Fanni (Mezzo-soprano)
Negro Spirituals
Evasion Disques LP613; 1974; LP

1357

De Gospel Train
Burleigh, Harry T.
Kennedy, Charles (Vocalist)
Heart & Soul: Songs of Harry T. Burleigh
Publisher not known; 1994; Cassette

1358

The Gospel Train
Walters, Richard (ed.)
Kruse, Tanya (Soprano)
*15 Easy Spiritual Arrangements for the
Progressing Singer*
Hal Leonard HL00000391 (high);
    HL00000392 (low); 2005; Score w/CD
Piano
Moderate dialect

1359

De Gospel Train
Composer not identified
Loiselle, Henri (Bass-baritone)
One Day at a Time
Hum Recordings HRHLCD001; 1996; CD
Piano

1360

The Gospel Train
Edwards, Leo
Matthews, Benjamin (Baritone)
A Spiritual Journey
Ebony Classic Recordings ECR 0001; 2000; CD
Piano

1361

The Gospel Train
Edwards, Leo
Matthews, Benjamin (Baritone)
A Balm in Gilead
Ebony Classic Recordings ECR 0001; 2000; CD
Piano

1362

De Gospel Train
Burleigh, Harry T.

Matthews, Inez (Mezzo-soprano)
Inez Matthews Sings Spirituals (Great New Voices of Today, v. 6)
Period SPL-580; [1950]; LP
Piano
Light dialect

Also released with *Inez Matthews Sings Spirituals* (Essential Media Group; 2011; CD)

1363

Gospel Train "Humoresque"
Kerr, Thomas H., Jr.
Mayes, Doris (Mezzo-soprano)
Deep River
La voix de son maître FDLP 1080; 1959; LP
Piano

1364

The Gospel Train
Welsh, Nicky
McCue, Bill (Bass-baritone)
Bill McCue Sings the Great Spirituals
Beltona SBE 173; 1974; LP
Orchestra

1365

Da Gospel Train
Johnson, Hall
Miller, Jeanette (Soprano)
No Man Canna Hinder Me
MiJon Record Productions MJ240; 1979; CD
Piano

1366

The Gospel Train
Composer not identified
Monzo, Oscar (Baritone)
Negro Spirituals
Dial Discos 50-2020; 1983; LP

1367

Gospel Train
Baldwin, Dalton; Jessye Norman; Patterson, Willis
Norman, Jessye (Soprano)
Negro Spirituals
Philips 9500 580; 1979; LP
Piano

Also released with *The Jessye Norman Collection* (Philips Classics 422 893-2; [1988]; CD) and *Spirituals* (Philips 416 462-2; 1990; CD)

1368

Gospel Train
Composer not identified
Norman, Jessye (Soprano)
The Jessye Norman Collection: Sacred Songs & Spirituals
Philips B0004506-02; 2005; CD
Piano
Heavy dialect

1369

Gospel Train
Composer not identified
Norman, Jessye (Soprano)
Bound for the Promised Land: Songs and Words of Equality and Freedom
Albany Records TROY1798; 2019; CD
Piano

1370

De Gospel Train
Burleigh, Harry T.
Philogene, Ruby (Soprano)
Steal Away
EMI Classics 7243 5 69707 2 4; 1997; CD
Piano

1371

Git on Board
Composer not identified
Porter, John (Bass)
No More Crying: Negro Spirituals
Pan Verlag OV-84; [1978]; LP

1372

De Gospel Train
[Burleigh, Harry T.]
Quivar, Florence (Mezzo-soprano)
Great American Spirituals
Angel CDM 7 64669 2; 1992; CD
Piano
Heavy dialect

Also released with *Great American Spirituals* (Musical Heritage Society 513725Z; 1994; CD); *Negro Spirituals* (EMI 7243 5 72790 2 4;

1998; CD) and *Ride On, King Jesus! Florence
Quivar Sings Black Music of America* (EMI
Classics 9 67138 2; 2010; CD)

1373
Gospel Train
Giesen, Hubert
Ray, William (Baritone)
Negro Spirituals
Intercord; [19--]; LP
Piano

1374
Gospel Train
Giesen, Hubert
Ray, William (Baritone)
*Sings Arias, Duets, Musical Selections and
   Negro Spirituals*
Intercord; [19--]; CD
Piano

1375
Git on Board Litle Chillen
Brown, Lawrence
Reese, Ruth (Contralto)
The Black Rose
His Master's Voice 7EGN 38; [19--]; 45 RPM

1376
Git on Bord, Li'l Children
Brown, Lawrence
Robeson, Paul (Bass-baritone)
The Complete EMI Sessions (1928–1939)
EMI Classics 50999 2 15586 2 7; 2008; CD
Piano
Heavy dialect

1377
Git on Board, Lil Children
[Brown, Lawrence]
Robeson, Paul (Bass-baritone)
Good News: Vintage Negro Spirituals
Living Era AJA 5622; 2006; CD
Piano
Moderate dialect

1378
Get on Board, Little Children
Brown, Lawrence
Robeson, Paul (Bass-baritone)

Paul Robeson in Live Performance
Columbia M 30424; 1971; LP
Piano
Light dialect

1379
Get on Board, Little Children
Brown, Lawrence
Robeson, Paul (Bass-baritone)
*A Lonesome Road: Paul Robeson Sings
   Spirituals and Songs*
ASV Living Era CD AJA 5027; 1984; CD
Piano
Heavy dialect

1380
Git on Board, Little Children
Brown, Lawrence
Robeson, Paul (Bass-baritone)
Paul Robeson Sings Negro Spirituals
Philips GBL 5584; [19--]; LP
Piano

1381
Get on Board, Little Children
Brown, Lawrence
Robeson, Paul (Bass-baritone)
Paul Robeson Collection
Hallmark Recordings 390692; 1998; CD

1382
Git on Board, Lil Children
Brown, Lawrence
Robeson, Paul (Bass-baritone)
Classic Gospel Songs
Emerald/K-Tel; 2013; Streaming audio
Piano

1383
Get on Board, Little Children
Brown, Lawrence
Robeson, Paul (Bass-baritone)
The Voice of Mississippi: 20 Great Tracks
Prism Leisure PLATCD 119; 1996; CD

1384
Git on Board, Little Children
Brown, Lawrence
Robeson, Paul (Bass-baritone)

Paul Robeson with Chorus, orchestra
Fontana BIG.417-1Y; 1958; LP

1385
Git on Board, Lil' Chillun
Brown, Lawrence
Robeson, Paul (Bass-baritone)
Weepin' Mary/I Want to Be Ready/Git on Board, Lil' Chillun/Dere's No Hidin' Place
Victor 22225; 1928; 78 RPM
Piano
Moderate dialect

1386
Git on Board, Little Chillen
Brown, Lawrence
Robeson, Paul (Bass-baritone)
Swing Low, Sweet Chariot
Columbia Masterworks MM-819; 1949; 78 RPM
Piano
Moderate dialect

1387
Get on Board, Little Children
Brown, Lawrence
Robeson, Paul (Bass-baritone)
The Essential Paul Robeson
Vanguard VSD 57/58; 1974; LP
Piano
Heavy dialect

1388
Git on Board Little Chillen
Brown, Lawrence
Robeson, Paul (Bass-baritone)
Paul Robeson Chante ... f16 Spirituals
Philips G 05.639 R; 1959; LP
Piano

1389
Get on Board, Little Children
[Brown, Lawrence]
Robeson, Paul (Bass-baritone)
Negro Spirituals (And More)
Discmedi DM-4674-02; 2009; CD

1390
Git on Board Lil' Children
[Brown, Lawrence]

Robeson, Paul (Bass-baritone)
Songs of My People
RCA Red Seal LM-3292; 1972; LP
Piano

1391
Get on Board, Little Children
[Brown, Lawrence]
Robeson, Paul (Bass-baritone)
Ballad for Americans and Great Songs of Faith, Love and Patriotism
Vanguard VCD-117/18; 1989; CD
Piano

1392
Get on Board, Little Children
[Brown, Lawrence]
Robeson, Paul (Bass-baritone)
Scandalize My Name
Classics Record Library 30-5647; 1976; LP
Piano
Light dialect

1393
Git on Board, Little Chillen
[Brown, Lawrence]
Robeson, Paul (Bass-baritone)
Swing Low, Sweet Chariot
Columbia Masterworks ML 2038; [195-]; LP
Piano

1394
Get on Board, Little Children
[Brown, Lawrence]
Robeson, Paul (Bass-baritone)
Robeson
Vanguard VSD 2015; 1958?; LP
Chorus, orchestra

1395
Git on Board, Lil' Chillun
[Brown, Lawrence]
Robeson, Paul (Bass-baritone)
Ol' Man River: His 56 Finest 1925–1945
Retrospective RTS 4116; 2008; CD

1396
Little Children, Get on Board
[Brown, Lawrence]

Robeson, Paul (Bass-baritone)
The Originals: "Spirituals"
Yoyo USA; 2006; Streaming audio

1397

Get on Board, Little Children
[Brown, Lawrence]
Robeson, Paul (Bass-baritone)
Ol Man River
Leverage; 2005; Streaming audio
Piano
Heavy dialect

1398

Get on Board, Little Children
[Brown, Lawrence]
Robeson, Paul (Bass-baritone)
Five Classic Albums Plus Bonus Tracks
Real Gone Music RGMCD287; 2017; CD
Piano
Light dialect

1399

Get on Board, Little Children
[Brown, Lawrence]
Robeson, Paul (Bass-baritone)
Ol' Man River: The Ultimate Collection
Roslin Records; 2011; Streaming audio
Piano
Moderate dialect

1400

Get on Board, Little Children
[Brown, Lawrence]
Robeson, Paul (Bass-baritone)
Complete Recordings
Universal Digital Enterprises; 2018;
　　Streaming audio

1401

De Gospel Train
Burleigh, Harry T.
Shanks, Donald (Bass)
Songs of Inspiration
ABC Classics Eloquence 426 803-2; 1989;
　　CD
Organ
Moderate dialect

1402

Git on Board
Kerr, Thomas H., Jr.
Taylor, Darryl (Countertenor)
How Sweet the Sound: A Charm of Spirituals
Albany TROY1244; 2011; CD
Piano

1403

Git on Board
Kerr, Thomas H., Jr.
Taylor, Richard (Baritone)
The New Negro Spiritual
W. C. Patterson; 2002; Score w/CD
Piano
Heavy dialect

1404

Git on Board
Kerr, Thomas H., Jr.
Toppin, Louise (Soprano)
Songs of Illumination
Centaur CRC 2375; 1998; CD
Piano

1405

De Gospel Train's a-Comin'
Composer not identified
Ventriglia, Franco (Baritone)
Franco Ventriglia Sings Negro Spirituals
Vedette Records; 2007; Streaming audio
Instrumental ensemble
Heavy dialect

1406

De Gospel Train's a-Comin'
Composer not identified
Ventriglia, Franco (Baritone)
Franco Ventriglia Sings Negro Spirituals
Vedette Records VRMS 316; [19--]; LP
Instrumental ensemble
Heavy dialect

1407

De Gospel Train (Git on Bo'd Li't Children)
Burleigh, Harry T.
Warfield, William (Bass-baritone)
*Spirituals: 200 Years of African-American
　　Spirituals*

ProArte CDD 3443; 1993; CD
Piano
Heavy dialect

1408

De Gospel Train
Composer not identified
Watts, Leonardo (Baritone)
*On Ma Journey: A Memorable Collection of
   Negro Spirituals*
Onyx Recording Associates ORA-101; 1961; LP
Chorus

1409

De Gospel Train
Burleigh, Harry T.
West, Lucretia (Mezzo-soprano)
Negro Spirituals III
Club français du disque 176; 1959; LP
Piano
Heavy dialect

1410

De Gospel Train
Burleigh, Harry T.
West, Lucretia (Mezzo-soprano)
Negro Spirituals mit Lukretia West
Opera 3408; [195-]; LP
Piano

1411

The Gospel Train
Composer not identified
West, Lucretia (Mezzo-soprano)
Lucretia West Sings Spirituals
Westminster WP 6063; [1957]; LP

1412

De Gospel Train
Morgenstern, Sam
West, Lucretia (Mezzo-soprano)
Spirituals
Westminster WL 5338; 1954; LP
Men's voices

1413

Gospel Train
Johnson, Hall
White, Willard (Bass-baritone)

*Willard White Sings: Copland; American
   Spirituals; Folk-Songs*
Chandos Records CHAN 8960; 1991; CD
Piano
Heavy dialect

1414

Git on Bo'd Lit'l Children
Burleigh, Harry T.
Winter, Georg (Vocalist)
Eine Kleine Hausmusik
Teldec 66.22670; 1981; LP
Piano

1415

Gospel Train
Schweizer, Rolf
Wolf, Lars (Vocalist)
Die Schwarze Stimme Europas
Cantate 666000; 1971; LP
Chorus, organ, percussion

. . . .

Great Day

1416

Great Day
Kerr, Thomas H., Jr.; Marsh, Don; Russ,
   Patrick
Battle, Kathleen (Soprano); Norman, Jessye
   (Soprano)
Spirituals in Concert
Deutsche Grammophon 429 790-2; 1991; CD
Chorus, orchestra
Heavy dialect

1417

Great Day
Hogan, Moses
Bazile, Bridget (Soprano)
Songs of Reflection
MGH Records 0800CD; 2020; CD

1418

Great Day
Ryan, Donald
Estes, Simon (Bass-baritone)
Steal Away: My Favorite Negro Spirituals
Deutsche Schallplatten DS 1041-2; 1994; CD

Piano
No dialect discerned

Also released with *Simon Sings His Favorite Gospels & Spirituals* (Praise Productions SMG-SE; 1999; CD) and *Save the Children, Save Their Lives* (CD Baby; 2020; Streaming audio)

1419

Great Day
Hogan, Moses
George, Roderick L. (Tenor)
The Spirit of the Holidays
American Spiritual Ensemble; 2009; CD

1420

Great Day
Hayes, Roland
Glover, Andre Solomon (Baritone)
Opera Ebony Sings Spirituals
Ebony Classic Recordings; 2002; CD

1421

Great Day!
Brown, Uzee, Jr.
Harris, Crystal (Mezzo-soprano)
Great Day!
Allgood; 2005; CD
Piano
Moderate dialect

1422

Great Day
Hogan, Moses
Hendricks, Barbara (Soprano)
Give Me Jesus
EMI Classics 7243 5 56788 2 9; 1998; CD
Chorus
Moderate dialect

1423

Great Day
Okpebholo, Shawn
Liverman, Will (Baritone)
Steal Away
Yellow Einstein; 2014; CD
Piano
Light dialect

1424

Great Day
Still, William Grant
More, Suzi (Vocalist)
Chords and Strings: Centuries of Songs for Voice and Guitar
Lil Red Hen Records; 2018; Streaming audio
Guitar

1425

Great Day
Still, William Grant
More, Suzi (Vocalist)
Chords and Strings: Centuries of Songs for Voice and Guitar
Lil Red Hen Records; [2018]; Streaming audio
Guitar
Heavy dialect

1426

Great Day
Composer not identified
Moses, Oral (Bass-baritone)
Extreme Spirituals
Cuneiform Record Rune 241; 2006; CD
Instrumental ensemble

1427

Great Day!
Traditional
Moses, Oral (Bass-baritone)
Spirituals in Zion: A Spiritual Heritage for the Soul
Albany Records TROY587; 2003; CD
A cappella

1428

Great Day
Baldwin, Dalton; Jessye Norman; Patterson, Willis
Norman, Jessye (Soprano)
Negro Spirituals
Philips 9500 580; 1979; LP
Piano

1429

Great Day
Composer not identified

Norman, Jessye (Soprano)
Lieder
Philips 422 048-2; 1988; CD
Piano

1430
Great Day
Composer not identified
Norman, Jessye (Soprano)
The Jessye Norman Collection: Sacred Songs & Spirituals
Philips B0004506-02; 2005; CD
Piano
Moderate dialect

1431
Great Day
Composer not identified
Norman, Jessye (Soprano)
Honor! A Celebration of the African American Cultural Legacy
Decca B0012660-02; 2009; CD
Piano

1432
Great Day
Kerr, Thomas H., Jr.
Norman, Jessye (Soprano)
Amazing Grace
Philips 432 546-2; 1990; CD
Piano
Moderate dialect

1433
Great Day
Kerr, Thomas H., Jr.
Norman, Jessye (Soprano)
Spirituals
Philips 416 462-2; 1990; CD
Piano
Moderate dialect

1434
Great Day
Kerr, Thomas H., Jr.
Norman, Jessye (Soprano)
Live
Philips 422 235-1; [1987]; CD
Piano

1435
Great Day
Lloyd, Charles, Jr.
Norman, Jessye (Soprano)
Great Day in the Morning
Philips 6769 104; 1982; LP
Chorus, other instrument(s)

1436
Great Day
Hogan, Moses
Ragin, Derek Lee (Countertenor); Bazile, Bridget (Soprano)
Negro Spirituals
Virgin Classics 0946 363305 2 5; 2006; CD
Chorus
Light dialect

1437
Great Day
Giesen, Hubert
Ray, William (Baritone)
Negro Spirituals
Intercord; [19--]; LP
Piano

1438
Great Day
Giesen, Hubert
Ray, William (Baritone)
Sings Arias, Duets, Musical Selections and Negro Spirituals
Intercord; [19--]; CD
Piano

1439
Great Day
Johnson, Hall
Thomas, Indra (Soprano)
Great Day: Indra Thomas Sings Spirituals
Delos DE 3427; 2012; CD
WoMen's voices, piano
Light dialect

1440
Great Day
Kerr, Thomas H., Jr.
Wade, Ray, Jr. (Tenor)
The New Negro Spiritual

W. C. Patterson; 2002; Score w/CD
Piano
Heavy dialect

1441

Great Day
Brown, Uzee, Jr.
Yovanovich, Amy (Mezzo-soprano)
Great Day!
Prince Productions 9808P; 2007; CD
Piano
No dialect discerned

. . . .

Guide My Feet

1442

Guide My Feet
Hairston, Jacqueline
Barnes, Sebronette (Soprano)
You Can Tell the World: Songs by African-American Women Composers
Senrab Record SRR7988; 2000; CD
Piano
Heavy dialect

1443

Guide My Feet
Hairston, Jacqueline
Cunningham-Fleming, Jeryl (Soprano)
The Spirituals: Featuring the American Spiritual Ensemble
LexArts; [20--]; CD

1444

Guide My Feet
Hairston, Jacqueline
Fernandez, Wilhelmenia (Soprano)
Negro Spirituals
Transart 131; 2005; CD
Piano

1445

Guide My Feet
Hairston, Jacqueline
Johnson, Karen (Soprano)
The New Negro Spiritual
W. C. Patterson; 2002; Score w/CD

Piano
Heavy dialect

1446

Guide My Feet
Composer not identified
Parks, Karen (Soprano)
Done Crossed Every River: Freedom's Journey
Arcadia ARC 2004-2; 1995; CD

1447

Guide My Feet
Hairston, Jacqueline
Parks, Karen (Soprano)
Opera Ebony Sings Spirituals
Ebony Classic Recordings; 2002; CD

1448

Guide My Feet
Hairston, Jacqueline
Rhodes, Yolanda (Soprano)
The Angels Bowed Down
Cambria Master Recordings CD-1237; 2019; CD

1449

Guide My Feet
Scharnberg, Kim
Robinson, Faye (Soprano)
Remembering Marian Anderson
d'Note Classics DND 1014; 1997; CD
Orchestra
No dialect discerned

1450

Guide My Feet
Hairston, Jacqueline
Taylor, Darryl (Countertenor)
How Sweet the Sound: A Charm of Spirituals
Albany TROY1244; 2011; CD
Piano

1451

Guide My Feet
Hairston, Jacqueline
Thomas, Indra (Soprano)
Great Day: Indra Thomas Sings Spirituals
Delos DE 3427; 2012; CD

Piano
Heavy dialect

1452
Guide My Feet
Lofton, David
Thomas, Indra (Soprano)
*Catch a Shining Star: A New Generation of
    Classical Artists*
National Association of Recording
    Merchandiers NARM 50008-2; 2003; CD
Piano

1453
Guide My Feet
Hairston, Jacqueline
Toppin, Louise (Soprano)
Ah! Love, But a Day
Albany Records/ Videmus TROY 385; 2000;
    CD
Piano
Heavy dialect

· · · · · · ·

Gwina Lay Down My Burden

1454
Gwine-a Lay Down Mah Burden
Thomas, Edna
Thomas, Edna (Soprano)
*Gwine-a Lay Down Mah Burden/Little
    Wheel a-Turnin' in my Heart; Keep
    a-Inchin' Erlong*
Columbia 1360-D; 1928; 78 RPM
Piano

· · · · · · ·

Gwina Lay Down My Life

1455
Gwina Lay Down My Life
Campbell, Colin M.
Thomas, Edna (Soprano)
Classic Gospel Songs
Emerald/K-Tel; 2013; Streaming audio
Piano

1456
Gwina Lay Down My Life
Composer not identified
Thomas, Edna (Soprano)
Negro Spirituals
Columbia 3361; 1928; 78 RPM
Piano

1457
Gwina Lay Down My Life
Thomas, Edna
Thomas, Edna (Soprano)
Good News: Vintage Negro Spirituals
Living Era AJA 5622; 2006; CD
Piano
Heavy dialect

· · · · · · ·

Gwinter Sing All Along de Way

1458
Gwinter Sing All Along de Way
Still, William Grant; Taylor, Vivian
Honeysucker, Robert (Baritone)
More Still: Music by William Grant Still
Cambria Master Recordings CD-1112; 1999;
    CD
Piano
Moderate dialect

· · · · · · ·

Hail de Crown

1459
Hail de Crown
Robinson, Avery
Robeson, Paul (Bass-baritone)
Spirituals: Original Recordings 1925–1936
Naxos Gospel Legends 8.120638; 2003; CD
Piano

· · · · · · ·

Hail de King of Babylon

1460
Hail de King of Babylon
Johnson, Hall

Brown, William (Tenor)
The Hall Johnson Collection
Carl Fischer VF5 CD1–VF5 CD2; 2003; Score
     w/CD
Piano

· · · · · · ·

Hallelujah

1461
Hallelujah
Composer not identified
McKelton, Samuel (Tenor)
*Done Crossed Every River: Freedom's
     Journey*
Arcadia ARC 2004-2; 1995; CD

1462
Hallelujah
Johnson, Hall
McKelton, Samuel (Tenor)
Opera Ebony Sings Spirituals
Ebony Classic Recordings; 2002; CD

1463
Hallelujah! [from *Green Pastures*]
Johnson, Hall
Toppin, Louise (Soprano)
The Hall Johnson Collection
Carl Fischer VF5 CD1–VF5 CD2; 2003; Score
     w/CD
Piano
Moderate dialect

· · · · · · ·

Hallelujah King Jesus

1464
Hallelujah! King Jesus [from *Green
     Pastures*]
Johnson, Hall
Toppin, Louise (Soprano)
The Hall Johnson Collection
Carl Fischer VF5 CD1–VF5 CD2; 2003; Score
     w/CD
Piano
Moderate dialect

· · · · · · ·

Hallelujah to the Lamb

1465
Hallelujah to the Lamb
Perry, Zenobia Powell
Taylor, Darryl (Tenor)
*Music of Zenobia Powell Perry: Art Songs
     and Piano Music*
Cambria CD-1138; 2010; CD
Piano
Heavy dialect

· · · · · · ·

Hard Trials

1466
Hard Trials
Burleigh, Harry T.
Anderson, Marian (Contralto)
The Best of Negro Spirituals
BMG BVCM-37416; 2003; CD
Piano
Heavy dialect

1467
Hard Trials
Burleigh, Harry T.
Anderson, Marian (Contralto)
*He's Got the Whole World in His Hands:
     Spirituals*
RCA Victor 09026-6[1960]2; 1994; CD
Piano
Light dialect

     Also released with *Marian Anderson:
Beyond the Music; Her Complete RCA Victor Recordings* (Sony Classical 19439836492;
2021; CD)

1468
Hard Trials
Burleigh, Harry T.
Anderson, Marian (Contralto)
The Lady from Philadelphia
Pearl GEMM CD 9069; 1993; CD
Piano
Heavy dialect

     Also released with *Marian Anderson:
Beyond the Music; Her Complete RCA Victor*

Recordings (Sony Classical 19439836492; 2021; CD)

1469

Hard Trials
Burleigh, Harry T.
Anderson, Marian (Contralto)
Marian Anderson: Portraits in Memory
Metropolitan Opera Guild MET 220; 1993; CD
Piano
Heavy dialect

1470

Hard Trials
Burleigh, Harry T.
Anderson, Marian (Contralto)
Spirituals
RCA Victor Red Seal 09026-63306-2; 1999; CD
Piano
Light dialect

1471

Hard Trials
Burleigh, Harry T.
Anderson, Marian (Contralto)
Rare Live Broadcast Performances
VAI VAIA 1275; 2013; CD
Orchestra
Heavy dialect

1472

Hard Trials
Burleigh, Harry T.
Anderson, Marian (Contralto)
Songs and Spirituals
RCA Victor M 986; [1945]; 78 RPM
Piano

1473

Hard Trials
[Burleigh, Harry T.]
Anderson, Marian (Contralto)
The Very Best of Marian Anderson
Master Classics Records; 2009; CD
Piano
Heavy dialect

1474

Hard Trials
Burleigh, Harry T.
Carnette, Count (Vocalist)
Count Carnette Sings Favorite Negro Spirituals
Carnette Archive Recordings; 1983; LP
Piano
Moderate dialect

1475

Hard Trials
Dadmun, Royal
Dadmun, Royal (Baritone)
I Want to Be Ready/Hard Trials
Gennett 4673; 1921; 78 RPM
Orchestra

1476

Hard Trials
Composer not identified
Green, Elnora E. (Contralto)
15 Spirituals
Private Label J3RS 2286; 1979; LP
Piano

1477

Hard Trials (from *Five Spirituals*)
Stucky, Rodney
Henderson, Mary (Mezzo-soprano)
Come Where the Aspens Quiver.... Bring Your Guitar
Fleur de Son Classics FDS 57955; 2002; CD
Guitar
Light dialect

1478

Hard Trials
Burleigh, Harry T.
Karle, Theo (Tenor)
Hard Trials/Nobody Knows de Trouble I've Seen
Brunswick 13071; 1921; 78 RPM
Orchestra

1479

Hard Trials
Meyer, Fredrich
London, George (Bass-baritone)

Spirituals
Deutsche Grammophon 00289 477 6193;
    2006; CD
Chorus
Heavy dialect

1480

Hard Trials
Burleigh, Harry T.
Moses, Oral (Bass-baritone)
*Deep River: Songs and Spirituals of Harry T.
    Burleigh*
Northeastern NR 252-CD; 1995; CD
Piano

1481

Hard Trials
[Burleigh, Harry T.]
Moyer, Del-Louise (Mezzo-soprano)
*He'll Bring to Pass: Spirituals &
    Americanegro Suite*
Alyssum ALY-9001; 1997; CD
Piano
No dialect discerned

1482

Hard Trials
Composer not identified
Pickens, Jo Ann (Soprano)
*My Heritage: American Melodies/Negro
    Spirituals*
Koch Schwann 3-1447-2; 1993; CD

1483

Hard Trials
Still, William Grant
Toppin, Louise (Soprano)
More Still: Music by William Grant Still
Cambria Master Recordings CD-1112; 1999;
    CD
Piano
Heavy dialect

- - - - - - -

He Arose

1484

He arose [from *The Life of Christ*]
[Hayes, Roland]

Jenkins, Isaiah (Tenor)
Lyric Tenor
Trans Radio TR 1010A; [195-]; LP
Piano

1485

He Arose
Composer not identified
Rustin, Bayard (Tenor)
*Bayard Rustin-The Singer: Negro Spirituals,
    Lute Songs & More*
Parnassus Records PACD 96083; 2022; CD
A cappella

- - - - - - -

He Is King of Kings

1486

He Is King of Kings
Composer not identified
Arroyo, Martina (Soprano); Lawrence, T.
    Ray (Vocalist)
There's a Meeting Here Tonight
Angel S-36072; 1974; LP
Chorus

- - - - - - -

He Raised Poor Lazarus

1487

He Raised Poor Lazarus [from *The Life of
    Christ*]
Hayes, Roland
Hayes, Roland (Tenor)
*Roland Hayes Sings the Life of Christ: As Told
    Through Aframerican Folksong*
Vanguard VRS-462; 1954; LP
Piano

Also released with *Aframerican Folk-
song: Telling the Story of The Life of Christ*
(Top Rank 39 620; [1961]; LP); *Roland Hayes
Sings the Life of Christ: As Told Through
Aframerican Folksong* (Vanguard SRV 352;
1976; LP); *Favorite Spirituals* (Vanguard
Classics OVC 6022; 1995; CD); *Charlton Hes-
ton Reads from The Life and Passion of Jesus
Christ* (Vanguard Classics ATM-CD-1259;
2003; CD) and *Big Psalms, Hymns and*

Spirituals Box (eOne Music/Vanguard Classics; 2015; Streaming audio)

· · · · · · ·

He Rose

1488

He Rose
Bledsoe, Jules
Bledsoe, Jules (Baritonc)
He Rose/Wake Up, Jacob
Royale 1701; [19--]; 78 RPM
Orchestra
   Also released with *Wake Up Jacob/He Rose/Poor Monah* (Ultraphone AP 393; 1931; 78 RPM)

· · · · · · ·

Hear the Lambs a-Crying

1489

Hear de Lam's a Cryin'
Composer not identified
Blackmon, Henry (Baritone)
Negro-Spirituals
ARC AG 1006; [19--]; 45 RPM
Piano

1490

Hear de Lam's a-Cryin'
Brown, Lawrence
Anderson, Marian (Contralto)
Great Spirituals
RCA Victor ERA 62; [195-]; 7" Vinyl
Piano

1491

Hear de Lam's a-Cryin'
Brown, Lawrence
Anderson, Marian (Contralto)
Spirituals
RCA Victor Red Seal 09026-63306-2; 1999; CD
Piano
No dialect discerned

1492

Hear de Lam's a-Aryin' (sic a-Crying)
Brown, Lawrence

Anderson, Marian (Contralto)
Negro Spirituals
La Voix de Son Maître FBLP1039; 1953; LP
Piano
Heavy dialect
   Also released with *Marian Anderson: Beyond the Music; Her Complete RCA Victor Recordings* (Sony Classical 19439836492; 2021; CD)

1493

Hear de Lam's a-Cryin'
Brown, Lawrence
Anderson, Marian (Contralto)
Marian Anderson Sings Negro Spirituals
His Master's Voice BLP 1060; [19--]; LP
Piano

1494

Hear de Lam's a-Cryin'
Brown, Lawrence
Anderson, Marian (Contralto)
Great Spirituals
Kipepeo Publishing; 2017; CD
Piano

1495

Hear de Lam's a-Cryin'
Brown, Lawrence
Anderson, Marian (Contralto)
Marian Anderson Sings Spirituals
RCA Victor Red Seal MO 1238; 1948; 78 RPM
Piano

1496

Hear de Lam's a-Cryin'
Brown, Lawrence
Anderson, Marian (Contralto)
Negro Spirituals
RCA Victor LM 2032; [1956]; LP
Piano

1497

Hear de Lam's a-Cryin'
[Brown, Lawrence]
Anderson, Marian (Contralto)
Alto Rhapsody; Selected Spirituals
Urania URN 22.328; 2007; CD
Piano

1498

Hear de Lam's a-Cryin'
[Brown, Lawrence]
Anderson, Marian (Contralto)
The Very Best of Marian Anderson
Master Classics Records; 2009; CD
Piano
Heavy dialect

1499

Hear de Lam's a-Cryin'
[Brown, Lawrence]
Anderson, Marian (Contralto)
Marian Anderson Sings Spirituals
RCA Victor LM 110; 1949; LP
Piano
Heavy dialect

   Also released with *Marian Anderson: Beyond the Music; Her Complete RCA Victor Recordings* (Sony Classical 19439836492; 2021; CD)

1500

Hear de Lam's a-Cryin'
[Brown, Lawrence]
Anderson, Marian (Contralto)
Negro Spirituals
RCA Gold Seal RVC-1570; [19--]; LP
Piano

1501

Hear de Lam's a-Cryin'
[Brown, Lawrence]
Anderson, Marian (Contralto)
Negro Spirituals
RCA Victor 630.396 A; [19--]; LP
Piano

1502

Hear the Lambs a-Cryin'
[Brown, Lawrence]
Anderson, Marian (Contralto)
Grandes Contraltos de la Musique Classique, Les: Marian Anderson, Vol. 2
Mon Patrimoine Musical Collection; 2017; Streaming audio
Piano

1503

Hear de Lambs a-Cryin'
Burleigh, Harry T.
Brown, Anthony (Baritone)
Spirituals
Brown/Smith Productions; 1995; CD
Piano
Heavy dialect

1504

Hear de Lambs a Cryin [from *The Life of Christ*]
Hayes, Roland
Caesar, Jackson (Tenor)
Spirituals: Celebrating the Music, Life, Legacy of Roland Hayes
CD Baby 7048606059; 2021; CD
Piano
Heavy dialect

1505

You Hear de Lambs
Composer not identified
Elzy, Ruby (Soprano)
Ruby Elzy in Song: Rare Recordings
Cambria Records CD-1154; 2006; CD
Piano
Heavy dialect

   Also released with *The 78 RPM Collection* (Master Classics Records; 2010; CD)

1506

Hear the Lambs
Robbiani, Mario
Fisher, Dorothy (Contralto)
Negro Spirituals
Edizione D'Arte Del Lions Club Milano Al Cenacolo; [19--]; LP
Orchestra
Light dialect

1507

You Hear the Lambs a-Cryin [from *The Life of Christ*]
Hayes, Roland
Hayes, Roland (Tenor)
Roland Hayes Sings the Life of Christ: As Told Through Aframerican Folksong
Vanguard VRS-462; 1954; LP

Piano
Light dialect

Also released with *Aframerican Folksong: Telling the Story of The Life of Christ* (Top Rank 39 620; [1961]; LP); *Roland Hayes Sings the Life of Christ: As Told Through Aframerican Folksong* (Vanguard SRV 352; 1976; LP); *Favorite Spirituals* (Vanguard Classics OVC 6022; 1995; CD); *Charlton Heston Reads from The Life and Passion of Jesus Christ* (Vanguard Classics ATM-CD-1259; 2003; CD) and *Big Psalms, Hymns and Spirituals Box* (eOne Music/Vanguard Classics; 2015; Streaming audio)

1508

Hear de Lambs a Cryin'
Hayes, Roland
Hayes, Roland (Tenor)
Were You There/Hear de Lambs a Cryin'/ Plenty Good Room
Columbia Masterworks 69812-D; 1940; 78 RPM
Piano

1509

Hear de Lambs a Cryin'
[Hayes, Roland]
Hayes, Roland (Tenor)
Art Songs and Spirituals
Veritas VM 112; 1967; LP
Piano
Heavy dialect

1510

Hear de Lambs a-Cryin' [from *The Life of Christ*]
Hayes, Roland
Holland, Charles (Tenor)
My Lord What a Mornin'
Musical Heritage Society MHS 512250K; 1988; CD
Piano
Moderate dialect

1511

Hear de Lambs a-Cryin' [from *The Life of Christ*]
Hayes, Roland

Holland, Charles (Tenor)
My Lord What a Mornin'
Musical Heritage Society MHS 912250X; 1982; LP
Piano
Moderate dialect

1512

Hear de lambs a-cryin [from *The Life of Christ*]
Hayes, Roland
Holland, Charles (Tenor)
Cinq Negro Spirituals
Pathé 45 ED. 28; 1954; 45 RPM
Piano

1513

Hear de Lambs a Cryin'? [from *The Life of Christ*]
Hayes, Roland
Matthews, Inez (Mezzo-soprano)
Inez Matthews Sings Spirituals (Great New Voices of Today, v. 6)
Period SPL-580; [1950]; LP
Piano
Heavy dialect

Also released with *Inez Matthews Sings Spirituals* (Essential Media Group; 2011; CD)

1514

Hear de Lambs a-Cryin'
Burleigh, Harry T.
Moses, Oral (Bass-baritone)
Deep River: Songs and Spirituals of Harry T. Burleigh
Northeastern NR 252-CD; 1995; CD
Piano

1515

Hear de Lambs a Cryin' [from *The Life of Christ*]
Hayes, Roland
Oby, Jason (Tenor)
The Life of Christ: Collected Spirituals
Private Label TSU4749; [200-]; CD
Piano
Moderate dialect

1516

Hear de Lambs a-Cryin'?
Brown, Lawrence
Peterson, Elwood (Baritone)
Negro Spirituals
Boîte à Musique LD 073; 1961; LP
Piano

1517

Hear de Lam's a Cryin'
Brown, Lawrence
Robeson, Paul (Bass-baritone)
Spirituals: Original Recordings 1925–1936
Naxos Gospel Legends 8.120638; 2003; CD
Piano

1518

Hear the Lambs a-Cryin
Brown, Lawrence
Robeson, Paul (Bass-baritone); Brown,
    Lawrence (Vocalist)
*A Lonesome Road: Paul Robeson Sings
    Spirituals and Songs*
ASV Living Era CD AJA 5027; 1984; CD
Piano
Moderate dialect

1519

Hear de Lams a Cryin'
Brown, Lawrence
Robeson, Paul (Bass-baritone)
Paul Robeson Sings Negro Spirituals
Philips GBL 5584; [19--]; LP
Piano

1520

Hear the Lambs a-Cryin'
Brown, Lawrence
Robeson, Paul (Bass-baritone)
Paul Robeson Collection
Hallmark Recordings 390692; 1998; CD

1521

Hear, de Lam's a-Cryin'
Brown, Lawrence
Robeson, Paul (Bass-baritone); Brown,
    Lawrence (Vocalist)
*Hear, De Lam's A-Cryin'/Ezekiel Saw de
    Wheel*

Victor 20604; 1927; 78 RPM
Piano

1522

Hear de Lam's a Cryin'
Brown, Lawrence
Robeson, Paul (Bass-baritone); Brown,
    Lawrence (Vocalist)
Songs of My People
RCA Red Seal LM-3292; 1972; LP
Piano

1523

Hear de Lam's a-Cryin'
Brown, Lawrence
Robeson, Paul (Bass-baritone)
Swing Low, Sweet Chariot
Columbia Masterworks MM-819; 1949; 78
    RPM
Piano

1524

Hear de Lam's a-Cryin'
Brown, Lawrence
Robeson, Paul (Bass-baritone); Brown,
    Lawrence (Vocalist)
*Hear, De Lam's A-Cryin'/Ezekiel Saw de
    Wheel*
His Master's Voice B 2838; 1928; 78 RPM
Piano

1525

Hear de Lam's a Cryin'
Brown, Lawrence
Robeson, Paul (Bass-baritone)
Paul Robeson Chante ... f16 Spirituals
Philips G 05.639 R; 1959; LP
Piano

1526

Hear de Lam's a-Cryin'
[Brown, Lawrence]
Robeson, Paul (Bass-baritone)
Negro Spirituals, v. 2
Philips NBE11102; 1956; 7" Vinyl

1527

Hear de Lam's a-Cryin'
[Brown, Lawrence]

Robeson, Paul (Bass-baritone)
Swing Low, Sweet Chariot
Columbia Masterworks ML 2038; [195-]; LP
Piano

1528

Hear da lam's a-cryin'
[Brown, Lawrence]
Robeson, Paul (Bass-baritone); Brown,
    Lawrence (Vocalist)
Ol' Man River: The Very Best of Paul Robeson
Memory Lane; 2012; CD

1529

Hear the Lambs a-Cryin'
[Brown, Lawrence]
Robeson, Paul (Bass-baritone); Brown,
    Lawrence (Vocalist)
Ol Man River
Leverage; 2005; Streaming audio
Piano
Moderate dialect

1530

Hear the Lambs a-Cryin'
[Brown, Lawrence]
Robeson, Paul (Bass-baritone); Brown,
    Lawrence (Vocalist)
Ol' Man River: The Ultimate Collection
Roslin Records; 2011; Streaming audio
Piano
Light dialect

1531

Hear de Lambs a-Cryin' [from *The Life of
    Christ*]
Hayes, Roland
Shirley, George (Tenor)
George Shirley at 80: My Time Has Come!
Videmus Records; 2014; CD
Piano

1532

Hear de Lambs a-Cryin' [from *The Life of
    Christ*]
Hayes, Roland
Sims, Robert (Baritone)
*Robert Sims Sings the Spirituals of Roland
    Hayes*

Canti Classics 2014-01; 2015; CD
Piano
Heavy dialect

1533

Hear de Lam's a-Cryin'
[Brown, Lawrence]
Spencer, Kenneth (Bass-baritone)
American Spirituals
Sonora MS-478; [1945]; 78 RPM
Piano
Light dialect

1534

Hear de Lams a'Cryin'
Composer not identified
Stuart, Avon (Baritone)
Avon Stuart Recital
Edition Rhodos ERS 1218; 1975; LP
Piano

1535

Hear de Lambs a-Cryin'?
Composer not identified
Verdejo, Awilda (Soprano)
Awilda Verdejo Sings Spirituals
Angeluz Performances; 1999; CD
Piano

1536

Hear de Lambs a Cryin? [from *The Life of
    Christ*]
Hayes, Roland
Williams, Willie (Vocalist)
My Tribute
Discovery V42227; 1974; LP
Piano

· · · · · · ·

Heaven, Heaven (Going to Shout All Over God's Heaven, I Got a Robe)

[Psalm 71:22, 144:9; Revelation 6:11]

"I've got a robe, you've got a robe, All of God's children got a robe; When I get to heaven, Going to play on my harp, Going to shout all over God's heaven. Heaven, heaven,

Everybody talking about heaven ain't going there...."

[Available in CW40, FHFN, HCTN, HLBS, HTBS, HTC1, JJAN, JSSp, LB6N, RHMF, RS12, SBFD, UBTM, WF10, WF70]

Folk spirituals often had hidden meanings in their texts intended to communicate to the enslaved who understood those meanings without conveying the meanings to those who enslaved them. To the ears of those who thought the words were merely child-like prose, they missed the condemnation—"Everybody talkin' 'bout Heav'n ain't goin' dere"—that was aimed at them for their acts of enslavement.

Numerous verses have survived through the oral tradition, giving composers many choices of what texts to use in their concert spirituals. The more successful settings seem to maintain the simplicity of the song's declaration in the vocal line and accompanying instrumental part(s). Correspondingly, the singer best serves the song by minimizing the amount of improvisation used and concentrating on communicating the joyous simplicity of the text.

1537

All God's Children Got Wings
Composer not identified
Adams, Robert (Vocalist)
All God's Children Got Wings/Scandalize My Name Scandalize My Name/It's Me O Lord/Joshua Fit de Battle of Jericho
Ultraphon C 18121; [19--]; 78 RPM

1538

Heav'n Heav'n
Burleigh, Harry T.
Anderson, Marian (Contralto)
Ev'Ry Time I Feel the Spirit (1930–1947)
Naxos Nostalgia 8.120779; 2004; CD
Piano

1539

Heav'n, Heav'n
Burleigh, Harry T.
Anderson, Marian (Contralto)
He's Got the Whole World in His Hands: Spirituals

RCA Victor 09026-6[1960]2; 1994; CD
Piano
Heavy dialect

1540

Heav'n, Heav'n
Burleigh, Harry T.
Anderson, Marian (Contralto)
The Lady
Magnum Music MCCD 017; 1996; CD
Piano

1541

Heaven, Heaven
Burleigh, Harry T.
Anderson, Marian (Contralto)
Prima Voce
Nimbus NI 7882; 1996; CD
Piano
Heavy dialect

1542

Heaven, Heaven
Burleigh, Harry T.
Anderson, Marian (Contralto)
Spirituals
RCA Victor Red Seal 09026-63306-2; 1999; CD
Piano
Moderate dialect

1543

Heaven, Heaven
Burleigh, Harry T.
Anderson, Marian (Contralto)
Tribute
Pro Arte CDD 3447; 1993; CD
Piano

1544

Heav'n, Heav'n
Burleigh, Harry T.
Anderson, Marian (Contralto)
When I Have Sung My Songs: The American Art Song, 1900–1940
New World NW 247; 1976; LP
Piano

1545

Heaven, Heaven (I Got a Robe)
Burleigh, Harry T.

Anderson, Marian (Contralto)
Great Voices of the Century
Memoir Classics CDMOIR 432; 1996; CD
Piano

1546

Heav'n, Heav'n
Burleigh, Harry T.
Anderson, Marian (Contralto)
Recital: Opera, Lieder, Oratorio
SYM1270.2; Symposium; 2005; CD
Piano

1547

Heaven, Heaven
Burleigh, Harry T.
Anderson, Marian (Contralto)
Lebendige Vergangenheit
Austro Mechana Historic Recordings
    MONO 89604; 2004; CD
Piano

1548

Heav'n Heav'n
Burleigh, Harry T.
Anderson, Marian (Contralto)
Met Stars in the New World
MET 216CD; 1992; CD

1549

Heav'n Heav'n
Burleigh, Harry T.
Anderson, Marian (Contralto)
Negro Spirituals: 1924–1949
Frémeaux & Associés FA 184; 2004; CD
Orchestra

1550

Heav'n Heav'n
Burleigh, Harry T.
Anderson, Marian (Contralto)
Heav'n, Heav'n
Victor 19370-B; 1924; 78 RPM
Orchestra
Light dialect

1551

Heav'n, Heav'n
Burleigh, Harry T.

Anderson, Marian (Contralto)
Jan Peerce and Marian Anderson Recital
Royale 1278; [195-]; LP
Piano
Moderate dialect

1552

Heav'n, Heav'n (I Got a Robe)
Burleigh, Harry T.
Anderson, Marian (Contralto)
Deep River/Heav'n, Heav'n
HMV B 2828; [19--]; 78 RPM
Piano

1553

Heav'n, Heav'n
Burleigh, Harry T.
Anderson, Marian (Contralto)
Let Freedom Ring!
JSP Records 683; 2016; CD
Piano
Heavy dialect

1554

Heav'n, Heav'n
Burleigh, Harry T.
Anderson, Marian (Contralto)
Negro Spirituals
La Voix de Son Maître 7 ERF 157; [19--];
    45 RPM

1555

Heaven, Heaven
Burleigh, Harry T.
Anderson, Marian (Contralto)
*City Called Heaven/Lord, I Can't Stay Away/
    Heaven, Heaven*
Victor Red Seal 8958; 1936; 78 RPM
Piano

1556

Heav'n, Heav'n (I Got a Robe)
Burleigh, Harry T.
Anderson, Marian (Contralto)
Deep River/Heav'n, Heav'n (I Got a Robe)
Victor 22015; [19--]; 78 RPM
Piano
Moderate dialect

1557
Heaven, Heaven
Burleigh, Harry T.
Anderson, Marian (Contralto)
Anderson Sings Negro Spirituals
Victor Golden Series EK-1007; [19--]; 45
    RPM
Piano

1558
Heav'n Heav'n
Burleigh, Harry T.
Anderson, Marian (Contralto)
Negro Spirituals, Vol. I
La Voix de Son Maître 7 ERF 17026; 1960;
    45 RPM

1559
Heav'n Heav'n
Burleigh, Harry T.
Anderson, Marian (Contralto)
Negro Spirituals
La Voix de Son Maître 7 EJF 3; 1955; 45 RPM
Piano

1560
Heav'n, Heav'n
Burleigh, Harry T.
Anderson, Marian (Contralto)
*Marian Anderson: Beyond the Music; Her
    Complete RCA Victor Recordings*
Sony Classical 19439836492; 2021; CD
Orchestra
Moderate dialect

1561
Heaven
Composer not identified
Anderson, Marian (Contralto)
American Negro Spirituals
Allegro LEG 9026; [19--]; LP

1562
Heav'n Heav'n (I Got a Robe)
[Burleigh, Harry T.]
Anderson, Marian (Contralto)
Deep River
Audio Book & Music; [20--]; CD

1563
Heaven, Heaven
[Burleigh, Harry T.]
Anderson, Marian (Contralto)
12 Outstanding American Singers, vol. 1
Legendary Recordings LR 139; 198-?; LP
Piano
Heavy dialect

1564
Heav'n Heav'n
[Burleigh, Harry T.]
Anderson, Marian (Contralto)
Marian Anderson Sings Spirituals
Flapper Past CD 7073; 1995; CD
Piano

1565
Heav'n Heav'n (I Got a Robe)
[Burleigh, Harry T.]
Anderson, Marian (Contralto)
Softly Awakes My Heart
ASV CD AJA 5262; 1999; CD
Piano

1566
Heaven, Heaven
[Burleigh, Harry T.]
Anderson, Marian (Contralto)
The Very Best of Marian Anderson
Master Classics Records; 2009; CD
Piano
Moderate dialect

1567
Heav'n Heav'n
[Burleigh, Harry T.]
Anderson, Marian (Contralto)
Marian Anderson, Volume 1
Pearl GEMM CD 9318; 1988; CD

1568
Heav'n, Heav'n
[Burleigh, Harry T.]
Anderson, Marian (Contralto)
Greats of the Gramophone, Vol. 1
Naxos Nostalgia 8.120569; 2001; CD
Piano

1569
Heav'n, Heav'n
[Burleigh, Harry T.]
Anderson, Marian (Contralto)
The First Recordings of Marian Anderson
Halo 50281; 1956; LP

1570
Heav'n, Heav'n
[Burleigh, Harry T.]
Anderson, Marian (Contralto)
Those Wonderful Stars of Yesterday
Columbia P6S 5334; [197-]; LP

1571
Heav'n, Heav'n
[Burleigh, Harry T.]
Anderson, Marian (Contralto)
*Marian Anderson Sings an International
    Concert*
Royale 1764; [194-]; 78 RPM
Piano

1572
Heav'n Heav'n (I Got a Robe!)
[Burleigh, Harry T.]
Anderson, Marian (Contralto)
Inspirations
Emerald Echoes; 2015; Streaming audio
Piano
Heavy dialect

1573
Heav'n, Heav'n
[Burleigh, Harry T.]
Anderson, Marian (Contralto)
*Heav'n, Heav'n/Sometimes I Feel Like a
    Motherless Child*
Masterpiece 8532; [1940]; 78 RPM
Piano
Moderate dialect

1574
Heav'n, Heav'n
[Burleigh, Harry T.]
Anderson, Marian (Contralto)
Marian Anderson
Davis Records 11749; [19--]; 78 RPM

Piano
Moderate dialect

1575
Heav'n Heav'n
[Burleigh, Harry T.]
Anderson, Marian (Contralto)
Those Wonderful Stars of Yesteryear
Columbia P6S 5334; [197-]; LP

1576
Heav'n, Heav'n
[Burleigh, Harry T.]
Anderson, Marian (Contralto)
*Sometimes I Feel Like a Motherless Child/
    Heav'n, Heav'n*
Ultraphone AP 1504; [193-]; 78 RPM
Piano

1577
Heav'n, Heav'n
[Burleigh, Harry T.]
Anderson, Marian (Contralto)
Marian Anderson and Elizabeth Wysor Sing
Allegro Royale 1589; 1955; LP
Piano
Heavy dialect

1578
Heav'n Heav'n
[Burleigh, Harry T.]
Anderson, Marian (Contralto)
The Rich Voice of Marian Anderson
Editions Audiovisuel Beulah; 2019;
    Streaming audio
Piano

1579
Heav'n Heav'n
[Burleigh, Harry T.]
Anderson, Marian (Contralto)
*Sometimes I Feel Like a Motherless Child/
    Heav'n, Heav'n*
Royale 1765; [1936]; 78 RPM
Piano

1580
Heav'n, Heav'n
[Burleigh, Harry T.]

Anderson, Marian (Contralto)
Ave Maria: And Other Schubert Songs
43 North Broadway, LLC; 2019; Streaming
    audio
Piano
Heavy dialect

1581

Heav'n, Heav'n
Composer not identified
Anonymous (Contralto)
*Heav'n, Heav'n/Sometimes I Feel Like a
    Motherless Child*
Concertone 318; [193-]; 78 RPM
Piano

1582

I Gotta Robe
Composer not identified
Arroyo, Martina (Soprano)
Negro Spirituals
EMI 7243 5 72790 2 4; 1998; CD
Chorus
Heavy dialect

1583

I Gotta Robe
Composer not identified
Arroyo, Martina (Soprano); Wallace,
    Mervin (Vocalist)
There's a Meeting Here Tonight
Angel S-36072; 1974; LP
Chorus

1584

I Got a Robe
Composer not identified
Arroyo, Martina (Soprano)
Martina Arroyo Singt Lieder der Welt
Eurodisc-Auslese [2000]3-241; 1979; LP

1585

I Got a Robe
Hogan, Moses
Simpson, Marietta (Mezzo-soprano)
Songs of Reflection
MGH Records 0800CD; 2020; CD

1586

I Gotta Robe
Sonntag, Stanley
Arroyo, Martina (Soprano)
Spirituals
Centaur CRC 2060; 1991; CD
Piano
Heavy dialect

1587

Goin' to Shout All Over God's Heaven
White, Clarence Cameron
Bledsoe, Jules (Baritone)
*Swing Low, Sweet Chariot/Goin' to Shout All
    Over God's Heaven*
Decca F.3486; 1935; 78 RPM
Piano
Heavy dialect

1588

Goin' to Shoot [Shout] All Over God's
    Heaven
[White, Clarence Cameron]
Bledsoe, Jules (Baritone)
*Brother, Can You Spare a Dime?: The Roots of
    American Song*
Pearl Gemm CD 9484; 1991; CD
Piano
Heavy dialect

1589

Heaven, Heaven
Hershberger, A. J.
Brown, Anthony (Baritone)
Toil and Triumph
Spirituals Project; 2002; CD
Chorus
Moderate dialect

1590

Heaven
Hayes, Roland
Caesar, Jackson (Tenor)
*Spirituals: Celebrating the Music, Life,
    Legacy of Roland Hayes*
CD Baby 7048606059; 2021; CD
Piano
Moderate dialect

1591

I Got a Robe
Burleigh, Harry T.
Carlsen, Svein (Bass)
Negro Spirituals
EuroMaster AS ECD19005; 1996; CD
Piano

1592

Heav'n, Heav'n
Credit, Roosevelt André
Credit, Roosevelt André (Bass-baritone)
Ol' Time Religion
CD Baby; 2007; CD, Streaming audio
Piano

1593

All God's Chillun Got Wings
Johnson, John Rosamond
Duncan, Todd (Baritone)
Negro Spirituals
Allegro ALG3022; [1952]; LP
Piano

1594

All God's Children Got Wings
Johnson, John Rosamond
Duncan, Todd (Baritone)
African American Spirituals
[Apple Music]; 2008; Streaming audio
Piano
Heavy dialect

1595

All God's Chillun Got Wings
[Johnson, John Rosamond]
Duncan, Todd (Baritone)
Spirituals
Royale 1810; [1950]; LP

1596

All God's Chillum Got Wings
[Johnson, John Rosamond]
Duncan, Todd (Baritone)
America's Great Baritone: Sings Folk Songs
Royale EP181; [195-]; 45 RPM

1597

Gonna Shout All Over God's Heaven
Brown, Uzee, Jr.
English-Robinson, Laura (Soprano)
Great Day!
Allgood; 2005; CD
Piano
Heavy dialect

1598

Heav'n, Heav'n
Ryan, Donald
Estes, Simon (Bass-baritone)
Steal Away: My Favorite Negro Spirituals
Deutsche Schallplatten DS 1041-2; 1994; CD
Piano
Moderate dialect

    Also released with *Simon Sings His Favorite Gospels & Spirituals* (Praise Productions SMG-SE; 1999; CD)

1599

Heav'n, Heav'n
Kaelin, Pierre
Evans, Allan (Bass-baritone)
Negro Spirituals
Electromusic Records EMCD 6885; 1985; CD
Chorus, other instrument(s)

1600

I Gotta Robe
Robbiani, Mario
Fisher, Dorothy (Contralto)
Negro Spirituals
Edizione D'Arte Del Lions Club Milano Al
    Cenacolo; [19--]; LP
Piano
Moderate dialect

1601

Heav'n, Heav'n
Burleigh, Harry T.
Forest, Michael (Tenor)
The Spirit Sings: American Spirituals
Shenandoah Conservatory SU003; [199-]; CD

1602

Heav'n, Heav'n
[Burleigh, Harry T.]

Hagen-William, Louis (Bass-baritone)
Negro Spirituals
Quantum QM 6909; 1993; CD
Piano
Heavy dialect

1603
Heav'n Heav'n
Burleigh, Harry T.
Harris, Hilda (Mezzo-soprano)
*From the Southland: Songs, Piano Sketches
    and Spirituals of Harry T. Burleigh*
Premier Recordings PRCD 1041; 1995; CD
Piano
Heavy dialect

1604
I Got a Robe
Composer not identified
Hayes, Roland (Tenor)
Afro-American Folksongs
Pelican Records LP 2028; 1983; LP
Piano

1605
Heaven [from *My Songs: Dream of Heaven*]
Hayes, Roland
Hayes, Roland (Tenor)
Roland Hayes: My Songs
Vanguard VRS-494; 1956; LP
Piano
Heavy dialect

    Also released with *Favorite Spirituals*
(Vanguard Classics OVC 6022; 1995; CD) and
Big Psalms, Hymns and Spirituals Box (eOne
Music/Vanguard Classics; 2015; Streaming
audio)

1606
I Got a Robe
Hogan, Moses
Hendricks, Barbara (Soprano)
Give Me Jesus
EMI Classics 7243 5 56788 2 9; 1998; CD
Chorus
Heavy dialect

1607
Heav'n Heav'n
Burleigh, Harry T.

Holmes, Eugene (Baritone)
Spirituals
Schubert Records SCH-102; [1988]; LP
Piano
Moderate dialect

1608
Heav'n
Composer not identified
Hunt, Arthur Billings (Baritone)
Hymns and Spirituals
Cook Laboratories 1090; [195-]; LP
Organ

1609
Heav'n, Heav'n
Burleigh, Harry T.
Jones, Arthur (Tenor)
Wade in the Water
Orbis Books; 1993; Book w/cass
Piano
Heavy dialect

1610
I've Got a Robe
Burleigh, Harry T.
Jones, Fanni (Mezzo-soprano)
Fanni Jones et Oswald Russell
Audio-Visual Enterprises AVE 30701; [19--];
    LP

1611
Hebb'n, Hebb'n
Meyer, Fredrich
London, George (Bass-baritone)
Spirituals
Deutsche Grammophon 00289 477 6193;
    2006; CD
Chorus, orchestra
Moderate dialect

1612
I Got a Robe [from *Feel the Spirit*]
Rutter, John
Marshall, Melanie (Mezzo-soprano)
Feel the Spirit
Collegium Records COLCD 128; 2001; CD
Chorus, orchestra

1613

Gonna Shout All Over God's Heaven
Brown, Uzee, Jr.
Moses, Oral (Bass-baritone)
Songs of America
Albany Records TROY1011; 2008; CD
Piano
Moderate dialect

Also released with *Sankofa: A Spiritual Reflection* (Albany Records TROY1802; 2019; CD)

1614

I've Got a Robe
Lloyd, Charles, Jr.; Norman, Jessye
Norman, Jessye (Soprano)
Great Day in the Morning
Philips 6769 104; 1982; LP
Chorus, other instrument(s)

1615

Heav'n Heav'n [from *Settings for Spirituals*]
Chadabe, Joel
Oliver, Irene (Soprano)
Settings for Spirituals; Solo
Lovely Music VR-3804; 1984; LP
Electronics

1616

Heav'n Heav'n
Composer not identified
Payne, John C. (Baritone)
Brother, Can You Spare a Dime?: The Roots of American Song
Pearl Gemm CD 9484; 1991; CD
Piano
Heavy dialect

1617

I Got Shoes
Composer not identified
Pickens, Jo Ann (Soprano)
My Heritage: American Melodies/Negro Spirituals
Koch Schwann 3-1447-2; 1993; CD

1618

Heaven
Composer not identified

Pleas III, Henry H. (Tenor)
Deep River: A Spiritual Journey
Rowe House Productions; 1999; CD

1619

I Got a Robe
Composer not identified
Porter, John (Bass)
No More Crying: Negro Spirituals
Pan Verlag OV-84; [1978]; LP

1620

Heaven
Hogan, Moses
Ragin, Derek Lee (Countertenor)
Ev'ry Time I Feel the Spirit: Spirituals
Channel Classics CCS 2991; 1991; CD
Chorus
Heavy dialect

1621

I Got a Robe
Giesen, Hubert
Ray, William (Baritone)
Negro Spirituals
Intercord; [19--]; LP
Piano

Also released with *Sings Arias, Duets, Musical Selections and Negro Spirituals* (Intercord; [19--]; CD)

1622

All God's Chillun Got Wings
Johnson, Hall
Robeson, Paul (Bass-baritone)
Legends of the 20th Century: Paul Robeson
EMI Records 7243 520140; 1999; CD
Piano

1623

All God's Chillun Got Wings
[Johnson, Hall]
Robeson, Paul (Bass-baritone)
The Very Best of Paul Robeson
Future Noise Music FVDD033; 2009; CD
Piano

1624

All God's Chillun Got Wings
[Johnson, Hall]

Robeson, Paul (Bass-baritone)
Spirituals/Folksongs/Hymns
Pearl GEMM CD 9382; 1989; CD

1625

All God's Chillun Got Wings
[Johnson, Hall]
Robeson, Paul (Bass-baritone)
Negro Spirituals, Blues, Songs
Saar CD 12519; 1995; CD

1626

All God's Chillun Got Wings
[Johnson, Hall]
Robeson, Paul (Bass-baritone)
Paul Robeson Collection
Hallmark Recordings 390692; 1998; CD

1627

All God's Chillun Got Wings
[Johnson, Hall]
Robeson, Paul (Bass-baritone)
Ol' Man River: His 56 Finest 1925–1945
Retrospective RTS 4116; 2008; CD

1628

All God's Chillum Got Wings
[Johnson, Hall]
Robeson, Paul (Bass-baritone)
Green Pastures
ASV Living Era CD AJA 5047; 1987; CD

1629

All God's Chillun Got Wings
[Johnson, Hall]
Robeson, Paul (Bass-baritone)
Voice of the People
Regis RRC 1056; 2011; CD
Piano
Heavy dialect

1630

All God's Chillun Got Wings
[Johnson, Hall]
Robeson, Paul (Bass-baritone)
Ol' Man River: The Ultimate Collection
Roslin Records; 2011; Streaming audio
Piano
Heavy dialect

1631

All God's Chillum Got Wings (I Gotta
    Robe)
[Johnson, Hall]
Robeson, Paul (Bass-baritone)
The Essential Collection
Primo PRMCD6233; 2018; CD

1632

I Got a Robe
Composer not identified
Spencer, Kenneth (Bass-baritone)
Negro Spirituals
Life Records C 1108; [19--]; LP

1633

I Got a Robe
Composer not identified
Spencer, Kenneth (Bass-baritone)
Kenneth Spencer Singt Neger-Spirituals
Garnet DG 2001; [19--]; 45 RPM
Orchestra

1634

I Got a Robe
Burleigh, Harry T.
Te Wiata, Inia (Bass)
A Popular Recital
Kiwi Pacific CD SLC-248; 1997; CD
Piano

1635

I Got Shoes
Golde, Walter
Thomas, Edna (Soprano)
*Way Down Upon the Swanee River/I Got
    Shoes*
Columbia 3345; 1923; 78 RPM
Piano

1636

I Got Shoes
Thomas, Edna
Thomas, Edna (Soprano)
*I Got Shoes/Way Down Upon the Swanee
    River*
Columbia 3345R; [1924]; 78 RPM
Piano

1637

I Got Shoes
Thomas, Edna
Thomas, Edna (Soprano)
I Got Shoes/Nobody Knows de Trouble I Sees
Columbia 1863-D; 1928; 78 RPM
Piano

1638

I-Got-a-Robe
Composer not identified
Webb, George (Tenor)
*Famous Negro Spirituals and Songs of
    Elizabethan England, Ireland & the
    Caribbean*
[Unknown] WLP7804; 1978; LP

1639

Heaven, Heaven
Burleigh, Harry T.
West, Lucretia (Mezzo-soprano)
Negro Spirituals III
Club français du disque 176; 1959; LP
Piano
Heavy dialect

1640

Heaven, Heaven
Burleigh, Harry T.
West, Lucretia (Mezzo-soprano)
Negro Spirituals mit Lukretia West
Opera 3408; [195-]; LP
Piano

1641

Heaven, Heaven
Burleigh, Harry T.
West, Lucretia (Mezzo-soprano)
Negro Spirituals
Club français du disque 215; [196-]; 7-in EP
Piano

1642

All God's Children Got Wings
Composer not identified
West, Lucretia (Mezzo-soprano)
Lucretia West Sings Spirituals
Westminster WP 6063; [1957]; LP

1643

All God's Chillun Got Wings
Morgenstern, Sam
West, Lucretia (Mezzo-soprano)
Spirituals
Westminster WL 5338; 1954; LP
Men's voices

1644

All God's children Got a Robe
Composer not identified
White, Willard (Bass-baritone)
The Paul Robeson Legacy
Linn AKD 190; 2015; CD
Instrumental ensemble

· · · · · · ·

Heaven's
a Beautiful Place

1645

Heaven's a Beautiful Place
Carter, Roland
Robinson-Oturo, Gail (Soprano)
*Sweetest Sound I Ever Heard: Spirituals for
    Solo Voice and Piano, Vol. 1*
CD Baby; 2020; Streaming audio
Piano
Light dialect

· · · · · · ·

He'll Bring It to Pass

1646

He'll Bring It to Pass
Johnson, Hall
Anderson, Marian (Contralto)
The Best of Negro Spirituals
BMG BVCM-37416; 2003; CD
Piano
Moderate dialect

1647

He'll Bring It to Pass
Johnson, Hall
Anderson, Marian (Contralto)
*He's Got the Whole World in His Hands:
    Spirituals*

RCA Victor 09026-6[1960]2; 1994; CD
Piano
Light dialect

1648

He'll Bring It to Pass
Johnson, Hall
Anderson, Marian (Contralto)
Jus' Keep on Singin'
RCA Victor LSC 2796; 1965; LP
Piano
Moderate dialect

    Also released with *Marian Anderson: Beyond the Music; Her Complete RCA Victor Recordings* (Sony Classical 19439836492; 2021; CD)

1649

He'll Bring It to Pass
[Johnson, Hall]
Moyer, Del-Louise (Mezzo-soprano)
He'll Bring to Pass: Spirituals &
    Americanegro Suite
Alyssum ALY-9001; 1997; CD
Piano
No dialect discerned

1650

He'll Bring It to Pass
Johnson, Hall; Joubert, Joseph
Toppin, Louise (Soprano)
He'll Bring It to Pass: The Spirituals of Hall
    Johnson for Voice and Piano
Albany Records TROY846; 2006; CD
Piano
Heavy dialect

· · · · · · ·

Here's a Pretty Little Baby

1651

Here's a Pretty Little Baby
Thomas, André J.
Slack, Karen (Soprano)
The Spirit of the Holidays
American Spiritual Ensemble; 2009; CD

· · · · · · ·

Here's One

1652

Here's One
Sneed, Damien
Brownlee, Lawrence (Tenor)
Spiritual Sketches
LeChateau Earl Records 888174029597; 2013;
    CD
Piano
No dialect discerned

1653

Here's One
Still, William Grant
Buggs, Claritha (Mezzo-soprano)
Ol' Time Religion
American Spiritual Ensemble ASE012; 2001;
    CD

1654

Here's One
Still, William Grant
Clemmons, François (Tenor)
Negro Spirituals Live! In Concert
American Negro Spiritual Research
    Foundation 8177 2048 3779; 1998; CD
Piano
Light dialect

1655

Here's One
Still, William Grant
Davis, Ollie Watts (Soprano)
Here's One: Spiritual Songs
KJAC Publishing KJAC0123; 2003; CD
Piano
Light dialect

1656

Here's One
Composer not identified
Green, Elnora E. (Contralto)
15 Spirituals
Private Label J3RS 2286; 1979; LP
Piano

1657

Here's One
Still, William Grant; Taylor, Vivian
Hamilton, Ruth (Contralto)
More Still: Music by William Grant Still
Cambria Master Recordings CD-1112; 1999;
 CD
Piano, saxophone
Moderate dialect

1658

Here's One
Still, William Grant
Harris, Inetta (Soprano)
*My Heritage Sings: A Selection of Spirituals
 & Hymns*
Private Label; [199-]; CD
Piano

1659

Here Is One
Mells, Herbert F.
Heard, Richard (Tenor)
*Ain't a That Good News: African-American
 Art Songs and Spirituals*
HM Classics HMC9602; 1998; CD
Piano
Heavy dialect

1660

Here's One
Still, William Grant
Honeysucker, Robert (Baritone)
Works by William Grant Still
New World Records 80399-2; 1990; CD
Piano

1661

Here's One
Still, William Grant
McFerrin, Robert (Baritone)
*Deep River and Other Classic Negro
 Spirituals*
Riverside Records RLP 12-812; 1959; LP
Piano
Heavy dialect
 Also released with *Classic Negro Spiri-
tuals* (Washington Records WLP 466; 1959;
LP)

1662

Here's One
Still, William Grant
Moses, Oral (Bass-baritone)
*Come Down Angels and Trouble the Water:
 Negro Spirituals, an American National
 Treasure!*
Albany Records TROY 1489; 2014; CD
Piano
Heavy dialect
 Also released with *Sankofa: A Spiritual
Reflection* (Albany Records TROY1802; 2019;
CD)

1663

Here's One
Still, William Grant
Pierson, Edward (Bass-baritone)
Edward Pierson Sings Hymns and Spirituals
Kemco 98-44; [19--]; LP

1664

Here's One
Still, William Grant
Price, Gwendolyn (Soprano)
Voices and piano
William Grant Still Music; 2000; CD

1665

Here's One
Still, William Grant
Quivar, Florence (Mezzo-soprano)
Negro Spirituals
EMI 7243 5 72790 2 4; 1998; CD
Piano
Heavy dialect
 Also released with *Ride On, King Jesus!
Florence Quivar Sings Black Music of Amer-
ica* (EMI Classics 9 67138 2; 2010; CD)

1666

Here's One
Still, William Grant
Rolle, Gilbert-Michel (Tenor)
Musical Voyage
Centaurus Classics; 2007; CD
Instrumental ensemble
No dialect discerned

1667

Here's One
Still, William Grant
Salters, Stephen (Baritone)
Spirit: Are You There, You Are There
HarmonizedDisharmony 0001; 2015; CD

1668

Here's One
Still, William Grant
Sims, Robert (Baritone)
*Soul of a Singer: Robert Sims Sings African-
   American Folk Songs*
Canti Classics 9801; 2013; CD
Piano
Heavy dialect

1669

Here's One
Still, William Grant
Wright, John Wesley (Tenor)
*The Spirituals: Featuring the American
   Spiritual Ensemble*
LexArts; [20--]; CD

• • • • • • •

He's Got the Whole World in His Hand

[Genesis 1:1; Job 12:10; Psalm 95:4]

"He's got the whole world in His hands,
He's got the big round world in His hands;
He's got the whole world in His hands, He's
got the whole world in His hands. He's got
the wind and the rain in His hands...."

[Available in ASSA, FHFN, HLBS, JB3a,
MBIH, MHDR, PLSY, RWSS, RW15, SOTS]

The text in various settings of this spiritual varies from version to version. Lovell listed six verses, and both the Bonds and Forrest settings each used four. This joyous spiritual is filled with reassurance that all are safe in God's Hands, even the gambler and other wrong-doers.

Forrest's setting was written for Marian Anderson and is well suited to the lower vocal range; whereas Bonds' setting, which the composer wrote for Leontyne Price, gives those with higher voices many opportunities

to shine vocally. The John Carter setting, from his *Cantata*, was also written for Price and originally for accompanying orchestra, though it is far easier to obtain the soprano and piano version.

The use of dialect in Forrest's published score is limited (roun,' gamblin,' lyin,' shootin,' an' me Brudder, ev'rybody), and only "ev'rybody" appears in the Bonds score, with no dialect in the printed text of the Carter score.

In an interview with musicologist Dominique-René de Lerma, Carter acknowledged that the history of the spiritual provided license for vocal improvisation. However, the harmonic density of the piano part throughout the song cycle does not seem to offer many opportunities for the vocalist to improvise.

1670

He's Got the Whole World in His Hand
Bonds, Margaret
Brown, Anthony (Baritone)
How Can I Keep from Singing?
Private label; 2013; CD
Piano
Light dialect

1671

He's Got the Whole World in His Hands
Forrest, Hamilton
Anderson, Marian (Contralto)
The Best of Negro Spirituals
BMG BVCM-37416; 2003; CD
Piano
Moderate dialect

1672

He's Got the Whole World in His Hands
Forrest, Hamilton
Anderson, Marian (Contralto)
Farewell Recital
RCA Victor LSC 2781; 1964; LP
Piano

Also released with *Marian Anderson: Beyond the Music; Her Complete RCA Victor Recordings* (Sony Classical 19439836492; 2021; CD)

1673

He's Got the Whole World in His Hands
Forrest, Hamilton
Anderson, Marian (Contralto)
He's Got the Whole World in His Hands: Spirituals
RCA Victor 09026-6[1960]2; 1994; CD
Piano
Light dialect

1674

He's Got the Whole World in His Hands
Forrest, Hamilton
Anderson, Marian (Contralto)
Spirituals
RCA Victor Red Seal 09026-63306-2; 1999; CD
Piano
Light dialect

1675

He's Got the Whole World in His Hands
Forrest, Hamilton
Anderson, Marian (Contralto)
Softly Awakes My Heart: Very Best of Marian Anderson
Alto ALN1955; 2016; CD
Piano
Heavy dialect

1676

He's Got the Whole World in His Hands
Forrest, Hamilton
Anderson, Marian (Contralto)
Let Freedom Ring!
JSP Records 683; 2016; CD
Piano
Moderate dialect

1677

He's Got the Whole World in His Hands (reprise)
Forrest, Hamilton
Anderson, Marian (Contralto)
Let Freedom Ring!
JSP Records 683; 2016; CD
Piano
Moderate dialect

1678

He's Got the Whole World in His Hands
Forrest, Hamilton
Anderson, Marian (Contralto)
Negro Spirituals
RCA Victor LM 2032; [1956]; LP
Piano
Moderate dialect

Also released with *Marian Anderson: Beyond the Music; Her Complete RCA Victor Recordings* (Sony Classical 19439836492; 2021; CD)

1679

He's Got the Whole World in His Hands
Forrest, Hamilton
Anderson, Marian (Contralto)
The President's Favorite Music
RCA Victor LM-2071; 1956; LP
Piano

1680

He's Got the Whole World
[Forrest, Hamilton]
Anderson, Marian (Contralto)
Marian Anderson and Dorothy Maynor in Concert
Eklipse Records EKR 49; 1995; CD
Piano

1681

He's Got the Whole World in His Hands
[Forrest, Hamilton]
Anderson, Marian (Contralto)
Marian Anderson Sings Eleven Great Spirituals
RCA Victor LRM 7006; 1955; LP
Piano

Also released with *Marian Anderson: Beyond the Music; Her Complete RCA Victor Recordings* (Sony Classical 19439836492; 2021; CD)

1682

He's Got the Whole World in His Hands
[Forrest, Hamilton]
Anderson, Marian (Contralto)
When Marian Sang: Selected Songs from Marian Anderson's Repertoire
BMG Special Products DPC13280; 2002; CD

1683

He's Got the Whole World in His Hands
[Forrest, Hamilton]
Anderson, Marian (Contralto)
*The Lord's Prayer and 24 Other Great Songs
    of Faith and Inspiration*
RCA Red Seal VCS-7083; 1971; LP
Piano

1684

He's Got the Whole World in His Hands
[Forrest, Hamilton]
Anderson, Marian (Contralto)
Alto Rhapsody; Selected Spirituals
Urania URN 22.328; 2007; CD
Piano

1685

He's Got the Whole World in His Hands
[Forrest, Hamilton]
Anderson, Marian (Contralto)
The Very Best of Marian Anderson
Master Classics Records; 2009; CD
Piano
Light dialect

1686

He's Got the Whole World in His Hands
[Forrest, Hamilton]
Anderson, Marian (Contralto)
Negro Spirituals
RCA Gold Seal RVC-1570; [19--]; LP
Piano

1687

He's Got the Whole World in His Hands
[Forrest, Hamilton]
Anderson, Marian (Contralto)
*Marian Anderson Sings Eleven Great
    Spirituals*
Kipepeo Publishing; 2017; CD
Piano

1688

He's Got the Whole World in His Hands
[Forrest, Hamilton]
Anderson, Marian (Contralto)
Marian Anderson & Dorothy Maynor
Parnassus Recordings PAR 1004; [19--]; LP

1689

He's Got the Whole World in His Hands
[Forrest, Hamilton]
Anderson, Marian (Contralto)
S. Hurok Presents
RCA Victor LM 2361; 1959; LP

1690

He's Got the Whole World in His Hands
[Forrest, Hamilton]
Anderson, Marian (Contralto)
Negro Spirituals
RCA Victor 630.396 A; [19--]; LP
Piano

1691

He's Got the Whole World in His Hands
[Forrest, Hamilton]
Anderson, Marian (Contralto)
American Anthem: Songs and Hymns
RCA Red Seal 09026-63888-2; 2001;
    Streaming audio
Piano
Heavy dialect

1692

He's Got the Whole World in His Hands
[Forrest, Hamilton]
Anderson, Marian (Contralto)
American Anthem: Songs and Hymns
RCA Red Seal 09026-63888-2; 2001; CD
Piano
Heavy dialect

1693

He's Got the Whole World in His Hands
[Forrest, Hamilton]
Anderson, Marian (Contralto)
50th Anniversary
RCA Victor PRS 287; 1969; LP
Piano

1694

He's Got the [Whole] World in His Hands
[Forrest, Hamilton]
Anderson, Marian (Contralto)
*Grandes Contraltos de la Musique Classique,
    Les: Marian Anderson, Vol. 14*

Mon Patrimoine Musical Collection; 2017;
    Streaming audio
Piano

1695

He's Got the Whole World in His Hands
[Forrest, Hamilton]
Anderson, Marian (Contralto)
The Rich Voice of Marian Anderson
Editions Audiovisuel Beulah; 2019;
    Streaming audio
Piano

1696

He's Got the Whole World in His Hands
[Forrest, Hamilton]
Anderson, Marian (Contralto)
*Marian Anderson: Beyond the Music; Her
    Complete RCA Victor Recordings*
Sony Classical 19439836492; 2021; CD
Piano
Moderate dialect

1697

He's Got the Whole World in His Hands
Forrest, Hamilton
Arroyo, Martina (Soprano)
Spirituals
Centaur CRC 2060; 1991; CD
Piano
Moderate dialect

1698

He's Got the Whole World in His Hand
Bonds, Margaret
Battle, Kathleen (Soprano)
Kathleen Battle in Concert
Deutsche Grammophon 445 524-2; 1994;
    CD
Piano
No dialect discerned

1699

He's Got the Whole World in His Hand
Bonds, Margaret; Marsh, Don; Russ, Patrick
Battle, Kathleen (Soprano); Norman, Jessye
    (Soprano)
Spirituals in Concert
Deutsche Grammophon 429 790-2; 1991; CD

Chorus, orchestra
Moderate dialect
    Also released with *The Best of Kathleen
Battle* (Deutsche Grammophon 000349502;
2004; CD)

1700

He's Got the Whole World in His Hands
Bonds, Margaret
Battle, Kathleen (Soprano)
Salzburg Recital
Deutsche Grammophon 415 361-2; 1986; CD
Piano
No dialect discerned

1701

He's Got the Whole World in His Hand
Johnson, Hall
Battle, Kathleen (Soprano)
Kathleen Battle at Carnegie Hall
Deutsche Grammophon 435 440-2; 1992; CD
Piano
Moderate dialect

1702

He's Got the Whole World in His Hands
[Bonds, Margaret]
Battle, Kathleen (Soprano)
12 Outstanding American Singers, vol. 1
Legendary Recordings LR 139; [198-]; LP
Piano
Light dialect

1703

He's Got the Whole World in His Hand
Bonds, Margaret
Benham, Dorothy (Soprano)
The Lord Is My Light
In His Light Productions; 2000; CD
Piano, violin

1704

He's Got the Whole World in His Hand
Bonds, Margaret
Black, Randall (Tenor)
*Then Sings My Soul: A Collection of Sacred
    Hymns and Spirituals*
Private label; 2006; CD
Piano

1705

He's Got the Whole World in His Hands
Boatwright, McHenry
Boatwright, McHenry (Bass-baritone)
Art of McHenry Boatwright: Spirituals
Golden Crest Records RE 7024; 1968; LP
Piano
Light dialect

1706

He's Got the Whole World in His Hands
Okpebholo, Shawn
Bridges, J'nai (Mezzo-soprano)
Lord How Come Me Here?
Navona Records NV6408; 2022; CD
Piano
No dialect discerned

1707

He's Got the Whole World in His Hands
Bonds, Margaret
Brown, Angela (Soprano)
Mosiac: A Collection of African-American Spirituals with Piano, guitar
Albany Records TROY721; 2004; CD
Piano
Light dialect

1708

He's Got the Whole World in His Hands
Brown, Angela; Webb, Charles
Brown, Angela (Soprano)
Soprano
Caboose Productions; 1995; CD
Piano
No dialect discerned

1709

He's Got the Whole World in His Hands
Bonds, Margaret
Brown, Anthony (Baritone)
Toil and Triumph
Spirituals Project; 2002; CD
Piano
Light dialect

1710

He's Got the Whole World in His Hands
Clark, Joe

Cabell, Nicole (Soprano); Cambridge, Alyson (Soprano)
Sisters in Song
Cedille Records CDR 90000 181; 2018; CD
Orchestra
Light dialect

1711

He's Got the Whole World in His Hands
Forrest, Hamilton
Carnette, Count (Vocalist)
Count Carnette Sings Favorite Negro Spirituals
Carnette Archive Recordings; 1983; LP
Piano
Light dialect

1712

He's Got the Whole World in His Hand
Bonds, Margaret; Hopkins, Gregory & Robert Wilson
Conrad, Barbara (Mezzo-soprano)
Spirituals
Naxos 8.553036; 1995; CD
Chorus, orchestra
Light dialect

1713

He's Got the Whole World in His Hands
Composer not identified
Cook, Dixon & Young (Tenor)
Triptych: A Celebration of the Negro Spiritual
CDY Records 649241879206; 2009; CD
Piano
No dialect discerned

1714

He's Got the Whole World in His Hand
Credit, Roosevelt André
Credit, Roosevelt André (Bass-baritone)
Ol' Time Religion
CD Baby; 2007; CD, Streaming audio
Piano

1715

He's Got the Whole World in His Hand
Bonds, Margaret
Davis, Ollie Watts (Soprano)
Here's One: Spiritual Songs

KJAC Publishing KJAC0123; 2003; CD
Piano
Light dialect

1716

He's Got the Whole World in His Hands
(after M.A. Bonds) [from *Four Spirituals for Soprano and String Quartet*]
Taylor, Stephen Andrew
Davis, Ollie Watts (Soprano)
Rootsongs
Azica AZI 71311; 2016; CD
Instrumental ensemble
No dialect discerned

1717

He's Got the Whole World in His Hands
Bonds, Margaret
Davis, Osceola (Soprano)
Negro Spirituals
Ondine ODE 715-2; 1988; CD
Piano

1718

He's Got the Whole World in His Hand
Bonds, Margaret; Link, Peter
Davis, Osceola (Soprano)
Climbing High Mountains
Watchfire Music; 2008; CD
Piano, orchestra
No dialect discerned

1719

He's Got the Whole World in His Hand
Bonds, Margaret
Dillard, Pamela (Mezzo-soprano)
Watch and Pray: Spirituals and Art Songs by African-American Women Composers
Koch International Classics 3-7247-2H1; 1994; CD
Piano
Light dialect

1720

He's Got the Whole World in His Hands
Bonds, Margaret
English-Robinson, Laura (Soprano)
Let It Shine!
ACA Digital Recording CM20020; 1994; CD

Piano
No dialect discerned

1721

He's Got the Whole World in His Hands
Roberts, Howard
Estes, Simon (Bass-baritone)
Spirituals
Philips 412 631-2; 1985; CD
Chorus, orchestra
No dialect discerned
  Also released with *Famous Spirituals* (Philips 462 062-2; 1997; CD)

1722

He's Got the Whole World in His Hand
Ryan, Donald
Estes, Simon (Bass-baritone)
Steal Away: My Favorite Negro Spirituals
Deutsche Schallplatten DS 1041-2; 1994; CD
Piano
Light dialect
  Also released with *Simon Sings His Favorite Gospels & Spirituals* (Praise Productions SMG-SE; 1999; CD) and *Save the Children, Save Their Lives* (CD Baby; 2010; CD)

1723

He's Got the Whole World in His Hand
Bonds, Margaret
Fernandez, Wilhelmenia (Soprano)
Spirituals
Tioch Digital Records TD 1009; 1982; LP
Piano
  Also released with *Sings Favorite Spirituals* (Phoenix PHCD 134; 1997; CD) and *Negro Spirituals* (Transart 131; 2005; CD)

1724

He's Got the Whole World in His Hand
Bonds, Margaret
Fernandez, Wilhelmenia (Soprano)
Negro Spirituals
Milan A 192; 1982; LP
Piano

1725

He's Got the Whole World
Robbiani, Mario

Fisher, Dorothy (Contralto)
Negro Spirituals
Edizione D'Arte Del Lions Club Milano Al
   Cenacolo; [19--]; LP
Orchestra
Light dialect

1726

He's Got the Whole World in His Hands
Bonds, Margaret
Gibson, Caroline (Soprano)
*On Ma Journey Now: Negro Spirituals in
   Concert*
Twin Productions; 2016; CD
Piano
No dialect discerned

1727

He's Got the Whole World in His Hands
Composer not identified
Green, Elnora E. (Contralto)
15 Spirituals
Private Label J3RS 2286; 1979; LP
Piano

1728

He's Got the Whole World in His Hand
Wheatley, Andres
Haniotis, Mario (Bass)
Negro Spirituals
Pastorale et Musique PM 17.047; [196-]; 45
   RPM
Piano
No dialect discerned

1729

He's Got the Whole World in His Hands
Hogan, Moses
Hendricks, Barbara (Soprano)
Give Me Jesus
EMI Classics 7243 5 56788 2 9; 1998; CD
Chorus
Moderate dialect

1730

He's Got the Whole World in His Hands
Composer not identified
Hines, Jerome (Bass)

*Sing! America! Sing!: Great Hymns of the
   Ages, Vol. 4*
Word Records W-4504-LP; [196-]; LP

1731

He's Got the Whole World in His Hand
Kaiser, Kurt
Hines, Jerome (Bass)
Great Moments of Sacred Music
Word Records W 3337; [196-]; LP

1732

He's Got the Whole World in His Hand
Bonds, Margaret
Hudson, Marlissa (Soprano)
Libera
AMP Records AGCD 2106; 2010; CD
Piano
No dialect discerned

1733

He's Got de Whole World
Composer not identified
Jones, Fanni (Mezzo-soprano)
Negro Spirituals
Phonotec 815; 1977; LP
Organ

1734

He's Got the Whole World in His Hands
Forrest, Hamilton
Jones, Fanni (Mezzo-soprano)
Fanni Jones et Oswald Russell
Audio-Visual Enterprises AVE 30701; [19--];
   LP

1735

He's Got de Whole World in His hands
Forrest, Hamilton
Jones, Fanni (Mezzo-soprano)
Negro Spirituals en Concert
Suisa; 1987; LP
Organ
Moderate dialect

1736

He's Got the Whole World in His Hand
Offenhauser, Deborah
Jones, Isola (Soprano)

Child of God: Sacred Songs by Deborah Offenhauser
Watchfire Music; 2015; CD
Orchestra
No dialect discerned

1737

He's Got the Whole World in His Hand
Bonds, Margaret
Jones, Randye (Soprano)
Come Down Angels
Ahhjay Records AHHJ-0001; 2003; CD
Piano
Light dialect

1738

He's Got the Whole World in His Hand
Composer not identified
Lord, Marie-Josée (Soprano)
Amazing Grace
ATMA Classique ACD2 2686; 2014; CD
Organ
No dialect discerned

1739

He's Got the Whole World in His Hands
Hairston, Jacqueline; Lynch, Lester & Noam Fairgold
Lynch, Lester (Baritone)
On My Journey Now: Spirituals & Hymns
Pentatone Music PTC 5186 57'; 2017; CD
Instrumental ensemble

1740

He's Got the Whole World
James, Willis
Matthews, Benjamin (Baritone)
A Balm in Gilead
Ebony Classic Recordings ECR 0001; 2000; CD
Piano

1741

He's Got the Whole World in His Hands
Forrest, Hamilton
Mayes, Doris (Mezzo-soprano)
Deep River
La voix de son maître FDLP 1080; 1959; LP
Piano

1742

He's Got the Whole World
Composer not identified
Maynor, Kevin (Bass)
Songs of America from Another American
Guild GMCD 7247; 2002; CD
Piano

1743

He's Got the Whole World in His Hands
Composer not identified
McDaniel, Yvette (Soprano)
Simply Spiritual
YM01 DIDX 046103; 1997; CD
Piano

1744

He's Got the Whole World in His Hand
Composer not identified
Miles, John (Tenor)
The Classic Spirituals
Epiphany 83-1027; 1983; LP
Instrumental ensemble

1745

He's Got the Whole World
Composer not identified
Moen, Judith (Soprano)
I Had a Dream About You
JAM Concerts JAM1001; 1996; CD

1746

He's Got the Whole World in His Hand
Bonds, Margaret
Moses, Oral (Bass-baritone)
Amen! African-American Composers of the 20th Century
Albany Records TROY459; 2001; CD
Piano
No dialect discerned

1747

He's Got the Whole World
Composer not identified
Nobles, NaGuanda (Soprano)
Homage to the Journey
Selbon Records; 2014; Streaming audio
Instrumental ensemble
No dialect discerned

1748

He's Got the Whole World
Bonds, Margaret
Norman, Jessye (Soprano)
Amazing Grace
Philips 432 546-2; 1990; CD
Piano
No dialect discerned

1749

He's Got the Whole World in His Hand
Bonds, Margaret
Norman, Jessye (Soprano)
Live
Philips 422 235-1; [1987]; CD
Piano

1750

He's Got the Whole World in His Hand
Bonds, Margaret
Norman, Jessye (Soprano)
*Bound for the Promised Land: Songs and
    Words of Equality and Freedom*
Albany Records TROY1798; 2019; CD
Piano

1751

He's Got the Whole World
Composer not identified
Norman, Jessye (Soprano)
Lieder
Philips 422 048-2; 1988; CD
Piano

1752

He's Got the Whole World in His Hands
Composer not identified
Norman, Jessye (Soprano)
Simply the Best
Philips Digital Classics 31 193 6; [1996];
    Streaming audio
Piano

1753

He's Got the Whole World in His Hands
Lloyd, Charles, Jr.; Norman, Jessye
Norman, Jessye (Soprano)
Great Day in the Morning

Philips 6769 104; 1982; LP
Chorus, other instrument(s)

1754

He's Got the Whole World in His Hands
[Bonds, Margaret]
Norman, Jessye (Soprano)
Brava, Jessye: The Very Best of Jessye Norman
Philips 442 157-2; 1993; CD
Piano
Light dialect

1755

He's Got the Whole World in His Hands
[Bonds, Margaret]
Norman, Jessye (Soprano)
The Jessye Norman Collection
Philips Classics 422 893-2; [1988]; CD
Piano
Heavy dialect

1756

He's Got the Whole World in His Hands
Composer not identified
Pickens, Jo Ann (Soprano)
*My Heritage: American Melodies/Negro
    Spirituals*
Koch Schwann 3-1447-2; 1993; CD

1757

He's Got the Whole World in His Hand
Composer not identified
Pleas III, Henry H. (Tenor)
Deep River: A Spiritual Journey
Rowe House Productions; 1999; CD

1758

He's Got the Whole World in His Hands
Bonds, Margaret
Price, Leontyne (Soprano)
The Essential Leontyne Price
BMG Classics 09026-68153-2; 1996; CD
Orchestra
Heavy dialect

Also released with *The Essential Leon-
tyne Price: Spirituals, Hymns & Sacred Songs*
(BMG Classics 09026-68157-2; 1996; CD);
*Complete Collection of Songs and Spiritual
Albums* (RCA Red Seal 88697940502; 2011;

CD) and *Leontyne Price Sings Spirituals* (RCA Red Seal 88691928242; 2012; CD)

1759

He's Got the Whole World in His Hands
Bonds, Margaret
Price, Leontyne (Soprano)
Swing Low, Sweet Chariot: Fourteen Spirituals
RCA Victor LSC 2600; 1962; LP
Orchestra
Heavy dialect

1760

He's Got the Whole World in His Hands
Bonds, Margaret
Price, Leontyne (Soprano)
Singers of the Century: Leontyne Price: Spiritual and Religious Songs
Jube Classic; 2016; Streaming audio
Orchestra
Heavy dialect

1761

He's Got the Whole World in His Hands
Composer not identified
Price, Leontyne (Soprano)
Great Moments at Carnegie Hall
RCA Red Seal 88985304202; 2016; CD
Piano
Light dialect

1762

He's Got the Whole World in His Hands
Composer not identified
Price, Leontyne (Soprano)
Golden Voices Sing Golden Favorites
Reader's Digest WCD4-5781–WCD4-5784; 1990; CD

1763

He's Got the Whole World in His Hand
Roberts, Howard
Price, Leontyne (Soprano)
The Voices of Living Stereo, vol. 2
RCA Victor Living Stereo 09026-68167-2; 1996; CD

1764

He's Got the Whole World in His Hands
[Bonds, Margaret]

Price, Leontyne (Soprano)
Leontyne Price reDiscovered
RCA Victor Red Seal 09026-63908-2; 2002; CD
Piano
Light dialect

1765

He's Got the Whole World in His Hands
Bonds, Margaret
Quivar, Florence (Mezzo-soprano)
Negro Spirituals
EMI 7243 5 72790 2 4; 1998; CD
Piano
Light dialect

1766

He's Got the Whole World in His Hands
[Bonds, Margaret]
Quivar, Florence (Mezzo-soprano)
Great American Spirituals
Angel CDM 7 64669 2; 1992; CD
Piano
Light dialect

1767

He's Got the Whole World in His Hands
[Bonds, Margaret]
Quivar, Florence (Mezzo-soprano)
Ride On, King Jesus! Florence Quivar Sings Black Music of America
EMI Classics 9 67138 2; 2010; CD
Piano
Light dialect

1768

He's Got the Whole World in His Hands
[Bonds, Margaret]
Quivar, Florence (Mezzo-soprano)
Great American Spirituals
Musical Heritage Society 513725Z; 1994; CD
Piano
Light dialect

1769

He's Got the Whole World in His Hand
Hogan, Moses
Ragin, Derek Lee (Countertenor)
Negro Spirituals

Virgin Classics 0946 363305 2 5; 2006; CD
Piano
Light dialect

1770

He's Got the Whole World in His Hands
Scharnberg, Kim
Robinson, Faye (Soprano)
Remembering Marian Anderson
d'Note Classics DND 1014; 1997; CD
Chorus, orchestra
No dialect discerned

1771

He's Got the Whole World in His Hand
Composer not identified
Robinson, Marie Hadley (Soprano)
Come Down Angels
Meyer Media; 2011; Streaming audio
Piano
Light dialect

1772

He's Got the Whole World in His Hands
Bonds, Margaret
Salters, Stephen (Baritone)
Stephen Salters/Shiela Kibbe
Musica Numeris CYP 9602; 2005; CD

1773

He's Got the Whole World in His Hand
Bonds, Margaret
Salters, Stephen (Baritone)
Spirit: Are You There, You Are There
HarmonizedDisharmony 0001; 2015; CD

1774

He's Got the Whole World in His Hands
Composer not identified
Lee, Seung Hyun (Soprano)
*Sweet Blessing: Spirituals & Hymns by
    Seung-Hyun Lee*
Seoul Records; [20--]; CD

1775

He's Got the Whole World in His Hand
Forrest, Hamilton
Simpson, Eugene Thamon (Bass)
Old American Songs

Black Heritage Publications; 2005; CD
Piano

    Also released with *Hall Johnson
Spirituals and Other Folk Songs* (Private
Label; 2016; CD)

1776

He's Got the Whole World in His Hands
Hogan, Moses
Simpson, Marietta (Mezzo-soprano)
Songs of Reflection
MGH Records 0800CD; 1997; CD

1777

He's Got the Whole World in His Hands
Hogan, Moses
Sims, Robert (Baritone)
*Deep River: Featuring 10 Spirituals Arranged
    for Solo Voice....*
MGH Records 5000; 2000; CD
Piano
No dialect discerned

1778

He's Got the Whole World in His Hands
Walters, Richard (ed.)
Stolen, Steven (Tenor)
*15 Easy Spiritual Arrangements for the
    Progressing Singer*
Hal Leonard HL00000391 (high) ;
    HL00000392 (low); 2005; Score w/CD
Piano
Light dialect

1779

He's Got the Whole World in His Hands
Swan, Walter
Swan, Walter (Baritone)
He's Got the Whole World in His Hands
Walter Swan; 2004; CD
Piano
No dialect discerned

1780

He's Got the Whole World in His Hands
Composer not identified
Sykes, Jubilant (Baritone)
Jubilation

EMI Classics/Angel 7243 5 57591 2 2; 2007;
    CD
Guitar

1781
He's Got the Whole World in His Hands
Bonds, Margaret
Thomas, Indra (Soprano)
Great Day: Indra Thomas Sings Spirituals
Delos DE 3427; 2012; CD
Piano
Light dialect

1782
He's Got the Whole World in His Hand
Composer not identified
Thompson, Derrick (Baritone)
Spirituals
Private Label; 2014; CD
Piano
No dialect discerned

1783
He's Got the Whole World in His Hands
Hogan, Moses
Tucker, Eric Hoy (Bass-baritone)
Southern Salute: Southern Songs & Spirituals
White Pine Music WPM218; 2012; CD
Piano
Light dialect

1784
He's Got the Whole World in His Hands
Composer not identified
Tyler, Veronica (Soprano)
Sings ... the Passion of Christ in Spirituals
BRC Productions; [19--]; LP
Piano

1785
He's Got the Whole World in His Hands
Composer not identified
Verdejo, Awilda (Soprano)
Awilda Verdejo Sings Spirituals
Angeluz Performances; 1999; CD
Piano

1786
He's Got the Whole World in His Hand
Composer not identified

White, Cassandra (Soprano)
Remembering the Spirituals
CBW Entertainment 837101334068; 2007;
    CD
Piano
No dialect discerned

1787
He's Got the Whole World in His Hand
Schweizer, Rolf
Wolf, Lars (Vocalist)
Die Schwarze Stimme Europas
Cantate 666000; 1971; LP
Chorus, organ, percussion

1788
He's Got the Whole World in His Hands
Bonds, Margaret
Yovanovich, Amy (Mezzo-soprano)
Great Day!
Prince Productions 9808P; 2007; CD
Piano
Light dialect

. . . .

He's Jus' de Same Today

1789
He's Jus' de Same Today
Composer not identified
Moyer, Del-Louise (Mezzo-soprano)
*He'll Bring to Pass: Spirituals &
    Americanegro Suite*
Alyssum ALY-9001; 1997; CD
Piano
Light dialect

. . . .

He's the Lily of the Valley

1790
He's the Lily of the Valley
Parker, Alice
Brown, Anthony (Baritone)
Spirituals
Brown/Smith Productions; 1995; CD
Piano
Light dialect

1791

He's the Lily of the Valley
Giesen, Hubert
Ray, William (Baritone)
Negro Spirituals
Intercord; [19--]; LP
Piano

1792

He's the Lily of the Valley
Giesen, Hubert
Ray, William (Baritone)
*Sings Arias, Duets, Musical Selections and
    Negro Spirituals*
Intercord; [19--]; CD
Piano

. . . .

His Name So Sweet

1793

His Name So Sweet
Johnson, Hall
Alexander, Roberta (Soprano)
Songs My Mother Taught Me
Etcetera KTC 1208; 1999; CD
Piano
Light dialect

1794

His Name So Sweet
Johnson, Hall
Battle, Kathleen (Soprano)
Kathleen Battle in Concert
Deutsche Grammophon 445 524-2; 1994;
    CD
Piano
Light dialect

1795

His Name So Sweet
Johnson, Hall
Battle, Kathleen (Soprano)
Salzburg Recital
Deutsche Grammophon 415 361-2; 1986;
    CD
Piano
Moderate dialect

1796

His Name So Sweet
Johnson, Hall
Brown, Anne (Soprano)
Anne Brown Sings Spirituals
Mercury EP-1-5038; [195-]; LP
Piano
Moderate dialect

1797

His Name So Sweet
[Johnson, Hall]
Brown, Anne (Soprano)
Black Swans: At Mid-Century
Parnassus PACD 96078/9; 2021; CD
Piano
Heavy dialect

1798

His Name So Sweet
Johnson, Hall
Brown, Anthony (Baritone)
Spirituals
Brown/Smith Productions; 1995; CD
Piano
Moderate dialect

1799

His Name So Sweet [from *Crossing Jordan*]
Corley, Maria Thompson
Clark, Maria (Soprano)
Soul Sanctuary: Spirituals & Hymns
Navona Records NV6406; 2022; CD
Piano, cello
Moderate dialect

1800

His Name So Sweet
Johnson, Hall
Davis, Osceola (Soprano)
Negro Spirituals
Ondine ODE 715-2; 1988; CD
Piano
Light dialect

1801

His Name So Sweet
Johnson, Hall
DuBose, Sequina (Soprano)

Swing Low, Sweet Chariot
American Spiritual Ensemble; 2011; CD

1802

His Name So Sweet
Johnson, Hall
Fernandez, Wilhelmenia (Soprano)
Negro Spirituals
Transart 131; 2005; CD
Piano

1803

His Name So Sweet
Johnson, Hall
Gibson, Caroline (Soprano)
On Ma Journey Now: Negro Spirituals in Concert
Twin Productions; 2016; CD
Piano
Heavy dialect

1804

His Name So Sweet
Composer not identified
Green, Elnora E. (Contralto)
15 Spirituals
Private Label J3RS 2286; 1979; LP
Piano

1805

His Name So Sweet
Johnson, Hall
Hall, Myrtle (Soprano)
Myrtle Hall, Lyric Soprano
Bella Voce Records 651P-2419; 1967; LP

1806

His Name So Sweet
Boatner, Edward
Heard, Richard (Tenor)
Ain't a That Good News: African-American Art Songs and Spirituals
HM Classics HMC9602; 1998; CD
Piano
Light dialect

1807

His Name So Sweet
Composer not identified

Hendricks, Barbara (Soprano)
Spirituals
EMI Classics 0946 346641 2 7; 2005; CD
Piano

1808

His Name So Sweet
Composer not identified
Hendricks, Barbara (Soprano)
Spirituals
EMI Classics 0946 346641 2 7; 2005; CD
Piano

1809

His Name So Sweet
Hendricks, Barbara; Alexeev, Dmitri
Hendricks, Barbara (Soprano)
Negro Spirituals
EMI CDC7470262; 1983; CD
Piano
Light dialect

　　　Also released with *Espirituales Negros* (EMI Classics/Altaya 01636; 1983; CD)

1810

His Name So Sweet
Composer not identified
Hendricks, Barbara (Soprano)
Schubert, Debussy, Fauré, Negro Spirituals
EMI Electrola CDZ 2523322; 1990; CD
Piano

1811

His Name So Sweet
Johnson, Hall
Holmes, Eugene (Baritone)
Eugene Holmes Sings Spirituals
Avant Garde AV-115; [1968]; LP
Piano
Moderate dialect

1812

His Name So Sweet
Johnson, Hall
Holmes, Eugene (Baritone)
Spirituals
Schubert Records SCH-102; [1988]; LP
Piano
Moderate dialect

1813

I've Just Come from the Fountain
Davis, Carl
Horne, Marilyn (Mezzo-soprano)
The Complete Decca Recitals
Decca 478 0165; 2008; CD
Chorus
Heavy dialect

1814

His Name So Sweet
Johnson, Hall
Matthews, Inez (Mezzo-soprano)
Inez Matthews Sings Spirituals (Great New Voices of Today, v. 6)
Period SPL-580; [1950]; LP
Piano
Moderate dialect

    Also released with *Inez Matthews Sings Spirituals* (Essential Media Group; 2011; CD)

1815

His Name So Sweet
Raphael, Michael
Maynor, Kevin (Bass)
The Spiritual: An Underground Railroad
Southeastern Virginia Arts Assoc.; [2000]; CD
Piano

1816

His Name Is So Sweet
Johnson, Hall
McFerrin, Robert (Baritone)
Deep River and Other Classic Negro Spirituals
Riverside Records RLP 12-812; 1959; LP
Piano
Light dialect

    Also released with *Classic Negro Spirituals* (Washington Records WLP 466; 1959; LP)

1817

His Name So Sweet
Johnson, Hall
Miller, Jeanette (Soprano)
No Man Canna Hinder Me

MiJon Record Productions MJ240; 1979; CD
Piano

1818

His Name So Sweet
Johnson, Hall
Mims, A. Grace Lee (Soprano)
Spirituals
H & GM Records HGM 8101; 1981; LP
Piano
Heavy dialect

1819

His Name So Sweet
Johnson, Hall
Oby, Jason (Tenor)
The Life of Christ: Collected Spirituals
Private Label TSU4749; [200-]; CD
Piano
Heavy dialect

1820

His Name So Sweet
Composer not identified
Price, Leontyne (Soprano)
Great Moments at Carnegie Hall
RCA Red Seal 88985304202; 2016; CD
Piano
Moderate dialect

1821

His Name So Sweet
Johnson, Hall; de Paur, Leonard
Price, Leontyne (Soprano)
Swing Low, Sweet Chariot: Fourteen Spirituals
RCA Victor LSC 2600; 1962; LP
Chorus, orchestra
Heavy dialect

    Also released with *The Essential Leontyne Price: Spirituals, Hymns & Sacred Songs* (BMG Classics 09026-68157-2; 1996; CD); *The Best of Negro Spirituals* (BMG BVCM-37416; 2003; CD); and *Leontyne Price Sings Spirituals* (RCA Red Seal 88691928242; 2012; CD)

1822

His Name So Sweet
Johnson, Hall; de Paur, Leonard

Price, Leontyne (Soprano)
*Complete Collection of Songs and Spiritual
    Albums*
RCA Red Seal 88697940502; 2011; CD
Orchestra

1823

His Name So Sweet
Johnson, Hall; de Paur, Leonard
Price, Leontyne (Soprano)
*Singers of the Century: Leontyne Price:
    Spiritual and Religious Songs*
Jube Classic; 2016; Streaming audio
Chorus, orchestra
Heavy dialect

1824

His Name Is So Sweet
[Johnson, Hall]
Price, Leontyne (Soprano)
Leontyne Price reDiscovered
RCA Victor Red Seal 09026-63908-2; 2002;
    CD
Piano
Moderate dialect

1825

His Name So Sweet
[Johnson, Hall; Roberts, Howard]
Quivar, Florence (Mezzo-soprano)
Great American Spirituals
Angel CDM 7 64669 2; 1992; CD
Chorus, piano
Heavy dialect

Also released with *Great American
Spirituals* (Musical Heritage Society
513725Z; 1994; CD); *Negro Spirituals* (EMI
7243 72790 2 4; 1998; CD) and *Ride On, King
Jesus! Florence Quivar Sings Black Music of
America* (EMI Classics 9 67138 2; 2010; CD)

1826

His Name So Sweet
Scharnberg, Kim
Robinson, Faye (Soprano)
Remembering Marian Anderson
d'Note Classics DND 1014; 1997; CD
Orchestra
Light dialect

1827

His Name So Sweet
Smith Moore, Undine
Simpson, Icy (Soprano)
I, Too
Longhorn Music; 2012; CD
Piano

1828

His Name So Sweet
Johnson, Hall
Straughter, Maralyn (Soprano)
Negro Spirituals of Hall Johnson
Variety Recording Service Var 0753; [196-];
    LP
Piano

1829

His Name So Sweet
Johnson, Hall
Thomas, Indra (Soprano)
Great Day: Indra Thomas Sings Spirituals
Delos DE 3427; 2012; CD
Piano
Heavy dialect

1830

His Name So Sweet
Johnson, Hall
Toppin, Louise (Soprano)
The Hall Johnson Collection
Carl Fischer VF5 CD1–VF5 CD2; 2003; Score
    w/CD
Piano
Moderate dialect

1831

His Name So Sweet
Johnson, Hall
Toppin, Louise (Soprano)
*He'll Bring It to Pass: The Spirituals of Hall
    Johnson for Voice and Piano*
Albany Records TROY846; 2006; CD
Piano
Moderate dialect

1832

His Name So Sweet
[Johnson, Hall]

Williams, Camilla (Soprano)
Camilla Williams Sings Spirituals
MGM Records M-G-M E-156; [195-]; LP
Piano
Heavy dialect

     Also released with *A Camilla Williams Recital* (MGM Records E-140; [1952]; LP)

1833

His Name So Sweet
Johnson, Hall
Wilson, Robin (Soprano)
Best of the Hall Johnson Centennial Festival Celebrating the 100th Anniversary of Hall Johnson's Birth
Hall Johnson Collection O33D2; 2002; CD
Piano

· · · · · · ·

Hold On

1834

Hold On!
Johnson, Hall
Anderson, Marian (Contralto)
Ev'Ry Time I Feel the Spirit (1930–1947)
Naxos Nostalgia 8.120779; 2004; CD
Piano

1835

Hold On!
Johnson, Hall
Anderson, Marian (Contralto)
He's Got the Whole World in His Hands: Spirituals
RCA Victor 09026-6[1960]2; 1994; CD
Piano
Light dialect

     Also released with *Marian Anderson: Beyond the Music; Her Complete RCA Victor Recordings* (Sony Classical 19439836492; 2021; CD)

1836

Hold On!
Johnson, Hall
Anderson, Marian (Contralto)
Spirituals

RCA Victor Red Seal 09026-63306-2; 1999; CD
Piano
Light dialect

     Also released with *Marian Anderson: Beyond the Music; Her Complete RCA Victor Recordings* (Sony Classical 19439836492; 2021; CD)

1837

Hold On
Johnson, Hall
Anderson, Marian (Contralto)
The Very Best of Marian Anderson
Master Classics Records; 2009; CD
Piano
No dialect discerned

1838

Hold On
Johnson, Hall
Anderson, Marian (Contralto)
Negro Spirituals: 1924–1949
Frémeaux & Associés FA 184; 2004; CD
Orchestra

1839

Hold On!
Johnson, Hall
Anderson, Marian (Contralto)
Poor Me/Hold On!
RCA Victor 10-1278; [1948]; 78 RPM
Piano
Moderate dialect

1840

Hold On!
Johnson, Hall
Anderson, Marian (Contralto)
Let Freedom Ring!
JSP Records 683; 2016; CD
Piano
Light dialect

1841

Hold On
Johnson, Hall
Blackmon, Henry (Baritone)
Negro Spirituals

Mirasound Records SGLP 6047; [19--]; LP
Organ

1842
Hold On
Johnson, Hall
Blackmon, Henry (Baritone)
Negro Spirituals
Vega 19179; [19--]; LP
Chorus, piano

1843
Hold On
Johnson, Hall
Brown, Anne (Soprano)
Anne Brown Sings Spirituals
Mercury EP-1-5038; [195-]; LP
Piano
Heavy dialect

    Also released with *Black Swans: At Mid-Century* (Parnassus PACD 96078/9; 2021; CD)

1844
Hold On!
Johnson, Hall
Brown, Anne (Soprano)
Sometimes I Feel Like a Motherless Child/ Hold On!
Tono L 28021; [19--]; 78 RPM
Piano
Moderate dialect

1845
Hold On
Traditional
Carey, Thomas (Baritone)
Go Down Moses
Da Camera Song SM 95028; 1970; LP
A cappella
Heavy dialect

1846
Hold On
Bonds, Margaret
Carnette, Count (Vocalist)
Count Carnette Sings Favorite Negro Spirituals
Carnette Archive Recordings; 1983; LP

Piano
Light dialect

1847
Hold On! (Haltet Aus Am Pflug)
Johnson, Hall
Foye, Hope (Soprano)
Haltet Aus Am Pflug!
Eterna A 192; [19--]; 78 RPM
Piano

1848
Hold On
[Burleigh, Harry T.]
Foye, Hope (Soprano)
Singing Her Song: The Story of Hope Foye
Union Bank of California; 2008; CD
Piano
Light dialect

1849
Hold On
Ching
Gormley, Clare (Soprano)
Where Morning Lies: Spiritual Songs
ABC Classics 461 766-2; 2002; CD
Piano
Light dialect

1850
Hold On
Composer not identified
Green, Elnora E. (Contralto)
15 Spirituals
Private Label J3RS 2286; 1979; LP
Piano

1851
Hold On
Johnson, Hall
Hamilton, Ruth (Contralto)
Good News
Videmus Records VIS735; 2007; CD
Piano
Heavy dialect

1852
Hold On
Composer not identified

Hendricks, Barbara (Soprano)
Spirituals
EMI Classics 0946 346641 2 7; 2005; CD
Piano

1853

Hold On
Composer not identified
Hendricks, Barbara (Soprano)
No Borders
Altara ALT 1010; 2005; CD
Chorus
Light dialect

1854

Hold On
Hendricks, Barbara; Alexeev, Dmitri
Hendricks, Barbara (Soprano)
Negro Spirituals
EMI CDC7470262; 1983; CD
Piano
Heavy dialect

　　　Also released with *Espirituales Negros* (EMI Classics/Altaya 01636; 1983; CD)

1855

Hold On!
Johnson, Hall
Holland, Charles (Tenor)
Negro Spirituals
Pathé 45 ED. 29; 1954; 45 RPM
Piano

1856

Hold On
Composer not identified
Jobson, Christine (Soprano)
By Faith: Hymns and Negro Spirituals
CD Baby; 2017; CD
Piano
Moderate dialect

1857

Keep Your Hands on the Plow (Hold On)
Composer not identified
Johnson, Yolanda F (Soprano)
Feel the Spirit!
Jublianti Artists; 2011; Streaming audio

Instrumental ensemble
Heavy dialect

1858

Hold On
Johnson, Hall
Matthews, Inez (Mezzo-soprano)
Inez Matthews Sings Spirituals (Great New Voices of Today, v. 6)
Period SPL-580; [1950]; LP
Piano
Moderate dialect

　　　Also released with *Inez Matthews Sings Spirituals* (Essential Media Group; 2011; CD)

1859

Hold On [from *Spiritual Songs for Tenor and Cello*]
Banfield, William C.
Melvin, Lee (Tenor)
Extensions of the Tradition
Innova 510; 1996; CD
Cello

1860

Hold On
Johnson, Hall
Miles, John (Tenor)
The Classic Spirituals
Epiphany 83-1027; 1983; LP
Instrumental ensemble

1861

Hold On
Composer not identified
Newby, Marion Crowley (Contralto)
Hymns and Spirituals for Canada's Centennial
A.T.C.M.; 1967; LP

1862

Hold On
Ching, Michael
Overton, Kenneth (Baritone)
Been in de Storm So Long (Songs My Fathers Taught Me)
American Spiritual Ensemble; 2012; CD
Piano, percussion
Light dialect

1863

Hold On
Pankey, Aubrey
Pankey, Aubrey (Baritone)
Negro Spirituals
Eterna 830010; 1983; LP
Piano
Moderate dialect

1864

Hold On
[Pankey, Aubrey]
Pankey, Aubrey (Baritone)
Aubrey Pankey Singt Negro-Spirituals
Eterna 7 30 005; 1959; LP
Piano
Moderate dialect

1865

Hold On!
Johnson, Hall
Quivar, Florence (Mezzo-soprano)
Negro Spirituals
EMI 7243 5 72790 2 4; 1998; CD
Piano
Heavy dialect

      Also released with *Ride On, King Jesus!*
Florence Quivar Sings Black Music of America
(EMI Classics 9 67138 2; 2010; CD)

1866

Hold On
Traditional
Sebron, Carolyn (Mezzo-soprano)
Resurrection, Pt. 1
Private Label; 2006; CD
A cappella
Light dialect

1867

Hold On
Berg,
Spencer, Kenneth (Bass-baritone)
Spirituals Sung by Kenneth Spencer
E.M.I. Records Ltd. SEG 7813; [19--]; 45 RPM

1868

Hold On
Composer not identified

Spencer, Kenneth (Bass-baritone)
Heimweh Nach Virginia
Music Tales 2087269; 2015; CD

1869

Hold On
Walberg, [Wladimir]
Spencer, Kenneth (Bass-baritone)
4 Negro Spirituals
Columbia ESRF 1067; 1957; 45 RPM
Orchestra

1870

Hold On
Paget, M.
Thompson, Jeanette (Soprano)
Negro Spirituals
Pavane Records ADW 7267; 1992; CD
Chorus
No dialect discerned

1871

Hold On
Bonds, Margaret
Tucker, Eric Hoy (Bass-baritone)
Southern Salute: Southern Songs & Spirituals
White Pine Music WPM218; 2012; CD
Piano
Light dialect

1872

Hold On!
Composer not identified
Verrett, Shirley (Soprano)
The Very Best of Gospel
Disconforme CDX7720; 2007; CD

1873

Hold On!
Johnson, Hall
Verrett, Shirley (Mezzo-soprano)
Shirley Verrett Recital
Suiza OSCD 223; 1991; CD
Piano

1874

Hold On!
[Johnson, Hall]
Verrett, Shirley (Mezzo-soprano)

Gospels & Spirituals Gold Collection
Retro R2CD 40-26; 1995; CD
Piano
Heavy dialect

1875

Hold On
Bonds, Margaret
Warfield, William (Bass-baritone)
Spirituals: 200 Years of African-American Spirituals
ProArte CDD 3443; 1993; CD
Piano
Heavy dialect

1876

Hold On
[Johnson, Hall]
Williams, Camilla (Soprano)
A Camilla Williams Recital
MGM Records E-140; [1952]; LP
Piano

. . . .

Hold Out Your Light

1877

Hold Out Your Light
McLin, Lena
Matthews, Benjamin (Baritone)
A Spiritual Journey
Ebony Classic Recordings ECR 0001; 2000; CD
Piano

1878

Hold Out Your Light
McLin, Lena
Matthews, Benjamin (Baritone)
A Balm in Gilead
Ebony Classic Recordings ECR 0001; 2000; CD
Piano

1879

Hold Out Your Light
McLin, Lena
Rucker, Mark (Baritone)
Mark Rucker Sings Lena McLin: Songs for Voice & Piano

Kjos Music Press KCD8; 2002; CD
Piano
Light dialect

1880

Hold Out Your Light
McLin, Lena
Warfield, William (Bass-baritone); Matthews, Benjamin Sims, Robert (Baritone)
Three Generations Live
Canti Records; 2000; CD
Piano

. . . .

Honor, Honor

[Matthew 3:11, 3:16; Acts 2:38, 22:16; 1 Peter 3:21; Romans 6:4; Galatians 3:27]

"King Jesus lit the candle by the waterside, To see the little children when they truly baptize. Honor, honor, Unto the dying Lamb. Oh run along children and be baptized, Mighty pretty meeting by the waterside...."

[Available in HJCO]

1881

Honor, Honor
Johnson, Hall
Anderson, Marian (Contralto)
Marian Anderson: Rare and Unpublished Recordings, 1936–1952
VAI Audio VAIA 1168; 1998; CD
Piano
Heavy dialect

1882

Honor, Honor
Johnson, Hall
Anderson, Marian (Contralto)
Spirituals
RCA Victor Red Seal 09026-63306-2; 1999; CD
Piano
Heavy dialect

1883

Honor, Honor
Johnson, Hall

Anderson, Marian (Contralto)
Negro Spirituals
La Voix de Son Maître FBLP1039; 1953; LP
Piano

1884

Honor, Honor
Johnson, Hall
Anderson, Marian (Contralto)
Marian Anderson Sings Negro Spirituals
His Master's Voice BLP 1060; [19--]; LP
Piano

1885

Honor, Honor
Johnson, Hall
Anderson, Marian (Contralto)
Marian Anderson Sings Spirituals
RCA Victor Red Seal MO 1238; 1948; 78
    RPM
Piano

1886

Honor, Honor
Johnson, Hall
Anderson, Marian (Contralto)
Negro Spirituals
RCA Victor LM 2032; [1956]; LP
Piano
Moderate dialect

Also released with *Marian Anderson: Beyond the Music; Her Complete RCA Victor Recordings* Sony Classical 19439836492; 2021; CD

1887

Honor, Honor
[Johnson, Hall]
Anderson, Marian (Contralto)
Alto Rhapsody; Selected Spirituals
Urania URN 22.328; 2007; CD
Piano

1888

Honor, Honor
[Johnson, Hall]
Anderson, Marian (Contralto)
The Very Best of Marian Anderson
Master Classics Records; 2009; CD

Piano
Light dialect

1889

Honor, Honor
[Johnson, Hall]
Anderson, Marian (Contralto)
Marian Anderson Sings Spirituals
RCA Victor LM 110; 1949; LP
Piano

Also released with *Marian Anderson: Beyond the Music; Her Complete RCA Victor Recordings* Sony Classical 19439836492; 2021; CD

1890

Honor, Honor
[Johnson, Hall]
Anderson, Marian (Contralto)
Negro Spirituals
RCA Gold Seal RVC-1570; [19--]; LP
Piano

1891

Honor, Honor
[Johnson, Hall]
Anderson, Marian (Contralto)
Negro Spirituals
RCA Victor 630.396 A; [19--]; LP
Piano

1892

Honor! honor!
Johnson, Hall
Arroyo, Martina (Soprano)
Spirituals
Centaur CRC 2060; 1991; CD
Piano
Moderate dialect

1893

Honor, Honor
Johnson, Hall
Battle, Kathleen (Soprano)
Kathleen Battle in Concert
Deutsche Grammophon 445 524-2; 1994;
    CD
Piano
Heavy dialect

1894

Honor, Honor
Johnson, Hall
Battle, Kathleen (Soprano)
Salzburg Recital
Deutsche Grammophon 415 361-2; 1986; CD
Piano
Heavy dialect

1895

Honor! Honor!
Johnson, Hall
Brown, Anthony (Baritone)
Spirituals
Brown/Smith Productions; 1995; CD
Piano
Heavy dialect

1896

Honor, Honor
Erb, Donald
Brown, William (Tenor)
Symphonic Spirituals
Columbia JC 36267; 1979; LP
Orchestra
Heavy dialect

　　　Also released with *Symphonic Spirituals*
(Spotify; [2019]; Streaming audio)

1897

Honor, Honor
Composer not identified
Charles, Lee (Tenor)
Swing Low Sweet Chariot: And Other Spirituals
Riverside RLP 12-651; 1957; LP
Piano, guitar

1898

Honor, Honor
Composer not identified
Cunningham-Fleming, Jeryl (Soprano)
*Stand the Storm: Anthems, Hymns, and
　　Spirituals of Faith and Hope*
Private Label; 2016; CD
Piano

1899

Honor, Honor
Johnson, Hall

Davis, Ollie Watts (Soprano)
Here's One: Spiritual Songs
KJAC Publishing KJAC0123; 2003; CD
Piano
Moderate dialect

1900

Honor, Honor
Johnson, Hall
Evans, Allan (Bass-baritone)
Negro Spirituals
Electromusic Records EMCD 6885; 1985; CD
Chorus, other instrument(s)

1901

Honor, Honor
Boatner, Edward
Fernandez, Wilhelmenia (Soprano)
Sings Favorite Spirituals
Phoenix PHCD 134; 1997; CD
Piano
Moderate dialect

　　　Also released with *Negro Spirituals*
(Transart 131; 2005; CD)

1902

Honor, Honor
Johnson, Hall
Fernandez, Wilhelmenia (Soprano)
Spirituals
Tioch Digital Records TD 1009; 1982; LP
Piano

　　　Also released with *Negro Spirituals*
(Milan A 192; 1982; LP)

1903

Honor, Honor
Laster, James
Forest, Michael (Tenor)
The Spirit Sings: American Spirituals
Shenandoah Conservatory SU003; [199-];
　　CD

1904

Honor, Honor
[Johnson, Hall]
Foye, Hope (Soprano)
Singing Her Song: The Story of Hope Foye
Union Bank of California; 2008; CD

Piano
Moderate dialect

1905

Honor, Honor
Johnson, Hall
Gibson, Caroline (Soprano)
On Ma Journey Now: Negro Spirituals in Concert
Twin Productions; 2016; CD
Piano
Heavy dialect

1906

Honor, Honor!
Johnson, Hall
Holland, Charles (Tenor)
Negro-Spirituals
Pathé 45 ED 29; [19--]; 45 RPM
Piano

1907

Honor! Honor!
Johnson, Hall
Holland, Charles (Tenor)
Honor! Honor!/Talk About a Child That Do Love Jesus
Victor Red Seal 4556; [19--]; 78 RPM
Piano

1908

Honor! Honor!
Johnson, Hall
Holland, Charles (Tenor)
Negro Spirituals
Pathé 45 ED. 29; 1954; 45 RPM
Piano

1909

Honor! Honor!
Johnson, Hall
Holland, Charles (Tenor)
Black Swans: At Mid-Century
Parnassus PACD 96078/9; 2021; CD
Piano
Heavy dialect

1910

Honor! Honor!
Johnson, Hall

Jones, Fanni (Mezzo-soprano)
Negro Spirituals en Concert
Suisa; 1987; LP
Organ
Moderate dialect

1911

King Jesus Lit a Candle
Johnson, Hall
Judkins, Edith (Soprano)
Sacred Recital, A
United Sound USR 3845; [19--]; LP

1912

Honor, Honor
Johnson, Hall
Little, Vera (Mezzo-soprano)
My Good Lord Done Been Here
Decca 123737; 1957; LP
Piano

1913

Honor, Honor
Johnson, Hall
Miller, Jeanette (Soprano)
No Man Canna Hinder Me
MiJon Record Productions MJ240; 1979; CD
Piano

1914

Honor, Honor
Composer not identified
Moen, Judith (Soprano)
I Had a Dream About You
JAM Concerts JAM1001; 1996; CD

1915

Honor, Honor
[Johnson, Hall]
Moyer, Del-Louise (Mezzo-soprano)
He'll Bring to Pass: Spirituals & Americanegro Suite
Alyssum ALY-9001; 1997; CD
Piano
Light dialect

1916

Honor! Honor!
Johnson, Hall

Philogene, Ruby (Soprano)
Steal Away
EMI Classics 7243 5 69707 2 4; 1997; CD
Chorus

1917

Honor, Honor
Composer not identified
Pickens, Jo Ann (Soprano)
*My Heritage: American Melodies/Negro
    Spirituals*
Koch Schwann 3-1447-2; 1993; CD

1918

Honor, Honor
Composer not identified
Pleas III, Henry H. (Tenor)
Deep River: A Spiritual Journey
Rowe House Productions; 1999; CD

1919

Honor! Honor!
Johnson, Hall; de Paur, Leonard
Price, Leontyne (Soprano)
The Essential Leontyne Price
BMG Classics 09026-68153-2; 1996; CD
Chorus
Heavy dialect

    Also released with *The Essential Leontyne
Price: Spirituals, Hymns & Sacred Songs*
(BMG Classics 09026-68157-2; 1996; CD);
Leontyne Price Sings Spirituals (RCA Red Seal
88691928242; 2012; CD)

1920

Honor! Honor!
Johnson, Hall; de Paur, Leonard
Price, Leontyne (Soprano)
*Swing Low, Sweet Chariot: Fourteen
    Spirituals*
RCA Victor LSC 2600; 1962; LP
Chorus
Heavy dialect

1921

Honor! Honor!
Johnson, Hall; de Paur, Leonard
Price, Leontyne (Soprano)

*Complete Collection of Songs and Spiritual
    Albums*
RCA Red Seal 88697940502; 2011; CD
Orchestra

1922

Honor! Honor!
Johnson, Hall; de Paur, Leonard
Price, Leontyne (Soprano)
*Singers of the Century: Leontyne Price:
    Spiritual and Religious Songs*
Jube Classic; 2016; Streaming audio
Chorus
Heavy dialect

1923

Honor, Honor
Johnson, Hall; Roberts, Howard
Quivar, Florence (Mezzo-soprano)
Great American Spirituals
Angel CDM 7 64669 2; 1992; CD
Chorus, piano
Heavy dialect

    Also released with *Great American
Spirituals* (Musical Heritage Society 513725Z;
1994; CD); *Negro Spirituals* (EMI 7243 5
72790 2 4; 1998; CD) and *Ride On, King Jesus!
Florence Quivar Sings Black Music of America*
(EMI Classics 9 67138 2; 2010; CD)

1924

Honor, Honor
Johnson, Hall
Sebron, Carolyn (Mezzo-soprano)
*Carolyn Sebron, Mezzo-soprano, Marie-
    Claude Arbaretaz, Piano*
Fondation Crédit Lyonnais; 1993; CD
Piano

1925

Honor, Honor
Johnson, Hall
Simpson, Eugene Thamon (Bass)
Hear Me, Ye Winds and Waves
Black Heritage Publications; 2005; CD
Piano
Heavy dialect

1926

Honor, Honor
Johnson, Hall
Simpson, Eugene Thamon (Bass)
Honors and Arms
Black Heritage Publications; 2005; CD
Piano

1927

Honor, Honor
Johnson, Hall
Simpson, Eugene Thamon (Bass)
*Hall Johnson Spirituals and Other Folk
    Songs*
Private Label; 2016; CD
Piano

1928

Honour, Honour!
Johnson, Hall
Smith, Muriel (Mezzo-soprano)
Negro Spirituals
Philips NBE11007; [195-]; 45 RPM
Piano

1929

Honour, Honour
Johnson, Hall
Spencer, Kenneth (Bass-baritone)
Volkslieder & Spirituals
Discoton 75546; [197-]; LP
Piano
Moderate dialect

1930

Honor, Honor
Johnson, Hall
Thomas, Indra (Soprano)
Great Day: Indra Thomas Sings Spirituals
Delos DE 3427; 2012; CD
Piano
Heavy dialect

1931

Honor! Honor!
Composer not identified
Thompson, Derrick (Baritone)
Spirituals
Private Label; 2014; CD
Piano
Light dialect

1932

Honor! Honor!
Johnson, Hall
Toppin, Louise (Soprano)
The Hall Johnson Collection
Carl Fischer VF5 CD1–VF5 CD2, 2003; Score
    w/CD
Piano
Heavy dialect

1933

Honor, Honor
Composer not identified
Verdejo, Awilda (Soprano)
Awilda Verdejo Sings Spirituals
Angeluz Performances; 1999; CD
Piano

1934

Honor, Honor
Composer not identified
Verrett, Shirley (Mezzo-soprano)
Great Moments at Carnegie Hall
RCA Red Seal 88985304202; 2016; CD
Piano
Heavy dialect

1935

Honor, Honor
Johnson, Hall
Verrett, Shirley (Mezzo-soprano)
Carnegie Hall Recital
Sony Music 82319; 2011; CD
Piano
Heavy dialect

    Also released with *Shirley Verrett: Edition*
(Newton Classics 8802167; 2013; CD)

1936

Honor, Honor
Johnson, Hall
West, Lucretia (Mezzo-soprano)
Negro Spirituals III
Club français du disque 176; 1959; LP
Piano
Heavy dialect

1937

Honor, Honor
Johnson, Hall
West, Lucretia (Mezzo-soprano)
Negro Spirituals mit Lukretia West
Opera 3408; [195-]; LP
Piano

1938

Honor, Honor
Johnson, Hall
Wilson, Robin (Soprano)
*Best of the Hall Johnson Centennial Festival
   Celebrating the 100th Anniversary of Hall
   Johnson's Birth*
Hall Johnson Collection O33D2; 2002; CD
Piano

1939

Honor, Honor
Johnson, Hall
Wright, John Wesley (Tenor)
*Wade in the Water: Songs of the River, the
   Lake, and the Sea*
Donald L. Robinson & Associates DLR-001;
   2004; CD
Piano

·······

Hush (Somebody's Calling My Name)

1940

Hush (Somebody's Calling My Name)
Battle, Kathleen; Sadin, Robert
Battle, Kathleen (Soprano)
So Many Stars
Sony Classical SK 68473; 1995; CD
Instrumental ensemble
Heavy dialect

   Also released with *The Complete Sony
Recordings* (Sony Classical 88985381362;
2016; CD)

1941

Hush, Hush
Robbiani, Mario
Fisher, Dorothy (Contralto)

Negro Spirituals
Edizione D'Arte Del Lions Club Milano Al
   Cenacolo; [19--]; LP
Piano

1942

Hush! Somebody's Callin' My Name
Lloyd, Charles, Jr.
Hobson, Richard (Baritone)
The Spiritual Art Song Collection
Warner Bros. SVBM00004; 2000; Score w/CD
Piano

1943

Hush (Somebody's Calling My Name)
Lloyd, Charles, Jr.
Jefferson, Othello (Tenor)
*Good News: African American Spirituals and
   Art Songs*
Cambria Records CD 1270; 2021; CD
Piano
Light dialect

1944

Hush! Somebody's Callin' My Name
Composer not identified
Norman, Jessye (Soprano)
*The Jessye Norman Collection: Sacred Songs
   & Spirituals*
Philips B0004506-02; 2005; CD
Chorus
Heavy dialect

1945

Hush! Somebody's Callin' My Name
Patterson. Willis
Norman, Jessye (Soprano)
Spirituals
Philips 416 462-2; 1990; CD
Chorus
Moderate dialect

1946

Hush! Somebody's Callin' My Name
Traditional
Norman, Jessye (Soprano)
Negro Spirituals
Philips 9500 580; 1979; LP
Chorus

1947
Hush (Somebody's Calling My Name)
Lloyd, Charles, Jr.
Sebron, Carolyn (Mezzo-soprano)
*Carolyn Sebron, Mezzo-soprano, Marie-
Claude Arbaretaz, Piano*
Fondation Crédit Lyonnais; 1993; CD
Piano

· · · · · · ·

I Ain't Got Weary Yet

1948
I Ain't Got Weary Yet
Composer not identified
Ingram, Paula Dione (Soprano)
*Art. Legacy. Celebration: A Salute to Black-
American Composers of Art Songs and
Spirituals, v. 1*
Private Label; 2014; CD
Piano

1949
I Ain't Got Weary Yet
Boatner, Edward
Jones, Arthur (Tenor)
Wade in the Water
Orbis Books; 1993; Book w/cass
Piano
Heavy dialect

· · · · · · ·

*I Am Bound
for the Kingdom*

1950
I Am Bound for de Kingdom
Price, Florence
Anderson, Marian (Contralto)
The Best of Negro Spirituals
BMG BVCM-37416; 2003; CD
Piano
Light dialect

1951
I Am Bound for de Kingdom
Price, Florence
Anderson, Marian (Contralto)

*He's Got the Whole World in His Hands:
Spirituals*
RCA Victor 09026-61960-2; 1994; CD
Piano
Moderate dialect

   Also released with *Marian Anderson:
Beyond the Music; Her Complete RCA Victor
Recordings* (Sony Classical 19439836492;
2021; CD)

1952
I Am Bound for the Kingdom
[Price, Florence]
Anderson, Marian (Contralto)
The Rich Voice of Marian Anderson
Editions Audiovisuel Beulah; 2019;
   Streaming audio
Piano

1953
I Am Bound for the Kingdom
Price, Florence
Matthews, Benjamin (Baritone)
A Spiritual Journey
Ebony Classic Recordings ECR 0001; 2000; CD
Piano

1954
I Am Bound for the Kingdom
Price, Florence
Matthews, Benjamin (Baritone)
A Balm in Gilead
Ebony Classic Recordings ECR 0001; 2000; CD
Piano

1955
I Am Bound for de Kingdom
Schweizer, Rolf
Wolf, Lars (Vocalist)
Die Schwarze Stimme Europas
Cantate 666000; 1971; LP
Chorus, organ, percussion

· · · · · · ·

I Am Seeking for a City

1956
I Am Seeking for a City
Miller, James

Forest, Michael (Tenor)
The Spirit Sings: American Spirituals
Shenandoah Conservatory SU003; [199-]; CD
Piano

1957

I Am Seeking for a City
Miller, James
Quivar, Florence (Mezzo-soprano)
Negro Spirituals
EMI 7243 5 72790 2 4; 1998; CD
Piano
Moderate dialect

   Also released with *Ride On, King Jesus!*
Florence Quivar Sings Black Music of America
(EMI Classics 9 67138 2; 2010; CD)

· · · · · · ·

I Bowed on My Knees and Cried, Holy

1958

I Bowed on My Knees and Cried, Holy!
Holmes, Charles
Price, Leontyne (Soprano)
Complete Collection of Songs and Spiritual Albums
RCA Red Seal 88697940502; 2011; CD
Chorus

· · · · · · ·

I Can Tell the World

1959

I Can Tell the World
Hayes, Roland; Boardman. Reginald
Hayes, Roland (Tenor); Hayes, Afrika (Soprano)
The Art of Roland Hayes
Smithsonian Collection RD 041; 1990; CD
Piano
Light dialect

· · · · · · ·

I Can't Stay Away

1960

Lord, I Can't Stay Away
Burleigh, Harry T.

Anderson, Marian (Contralto)
Great Voices of the Century
Memoir Classics CDMOIR 432; 1996; CD
Piano

1961

I Can't Stay Away
Hayes, Roland
Anderson, Marian (Contralto)
Ev'Ry Time I Feel the Spirit (1930–1947)
Naxos Nostalgia 8.120779; 2004; CD
Piano

1962

Lord, I Can't Stay Away
Hayes, Roland
Anderson, Marian (Contralto)
Farewell Recital
RCA Victor LSC 2781; 1964; LP
Piano

   Also released with *Marian Anderson: Beyond the Music; Her Complete RCA Victor Recordings* (Sony Classical 19439836492; 2021; CD)

1963

Lord, I Can't Stay Away
Hayes, Roland
Anderson, Marian (Contralto)
Good News: Vintage Negro Spirituals
Living Era AJA 5622; 2006; CD
Piano
Light dialect

1964

Lord, I Can't Stay Away
Hayes, Roland
Anderson, Marian (Contralto)
He's Got the Whole World in His Hands: Spirituals
RCA Victor 09026-6[1960]2; 1994; CD
Piano
Light dialect

1965

I Can't Stay Away
Hayes, Roland
Anderson, Marian (Contralto)

*The Art of Marian Anderson: Arias, Songs
    and Spirituals*
His Master's Voice EG 29001614; 1986; LP
Piano

        Also released with *Marian Anderson:
Beyond the Music; Her Complete RCA Victor
Recordings* (Sony Classical 19439836492; 2021;
CD)

1966

Lord, I Can't Stay Away
Hayes, Roland
Anderson, Marian (Contralto)
Marian Anderson: Portraits in Memory
Metropolitan Opera Guild MET 220; 1993;
    CD
Piano
Heavy dialect

1967

I Can't Stay Away
Hayes, Roland
Anderson, Marian (Contralto)
Negro Spirituals
EMI 7243 5 72790 2 4; 1998; CD
Piano
Light dialect

1968

Lord, I Can't Stay Away
Hayes, Roland
Anderson, Marian (Contralto)
Prima Voce
Nimbus NI 7882; 1996; CD
Piano
Moderate dialect

1969

Lord I Can't Stay Away
Hayes, Roland
Anderson, Marian (Contralto)
Rarities: Broadcast Performances 1943–1952
Video Artists International VAIA 1200;
    1998; CD
Orchestra

1970

Lord, I Can't Stay Away
Hayes, Roland

Anderson, Marian (Contralto)
Spirituals
RCA Victor Red Seal 09026-63306-2; 1999;
    CD
Piano
Moderate dialect

1971

Lord, I Can't Stay Away
Hayes, Roland
Anderson, Marian (Contralto)
Tribute
Pro Arte CDD 3447; 1993; CD
Piano

1972

I Can't Stay Away
Hayes, Roland
Anderson, Marian (Contralto)
Lebendige Vergangenheit
Austro Mechana Historic Recordings
    MONO 89604; 2004; CD
Piano

1973

Lord I Can't Stay Away
Hayes, Roland
Anderson, Marian (Contralto)
Marian Anderson in Concert 1943–1952
Eklipse Records EKR CD19; 1993; CD
Orchestra

1974

I Can't Stay Away
Hayes, Roland
Anderson, Marian (Contralto)
Negro Spirituals: 1924–1949
Frémeaux & Associés FA 184; 2004; CD
Orchestra

1975

Lord I Can't Stay Away
Hayes, Roland
Anderson, Marian (Contralto)
*City Called Heaven/Lord, I Can't Stay Away/
    Heaven, Heaven*
Victor Red Seal 8958; 1936; 78 RPM
Piano

1976
I Can't Stay Away
Hayes, Roland
Anderson, Marian (Contralto)
I Can't Stay Away/Were You There
Victor Red Seal 1966; 1939; 78 RPM
Piano

1977
I Can't Stay Away
Hayes, Roland
Anderson, Marian (Contralto)
Negro Spirituals, Vol. I
La Voix de Son Maître 7 ERF 17026; 1960;
    45 RPM

1978
I Can't Stay Away
Hayes, Roland
Anderson, Marian (Contralto)
Negro Spirituals
La Voix de Son Maître 7 EJF 3; 1955; 45 RPM
Piano

1979
Lord, I Can't Stay Away
Hayes, Roland
Anderson, Marian (Contralto)
Piano
Moderate dialect

1980
Lord, I Can't Stay Away
Hayes, Roland
Anderson, Marian (Contralto)
*Marian Anderson: Beyond the Music; Her
    Complete RCA Victor Recordings*
Sony Classical 19439836492; 2021; CD
Piano
Moderate dialect

1981
Lord I Can't Stay Away
Johnson, Hall
Anderson, Marian (Contralto)
Anderson Sings Negro Spirituals
Victor Golden Series EK-1007; [19--]; 45
    RPM
Piano

1982
I Can't Stay Away
[Hayes, Roland]
Anderson, Marian (Contralto)
The Lady from Philadelphia
Pearl GEMM CD 9069; 1993; CD
Piano

1983
Lord, I Can't Stay Away
[Hayes, Roland]
Anderson, Marian (Contralto)
Marian Anderson Sings Spirituals
Flapper Past CD 7073; 1995; CD
Piano

1984
Lord, I Can't Stay Away
[Hayes, Roland]
Anderson, Marian (Contralto)
The Very Best of Marian Anderson
Master Classics Records; 2009; CD
Piano
Light dialect

1985
Lord I Can't Stay Away
[Hayes, Roland]
Anderson, Marian (Contralto)
Classic Gospel Songs
Emerald/K-Tel; 2013; Streaming audio
Piano

1986
I Can't Stay Away
[Hayes, Roland]
Anderson, Marian (Contralto)
Negro Spirituals
La Voix de Son Maître 7 ERF 157; [19--];
    45 RPM

1987
Lord I Can't Stay Away
[Hayes, Roland]
Anderson, Marian (Contralto)
The Rich Voice of Marian Anderson
Editions Audiovisuel Beulah; 2019;
    Streaming audio
Piano

1988

Я не могу быть в стороне (YA ne mogu
   byt' v storone)
Composer not identified
Filatova, Ludmila (Mezzo-soprano)
Негритянские Спиричузлс (Negrityanskiye
   Spirichuzls—Negro Spirituals)
Melodiâ S10 21833 009; 1985; LP
Organ
Light dialect

1989

Lord I Can't Stay Away
Hayes, Roland; Pankey, Aubrey
Pankey, Aubrey (Baritone)
Negro Spirituals
Eterna 830010; 1983; LP
Piano

1990

Lord I Can't Stay Away
[Hayes, Roland]
Pankey, Aubrey (Baritone)
Aubrey Pankey Singt Negro-Spirituals
Eterna 7 30 005; 1959; LP
Piano
Heavy dialect

1991

Lord I Can't Stay Away
[Hayes, Roland]
Pankey, Aubrey (Baritone)
Negro-Spirituals
Eterna 5 30 022; [19--]; 45 RPM
Piano
Heavy dialect

1992

Lord I Can't Stay Away
Hayes, Roland
Sims, Robert (Baritone)
Robert Sims Sings the Spirituals of Roland
   Hayes
Canti Classics 2014-01; 2015; CD
Piano
Heavy dialect

1993

I Can't Stay Away [from *Green Pastures*]
Johnson, Hall

Toppin, Louise (Soprano)
The Hall Johnson Collection
Carl Fischer VF5 CD1–VF5 CD2; 2003; Score
   w/CD
Piano
Heavy dialect

• • • • • • •

I Can't Stay
Here by Myself

1994

I Can Not Stay Here by Myself
Johnson, Hall
Matthews, Benjamin (Baritone)
A Balm in Gilead
Ebony Classic Recordings ECR 0001; 2000;
   CD
Piano

1995

I Cannot Stay Here by Myself
Johnson, Hall
Mims, A. Grace Lee (Soprano)
Spirituals
H & GM Records HGM 8101; 1981; LP
Piano
Heavy dialect

1996

I Can't Stay Here by Myself
Pankey, Aubrey
Pankey, Aubrey (Baritone)
Negro Spirituals
Eterna 830010; 1983; LP
Piano

1997

I Cannot Stay Here by Myself
Johnson, Hall
Taylor, Darryl (Countertenor)
How Sweet the Sound: A Charm of
   Spirituals
Albany TROY1244; 2011; CD
Piano

· · · · · · ·
I Don't Feel No Ways Tired

1998

I Don't Feel No-ways Tired
Burleigh, Harry T.
Anderson, Marian (Contralto)
The Lady
Magnum Music MCCD 017; 1996; CD
Piano

1999

I Don't Feel No Ways Tired
Burleigh, Harry T.
Anderson, Marian (Contralto)
The Lady from Philadelphia
Pearl GEMM CD 9069; 1993; CD
Piano

2000

I Don't Feel No Ways Tired
Burleigh, Harry T.
Anderson, Marian (Contralto)
*The Art of Marian Anderson: Arias, Songs
    and Spirituals*
His Master's Voice EG 29001614; 1986; LP
Piano

2001

I Don't Feel No-ways Tired
Burleigh, Harry T.
Anderson, Marian (Contralto)
Prima Voce
Nimbus NI 7882; 1996; CD
Piano
Heavy dialect

2002

I Don't Feel No Ways Tired
Burleigh, Harry T.
Anderson, Marian (Contralto)
*Softly Awakes My Heart: Arias, Songs and
    Spirituals, Original Recordings [1924]
    1944*
Naxos Nostalgia 8.120566; 2001; CD
Piano
Heavy dialect

2003

I Don't Feel No Ways Tired
Burleigh, Harry T.
Anderson, Marian (Contralto)
Lebendige Vergangenheit
Austro Mechana Historic Recordings
    MONO 89604; 2004; CD
Piano

2004

I Don't Feel No Ways Tired
Burleigh, Harry T.
Anderson, Marian (Contralto)
Negro Spirituals: 1924–1949
Frémeaux & Associés FA 184; 2004; CD
Orchestra

2005

I Don't Feel No-ways Tired
Burleigh, Harry T.
Anderson, Marian (Contralto)
*Sometimes I Feel Like a Motherless Child/I
    Don't Feel No-ways Tired*
Victor Red Seal; [19--]; 78 RPM
Piano
Light dialect

2006

I Don't Feel No-ways Tired
Burleigh, Harry T.
Anderson, Marian (Contralto)
Deep River/I Don't Feel No Ways Tired
D.A. 1676; 1925; 78 RPM
Piano
Light dialect

2007

I Don't Feel No Ways Tired
[Burleigh, Harry T.]
Anderson, Marian (Contralto)
Deep River
Audio Book & Music; [20--]; CD

2008

I Don't Feel No Ways Tir'd
[Burleigh, Harry T.]
Anderson, Marian (Contralto)
Marian Anderson Sings Spirituals

Flapper Past CD 7073; 1995; CD
Piano

2009

I Don't Feel No-ways Tired
[Burleigh, Harry T.]
Anderson, Marian (Contralto)
Ave Maria: And Other Schubert Songs
43 North Broadway, LLC; 2019; Streaming
    audio
Piano
Light dialect

2010

I Don't Feel No-ways Tired
Burleigh, Harry T.
Boatner, Edward H.S. (Bass-baritone)
Black Swans
Parnassus Recordings PACD 96067; 2019;
    CD
Piano
No dialect discerned

2011

Lord I Don't Feel No-ways Tired
Simpson-Currenton, Evelyn
Chandler-Eteme, Janice (Soprano); Dixon,
    Rodrick (Tenor)
Devotions
Sligo Records; 2007; CD
Piano

2012

I Don't Feel No-ways Tired
Burleigh, Harry T.
Cheatham, Kitty (Soprano)
*Swing Low, Sweet Chariot/I Don't Feel
    No-ways Tired or "I Am Seeking for
    a City"/Walk in Jerusalem Just Like
    John/Sinner Please Don't Let This
    Harvest Pass*
Victor 45086; 1916; 78 RPM
Piano
Heavy dialect

2013

No Ways Tired
Composer not identified
Jobson, Christine (Soprano)

By Faith: Hymns and Negro Spirituals
CD Baby; 2017; CD
Piano
Heavy dialect

2014

Lord, I Don't Feel No-ways Tired
Composer not identified
McDaniel, Yvette (Soprano)
Simply Spiritual
YM01 DIDX 046103; 1997; CD
Piano

2015

I Don't Feel No Ways Tired
Composer not identified
McKelton, Samuel (Tenor); Parks, Karen
    (Soprano)
*Done Crossed Every River: Freedom's
    Journey*
Arcadia ARC 2004-2; 1995; CD

2016

Lord, I Don't Feel Noways Tired
Johnson, Hall; Appling, William
Mims, A. Grace Lee (Soprano)
Spirituals
H & GM Records HGM 8101; 1981; LP
Piano
Heavy dialect

2017

I Don't Feel No-ways Tired
Burleigh, Harry T.
Moses, Oral (Bass-baritone)
*Amen! African-American Composers of the
    20th Century*
Albany Records TROY459; 2001; CD
Piano
Light dialect

2018

I Don't Feel No-ways Tired
Burleigh, Harry T.
Moses, Oral (Bass-baritone)
Sankofa: A Spiritual Reflection
Albany Records TROY1802; 2019; CD
Piano
Moderate dialect

2019

I Don't Feel No Ways Tired
Hogan, Moses
Ragin, Derek Lee (Countertenor)
Ev'ry Time I Feel the Spirit: Spirituals
Channel Classics CCS 2991; 1991; CD
Piano
Heavy dialect

2020

I Don't Feel No Ways Tired
Burleigh, Harry T.
Seagle, Oscar (Baritone)
Nobody Knows de Trouble I've Seen/I Don't Feel No Ways Tired
Columbia Record A2469; 1917; 78 RPM
Orchestra
Light dialect

    Also released with *Nobody Knows de Trouble I've Seen/I Don't Feel No Ways Tired* (Columbia 71-M; 1917; 78 RPM)

2021

Don't Feel No Ways Tired
Composer not identified
Thompson, Derrick (Baritone)
Spirituals
Private Label; 2014; CD
Piano
Light dialect

2022

Lord, I Don't Feel Noways Tired [from *Green Pastures*]
Johnson, Hall
Toppin, Louise (Soprano)
The Hall Johnson Collection
Carl Fischer VF5 CD1–VF5 CD2; 2003; Score w/CD
Piano
Moderate dialect

2023

Lord, I Don't Feel Noways Tired
Johnson, Hall
West, Lucretia (Mezzo-soprano)
Negro Spirituals III
Club français du disque 176; 1959; LP

Piano
Heavy dialect

. . . .

I Got a Home in That Rock

2024

I Got a Home in Dat Rock
[Brown, Lawrence]
Robeson, Paul (Bass-baritone)
Complete Recordings
Universal Digital Enterprises; 2018; Streaming audio

2025

I Got a Home in-a Dat Rock
Hogan, Moses
Brown, Anthony (Baritone)
Toil and Triumph
Spirituals Project; 2002; CD
Chorus
Moderate dialect

2026

I Got a Home in That Rock
Composer not identified
Charles, Lee (Tenor)
Swing Low Sweet Chariot: And Other Spirituals
Riverside RLP 12-651; 1957; LP
Piano, guitar

2027

Приют на камне обрел я (Priyut na kamne obrel ya)
Composer not identified
Filatova, Ludmila (Mezzo-soprano)
Негритянские Спиричуэлс (Negrityanskiye Spirichuzls—Negro Spirituals)
Melodiâ S10 21833 009; 1985; LP
Organ
Light dialect

2028

I Got a Home in That Rock
Bonds, Margaret
Forest, Michael (Tenor)

The Spirit Sings: American Spirituals
Shenandoah Conservatory SU003; [199-];
　　CD

2029

I Got a Home in That Rock
Composer not identified
Green, Elnora E. (Contralto)
This Is My Task
Private Label NR 18650; 1991; LP

2030

I Got a Home in a-Dat Rock
[Brown, Lawrence]
Hagen-William, Louis (Bass-baritone)
Negro Spiritual
Quantum QM 6909; 1993; CD
Piano
Light dialect

2031

I Gotta Home ina Dat Rock
Burleigh, Harry T.; Taylor, Vivian
Honeysucker, Robert (Baritone); Dry,
　　Marion (Contralto)
Let's Have a Union
Brave Records BRAV-0923; 2009; CD
Piano
Moderate dialect

2032

Got a Home in-a Dat Rock [from *Five
　　Spirituals for Baritone and Cello*]
Balentine, James Scott
Jones, Timothy (Baritone)
Love Comes in at the Eye
Albany TROY1734; 2018; CD
Cello
Heavy dialect

2033

I Gotta Home inna Dat Rock
Still, William Grant
More, Suzi (Vocalist)
*Chords and Strings: Centuries of Songs for
　　Voice and Guitar*
Lil Red Hen Records; [2018]; Streaming
　　audio

Guitar
Moderate dialect

2034

I Got a Home in-a Dat Rock [from Cycle of
　　Six Spirituals]
Owens, Robert
Moses, Oral (Bass-baritone)
*Come Down Angels and Trouble the Water:
　　Negro Spirituals, an American National
　　Treasure!*
Albany Records TROY 1489; 2014; CD
Piano
Moderate dialect

2035

I Got a Home in Dat Rock
Brown, Lawrence
Robeson, Paul (Bass-baritone)
Spirituals: Original Recordings 1925–1936
Naxos Gospel Legends 8.120638; 2003; CD
Piano

2036

I Got a Home in Dat Rock /Gimme Your
　　Han'
Brown, Lawrence
Robeson, Paul (Bass-baritone); Brown,
　　Lawrence (Vocalist)
The Power and the Glory
Columbia/Legacy CK 47337; 1991; CD
Piano
Moderate dialect

2037

I Got a Home in-a Dat Rock!
Brown, Lawrence
Robeson, Paul (Bass-baritone)
Songs of My People
RCA Red Seal LM-3292; 1972; LP
Piano

2038

I Got a Home in That Rock
Brown, Lawrence
Robeson, Paul (Bass-baritone)
*A Lonesome Road: Paul Robeson Sings
　　Spirituals and Songs*

ASV Living Era CD AJA 5027; 1984; CD
Piano
Moderate dialect

2039

I Got a Home in Dat Rock
Brown, Lawrence
Robeson, Paul (Bass-baritone)
Paul Robeson Sings Negro Spirituals
Philips GBL 5584; [19--]; LP
Piano

2040

I Got a Home in That Rock
Brown, Lawrence
Robeson, Paul (Bass-baritone)
Paul Robeson Collection
Hallmark Recordings 390692; 1998; CD

2041

I Got a Home in Dat Rock /Gimme Your
     Han'
Brown, Lawrence
Robeson, Paul (Bass-baritone)
They Sing Praises
Columbia CK 67007; 1995; CD
Piano

2042

I Got a Home in Dat Rock
Brown, Lawrence
Robeson, Paul (Bass-baritone)
Swing Low, Sweet Chariot
Columbia Masterworks MM-819; 1949; 78
     RPM
Piano

2043

I Got a Home in Dat Rock
Brown, Lawrence
Robeson, Paul (Bass-baritone)
I Got a Home in Dat Rock /Witness
His Master's Voice B 2727; 1928; 78 RPM
Piano

2044

I Got a Home in-a Dat Rock
Brown, Lawrence
Robeson, Paul (Bass-baritone)

I Got a Home in-a Dat Rock /Witness
Victor 21109; 1927; 78 RPM
Piano
Heavy dialect

2045

I Got a Home in Dat Rock
Brown, Lawrence
Robeson, Paul (Bass-baritone)
Paul Robeson Chante ... f16 Spirituals
Philips G 05.639 R; 1959; LP
Piano

2046

I Got a Home in That Rock
[Brown, Lawrence]
Robeson, Paul (Bass-baritone)
Scandalize My Name
Classics Record Library 30-5647; 1976; LP
Piano
Light dialect

2047

I Got a Home in Dat Rock
[Brown, Lawrence]
Robeson, Paul (Bass-baritone)
Swing Low, Sweet Chariot
Columbia Masterworks ML 2038; [195-];
     LP
Piano

2048

I Got a Home in Dat Rock
[Brown, Lawrence]
Robeson, Paul (Bass-baritone)
*Ol' Man River: The Very Best of Paul
     Robeson*
Memory Lane; 2012; CD

2049

I Got a Home in Dat Rock
[Brown, Lawrence]
Robeson, Paul (Bass-baritone)
Five Classic Albums Plus Bonus Tracks
Real Gone Music RGMCD287; 2017; CD

2050

I Got a Home in That Rock
[Brown, Lawrence]

Robeson, Paul (Bass-baritone)
Ol' Man River: The Ultimate Collection
Roslin Records; 2011; Streaming audio
Piano
Light dialect

2051

Gotta Home in a-Dat Rock
Hogan, Moses
Sims, Robert (Baritone)
*In the Spirit: Spirituals and American Songs
    with Orchestra and Chorus*
Canti Classics; 2009; CD
Chorus
Heavy dialect

2052

I Got a Home
Composer not identified
Spencer, Kenneth (Bass-baritone)
Kenneth Spencer Singt Neger-Spirituals
Garnet DG 2001; [19--]; 45 RPM
Orchestra

2053

I Got a Home in-a Dat Rock
Walberg, Wladimir
Spencer, Kenneth (Bass-baritone)
*I Got a Home in-a Dat Rock /Go Down,
    Moses*
Columbia LF 274; 1957; 78 RPM
Orchestra

   Also released with *4 Negro Spirituals*
(Columbia ESRF 1067; 1957; 45 RPM)

2054

I Got a Home in-a Dat Rock!
Owens, Robert
Taylor, Darryl (Tenor)
Fields of Wonder
Albany TROY897; 2006; CD
Instrumental ensemble

2055

I Got a Home in That Rock
Bonds, Margaret
Toppin, Louise (Soprano)
Good News
Videmus Records VIS735; 2007; CD

Piano
Heavy dialect

· · · · · · ·

I Got to Lie Down

2056

I Got to Life (sic) Down
Johnson, Hall
Blackmon, Henry (Baritone)
Geestelijke Liederen En Negro Spirituals
Mirasound Records SGLP 6047; 1974; LP
Piano

2057

I Got to Lie Down [from *Son of Man*]
Johnson, Hall
Brown, Anthony (Baritone)
Spirituals
Brown/Smith Productions; 1995; CD
Piano
Heavy dialect

2058

I Got to Lie Down [from *Son of Man*]
Johnson, Hall
Foreman, Blanche (Contralto)
*Best of the Hall Johnson Centennial Festival
    Celebrating the 100th Anniversary of Hall
    Johnson's Birth*
Hall Johnson Collection O33D2; 2002; CD
Piano

2059

I Got to Lie Down [from *Son of Man*]
Johnson, Hall
Holland, Charles (Tenor)
My Lord What a Mornin'
Musical Heritage Society MHS 912250X;
    1982; LP
Piano
Moderate dialect

   Also released with *My Lord What a
Mornin'* (Musical Heritage Society MHS
512250K; 1988; CD)

2060

I Got to Lie Down [from *Son of Man*]
Johnson, Hall

Holmes, Eugene (Baritone)
Spirituals
Schubert Records SCH-102; [1988]; LP
Piano
Light dialect

2061

I Got to Lie Down
Meyer, Fredrich
London, George (Bass-baritone)
Spirituals
Deutsche Grammophon 00289 477 6193;
    2006; CD
Piano, trumpet
Heavy dialect

2062

I Got to Lie Down [from *Son of Man*]
Johnson, Hall
McFerrin, Robert (Baritone)
Deep River and Other Classic Negro Spirituals
Riverside Records RLP 12-812; 1959; LP

    Also released with *Classic Negro Spiritu-
als* (Washington Records WLP 466; 1959; LP)

2063

I Got to Lie Down [from *Son of Man*]
Johnson, Hall
Overton, Kenneth (Baritone)
*Been in de Storm So Long (Songs My Fathers
    Taught Me)*
American Spiritual Ensemble; 2012; CD
Piano
Heavy dialect

2064

I Got to Lie Down [from *Son of Man*]
Johnson, Hall
Overton, Kenneth (Baritone)
Swing Low, Sweet Chariot
American Spiritual Ensemble; 2011; CD

2065

I Got to Lie Down [from *Son of Man*]
Johnson, Hall
Simpson, Eugene Thamon (Bass)
Honors and Arms
Black Heritage Publications; 2005; CD
Piano

2066

I Got to Lie Down [from *Son of Man*]
Johnson, Hall
Simpson, Eugene Thamon (Bass)
*Hall Johnson Spirituals and Other Folk
    Songs*
Private Label; 2016; CD
Piano

2067

I Got to Lie Down [from *Son of Man*]
Johnson, Hall
Taylor, Darryl (Countertenor)
How Sweet the Sound: A Charm of Spirituals
Albany TROY1244; 2011; CD
Piano

2068

I Got to Lie Down [from *Son of Man*]
Johnson, Hall
Toppin, Louise (Soprano)
The Hall Johnson Collection
Carl Fischer VF5 CD1–VF5 CD2; 2003; Score
    w/CD
Piano
Moderate dialect

2069

I Got to Lie Down [from *Son of Man*]
Johnson, Hall
Toppin, Louise (Soprano)
*He'll Bring It to Pass: The Spirituals of Hall
    Johnson for Voice and Piano*
Albany Records TROY846; 2006; CD
Piano
Moderate dialect

2070

I Got to Lie Down
Composer not identified
Verdejo, Awilda (Soprano)
Awilda Verdejo Sings Spirituals
Angeluz Performances; 1999; CD
Piano

2071

I Got to Lie Down [from *Son of Man*]
Johnson, Hall
Warfield, William (Bass-baritone)

*Spirituals: 200 Years of African-American
    Spirituals*
ProArte CDD 3443; 1993; CD
Piano
Heavy dialect

. . . .

I Gotta Move When
the Spirit Say Move

2072

I Gotta Move When the Spirit Say Move
Perry, Zenobia Powell
Jefferson, Othello (Tenor)
*Good News: African American Spirituals and
    Art Songs*
Cambria Records CD 1270; 2021; CD
Vocal ensemble, piano
Light dialect

. . . .

I Heard the Preachin'
of de Elder

2073

I Heard de Preachin' of de Elder
Brown, Charles
Griffin, Ivan (Bass-baritone)
The New Negro Spiritual
W. C. Patterson; 2002; Score w/CD
Piano
Heavy dialect

. . . .

I Know the Lord Laid
His Hands on Me

2074

I Know the Lord Laid His Hands on Me
Brown, Lawrence
Anderson, Marian (Contralto)
Negro Spirituals: 1924–1949
Frémeaux & Associés FA 184; 2004; CD
Orchestra

2075

I Know de Lord's Laid His Hands on Me
Brown, Lawrence

Anderson, Marian (Contralto)
Negro Spirituals
La Voix de Son Maître 7EJF2; 1955; 45 RPM
Orchestra

2076

I Know de Lord's Laid His Hands on Me
Brown, Lawrence
Anderson, Marian (Contralto)
*Tramping/I Know de Lord's Laid His Hands
    on Me*
His Master's Voice D.A. 1669; [19--]; 78 RPM
Piano
Light dialect

2077

I Know de Lord's Laid His Hands on Me
Brown, Lawrence
Anderson, Marian (Contralto)
Negro Spirituals, vol. II
La Voix de Son Maître 7 ERF 17025; 1962;
    EP 45 RPM
Orchestra

2078

I Know the Lord's Laid
[Brown, Lawrence]
Anderson, Marian (Contralto)
The Lady from Philadelphia
Pearl GEMM CD 9069; 1993; CD
Piano

2079

I Know the Lord Laid His Hands on Me
[Brown, Lawrence]
Anderson, Marian (Contralto)
Marian Anderson: Portraits in Memory
Metropolitan Opera Guild MET 220; 1993;
    CD
Piano
Moderate dialect

2080

I Know de Lord's Laid
[Brown, Lawrence]
Anderson, Marian (Contralto)
Marian Anderson Sings Spirituals
Flapper Past CD 7073; 1995; CD
Piano

2081

I Know de Lord's Laid His Hand on Me
[Brown, Lawrence]
Anderson, Marian (Contralto)
Softly Awakes My Heart
ASV CD AJA 5262; 1999; CD
Piano

2082

I Know the Lord's Laid His Hands on Me
[Brown, Lawrence]
Anderson, Marian (Contralto)
Inspirations
Emerald Echoes; 2015; Streaming audio
Piano
Moderate dialect

2083

I know Lord Laid His Hands on Me
[Brown, Lawrence]
Anderson, Marian (Contralto)
Trampin'/I Know Lord Laid His Hands on Me
Victor 1896; [19--]; 78 RPM
Piano
Light dialect

2084

I Know de Lord's Laid His Hands on Me
Burleigh, Harry T.
Brown, Anthony (Baritone)
Toil and Triumph
Spirituals Project; 2002; CD
Chorus, piano
Light dialect

2085

I Know de Lord's Laid His Hands on Me
Burleigh, Harry T.
Davis, Ollie Watts (Soprano)
Here's One: Spiritual Songs
KJAC Publishing KJAC0123; 2003; CD
Piano
Light dialect

2086

I Know de Lord's Laid His Hands on Me
Brown, Lawrence
Duncan, Todd (Baritone)
Negro Spirituals

Allegro ALG3022; [1952]; LP
Piano

Also released with *American Negro Spirituals* (Allegro LEG 9026; [19--]; LP)

2087

I Know de Lord's Laid His Hands on Me
Brown, Lawrence
Duncan, Todd (Baritone)
African American Spirituals
[Apple Music]; 2008; Streaming audio
Piano
Moderate dialect

2088

I Know de Lord's Laid His Hands on Me
[Brown, Lawrence]
Duncan, Todd (Baritone)
Spirituals
Royale 1810; [1950]; LP

2089

I Know the Lord
Brown, Lawrence
Elzy, Ruby (Soprano)
Ruby Elzy in Song: Rare Recordings
Cambria Records CD-1154; 2006; CD
Piano
Heavy dialect

Also released with *The 78 RPM Collection* (Master Classics Records; 2010; CD)

2090

I Know de Lord's Laid His Hands on Me
[Boatner, Edward]
Hagen-William, Louis (Bass-baritone)
Negro Spirituals
Quantum QM 6909; 1993; CD
Piano

2091

I Know the Lord Laid His Hands on Me
Boatner, Edward
Ingram, Paula Dione (Soprano)
Art. Legacy. Celebration: A Salute to Black-American Composers of Art Songs and Spirituals, v. 1
Private Label; 2014; CD
Piano

2092

I Know the Lord's Laid His Hands on Me
Welsh, Nicky
McCue, Bill (Bass-baritone)
Bill McCue Sings the Great Spirituals
Beltona SBE 173; 1974; LP
Orchestra

2093

I Know de Lord's Laid His Hands on Me
Burleigh, Harry T.
Mims, A. Grace Lee (Soprano)
Spirituals
H & GM Records HGM 8101; 1981; LP
Piano
Heavy dialect

2094

I Know de Lord's Laid His Hands on Me
[Burleigh, Harry T.]
Moyer, Del-Louise (Mezzo-soprano)
He'll Bring to Pass: Spirituals &
Americanegro Suite
Alyssum ALY-9001; 1997; CD
Piano
Light dialect

2095

I Know de Lord
Brown, Lawrence
Robeson, Paul (Bass-baritone)
Paul Robeson Sings Negro Spirituals
Philips GBL 5584; [19--]; LP
Piano

2096

I Know de Lord
Brown, Lawrence
Robeson, Paul (Bass-baritone)
Swing Low, Sweet Chariot
Columbia Masterworks MM-819; 1949; 78
    RPM
Piano

2097

I Know de Lord
Brown, Lawrence
Robeson, Paul (Bass-baritone); Brown,
    Lawrence (Vocalist)

Paul Robeson Chante ... 16 Spirituals
Philips G 05.639 R; 1959; LP
Piano

2098

I Know the Lord
[Brown, Lawrence]
Robeson, Paul (Bass-baritone); Brown,
    Lawrence (Vocalist)
Scandalize My Name
Classics Record Library 30-5647; 1976; LP
Piano
Moderate dialect

2099

I Know de Lord
[Brown, Lawrence]
Robeson, Paul (Bass-baritone)
Swing Low, Sweet Chariot
Columbia Masterworks ML 2038; [195-]; LP
Piano

2100

I Know the Lord's Laid His Hand on Me
McLin, Lena
Rucker, Mark (Baritone)
Mark Rucker Sings Lena McLin: Songs for
    Voice & Piano
Kjos Music Press KCD8; 2002; CD
Piano
No dialect discerned

2101

I Know the Lord Laid His Hands on Me
Composer not identified
Rustin, Bayard (Tenor)
Bayard Rustin, the Singer
Bayard Rustin Fund; 1992; CD
Piano

2102

I Know the Lord Laid His Hands on Me
Traditional
Rustin, Bayard (Tenor)
Bayard Rustin Sings Twelve Spirituals on the
    Life of Christ
Fellowship Records E2-KL 1771; [195-]; LP
A cappella
Heavy dialect

Also released with *Bayard Rustin, the Singer* (Black Swan Series; Parnassus Records PACD 96083; 2022; CD)

2103

I Must Walk That Lonesome Valley
Shaw, Clifford
Alexander, Roberta (Soprano)
Songs My Mother Taught Me
Etcetera KTC 1208; 1999; CD
Piano
No dialect discerned

Also released with *Roberta Alexander... A Retrospective* (Etcetera KTC1222; 2013; CD)

· · · · · · ·

I Stood on the River of Jordan

2104

I Stood on de Ribber ob Jerdon
Burleigh, Harry T.
Anderson, Marian (Contralto)
He's Got the Whole World in His Hands: Spirituals
RCA Victor 09026-6[1960]2; 1994; CD
Piano
Moderate dialect

2105

I Stood on de Ribber ob Jerdon
Burleigh, Harry T.
Anderson, Marian (Contralto)
Marian Anderson: Beyond the Music; Her Complete RCA Victor Recordings
Sony Classical 19439836492; 2021; CD
Piano
Heavy dialect

2106

I Stood on de Ribber ob Jerdon
[Burleigh, Harry T.]
Anderson, Marian (Contralto)
The Rich Voice of Marian Anderson
Editions Audiovisuel Beulah; 2019; Streaming audio
Piano

2107

I Stood on de Ribber ob Jerdon
Burleigh, Harry T.
Arroyo, Martina (Soprano)
Spirituals
Centaur CRC 2060; 1991; CD
Piano
Heavy dialect

2108

I Stood on de Ribber of Jerdon
Burleigh, Harry T.
Arroyo, Martina (Soprano)
There's a Meeting Here Tonight
Angel S-36072; 1974; LP
Chorus

2109

I Stood on de Ribber of Jerdon
Burleigh, Harry T.; Vené, R.
Arroyo, Martina (Soprano)
Negro Spirituals
EMI 7243 5 72790 2 4; 1998; CD
Chorus
Heavy dialect

2110

I Stood on the River of Jordan
[Burleigh, Harry T.]
Arroyo, Martina (Soprano)
Liederabend 1968
Hänssler Classic 93.719; 2012; CD
Piano
Light dialect

2111

I Stood on de Ribber ob Jerdon
[Burleigh, Harry T.]
Arroyo, Martina (Soprano)
Martina Arroyo Singt Lieder der Welt
Eurodisc-Auslese [2000]3-241; 1979; LP

2112

I Stood on the Ribber ob Jerdon
Burleigh, Harry T.
Blackmon, Henry (Baritone)
Negro Spirituals
Jubilate JB 1716; 1961; 45 RPM
Organ

2113
I Stood on de Ribber ob Jerdon
Burleigh, Harry T.
Carnette, Count (Vocalist)
Count Carnette Sings Favorite Negro Spirituals
Carnette Archive Recordings; 1983; LP
Piano
Heavy dialect

2114
I Stood on de Ribber ob Jordan
Composer not identified
Clark, Clarence Carroll (Baritone)
Swing Low, Sweet Chariot/I Stood on de Ribber ob Jordan
Paramount 12038; 1924; 78 RPM
Piano

2115
I Stood on de Ribber ob Jordan
Burleigh, Harry T.
Davis, Ellabelle (Soprano)
Ellabelle Davis Sings Negro Spirituals
London LPS 182; [1950]; LP
Orchestra
Heavy dialect

Also released with *First Time Buyer's Guide to American Negro Spirituals* (Primo Collection PRMCD6038; 2006; CD) and *Negro Spirituals: The Concert Tradition 1909–1948* (Frémeaux & Associés FA 168; 1999; CD)

2116
I Stood on de Ribber ob Jerdon
Burleigh, Harry T.
Davis, Ellabelle (Soprano)
I Stood on de Ribber ob Jordan/Plenty Good Room
Decca 14624; [19--]; 78 RPM
Orchestra

2117
I Stood on de Ribber ob Jordan
Burleigh, Harry T.
Davis, Ellabelle (Soprano)
Recital of Negro Spirituals by Ellabelle Davis
Decca LM.4504; [1950]; LP
Orchestra

2118
I Stood on de Ribber ob Jordan
Burleigh, Harry T.
Davis, Ellabelle (Soprano)
I Stood on de Ribber ob Jordan
Decca M.653; [19--]; 78 RPM
Orchestra

2119
I Stood on de Ribber ob Jerden
[Burleigh, Harry T.]
Davis, Ellabelle (Soprano)
Spirituals
Past Classics; 2013; Streaming audio
Orchestra
Heavy dialect

2120
I Stood on de Ribber
[Burleigh, Harry T.]
Davis, Ellabelle (Soprano)
Were You There?
Decca DFE 8618; 1965; 45 RPM
Orchestra

2121
I Stood on de Ribber of Jordan
[Burleigh, Harry T.]
Davis, Ellabelle (Soprano)
Great Negro Spirituals
Replay Record; 2013; Streaming audio
Orchestra
Heavy dialect

2122
I Stood on the River of Jordan
[Burleigh, Harry T.]
Davis, Ellabelle (Soprano)
The Concerto: African American Spirituals
Orange Amaro; 2019; Streaming audio
Orchestra

2123
I Stood on de Ribber ob Jerden
[Burleigh, Harry T.]
Hampton, Jonathon (Vocalist)
Negro Spirituals: Songs of Trial and Triumph
Private Label; 2017; Streaming audio

Piano
Light dialect

2124

I Stood on the River of Jordan
Hogan, Moses
Hendricks, Barbara (Soprano)
Give Me Jesus
EMI Classics 7243 5 56788 2 9; 1998; CD
Chorus
Light dialect

2125

I Stood on de Ribber of Jerden
Burleigh, Harry T.
Holland, Charles (Tenor)
Negro-Spirituals
Pathé 45 ED 29; [19--]; 45 RPM
Piano

     Also released with *Negro Spirituals*
(Pathé 45 ED. 29; 1954; 45 RPM)

2126

I Stood on de Ribber ob Jerdon
Burleigh, Harry T.
Holmes, Eugene (Baritone)
Eugene Holmes Sings Spirituals
Avant Garde AV-115; [1968]; LP
Piano
Heavy dialect

2127

I Stood on the Ribber ob Jerdon
Clinton, Irving
Irving, Clinton (Bass-baritone)
Clinton Irving Sings Spirituals: A Tribute
Rogers; 2001; CD

2128

I Stood on de Ribber ob Jerdon
Burleigh, Harry T.
Little, Vera (Mezzo-soprano)
My Good Lord Done Been Here
Decca 123737; 1957; LP
Piano

2129

I Stood on the River of Jordan
Burleigh, Harry T.

Oby, Jason (Tenor)
The Life of Christ: Collected Spirituals
Private Label TSU4749; [200-]; CD
Piano
Moderate dialect

2130

I Stood on de River of Jordan
Burleigh, Harry T.
Reese, Ruth (Contralto)
Motherless Child
OPS 1006/79; 1979; LP

2131

I Stood on the River
[Burleigh, Harry T.]
Robeson, Paul (Bass-baritone)
Paul Robeson
Music Video Dist. MDGC23420.2; 2007;
  CD

2132

I Stood on the Ribber ob Jerdon
Burleigh, Harry T.
Spencer, Kenneth (Bass-baritone)
*Nobody Knows de Trouble I've Seen/I Stood
  on the Ribber ob Jerdon*
Supraphon G 23272; [19--]; 78 RPM
Organ, piano

. . . .

I Want Jesus
to Walk with Me

2133

I Want Jesus to Walk with Me
Boatner, Edward
Anderson, Marian (Contralto)
*He's Got the Whole World in His Hands:
  Spirituals*
RCA Victor 09026-6[1960]2; 1994; CD
Piano
Moderate dialect

2134

I Must Walk That Lonesome Valley
Shaw, Clifford
Alexander, Roberta (Soprano)

Roberta Alexander... A Retrospective
Etcetera KTC1222; 2013; CD
Piano
No dialect discerned

2135

I Want Jesus to Walk with Me
Boatner, Edward
Anderson, Marian (Contralto)
Marian Anderson: Beyond the Music;
   Her Complete RCA Victor Recordings
Sony Classical 19439836492; 2021; CD
Piano
Heavy dialect

2136

I Want Jesus to Walk with Me
[Boatner, Edward]
Anderson, Marian (Contralto)
The Rich Voice of Marian Anderson
Editions Audiovisuel Beulah; 2019;
   Streaming audio
Piano

2137

I Want Jesus to Walk with Me
Composer not identified
Arroyo, Martina (Soprano)
Negro Spirituals
EMI 7243 5 72790 2 4; 1998; CD
Chorus
Moderate dialect

2138

I Want Jesus to Walk with Me
Composer not identified
Arroyo, Martina (Soprano)
There's a Meeting Here Tonight
Angel S-36072; 1974; LP
Chorus

2139

I Want Jesus to Walk with Me
Boatner, Edward
Blackmon, Henry (Baritone)
Negro Spirituals
Mirasound Records SGLP 6047; [19--]; LP
Organ

2140

I Want Jesus to Walk with Me
Boatner, Edward
Blackmon, Henry (Baritone)
Negro Spirituals
Vega 19179; [19--]; LP
Chorus, piano

2141

I Want Jesus to Walk with Me
Boatner, Edward
Blackmon, Henry (Baritone)
Negro Spirituals
Stichting St. Josefkerk Discofonds
   Leidschendam JK 1006; [1964]; 45 RPM
Organ

2142

I Want Jesus to Walk with Me
Composer not identified
Carey, Thomas (Baritone)
Go Down Moses
Da Camera Song SM 95028; 1970; LP
Piano

2143

I Want Jesus to Walk with Me
Corley, Maria Thompson
Clark, Maria (Soprano)
Soul Sanctuary: Spirituals & Hymns
Navona Records NV6406; 2022; CD
Piano
Light dialect

2144

I Want Jesus to Walk with Me
Boatner, Edward
Conrad, Barbara (Mezzo-soprano)
Spirituals
Naxos 8.553036; 1995; CD
Piano
Heavy dialect

2145

I Want Jesus to Walk with Me
Cooke, Barbara Logan
Cooke, Barbara (Vocalist)
*Sometimes I Feel: A Collection of Negro
   Spirituals for Voice and Instruments*

Private Label KDISC420; 2002; CD
Instrumental ensemble

2146

I Want Jesus to Walk with Me
Composer not identified
Credit, Roosevelt André (Bass-baritone)
Get on Board
Private label; 2016; Streaming audio
Piano
Moderate dialect

2147

I Want Jesus to Walk with Me
Boatner, Edward
Davis, Osceola (Soprano)
Negro Spirituals
Ondine ODE 715-2; 1988; CD
Piano
No dialect discerned

2148

I Want Jesus to Walk with Me
Boatner, Edward
Evans, Allan (Bass-baritone)
Negro Spirituals
Electromusic Records EMCD 6885; 1985; CD
Chorus, other instrument(s)

2149

I Want Jesus to Walk with Me
Boatner, Edward
Fernandez, Wilhelmenia (Soprano)
Negro Spirituals
Transart 131; 2005; CD
Piano

2150

I Want Jesus to Walk with Me
Composer not identified
Green, Elnora E. (Contralto)
This Is My Task
Private Label NR 18650; 1991; LP

2151

I Want Jesus to Walk with Me
[Boatner, Edward]
Hagen-William, Louis (Bass-baritone)
Negro Spiritual

Quantum QM 6909; 1993; CD
Piano
Light dialect

2152

I Want Jesus to Walk with Me
Hicks, Lori
Hicks, Lori (Soprano)
Music of My Voice
CelestialSong Productions; 2015; CD
Piano

2153

I Want Jesus to Walk with Me
Boatner, Edward
Honeysucker, Robert (Baritone)
Let's Have a Union
Brave Records BRAV-0923; 2009; CD
Piano
Moderate dialect

2154

I Want Jesus
Composer not identified
Jobson, Christine (Soprano)
By Faith: Hymns and Negro Spirituals
CD Baby; 2017; CD
Piano
Heavy dialect

2155

I Want Jesus to Walk with Me
Traditional
Jones, Arthur (Tenor)
Wade in the Water
Orbis Books; 1993; Book w/cass
A cappella
Moderate dialect

2156

I Want Jesus to Walk with Me
Boatner, Edward
Kimbrough, Steven (Baritone)
The Life of Christ in Song
[Private label]; 2011; CD

2157

I Want Jesus to Walk with Me
Lindsay, Tedrin Blair; Little, Ricky

Little, Ricky (Baritone)
The Spirituals: Featuring the American
    Spiritual Ensemble
LexArts; [20--]; CD

2158

I Want Jesus to Walk wid Me
Johnson, Hall
Mayes, Doris (Mezzo-soprano)
Deep River
La voix de son maître FDLP 1080; 1959; LP
Piano

2159

I Want Jesus to Walk with Me
Composer not identified
McDaniel, Yvette (Soprano)
Simply Spiritual
YM01 DIDX 046103; 1997; CD
Piano

2160

I Want Jesus to Walk with Me
Lloyd, Charles, Jr.
Paige-Green, Jacqueline (Soprano)
The Spiritual Art Song Collection
Warner Bros. SVBM00004; 2000; Score w/
    CD
Piano

2161

I Want Jesus to Walk with Me
Boatner, Edward
Pierson, Edward (Bass-baritone)
Edward Pierson Sings Hymns and Spirituals
Kemco 98-44; [19--]; LP

2162

I Want Jesus to Walk with Me
Composer not identified
Price, Eudora (Vocalist)
Classic Duo Serbia Meets New York: From
    Handel to Spirituals
Private Label; 2007; CD
Piano

2163

Walk with Me
Sadin, Robert

Robinson, Morris (Bass)
Going Home
Decca B0008277-02; 2007; CD
Instrumental ensemble
Moderate dialect

2164

I Want Jesus to Walk with Me
Traditional
Sebron, Carolyn (Mezzo-soprano)
Resurrection, Pt. 1
Private Label; 2006; CD
A cappella
Light dialect

2165

I Want Jesus to Walk with Me
Boatner, Edward
Shirley, George (Tenor)
George Shirley at 80: My Time Has Come!
Videmus Records; 2014; CD
Piano

2166

U [sic I] Want Jesus to Walk with Me
Boatner, Edward
Simpson, Eugene Thamon (Bass)
Hear Me, Ye Winds and Waves
Black Heritage Publications; 2005; CD
Piano
Light dialect

2167

I Want Jesus to Walk with Me
Boatner, Edward
Simpson, Eugene Thamon (Bass)
Hall Johnson Spirituals and Other Folk
    Songs
Private Label; 2016; CD
Piano

2168

I Want Jesus to Walk with Me
Boatner, Edward
Spencer, Kenneth (Bass-baritone)
Volkslieder & Spirituals
Discoton 75546; [197-]; LP
Piano
Light dialect

2169

I Want Jesus to Walk with Me
Traditional
Swan, Walter (Baritone)
He's Got the Whole World in His Hands
Walter Swan; 2004; CD
A cappella
Heavy dialect

2170

I Want Jesus to Walk with Me
Composer not identified
West, Lucretia (Mezzo-soprano)
Spirituals
Westminster WL 5338; 1954; LP
Piano

2171

I Want Jesus to Walk with Me
Composer not identified
West, Lucretia (Mezzo-soprano)
Lucretia West Sings Spirituals
Westminster WP 6063; [1957]; LP

· · · · · · ·

I Want
to Be Like Jesus

2172

I Want to Be Like Jesus
Payne, John C.
Evans, Charlie (Vocalist)
Sing God's Plan
Private Label; 2005; CD
Piano
Heavy dialect

· · · · · · ·

I Want
to Be Ready

2173

I Want to Be Ready
Johnson, Hall
Blackmon, Henry (Baritone)
Negro Spirituals
Jubilate JB 1716; 1961; 45 RPM
Organ

2174

I Want to Be Ready
Burleigh, Harry T.
Burton, Dashon (Bass-baritone)
*Songs of Struggle & Redemption: We Shall
    Overcome*
Acis Productions APL08685; 2015; CD
Piano
Heavy dialect

2175

Walk in Jerusalem Just Like John
Traditional
Cheatham, Kitty (Soprano)
*Swing Low, Sweet Chariot/I Don't Feel No-
    ways Tired or "I Am Seeking for a City"/
    Walk in Jerusalem Just Like John/Sinner
    Please Don't Let This Harvest Pass*
Victor 45086; 1916; 78 RPM
A cappella
Heavy dialect

2176

I Want to Be Ready
Burleigh, Harry T.
Dadmun, Royal (Baritone)
I Want to Be Ready/Hard Trials
Gennett 4673; 1921; 78 RPM
Orchestra

2177

I Want to Be Ready
Kaelin, Pierre
Evans, Allan (Bass-baritone)
Negro Spirituals
Electromusic Records EMCD 6885; 1985; CD
Chorus, other instrument(s)

2178

I Want to Be Ready
McIntyre, Philip
Forest, Michael (Tenor)
The Spirit Sings: American Spirituals
Shenandoah Conservatory SU003; [199-]; CD

2179

I Want to Be Ready
Composer not identified
Hagen-William, Louis (Bass-baritone)

Negro Spiritual
Quantum QM 6909; 1993; CD
Piano
Light dialect

2180

I Want to Be Ready
Clinton, Irving
Irving, Clinton (Bass-baritone)
Clinton Irving Sings Spirituals: A Tribute
Rogers; 2001; CD

2172
I Want to Be Ready
Composer not identified
Jones, Fanni (Mezzo-soprano)
Negro Spirituals
Evasion Disques LP613; 1974; LP

2181

I Want to Be Ready
Miller, James
Koehler, Hope (Soprano)
The Lily of the Valley
American Spiritual Ensemble; [2003]; CD

2182

I Want to Be Ready
Simpson, Elmur
Matthews, Benjamin (Baritone)
Bon Voyage Recital @ McCormick Place
S.P.S. SS-8993-018; 1966; LP
Piano

2183

I Want to Be Ready
Composer not identified
Monzo, Oscar (Baritone)
Negro Spirituals
Dial Discos 50-2020; 1983; LP

2184

I Want to Be Ready, or, Walk in Jerusalem
   just like John
Traditional
Moses, Oral (Bass-baritone)
*Spirituals in Zion: A Spiritual Heritage for
   the Soul*
Albany Records TROY587; 2003; CD

A cappella
Light dialect

2185

I Wanna Be Ready
Miller, James
Philogene, Ruby (Soprano)
Steal Away
EMI Classics 7243 5 69707 2 4; 1997; CD
Chorus

2186

I Want to Be Ready
Composer not identified
Pickens, Jo Ann (Soprano)
*My Heritage: American Melodies/Negro
   Spirituals*
Koch Schwann 3-1447-2; 1993; CD

2187

I Want to Be Ready
Burleigh, Harry T.
Robeson, Paul (Bass-baritone)
The Complete EMI Sessions (1928–1939)
EMI Classics 50999 2 15586 2 7; 2008; CD
Piano
Heavy dialect

2188

I Want to Be Ready
Burleigh, Harry T.
Robeson, Paul (Bass-baritone)
Songs of My People
RCA Red Seal LM-3292; 1972; LP
Piano

2189

I Want to Be Ready
Burleigh, Harry T.
Robeson, Paul (Bass-baritone)
Paul Robeson Collection
Hallmark Recordings 390692; 1998; CD

2190

I Want to Be Ready
Burleigh, Harry T.
Robeson, Paul (Bass-baritone)
*Weepin' Mary/I Want to Be Ready/Git on
   Board, Lil' Chillun/Dere's No Hidin' Place*

Victor 22225; 1928; 78 RPM
Piano
Light dialect

2191

I Want to Be Ready
[Burleigh, Harry T.]
Robeson, Paul (Bass-baritone)
Ol Man River
Leverage; 2005; Streaming audio
Piano
Moderate dialect

2192

I Want to Be Ready
[Burleigh, Harry T.]
Robeson, Paul (Bass-baritone)
Ol' Man River: The Ultimate Collection
Roslin Records; 2011; Streaming audio
Piano
Moderate dialect

2193

Walk in Jerusalem Just Like John
Traditional
Sebron, Carolyn (Mezzo-soprano)
Resurrection, Pt. 1
Private Label; 2006; CD
A cappella
Light dialect

2194

I Want to Be Ready
Davis, Sam
Shelhart, John (Bass-baritone)
*Ain't Got Time to Die: Songs of the American
    Spirit*
First Presbyterian Church in the City of
    New York FPC 1002; 1997; CD
Chorus

2195

I Wanna Be Ready
Miller, John
Thompson, Jeanette (Soprano)
Negro Spirituals
Pavane Records ADW 7267; 1992; CD
Chorus
No dialect discerned

2196

I Want to Be Ready [from *Green Pastures*]
Johnson, Hall
Toppin, Louise (Soprano)
The Hall Johnson Collection
Carl Fischer VF5 CD1–VF5 CD2; 2003; Score
    w/CD
Piano
Heavy dialect

2197

I Want to Be Ready
Coil, Pat; Wilson-Felder, Cynthia
Wilson-Felder, Cynthia (Soprano)
*Spirituals: Songs from the American
    Experience*
GBGMusik CD 1-005; 1996; CD
Instrumental ensemble

2198

I Want to Be Ready
Burleigh, Harry T.
Winter, Georg (Vocalist)
Eine Kleine Hausmusik
Teldec 66.22670; 1981; LP
Piano

. . . .

I Want to Die Easy

2199

I Want to Die Easy
Smith, Hale
Albert, Donnie Ray (Baritone)
Donnie Ray Albert in Recital
Cinnabar Records CNB1402; 2003; CD
Piano
No dialect discerned

2200

I Want to Die Easy
Smith, Hale
Dry, Marion (Contralto)
Let's Have a Union
Brave Records BRAV-0923; 2009; CD
Piano
Light dialect

2201
I Want to Die Easy When I Die
Brown, Uzee, Jr.
Harris, Crystal (Mezzo-soprano)
Great Day!
Allgood; 2005; CD
Piano
Moderate dialect

2202
I Wanna Die Easy
Hicks, Lori
Hicks, Lori (Soprano)
Music of My Voice
CelestialSong Productions; 2015; CD
Piano

2203
I Want to Die Easy
Smith, Hale
Ishmael, Darnel (Bass-baritone)
The New Negro Spiritual
W. C. Patterson; 2002; Score w/CD
Piano
Heavy dialect

2204
I Want to Die Easy When I Die
Johnson, John Rosamond; Appling, William
Mims, A. Grace Lee (Soprano)
Spirituals
H & GM Records HGM 8101; 1981; LP
Piano
Moderate dialect

2205
I Want to Die Easy
Smith, Hale
Taylor, Darryl (Countertenor)
How Sweet the Sound: A Charm of Spirituals
Albany TROY1244; 2011; CD
Piano

. . . .

I Want to Go Home

2206
I Want to Go Home
Hayes, Roland

Hayes, Roland (Tenor)
Lit'l Boy/I Want to Go Home/You're Tired, Chile!
Columbia 17275-D; [1941]; 78 RPM
A cappella

2207
I Want to Go Home
[Hayes, Roland]
Hayes, Roland (Tenor)
Art Songs and Spirituals
Veritas VM 112; 1967; LP
A cappella
Light dialect

. . . .

I Want to Go to Heaven

2208
Я хочу попасть на небо (YA khochu popast' na nebo)
Composer not identified
Filatova, Ludmila (Mezzo-soprano)
Негритянские Спиричуэлс (Negrityanskiye Spirichuzls—Negro Spirituals)
Melodiâ S10 21833 009; 1985; LP
Organ
No dialect discerned

. . . .

I Was There When They Crucified My Lord

2209
I Was There When They Crucified My Lord
Composer not identified
Anderson, Marian (Contralto)
Rarities: Broadcast Performances 1943–1952
Video Artists International VAIA 1200; 1998; CD
Orchestra

2210
I Was There When They Crucified My Lord
Composer not identified
Anderson, Marian (Contralto)
Marian Anderson in Concert 1943–1952
Eklipse Records EKR CD19; 1993; CD
Orchestra

2211

I Was There When They Crucified My Lord
Composer not identified
Treigle, Norman (Bass-baritone)
I Believe
New York City Opera Guild COG 1001;
    [197-]; LP
Keyboard

. . . .

I Wish I Knew How It Would Feel to Be Free

2212

Chorus
Heavy dialect

2213

I Wish I Knew How It Would Feel to Be Free
Dallas, Dick
Price, Leontyne (Soprano)
The Essential Leontyne Price
BMG Classics 09026-68153-2; 1996; CD
Chorus
Heavy dialect

    Also released with *The Essential Leon-
tyne Price: Spirituals, Hymns & Sacred Songs*
(BMG Classics 09026-68157-2; 1996; CD) and
Leontyne Price Sings Spirituals (RCA Red
Seal 88691928242; 2012; CD)

2214

I Wish I Knew How It Would Feel to Be
    Free
Johnson, Hall
Price, Leontyne (Soprano)
I Wish I Knew How It Would Feel to Be Free
RCA Red Seal LSC 3183; 2011; CD
Chorus
Heavy dialect

2215

I Wish I Knew How It Would Feel to Be
    Free
Taylar, Billy; Bonds, Margaret
Price, Leontyne (Soprano)
The Best of Negro Spirituals
BMG BVCM-37416; 2003; CD

Chorus
Moderate dialect

. . . .

If He Change My Name

2216

If He Change My Name
MacGimsey, Robert
Anderson, Marian (Contralto)
Spirituals
RCA Victor Red Seal 09026-63306-2; 1999;
    CD
Piano
Heavy dialect

2217

If He Change My Name
MacGimsey, Robert
Anderson, Marian (Contralto)
Negro Spirituals
RCA Victor LM 2032; [1956]; LP
Piano
Light dialect

    Also released with *Marian Anderson:
Beyond the Music; Her Complete RCA Victor
Recordings* Sony Classical 19439836492; 2021;
CD

2218

If He Change My Name
[MacGimsey, Robert]
Anderson, Marian (Contralto)
*Marian Anderson Sings Eleven Great
    Spirituals*
RCA Victor LRM 7006; 1955; LP
Piano

    Also released with *Marian Anderson
Sings Eleven Great Spirituals* (Kipepeo Publishing; 2017; CD)

2219

If He Change My Name
[MacGimsey, Robert]
Anderson, Marian (Contralto)
Alto Rhapsody; Selected Spirituals
Urania URN 22.328; 2007; CD
Piano

2220

If He Change My Name
[MacGimsey, Robert]
Anderson, Marian (Contralto)
The Very Best of Marian Anderson
Master Classics Records; 2009; CD
Piano
Light dialect

2221

If He Change My Name
[MacGimsey, Robert]
Anderson, Marian (Contralto)
Negro Spirituals
RCA Victor 630.396 A; [19--]; LP
Piano

2222

If He Change My Name
[MacGimsey, Robert]
Anderson, Marian (Contralto)
Grandes Contraltos de la Musique Classique, Les: Marian Anderson, Vol. 3
Mon Patrimoine Musical Collection; 2017; Streaming audio
Piano

2223

If He Changes My Name
Robbiani, Mario
Fisher, Dorothy (Contralto)
Negro Spirituals
Edizione D'Arte Del Lions Club Milano Al Cenacolo; [19--]; LP
Orchestra
Moderate dialect

2224

If He Changed Mah Name
Composer not identified
Matthews, Benjamin (Baritone)
Opera Ebony Sings Spirituals
Ebony Classic Recordings; 2002; CD

2225

If He Changed My Name
Thomas, André J.
Tucker, Eric Hoy (Bass-baritone)
Southern Salute: Southern Songs & Spirituals
White Pine Music WPM218; 2012; CD
Piano
Light dialect

. . . .

I'll Hear de Trumpet

2226

I'll Hear de Trumpet
Brown, Lawrence
Robeson, Paul (Bass-baritone)
Paul Robeson Sings Negro Spirituals
Philips GBL 5584; [19--]; LP
Piano

2227

I'll Hear de Trumpet
Brown, Lawrence
Robeson, Paul (Bass-baritone)
Swing Low, Sweet Chariot
Columbia Masterworks MM-819; 1949; 78 RPM
Piano

2228

I'll Hear de Trumpet
Brown, Lawrence
Robcson, Paul (Bass-baritone)
Paul Robeson Chante ... f16 Spirituals
Philips G 05.639 R; 1959; LP
Piano

2229

I'll Hear de Trumpet
[Brown, Lawrence]
Robeson, Paul (Bass-baritone)
Swing Low, Sweet Chariot
Columbia Masterworks ML 2038; [195-]; LP
Piano

2230

I'll Hear the Trumpet Sound
Brown, Lawrence
Robeson, Paul (Bass-baritone)
Paul Robeson in Live Performance

Columbia M 30424; 1971; LP
Piano
Light dialect

. . . .

I'll Make Me a Man

2231

I'll Make Me a Man
Hayes, Roland
Caesar, Jackson (Tenor)
*Spirituals: Celebrating the Music, Life,
    Legacy of Roland Hayes*
CD Baby 7048606059; 2021; CD
Piano, percussion
No dialect discerned

2232

I'll Make Me a Man
Hayes, Roland
Caesar, Jackson (Tenor)
*Spirituals: Celebrating the Music, Life,
    Legacy of Roland Hayes*
CD Baby 7048606059; 2021; CD
Piano [no percussion]
No dialect discerned

2233

I'll Make Me a Man
Hayes, Roland
Hayes, Roland (Tenor)
Roland Hayes: My Songs
Vanguard VRS-494; 1956; LP
Piano

2234

I'll Make Me a Man [from *My Songs: Dream
    of Heaven*]
Hayes, Roland
Hayes, Roland (Tenor)
Favorite Spirituals
Vanguard Classics OVC 6022; 1995; CD
Piano
Heavy dialect

    Also released with *Big Psalms, Hymns
and Spirituals Box* (eOne Music/Vanguard
Classics; 2015; Streaming audio)

. . . .

I'll Never Turn Back
No More

2235

Never Turn Back
Santiago, Jeanette
Burton, Marta (Vocalist)
They Slice the Air
Spirituals Project; 2007; CD
Flute, guitar
No dialect discerned

2236

Never Turn Back No More
Handy, W. C.
Davis, Osceola (Soprano)
Negro Spirituals
Ondine ODE 715-2; 1988; CD
Piano

2237

I'll Never Turn Back
Handy, William C.
Heard, Richard (Tenor)
*Ain't a That Good News: African-American
    Art Songs and Spirituals*
HM Classics HMC9602; 1998; CD
Piano
No dialect discerned

2238

I'll Never Turn Back
Simpson, Elmer A.
Matthews, Benjamin (Baritone)
A Balm in Gilead
Ebony Classic Recordings ECR 0001; 2000;
    CD
Piano

. . . .

I'll Reach to Heaven

2239

I'll Reach to Heaven [from *Five Creek-
    Freedmen Spirituals*]
Bonds, Margaret
Blackmon, Henry (Baritone)

Geestelijke Liederen En Negro Spirituals
Mirasound Records SGLP 6047; 1974; LP
Piano

2240
I'll Reach to Heaven [from *Five Creek-Freedmen Spirituals*]
Bonds, Margaret
Honeysucker, Robert (Baritone)
Good News
Videmus Records VIS735; 2007; CD
Piano
Light dialect

2241
I'll Reach to Heaven [from *Five Creek-Freedmen Spirituals*]
Bonds, Margaret
Taylor, Darryl (Countertenor)
How Sweet the Sound: A Charm of Spirituals
Albany TROY1244; 2011; CD
Piano

. . . .

I'm a Poor Lil' Orphan

2242
I'm a Poor Lil' Orphan
Perry, Julia
Hamilton, Ruth (Contralto)
Watch and Pray: Spirituals and Art Songs by African-American Women Composers
Koch International Classics 3-7247-2H1; 1994; CD
Piano
Heavy dialect

2243
I'm a Po' Lil' Orphan in Dis Worl'
Perry, Julia
Harris, Inetta (Soprano)
My Heritage Sings: A Selection of Spirituals & Hymns
Private Label; [199-]; CD
Piano

2244
I'm a Po' Lil' Orphan
Composer not identified

McKelton, Samuel (Tenor)
Done Crossed Every River: Freedom's Journey
Arcadia ARC 2004-2; 1995; CD

2245
I'm a Po' Lil' Orphan
Jessye, Eva
McKelton, Samuel (Tenor)
Opera Ebony Sings Spirituals
Ebony Classic Recordings; 2002; CD

2246
I'm a Po' Lil Orphan in Dis Worl
Perry, Julia
Oglesby, Isador (Tenor)
Negro Spirituals: The Musical Roots of American Folk Songs
Praise PR 658; 1978; LP
Piano

2247
I'm a Poor Lil' Orphan
Perry, Julia
Pleas III, Henry H. (Tenor)
Come Down Angels!
The Unveiled Voices Project; 2017; Streaming audio
Piano
Light dialect

2248
I'm a Poor Lil' Orphan
Perry, Julia
Pleas III, Henry H. (Tenor)
Come Down Angels: A Program of Vocal Works by Women Composers
The Unveiled Voices Project; 2016; CD
Piano
Light dialect

2249
I'm a Poor Little Orphan in This World!
Composer not identified
Verrett, Shirley (Soprano)
The Very Best of Gospel
Disconforme CDX7720; 2007; CD

2250
I'm a Poor Little Orphan in This World!
Perry, Julia

Verrett, Shirley (Mezzo-soprano)
Shirley Verrett Recital
Suiza OSCD 223; 1991; CD
Piano

2251

I'm a Poor Little Orphan in This World!
Perry, Julia
Verrett, Shirley (Mezzo-soprano)
Gospels & Spirituals Gold Collection
Retro R2CD 40-26; 1995; CD
Piano
Heavy dialect

. . . .

I'm a-Rollin'

2252

I'm a-Rollin'
Composer not identified
Chaiter, Yoram (Bass)
Spirituals & Other Songs
Romeo Records 7311; 2014; CD
Piano
Light dialect

2253

I'm a-Rollin'
Composer not identified
Corbett, Patricia (Soprano)
Patricia Corbett Sings…. Best Loved Songs
RCA Victor Custom GO8P-0267; [1956]; LP

2254

I'm a' Rolling through an Unfriendly
    World
Composer not identified
Davis, Frank (Bass-baritone)
16 Spirituals My Father Taught Me
DeWitt Records 601; 1960; LP

2255

I'm a Rollin'
Composer not identified
Essin, Sonia (Contralto)
The Art of Sonia Essin
Orion ORS 77271; 1977; LP
Piano
Light dialect

2256

I'm a Rollin'
Composer not identified
Moses, Oral (Bass-baritone)
Extreme Spirituals
Cuneiform Record Rune 241; 2006; CD
Instrumental ensemble

2257

I'm a Rollin'
Traditional
Moses, Oral (Bass-baritone)
*Spirituals in Zion: A Spiritual Heritage for
    the Soul*
Albany Records TROY587; 2003; CD
A cappella
Light dialect

2258

I'm a Rolling
Composer not identified
Porter, John (Bass)
No More Crying: Negro Spirituals
Pan Verlag OV-84; [1978]; LP

. . . .

I'm Buildin' Me a Home

2259

I'm Buildin' Me a Home
Composer not identified
McCoy, Claurice (Vocalist); Comstock,
    Anne (Vocalist)
They Slice the Air
Spirituals Project; 2007; CD
Chorus
Light dialect

. . . .

I'm Goin' Home on Mornin' Train

2260

I'm Goin' Home on Mornin' Train
Sims, Robert
Sims, Robert (Baritone)
*Soul of a Singer: Robert Sims Sings African-
    American Folk Songs*

Canti Classics 9801; 2013; CD
A cappella
Heavy dialect

. . . .

I'm Goin' to March Down to Jordan

2261

I'm Goin' to March Down to Jordan
Work, John Wesley
Davis, Ellabelle (Soprano)
Soon I Will Be Done/I'm Goin' to March Down to Jordan
Philips A 56002 H; 1952; 78 RPM
Piano

2262

I'm Goin' to March Down to Jordan
Work, J[ohn Wesley]
Peete, Jerry (Tenor)
Songs of Schubert, Lassen, Ives, McDowell and others
Silver Crest CRS 72280; [197-]; LP
Piano

. . . .

I'm Goin' to Thank God

2263

I'm Goin' to Thank God
Dett, Robert Nathaniel
Mims, A. Grace Lee (Soprano)
Spirituals
H & GM Records HGM 8101; 1981; LP
Piano
Heavy dialect

. . . .

I'm Going Down to the Ribber of Jordan

2264

I'm Going Down to the Ribber of Jordan
Composer not identified
Spencer, Kenneth (Bass-baritone)
Negro Spirituals
Life Records C 1108; [19--]; LP

. . . .

I'm Going to Tell God All My Troubles

2265

I'm Goin' to Tell God All My Troubles
Brown, Lawrence
Blackmon, Henry (Baritone)
Negro Spirituals
Mirasound Records SGLP 6047; [19--]; LP
Organ

2266

I'm Goin' to Tell God All My Troubles
Brown, Lawrence
Blackmon, Henry (Baritone)
Negro Spirituals
Vega 19179; [19--]; LP
Chorus, piano

2267

I'm Go'n'ter Tell God All o' My Troubles
Johnson, Hall
Brown, William (Tenor)
The Hall Johnson Collection
Carl Fischer VF5 CD1–VF5 CD2; 2003; Score w/CD
Piano
Moderate dialect

2268

I'm Gonna Tell God All o' My Troubles
Composer not identified
Carey, Thomas (Baritone)
Sechs Amerikanische Volkslieder/Sechs Negro Spirituals
Colosseum SM 3003; 1970; LP
Orchestra

2269

I'm Gonna Tell God All'a My Troubles
[Brown, Lawrence]
Duncan, Todd (Baritone)
American Negro Spirituals
Allegro LEG 9026; [19--]; LP

2270

I'm Gonna Tell God All My Troubles
[Brown, Lawrence]

Duncan, Todd (Baritone)
America's Great Baritone: Sings Folk Songs
Royale EP181; [195-]; 45 RPM

2271

I'm Goin' to Tell God All My Troubles
Brown, Lawrence
Duncan, Todd (Baritone)
Negro Spirituals
Allegro ALG3022; [1952]; LP
Piano
Light dialect

     Also released with *African American Spirituals* ([Apple Music]; 2008; Streaming audio)

2272

I'm Gonna Tell God All o' My Troubles
Johnson, Hall
Foreman, Blanche (Contralto)
Best of the Hall Johnson Centennial Festival Celebrating the 100th Anniversary of Hall Johnson's Birth
Hall Johnson Collection O33D2; 2002; CD
Piano

2273

I'm Gonter Tell God All of My Troubles
Johnson, Hall
Kirkham, Robert (Baritone)
Song Recital by Robert Kirkham
Epworth EP 8521; [197-]; LP
Piano

2274

I'm Go'n'ter Tell God All o' My Troubles
Johnson, Hall
Lewis, Cheryse McLeod (Mezzo-soprano)
Spirituals
CheryseMusic; 2012; CD
Piano

2275

I'm Goin' to Tell God All My Troubles
Brown, Lawrence
Matthews, Inez (Mezzo-soprano)
Inez Matthews Sings Spirituals
Essential Media Group; 2011; CD

Piano
Moderate dialect

2276

I'm Goin' to Tell God All My Troubles
Brown, Lawrence
Matthews, Inez (Mezzo-soprano)
Inez Matthews Sings Spirituals (Great New Voices of Today, v. 6)
Period SPL-580; [1950]; LP
Piano
Moderate dialect

2277

I'm Gonter Tell God All o' My Troubles
Johnson, Hall
Mayes, Doris (Mezzo-soprano)
Deep River
La voix de son maître FDLP 1080; 1959; LP
Piano

2278

I'm Goin' to Tell God All My Troubles
Dett, Robert Nathaniel
Maynor, Dorothy (Soprano)
Dorothy Maynor in Concert at Library of Congress
Library of Congress, Music Division LCM 2141; 2007; CD
Piano
Heavy dialect

2279

I'm Goin' to Tell God All My Troubles
Dett, Robert Nathaniel
Maynor, Dorothy (Soprano)
Dorothy Maynor, Soprano
Bridge Records 9233; 2007; CD
Piano
Heavy dialect

2280

I'm Gonter Tell God All o' My Troubles
Johnson, Hall
McFerrin, Robert (Baritone)
Deep River and Other Classic Negro Spirituals
Riverside Records RLP 12-812; 1959; LP

Piano
Heavy dialect

2281

I'm Gonter Tell God All o' My Troubles
Johnson, Hall
McFerrin, Robert (Baritone)
Classic Negro Spirituals
Washington Records WLP 466; 1959; LP
Piano
Heavy dialect

2282

I'm Gonna Tell God All My Troubles
Johnson, Hall
Miles, John (Tenor)
The Classic Spirituals
Epiphany 83-1027; 1983; LP
Instrumental ensemble

2283

I'm Gonna Tell God
Johnson, Hall
Pierson, Edward (Bass-baritone)
Edward Pierson Sings Hymns and Spirituals
Kemco 98-44; [19--]; LP

2284

I'm Gonter Tell God All o' My Troubles
Johnson, Hall
Quivar, Florence (Mezzo-soprano)
Negro Spirituals
EMI 7243 5 72790 2 4; 1998; CD
Piano
Heavy dialect
    Also released with *Ride On, King Jesus!*
Florence Quivar Sings Black Music of America (EMI Classics 9 67138 2; 2010; CD)

2285

I'm Goin' to Tell God All o' My Troubles
Brown, Lawrence
Robeson, Paul (Bass-baritone)
Songs of My People
RCA Red Seal LM-3292; 1972; LP
Piano

2286

I'm Goin' to Tell God All o' My Troubles
Brown, Lawrence

Robeson, Paul (Bass-baritone)
Spirituals: Original Recordings 1925–1936
Naxos Gospel Legends 8.120638; 2003; CD
Piano

2287

I'm Goin' to Tell God All o' My Troubles
Brown, Lawrence
Robeson, Paul (Bass-baritone)
*A Lonesome Road: Paul Robeson Sings
    Spirituals and Songs*
ASV Living Era CD AJA 5027; 1984; CD
Piano
Moderate dialect

2288

I'm Goin to Tell God All o My Troubles
Brown, Lawrence
Robeson, Paul (Bass-baritone)
*Deep River/I'm Goin to Tell God All o My
    Troubles*
Victor 20793; 1927; 78 RPM
Piano

2289

I'm Goin' to Tell God All o' My Troubles
Brown, Lawrence
Robeson, Paul (Bass-baritone)
Paul Robeson Collection
Hallmark Recordings 390692; 1998; CD

2290

I'm Goin' to Tell God All o' My Troubles
Brown, Lawrence
Robeson, Paul (Bass-baritone)
*Deep River/I'm Goin' to Tell God All o' My
    Troubles*
His Master's Voice B 2619; 1928; 78 RPM
Piano
Light dialect

2291

I'm Goin' to Tell God All My Troubles
Brown, Lawrence
Robeson, Paul (Bass-baritone)
*V-Disc: The Songs That Went to War (World
    War II 50th Anniversary Collector's Edition)*
Time-Life Music R139-39/OPCD-4537; 1992;
    CD

Piano
Light dialect

2292
I'm Gonna Tell God All o' My Troubles
[Brown, Lawrence]
Robeson, Paul (Bass-baritone)
Paul Robeson: Great Voices of the Century,
    v. 1
Memoir Classics CDMOIR 415; 1992; CD
Piano

2293
I'm Goin to Tell God All o My Troubles
[Brown, Lawrence]
Robeson, Paul (Bass-baritone)
Ol Man River
Leverage; 2005; Streaming audio
Piano
Light dialect

2294
I'm Going to Tell God All o' My Troubles
[Brown, Lawrence]
Robeson, Paul (Bass-baritone)
Ol' Man River: The Ultimate Collection
Roslin Records; 2011; Streaming audio
Piano
Moderate dialect

2295
I'm Gonna Tell God All My Troubles
Johnson, Hall
Shirley, George (Tenor)
George Shirley at 80: My Time Has Come!
Videmus Records; 2014; CD
Piano

2296
I'm Gonter Tell God All o' My Troubles
Johnson, Hall
Simpson, Eugene Thamon (Bass)
Thanks Be to Thee
Black Heritage Publications; 2005; CD
Piano

2297
I'm Gonter Tell God All of My Troubles
Johnson, Hall

Simpson, Eugene Thamon (Bass)
Hall Johnson Spirituals and Other Folk
    Songs
Private Label; 2016; CD
Piano

2298
I'm Goin' to Tell God All o' My Troubles
Brown, [Lawrence]
Spencer, Kenneth (Bass-baritone)
Volkslieder & Spirituals
Discoton 75546; [197-]; LP
Piano
Heavy dialect

2299
I'm Gonna Tell God All My Troubles
Johnson, Hall
Toppin, Louise (Soprano)
He'll Bring It to Pass: The Spirituals of Hall
    Johnson for Voice and Piano
Albany Records TROY846; 2006; CD
Piano
Heavy dialect

2300
I'm Goin' to Tell God All My Troubles
Robeson, Paul (Bass-baritone)
Head Like a Rock/Lindy Lou/Deep
    River/I'm Goin' to Tell God All My
    Troubles
V Disc 51; 1943; 78 RPM

. . . .

I'm Gonna Sing When the Spirit Says Sing

2301
I'm Gonna Sing When the Spirit Says-a
    Sing
Traditional
Jones, Arthur (Tenor)
Wade in the Water
Orbis Books; 1993; Book w/cass
A cappella
Moderate dialect

. . . .

I'm Just Goin' Over Jordan

2302

I'm Just a-Goin' Over Jordan
Suben, Joel Eric
Lennick, Jessica (Soprano)
*Five Spirituals for Soprano and
     Orchestra*
Private label; 2018; Streaming audio
Orchestra
Light dialect

. . . .

I'm Seekin' for a City

2303

I'm Seekin' for a City
Johnson, Hall
Bryant, Peter (Vocalist)
I Will Pass This Way but Once
Facts of Faith Records WR 5161; 1977;
     LP
Organ

2304

I'm Seckin' for a City
Hayes, Roland
Maynor, Dorothy (Soprano)
*Dorothy Maynor in Concert at Library of
     Congress*
Library of Congress, Music Division LCM
     2141; 2007; CD
Piano
Light dialect

2305

I'm Seekin' for a City
Haycs, Roland
Maynor, Dorothy (Soprano)
Dorothy Maynor, Soprano
Bridge Records 9233; 2007; CD
Piano
Light dialect

. . . .

I'm So Glad Trouble Don't Last Always

2306

I'm So Glad Trouble Don't Last Always
Sanders, Wayne
Anonymous (Vocalist)
Opera Ebony Sings Spirituals
Ebony Classic Recordings; 2002; CD

2307

I'm So Glad Trouble Don't Last Always
Composer not identified
Ayers, Vanessa (Mezzo-soprano); Matthews,
     Benjamin (Baritone)
Done Crossed Every River: Freedom's Journey
Arcadia ARC 2004-2; 1995; CD

2308

I'm So Glad Trouble Don't Last Alway
Dett, Robert Nathaniel
Clark, Clarence Carroll (Baritone)
*Deep River/I'm So Glad Trouble Don't Last
     Alway*
Columbia 128D; 1924; 78 RPM
Piano
No dialect discerned

2309

I'm So Glad Trouble Don't Last Always
[Dett, Robert Nathaniel]
Clark, Clarence Carroll (Baritone)
*The Road Beyond/I'm So Glad Trouble Don't
     Last Always*
Paramount 33137; 1924; 78 RPM
Piano
No dialect discerned

2310

I'm So Glad Trouble Don't Last Alway
Dett, Robert Nathaniel
Delmore, Harry A. (Tenor)
*Swing Low, Sweet Chariot/I'm So Glad
     Trouble Don't Last Alway*
Grey Gull 9001; [1924]; 78 RPM
Piano
No dialect discerned

2311

I'm So Glad Trouble Don't Last Always
Composer not identified
Hayes, Roland (Tenor)
Afro-American Folksongs
Pelican Records LP 2028; 1983; LP
Piano

2312

I'm So Glad Trouble Don't Last Always
Dett, Robert Nathaniel
Hayes, Roland (Tenor)
The Art of Roland Hayes
Smithsonian Collection RD 041; 1990; CD
Piano
Light dialect

2313

I'm So Glad Trouble Don't Last Alway
Dett, Robert Nathaniel
Reavis, Hattie King (Soprano)
*There Is a Green Hill Far Away/I'm So Glad
    Trouble Don't Last Always*
Black Swan 7106; [1921]; 78 RPM
Orchestra

. . . .

I'm Traveling
to the Grave

2314

I'm a Trav'ling to the Grave
Hershberger, A. J.
Brown, Anthony (Baritone)
Toil and Triumph
Spirituals Project; 2002; CD
Chorus
Moderate dialect

2315

I'm a-Travelin' to the Grave
Dett, Robert Nathaniel
Brown, William (Tenor)
*Fi-Yer!: a century of African American
    song*
Albany Records TROY 329; 1999; CD
Piano
Heavy dialect

2316

I'm a Travelling to the Grave
Dett, Robert Nathaniel
Davis, Ellabelle (Soprano)
Ellabelle Davis Sings Negro Spirituals
London LPS 182; [1950]; LP
Piano
Moderate dialect

> Also released with *Recital of Negro Spirituals by Ellabelle Davis* (Decca LM.4504; [1950]; LP) and *Great Negro Spirituals* (Replay Record; 2013; Streaming audio)

2317

Travelin' to de Grave
Dett, Robert Nathaniel
Oglesby, Isador (Tenor)
*Negro Spirituals: The Musical Roots of
    American Folk Songs*
Praise PR 658; 1978; LP
Piano

. . . .

I'm Troubled

2318

I'm Troubled [from *My Songs: Dream of
    Heaven*]
Hayes, Roland
Hayes, Roland (Tenor)
Roland Hayes: My Songs
Vanguard VRS-494; 1956; LP
Piano

> Also released with *Favorite Spirituals* (Vanguard Classics OVC 6022; 1995; CD) and
>
> *Big Psalms, Hymns and Spirituals Box* (eOne Music/Vanguard Classics; 2015; Streaming audio)

2319

I'm Troubled in Mind
Boatner, Edward
Hendricks, Barbara (Soprano)
Give Me Jesus
EMI Classics 7243 5 56788 2 9; 1998; CD
A cappella
Moderate dialect

2320

I'm Troubled
Composer not identified
Pleas III, Henry H. (Tenor)
Deep River: A Spiritual Journey
Rowe House Productions; 1999; CD

· · · · · · ·

I'm Working on My Building

2321

I'm Working on My Building
Price, Florence
Heard, Richard (Tenor)
My Dream: Art Songs and Spirituals
Percentage Records/Sound of Art
    Recordings CD147597; 2012; CD
Piano
Heavy dialect

2322

I'm Workin' on My Buildin'
Price, Florence
Rhodes, Yolanda (Soprano)
The Angels Bowed Down
Cambria Master Recordings CD-1237; 2019;
    CD

2323

I'm Workin' on My Buildin'
Composer not identified
Robinson, Marie Hadley (Soprano)
Come Down Angels
Meyer Media; 2011; Streaming audio
Piano
Heavy dialect

· · · · · · ·

In a' Dat Mornin'

2324

In a' Dat Mornin'
Hayes, Roland
Jenkins, Isaiah (Tenor)
Lyric Tenor
Trans Radio TR 1010A; [195-]; LP
Piano

· · · · · · ·

In Bright Mansions

2325

In Bright Mansions
Johnson, Hall
Clemmons, François (Tenor)
Negro Spirituals Live! In Concert
American Negro Spiritual Research
    Foundation 8177 2048 3779; 1998; CD
Piano
No dialect discerned

2326

In Bright Mansions Above
de Paur, Leonard; Roberts, Howard
Quivar, Florence (Mezzo-soprano)
Great American Spirituals
Angel CDM 7 64669 2; 1992; CD
Chorus
Light dialect

    Also released with *Great American Spir-
    ituals* (Musical Heritage Society 513725Z;
    1994; CD); *Negro Spirituals* (EMI 7243 5
    72790 2 4; 1998; CD) and *Ride On, King Jesus!
    Florence Quivar Sings Black Music of America*
    (EMI Classics 9 67138 2; 2010; CD)

2327

In Bright Mansions Above [from *Green
    Pastures*]
Johnson, Hall
Toppin, Louise (Soprano)
The Hall Johnson Collection
Carl Fischer VF5 CD1–VF5 CD2; 2003; Score
    w/CD
Piano
Moderate dialect

· · · · · · ·

In That Great Getting Up Morning

2328

Great Gittin' Up Mornin'
Composer not identified
Allen, Betty (Mezzo-soprano)
On Wings of Song

RCA Custom Reader's Digest RDA43-A;
[1960]; LP
Chorus, instrumental ensemble
Moderate dialect

2329

Great Gittin' Up Mornin'
Brown, Lawrence
Anderson, Marian (Contralto)
*He's Got the Whole World in His Hands:
Spirituals*
RCA Victor 09026-6[1960]2; 1994; CD
Piano
Heavy dialect

2330

Great Gittin' Up Mornin'
Brown, Lawrence
Anderson, Marian (Contralto)
*Marian Anderson: Beyond the Music; Her
Complete RCA Victor Recordings*
Sony Classical 19439836492; 2021; CD
Piano
Heavy dialect

2331

In That Great Getting Up Morning
Marsh, Don; Russ, Patrick
Battle, Kathleen (Soprano); Norman, Jessye
(Soprano)
Spirituals in Concert
Deutsche Grammophon 429 790-2; 1991; CD
Chorus, orchestra
Heavy dialect

2332

Утро великого воскресенья (Utro velikogo
voskresen'ya)
Composer not identified
Filatova, Ludmila (Mezzo-soprano)
*Негритянские Спиричуэлс (Negrityanskiye
Spirichuzls—Negro Spirituals)*
Melodiâ S10 21833 009; 1985; LP
Organ
Light dialect

2333

In Dat Great Gittin' Up Mornin'
Composer not identified

Heard, William N. (Vocalist)
*Songs from the Sanctuary: Hymns, Spirituals
& Classic Gospels, Volume II*
Heardsong Productions; 2012; CD
Chorus

2334

In Dat Great Gittin' Up Morning
Composer not identified
Maynor, Dorothy (Soprano)
The Art of Dorothy Maynor
RCA Red Seal LM 3086; 1969; LP
Men's voices

2335

In Dat Great Gittin' Up Morning
Composer not identified
Maynor, Dorothy (Soprano)
Spirituals, Arias, Songs ([1940]1943)
Claremont CD GSE 78-50-59; 1994; CD
Chorus

2336

In Dat Great Gittin' Up Morning
Composer not identified
Maynor, Dorothy (Soprano)
Negro Spirituals
RCA Victor M879; 1942; 78 RPM
Men's voices

Also released with *Dorothy Maynor
Sings Spirituals and Sacred Songs* (RCA
Camden CAL-344; 1957; LP) and *Negro Spir-
ituals* (Kipepeo Publishing; 2018; CD)

2337

Great Gittin Up Morning
Pankey, Aubrey
Pankey, Aubrey (Baritone)
Negro Spirituals
Eterna 830010; 1983; LP
Piano

2338

Great Gittin' Up Mornin'
Brown, Lawrence
Robeson, Paul (Bass-baritone)
Paul Robeson Sings Negro Spirituals
Philips GBL 5584; [19--]; LP
Piano

2339

Great Gittin' Up Mornin'
Brown, Lawrence
Robeson, Paul (Bass-baritone)
Swing Low, Sweet Chariot
Columbia Masterworks MM-819; 1949; 78
    RPM
Piano

2340

Great Gittin' Up Mornin
Brown, Lawrence
Robeson, Paul (Bass-baritone); Brown,
    Lawrence (Vocalist)
Paul Robeson Chante ... f16 Spirituals
Philips G 05.639 R; 1959; LP
Piano

2341

Great Gittin' Up Mornin'
[Brown, Lawrence]
Robeson, Paul (Bass-baritone)
Swing Low, Sweet Chariot
Columbia Masterworks ML 2038; [195-]; LP
Piano

· · · · · · ·

In That Morning

2342

In That Morning
Composer not identified
Charles, Lee (Tenor)
*Swing Low Sweet Chariot: And Other
    Spirituals*
Riverside RLP 12-651; 1957; LP
Piano, guitar

2343

In-a Dat Mornin'
Hayes, Roland
Hayes, Roland (Tenor)
Roland Hayes: My Songs
Vanguard VRS-494; 1956; LP
Piano

2344

In-a-da-Morning
[Hayes, Roland]

Hayes, Roland (Tenor)
Big Psalms, Hymns and Spirituals Box
eOne Music/Vanguard Classics; 2015;
    Streaming audio
Piano

2345

In That Mornin'
Dett, Robert Nathaniel
Peterson, Elwood (Baritone)
Negro Spirituals
Boîte à Musique LD 073; 1961; LP
Piano

· · · · · · ·

*Is Massa Gonna
Sell Us Tomorrow*

2346

Is Massa Gonna Sell Us Tomorrow?
Composer not identified
Carlsen, Svein (Bass)
Negro Spirituals
EuroMaster AS ECD19005; 1996; CD
Piano

2347

Is Massa Gonna Sell Us Tomorrow?
Composer not identified
Foye, Hope (Soprano)
*The Best of Hope Foye: 20th and 21st Century
    Legendary Song Collection*
Permanent Productions PP00115; 2010; CD

· · · · · · ·

*Is There Anybody
Here That Loves
My Jesus*

2348

Is There Anybody Here Who Loves My
    Jesus?
Byler, L & M
Brown, Anthony (Baritone)
Toil and Triumph
Spirituals Project; 2002; CD
Piano
Light dialect

2349

Is There Anybody Here That Loves My
    Jesus
Smith Moore, Undine
Dillard, Pamela (Mezzo-soprano)
*Watch and Pray: Spirituals and Art Songs by
    African-American Women Composers*
Koch International Classics 3-7247-2H1;
    1994; CD
Piano
Heavy dialect

2350

Is There Anybody Here?
Carter, Roland
Lee, Albert R. (Tenor)
The Lily of the Valley
American Spiritual Ensemble; [2003]; CD
Piano

2351

Is There Anybody Here Love My Jesus?
Carter, Roland
Matthews, Benjamin (Baritone)
A Balm in Gilead
Ebony Classic Recordings ECR 0001; 2000;
    CD
Piano

2352

Is There Anybody Here?
[Carter, Roland]
Miller-Sydney, Audrey (Soprano)
*Climbing High Mountains: African
    American Art Songs and Spirituals*
Private Label; 2004; CD
Piano
No dialect discerned

2353

Is There Anybody Here That Loves My Jesus
Smith Moore, Undine
Moses, Oral (Bass-baritone)
*Come Down Angels and Trouble the Water:
    Negro Spirituals, an American National
    Treasure!*
Albany Records TROY 1489; 2014; CD
Piano
Light dialect

Also released with *Sankofa: A Spiritual
Reflection* (Albany Records TROY1802; 2019;
CD)

2354

Is There Anybody Here?
Carter, Roland
Robinson-Oturo, Gail (Soprano)
*Sweetest Sound I Ever Heard: Spirituals for
    Solo Voice and Piano, Vol. 1*
CD Baby; 2020; Streaming audio
Piano
Light dialect

2355

Is There Anybody Here
Carter, Roland
Salters, Stephen (Baritone)
Spirit: Are You There, You Are There
HarmonizedDisharmony 0001; 2015; CD

2356

Is There Anybody Here Who Loves My
    Jesus
Carter, Roland
Sims, Robert (Baritone)
*Soul of a Singer: Robert Sims Sings African-
    American Folk Songs*
Canti Classics 9801; 2013; CD
Piano
Heavy dialect

2357

Is There Anybody Here Who Loves My
    Jesus
Carter, Roland
Sims, Robert (Baritone)
*In the Spirit: Spirituals and American Songs
    with Orchestra and Chorus*
Canti Classics; 2009; CD
Orchestra
Heavy dialect

2358

Is There Anybody Here?
Carter, Roland
Taylor, Darryl (Countertenor)
*How Sweet the Sound: A Charm of
    Spirituals*

Albany TROY1244; 2011; CD
Piano

. . . .

Is There Anybody Waitin' for Me

2359

Is There Anybody Waitin' for Me
Composer not identified
Oglesby, Isador (Tenor)
Life of Jesus in Negro Spirituals
Oglesby Recordings Album 2; 1980; LP
Piano

. . . .

I've Been 'Buked

2360

I've Been 'Buked
Johnson, Hall
Anderson, Marian (Contralto)
He's Got the Whole World in His Hands:
Spirituals
RCA Victor 09026-6[1960]2; 1994; CD
Piano
Heavy dialect

2361

I've Been 'Buked
Johnson, Hall
Anderson, Marian (Contralto)
Jus' Keep on Singin'
RCA Victor LSC 2796; 1965; LP
Piano
Moderate dialect

Also released with *Marian Anderson:*
Beyond the Music; Her Complete RCA Victor
Recordings Sony Classical 19439836492; 2021;
CD

2362

I've Been Buked
Cooke, Barbara Logan
Cooke, Barbara (Vocalist)
Sometimes I Feel: A Collection of Negro
Spirituals for Voice and Instruments

Private Label KDISC420; 2002; CD
Instrumental ensemble

2363

I've Been 'Buked
Johnson, Hall; Roberts, Howard
Quivar, Florence (Mezzo-soprano)
Great American Spirituals
Angel CDM 7 64669 2; 1992; CD
Chorus
Moderate dialect

Also released with *Great American Spir-*
ituals (Musical Heritage Society 513725Z;
1994; CD); *Negro Spirituals* (EMI 7243 5
72790 2 4; 1998; CD) and *Ride On, King Jesus!*
Florence Quivar Sings Black Music of America
(EMI Classics 9 67138 2; 2010; CD)

2364

I've Been 'Buked
Composer not identified
Rustin, Bayard (Tenor)
Bayard Rustin Sings Spirituals, Work &
Freedom Songs
Bayard Rustin Fund; 1988; Cassette
Piano
Heavy dialect

Also released with *Bayard Rustin Sings*
Spirituals, Work & Freedom Songs (Bayard
Rustin Fund; 2003; CD)

2365

I'se Been Buked/Gonna Lay Down My Life
Campbell, Colin M.
Thomas, Edna (Soprano)
Classic Gospel Songs
Emerald/K-Tel; 2013; Streaming audio
Piano
Heavy dialect

2366

I'se Been Buked/Gonna Lay Down My Life
[Campbell, Colin M.]
Thomas, Edna (Soprano)
Negro Spirituals
Columbia 3361; 1928; 78 RPM
Piano
Heavy dialect

2367

I'se Been Buked/Gonna Lay Down My Life
[Campbell, Colin M.]
Thomas, Edna (Soprano)
Good News: Vintage Negro Spirituals
Living Era AJA 5622; 2006; CD
Piano
Heavy dialect

2368

I'se Been Buked/Gonna Lay Down My Life
[Campbell, Colin M.]
Thomas, Edna (Soprano)
Religious Music, vol. 2
Document Records; [1999]; CD
Piano
Heavy dialect

· · · · · · ·

I've Been in the Storm So Long

2369

I Been in de Storm So Long
Johnson, Hall
Anderson, Marian (Contralto)
He's Got the Whole World in His Hands: Spirituals
RCA Victor 09026-61960-2; 1994; CD
Piano
Moderate dialect

2370

I Been in de Storm So Long
Johnson, Hall
Anderson, Marian (Contralto)
Jus' Keep on Singin'
RCA Victor LSC 2796; 1965; LP
Piano
Moderate dialect

    Also released with *Marian Anderson: Beyond the Music; Her Complete RCA Victor Recordings* Sony Classical 19439836492; 2021; CD

2371

I Been in the Storm So Long
Traditional

Brown, Anthony (Baritone)
Toil and Triumph
Spirituals Project; 2002; CD
Chorus
Moderate dialect

2372

I've Been in de Storm
Burleigh, Harry T.
Burton, Dashon (Bass-baritone)
Songs of Struggle & Redemption: We Shall Overcome
Acis Productions APL08685; 2015; CD
Piano
Light dialect

2373

I Been in de Storm
Traditional
Conrad, Barbara (Mezzo-soprano)
Spirituals
Naxos 8.553036; 1995; CD
A cappella
Heavy dialect

2374

I've Been in the Storm So Long
Composer not identified
Davis, Frank (Bass-baritone)
16 Spirituals My Father Taught Me
DeWitt Records 601; 1960; LP

2375

I've Been in de Storm So Long
Johnson, Hall
Foreman, Blanche (Contralto)
Best of the Hall Johnson Centennial Festival Celebrating the 100th Anniversary of Hall Johnson's Birth
Hall Johnson Collection O33D2; 2002; CD
Piano

2376

I've Been in the Storm So Long
Composer not identified
Green, Elnora E. (Contralto)
This Is My Task
Private Label NR 18650; 1991; LP

2377
I've Been in the Storm So Long
[Johnson, Hall]
Hampton, Jonathon (Vocalist)
Negro Spirituals: Songs of Trial and Triumph
Private Label; 2017; Streaming audio
Piano
Light dialect

2378
I've Been in de Storm So Long
Burleigh, Harry T.
Hendricks, Barbara (Soprano)
Give Me Jesus
EMI Classics 7243 5 56788 2 9; 1998; CD
A cappella
Heavy dialect

2379
I Been in the Storm So Long
Clinton, Irving
Irving, Clinton (Bass-baritone)
Clinton Irving Sings Spirituals: A Tribute
Rogers; 2001; CD

2380
I've Been in the Storm So Long
Suben, Joel Eric
Lennick, Jessica (Soprano)
Five Spirituals for Soprano and Orchestra
Private label; 2018; Streaming audio
Orchestra
No dialect discerned

2381
I've Been in de Storm So Long
Burleigh, Harry T.
Moses, Oral (Bass-baritone)
Songs of America
Albany Records TROY1011; 2008; CD
Piano
Light dialect

    Also released with *Sankofa: A Spiritual Reflection* (Albany Records TROY1802; 2019; CD)

2382
Been in de Storm So Long
Sanders, Wayne

Overton, Kenneth (Baritone)
Been in de Storm So Long (Songs My Fathers Taught Me)
American Spiritual Ensemble; 2012; CD
A cappella

2383
I've Been in de Storm So Long
Burleigh, Harry T.
Parks, Karen (Soprano)
Nobody Knows
Ottimavoce 52736; 2007; CD
A cappella
Light dialect

2384
I've Been in the Storm
Burleigh, Harry T.
Powell, Angela (Soprano)
City Called Heaven
Private Label AP6957; 2003; CD
Piano

2385
I've Been in de Storm
Burleigh, Harry T.
Salters, Stephen (Baritone)
Spirit: Are You There, You Are There
HarmonizedDisharmony 0001; 2015; CD

2386
Been in de Storm So Long
Brown, Charles
Taylor, Richard (Baritone)
The New Negro Spiritual
W. C. Patterson; 2002; Score w/CD
Piano
Heavy dialect

2387
I Been in de Storm So Long
de Paur, Leonard
Verrett, Shirley (Mezzo-soprano)
Singin' in the Storm
Sony 82318; 2011; CD
Orchestra

2388
I Been in de Storm So Long
Johnson, Hall

Verrett, Shirley (Mezzo-soprano)
Shirley Verrett: Edition
Newton Classics 8802167; 2013; CD
Instrumental ensemble

· · · · · · ·

I've Got a Home
in That Rock

2389

I've Got a Home in-a That Rock
Composer not identified
Newby, Marion Crowley (Contralto)
A Motherless Child
Compassion; [19--]; LP

· · · · · · ·

I've Got Religion

2390

I've Got Religion
Mells, Herbert F.
Heard, Richard (Tenor)
*Ain't a That Good News: African-American
    Art Songs and Spirituals*
HM Classics HMC9602; 1998; CD
Piano
No dialect discerned

2391

I've Got Religion
Mells, Herbert F.
Oglesby, Isador (Tenor)
Isador Sings Negro Spirituals
Oglesby Recordings Album 3; 1983; LP
Piano

2392

Jesus Lay Your Head in the Window
Hogan, Moses
Bazile, Bridget (Soprano); Walker, Alfred
    (Bass)
Songs of Reflection
MGH Records 0800CD; 1997; CD
Piano

· · · · · · ·

Jesus Lay Your Head
in the Window

2393

Jesus, Lay Your Head in the Window
Johnson, John Rosamond; Smith, Hale
Brown, William (Tenor)
Symphonic Spirituals
Columbia JC 36267; 1979; LP
Orchestra
Moderate dialect

2394

Jesus, Lay Your Head in the Window
Smith, Hale
Fernandez, Wilhelmenia (Soprano)
Negro Spirituals
Transart 131; 2005; CD
Piano

2395

Jesus, Lay Your Head
Johnson, Hall
Hamilton, Ruth (Contralto)
Good News
Videmus Records VIS735; 2007; CD
Piano
Heavy dialect

2396

Jesus, Lay Your Head in the Window
Smith, Hale
Jones, Randye (Soprano)
Come Down Angels
Ahhjay Records AHHJ-0001; 2003; CD
Piano
No dialect discerned

2397

Jesus, Lay Your Head in the Window
Composer not identified
McDaniel, Yvette (Soprano)
Simply Spiritual
YM01 DIDX 046103; 1997; CD
Piano

2398

Jesus Lay Your Head in the Window
Composer not identified
Miller-Sydney, Audrey (Soprano)
*Climbing High Mountains: African
    American Art Songs and Spirituals*
Private Label; 2004; CD
Piano
No dialect discerned

2399

Jesus, Lay Your Head in the Window
Scharnberg, Kim
Robinson, Faye (Soprano)
Remembering Marian Anderson
d'Note Classics DND 1014; 1997; CD
Orchestra
No dialect discerned

2400

Jesus Lay Your Head in the Window
Smith, Hale
Salters, Stephen (Baritone)
Spirit: Are You There, You Are There
HarmonizedDisharmony 0001; 2015; CD

2401

Jesus, Lay Your Head in the Window
Smith, Hale
Shirley, George (Tenor)
George Shirley at 80: My Time Has Come!
Videmus Records; 2014; CD
Piano

2402

Jesus, Lay Your Head in the Window
Smith, Hale
Taylor, Richard (Baritone)
The New Negro Spiritual
W. C. Patterson; 2002; Score w/CD
Piano
Heavy dialect

2403

Jesus Lay Your Head in the Window
Smith, Hale
Toppin, Louise (Soprano)
Songs of Illumination

Centaur CRC 2375; 1998; CD
Piano

2404

Jesus Lay Your Head in the Window [from
    Four Negro Spirituals]
Smith, Hale
Toppin, Louise (Soprano)
Witness
Albany Records TROY868; 2006; CD
Orchestra
Heavy dialect

2405

Jesus Lay Your Head in de Winder
Johnson, [Hall]
Weathers, Felicia (Soprano)
Arias and Spirituals
Belart/Universal Classics 461 5922; 1999; CD
Piano
Light dialect

2406

Jesus, Lay Your Head in the Window
Johnson, Hall
Weathers, Felicia (Soprano)
Spirituals & Kodály Folk Songs
Decca SXL 6245; 1966; LP
Piano
Light dialect

2407

Jesus, Lay Your Head in de Winder
Johnson, Hall
Wilson, Robin (Soprano)
*Best of the Hall Johnson Centennial Festival
    Celebrating the 100th Anniversary of Hall
    Johnson's Birth*
Hall Johnson Collection O33D2; 2002; CD
Piano

· · · · · · ·

Jesus Walked This
Lonesome Valley

2408

Jesus Walked This Lonesome Valley
Cooke, Barbara Logan

Cooke, Barbara (Vocalist)
*Sometimes I Feel: A Collection of
    Negro Spirituals for Voice and
    Instruments*
Private Label KDISC420; 2002; CD
Instrumental ensemble

2409

Jesus Walked This Lonesome Valley
[Dawson, William L.]
Hagen-William, Louis (Bass-baritone)
Negro Spiritual
Quantum QM 6909; 1993; CD
Piano
Light dialect

2410

Jesus Walked This Lonesome Vallee
Dawson, William L.
Little, Vera (Mezzo-soprano)
My Good Lord Done Been Here
Decca 123737; 1957; LP
Piano

2411

Jesus Walked This Lonesome Valley
Dawson, William L.
Oglesby, Isador (Tenor)
Life of Jesus in Negro Spirituals
Oglesby Recordings Album 2; 1980; LP
Piano

2412

Jesus Walked This Lonesome Valley
Dawson, William L.
Patton. John (Tenor)
Black Spirituals and Art Songs
Narthex Recording 827N-4581; 1970; LP
Piano
No dialect discerned

2413

Lonesome Valley
Composer not identified
Rustin, Bayard (Tenor)
Bayard Rustin, the Singer
Bayard Rustin Fund; 1992; CD
Piano

2414

Jesus Walked His Lonesome Valley
Traditional
Rustin, Bayard (Tenor)
*Bayard Rustin Sings Twelve Spirituals on the
    Life of Christ*
Fellowship Records E2-KL 1771; [195-]; LP
A cappella
Moderate dialect

        Also released with *Bayard Rustin-The
Singer* (Black Swan Series; Parnassus Records
PACD 96083; 2022; CD)

2415

Jesus Walked This Lonesome Valley
Myers, Gordon
Salters, Stephen (Baritone)
Spirit: Are You There, You Are There
HarmonizedDisharmony 0001; 2015; CD

. . . .

John's Gone Down on the Island in the Mornin

2416

John's Gone Down on the Island in the
    Mornin
Burleigh, Harry T.
Oby, Jason (Tenor)
The Life of Christ: Collected Spirituals
Private Label TSU4749; [200-]; CD
Piano
Moderate dialect

. . . .

Joshua Fit the Battle of Jericho

[Joshua 6:1-27]
        Joshua fit the battle of Jericho, Jericho,
Jericho, Joshua fit the battle of Jericho,
        And the walls come a tumbling down.
You may talk about your king of Gideon,
        You may talk about your man of Saul;
There's none like good ol' Joshua....
        [Available in AAGS, AB10, EM34,

HCTN, HJCO, HLBS, HTBS, JARS, JBES, JJAN, JJBA, JSSp, LLS2, MBIH, PLSY]

2417

Joshua Fit de Battle of Jericho
Composer not identified
Adams, Robert (Vocalist)
All God's Children Got Wings/Scandalize My Name Scandalize My Name/It's Me O Lord/Joshua Fit de Battle of Jericho
Ultraphon C 18121; [19--]; 78 RPM
Piano

2418

Joshua Fit de Battle
Allen, LaShelle
Allen, LaShelle (Mezzo-soprano)
Swing Low, Sweet Chariot
American Spiritual Ensemble; 2011; CD

2419

Joshua Fit de Battle ob Jericho
Brown, Lawrence
Aluko, Tayo (Baritone)
Recalling Robeson: Songs from Call Mr. Robeson
Tayo Aluko and Friends TAAF CD 001; 2007; CD
Piano

2420

Joshua
Venanzi, Henri
Arroyo, Martina (Soprano)
Spirituals
Centaur CRC 2060; 1991; CD
Piano
Light dialect

2421

Joshua Fit de Battle of Jericho [from *Green Pastures*]
Johnson, Hall
Brown, William (Tenor)
The Hall Johnson Collection
Carl Fischer VF5 CD1–VF5 CD2; 2003; Score w/CD
Piano
Heavy dialect

2422

Joshua Fit de Battle of Jericho
Johnson, Hall
Burton, Dashon (Bass-baritone)
Songs of Struggle & Redemption: We Shall Overcome
Acis Productions APL08685; 2015; CD
Piano
Heavy dialect

2423

Joshua Fit the Battle of Jericho
Composer not identified
Carey, Thomas (Baritone)
Go Down Moses
Da Camera Song SM 95028; 1970; LP
Piano

2424

Joshua Fit the Battle of Jerico
Composer not identified
Carlsen, Svein (Bass)
Negro Spirituals
EuroMaster AS ECD19005; 1996; CD
Piano

2425

Joshua Fit de Battle of Jericho
[Burleigh, Harry T.]
Chaiter, Yoram (Bass)
Spirituals & Other Songs
Romeo Records 7311; 2014; CD
Piano
Light dialect

2426

Joshua
Composer not identified
Charles, Lee (Tenor)
Swing Low Sweet Chariot: And Other Spirituals
Riverside RLP 12-651; 1957; LP
Piano, guitar

2427

Joshua Fit duh Battle
Clemmons, François; Marder, Jeffrey
Clemmons, François (Tenor)
Negro Spirituals Live! In Concert

American Negro Spiritual Research
   Foundation 8177 2048 3779; 1998; CD
Piano
Light dialect

2428

Joshua Fit de Battle of Jericho
Brown, Lawrence
Duncan, Todd (Baritone)
African American Spirituals
[Apple Music]; 2008; Streaming audio
Piano
Moderate dialect

2429

Joshua Fit de Battle of Jericho
Brown, Lawrence
Duncan, Todd (Baritone)
Negro Spirituals
Allegro ALG3022; [1952]; LP
Piano

2430

Joshua Fit de Battle of Jerico
[Brown, Lawrence]
Duncan, Todd (Baritone)
America's Great Baritone: Sings Folk Songs
Royale EP181; [195-]; 45 RPM

2431

Joshua Fit de Battle ob Jerico [sic]
[Brown, Lawrence]
Duncan, Todd (Baritone)
Spirituals
Royale 1810; [1950]; LP

2432

Joshua Fought the Battle of Jericho
Ryan, Donald
Estes, Simon (Bass-baritone)
Steal Away: My Favorite Negro Spirituals
Deutsche Schallplatten DS 1041-2; 1994; CD
Piano
Light dialect

    Also released with *Simon Sings His Favorite Gospels & Spirituals* (Praise Productions SMG-SE; 1999; CD) and *Save the Children, Save Their Lives* (CD Baby; 2010; CD)

2433

Joshua Fit the Battle of Jericho
Johnson, Hall
Evans, Allan (Bass-baritone)
Negro Spirituals
Electromusic Records EMCD 6885; 1985;
   CD
Chorus, other instrument(s)

2434

Joshua Fit the Battle of Jericho
Composer not identified
Franklin, Lavinia A. (Vocalist)
*Historical Interpretation of Negro Spirituals
   and Lift Every Voice and Sing*
Recorded Publications JZB-02591; 1970; LP
Organ

2435

Joshua Fit the Battle ob Jericho
[Brown, Lawrence]
Hagen-William, Louis (Bass-baritone)
Negro Spirituals
Quantum QM 6909; 1993; CD
Piano
Light dialect

2436

Joshua Fit the Battle of Jericho
Wheatley, Andres
Haniotis, Mario (Bass)
Negro Spirituals
Pastorale et Musique PM 17.047; [196-]; 45
   RPM
Piano
No dialect discerned

2437

Joshua Fought the Battle of Jericho
Composer not identified
Harris, Lloyd (Bass)
Negro Spirituals
Pléiade P45301; 1960; 45 RPM
Piano

2438

Joshua Fit de Battle of Jericho
Composer not identified

Hendricks, Barbara (Soprano)
Espirituales Negros
EMI Classics/Altaya 01636; 1983; CD
Piano

2439

Joshua Fit the Battle of Jericho
Composer not identified
Hendricks, Barbara (Soprano)
Schubert, Debussy, Fauré, Negro Spirituals
EMI Electrola CDZ 2523322; 1990; CD
Piano

2440

Joshua Fit de Battle of Jericho
Composer not identified
Hendricks, Barbara (Soprano)
Spirituals
EMI Classics 0946 346641 2 7; 2005; CD
Piano

2441

Joshua Fit de Battle of Jericho
Composer not identified
Hendricks, Barbara (Soprano)
Piano

2442

Joshua Fit de Battle of Jericho
Hendricks, Barbara; Alexeev, Dmitri
Hendricks, Barbara (Soprano)
Negro Spirituals
EMI CDC7470262; 1983; CD
Piano
Moderate dialect

    Also released with *Spirituals* (EMI Classics 0946 346641 2 7; 2005; CD) and *The Very Best of Barbara Hendricks* (EMI Classics 7243 5 86323 2 3; 2005; CD)

2443

Joshua Fit the Battle of Jericho
Hayes, Mark
Hudson, Marlissa (Soprano)
Libera
AMP Records AGCD 2106; 2010; CD
Piano
No dialect discerned

2444

Joshua Fit the Battle of Jericho
Clinton, Irving
Irving, Clinton (Bass-baritone)
Clinton Irving Sings Spirituals: A Tribute
Rogers; 2001; CD

2445

Joshua Fit in the Battle of Jericho
Burleigh, Harry T.
Jones, Arthur (Tenor)
Wade in the Water
Orbis Books; 1993; Book w/cass
Piano
Moderate dialect

2446

Joshua Fit de Battle of Jericho
Burleigh, Harry T.
Jones, Fanni (Mezzo-soprano)
Fanni Jones et Oswald Russell
Audio-Visual Enterprises AVE 30701; [19--];
    LP

2447

Joshua Fit de Battle ob Jericho
Composer not identified
Jones, Fanni (Mezzo-soprano)
Negro Spirituals
Phonotec 815; 1977; LP
Organ

2448

Joshua Fit de Battle of Jericho
Burleigh, Harry T.
Kennedy, Charles (Vocalist)
Heart & Soul: Songs of Harry T. Burleigh
Publisher not known; 1994; Cassette

2449

Joshua Fit the Battle of Jericho
Hayes, Mark
Lima, Philip (Baritone)
Songs of a Wayfarer
Private Label; 2017; Streaming audio
Piano
No dialect discerned

2450

Joshua Fit de Battle of Jericho
Meyer, Fredrich
London, George (Bass-baritone)
Spirituals
Deutsche Grammophon 00289 477 6193;
2006; CD
Chorus, orchestra
Heavy dialect

2451

Joshua Fought the Battle of Jericho
Simonson, Victor; Lynch, Lester
Lynch, Lester (Baritone)
On My Journey Now: Spirituals & Hymns
Pentatone Music PTC 5186 57'; 2017; CD
Piano

2452

Joshua Fit de Battle ob Jericho [from
Journey Beyond Time]
Crumb, George
Martin, Barbara Ann (Soprano)
American Songbooks II & IV
BRIDGE 9275A/B; 2008; CD
Piano, percussion

2453

Joshua Fit de Battle of Jericho
Brown, Lawrence
Maynor, Kevin (Bass)
Paul Robeson Remembered
Fleur de Son Classics FDS 57929; 1998;
CD
Piano
Moderate dialect

2454

Joshua Fought the Battle of Jericho
Welsh, Nicky
McCue, Bill (Bass-baritone)
Bill McCue Sings the Great Spirituals
Beltona SBE 173; 1974; LP
Orchestra

2455

Joshua Fit the Battle of Jericho
Bagley, Christopher

McKinney, Jason (Bass-baritone)
Songs Inspired by Paul Robeson
United in Music; 2014; CD
Piano
Moderate dialect

2456

Joshua Fit da Battle
Winchell, Jane
Miller, Jeanette (Soprano)
No Man Canna Hinder Me
MiJon Record Productions MJ240; 1979;
CD
Piano

2457

Joshua Fit the Battle of Jericho
Composer not identified
Moses, Oral (Bass-baritone)
Extreme Spirituals
Cuneiform Record Rune 241; 2006; CD
Instrumental ensemble

2458

Joshua Fit de Battle ob Jericho
Traditional
Moses, Oral (Bass-baritone)
*Spirituals in Zion: A Spiritual Heritage for
the Soul*
Albany Records TROY587; 2003; CD
A cappella

2459

Joshua Fit the Battle of Jericho
Edwards, Leo
Overton, Kenneth (Baritone)
*Been in de Storm So Long (Songs My Fathers
Taught Me)*
American Spiritual Ensemble; 2012; CD
Piano
Light dialect

2460

Joshua Fit de Battle of Jericho
Brown, Lawrence
Pankey, Aubrey (Baritone)
Negro Spirituals
Eterna 830010; 1983; LP
Piano

2461

Joshua Fit de Battle ob Jericho
Composer not identified
Pickens, Jo Ann (Soprano)
*My Heritage: American Melodies/Negro
    Spirituals*
Koch Schwann 3-1447-2; 1993; CD

2462

Joshua Fit the Battle
Composer not identified
Porter, John (Bass)
No More Crying: Negro Spirituals
Pan Verlag OV-84; [1978]; LP

2463

Joshua Fit the Battle of Jericho
Hayes, Mark
Powell, Angela (Soprano)
City Called Heaven
Private Label AP6957; 2003; CD
Piano

2464

Joshua Fit da Battle of Jericho
Bonds, Margaret
Quivar, Florence (Mezzo-soprano)
Great American Spirituals
Musical Heritage Society 513725Z; 1994; CD
Piano
Heavy dialect

    Also released with *Great American
Spirituals* (Angel CDM 7 64669 2; 1992; CD);
Negro Spirituals (EMI 7243 5 72790 2 4; 1998;
CD) and *Ride On, King Jesus! Florence Qui-
var Sings Black Music of America* (EMI Clas-
sics 9 67138 2; 2010; CD)

2465

Joshua Fit the Battle of Jericho
Giesen, Hubert
Ray, William (Baritone)
Negro Spirituals
Intercord; [19--]; LP
Piano

2466

Joshua Fit the Battle of Jericho
Giesen, Hubert

Ray, William (Baritone)
*Sings Arias, Duets, Musical Selections and
    Negro Spirituals*
Intercord; [19--]; CD
Piano

2467

Joshua Fit the Battle of Jerico
Brown, Lawrence
Reese, Ruth (Contralto)
Motherless Child
OPS 1006/79; 1979; LP

2468

Joshua Fit de Battle ob Jerico
Brown, Lawrence
Reese, Ruth (Contralto)
The Black Rose
His Master's Voice 7EGN 38; [19--]; 45 RPM

2469

Joshua Fit de Battle ob Jericho
Brown, Lawrence
Robeson, Paul (Bass-baritone); Brown,
    Lawrence (Vocalist)
*Swing Low, Sweet Chariot/Joshua Fit de
    Battle ob Jericho*
His Master's Voice B 2339; 1926; 78 RPM
Piano
Moderate dialect

2470

Joshua Fit de Battle of Jericho
Brown, Lawrence
Robeson, Paul (Bass-baritone); Brown,
    Lawrence (Vocalist)
Spirituals
Columbia Masterworks 17379-D; 1945; 78
    RPM
Piano
Heavy dialect

2471

Joshua Fit de Battle of Jericho
Brown, Lawrence
Robeson, Paul (Bass-baritone); Brown,
    Lawrence (Vocalist)
*Joshua Fit de Battle of Jericho/Nobody Knows
    de Trouble I've Seen*

Columbia Masterworks 17470-D; 1946; 78
   RPM
Piano
Moderate dialect

2472

Joshua Fit de Battle of Jericho
Brown, Lawrence
Robeson, Paul (Bass-baritone)
Paul Robeson with Chorus, orchestra
Fontana BIG.417-1Y; 1958; LP

2473

Joshua Fit de Battle of Jericho
Brown, Lawrence
Robeson, Paul (Bass-baritone)
Spirituals
Philips 409.115 AE; 1959; 45 RPM
Piano

2474

Joshua Fit de Battle ob Jericho
Brown, Lawrence
Robeson, Paul (Bass-baritone)
Songs of My People
RCA Red Seal LM-3292; 1972; LP
Piano

2475

Joshua Fit de Battle ob Jericho
Brown, Lawrence
Robeson, Paul (Bass-baritone)
The Best of Paul Robeson
EMI NTS 181; 1979; LP
Piano

2476

Joshua Fit de Battle ob Jericho
Brown, Lawrence
Robeson, Paul (Bass-baritone)
Golden Voice of Paul Robeson
EMI Music PLAY-1020; 1983; CD

2477

Joshua Fit de Battle of Jericho
Brown, Lawrence
Robeson, Paul (Bass-baritone)
Songs for Free Men, 1940–45

Pearl GEMM CD 9264; 1997; CD
Piano

2478

Joshua, Fit de Battle ob Jericho
Brown, Lawrence
Robeson, Paul (Bass-baritone)
Paul Robeson Collection
Hallmark Recordings 390692; 1998; CD

2479

Joshua Fit de Battle ob Jericho
Brown, Lawrence
Robeson, Paul (Bass-baritone)
Legends of the 20th Century: Paul Robeson
EMI Records 7243 520140; 1999; CD
Piano

2480

Joshua Fit de Battle ob Jericho
Brown, Lawrence
Robeson, Paul (Bass-baritone)
The Great Paul Robeson
Pegasus PGN CD 811; 2000; CD

2481

Joshua Fit de Battle of Jericho
Brown, Lawrence
Robeson, Paul (Bass-baritone)
Spirituals: Original Recordings 1925–1936
Naxos Gospel Legends 8.120638; 2003; CD
Piano

2482

Joshua Fit de Battle ob Jericho
Brown, Lawrence
Robeson, Paul (Bass-baritone); Brown,
   Lawrence (Vocalist)
Good News: Vintage Negro Spirituals
Living Era AJA 5622; 2006; CD
Piano
Moderate dialect

2483

Joshua Fit de Battle ob Jericho
Brown, Lawrence
Robeson, Paul (Bass-baritone); Brown,
   Lawrence (Vocalist)

The Complete EMI Sessions (1928–1939)
EMI Classics 50999 2 15586 2 7; 2008; CD
Piano
Heavy dialect

2484

Joshua Fit de Battle of Jericho
Brown, Lawrence
Robeson, Paul (Bass-baritone)
Paul Robeson Sings Negro Spirituals
Philips GBL 5584; [19--]; LP
Piano

2485

Joshua Fit de Battle ob Jericho
Brown, Lawrence
Robeson, Paul (Bass-baritone); Brown,
    Lawrence (Vocalist)
Negro Spirituals
His Master's Voice 7EG 8422; [19--]; 45 RPM
Piano

2486

Joshua Fit de Battle ob Jericho
Brown, Lawrence
Robeson, Paul (Bass-baritone); Brown,
    Lawrence (Vocalist)
Paul Robeson
World Record Club W9648/EMI SM 431;
    [19--]; LP
Piano

2487

Joshua Fit the Battle of Jericho
Brown, Lawrence
Robeson, Paul (Bass-baritone); Brown,
    Lawrence (Vocalist)
By an' By/Joshua Fit the Battle of Jericho
Columbia DS 1785; [19--]; 78 RPM
Piano
Moderate dialect

2488

Joshua Fit de Battle of Jericho
Brown, Lawrence
Robeson, Paul (Bass-baritone)
Spirituals
Columbia Masterworks ML 4105 ; CBS
    62483; [1948]; LP

2489

Joshua Fit de Battle of Jericho
Brown, Lawrence
Robeson, Paul (Bass-baritone)
Spirituals
Philips 429 395 BE; [195-]; 45 RPM

2490

Joshua Fit de Battle ob Jericho
[Brown, Lawrence]
Robeson, Paul (Bass-baritone); Brown,
    Lawrence (Vocalist)
*Joshua Fit de Battle ob Jericho/Bye and Bye
    (I'm Goin' to Lay Down Dis Heavy Load)*
Victor 19743; 1925; 78 RPM
Piano

2491

Joshua Fit de Battle of Jericho
[Brown, Lawrence]
Robeson, Paul (Bass-baritone); Brown,
    Lawrence (Vocalist)
Spirituals
Columbia Masterworks M-610; 1946; 78
    RPM
Piano

2492

Joshua Fought the Battle of Jericho
[Brown, Lawrence]
Robeson, Paul (Bass-baritone)
The Essential Paul Robeson
Vanguard VSD 57/58; 1974; LP
Piano
Heavy dialect

2493

Joshua Fit de Battle of Jericho
[Brown, Lawrence]
Robeson, Paul (Bass-baritone)
Scandalize My Name
Classics Record Library 30-5647; 1976; LP
Piano
Moderate dialect

2494

Joshua Fought the Battle of Jericho
[Brown, Lawrence]
Robeson, Paul (Bass-baritone)

*Ballad for Americans and Great Songs of
　Faith, Love and Patriotism*
Vanguard VCD-117/18; 1989; CD
Piano

2495

Joshua Fit de Battle of Jericho
[Brown, Lawrence]
Robeson, Paul (Bass-baritone); Brown,
　Lawrence (Vocalist)
Spirituals/Folksongs/Hymns
Pearl GEMM CD 9382; 1989; CD

2496

Joshua Fit the Battle on Jericho
[Brown, Lawrence]
Robeson, Paul (Bass-baritone)
The Essential History of Gospels & Spirituals
Deja Vu; 1990; CD

2497

Joshua Fit de Battle of Jericho
[Brown, Lawrence]
Robeson, Paul (Bass-baritone); Brown,
　Lawrence (Vocalist)
The Power and the Glory
Columbia/Legacy CK 47337; 1991; CD
Piano
Moderate dialect

2498

Joshua Fit de' Battle of Jericho
[Brown, Lawrence]
Robeson, Paul (Bass-baritone)
*Paul Robeson: Great Voices of the Century,
　v. 1*
Memoir Classics CDMOIR 415; 1992; CD
Piano

2499

Joshua Fit the Battle of Jericho
[Brown, Lawrence]
Robeson, Paul (Bass-baritone)
The Essential Spirituals
Columbia 473788 2; 1993; CD

2500

Joshua Fit de Battle ob Jericho
[Brown, Lawrence]

Robeson, Paul (Bass-baritone); Brown,
　Lawrence (Vocalist)
Gospels & Spirituals Gold Collection
Retro R2CD 40-26; 1995; CD
Piano
Moderate dialect

2501

Joshua Fit de Battle ob Jericho
[Brown, Lawrence]
Robeson, Paul (Bass-baritone)
Ol' Man River: His 25 Greatest 1925–1939
ASV Ltd. CD AJA 5276; 1998; CD

2502

Joshua Fit the Battle of Jericho
[Brown, Lawrence]
Robeson, Paul (Bass-baritone); Brown,
　Lawrence (Vocalist)
Deep River
Great Voices of the Century GVC 2004;
　1999; CD
Piano

2503

Joshua Fit de Battle ob Jericho
[Brown, Lawrence]
Robeson, Paul (Bass-baritone)
The Essential Paul Robeson
ASV CD AJS 244; 2000; CD

2504

Joshua Fit the Battle of Jericho
[Brown, Lawrence]
Robeson, Paul (Bass-baritone)
Paul Robeson
Forever Gold FG019; 2001; CD
Piano

2505

Joshua Fit de Battle ob Jericho
[Brown, Lawrence]
Robeson, Paul (Bass-baritone); Brown,
　Lawrence (Vocalist)
Ol Man River
Leverage; 2005; Streaming audio
Piano
Light dialect

2506

Joshua Fit the Battle of Jericho
[Brown, Lawrence]
Robeson, Paul (Bass-baritone)
The Originals: "Spirituals"
Yoyo USA; 2006; Streaming audio

2507

Joshua Fit de Battle of Jericho
[Brown, Lawrence]
Robeson, Paul (Bass-baritone)
Paul Robeson
Music Video Dist. MDGC23420.2; 2007; CD

2508

Joshua Fit de Battle of Jericho
[Brown, Lawrence]
Robeson, Paul (Bass-baritone)
Collection
RGS Music 1404-2; 2007; CD

2509

Joshua Fit the Battle of Jericho
[Brown, Lawrence]
Robeson, Paul (Bass-baritone)
The Very Best of Gospel
Disconforme CDX7720; 2007; CD

2510

Joshua Fit de Battle of Jericho
[Brown, Lawrence]
Robeson, Paul (Bass-baritone)
Man They Couldn't Silence
Rev-Ola CR REV 208; 2007; CD

2511

Joshua Fit de Battle ob Jericho
[Brown, Lawrence]
Robeson, Paul (Bass-baritone)
The Best of Paul Robeson
Delta Music Group CD6252; 2008; CD

2512

Joshua Fit de Battle ob Jericho
[Brown, Lawrence]
Robeson, Paul (Bass-baritone)
Ol' Man River: His 56 Finest 1925–1945
Retrospective RTS 4116; 2008; CD

2513

Joshua Fit the Battle of Jericho
[Brown, Lawrence]
Robeson, Paul (Bass-baritone)
Negro Spirituals (And More)
Discmedi DM-4674-02; 2009; CD

2514

Joshua Fit de Battle ob Jericho
[Brown, Lawrence]
Robeson, Paul (Bass-baritone); Brown,
   Lawrence (Vocalist)
The Ultimate Collection
Burning Fire; 2009; Streaming audio
Piano
Moderate dialect

2515

Joshua Fit de Battle of Jericho
[Brown, Lawrence]
Robeson, Paul (Bass-baritone)
*Oh, Happy Day! Gospels & Spirituals: The
   Ultimate CD*
Ultimate; 2010; CD

2516

Joshua Fit de Battle of Jericho
[Brown, Lawrence]
Robeson, Paul (Bass-baritone); Brown,
   Lawrence (Vocalist)
Drink to Me Only with Thine Eyes
MD Music; 2010; Streaming audio
Piano
Heavy dialect

2517

Joshua Fit the Battle of Jericho
[Brown, Lawrence]
Robeson, Paul (Bass-baritone); Brown,
   Lawrence (Vocalist)
Voice of the People
Regis RRC 1056; 2011; CD
Piano
Moderate dialect

2518

Joshua Fit de Battle of Jericho
[Brown, Lawrence]

Robeson, Paul (Bass-baritone); Brown,
    Lawrence (Vocalist)
Ol' Man River: The Ultimate Collection
Roslin Records; 2011; Streaming audio
Piano
Light dialect

2519

Joshua Fit de Battle ob Jericho
[Brown, Lawrence]
Robeson, Paul (Bass-baritone); Brown,
    Lawrence (Vocalist)
Ol' Man River: The Very Best of Paul Robeson
Memory Lane; 2012; CD

2520

Joshua Fit de Battle ob Jericho
[Brown, Lawrence]
Robeson, Paul (Bass-baritone); Brown,
    Lawrence (Vocalist)
Classic Gospel Songs
Emerald/K-Tel; 2013; Streaming audio
Piano

2521

Joshua Fit de Battle ob Jericho
[Brown, Lawrence]
Robeson, Paul (Bass-baritone); Brown,
    Lawrence (Vocalist)
Ol' Man River: The Best of Paul Robeson
Emerald Echoes; 2015; Streaming audio
Piano

2522

Joshua Fit the Battle of Jericho
[Brown, Lawrence]
Robeson, Paul (Bass-baritone)
Five Classic Albums Plus Bonus Tracks
Real Gone Music RGMCD287; 2017; CD

2523

Joshua Fit de Battle of Jericho
[Brown, Lawrence]
Robeson, Paul (Bass-baritone)
The Essential Collection
Primo PRMCD6233; 2018; CD

2524

Joshua Fit the Battle of Jericho
[Brown, Lawrence]

Robeson, Paul (Bass-baritone)
Complete Recordings
Universal Digital Enterprises; 2018;
    Streaming audio

2525

Joshua Fit the Battle of Jericho
[Brown, Lawrence]
Robeson, Paul (Bass-baritone)
The Paul Robeson Story
Columbia 5C 052-04830; [19--]; LP

2526

Joshua Fit the Battle of Jericho
[Brown, Lawrence]
Robeson, Paul (Bass-baritone)
Ol' Man River
Golden Options GO 3820; [2000]; CD

2527

Joshua Fought the Battle of Jericho
[Brown, Lawrence]
Robeson, Paul (Bass-baritone)
Robeson
Vanguard VSD-2015; 1958?; LP
Chorus, orchestra

2528

Joshua Fit the Battle of Jericho
Composer not identified
Spencer, Kenneth (Bass-baritone)
Negro Spirituals
Life Records C 1108; [19--]; LP

2529

Joshua Fit the Battle of Jericho
Nagel, [Otto]
Spencer, Kenneth (Bass-baritone)
Volkslieder & Spirituals
Discoton 75546; [197-]; LP
Chorus
Heavy dialect

2530

Joshua Fit the Battle of Jericho
[Brown, Lawrence]
Spencer, Kenneth (Bass-baritone)
American Spirituals

Sonora MS-478; [1945]; 78 RPM
Piano
Moderate dialect

2531

Joshua Fit the Battle of Jericho
Hayes, Mark
Thomas, Indra (Soprano)
Great Day: Indra Thomas Sings Spirituals
Delos DE 3427; 2012; CD
Piano
Moderate dialect

2532

Joshua Fit de Battle ob Jericho
Composer not identified
Ventriglia, Franco (Baritone)
Instrumental ensemble
Heavy dialect

2533

Joshua Fit de Battle ob Jericho
Composer not identified
Ventriglia, Franco (Baritone)
Franco Ventriglia Sings Negro Spirituals
Vedette Records VRMS 316; [19--]; LP
Instrumental ensemble
Heavy dialect

 Also released with *Franco Ventriglia Sings Negro Spirituals* (Vedette Records; 2007; Streaming audio)

2534

Joshua Fit de Battle ob Jericho
Burleigh, Harry T.
Warfield, William (Bass-baritone)
Spirituals: 200 Years of African-American Spirituals
ProArte CDD 3443; 1993; CD
Piano
Moderate dialect

2535

Joshua Fit de Battle of Jericho
Composer not identified
Webb, George (Tenor)
Famous Negro Spirituals and Songs of Elizabethan England, Ireland & the Caribbean
[Unknown] WLP7804; 1978; LP

2536

Joshua Fit de Battle of Jericho
Schweizer, Rolf
Wolf, Lars (Vocalist)
Die Schwarze Stimme Europas
Cantate 666000; 1971; LP
Chorus, organ, percussion

· · · · · · ·

Just Keep on Singing

2537

Jus' Keep on Singin'
Johnson, Hall
Anderson, Marian (Contralto)
Jus' Keep on Singin'
RCA Victor LSC 2796; 1965; LP
Piano

2538

Jus' Keep on Singin'
Johnson, Hall
Anderson, Marian (Contralto)
He's Got the Whole World in His Hands: Spirituals
RCA Victor 09026-61960-2; 1994; CD
Piano
Heavy dialect

2539

Jus' Keep on Singin'
Johnson, Hall
Anderson, Marian (Contralto)
Marian Anderson: Beyond the Music; Her Complete RCA Victor Recordings
Sony Classical 19439836492; 2021; CD
Piano
Light dialect

· · · · · · ·

Keep a-Inchin' Along

2540

Keep an 'Inchin' Along
Composer not identified

Jones, Fanni (Mezzo-soprano)
Negro Spirituals
Evasion Disques LP613; 1974; LP

2541
Keep a-Inchin' Along
Composer not identified
Jones, Fanni (Mezzo-soprano)
Negro Spirituals
Phonotec 815; 1977; LP
Organ

2542
Keep a-Inchin' Along
Johnson, Hall
Jones, Fanni (Mezzo-soprano)
Negro Spirituals en Concert
Suisa; 1987; LP
Organ
Heavy dialect

. . . .

Keep Me from Sinking Down

2543
Keep Me from Sinking Down
Composer not identified
Hayes, Roland (Tenor)
Afro-American Folksongs
Pelican Records LP 2028; 1983; LP
Piano

2544
Keep Me f'om Sinking Down
Still, William Grant
Hill, Christin-Marie (Mezzo-soprano)
Songs of William Grant Still
White Pine Music WPM224; 2015; CD
Piano

2545
Keep Me from Sinkin' Down
Still, William Grant
More, Suzi (Vocalist)
*Chords and Strings: Centuries of Songs for
    Voice and Guitar*

Lil Red Hen Records; 2018; Streaming audio
Guitar

. . . .

Keep Your Lamps Trimmed and Burning

2546
Keep Me from Sinkin' Down
Sims, Robert
Sims, Robert (Baritone); Hayes, Roland (Tenor)
*Robert Sims Sings the Spirituals of Roland
    Hayes*
Canti Classics 2014-01; 2015; CD
A cappella
Light dialect

2547
Keep Your Lamps Trimmed and Burning
Brown, Uzee, Jr.
Brown, Uzee, Jr. (Baritone)
Great Day!
Allgood; 2005; CD
Piano
Light dialect

2548
Keep Your Lamps Trimmed and Burning!
Brown, Uzee, Jr.
Moses, Oral (Bass-baritone)
Songs of America
Albany Records TROY1011; 2008; CD
Piano
Light dialect

2549
Keep Your Lamps Trimmed and Burning!
Brown, Uzee, Jr.
Moses, Oral (Bass-baritone)
Sankofa: A Spiritual Reflection
Albany Records TROY1802; 2019; CD
Piano
Light dialect

. . . .

King Jesus Is a Listenin'

2550
King Jesus Is a Listenin'
Composer not identified

Kaskas, Anna (Contralto)
Sacred Songs
SESAC YTNY 5735-YTNY 5736; [19--]; LP

· · · · · · ·

King of Kings

2551
King of Kings
Composer not identified
Rustin, Bayard (Tenor)
Bayard Rustin, the Singer
Bayard Rustin Fund; 1992; CD
Piano

· · · · · · ·

Kum Ba Yah

2552
Kum Ba Yah
Composer not identified
Brown, Anthony (Baritone)
*Each Other's Light: Songs of Peace, Hope &
    Justice*
Private label AB0906; [2017]; CD
Chorus
No dialect discerned

2553
Come by Here Good Lord
Sneed, Damien
Brownlee, Lawrence (Tenor)
Spiritual Sketches
LeChateau Earl Records 888174029597; 2013;
    CD
Piano
Light dialect

2554
Kumbaya
Composer not identified
Thompson, Jeanette (Soprano)
Negro Spirituals
Pavane Records ADW 7267; 1992; CD
Chorus
No dialect discerned

· · · · · · ·

Laid Down My Burdens

2555
Laid Down My Burdens
Becton, Shelton
Graves, Denyce (Mezzo-soprano)
Angels Watching Over Me
NPR Classics CD 0006; 1997; CD
Chorus, piano
Heavy dialect

· · · · · · ·

Last Supper

2556
The Last Supper [from *The Life of Christ*]
Hayes, Roland
Holland, Charles (Tenor)
My Lord What a Mornin'
Musical Heritage Society MHS 912250X;
    1982; LP
Piano
Light dialect

2557
The Last Supper [from *The Life of Christ*]
Hayes, Roland
Holland, Charles (Tenor)
My Lord What a Mornin'
Musical Heritage Society MHS 512250K;
    1988; CD
Piano
Light dialect

2558
The Last Supper [from *The Life of Christ*]
[Hayes, Roland]
Jenkins, Isaiah (Tenor)
Lyric Tenor
Trans Radio TR 1010A; [195-]; LP
Piano

2559
The Last Supper [from *The Life of Christ*]
Hayes, Roland
Oby, Jason (Tenor)
The Life of Christ: Collected Spirituals

Private Label TSU4749; [200-]; CD
Piano
Moderate dialect

2560

The Last Supper [from *The Life of Christ*]
Hayes, Roland
Shirley, George (Tenor)
George Shirley at 80: My Time Has Come!
Videmus Records; 2014; CD
Piano

2561

The Last Supper [from *The Life of Christ*]
Hayes, Roland
Williams, Willie (Vocalist)
My Tribute
Discovery V42227; 1974; LP
Piano

· · · · · · ·

The Last Supper

2562

The Last Supper [from *The Life of Christ*]
Hayes, Roland
Sims, Robert (Baritone)
Robert Sims Sings the Spirituals of Roland Hayes
Canti Classics 2014-01; 2015; CD
Piano
Heavy dialect

· · · · · · ·

Lay Dis Body Down

2563

Lay Dis Body Down
Composer not identified
Hayes, Roland (Tenor)
Afro-American Folksongs
Pelican Records LP 2028; 1983; LP
Piano

2564

Lay Dis Body Down
Hayes, Roland; Boardman. Reginald
Hayes, Roland (Tenor)

The Art of Roland Hayes
Smithsonian Collection RD 041; 1990; CD
Piano
Moderate dialect

· · · · · · ·

Lead Me to the Water

2565

Lead Me to the Water
Lawrence, William
Maynor, Dorothy (Soprano)
Dorothy Maynor in Concert at Library of Congress
Library of Congress, Music Division LCM 2141; 2007; CD
Piano
No dialect discerned

2566

Lead Me to the Water
Lawrence, William
Maynor, Dorothy (Soprano)
Dorothy Maynor, Soprano
Bridge Records 9233; 2007; CD
Piano
No dialect discerned

· · · · · · ·

Leanin' on Dat Lamb

2567

Leanin' on Dat Lamb
Johnson, Hall
Jefferson, Othello (Tenor)
Good News: African American Spirituals and Art Songs
Cambria Records CD 1270; 2021; CD
Piano
Heavy dialect

2568

Leanin' on That Lamb
Rice, Mark; Sykes, Jubilant
Sykes, Jubilant (Baritone)
Jubilant Sykes Sings Copland and Spirituals
Arioso Classics AC 00011; 2008; CD
Orchestra

· · · · · · ·
Le's Have a Union

2569
Le's Have a Union
Johnson, Hall
Anderson, Marian (Contralto)
Jus' Keep on Singin'
RCA Victor LSC 2796; 1965; LP
Piano
Moderate dialect

Also released with *Marian Anderson: Beyond the Music; Her Complete RCA Victor Recordings* Sony Classical 19439836492; 2021; CD

2570
Le's Have a Union
Johnson, Hall
Anderson, Marian (Contralto)
He's Got the Whole World in His Hands: Spirituals
RCA Victor 09026-61960-2; 1994; CD
Piano
Moderate dialect

Also released with *Marian Anderson: Beyond the Music; Her Complete RCA Victor Recordings* Sony Classical 19439836492; 2021; CD

2571
Le's Have a Union
Johnson, Hall
Graves, Denyce (Mezzo-soprano)
Angels Watching Over Me
NPR Classics CD 0006; 1997; CD
Piano
Moderate dialect

2572
Let's Have a Union
Johnson, [Hall]
Honeysucker, Robert (Baritone)
Let's Have a Union
Brave Records BRAV-0923; 2009; CD
Piano
Moderate dialect

2573
Le's Have a Union
Johnson, Hall
Honeysucker, Robert (Baritone)
Good News
Videmus Records VIS735; 2007; CD
Piano
Heavy dialect

2574
Le's Have a Union
Johnson, Hall
Hopkins, Gregory (Tenor)
Best of the Hall Johnson Centennial Festival Celebrating the 100th Anniversary of Hall Johnson's Birth
Hall Johnson Collection O33D2; 2002; CD
Piano

2575
Le's Have a Union
Johnson, Hall
Simpson, Eugene Thamon (Bass)
Thanks Be to Thee
Black Heritage Publications; 2005; CD
Piano

2576
Le's Have a Union
Johnson, Hall
Simpson, Eugene Thamon (Bass)
Hall Johnson Spirituals and Other Folk Songs
Private Label; 2016; CD
Piano

2577
Le's Have a Union
Johnson, Hall
Toppin, Louise (Soprano)
He'll Bring It to Pass: The Spirituals of Hall Johnson for Voice and Piano
Albany Records TROY846; 2006; CD
Piano
Heavy dialect

2578
Le's Have a Union
Johnson, Hall

Warfield, William (Bass-baritone)
*Spirituals: 200 Years of African-American
    Spirituals*
ProArte CDD 3443; 1993; CD
Piano
Heavy dialect

• • • • • • •

Let Us All Work Together

2579

Let Us All Work Together
Hayes, Roland
Jenkins, Isaiah (Tenor)
Lyric Tenor
Trans Radio TR 1010A; [195-]; LP
Piano

• • • • • • •

*Let Us Break Bread
Together*

[Psalm 4:1; Matthew 26:27; Mark 14:23;
Luke 22:17; Acts 20:7; I Corinthians 11:23,
11:25-26]

"Let us break bread together on our
knees; Let us break bread together on our
knees; / When I fall on my knees, with my
face to the rising sun; O Lord, have mercy
on me. / Let us drink wine together on our
knees; ... Let us praise God together on our
knees; ...." [Available in CLSA, JAS1, JBBS,
JCCA, JSSp, MHDR, RWSC, RW15]

Although the life and miraculous works
of Jesus Christ have often been the subject of
folk spirituals, his celebration of Commu-
nion has rarely been included. "Let Us Break
Bread Together on Our Knees" is that rare
exception. The spiritual is also structured in
the more rare group using a slow, sustained
vocal line, repeating the text as a means to
emphasize its importance. This use of repeti-
tion has its roots in African music.

It is believed that the words "when I fall
on my knees, with my face to the rising sun"
were a "secret signal" of an impending gath-
ering, indeed a call to "praise God together."

The numerous recordings of this spiritual present a vast range of compositional

approaches, from the Neo-Romanticism of
William Lawrence's setting to the Gospel
musical style of Moses Hogan's. While John
Carter's setting is part of the cycle, "Cantata," it is often performed alone.

2580

Let Us Break Bread Together
Composer not identified
Addison, Adele (Soprano)
Little David Play on Your Harp
Kapp Records KL 1109; 1959; LP
Men's voices
Moderate dialect

2581

Let Us Break Bread Together
Composer not identified
Allen, Betty (Mezzo-soprano)
On Wings of Song
RCA Custom Reader's Digest RDA43-A;
    [1960]; LP
Chorus, organ
Moderate dialect

2582

Let Us Break Bread Together
Lawrence, William
Anderson, Marian (Contralto)
Negro Spirituals: 1924–1949
Frémeaux & Associés FA 184; 2004; CD
Orchestra

2583

Let Us Break Bread Together
Lawrence, William
Anderson, Marian (Contralto)
Farewell Recital
RCA Victor LSC 2781; 1964; LP
Piano

Also released with *Marian Anderson:
Beyond the Music; Her Complete RCA Victor
Recordings* Sony Classical 19439836492; 2021;
CD

2584

Let Us Break Bread Together
Lawrence, William
Anderson, Marian (Contralto)

Marian Anderson: Rare and Unpublished Recordings, 1936–1953
VAI Audio VAIA 1168; 1998; CD
Piano
Heavy dialect

2585

Let Us Break Bread Together
Lawrence, William
Anderson, Marian (Contralto)
Spirituals
RCA Victor Red Seal 09026-63306-2; 1999; CD
Piano
Light dialect

2586

Let Us Break Bread Together
Lawrence, William
Anderson, Marian (Contralto)
Softly Awakes My Heart: Arias, Songs and Spirituals, Original Recordings 1924–1945
Naxos Nostalgia 8.120566; 2001; CD
Piano
Heavy dialect

2587

Let Us Break Bread Together
Lawrence, William
Anderson, Marian (Contralto)
Let Us Break Bread Together/Oh! What a Beautiful City
Victor 10-1040; [19--]; 78 RPM
Piano
Moderate dialect

2588

Let Us Break Bread Together
Lawrence, William
Anderson, Marian (Contralto)
Negro Spirituals
RCA Victor LM 2032; [1956]; LP
Piano

Also released with *Marian Anderson: Beyond the Music; Her Complete RCA Victor Recordings* Sony Classical 19439836492; 2021; CD

2589

Let Us Break Bread Together
[Lawrence, William]
Anderson, Marian (Contralto)
Marian Anderson Sings Eleven Great Spirituals
RCA Victor LRM 7006; 1955; LP
Piano

Also released with *Marian Anderson: Beyond the Music; Her Complete RCA Victor Recordings* Sony Classical 19439836492; 2021; CD

2590

Let Us Break Bread Together
[Lawrence, William]
Anderson, Marian (Contralto)
Marian Anderson Sings Spirituals
Flapper Past CD 7073; 1995; CD
Piano

2591

Let Us Break Bread Together
[Lawrence, William]
Anderson, Marian (Contralto)
The Lady
Magnum Music MCCD 017; 1996; CD
Piano

2592

Let Us Break Bread Together
[Lawrence, William]
Anderson, Marian (Contralto)
Alto Rhapsody; Selected Spirituals
Urania URN 22.328; 2007; CD
Piano

2593

Let Us Break Bread Together
[Lawrence, William]
Anderson, Marian (Contralto)
The Very Best of Marian Anderson
Master Classics Records; 2009; CD
Piano
Moderate dialect

2594

Let Us Break Bread Together
[Lawrence, William]

Anderson, Marian (Contralto)
*Marian Anderson Sings Eleven Great
   Spirituals*
Kipepeo Publishing; 2017; CD
Piano

2595

Let Us Break Bread Together
[Lawrence, William]
Anderson, Marian (Contralto)
*Grandes Contraltos de la Musique Classique,
   Les: Marian Anderson, Vol. 6*
Mon Patrimoine Musical Collection; 2017;
   Streaming audio
Piano

2596

Let Us Break Bread Together
[Lawrence, William]
Anderson, Marian (Contralto)
Ave Maria: And Other Schubert Songs
43 North Broadway, LLC; 2019; Streaming
   audio
Piano
Moderate dialect

2597

Let Us Break Bread Together
[Lawrence, William]
Anderson, Marian (Contralto)
Negro Spirituals
RCA Gold Seal RVC-1570; [19--]; LP
Piano

2598

Let Us Break Bread Together
[Lawrence, William]
Anderson, Marian (Contralto)
Negro Spirituals
RCA Victor 630.396 A; [19--]; LP
Piano

2599

Let Us Break Bread Together
[Lawrence, William]
Anderson, Marian (Contralto)
Deep River
Audio Book & Music; [20--]; CD

2600

Let Us Break Bread Together
Lawrence, William
Arroyo, Martina (Soprano)
There's a Meeting Here Tonight
Angel S-36072; 1974; LP
Chorus

2601

Let Us Break Bread Together
Lawrence, William
Arroyo, Martina (Soprano)
Negro Spirituals
EMI 7243 5 72790 2 4; 1998; CD
Chorus
Heavy dialect

2602

Let Us Break Bread Together
Kirk, Theron W.
Blackmon, Henry (Baritone)
Negro Spirituals
Mirasound Records SGLP 6047; [19--]; LP
Organ

2603

Let Us Break Bread Together
Kirk, Theron W.
Blackmon, Henry (Baritone)
Negro Spirituals
Vega 19179; [19--]; LP
Chorus, piano

2604

Let Us Break Bread Together
Boatwright, McHenry
Boatwright, McHenry (Bass-baritone)
Art of McHenry Boatwright: Spirituals
Golden Crest Records RE 7024; 1968; LP
Piano
Light dialect

2605

Let Us Break Bread (Air) [from *Cantata*]
Carter, John D.
Brewer, Christine (Soprano)
Saint Louis Woman
Opera Theatre of Saint Louis OTSL CD93;
   1993; CD

Piano
Moderate dialect

2606

Let Us Break Bread (Air) [from *Cantata*]
Carter, John D.
Brewer, Christine (Soprano)
*Songs by Wagner, Wolf, Britten and John
    Carter*
Wigmore Hall Live WHLive0022; 2008;
    CD
Piano
Moderate dialect

2607

Let Us Break Bread Together
Hogan, Moses
Brown, Anthony (Baritone)
Toil and Triumph
Spirituals Project; 2002; CD
Piano
Moderate dialect

2608

Let Us Break Bread Together
Hogan, Moses
Brown, Anthony (Baritone)
How Can I Keep from Singing?
Private label; 2013; CD
Piano
Light dialect

2609

Let Us Break Bread Together
Smith, Hale
Brown, William (Tenor)
Symphonic Spirituals
Columbia JC 36267; 1979; LP
Orchestra
Light dialect

2610

Let Us Break Bread Together
Smith, Hale
Brown, William (Tenor)
Symphonic Spirituals
Spotify; [2019]; Streaming audio
Orchestra
Light dialect

2611

Let Us Break Bread Together
Composer not identified
Carey, Thomas (Baritone)
Go Down Moses
Da Camera Song SM 95028; 1970; LP
Piano

2612

Let Us Break Bread Together
Composer not identified
Charles, Lee (Tenor)
*Swing Low Sweet Chariot: And Other
    Spirituals*
Riverside RLP 12-651; 1957; LP
Piano, guitar

2613

Let Us Break Bread Together (Air) [from
    Cantata]
Carter, John D.
Danrich, Adrienne (Soprano)
A Tribute to William Warfield
Mark Records MCD-1409; 1994; CD
Piano

2614

Air [from *Cantata*]
Carter, John D.; Link, Peter
Davis, Osceola (Soprano)
Climbing High Mountains
Watchfire Music; 2008; CD
Piano, orchestra
No dialect discerned

2615

Let Us Break Bread Together
Lawrence, William; Reilly, McLaughlin
Davy, Gloria (Soprano)
Spirituals
Decca LW 5215; 1959; LP

2616

We'll Crush Grain Together (Let Us Break
    Bread Together)
Composer not identified
Dobbs, Mattiwilda (Soprano)
M. Dobbs Sings (U.S.A.)

Soviet Gramophone Records (Melodiya)
GOST 5289-56; 1960; LP
Piano

2617

We'll Crush Grain Together (Let Us Break
Bread Together)
Composer not identified
Dobbs, Mattiwilda (Soprano)
*Mattiwilda Dobbs Sings Franz Schubert/
American Negro Spirituals*
Aprelevsky 5846; [1961]; LP
Piano

2618

Let Us Break Bread Together
Lawrence, William
Dobbs, Mattiwilda (Soprano)
*Tva Sidor Av Mattiwilda Dobbs Och
Gotthard Arner*
Proprius 25 04-02-0004; [19--]; LP
Organ

2619

Let Us Break Bread Together
Composer not identified
Duckworth, Zorita (Mezzo-soprano)
Forget Me Not.... Negro Spirituals
Private Label; [20--]; CD

2620

Let Us Break Bread Together
Lawrence, William
Duncan, Todd (Baritone)
*Let Us Break Bread Together/My Lord, What
a Mornin'*
Philips A 56008 H; [195-]; 78 RPM
Piano
Light dialect

2621

Let Us Break Bread (Air) [from *Cantata*]
Carter, John D.
English-Robinson, Laura (Soprano)
Let It Shine!
ACA Digital Recording CM20020; 1994;
CD
Piano
No dialect discerned

2622

Let Us Break Bread Together
Roberts, Howard
Estes, Simon (Bass-baritone)
Spirituals
Philips 412 631-2; 1985; CD
Chorus
Light dialect

2623

Let Us Break Bread Together
Roberts, Howard
Estes, Simon (Bass-baritone)
Met Stars in the New World
MET 216CD; 1992; CD

2624

Let Us Break Bread Together
Roberts, Howard
Estes, Simon (Bass-baritone)
Famous Spirituals
Philips 462 062-2; 1997; CD
Chorus
Light dialect

2625

Let Us Break Bread Together
Robbiani, Mario
Fisher, Dorothy (Contralto)
Negro Spirituals
Edizione D'Arte Del Lions Club Milano Al
Cenacolo; [19--]; LP
Instrumental ensemble
Heavy dialect

2626

Let Us Break Bread Together
Composer not identified
Foye, Hope (Soprano)
*Scandalize My Name/Merry-Go-Round/Let
Us Break Bread Together*
CCCP Lighthouse B 20667/20669; 1951; 78
RPM
Piano

2627

Let Us Break Bread (Air) [from *Cantata*]
Carter, John D.
Givens, Melissa (Soprano)

Let the Rain Kiss You
Divameg Productions 141434; 2001; CD
Piano

2628
Air [from *Cantata*]
Carter, John D.
Gormley, Clare (Soprano)
Where Morning Lies: Spiritual Songs
ABC Classics 461 766-2; 2002; CD
Piano
Moderate dialect

2629
Let Us Break Bread Together
Kaiser, Kurt
Hines, Jerome (Bass)
Great Moments of Sacred Music
Word Records W 3337; [196-]; LP

2630
Let Us Break Bread Together
Hirtz, Gerd
Holmes, Eugene (Baritone)
Spirituals
Schubert Records SCH-102; [1988]; LP
Piano
Heavy dialect

2631
Let Us Break Bread Together
Lawrence, William
Holmes, Eugene (Baritone)
Eugene Holmes Sings Spirituals
Avant Garde AV-115; [1968]; LP
Piano
Heavy dialect

2632
Let Us Break Bread Together
Lawrence, William
Jones, Fanni (Mezzo-soprano)
Negro Spirituals en Concert
Suisa; 1987; LP
Organ
Heavy dialect

2633
Air (Let Us Break Bread) [from *Cantata*]
Carter, John D.

Jones, Randye (Soprano)
Come Down Angels
Ahhjay Records AHHJ-0001; 2003; CD
Piano
Light dialect

2634
Let Us Break Bread Together
Hogan, Moses
Lynch, Lester (Baritone)
On My Journey Now: Spirituals & Hymns
Pentatone Music PTC 5186 57'; 2017; CD
Piano

2635
Let Us Break Bread Together on Our Knees
Lawrence, William
Mayes, Doris (Mezzo-soprano)
Deep River
La voix de son maître FDLP 1080; 1959; LP
Piano

2636
Let Us Break Breat [sic Bread] Together
Composer not identified
Maynor, Kevin (Bass)
Songs of America from Another American
Guild GMCD 7247; 2002; CD
Piano

2637
Let Us Break Bread
Composer not identified
McDaniel, Yvette (Soprano)
Simply Spiritual
YM01 DIDX 046103; 1997; CD
Piano

2638
Let Us Break Bread Together
Lawrence, William
McFerrin, Robert (Baritone)
Deep River and Other Classic Negro Spirituals
Riverside Records RLP 12-812; 1959; LP
Piano
Light dialect

2639
Let Us Break Bread Together
Lawrence, William

McFerrin, Robert (Baritone)
Classic Negro Spirituals
Washington Records WLP 466; 1959; LP
Piano
Light dialect

2640

Let Us Break Bread Together
Composer not identified
Miles, John (Tenor)
The Classic Spirituals
Epiphany 83-1027; 1983; LP
Instrumental ensemble

2641

Let Us Break Bread Together
Hogan, Moses
Moses, Oral (Bass-baritone)
Songs of America
Albany Records TROY1011; 2008; CD
Piano
Light dialect

2642

Let Us Break Bread
Composer not identified
Norman, Jessye (Soprano)
*The Jessye Norman Collection: Sacred Songs
    & Spirituals*
Philips B0004506-02; 2005; CD
Orchestra
Light dialect

2643

Let Us Break Bread Together
Hope, Peter
Norman, Jessye (Soprano)
Amazing Grace
Philips 432 546-2; 1990; CD
Orchestra
Light dialect

2644

Let Us Break Bread Together
[Hope, Peter]
Norman, Jessye (Soprano)
Sacred Songs
Philips 400 019-2; 1983; CD

Orchestra
Light dialect

2645

Break Bread Together
Dett, Robert Nathaniel
Oglesby, Isador (Tenor)
Life of Jesus in Negro Spirituals
Oglesby Recordings Album 2; 1980; LP
Piano

2646

Let Us Break Bread Together [from *Settings
    for Spirituals*]
Chadabe, Joel
Oliver, Irene (Soprano)
Settings for Spirituals; Solo
Lovely Music VR-3804; 1984; LP
Piano

2647

Let Us Break Bread Together
Lloyd, Charles, Jr.
Paige-Green, Jacqueline (Soprano)
The Spiritual Art Song Collection
Warner Bros. SVBM00004; 2000; Score w/
    CD
Piano

2648

Let Us Break Bread (Air) [from *Cantata*]
Carter, John D.
Pickens, Jo Ann (Soprano)
*My Heritage: American Melodies/Negro
    Spirituals*
Koch Schwann 3-1447-2; 1993; CD

2649

Let Us Break Bread Together
Composer not identified
Pierson, Edward (Bass-baritone)
Edward Pierson Sings Hymns and Spirituals
Kemco 98-44; [19--]; LP

2650

Let Us Break Bread (Air) [from *Cantata*]
[Carter, John D.]
Pleas III, Henry H. (Tenor)
Cantata

Private Label; 2003; CD
Piano

2651

Let Us Break Bread
Collingwood, Lawrence
Price, Leontyne (Soprano)
The Essential Leontyne Price
BMG Classics 09026-68153-2; 1996; CD
Orchestra
Heavy dialect

2652

Let Us Break Bread Together on Our Knees
Lawrence, William; de Paur, Leonard
Price, Leontyne (Soprano)
*Swing Low, Sweet Chariot: Fourteen
    Spirituals*
RCA Victor LSC 2600; 1962; LP
Orchestra
Heavy dialect

Also released with *The Essential Leontyne Price: Spirituals, Hymns & Sacred Songs* (BMG Classics 09026-68157-2; 1996; CD); *The Best of Negro Spirituals* (BMG BVCM-37416; 2003; CD); *Complete Collection of Songs and Spiritual Albums* (RCA Red Seal 88697940502; 2011; CD); *Leontyne Price Sings Spirituals* (RCA Red Seal 88691928242; 2012; CD) and *Singers of the Century: Leontyne Price: Spiritual and Religious Songs* (Jube Classic; 2016; Streaming audio)

2653

Let Us Break Bread Together on Our Knees
Hogan, Moses
Ragin, Derek Lee (Countertenor)
Negro Spirituals
Virgin Classics 0946 363305 2 5; 2006; CD
Piano
Heavy dialect

2654

Let Us Break Bread Together
Lawrence, William
Reese, Ruth (Contralto)
The Black Rose
His Master's Voice 7EGN 38; [19--]; 45
    RPM

2655

Let Us Break Bread Together on Our Knees
Composer not identified
Robeson, Paul (Bass-baritone)
The Collector's Paul Robeson
Monitor MCD-61580; 1989; CD
Piano
Moderate dialect

2656

Let Us Break Bread Together on Our Knees
Composer not identified
Robeson, Paul (Bass-baritone)
American Balladeer
Collectables Records COL-CD-6502; 1990;
    CD
Chorus

2657

Let Us Break Bread Together on Our Knees
Composer not identified
Robeson, Paul (Bass-baritone)
*On My Journey: Paul Robeson's Independent
    Recordings*
Smithsonian Folkways Recordings SFW CD
    40178; 2007; CD
Piano
Moderate dialect

2658

Let Us Break Bread Together on Our Knees
Composer not identified
Robeson, Paul (Bass-baritone)
Negro Spirituals (And More)
Discmedi DM-4674-02; 2009; CD

2659

Let Us Break Bread Together on Knees
Composer not identified
Robeson, Paul (Bass-baritone)
Negro Spirituals
Chant du Monde LDX 74376; 1982; LP
Piano

2660

Let Us Break Bread Together
Wertsch, Nancy
Shelhart, John (Bass-baritone); Fox, David
    (Tenor)

Ain't Got Time to Die: Songs of the American Spirit
First Presbyterian Church in the City of New York FPC 1002; 1997; CD
Chorus, piano, organ

2661

Let Us Break Bread Together
Hogan, Moses
Sims, Robert (Baritone)
Deep River: Featuring 10 Spirituals Arranged for Solo Voice....
MGH Records 5000; 2000; CD
Piano
Heavy dialect

2662

Let Us Break Bread Together
Walters, Richard (ed.)
Stolen, Steven (Tenor)
15 Easy Spiritual Arrangements for the Progressing Singer
Hal Leonard HL00000391 (high) ; HL00000392 (low); 2005; Score w/CD
Piano
Light dialect

2663

Let Us Break Bread Together on Our Knees
Hogan, Moses
Stratton, Brian (Tenor)
Songs of Reflection
MGH Records 0800CD; 2020; CD

2664

Let Us Break Bread Together
Blanchard, Terence
Sykes, Jubilant (Baritone)
Jubilant Sykes
Sony Classical SK 63294; 1998; CD
Instrumental ensemble

2665

Let Us Break Bread Together (from *Cantata*)
Carter, John D.
Thomas, Indra (Soprano)
Great Day: Indra Thomas Sings Spirituals

Delos DE 3427; 2012; CD
Piano
Light dialect

2666

Air: Let Us Break Bread Together
[Carter, John D.]
Thoms, Treva (Soprano)
Come Sunday: Sacred American Songs
Private Label; 2007; CD
Piano

2667

Let Us Break Bread Together [from *Four Negro Spirituals*]
Smith, Hale
Toppin, Louise (Soprano)
Witness
Albany Records TROY868; 2006; CD
Orchestra
Moderate dialect

2668

Let Us Break Bread
Composer not identified
Tyler, Veronica (Soprano)
Sings ... the Passion of Christ in Spirituals
BRC Productions; [19--]; LP
Piano

2669

Let Us Break Bread Together (Air) [from *Cantata*]
[Carter, John D.]
Verdejo, Awilda (Soprano)
Awilda Verdejo Sings Spirituals
Angeluz Performances; 1999; CD
Piano

2670

Let Us Break Bread (Air) [from *Cantata*]
Carter, John D.
Wade, Ray, Jr. (Tenor)
Sence You Went Away
Albany Records TROY 387; 1998; CD
Piano
Moderate dialect

2671

Let Us Break Bread
Composer not identified
Webb, George (Tenor)
*Famous Negro Spirituals and Songs of
    Elizabethan England, Ireland & the
    Caribbean*
[Unknown] WLP7804; 1978; LP

2672

Let Us Break Bread Together on Our Knees
Composer not identified
West, Lucretia (Mezzo-soprano)
Negro Spirituals III
Club français du disque 176; 1959; LP
Piano
Heavy dialect

2673

Let Us Break Bread Together
Composer not identified
West, Lucretia (Mezzo-soprano)
Lucretia West Sings Spirituals
Westminster WP 6063; [1957]; LP

2674

Let Us Break Bread Together
Morgenstern, Sam
West, Lucretia (Mezzo-soprano)
Spirituals
Westminster WL 5338; 1954; LP
Orchestra

2675

Let Us Break Bread Together
[Hogan, Moses]
White, Cassandra (Soprano)
Remembering the Spirituals
CBW Entertainment 837101334068; 2007;
    CD
Piano
No dialect discerned

2676

Let Us Break Bread Together on Our Knees
    (Air) [from *Cantata*]
Carter, John D.
Williams, Wayne (Tenor)
Music from My Life

Movideo Productions 02-1993; 1993; CD
Piano

2677

Let Us Break Bread Together
Schweizer, Rolf
Wolf, Lars (Vocalist)
Die Schwarze Stimme Europas
Cantate 666000; 1971; LP
Chorus, organ, percussion

2678

Let Us Break Bread Together
[Lawrence, William]
Dobbs, Mattiwilda (Soprano)
Rarities
House of Opera CD96547; [20--]; CD
Piano
Moderate dialect

2679

Let Us Break Bread Together on Our Knees
Composer not identified
Robeson, Paul (Bass-baritone)
Encore, Robeson!
Monitor MP 581; 1960; LP

· · · · · · ·

Let Us Cheer
the Weary Traveler

2680

Let Us Cheer the Weary Traveler
Burleigh, Harry T.; Vene, Ruggero
Price, Leontyne (Soprano)
*The Essential Leontyne Price: Spirituals,
    Hymns & Sacred Songs*
BMG Classics 09026-68157-2; 1996; CD
Chorus
Moderate dialect

Also released with *The Essential Leontyne Price* (BMG Classics 09026-68153-2; 1996;
CD); *Complete Collection of Songs and Spiritual Albums* (RCA Red Seal 88697940502;
2011; CD); *I Wish I Knew How It Would Feel
to Be Free* (RCA Red Seal LSC 3183; 2011; CD)
and *Leontyne Price Sings Spirituals* (RCA Red
Seal 88691928242; 2012; CD)

· · · · · · ·

Let Us Go Down to Jordan

2681

Let Us Go Down to Jordan
Composer not identified
Davis, Frank (Bass-baritone)
16 Spirituals My Father Taught Me
DeWitt Records 601; 1960; LP

· · · · · · ·

Listen to the Angels

2682

Listen to the Angel's Shoutin'
Composer not identified
Martin, Vivian (Soprano)
Sings Spirituals and Songs
Halo 50277; 1957; LP

2683

Listen to the Angels Shoutin'
Composer not identified
Moses, Oral (Bass-baritone)
Extreme Spirituals
Cuneiform Record Rune 241; 2006; CD
Instrumental ensemble

2684

Listen to the Angels Shouting
Traditional
Moses, Oral (Bass-baritone)
Spirituals in Zion: A Spiritual Heritage for the Soul
Albany Records TROY587; 2003; CD
A cappella
Moderate dialect

2685

Listen to the Angels
Lloyd, Charles, Jr.
Paige-Green, Jacqueline (Soprano)
The Spiritual Art Song Collection
Warner Bros. SVBM00004; 2000; Score w/ CD
Piano

· · · · · · ·

Listen to the Lambs

2686

Listen to the Lambs
Venanzi, Henri
Arroyo, Martina (Soprano)
Spirituals
Centaur CRC 2060; 1991; CD
Piano
Heavy dialect

2687

Listen to the Lamb
Composer not identified
Duckworth, Zorita (Mezzo-soprano)
Forget Me Not.... Negro Spirituals
Private Label; [20--]; CD

2688

Listen to the Lambs
Henderson, Skitch
Hines, Jerome (Bass)
Standin' in the Need of Prayer
RCA Victor LPM-2047; [1960]; LP

2689

Listen to the Lambs
Composer not identified
Putkonen, Marko (Bass)
Deep River: Negro Spirituals
Lilium LILP 101; 1991; LP

· · · · · · ·

Little Boy

2690

Lit'l Boy [from *The Life of Christ*]
Hayes, Roland
Young, Thomas (Tenor)
A Spiritual Christmas
Musical Heritage Society 5167448; 2002; CD
Piano
Moderate dialect

2691

Lit'l Boy [from *The Life of Christ*]
Hayes, Roland

Caesar, Jackson (Tenor)
Spirituals: Celebrating the Music, Life,
  Legacy of Roland Hayes
CD Baby 7048606059; 2021; CD
Piano
Light dialect

2692

Little Boy
Composer not identified
Carey, Thomas (Baritone)
Go Down Moses
Da Camera Song SM 95028; 1970; LP
Piano

2693

Little Boy
Hayes, Roland
Carey, Thomas (Baritone)
Black Swans: At Mid-Century
Parnassus PACD 96078/9; 2021; CD
Piano
Heavy dialect

2694

Li'l Boy
Hayes, Roland
Clemmons, François (Tenor)
Negro Spirituals Live! In Concert
American Negro Spiritual Research
  Foundation 8177 2048 3779; 1998; CD
Piano
Light dialect

2695

Little Boy How Old Are You?
[Hayes, Roland]
Cook, Dixon & Young (Tenor)
Triptych: A Celebration of the Negro Spiritual
CDY Records 649241879206; 2009; CD
Piano
Moderate dialect

2696

Lit'l Boy [from *The Life of Christ*]
Hayes, Roland
Forrester, Maureen (Contralto)
An Evening with Maureen Forrester and
  Andrew Davis

Fanfare DFCD-9024; 1987; CD
Piano

2697

L'il Boy [from *The Life of Christ*]
Hayes, Roland
Forrester, Maureen (Contralto)
The Art of Maureen Forrester
Mastersound IMP 70170; 1997; CD
Piano

2698

Little Boy, How Old Are You?
Composer not identified
Hayes, Roland (Tenor)
Afro-American Folksongs
Pelican Records LP 2028; 1983; LP
Piano

2699

Lit'l Boy
Composer not identified
Hayes, Roland (Tenor)
Roland Hayes Sings: Negro Spirituals,
  Aframerican Folk Songs
Amadeo Records AVRS 6033; [19--]; LP
Piano

2700

Lit'l Boy [from *The Life of Christ*]
Hayes, Roland
Hayes, Roland (Tenor)
Roland Hayes Sings the Life of Christ: As Told
  Through Aframerican Folksong
Vanguard VRS-462; 1954; LP
Piano

2701

Lit'l Boy [from *The Life of Christ*]
Hayes, Roland
Hayes, Roland (Tenor)
Roland Hayes Sings the Life of Christ: As Told
  Through Aframerican Folksong
Vanguard SRV 352; 1976; LP
Piano

2702

Lit'l Boy [from *The Life of Christ*]
Hayes, Roland

Hayes, Roland (Tenor)
Favorite Spirituals
Vanguard Classics OVC 6022; 1995; CD
Piano
Light dialect

2703

Lit'l Boy (Christ in the Temple) [from *The Life of Christ*]
Hayes, Roland
Hayes, Roland (Tenor)
Negro Spirituals: The Concert Tradition 1909–1948
Frémeaux & Associés FA 168; 1999; CD
Piano
Light dialect

2704

Lit'l Boy [from *The Life of Christ*]
Hayes, Roland
Hayes, Roland (Tenor)
Charlton Heston Reads from The Life and Passion of Jesus Christ
Vanguard Classics ATM-CD-1259; 2003; CD
Piano

2705

Lit'l Boy (Christ in the Temple) [from *The Life of Christ*]
Hayes, Roland
Hayes, Roland (Tenor)
First Time Buyer's Guide to American Negro Spirituals
Primo Collection PRMCD6038; 2006; CD
Piano
No dialect discerned

2706

Lit'l Boy [from *The Life of Christ*]
Hayes, Roland
Hayes, Roland (Tenor)
The Art of Roland Hayes: Six Centuries of Song
Preiser Records; 2010; CD
Piano
Light dialect

2707

Lit'l Boy: Christ in the Temple before the Scribes [from *The Life of Christ*]

Hayes, Roland
Hayes, Roland (Tenor)
Lit'l Boy/I Want to Go Home/You're Tired, Chile!
Columbia 17275-D; [1941]; 78 RPM

2708

Lit'l Boy [from *The Life of Christ*]
Hayes, Roland
Hayes, Roland (Tenor)
Lit'l Boy/Were You There
Angel-Mo' AN 3122 E; [1941]; 78 RPM
Piano

2709

Lit'l Boy [from *The Life of Christ*]
Hayes, Roland
Hayes, Roland (Tenor)
Aframerican Folksong: Telling the Story of The Life of Christ
Top Rank 39 620; [1961]; LP
Piano

    Also released with *Art Songs and Spirituals* (Veritas VM 112; 1967; LP) and *Big Psalms, Hymns and Spirituals Box* (eOne Music/Vanguard Classics; 2015; Streaming audio)

2710

Lit'l Boy [from *The Life of Christ*]
[Hayes, Roland]
Hayes, Roland (Tenor)
The Concerto: African American Spirituals
Orange Amaro; 2019; Streaming audio
Piano

2711

Lit'l Boy [from *The Life of Christ*]
Hayes, Roland
Hazell, Earl (Bass)
Swing Low, Sweet Chariot
American Spiritual Ensemble; 2011; CD

2712

Lit'l Boy [from *The Life of Christ*]
Hayes, Roland
Holland, Charles (Tenor)
Cinq Negro Spirituals
Pathé 45 ED. 28; 1954; 45 RPM
Piano

2713

Lit'l Boy (Christ in the Temple) [from *The Life of Christ*]
Hayes, Roland
Holland, Charles (Tenor)
My Lord What a Mornin'
Musical Heritage Society MHS 912250X; 1982; LP
Piano
No dialect discerned

Also released with *My Lord What a Mornin'* (Musical Heritage Society MHS 512250K; 1988; CD)

2714

Lit'l Boy [from *The Life of Christ*]
Hayes, Roland
Jefferson, Othello (Tenor)
Good News: African American Spirituals and Art Songs
Cambria Records CD 1270; 2021; CD
Piano
Light dialect

2715

Lit'l Boy How Old Are You? [from *The Life of Christ*]
[Hayes, Roland]
Jenkins, Isaiah (Tenor)
Lyric Tenor
Trans Radio TR 1010A; [195-]; LP
Piano

2716

Lil' Boy, How Old Are You? [from *The Life of Christ*]
Hayes, Roland
Matthews, Benjamin (Baritone)
A Balm in Gilead
Ebony Classic Recordings ECR 0001; 2000; CD
Piano

2717

Litl' Boy [from *The Life of Christ*]
Hayes, Roland
Matthews, Inez (Mezzo-soprano)
Inez Matthews Sings Spirituals
Essential Media Group; 2011; CD

Piano
Heavy dialect

2718

Litl' Boy [from *The Life of Christ*]
Hayes, Roland
Matthews, Inez (Mezzo-soprano)
Inez Matthews Sings Spirituals (Great New Voices of Today, v. 6)
Period SPL-580; [1950]; LP
Piano
Heavy dialect

2719

Lit'l Boy [from *The Life of Christ*]
Hayes, Roland
Moses, Oral (Bass-baritone)
Songs of America
Albany Records TROY1011; 2008; CD
Piano
Light dialect

Also released with *Sankofa: A Spiritual Reflection* (Albany Records TROY1802; 2019; CD)

2720

Lit'l Boy [from *The Life of Christ*]
Hayes, Roland
Oby, Jason (Tenor)
The Life of Christ: Collected Spirituals
Private Label TSU4749; [200-]; CD
Piano
Light dialect

2721

Lit'l Boy [from *The Life of Christ*]
Hayes, Roland
Oglesby, Isador (Tenor)
Life of Jesus in Negro Spirituals
Oglesby Recordings Album 2; 1980; LP
Piano

2722

Lit'l Boy How Old Are You? [from *The Life of Christ*]
Hayes, Roland
Patton. John (Tenor)
Black Spirituals and Art Songs
Narthex Recording 827N-4581; 1970; LP

Piano
Moderate dialect

2723

Lt'l Boy [from *The Life of Christ*]
Hayes, Roland
Quivar, Florence (Mezzo-soprano)
Negro Spirituals
EMI 7243 5 72790 2 4; 1998; CD
Piano
Light dialect

2724

Lit'l Boy [from *The Life of Christ*]
Hayes, Roland
Quivar, Florence (Mezzo-soprano)
*Ride On, King Jesus! Florence Quivar Sings
    Black Music of America*
EMI Classics 9 67138 2; 2010; CD
Piano

2725

Little Boy, How Old Are You?
Traditional
Rustin, Bayard (Tenor)
*Bayard Rustin Sings Spirituals, Work &
    Freedom Songs*
Bayard Rustin Fund; 1988; Cassette
A cappella
Moderate dialect

2726

Little Boy, How Old Are You?
Traditional
Rustin, Bayard (Tenor)
*Bayard Rustin Sings Spirituals, Work &
    Freedom Songs*
Bayard Rustin Fund; 2003; CD
A cappella
Moderate dialect

2727

Lit'l Boy [from *The Life of Christ*]
Hayes, Roland
Salters, Stephen (Baritone)
Stephen Salters/Shiela Kibbe
Musica Numeris CYP 9602; 2005; CD

2728

Lit'l Boy [from *The Life of Christ*]
Hayes, Roland
Salters, Stephen (Baritone)
Spirit: Are You There, You Are There
HarmonizedDisharmony 0001; 2015; CD

2729

Lit'l Boy [from *The Life of Christ*]
Hayes, Roland
Shirley, George (Tenor)
George Shirley at 80: My Time Has Come!
Videmus Records; 2014; CD
Piano

2730

Lit'l Boy [from *The Life of Christ*]
Hayes, Roland
Sims, Robert (Baritone)
*In the Spirit: Spirituals and American Songs
    with Orchestra and Chorus*
Canti Classics; 2009; CD
Piano
Heavy dialect

2731

Lit'l Boy [from *The Life of Christ*]
Hayes, Roland
Sims, Robert (Baritone)
*Robert Sims Sings the Spirituals of Roland
    Hayes*
Canti Classics 2014-01; 2015; CD
Piano
Heavy dialect

2732

Lit'l Boy [from *The Life of Christ*]
Hayes, Roland
Sims, Robert (Baritone)
*Soul of a Singer: Robert Sims Sings African-
    American Folk Songs*
Canti Classics 9801; 2013; CD
Piano
Heavy dialect

2733

Li'l Boy How Ol' Are You?
Composer not identified

Smith, Muriel (Mezzo-soprano)
The Glory of Christmas
Philips BL 7586; [196-]; LP
Chorus, orchestra

2734

Lit'l Boy [from *The Life of Christ*]
Hayes, Roland
Warfield, William (Bass-baritone)
*Spirituals: 200 Years of African-American
    Spirituals*
ProArte CDD 3443; 1993; CD
Piano
Light dialect

2735

Lit'l Boy [from *The Life of Christ*]
Hayes, Roland
Williams, Willie (Vocalist)
My Tribute
Discovery V42227; 1974; LP
Piano

2736

Lit'l Boy (Christ in the Temple)
Young, Thomas J.
Young, Thomas (Tenor)
*Black Christmas: Spirituals in the African-
    American Tradition*
Essay Recordings CD1011; 1990; CD
Piano
No dialect discerned

· · · · · · ·

Little David Play
on Your Harp

2737

Little David, Play on Your Harp
Burleigh, Harry T.
Arroyo, Martina (Soprano)
Spirituals
Centaur CRC 2060; 1991; CD
Piano
Heavy dialect

2738

Little David, Play on Your Harp
Composer not identified

Arroyo, Martina (Soprano); Lane, Betty
    (Vocalist)
There's a Meeting Here Tonight
Angel S-36072; 1974; LP
Chorus

2739

Li'l David Play on Your Harp
Composer not identified
Arroyo, Martina (Soprano)
Liederabend 1968
Hänssler Classic 93.719; 2012; CD
Piano
No dialect discerned

2740

Little David, Play on Your Harp
[Burleigh, Harry T.]
Arroyo, Martina (Soprano)
Negro Spirituals
EMI 7243 5 72790 2 4; 1998; CD
Chorus
Moderate dialect

2741

Lit'l David Play on Your Harp
Hayes, Roland
Caesar, Jackson (Tenor)
*Spirituals: Celebrating the Music, Life,
    Legacy of Roland Hayes*
CD Baby 7048606059; 2021; CD
Piano
No dialect discern

2742

Lil' David [from Songs for Joy (A Suite of
    Spirituals)]
Simpson-Currenton, Evelyn
Chandler-Eteme, Janice (Soprano)
Devotions
Sligo Records; 2007; CD
Piano

2743

Little David, Play on Your Harp
Ryan, Donald
Estes, Simon (Bass-baritone)
Steal Away: My Favorite Negro Spirituals
Deutsche Schallplatten DS 1041-2; 1994; CD

Piano
No dialect discerned

Also released with *Simon Sings His Favorite Gospels & Spirituals* (Praise Productions SMG-SE; 1999; CD) and *Save the Children, Save Their Lives* (CD Baby; 2010; CD)

2744
Li'l David
Simpson-Curenton, Evelyn
Graves, Denyce (Mezzo-soprano)
Angels Watching Over Me
NPR Classics CD 0006; 1997; CD
Piano
Moderate dialect

2745
Little David
Composer not identified
Hayes, Roland (Tenor)
Afro-American Folksongs
Pelican Records LP 2028; 1983; LP
Piano

2746
Lit'l David
Hayes, Roland
Hayes, Roland (Tenor)
Roland Hayes: My Songs
Vanguard VRS-494; 1956; LP
Piano
Moderate dialect

Also released with *The Art of Roland Hayes* (Smithsonian Collection RD 041; 1990; CD); *Favorite Spirituals* (Vanguard Classics OVC 6022; 1995; CD) and *Big Psalms, Hymns and Spirituals Box* (eOne Music/Vanguard Classics; 2015; Streaming audio)

2747
Little David, Play on Your Harp [from Five Spirituals]
Stucky, Rodney
Henderson, Mary (Mezzo-soprano)
Come Where the Aspens Quiver.... Bring Your Guitar
Fleur de Son Classics FDS 57955; 2002; CD
Guitar
No dialect discerned

2748
Little David Play on Your Harp
Burleigh, Harry T.
Holmes, Eugene (Baritone)
Eugene Holmes Sings Spirituals
Avant Garde AV-115; [1968]; LP
Piano
Light dialect

2749
Lit'le David Play on Yo' Harp
Johnson, John Rosamond
Honeysucker, Robert (Baritone)
Let's Have a Union
Brave Records BRAV-0923; 2009; CD
Piano
Moderate dialect

2750
Little David
Browne, George
Lawrence, Martin (Bass-baritone)
Negro Spirituals
P&R; 2011; Streaming audio
Orchestra
Moderate dialect

2751
Little David
Browne, George
Lawrence, Martin (Bass-baritone)
Negro Spirituals
Marathon Media International; 2013; Streaming audio
Orchestra
Moderate dialect

2752
Little David
Browne, George
Lawrence, Martin (Bass-baritone)
Negro Spirituals
World Record Club MW-2005; [196-]; LP
Orchestra
Moderate dialect

2753
Little David, Play on Your Harp
Welsh, Nicky

McCue, Bill (Bass-baritone)
Bill McCue Sings the Great Spirituals
Beltona SBE 173; 1974; LP
Orchestra

2754

Lil' David
Simpson-Curenton, Evelyn
Moses, Oral (Bass-baritone)
Come Down Angels and Trouble the Water:
Negro Spirituals, an American National
Treasure!
Albany Records TROY 1489; 2014; CD
Piano
Light dialect

2755

Lit'le David Play on Yo' Harp
Flynn, William
Paris, Virginia (Contralto)
Spirituals
Spotlight Classic SC 1008; 1957; LP
Orchestra

2756

Little David, Play on Yo' Harp
Flynn, William
Paris, Virginia (Contralto)
Virginia Paris in Australia
Lyric Records CD 178; [2005]; CD
Orchestra

2757

Little David, Play on Your Harp
Burleigh, Harry T.
Parks, Karen (Soprano)
Nobody Knows
Ottimavoce 52736; 2007; CD
Piano
Light dialect

2758

Little David Play on Your Harp
Hayes, Roland
Patton. John (Tenor)
Black Spirituals and Art Songs
Narthex Recording 827N-4581; 1970; LP
Piano
Moderate dialect

2759

Little David, Play on Your Harp
Johnson, Hall
Ragin, Derek Lee (Countertenor)
Ev'ry Time I Feel the Spirit: Spirituals
Channel Classics CCS 2991; 1991; CD
Piano
Heavy dialect

2760

Little David, Play on Yo' Harp
Giesen, Hubert
Ray, William (Baritone)
Negro Spirituals
Intercord; [19--]; LP
Piano

2761

Little David, Play on Yo' Harp
Giesen, Hubert
Ray, William (Baritone)
Sings Arias, Duets, Musical Selections and
Negro Spirituals
Intercord; [19--]; CD
Piano

2762

Lil' David
Brown, Lawrence
Robeson, Paul (Bass-baritonc); Brown,
Lawrence (Vocalist)
Swing Low, Sweet Chariot
Columbia Masterworks MM-819; 1949; 78
RPM
Piano
Moderate dialect

2763

Lil' David
Brown, Lawrence
Robeson, Paul (Bass-baritone); Brown,
Lawrence (Vocalist)
Paul Robeson Chante ... 16 Spirituals
Philips G 05.639 R; 1959; LP
Piano

2764

Li'l David
Brown, Lawrence

Robeson, Paul (Bass-baritone); Brown,
    Lawrence (Vocalist)
Paul Robeson
Pearl GEMM CD 9356; 1989; CD

2765
Li'l David
Brown, Lawrence
Robeson, Paul (Bass-baritone); Brown,
    Lawrence (Vocalist)
The Complete EMI Sessions (1928–1939)
EMI Classics 50999 2 15586 2 7; 2008; CD
Piano
Heavy dialect

2766
Lil David
Brown, Lawrence
Robeson, Paul (Bass-baritone)
Paul Robeson Sings Negro Spirituals
Philips GBL 5584; [19--]; LP
Piano

2767
Little David, Play on Your Harp
[Brown, Lawrence]
Robeson, Paul (Bass-baritone); Brown,
    Lawrence (Vocalist)
Scandalize My Name
Classics Record Library 30-5647; 1976; LP
Piano
Light dialect

2768
Lil' David
[Brown, Lawrence]
Robeson, Paul (Bass-baritone); Brown,
    Lawrence (Vocalist)
The Ultimate Collection
Burning Fire; 2009; Streaming audio
Piano
Heavy dialect

2769
Lil' David
[Brown, Lawrence]
Robeson, Paul (Bass-baritone)
Swing Low, Sweet Chariot

Columbia Masterworks ML 2038; [195-];
    LP
Piano

2770
Lit'l David
Hayes, Roland
Sims, Robert (Baritone)
*Robert Sims Sings the Spirituals of Roland
    Hayes*
Canti Classics 2014-01; 2015; CD
Piano
Heavy dialect

2771
Little David, Play on Yo Harp
Composer not identified
Spencer, Kenneth (Bass-baritone)
American Spirituals
Sonora MS-478; [1945]; 78 RPM
Piano
Heavy dialect

2772
Little David Play on Yo Harp
Composer not identified
Spencer, Kenneth (Bass-baritone)
Negro Spirituals
Life Records C 1108; [19--]; LP

2773
Little David Play on Yo' Harp
Nagel, [Otto]
Spencer, Kenneth (Bass-baritone)
Volkslieder & Spirituals
Discoton 75546; [197-]; LP
Chorus
Light dialect

2774
Little David Play on Your Harp
Bonds, Margaret
Toppin, Louise (Soprano)
Ah! Love, But a Day
Albany Records/ Videmus TROY 385; 2000;
    CD
Piano
Heavy dialect

2775

Lit'le David Play on Yo' Harp
Composer not identified
West, Lucretia (Mezzo-soprano)
Spirituals
Westminster WL 5338; 1954; LP
Piano

2776

Little David Play on Your Harp
Composer not identified
West, Lucretia (Mezzo-soprano)
Lucretia West Sings Spirituals
Westminster WP 6063; [1957]; LP

2777

Little David Play on Your Harp
Composer not identified
Williams, Wayne (Tenor)
Music from My Life
Movideo Productions 02-1993; 1993; CD
Piano

· · · · · · ·

Little More Faith in Jesus

2778

A Little More Faith in Jesus
Traditional
Moses, Oral (Bass-baritone)
Spirituals in Zion: A Spiritual Heritage for the Soul
Albany Records TROY587; 2003; CD
A cappella
Heavy dialect

· · · · · · ·

Live a-Humble

2779

Live a-Humble
Boatwright, McHenry
Boatwright, McHenry (Bass-baritone)
Art of McHenry Boatwright: Spirituals
Golden Crest Records RE 7024; 1968; LP
Piano
Light dialect

2780

Live-a-Humble [from *The Life of Christ*]
Hayes, Roland
Caesar, Jackson (Tenor)
Spirituals: Celebrating the Music, Life, Legacy of Roland Hayes
CD Baby 7048606059; 2021; CD
Piano
Moderate dialect

2781

Live-a-Humble
Mills, Marvin
Graves, Denyce (Mezzo-soprano)
Angels Watching Over Me
NPR Classics CD 0006; 1997; CD
Chorus, piano
Heavy dialect

2782

Live a-Humble [from *The Life of Christ*]
Hayes, Roland
Hayes, Roland (Tenor)
Roland Hayes Sings the Life of Christ: As Told Through Aframerican Folksong
Vanguard VRS-462; 1954; LP
Piano

2783

Live a-Humble [from *The Life of Christ*]
Hayes, Roland
Hayes, Roland (Tenor)
Roland Hayes Sings the Life of Christ: As Told Through Aframerican Folksong
Vanguard SRV 352; 1976; LP
Piano

2784

Live a-Humble [from *The Life of Christ*]
Hayes, Roland
Hayes, Roland (Tenor)
Favorite Spirituals
Vanguard Classics OVC 6022; 1995; CD
Piano
Light dialect

2785

Live a-Humble [from *The Life of Christ*]
Hayes, Roland

Hayes, Roland (Tenor)
Charlton Heston Reads from The Life and Passion of Jesus Christ
Vanguard Classics ATM-CD-1259; 2003; CD
Piano

2786

Live a-Humble [from *The Life of Christ*]
Hayes, Roland
Hayes, Roland (Tenor)
Aframerican Folksong: Telling the Story of The Life of Christ
Top Rank 39 620; [1961]; LP
Piano

2787

Live a-Humble
[Hayes, Roland]
Hayes, Roland (Tenor)
Big Psalms, Hymns and Spirituals Box
eOne Music/Vanguard Classics; 2015; Streaming audio
Piano

2788

Live Humble [from *The Life of Christ*]
Hayes, Roland
Holland, Charles (Tenor)
Cinq Negro Spirituals
Pathé 45 ED. 28; 1954; 45 RPM
Piano

2789

Live A-Humble (Healed the sick) [from *The Life of Christ*]
Hayes, Roland
Holland, Charles (Tenor)
My Lord What a Mornin'
Musical Heritage Society MHS 912250X; 1982; LP
Piano
No dialect discerned

2790

Live A-Humble (Healed the sick) [from *The Life of Christ*]
Hayes, Roland
Holland, Charles (Tenor)
My Lord What a Mornin'

Musical Heritage Society MHS 512250K; 1988; CD
Piano
No dialect discerned

2791

Live a-Humble [from *The Life of Christ*]
[Hayes, Roland]
Jenkins, Isaiah (Tenor)
Lyric Tenor
Trans Radio TR 1010A; [195-]; LP
Piano

2792

Live a Humble [from *The Life of Christ*]
Hayes, Roland
Matthews, Benjamin (Baritone)
A Spiritual Journey
Ebony Classic Recordings ECR 0001; 2000; CD
Piano

2793

Live a-Humble [from *The Life of Christ*]
Hayes, Roland
Matthews, Inez (Mezzo-soprano)
Inez Matthews Sings Spirituals
Essential Media Group; 2011; CD
Piano
Moderate dialect

2794

Live a-Humble [from *The Life of Christ*]
Hayes, Roland
Matthews, Inez (Mezzo-soprano)
Inez Matthews Sings Spirituals (Great New Voices of Today, v. 6)
Period SPL-580; [1950]; LP
Piano
Moderate dialect

2795

Live a-Humble
Composer not identified
Norman, Jessye (Soprano)
Negro Spirituals
Philips 9500 580; 1979; LP
Chorus
Light dialect

Also released with *The Jessye Norman Collection: Sacred Songs & Spirituals* (Philips B0004506-02; 2005; CD)

2796

Live a Humble
Patterson. Willis
Norman, Jessye (Soprano)
Spirituals
Philips 416 462-2; 1990; CD
Chorus
Light dialect

2797

Live a-Humble [from *The Life of Christ*]
Hayes, Roland
Oby, Jason (Tenor)
The Life of Christ: Collected Spirituals
Private Label TSU4749; [200-]; CD
Piano
Heavy dialect

2798

Live a-Humble
Hogan, Moses
Ragin, Derek Lee (Countertenor)
Ev'ry Time I Feel the Spirit: Spirituals
Channel Classics CCS 2991; 1991; CD
Piano
Heavy dialect

2799

Live a-Humble [from *The Life of Christ*]
Hayes, Roland
Shirley, George (Tenor)
George Shirley at 80: My Time Has Come!
Videmus Records; 2014; CD
Piano

2800

Live a-Humble [from *The Life of Christ*]
Hayes, Roland
Sims, Robert (Baritone)
Robert Sims Sings the Spirituals of Roland Hayes
Canti Classics 2014-01; 2015; CD
Piano
Heavy dialect

2801

Live a Humble
Blanchard, Terence
Sykes, Jubilant (Baritone)
Jubilant Sykes
Sony Classical SK 63294; 1998; CD
Instrumental ensemble

2802

Live a-Humble
Composer not identified
Verdejo, Awilda (Soprano)
Awilda Verdejo Sings Spirituals
Angeluz Performances; 1999; CD
Piano

2803

Live a-Humble [from *The Life of Christ*]
Hayes, Roland
Williams, Willie (Vocalist)
My Tribute
Discovery V42227; 1974; LP
Piano

. . . .

Lord, Guide My Feet

2804

Lord Guide My Feet
Composer not identified
Davis, Frank (Bass-baritone)
16 Spirituals My Father Taught Me
DeWitt Records 601; 1960; LP

. . . .

Lord, How Come Me Here

2805

Lord, How Come Me Here?
Johnson, Hall
Anderson, Marian (Contralto)
Jus' Keep on Singin'
RCA Victor LSC 2796; 1965; LP
Piano

Also released with *Marian Anderson: Beyond the Music; Her Complete RCA Victor*

Recordings Sony Classical 19439836492; 2021; CD

2806
Lord, How Come Me Here?
Johnson, Hall
Anderson, Marian (Contralto)
He's Got the Whole World in His Hands: Spirituals
RCA Victor 09026-61960-2; 1994; CD
Piano
Moderate dialect

2807
Lord, How Come Me Here
Olden Lee, Sylvia; Simpson-Curenton, Evelyn
Battle, Kathleen (Soprano)
Spirituals in Concert
Deutsche Grammophon 429 790-2; 1991; CD
Flute
Heavy dialect

2808
Lord, How Come Me Here?
Okpebholo, Shawn
Bridges, J'nai (Mezzo-soprano)
Lord How Come Me Here?
Navona Records NV6408; 2022; CD
Cello
Light dialect

2809
Lord, How Come Me Here?
Brown, Angela
Brown, Angela (Soprano)
Soprano
Caboose Productions; 1995; CD
A cappella
Heavy dialect

2810
Lord, How Come Me Here
Composer not identified
Brown, Angela (Soprano)
Ol' Time Religion
American Spiritual Ensemble ASE012; 2001; CD

2811
Lord, How Come Me Here
Simpson-Curenton, Evelyn; Brown, Angela
Brown, Angela (Soprano)
Mosiac: A Collection of African-American Spirituals with Piano, guitar
Albany Records TROY721; 2004; CD
A cappella
Moderate dialect

2812
Lord How Come Me Here?
Composer not identified
Chatham, Joyce (Vocalist)
They Slice the Air
Spirituals Project; 2007; CD
Guitar
Heavy dialect

2813
Lord. How Come Me Here? [from *Five Negro Worksongs*]
Composer not identified
Hayes, Roland (Tenor)
Evening with Roland Hayes, Tenor
Heritage LP-SS-1204; 1953; LP
Piano
Heavy dialect

   Also released with *A Roland Hayes Recital* (A 440 Records AC1203; [19--]; LP) and *The Art of Roland Hayes: Six Centuries of Song* (Preiser Records; 2010; CD)

2814
Lord, How Come Me Here?
Traditional
Nobles, NaGuanda (Soprano)
Homage to the Journey
Selbon Records; 2014; Streaming audio
A cappella
Moderate dialect

. . . .

Lord, I Can't Turn Back

2815
Lord, I Can't Turn Back
Williams, Robert E.

Blackmon, Henry (Baritone)
Negro Spirituals
Mirasound Records SGLP 6047; [19--]; LP
Organ

2816
Lord, I Can't Turn Back
Williams, Robert E.
Blackmon, Henry (Baritone)
Negro Spirituals
Vega 19179; [19--]; LP
Chorus, piano

2817
Lord, I Can't Turn Back
Lloyd, Charles, Jr.
Paige-Green, Jacqueline (Soprano)
The Spiritual Art Song Collection
Warner Bros. SVBM00004; 2000; Score w/
    CD
Piano

2818
Lord, I Can't Turn Back
Williams, R. E.
Ragin, Derek Lee (Countertenor)
Negro Spirituals
Virgin Classics 0946 363305 2 5; 2006; CD
Chorus
Light dialect

· · · · · · ·
Lord, I Didn't Know

2819
Lord I Didn't Know
Plinton, [Ursula]; Matthews
Matthews, Inez (Mezzo-soprano)
*Inez Matthews Sings Spirituals (Great New
    Voices of Today, v. 6)*
Period SPL-580; [1950]; LP
Piano
Moderate dialect

    Also released with *Inez Matthews Sings
Spirituals* (Essential Media Group; 2011;
CD)

· · · · · · ·
Lord, I Don't Care Where You Bury My Body

2820
Lord, I Don't Care Where You Bury My
    Body
Composer not identified
Rustin, Bayard (Tenor)
Bayard Rustin, the Singer
Bayard Rustin Fund; 1992; CD
Piano

2821
Lord I Don't Care Where You Bury My Body
Traditional
Rustin, Bayard (Tenor)
*Bayard Rustin Sings Twelve Spirituals on the
    Life of Christ*
Fellowship Records E2-KL 1771; [195-]; LP
A cappella
Moderate dialect

    Also released with *Bayard Rustin-The
Singer* (Black Swan Series; Parnassus Records
PACD 96083; 2022; CD)

· · · · · · ·
Lord, I Don't Feel

2822
Lord, I don't feel
Johnson, Hall
West, Lucretia (Mezzo-soprano)
Negro Spirituals mit Lukretia West
Opera 3408; [195-]; LP
Piano

· · · · · · ·
Lord, I Don't Feel Noways Tired

2823
Lord, I Don't Feel Noways Tired
Johnson, Hall
Blackmon, Henry (Baritone)
Negro Spirituals
Jubilate JB 1716; 1961; 45 RPM
Organ

·······
Lord, I Have Seen

2824

Lord, I Have Seen
Cooper, John D.
Jones, Andrea (Soprano)
Ol' Time Religion
American Spiritual Ensemble ASE012; 2001;
CD

·······
Lord, I Just Can't Keep from Cryin'

2825

Lord, I Just Can't Keep from Cryin' [from
    Five Creek-Freedmen Spirituals]
Bonds, Margaret; Brown, Angela; Cooper,
    Tyron
Brown, Angela (Soprano)
*Mosiac: A Collection of African-American
    Spirituals with Piano, guitar*
Albany Records TROY721; 2004; CD
Guitar
Light dialect

2826

Lord, I Just Can't Keep from Cryin' [from
    Five Creek-Freedmen Spirituals]
Bonds, Margaret
Hamilton, Ruth (Contralto)
*Watch and Pray: Spirituals and Art Songs by
    African-American Women Composers*
Koch International Classics 3-7247-2H1;
    1994; CD
Piano
Heavy dialect

2827

Lord, I Just Can't Keep from Crying [from
    Settings for Spirituals]
Chadabe, Joel
Oliver, Irene (Soprano)
Settings for Spirituals; Solo
Lovely Music VR-3804; 1984; LP
Electronics

2828

Lord, I Just Can't Keep from Cryin' [from
    Five Creek-Freedmen Spirituals]
Bonds, Margaret
Price, Leontyne (Soprano)
*Complete Collection of Songs and Spiritual
    Albums*
RCA Red Seal 88697940502; 2011; CD

2829

Lord, I Just Can't Keep from Cryin' [from
    Five Creek-Freedmen Spirituals]
[Bonds, Margaret]
Price, Leontyne (Soprano)
Leontyne Price reDiscovered
RCA Victor Red Seal 09026-63908-2; 2002;
    CD
Piano
Heavy dialect

2830

Lord, I Just Can't Keep from Cryin' [from
    Five Creek-Freedmen Spirituals]
[Bonds, Margaret]
Price, Leontyne (Soprano)
Great Moments at Carnegie Hall
RCA Red Seal 88985304202; 2016; CD
Piano
Heavy dialect

2831

Lord, I Just Can't Keep from Cryin' [from
    Five Creek-Freedmen Spirituals]
Bonds, Margaret
Rhodes, Yolanda (Soprano)
The Angels Bowed Down
Cambria Master Recordings CD-1237; 2019;
    CD

2832

Lord, I Just Can't Keep from Cryin' [from
    Five Creek-Freedmen Spirituals]
[Bonds, Margaret]
Verdejo, Awilda (Soprano)
Awilda Verdejo Sings Spirituals
Angeluz Performances; 1999; CD
Piano

2833
Lord I Just Can't Keep from Crying
Composer not identified
Green, Elnora E. (Contralto)
This Is My Task
Private Label NR 18650; 1991; LP

· · · · · · ·

Lord, I Want to Be a Christian

2834
Lord I Want to Be a Christian
Composer not identified
Hendricks, Barbara (Soprano)
100 Plus Beaux Airs de Barbara Hendricks, Les
EMI Classics 50999 085683 2 8; 2012; CD
Chorus
Moderate dialect

2835
Lord, I Want to Be a Christian
Composer not identified
Credit, Roosevelt André (Bass-baritone)
Get on Board
Private label; 2016; Streaming audio
Piano
Light dialect

2836
Lord I Want to Be a Christian
Composer not identified
Jones, Fanni (Mezzo-soprano)
Negro Spirituals
Phonotec 815; 1977; LP
Organ

2837
Lord I Want to Be a Christian
Composer not identified
Nobles, NaGuanda (Soprano)
Homage to the Journey
Selbon Records; 2014; Streaming audio
Piano
No dialect discerned

2838
I Want to Be a Christian
Johnson, Hall

Oglesby, Isador (Tenor)
Life of Jesus in Negro Spirituals
Oglesby Recordings Album 2; 1980; LP
Piano

2839
Lord, I Want to Be a Christian
Sadin, Robert
Robinson, Morris (Bass)
Going Home
Decca B0008277-02; 2007; CD
Instrumental ensemble
No dialect discerned

2840
Lord I Want to Be More Humble in My
    Heart
Composer not identified
Hunt, Arthur Billings (Baritone)
Hymns and Spirituals
Cook Laboratories 1090; [195-]; LP
Organ

2841
Lord, I Want to Be a Christian
Corley, Maria Thompson
Clark, Maria (Soprano)
Soul Sanctuary: Spirituals & Hymns
Navona Records NV6406; 2022; CD
Piano
Heavy dialect

2842
Lord, I Want to Be a Christian
Ryan, Donald
Estes, Simon (Bass-baritone)
Steal Away: My Favorite Negro Spirituals
Deutsche Schallplatten DS 1041-2; 1994; CD
Piano
No dialect discerned

2843
Lawd Ah Wants to Be a Christian
Still, William Grant
Harris, Inetta (Soprano)
*My Heritage Sings: A Selection of Spirituals
    & Hymns*
Private Label; [199-]; CD
Piano

2844

Lord, I Want to Be a Christian
Hogan, Moses
Hendricks, Barbara (Soprano)
Give Me Jesus
EMI Classics 7243 5 56788 2 9; 1998; CD
Chorus
Moderate dialect

2845

Lawd, Ah Wants to Be a Christian
Still, William Grant
Hill, Christin-Marie (Mezzo-soprano)
Songs of William Grant Still
White Pine Music WPM224; 2015; CD
Piano

2846

Lord, I Want to Be a Christian
Suben, Joel Eric
Lennick, Jessica (Soprano)
Five Spirituals for Soprano and Orchestra
Private label; 2018; Streaming audio
Orchestra
Heavy dialect

2847

Lord, I Want to Be a Christian
Composer not identified
McDaniel, Yvette (Soprano)
Simply Spiritual
YM01 DIDX 046103; 1997; CD
Piano

2848

Lawd I Wants to Be a Christian in my Heart
Still, William Grant
Patton. John (Tenor)
Black Spirituals and Art Songs
Narthex Recording 827N-4581; 1970; LP
Piano
Heavy dialect

2849

Lord, I Want to Be a Christian
Composer not identified
Ragin, Derek Lee (Countertenor)
Negro Spirituals
Virgin Classics 0946 363305 2 5; 2006; CD
Chorus
Light dialect

2850

Lord, I Want to Be a Christian
Walters, Richard (ed.)
Stolen, Steven (Tenor)
*15 Easy Spiritual Arrangements for the
    Progressing Singer*
Hal Leonard HL00000391 (high);
    HL00000392 (low); 2005; Score w/CD
Piano
No dialect discerned

2851

Lord, I Want to Be a Christian
Coil, Pat; Wilson-Felder, Cynthia
Wilson-Felder, Cynthia (Soprano)
*Spirituals: Songs from the American
    Experience*
GBGMusik CD 1-005; 1996; CD
Piano

. . . .

Lord, I'll Go

2852

Lord, I'll Go
Hairston, Jacqueline
Taylor, Darryl (Countertenor)
How Sweet the Sound: A Charm of Spirituals
Albany TROY1244; 2011; CD
Piano

. . . .

Lord, Is This Heaven

2853

Lord, is this Heaven? [from *My Songs:
    Dream of Heaven*]
Hayes, Roland
Hayes, Roland (Tenor)
Favorite Spirituals
Vanguard Classics OVC 6022; 1995; CD
Piano
Heavy dialect

Also released with *Big Psalms, Hymns
and Spirituals Box* (eOne Music/Vanguard
Classics; 2015; Streaming audio)

········

Mah Brudder's Died an' Gone to Hebben

2854

Mah Brudder's Died an' Gone to Hebben
Suben, Joel Eric
Lennick, Jessica (Soprano)
Five Spirituals for Soprano and Orchestra
Private label; 2018; Streaming audio
Orchestra
Moderate dialect

········

Make More Room

2855

Make More Room
Dett, Robert Nathaniel
Reavis, Hattie King (Contralto)
Black Swans
Parnassus Recordings PACD 96067; 2019; CD

········

Man Goin' Round

2856

A Man Goin' Round
Dett, Robert Nathaniel
Pankey, Aubrey (Baritone)
Negro Spirituals
Eterna 830010; 1983; LP
Piano

········

March Down to Jordan

2857

March Down to Jordan
Hairston, Jacqueline
Matthews, Benjamin (Baritone)
A Spiritual Journey
Ebony Classic Recordings ECR 0001; 2000; CD
Piano

2858

March Down to Jordan
Hairston, Jacqueline

Overton, Kenneth (Baritone)
Been in de Storm So Long (Songs My Fathers Taught Me)
American Spiritual Ensemble; 2012; CD
Piano
Heavy dialect

········

March On

2859

March On! [from *Green Pastures*]
Johnson, Hall
Brown, William (Tenor)
The Hall Johnson Collection
Carl Fischer VF5 CD1–VF5 CD2; 2003; Score w/CD
Piano
Moderate dialect

2860

March On
Composer not identified
Franklin, Lavinia A. (Vocalist)
Historical Interpretation of Negro Spirituals and Lift Every Voice and Sing
Recorded Publications JZB-02591; 1970; LP
Organ

········

Mary and Her Baby Chile

2861

Mary and Her Baby Chile
Hairston, Jacqueline
Battle, Kathleen (Soprano)
The Complete Sony Recordings
Sony Classical 88985381362; 2016; CD
Guitar

········

Mary Had a Baby

[Isaiah 9:6; Matthew 1:18-25; Luke 1:26-38, 2:1-21]

"Mary had a baby, Yes, Lord! The people keep a-coming, but the train done gone. / What did she name him? Where did she lay him? Laid in a manager, Wrapped him in swaddling...." [Available in HJTS, RW15]

The Christmas season was the one time of the year when the burdens borne by the enslaved were lightened and they were allowed to celebrate, though slave narratives and research on the period suggested celebrations that tended more towards the profane than the sacred. This folk spiritual is one of the few that remain of the era. Its verses tell the story of Christ's birth through the actions of His mother, Mary.

The choral versions composed by Hall Johnson and William Levi Dawson of the concert spiritual are more regularly featured than the solo vocal setting by Johnson. The Johnson settings include the text "The people keep a-coming, but the train done gone," raising the question about whether the intent of the text is a possible "secret signal" of an impending escape. Rather, the text suggests a cautionary that the opportunity for redemption from sin has already departed, a sentiment similarly expressed in the spiritual, "Heav'n, Heav'n" (Ev'rybody talkin' bout Heav'n ain't goin' dere).

2862

Mary Had a Baby
Johnson, Hall
Ayers, Vanessa (Mezzo-soprano)
Black Christmas: Spirituals in African-American Tradition
Essay Recordings CD1011; 1990; CD
Piano
Heavy dialect

Also released with *A Spiritual Christmas* (Musical Heritage Society 5167448; 2002; CD)

2863

Mary Had a Baby (Yes, Lord)
[Dawson, William L.]
Battle, Kathleen (Soprano)
A Christmas Celebration
EMI CDC-7 47587 2; 1986; CD
Chorus
No dialect discerned

2864

Mary Had a Baby
[Dawson, William L.]
Battle, Kathleen (Soprano)
Victoria Christmas in Song, A
Angel CDM 7 64896 2 9; 1993; CD
Chorus

2865

Mary Had a Baby
Dawson, William L.
Battle, Kathleen (Soprano)
Negro Spirituals
EMI 7243 5 72790 2 4; 1998; CD
Chorus, orchestra
No dialect discerned

2866

Mary Had a Baby
Hairston, Jacqueline
Battle, Kathleen (Soprano)
Angels' Glory
Sony Classical SK 62723; 1996; CD
Guitar
No dialect discerned

Also released with *The Complete Sony Recordings* (Sony Classical 88985381362; 2016; CD)

2867

Mary Had a Baby
Dawson, William L.
Bryant, Peter (Vocalist)
I Will Pass This Way but Once
Facts of Faith Records WR 5161; 1977; LP
Organ

2868

Mary Had a Baby
Composer not identified
Forrester, Maureen (Contralto)
The Art of Maureen Forrester
Mastersound IMP 70170; 1997; CD
Piano

2869

Mary Had a Baby
Traditional
Hendricks, Barbara (Soprano)

Shout for Joy: Spiritual Christmas (Noël sacré)
Arte Verum ARV-009; 2010; CD
A cappella
Heavy dialect

2870

Mary Had a Baby
Johnson, Hall
Jones, Arthur (Tenor)
Wade in the Water
Orbis Books; 1993; Book w/cass
Piano
Moderate dialect

2871

Mary Had a Baby
Johnson, Hall
Jones, Fanni (Mezzo-soprano)
Negro Spirituals en Concert
Suisa; 1987; LP
Organ
Moderate dialect

2872

Mary Had a Baby
Dawson, William L.
Jones-Sojola, Andrea (Soprano)
The Spirit of the Holidays
American Spiritual Ensemble; 2009; CD

2873

Mary Had a Baby
Hengeveld, G.
Judkins, Edith (Soprano)
Sacred Recital, A
United Sound USR 3845; [19--]; LP

2874

Mary Had a Baby
Walters, Richard (ed.)
Kruse, Tanya (Soprano)
15 Easy Spiritual Arrangements for the Progressing Singer
Hal Leonard HL00000391 (high) ; HL00000392 (low); 2005; Score w/CD
Piano
No dialect discerned

2875

Mary Had a Baby
Composer not identified
Lord, Marie-Josée (Soprano)
Amazing Grace
ATMA Classique ACD2 2686; 2014; CD
Chorus, organ

2876

Mary Had a Baby
Dawson, William L.
Martin, Marvis (Soprano)
The Spirituals of William L. Dawson
St. Olaf Records E-2159; 1997; CD
Chorus

2877

Mary Had a Baby
Composer not identified
Norman, Jessye (Soprano)
The Jessye Norman Collection: Sacred Songs & Spirituals
Philips B0004506-02; 2005; CD
Chorus
Light dialect

2878

Mary Had a Baby
Kerr, Thomas H., Jr.
Norman, Jessye (Soprano)
Negro Spirituals
Philips 9500 580; 1979; LP
Chorus

2879

Mary Had a Baby
Patterson. Willis
Norman, Jessye (Soprano)
Amazing Grace
Philips 432 546-2; 1990; CD
Chorus
No dialect discerned

Also released with *Spirituals* (Philips 416 462-2; 1990; CD) and *In the Spirit—Sacred Music for Christmas* (Philips B0005508-02; 2005; CD)

2880
Mary Had a Baby
Giesen, Hubert
Ray, William (Baritone)
Negro Spirituals
Intercord; [19--]; LP
Piano

     Also released with *Sings Arias, Duets, Musical Selections and Negro Spirituals* (Intercord; [19--]; CD)

2881
Mary Had a Baby, Yes Lord
Jackson
Robeson, Paul (Bass-baritone)
Paul Robeson Collection
Hallmark Recordings 390692; 1998; CD

2882
Mary Had a Baby, Yes Lord
Jackson
Robeson, Paul (Bass-baritone)
Paul Robeson
World Record Club W9648/EMI SM 431;
    [19--]; LP
Piano

     Also released with The *Complete EMI Sessions (1928–1939)* (EMI Classics 50999 2 15586 2 7; 2008; CD)

2883
Mary Had a Baby, Yes Lord
Jackson
Robeson, Paul (Bass-baritone)
Bear de Burden; All God's Chillun Got Wings/Mary Had a Baby, Yes, Lord
His Master's Voice B. 4336; [1933]; 78 RPM
Piano
Moderate dialect

2884
Mary Had a Baby, Yes Lord
[Johnson, Hall]
Robeson, Paul (Bass-baritone)
Green Pastures
ASV Living Era CD AJA 5047; 1987; CD

2885
Mary Had a Baby, Yes Lord
[Johnson, Hall]
Robeson, Paul (Bass-baritone)
Negro Spirituals, Blues, Songs
Saar CD 12519; 1995; CD

2886
Mary Had a Baby, Yes Lord
[Johnson, Hall]
Robeson, Paul (Bass-baritone)
Ol' Man River: His 56 Finest 1925–1945
Retrospective RTS 4116; 2008; CD

2887
Mary Had a Baby, Yes Lord
[Johnson, Hall]
Robeson, Paul (Bass-baritone)
The Very Best of Paul Robeson
Future Noise Music FVDD033; 2009; CD
Piano

2888
Mary Had a Baby
[Johnson, Hall]
Robeson, Paul (Bass-baritone)
The Ultimate Collection
Burning Fire; 2009; Streaming audio

2889
Mary Had a Baby, Yes Lord
[Johnson, Hall]
Robeson, Paul (Bass-baritone)
Ol' Man River: The Ultimate Collection
Roslin Records; 2011; Streaming audio
Piano
Light dialect

2890
Mary Had a Baby, Yes Lord
[Johnson, Hall]
Robeson, Paul (Bass-baritone)
Sometimes I Feel Like a Motherless Child
JazzAge; 2012; Streaming audio
Piano

2891
Mary Had a Baby
Traditional

Sebron, Carolyn (Mezzo-soprano)
Carolyn Sebron, Mezzo-soprano, Marie-Claude Arbaretaz, Piano
Fondation Crédit Lyonnais; 1993; CD
A cappella

·······

Mary Was Queen of Galilee

2892

Mary Was Queen of Galilee
Whalum, Wendell
Ayers, Vanessa (Mezzo-soprano)
Black Christmas: Spirituals in the African-American Tradition
Essay Recordings CD1011; 1990; CD
Chorus
No dialect discerned

·······

Mary, What You Goin' to Name Your Pretty Little Baby?

2893

Mary, What You Gonna Name Your Pretty
    Little Baby?
Composer not identified
Rustin, Bayard (Tenor)
Bayard Rustin, the Singer
Bayard Rustin Fund; 1992; CD
Piano

2894

Mary, What You Gonna Name Your Pretty
    Little Baby?
Traditional
Rustin, Bayard (Tenor)
*Bayard Rustin Sings Spirituals, Work &
    Freedom Songs*
Bayard Rustin Fund; 1988; Cassette
A cappella
Heavy dialect

2895

Mary, What You Gonna Name Your Pretty
    Little Baby?

Traditional
Rustin, Bayard (Tenor)
*Bayard Rustin Sings Twelve Spirituals on the
    Life of Christ*
Fellowship Records E2-KL 1771; [195-]; LP
A cappella
No dialect discerned

     Also released with *Bayard Rustin Sings
Spirituals, Work & Freedom Songs* (Bayard
Rustin Fund; 2003; CD); *Bayard Rustin-The
Singer* (Black Swan Series; Parnassus Records
PACD 96083; 2022; CD)

·······

Mary Wore Three Links of Chain

2896

Mary Wore Three Links of Chain
Walker, George
Buchanan, Alison (Soprano)
Great American Concert Music
Albany Records TROY1370; 2012; CD
Piano
Light dialect

2897

Mary Wore Three Links of Chain
Walker, George
Taylor, Darryl (Countertenor)
How Sweet the Sound: A Charm of Spirituals
Albany TROY1244; 2011; CD
Piano

·······

Mary's Boy Child

2898

Mary's Boy Child
Hairston, Jester
Balthrop, Carmen (Soprano)
The Art of Christmas, Volume 1
Private label cb5893; 2004; CD
Piano
Light dialect

2899

Mary's Boy Child
Hairston, Jester

Domingo, Plácido (Tenor)
Christmas with Placido Domingo
Sony Music Entertainment SFK 63304; 1984;
    CD
Orchestra
No dialect discerned

2900

Mary's Boy Child
Hairston, Jester
Domingo, Plácido (Tenor)
A Tenors Christmas
Sony Music Entertainment SFK 63304; 1997;
    CD
Orchestra
No dialect discerned

2901

Mary's Boy Child
Hairston, Jester
Evans, Allan (Bass-baritone)
Negro Spirituals
Electromusic Records EMCD 6885; 1985; CD
Chorus, other instrument(s)

2902

Mary's Boy Child
Hairston, Jester; Rutter, John
Marshall, Melanie (Mezzo-soprano)
A Christmas Festival
Collegium Records COLCD 133; 2008; CD
Orchestra

2903

Mary's Boy Child
Hairston, Jester
Te Kanawa, Kiri (Soprano)
Simply Christmas
Decca B000123-02; 2003; CD
Chorus, orchestra

2904

Mary's Boy Child
Hairston, Jester
Terfel, Bryn (Baritone)
The All-Star Christmas Album
Deutsche Grammophon 289 457 357-2; 1997;
    CD
Piano

. . . .

Mary's Little Boy Chile

2905

Mary's Little Boy Chile
Hairston, Jester; Smith, Hale
Battle, Kathleen (Soprano); Von Stade,
    Frederica (Mezzo-soprano)
A Carnegie Hall Christmas Concert
Sony SK 48235; 1992; CD
Chorus, orchestra
Heavy dialect

2906

Mary's Little Boy Chile
Hairston, Jester; Smith, Hale
Battle, Kathleen (Soprano); Von Stade,
    Frederica (Mezzo-soprano)
The Complete Sony Recordings
Sony Classical 88985381362; 2016; CD
Chorus, orchestra
Heavy dialect

. . . .

Medleys

2907

Mary's Little Boy Chile
Hairston, Jester; Smith, Hale
Battle, Kathleen (Soprano); Von Stade,
    Frederica (Mezzo-soprano)
Complete Columbia Recital Albums
Sony Classical 88875183412; 2016; CD
Chorus, orchestra
Heavy dialect

2908

Hard Trials/Dere's No Hidin' Place Down
    Dere
Burleigh, Harry T.; Brown, Lawrence
Anderson, Marian (Contralto)
Songs and Spirituals by Marian Anderson
RCA Victor 10-1122--10-1125; 1944; 78 RPM
Piano
Heavy dialect

2909

Jus' Keep On Singin'/Ride On, King Jesus!
Burleigh, Harry T.

Anderson, Marian (Contralto)
He's Got the Whole World in His Hands:
Spirituals
RCA Victor 09026-61960-2; 1994; CD
Piano
Light dialect

2910

Hard Trials/Dere's No Hidin' Place
Burleigh, Harry T.
Anderson, Marian (Contralto)
Marian Anderson Sings Spirituals
Flapper Past CD 7073; 1995; CD
Piano

2911

Lord, I Can't Stay/Heaven, Heaven
Burleigh, Harry T.
Anderson, Marian (Contralto)
Softly Awakes My Heart: Arias, Songs and
Spirituals, Original Recordings [1924]1946
Naxos Nostalgia 8.120566; 2001; CD
Piano

2912

Lord, I Can't Stay Away/Heav'n, Heav'n
Hayes, Roland
Anderson, Marian (Contralto)
Negro Spirituals: The Concert Tradition
1909–1948
Frémeaux & Associés FA 168; 1999; CD
Piano
Moderate dialect

2913

Lord I Can't Stay Away/Heaven, Heaven (I
Got a Robe)
Hayes, Roland; Burleigh, Harry T.
Anderson, Marian (Contralto)
Softly Awakes My Heart: Very Best of Marian
Anderson
Alto ALN1955; 2016; CD
Piano
Moderate dialect

2914

Jus' Keep on Singin'/Ride On, King Jesus
Johnson, Hall
Anderson, Marian (Contralto)

Marian Anderson: Beyond the Music; Her
Complete RCA Victor Recordings
Sony Classical 19439836492; 2021; CD
Light dialect

2915

Lord I Can't Stay Away/Heav'n, Heav'n
[Hayes, Roland]
Anderson, Marian (Contralto)
The Concerto: African American Spirituals
Orange Amaro; 2019; Streaming audio
Piano

2916

Mary and Her Baby Chile (O Mary, Where Is
Your Baby?/O, Mary and the Baby, Sweet
Lamb/Ain't That a-Rockin' All Night)
Hairston, Jacqueline
Battle, Kathleen (Soprano)
Angels' Glory
Sony Classical SK 62723; 1996; CD
Guitar

2917

I Believe I'll Go Back Home/Lordy, Won't
You Help Me
Lloyd, Charles, Jr.
Battle, Kathleen (Soprano); Norman, Jessye
(Soprano)
Spirituals in Concert
Deutsche Grammophon 429 790-2; 1991; CD
Orchestra
Heavy dialect

2918

American Songs: I Wonder as I Wander;
Mary Had a Baby; Oh Mary, What You
Gonna Name That Pretty Little Baby?;
Who Was Mary? Mary was Queen of
Galilee; Sister Mary Had-a But One
Child; Go Tell It on the Mountain
Sadin, Robert / Olden Lee, Sylvia / Whalum,
Wendell / Hayes, Roland / Allen, Nancy /
Marsh, Don / Harris, Arthur
Battle, Kathleen (Soprano); Von Stade,
Frederica (Mezzo-soprano)
A Carnegie Hall Christmas Concert
Sony SK 48235; 1992; CD
Chorus, orchestra

2919

American Songs: I Wonder as I Wander;
    Mary Had a Baby; Oh Mary, What You
    Gonna Name That Pretty Little Baby?;
    Who Was Mary? Mary was Queen of
    Galilee; Sister Mary Had-a But One
    Child; Go Tell It on the Mountain
Sadin, Robert / Olden Lee, Sylvia / Whalum,
    Wendell / Hayes, Roland / Allen, Nancy /
    Marsh, Don / Harris, Arthur
Battle, Kathleen (Soprano); Von Stade,
    Frederica (Mezzo-soprano)
Complete Columbia Recital Albums
Sony Classical 88875183412; 2016; CD
Chorus, orchestra

2920

Over My Head/Lil' David
Simpson-Curenton, Evelyn
Battle, Kathleen (Soprano)
Spirituals in Concert
Deutsche Grammophon 429 790-2; 1991; CD
Flute, harp
Heavy dialect

2921

Swing Low, Sweet Chariot/Ride Up in the
    Chariot
Simpson-Curenton, Evelyn
Battle, Kathleen (Soprano)
Spirituals in Concert
Deutsche Grammophon 429 790-2; 1991; CD
Chorus, orchestra
Heavy dialect

2922

Motherless Child/Swing Low, Sweet Chariot
Corley, Maria Thompson
Clark, Maria (Soprano)
Soul Sanctuary: Spirituals & Hymns
Navona Records NV6406; 2022; CD
Piano
Heavy dialect

2923

I Am Seeking for a City/Don't Feel No-ways
    Tired
Hairston, Jester; Clemmons, François,
    Marder, Jeffrey

Clemmons, François (Tenor)
Negro Spirituals Live! In Concert
American Negro Spiritual Research
    Foundation 8177 2048 3779; 1998; CD
Piano
Moderate dialect

2924

Calvary Medley
Kilby III, Shelton E.
Conrad, Barbara (Mezzo-soprano)
Spirituals
Naxos 8.553036; 1995; CD
Chorus, orchestra
Heavy dialect

2925

Have You Heard About the Baby/Glory to
    the Newborn King
Becton, Shelton
Cook, Victor Trent (Tenor); Dixon, Roderick
    (Tenor), Young, Thomas (Tenor)
Three Mo' Tenors
RCA Victor 09026-63827-2; 2001; CD
Orchestra

2926

Sweet Little Jesus Boy/Mary Had a Baby
MacGimsey, Robert; Mills, Marvin; Floyd,
    Charles
Graves, Denyce (Mezzo-soprano)
*PBS Presents Denyce Graves, A Cathedral
    Christmas*
PBS DGCC-957; 1997; CD
Chorus, piano
Light dialect

2927

Hear de Lambs/Plenty Good Room
Composer not identified
Hayes, Roland (Tenor)
*Brother, Can You Spare a Dime?: The Roots of
    American Song*
Pearl Gemm CD 9484; 1991; CD
Piano
Moderate dialect

2928

Hear de Lambs a Cryin'/Plenty Good Room
Hayes, Roland

Hayes, Roland (Tenor)
*Negro Spirituals: The Concert Tradition
    1909–1948*
Frémeaux & Associés FA 168; 1999; CD
Piano
Moderate dialect

2929

Hear de Lambs a Cryin'/Plenty Good Room
Hayes, Roland
Hayes, Roland (Tenor)
*First Time Buyer's Guide to American Negro
    Spirituals*
Primo Collection PRMCD6038; 2006; CD
Piano
Moderate dialect

2930

Hear de Lambs a Cryin'/Plenty Good Room
    [Hayes, Roland]
Hayes, Roland (Tenor)
The Concerto: African American Spirituals
Orange Amaro; 2019; Streaming audio
Piano

2931

Come to Jesus/Hard Trials/Come to Jesus
    [from *Conversion* (Invitation 1)]
Cornelius, II, John
Heaston, Nicole (Soprano)
*Marilyn Horne Foundation Presents on
    Wings of Song. Recital No. 9*
Marilyn Horne Foundation DCD 5028;
    2001; CD
Piano

2932

Heaven Spirituals
Hicks, Lori
Hicks, Lori (Soprano)
Music of My Voice
CelestialSong Productions; 2015; CD
Piano

2933

Steal Away to Heaven (Medley: Nobody
    Knows the Trouble I've Seen /Sometimes
    I Feel Like a Motherless Child /Steal
    Away)

Hayes, Mark
Lima, Philip (Baritone)
Songs of a Wayfarer
Private Label; 2017; Streaming audio
Piano
No dialect discerned

2934

I Feel the Spirit Moving (Medley: Old
    Time Religion /Every Time I Feel the
    Spirit)
Hayes, Mark
Lima, Philip (Baritone)
Songs of a Wayfarer
Private Label; 2017; Streaming audio
Piano
Moderate dialect

2935

Couldn't Hear Nobody Pray/Standin' in the
    Need of Prayer
Okpebholo, Shawn
Liverman, Will (Baritone); Bridges, J'nai
    (Mezzo-soprano)
Steal Away
Yellow Einstein; 2014; CD
Piano
Light dialect

2936

I Want to Die Easy When I Die/Sometimes I
    Feel Like a Motherless Child
Okpebholo, Shawn
Liverman, Will (Baritone); Bridges, J'nai
    (Mezzo-soprano)
Steal Away
Yellow Einstein; 2014; CD
Piano
No dialect discerned

2937

Lord, I Want to Be a Christian/Give Me
    Jesus
Okpebholo, Shawn
Liverman, Will (Baritone)
Steal Away
Yellow Einstein; 2014; CD
Piano, flute
No dialect discerned

2938

There Is a Balm in Gilead/The Storm Is
  Passing Over
Composer not identified
Matthews, Benjamin (Baritone)
Done Crossed Every River: Freedom's Journey
Arcadia ARC 2004-2; 1995; CD

2939

Balm in Gilead/the Storm is passing over
Tindley, Charles
Matthews, Benjamin (Baritone)
A Balm in Gilead
Ebony Classic Recordings ECR 0001; 2000;
  CD
Piano

2940

There Is a Balm in Gilead/Sometimes I Feel
  Like a Motherless Child
Composer not identified
Norman, Jessye (Soprano)
Spirituals: Great Day in the Morning
Philips 412 240-1; 1982; LP
Chorus, other instrument(s)

2941

Crucifixion/Hear the Lamb's a-Crying
Composer not identified
Norman, Jessye (Soprano)
Spirituals: Great Day in the Morning
Philips 412 240-1; 1982; LP
Chorus, other instrument(s)

2942

I Believe I'll Go Back Home/In This Field
Lloyd, Charles, Jr.
Norman, Jessye (Soprano)
Spirituals: Great Day in the Morning
Philips 412 240-1; 1982; LP
Chorus, other instrument(s)

2943

Walk About Elders/Ride On, King Jesus
Lloyd, Charles, Jr.
Norman, Jessye (Soprano)
Spirituals: Great Day in the Morning
Philips 412 240-1; 1982; LP
Chorus, other instrument(s)

2944

I Believe I'll Go Back Home-In This Field
Lloyd, Charles, Jr.
Norman, Jessye (Soprano)
Great Day in the Morning
Philips 6769 104; 1982; LP
A cappella

2945

Walk About Elders/Ride On, King Jesus
Lloyd, Charles, Jr.
Norman, Jessye (Soprano)
Great Day in the Morning
Philips 6769 104; 1982; LP
Chorus

2946

Little David, Play on Your Harp/Ezekiel Saw
  the Wheel
Lloyd, Charles, Jr.
Norman, Jessye (Soprano)
Great Day in the Morning
Philips 6769 104; 1982; LP
Chorus, other instrument(s)

2947

There Is a Balm in Gilead/Sometimes I Feel
  Like a Motherless Child
Lloyd, Charles, Jr.; Norman, Jessye
Norman, Jessye (Soprano)
Great Day in the Morning
Philips 6769 104; 1982; LP
A cappella

2948

Crucifixion/Hear the Lamb's a-Crying
Norman, Jessye
Norman, Jessye (Soprano)
Great Day in the Morning
Philips 6769 104; 1982; LP
Chorus, other instrument(s)
Heavy dialect

2949

Calvary/They Crucified My Lord
Simpson-Curenton, Evelyn
Norman, Jessye (Soprano)
Spirituals in Concert
Deutsche Grammophon 429 790-2; 1991; CD

Men's voices, Orchestra
Moderate dialect

2950

Christmas Medley (Amen)
Dean, Johnie
Overton, Kenneth (Baritone); Harmon,
    Jondra (Mezzo-soprano); Helm, Alicia
    Marie (Soprano); Cunningham-Fleming,
    Jeryl (Soprano); Slack, Karen (Soprano)
The Spirit of the Holidays
American Spiritual Ensemble; 2009; CD
Chorus, piano

2951

The Virgin Mary Had a Baby Boy/Mary's
    Little Boy Child
Dean, Johnie
Overton, Kenneth (Baritone); Brown, Jason
    (Tenor); George, Roderick (Tenor)
The Spirit of the Holidays
American Spiritual Ensemble; 2009; CD

2952

Negro Spiritual Medley: I will pray/Lord I
    Want to Be a Christian/Gwine ride up in
    a chariot....
Composer not identified
Payne, John C. (Baritone)
*Brother, Can You Spare a Dime?: The Roots of
    American Song*
Pearl Gemm CD 9484; 1991; CD
Chorus, organ

2953

I Will Pray/I Want to Be a Christian/Gwine
    Ride Up in a Chariot
Composer not identified
Payne, John C. (Baritone)
Good News: Vintage Negro Spirituals
Living Era AJA 5622; 2006; CD
Chorus, organ

2954

Go Down Moses/Deep River
Composer not identified
Payne, John C. (Baritone)
The Concerto: African American Spirituals

Orange Amaro; 2019; Streaming audio
Piano

2955

I Will Pray/Lord, I Want to Be a Christian/
    Gwine Ride in a Chariot/Witness/Were
    You There/He Moves
Composer not identified
Payne, John C. (Baritone)
Negro Spiritual Medley
Regal Zonophone MR 1886; [193-]; 78 RPM
Chorus, organ

2956

Free at Last/Somebody's Knockin' at Your
    Door/You Must Have That True Religion/
    Daniel/You rock me when I rock.; Go
    Down, Moses
Composer not identified
Payne, John C. (Baritone)
Negro Spiritual Medley
Pathé 1137; [193-]; 78 RPM
Chorus, organ

2957

Go Down, Moses/Deep River
[Burleigh, Harry T.]
Payne, John C. (Baritone)
*Brother, Can You Spare a Dime?: The Roots of
    American Song*
Pearl Gemm CD 9484; 1991; CD
Piano
No dialect discerned

2958

Go Down Moses/Deep River
[Burleigh, Harry T.]
Payne, John C. (Baritone)
*Negro Spirituals: The Concert Tradition
    1909–1948*
Frémeaux & Associés FA 168; 1999; CD
Piano
No dialect discerned

2959

Git on Board, Lil' Chillun/Dere's No Hidin'
    Place
Brown, Lawrence
Robeson, Paul (Bass-baritone)

*Git on Board, Lil' Chillun/Dere's No Hidin'
    Place/Oh! Rock Me, Julie/Oh! Didn't It
    Rain*
His Master's Voice B 3033; 1929; 78 RPM
Piano
Moderate dialect

2960

Goin' to Ride Up in de Chariot/Ev'ry Time I
    Feel de Spirit
Brown, Lawrence; Brown, Lawrence
Robeson, Paul (Bass-baritone); Brown,
    Lawrence (Vocalist)
*Goin' to Ride Up in de Chariot/ Ev'ry Time I
    Feel de Spirit/Lay Down Late*
His Master's Voice B.8813; 1938; 78 RPM
Piano
Heavy dialect

2961

I'll Hear de Trumpet/Ezekial Saw de Wheel
Brown, Lawrence
Robeson, Paul (Bass-baritone); Brown,
    Lawrence (Vocalist)
The Power and the Glory
Columbia/Legacy CK 47337; 1991; CD
Piano
Moderate dialect

2962

No More Auction Block/Great Gettin' Up
    Morning
Brown, Lawrence
Robeson, Paul (Bass-baritone); Brown,
    Lawrence (Vocalist)
The Power and the Glory
Columbia/Legacy CK 47337; 1991; CD
Light dialect

2963

Swing Low, Sweet Chariot/Every Time I Feel
    the Spirit
Brown, Lawrence
Robeson, Paul (Bass-baritone); Brown,
    Lawrence (Vocalist)
The Power and the Glory
Columbia/Legacy CK 47337; 1991; CD
Piano
Light dialect

2964

Hear da Lam's a Cryin'/Going to Ride Up in
    de Chariot
Brown, Lawrence; Brown, Lawrence
Robeson, Paul (Bass-baritone); Brown,
    Lawrence (Vocalist)
The Power and the Glory
Columbia/Legacy CK 47337; 1991; CD
Piano
Heavy dialect

2965

Git on Board, Little Chillun/L'il David
Brown, Lawrence
Robeson, Paul (Bass-baritone); Brown,
    Lawrence (Vocalist)
The Power and the Glory
Columbia/Legacy CK 47337; 1991; CD
Piano
Moderate dialect

2966

Dere's a Man Goin' Round/I Know de Lord
Brown, Lawrence
Robeson, Paul (Bass-baritone)
They Sing Praises
Columbia CK 67007; 1995; CD
Piano

2967

Git on Board Lil' Children/Dere's No
    Hiding Place Down Dere
Brown, Lawrence
Robeson, Paul (Bass-baritone)
Spirituals: Original Recordings 1925–1936
Naxos Gospel Legends 8.120638; 2003;
    CD
Piano

2968

Git on Board, Little Chillun/Dere's No
    Hidin' Place
Brown, Lawrence
Robeson, Paul (Bass-baritone)
Paul Robeson
World Record Club W9648/EMI SM 431;
    [19--]; LP
Piano

2969

Hammer Song/L'il David
Brown, Lawrence
Robeson, Paul (Bass-baritone); Brown,
    Lawrence (Vocalist)
Paul Robeson
World Record Club W9648/EMI SM 431;
    [19--]; LP
Piano

2970

Weepin' Mary/I Want to Be Ready
Burleigh, Harry T.
Robeson, Paul (Bass-baritone)
*My Lord, What a Mornin'/Weepin' Mary/I
    Want to Be Ready*
His Master's Voice B 2897; 1929; 78 RPM
Piano
Light dialect/Heavy dialect

2971

Weepin' Mary/I Want to Be Ready
Burleigh, Harry T.
Robeson, Paul (Bass-baritone)
Spirituals: Original Recordings 1925–1936
Naxos Gospel Legends 8.120638; 2003; CD
Piano

2972

Oh Rock Me Julie/Oh Didn't It Rain
Burleigh, Harry T.
Robeson, Paul (Bass-baritone)
Spirituals: Original Recordings 1925–1936
Naxos Gospel Legends 8.120638; 2003; CD
Piano

2973

I Stood on de Ribber/Peter Go Ring Dem
    Bells
Burleigh, Harry T.
Robeson, Paul (Bass-baritone)
Spirituals: Original Recordings 1925–1936
Naxos Gospel Legends 8.120638; 2003; CD
Piano

2974

I Stood on the Ribber Jordan/Peter Go Ring
    Dem Bells
Burleigh, Harry T.

Robeson, Paul (Bass-baritone)
The Complete EMI Sessions (1928–1939)
EMI Classics 50999 2 15586 2 7; 2008; CD
Piano
Heavy dialect

2975

I Stood on de Ribber/Peter, Go Ring Dem Bells
Burleigh, Harry T.
Robeson, Paul (Bass-baritone)
*I Stood on de Ribber/Peter, Go Ring Dem
    Bells/Go Down, Moses*
His Master's Voice B3381; [193-]; 78 RPM
Piano
Heavy dialect

2976

Oh! Rock Me Julie/Oh! Didn't It Rain
Burleigh, Harry T.
Robeson, Paul (Bass-baritone)
Paul Robeson
World Record Club W9648/EMI SM 431;
    [19--]; LP
Piano

2977

Medley of Spirituals (Black Sheep/Heav'n
    Bells Are Ringin'/I'll Hear de Trumpet
    Sound/Swing Low, Sweet Chariot/Walk
    Together, Children)
Composer not identified
Robeson, Paul (Bass-baritone)
The Complete EMI Sessions (1928–1939)
EMI Classics 50999 2 15586 2 7; 2008; CD
Chorus, orchestra

2978

Paul Robeson medley (pt. 1) (Roll de Ole
    Chariot/Mary Had a Baby/Swing Low,
    Sweet Chariot/Heav'n, Heav'n)
Composer not identified
Robeson, Paul (Bass-baritone)
The Complete EMI Sessions (1928–1939)
EMI Classics 50999 2 15586 2 7; 2008; CD
Orchestra

2979

Medley of Spirituals (Black Sheep/Heav'n
    Bells Are Ringin'/I'll Hear de Trumpet

Sound/Swing Low, Sweet Chariot/Walk
　　Together, Children)
Composer not identified
Robeson, Paul (Bass-baritone)
Negro Spirituals (And More)
Discmedi DM-4674-02; 2009; CD

2980

I'm Rolling and Sing-a-Ho/Hail de Crown/
　　Joshua Fit de Battle of Jericho/I Got a
　　Robe/Oh Lord I Done/De Gospel Train
Composer not identified
Robeson, Paul (Bass-baritone)
Negro Spiritual Medley
His Master's Voice C 2287; [1931]; 78 RPM
Men's voices, orchestra

2981

Black Sheep/Heav'n Bells Are Ringin'/I'll
　　Hear de Trumpet Sound/Swing Low,
　　Sweet Chariot/Walk Together, Children
Composer not identified
Robeson, Paul (Bass-baritone)
Negro Spiritual Medley
His Master's Voice C 2287; [1931]; 78 RPM
Men's voices, orchestra

2982

De Ole Ark's a-Movering/Ezekiel Saw de
　　Wheel
Johnson, [John Rosamond]; Brown,
　　Lawrence
Robeson, Paul (Bass-baritone); Brown,
　　Lawrence (Vocalist)
*The Negro Spirituals Concert Tradition,
　　1909–1948*
Frémeaux & Associés FA 168; 1999; CD
Piano
Moderate dialect

2983

De Ole Ark's a-Movering/Ezekiel Saw de
　　Wheel
Johnson, [John Rosamond]; Brown,
　　Lawrence
Robeson, Paul (Bass-baritone)
Paul Robeson
World Record Club W9648/EMI SM 431;
　　[19--]; LP

Piano
Moderate dialect
　　Also released with *First Time Buyer's
Guide to American Negro Spirituals* (Primo
Collection PRMCD6038; 2006; CD)

2984

Roll de Ole Chariot (Clapham & Robeson);
　　Mary Had a Baby (Jackson); Swing Low,
　　Sweet Chariot (L. Brown); Heav'n, Heav'n
　　(I Got a Robe) (Burleigh)
Various
Robeson, Paul (Bass-baritone)
Spirituals: Original Recordings 1925–1936
Naxos Gospel Legends 8.120638; 2003; CD
Piano

2985

Roll de Ole Chariot (Clapham & Robeson);
　　Mary Had a Baby (Jackson); Swing Low,
　　Sweet Chariot (L. Brown); Heav'n, Heav'n
　　(I Got a Robe) (Burleigh)
Various
Robeson, Paul (Bass-baritone)
Paul Robeson Medley
His Master's Voice C .2621; [1933]; 78 RPM
Orchestra
Moderate dialect

2986

Bear de Burden/All God's Chillun Got
　　Wings
White, [Walter]; Johnson, [John Rosamond]
Robeson, Paul (Bass-baritone)
*Bear de Burden; All God's Chillun Got
　　Wings/Mary Had a Baby, Yes, Lord*
His Master's Voice B. 4336; [1933]; 78 RPM
Piano
Heavy dialect

2987

Bear de Burden/All God's Chillun Got
　　Wings
White, [Walter]; Johnson, [John Rosamond]
Robeson, Paul (Bass-baritone)
Paul Robeson
World Record Club W9648/EMI SM 431;
　　[19--]; LP
Piano

Also released with *The Essential Paul Robeson* (ASV CD AJS 244; 2000; CD); *The Complete EMI Sessions (1928–1939)* (EMI Classics 50999 2 15586 2 7; 2008; CD); *The Ultimate Collection* (Burning Fire; 2009; Streaming audio) and *Ol' Man River: The Very Best of Paul Robeson* (Memory Lane; 2012; CD)

2988

Swing Low Sweet Chariot/Everytime I Feel the Spirit
[Brown, Lawrence]
Robeson, Paul (Bass-baritone)
The Essential Spirituals
Columbia 473788 2; 1993; CD

2989

Git on Board, Li'l Children/Dere's No Hidin' Place
[Brown, Lawrence]
Robeson, Paul (Bass-baritone)
The Essential Paul Robeson
ASV CD AJS 244; 2000; CD

2990

I Stood on the Ribber Jordan/Peter Go Ring Dem Bells
[Burleigh, Harry T.]
Robeson, Paul (Bass-baritone)
The Ultimate Collection
Burning Fire; 2009; Streaming audio

2991

Roll de Ole Chariot/Mary Had a Baby, yes, Lord/Swing Low, Sweet Chariot/Heav'n, Heav'n (I Got a Robe)
Robeson, Paul (Bass-baritone)
Ol' Man River: The Very Best of Paul Robeson
Memory Lane; 2012; CD

2992

Git on Board, Li'l Children/Dere's No Hidin' Place down there
[Brown, Lawrence]
Robeson, Paul (Bass-baritone)
Ol' Man River: The Very Best of Paul Robeson
Memory Lane; 2012; CD

2993

Weepin' Mary/I Want to Be Ready
[Burleigh, Harry T.]
Robeson, Paul (Bass-baritone)
Ol' Man River: The Very Best of Paul Robeson
Memory Lane; 2012; CD

2994

De Ole Ark's a-Movering/Ezekiel Saw de Wheel
[Johnson, John Rosamond]
Robeson, Paul (Bass-baritone); Brown, Lawrence (Vocalist)
The Concerto: African American Spirituals
Orange Amaro; 2019; Streaming audio
Piano

2995

Swing low/Mornin' train
Hayes, Roland
Sims, Robert (Baritone)
Robert Sims Sings the Spirituals of Roland Hayes
Canti Classics 2014-01; 2015; CD
A cappella
Heavy dialect

2996

Glory, Glory Hallelujah/I'm a Soldier/ Don't Ya Let Nobody Turn You 'Round [from *Spiritual Suite for Baritone and Orchestra*]
McLin, Lena
Sims, Robert (Baritone)
In the Spirit: Spirituals and American Songs with Orchestra and Chorus
Canti Classics; 2009; CD
Chorus
Heavy dialect

2997

Glory, Glory Hallelujah/I'm a Soldier/ Don't Ya Let Nobody Turn You 'Round [from *Spiritual Suite for Baritone and Orchestra*]
McLin, Lena
Sims, Robert (Baritone)
Soul of a Singer: Robert Sims Sings African-American Folk Songs

Canti Classics 9801; 2013; CD
Orchestra
Heavy dialect

2998

Ship of Zion/Old Time Religion
Burleigh, Harry T.
Spencer, Kenneth (Bass-baritone)
Negro Spirituals
Life Records C 1108; [19--]; LP

2999

Ship of Zion/Ol' Time Religion
Nagel, [Otto]
Spencer, Kenneth (Bass-baritone)
Volkslieder & Spirituals
Discoton 75546; [197-]; LP
Chorus
Light dialect

3000

I Wanna Be Ready/Tone de Bell
Golde, Walter
Thomas, Edna (Soprano)
*Carry Me Back to Old Virginnie/I Wanna Be
    Ready/Tone de Bell*
Columbia 3370; 1924; 78 RPM
Piano

3001

Little Wheel a-Turnin' in my Heart/Keep
    a-Inchin' Along
Golde, Walter
Thomas, Edna (Soprano)
*Were You There?/Little Wheel A-Turnin' in
    my Heart/Keep A-Inching Along*
Columbia 3398; 1924; 78 RPM
Piano

3002

Little Wheel a-Turnin' in my Heart/Keep
    a-Inchin' Along
Thomas, Edna
Thomas, Edna (Soprano)
*Gwine-a Lay Down Mah Burden/Little
    Wheel a-Turnin' in my Heart; Keep
    a-Inchin' Erlong*
Columbia 1360-D; 1928; 78 RPM
Piano

3003

I'se Been Buked/Gonna Lay Down My Life
[Campbell, Colin M.]
Thomas, Edna (Soprano)
I'se Been Buked
Suncoast Music; 2015; Streaming audio
Piano
Heavy dialect

3004

Oh Freedom/Sometime I Feel Like a
    Motherless Child
Carter, John D.
Thompson, Jeanette (Soprano)
Negro Spirituals
Pavane Records ADW 7267; 1992; CD
Piano
No dialect discerned

3005

Spiritual Quodlibet
Johnson, Hall; Taylor, Vivian
Toppin, Louise (Soprano); Honeysucker,
    Robert (Baritone)
Good News
Videmus Records VIS735; 2007; CD
Piano
Heavy dialect

3006

American Songs: I Wonder as I Wander;
    Mary Had a Baby; Oh Mary, What You
    Gonna Name That Pretty Little Baby?;
    Who Was Mary? Mary was Queen of
    Galilee; Sister Mary Had-a But One
    Child; Go Tell It on the Mountain
Sadin, Robert / Olden Lee, Sylvia / Whalum,
    Wendell / Hayes, Roland / Allen, Nancy /
    Marsh, Don / Harris, Arthur
Von Stade, Frederica (Mezzo-soprano);
    Battle, Kathleen (Soprano)
The Complete Sony Recordings
Sony Classical 88985381362; 2016; CD
Chorus, orchestra

3007

Everytime I Feel the Spirit [from *Spirituals
    Suite*]
Hailstork, Adolphus

Ward, Frank (Bass-baritone)
*Amazing Grace: Organ Music of Adolphus
   Hailstork*
Albany Records TROY873; 2006; CD
A cappella (1st part), organ solo (2nd part)
Heavy dialect

3008

There Is a Balm in Gilead [from *Spirituals
   Suite*]
Hailstork, Adolphus
Ward, Frank (Bass-baritone)
*Amazing Grace: Organ Music of Adolphus
   Hailstork*
Albany Records TROY873; 2006; CD
A cappella (1st part), organ solo (2nd part)
Moderate dialect

3009

Wade in the Water [from *Spirituals Suite*]
Hailstork, Adolphus
Ward, Frank (Bass-baritone)
*Amazing Grace: Organ Music of Adolphus
   Hailstork*
Albany Records TROY873; 2006; CD
Percussion, organ
Heavy dialect

3010

Oh Freedom [from *Spirituals Suite*]
Hailstork, Adolphus
Ward, Frank (Bass-baritone)
*Amazing Grace: Organ Music of Adolphus
   Hailstork*
Albany Records TROY873; 2006; CD
A cappella (1st part), organ solo (2nd part)
Moderate dialect

3011

Three Spirituals for Three Baritones (Run
   Mary Run/Beulah Land/Wade in the
   Water)
Hairston, Jacqueline
Warfield, William (Bass-baritone); Matthews,
   Benjamin Sims, Robert (Baritone)
Three Generations Live
Canti Records; 2000; CD
Piano
Heavy dialect

3012

I Got a Robe/Plenty Good Room
Coil, Pat; Wilson-Felder, Cynthia
Wilson-Felder, Cynthia (Soprano)
*Spirituals: Songs from the American
   Experience*
GBGMusik CD 1-005; 1996; CD
Instrumental ensemble

3013

Swing Low, Sweet Chariot/Ride Up in the
   Chariot
Composer not identified
Battle, Kathleen (Soprano)
The Best of Kathleen Battle
Deutsche Grammophon 000349502; 2004;
   CD
Chorus, orchestra
Heavy dialect

3014

Swing Low, Sweet Chariot/Ride Up in the
   Chariot
Composer not identified
Battle, Kathleen (Soprano)
The Best of Kathleen Battle
Deutsche Grammophon 000349502; 2004;
   CD
Chorus, orchestra
Heavy dialect

· · · · · · ·

My God Is So High

3015

My God Is So High
Johnson, Hall; Smith, Hale
Battle, Kathleen (Soprano)
Spirituals in Concert
Deutsche Grammophon 429 790-2; 1991; CD
Orchestra
Heavy dialect

3016

My God Is So High
Brown, Uzee, Jr.
Brown, Uzee, Jr. (Baritone)
Great Day!
Allgood; 2005; CD

Piano
Heavy dialect

3017

My God Is So High
Johnson, Hall
Bryant, Peter (Vocalist)
I Will Pass This Way but Once
Facts of Faith Records WR 5161; 1977; LP
Organ

3018

You Mus Come In by an thro de Lamb
Hayes, Roland
Caesar, Jackson (Tenor)
*Spirituals: Celebrating the Music, Life,
    Legacy of Roland Hayes*
CD Baby 7048606059; 2021; CD
Piano
Moderate dialect

3019

My God Is So High
Cooke, Barbara Logan
Cooke, Barbara (Vocalist); Deloatch, Lois
    (Vocalist)
*Sometimes I Feel: A Collection of Negro
    Spirituals for Voice and Instruments*
Private Label KDISC420; 2002; CD
Piano

3020

My God Is So High
Johnson, Hall
Foreman, Blanche (Contralto)
*Best of the Hall Johnson Centennial Festival
    Celebrating the 100th Anniversary of Hall
    Johnson's Birth*
Hall Johnson Collection O33D2; 2002; CD
Piano

3021

My God Is So High
Johnson, Hall
Harris, Inetta (Soprano)
*My Heritage Sings: A Selection of Spirituals
    & Hymns*
Private Label; [199-]; CD
Piano

3022

My God Is So High
Composer not identified
Hayes, Roland (Tenor)
Evening with Roland Hayes, Tenor
Heritage LP-SS-1204; 1953; LP
Piano

3023

My God Is So High
Composer not identified
Hayes, Roland (Tenor)
Afro-American Folksongs
Pelican Records LP 2028; 1983; LP
Piano

3024

My God Is So High
Composer not identified
Hayes, Roland (Tenor)
The Art of Roland Hayes: Six Centuries of Song
Preiser Records; 2010; CD
Piano
Light dialect

3025

You Must Come In
Hayes, Roland
Hayes, Roland (Tenor)
Roland Hayes: My Songs
Vanguard VRS-494; 1956; LP
Piano

3026

You Must Come in by and through the Lamb
    [from *My Songs*]
Hayes, Roland
Hayes, Roland (Tenor)
Favorite Spirituals
Vanguard Classics OVC 6022; 1995; CD
Piano
Moderate dialect

3027

My God Is So High [from *Three Aframerican
    Religious Folksongs*]
Hayes, Roland
Hayes, Roland (Tenor)
Roland Hayes Recital, A

A 440 Records AC1203; [19--]; LP
Piano

3028
You Must Come in by and through the Lamb
    [from *My Song*]
[Hayes, Roland]
Hayes, Roland (Tenor)
Big Psalms, Hymns and Spirituals Box
eOne Music/Vanguard Classics; 2015;
    Streaming audio
Piano

3029
My God Is So High
Hogan, Moses
Hendricks, Barbara (Soprano)
Give Me Jesus
EMI Classics 7243 5 56788 2 9; 1998; CD
Chorus
Heavy dialect

3030
You Mus' Come in by an' thro' the Lamb
Hayes, Roland
Jefferson, Othello (Tenor)
*Good News: African American Spirituals and
    Art Songs*
Cambria Records CD 1270; 2021; CD
Piano
Light dialect

3031
You Mus' Come in by an' thro' de Lamb
Hayes, Roland
Jenkins, Isaiah (Tenor)
Lyric Tenor
Trans Radio TR 1010A; [195-]; LP
Piano

3032
You Mus' Come in by an' thro' de Lamb
Hayes, Roland
Matthews, Inez (Mezzo-soprano)
*Inez Matthews Sings Spirituals (Great New
    Voices of Today, v. 6)*
Period SPL-580; [1950]; LP
Piano
Light dialect

Also released with *Inez Matthews Sings
Spirituals* (Essential Media Group; 2011;
CD)

3033
You Must Come in by and thru de Lamb
Hayes, Roland
Salters, Stephen (Baritone)
Spirit: Are You There, You Are There
HarmonizedDisharmony 0001; 2015; CD

· · · · · · ·

My God Is So High

3034
My God Is So High
Clemmons, François; Marder, Jeffrey
Clemmons, François (Tenor)
Negro Spirituals Live! In Concert
American Negro Spiritual Research
    Foundation 8177 2048 3779; 1998; CD
Piano
Moderate dialect

3035
My God Is So High
Hayes, Roland
Sims, Robert (Baritone)
*Robert Sims Sings the Spirituals of Roland
    Hayes*
Canti Classics 2014-01; 2015; CD
Piano
Heavy dialect

3036
My God Is So High
Rice, Mark; Marsh, Don
Sykes, Jubilant (Baritone)
Jubilant Sykes Sings Copland and Spirituals
Arioso Classics AC 00011; 2008; CD
Orchestra

3037
My God Is So High [from *Green Pastures*]
Johnson, Hall
Toppin, Louise (Soprano)
The Hall Johnson Collection
Carl Fischer VF5 CD1–VF5 CD2; 2003; Score
    w/CD

Piano
Moderate dialect

3038

My God Is So High
Johnson, Hall
Toppin, Louise (Soprano)
*He'll Bring It to Pass: The Spirituals of Hall
    Johnson for Voice and Piano*
Albany Records TROY846; 2006; CD
Piano
Moderate dialect

3039

My Good Lord's Done Been Here
Hogan, Moses
Albert, Donnie Ray (Baritone)
Donnie Ray Albert in Recital
Cinnabar Records CNB1402; 2003; CD
Piano
No dialect discerned

3040

My Good Lord's Done Been There
Hogan, Moses
Black, Randall (Tenor)
*Then Sings My Soul: A Collection of Sacred
    Hymns and Spirituals*
Private label; 2006; CD
Piano

3041

My Good Lord Done Been Here
Johnson, Hall
Brice, Carol (Contralto)
A Carol Brice Recital
Columbia ML 2108; 1950; LP
Piano
Heavy dialect

3042

My Good Lord Done Been Here
Johnson, Hall
Brice, Carol (Contralto)
On Ma Journey/My Good Lord Done Been Here
Columbia Masterworks 17524-D; [1948]; 78
    RPM
Piano
Heavy dialect

3043

My Good Lord Done Been Here
Johnson, Hall
Brown, William (Tenor)
The Hall Johnson Collection
Carl Fischer VF5 CD1–VF5 CD2; 2003; Score
    w/CD
Piano
Moderate dialect

3044

My Good Lord Done Been Here
Johnson, Hall
Foreman, Blanche (Contralto)
*Best of the Hall Johnson Centennial Festival
    Celebrating the 100th Anniversary of Hall
    Johnson's Birth*
Hall Johnson Collection O33D2; 2002; CD
Piano

3045

My Good Lord Done Been Here
Johnson, Hall
Little, Vera (Mezzo-soprano)
My Good Lord Done Been Here
Decca 123737; 1957; LP
Piano

3046

My Good Lord Done Been Here
Hairston, Jacqueline
Matthews, Benjamin (Baritone)
A Balm in Gilead
Ebony Classic Recordings ECR 0001; 2000;
    CD
Piano

3047

My Good Lord Done Been Here
Johnson, Hall
Matthews, Benjamin (Baritone)
Bon Voyage Recital @ McCormick Place
S.P.S. SS-8993-018; 1966; LP
Piano

3048

My Good Lord Done Been Here
Johnson, Hall

Mayes, Doris (Mezzo-soprano)
Deep River
La voix de son maître FDLP 1080; 1959; LP
Piano

3049

My Good Lord's Done Been Here
Composer not identified
Melton, James (Tenor)
James Melton
Rococo 5310; [1970]; LP

3050

Bles' My Soul an' Gone
Jessye, Eva
Mims, A. Grace Lee (Soprano)
Spirituals
H & GM Records HGM 8101; 1981; LP
Piano
Heavy dialect

3051

My Good Lord's Done Been Here
Hogan, Moses
Overton, Kenneth (Baritone)
*Been in de Storm So Long (Songs My Fathers
    Taught Me)*
American Spiritual Ensemble; 2012; CD
Piano
Heavy dialect

3052

My Good Lord Done Been Here
Johnson, Hall
Simpson, Eugene Thamon (Bass)
*Hall Johnson Spirituals and Other Folk
    Songs*
Private Label; 2016; CD
Piano

3053

My Good Lord's Done Been Here
Hairston, Jacqueline
Sims, Robert (Baritone)
*In the Spirit: Spirituals and American Songs
    with Orchestra and Chorus*
Canti Classics; 2009; CD
Piano
Heavy dialect

3054

My Good Lord's Done Been Here
Hogan, Moses
Sims, Robert (Baritone)
*Deep River: Featuring 10 Spirituals Arranged
    for Solo Voice....*
MGH Records 5000; 2000; CD
Piano
Heavy dialect

3055

My Good Lord's Done Been Here
Hogan, Moses
Tucker, Eric Hoy (Bass-baritone)
*Southern Salute: Southern Songs &
    Spirituals*
White Pine Music WPM218; 2012; CD
Piano
Light dialect

3056

My Good Lord Done Been Here
Johnson, Hall
Warfield, William (Bass-baritone)
*Spirituals: 200 Years of African-American
    Spirituals*
ProArte CDD 3443; 1993; CD
Piano
Heavy dialect

3057

My Good Lord Done Been Here
Johnson, [Hall]
Weathers, Felicia (Soprano)
Arias and Spirituals
Belart/Universal Classics 461 5922; 1999;
    CD
Piano
Light dialect

3058

My Good Lord's Done Been Here
Johnson, Hall
Weathers, Felicia (Soprano)
Spirituals & Kodály Folk Songs
Decca SXL 6245; 1966; LP
Piano
Light dialect

3059

My Journey
Dett, Robert Nathaniel
Oglesby, Isador (Tenor)
Negro Spirituals: The Musical Roots of American Folk Songs
Praise PR 658; 1978; LP
Piano

· · · · · · ·

My Little Soul's Goin' to Shine

3060

My Little Soul's Goin to Shine
Price, Florence
Heard, Richard (Tenor)
My Dream: Art Songs and Spirituals
Percentage Records/Sound of Art Recordings CD147597; 2012; CD
Piano
Moderate dialect

· · · · · · ·

My Lord What a Morning

[Matthew 24:29-31]

"My Lord, what a morning, My Lord, what a morning; My Lord, what a morning; When the stars begin to fall. You'll hear the trumpet sound, To wake the nations underground,...."

[Available in CW40, EM34, FH25, HCTN, HJTS, HLBS, HTBS, HT25, JAS1, JBTS, JJBA, MH10, PLSY, RWSC, SBFD, WF70]

3061

My Lord, What a Mornin'
Burleigh, Harry T.
Cantril, Kenneth (Baritone)
My Lord, What a Mornin'/Deep River
London 290; [19--]; 78 RPM
Piano

3062

My Lord, What a Mornin'
Burleigh, Harry T.

D'Alvarez, Marguerite (Contralto)
Nobody Knows de Trouble I've Seen/My Lord, What a Mornin'
Gramophone DA-796; [1927]; 78 RPM
Piano

3063

My Lord, What a Mornin'
Burleigh, Harry T.
Alexander, Roberta (Soprano)
Songs My Mother Taught Me
Etcetera KTC 1208; 1999; CD
Piano
Moderate dialect

3064

My Lord, What a Mornin'
Burleigh, Harry T.
Anderson, Marian (Contralto)
My Lord, What a Mornin'
Victor [1956]-B; 1924; 78 RPM
Orchestra
Heavy dialect

3065

My Lord, What a Morning
Burleigh, Harry T.
Anderson, Marian (Contralto)
Marian Anderson Sings Spirituals
RCA Victor Red Seal MO 1238; 1948; 78 RPM
Piano

3066

My Lord, What a Morning
Burleigh, Harry T.
Anderson, Marian (Contralto)
Negro Spirituals
La Voix de Son Maître FBLP1039; 1953; LP
Piano

3067

My Lord, What a Morning
Burleigh, Harry T.
Anderson, Marian (Contralto)
Bach, Brahms, Schubert
RCA Victor 7911-2-RG; 1989; CD
Piano
Light dialect

3068

My Lord, What a Morning
Burleigh, Harry T.
Anderson, Marian (Contralto)
Negro Spirituals: The Concert Tradition
  1909–1948
Frémeaux & Associés FA 168; 1999; CD
Orchestra
Moderate dialect

3069

My Lord, What a Morning
Burleigh, Harry T.
Anderson, Marian (Contralto)
Spirituals
RCA Victor Red Seal 09026-63306-2; 1999;
  CD
Piano
No dialect discerned

3070

My Lord, What a Morning
Burleigh, Harry T.
Anderson, Marian (Contralto)
First Time Buyer's Guide to American Negro
  Spirituals
Primo Collection PRMCD6038; 2006; CD
Orchestra
Moderate dialect

3071

My Lord What a Morning
Burleigh, Harry T.
Anderson, Marian (Contralto)
Softly Awakes My Heart: Very Best of Marian
  Anderson
Alto ALN1955; 2016; CD
Piano
Light dialect

3072

My Lord, What a Mornin'
Burleigh, Harry T.
Anderson, Marian (Contralto)
Marian Anderson: Beyond the Music; Her
  Complete RCA Victor Recordings
Sony Classical 19439836492; 2021; CD
Orchestra
No dialect discerned

3073

My Lord, What a Mornin'
Burleigh, Harry T.
Anderson, Marian (Contralto)
Marian Anderson: Beyond the Music; Her
  Complete RCA Victor Recordings
Sony Classical 19439836492; 2021; CD
Piano
Light dialect

3074

My Lord, What a Morning
Burleigh, Harry T.
Anderson, Marian (Contralto)
Marian Anderson Sings Negro Spirituals
His Master's Voice BLP 1060; [19--]; LP
Piano

3075

My Lord, What a Morning
Burleigh, Harry T.
Anderson, Marian (Contralto)
Negro Spirituals
RCA Victor LM 2032; [1956]; LP
Piano

3076

My Lord, What a Morning
[Burleigh, Harry T.]
Anderson, Marian (Contralto)
Marian Anderson Sings Spirituals
RCA Victor LM 110; 1949; LP
Piano

3077

My Lord, What a Mornin'!
[Burleigh, Harry T.]
Anderson, Marian (Contralto)
Alto Rhapsody; Selected Spirituals
Urania URN 22.328; 2007; CD
Piano

3078

My Lord, What a Morning
[Burleigh, Harry T.]
Anderson, Marian (Contralto)
The Very Best of Marian Anderson
Master Classics Records; 2009; CD

Piano
Moderate dialect

3079

My Lord, What a Morning
[Burleigh, Harry T.]
Anderson, Marian (Contralto)
Spirituals
Past Classics; 2013; Streaming audio
Orchestra
No dialect discerned

3080

What a Morning
[Burleigh, Harry T.]
Anderson, Marian (Contralto)
*Grandes Contraltos de la Musique Classique,
    Les: Marian Anderson, Vol. 1*
Mon Patrimoine Musical Collection; 2017;
    Streaming audio
Piano

3081

My Lord What a Morning
[Burleigh, Harry T.]
Anderson, Marian (Contralto)
The Concerto: African American Spirituals
Orange Amaro; 2019; Streaming audio
Orchestra

3082

My Lord, What a Morning
[Burleigh, Harry T.]
Anderson, Marian (Contralto)
Negro Spirituals
RCA Gold Seal RVC-1570; [19--]; LP
Piano

3083

My Lord, What a Morning!
[Burleigh, Harry T.]
Anderson, Marian (Contralto)
Negro Spirituals
RCA Victor 630.396 A; [19--]; LP
Piano

3084

My Lord, What a Mornin'
Burleigh, Harry T.

Arroyo, Martina (Soprano)
Spirituals
Centaur CRC 2060; 1991; CD
Piano
Heavy dialect

3085

My Lord, What a Morning!
[Burleigh, Harry T.]
Arroyo, Martina (Soprano)
There's a Meeting Here Tonight
Angel S-36072; 1974; LP
Chorus

3086

My Lord, What a Morning!
[Burleigh, Harry T.]
Arroyo, Martina (Soprano)
Negro Spirituals
EMI 7243 5 72790 2 4; 1998; CD
Chorus
Moderate dialect

3087

My Lord What a Mornin'
Burleigh, Harry T.
Brown, Anthony (Baritone)
Spirituals
Brown/Smith Productions; 1995; CD
Piano
Heavy dialect

3088

My Lord, What a Mornin'
Burleigh, Harry T.
Burton, Dashon (Bass-baritone)
*Songs of Struggle & Redemption: We Shall
    Overcome*
Acis Productions APL08685; 2015; CD
Piano
Heavy dialect

3089

My Lord, What a Mornin'
[Burleigh, Harry T.]
Cantril, Kenneth (Baritone)
Spirituals
London LA 52; 1948; 78 RPM
Piano

3090

My Lord, What a Mornin'
Burleigh, Harry T.
Carlsen, Svein (Bass)
Negro Spirituals
EuroMaster AS ECD19005; 1996; CD
Piano

3091

My Lord, What a Mornin'
Burleigh, Harry T.
Carnette, Count (Vocalist)
*Count Carnette Sings Favorite Negro
    Spirituals*
Carnette Archive Recordings; 1983; LP
Piano
Light dialect

3092

My Lord What a Morning
Joubert, Joseph
Conrad, Barbara (Mezzo-soprano); Parks,
    Karen (Soprano)
Spirituals
Naxos 8.553036; 1995; CD
Orchestra
Moderate dialect

3093

O Lord What a Mornin
Composer not identified
Cuénod, Hugues (Tenor)
Prima Voce Party
Nimbus Records NI 7838; 1992; CD
Piano
Light dialect

3094

My Lord What a Morning
[Harry T. Burleigh]
Delmore, Harry A. (Tenor)
By and By/My Lord What a Morning
Grey Gull 4165; [1927]; 78 RPM

3095

My Lord, What a Mornin'
Burleigh, Harry T.
Duncan, Todd (Baritone)

African American Spirituals
[Apple Music]; 2008; Streaming audio
Piano
Moderate dialect

3096

My Lord, What a Mornin'
Burleigh, Harry T.
Duncan, Todd (Baritone)
*Let Us Break Bread Together/My Lord, What
    a Mornin'*
Philips A 56008 H; [195-]; 78 RPM
Piano
Light dialect

3097

My Lord, What a Mornin'
Burleigh, Harry T.
Duncan, Todd (Baritone)
Negro Spirituals
Allegro ALG3022; [1952]; LP
Piano

3098

My Lord What a Mornin'
Darden, George
Fernandez, Wilhelmenia (Soprano)
Spirituals
Tioch Digital Records TD 1009; 1982; LP
Piano
Heavy dialect

3099

My Lord What a Mornin'
Darden, George
Fernandez, Wilhelmenia (Soprano)
Negro Spirituals
Milan A 192; 1982; LP
Piano

3100

My Lord What a Mornin'
Darden, George
Fernandez, Wilhelmenia (Soprano)
Sings Favorite Spirituals
Phoenix PHCD 134; 1997; CD
Piano
Heavy dialect

3101

My Lord What a Morning
Burleigh, Harry T.
Forest, Michael (Tenor)
The Spirit Sings: American Spirituals
Shenandoah Conservatory SU003; [199-];
    CD

3102

My Lord What a Morning
Page, Sue Ellen
Forest, Michael (Tenor)
The Spirit Sings: American Spirituals
Shenandoah Conservatory SU003; [199-];
    CD

3103

My Lord What a Morning
Composer not identified
Franklin, Lavinia A. (Vocalist)
*Historical Interpretation of Negro Spirituals
    and Lift Every Voice and Sing*
Recorded Publications JZB-02591; 1970;
    LP
Organ

3104

My Lord, What a Mornin'
Composer not identified
Green, Elnora E. (Contralto)
15 Spirituals
Private Label J3RS 2286; 1979; LP
Piano

3105

My Lord What a Mornin'
Burleigh, Harry T.
Hamilton, Ruth (Contralto)
Good News
Videmus Records VIS735; 2007; CD
Piano
Heavy dialect

3106

My Lord, What a Mornin'
Burleigh, Harry T.
Hendricks, Barbara (Soprano)
Give Me Jesus
EMI Classics 7243 5 56788 2 9; 1998; CD

A cappella
Moderate dialect

3107

My Lord What a Mornin'
Johnson, Hall
Holland, Charles (Tenor)
My Lord What a Mornin'
Musical Heritage Society MHS 912250X;
    1982; LP
Piano
Heavy dialect

3108

My Lord What a Mornin'
Johnson, Hall
Holland, Charles (Tenor)
My Lord What a Mornin'
Musical Heritage Society MHS 512250K;
    1988; CD
Piano
Heavy dialect

3109

My Lord What a Mornin'
Clinton, Irving
Irving, Clinton (Bass-baritone)
Clinton Irving Sings Spirituals: A Tribute
Rogers; 2001; CD

3110

My Lord What a Morning
Composer not identified
Jones, Fanni (Mezzo-soprano)
Negro Spirituals
Evasion Disques LP613; 1974; LP

3111

My Lord, What a Mornin'
Composer not identified
Jones, Fanni (Mezzo-soprano)
Negro Spirituals
Phonotec 815; 1977; LP
Organ

3112

My Lord, What a Mornin'
Burleigh, Harry T.

Lewis, Cheryse McLeod (Mezzo-soprano)
Spirituals
CheryseMusic; 2012; CD
Piano

3113

My Lord, What a Mornin'
Hayes, Mark
Lima, Philip (Baritone)
Songs of a Wayfarer
Private Label; 2017; Streaming audio
Piano
Light dialect

3114

My Lord, What a Mornin'
Meyer, Fredrich
London, George (Bass-baritone)
Spirituals
Deutsche Grammophon 00289 477 6193;
   2006; CD
Orchestra
Heavy dialect

3115

My Lord, What a Morning
Burleigh, Harry T.; Simonson, Victor, Lester
   Lynch & Noam Fairgold
Lynch, Lester (Baritone)
On My Journey Now: Spirituals & Hymns
Pentatone Music PTC 5186 57'; 2017; CD
Chorus, piano, organ, violin

3116

My Lord What a Mornin'
Burleigh, Harry T.
Mann, Celeste (Mezzo-soprano)
*Songs in the Spirit: A Concert of Sacred
   Music*
Private Label; [2012]; CD
Piano
Light dialect

3117

My Lawd What a Morning
Raphael, Michael
Maynor, Kevin (Bass)
The Spiritual: An Underground Railroad

Southeastern Virginia Arts Assoc.; [2000]; CD
Piano

3118

My Lord What a Morning
Composer not identified
Miles, John (Tenor)
The Classic Spirituals
Epiphany 83-1027; 1983; LP
Instrumental ensemble

3119

My Lord, What a Mornin'
Composer not identified
Monzo, Oscar (Baritone)
Negro Spirituals
Dial Discos 50-2020; 1983; LP

3120

My Lord, What a Mourning
Traditional
Moses, Oral (Bass-baritone)
*Spirituals in Zion: A Spiritual Heritage for
   the Soul*
Albany Records TROY587; 2003; CD
A cappella

3121

My Lord, What a Mornin'
[Burleigh, Harry T.]
Moyer, Del-Louise (Mezzo-soprano)
*He'll Bring to Pass: Spirituals &
   Americanegro Suite*
Alyssum ALY-9001; 1997; CD
Piano
No dialect discerned

3122

My Lord, What a Morning
[Burleigh, Harry T.]
Norman, Jessye (Soprano)
An Evening with Jessye Norman
Opera D'Oro Recitals OPD-2011; 1999; CD
Piano
Light dialect

3123

My Lord What a Morning
Composer not identified

Norman, Jessye (Soprano)
Oh, Happy Day! Gospels & Spirituals: The Ultimate CD
Ultimate; 2010; CD

3124
My Lord, What a Morning
Patterson. Willis
Norman, Jessye (Soprano)
Negro Spirituals
Philips 9500 580; 1979; LP
Chorus

3125
My Lord, What a Morning
Patterson. Willis
Norman, Jessye (Soprano)
Spirituals
Philips 416 462-2; 1990; CD
Chorus
Light dialect

3126
My Lord What a Morning
[Burleigh, Harry T.]
Norman, Jessye (Soprano)
Gospels & Spirituals Gold Collection
Retro R2CD 40-26; 1995; CD
Piano
Moderate dialect

3127
My Lord, What a Morning
[Burleigh, Harry T.]
Norman, Jessye (Soprano)
The Jessye Norman Collection: Sacred Songs & Spirituals
Philips B0004506-02; 2005; CD
Chorus
Moderate dialect

3128
My Lord, What a Morning
[Burleigh, Harry T.]
Norman, Jessye (Soprano)
Honor! A Celebration of the African American Cultural Legacy
Decca B0012660-02; 2009; CD

Chorus
Moderate dialect

3129
My Lord, What a Mornin'
Burleigh, Harry T.
Parks, Karen (Soprano)
Nobody Knows
Ottimavoce 52736; 2007; CD
Piano
Light dialect

3130
My Lord What a Morning
Burleigh, Harry T.
Payne, John C. (Baritone)
My Lord What a Morning/My Way Is Cloudy
Columbia 3644; 1925; 78 RPM
Piano

3131
My Lord, What a Morning
[Burleigh, Harry T.]
Payne, John C. (Baritone)
Black Europe: Sounds & Images of Black People in Europe pre–1927
Bear Family Productions BCD 16095; 2013; CD
Piano
Moderate dialect

3132
My Lord, What a Mornin'
Composer not identified
Pickens, Jo Ann (Soprano)
My Heritage: American Melodies/Negro Spirituals
Koch Schwann 3-1447-2; 1993; CD

3133
My Lord What a Morning
Composer not identified
Pleas III, Henry H. (Tenor)
Deep River: A Spiritual Journey
Rowe House Productions; 1999; CD

3134
My Lord What a Morning
Burleigh, Harry T.

Powell, Angela (Soprano)
City Called Heaven
Private Label AP6957; 2003; CD
Piano

3135

Oi Herra, Uuteen Aamuun (My Lord, What a Morning)
Composer not identified
Putkonen, Marko (Bass)
Deep River: Negro Spirituals
Lilium LILP 101; 1991; LP

3136

My Lord, What a Morning
Hogan, Moses
Ragin, Derek Lee (Countertenor)
Negro Spirituals
Virgin Classics 0946 363305 2 5; 2006; CD
Piano
Heavy dialect

3137

My Lord, What a Mornin'
Burleigh, Harry T.
Robeson, Paul (Bass-baritone)
My Lord, What a Mornin'/Weepin' Mary/ I Want to Be Ready
His Master's Voice B 2897; 1929; 78 RPM
Piano
Light dialect

3138

My Lord What a Mornin'
Burleigh, Harry T.
Robeson, Paul (Bass-baritone)
Spirituals: Original Recordings 1925–1936
Naxos Gospel Legends 8.120638; 2003; CD
Piano

3139

My Lord, What a Mornin'
Burlcigh, Harry T.
Robeson, Paul (Bass-baritone)
The Complete EMI Sessions (1928–1939)
EMI Classics 50999 2 15586 2 7; 2008; CD
Piano
Heavy dialect

3140

My Lord, What a Morning!
Composer not identified
Rustin, Bayard (Tenor)
Bayard Rustin Sings Spirituals, Work & Freedom Songs
Bayard Rustin Fund; 1988; Cassette
Piano
Moderate dialect

3141

My Lord, What a Morning!
Composer not identified
Rustin, Bayard (Tenor)
Bayard Rustin Sings Spirituals, Work & Freedom Songs
Bayard Rustin Fund; 2003; CD
Piano
Moderate dialect

3142

My Lord, What a Morning'
Johnson, Hall
Straughter, Maralyn (Soprano)
Negro Spirituals of Hall Johnson
Variety Recording Service Var 0753; [196-]; LP
Piano

3143

My Lord, What a Mornin'
Burleigh, Harry T.
Thompson, Jeanette (Soprano)
Negro Spirituals
Pavane Records ADW 7267; 1992; CD
Chorus
No dialect discerned

3144

My Lord What a Morning [from *Witness: Original Compositions in Spiritual Style*]
Baker, David
Toppin, Louise (Soprano)
Witness
Albany Records TROY868; 2006; CD
Orchestra
Moderate dialect

3145

My Lord What a Morning
Composer not identified
Tyler, Veronica (Soprano)
Sings ... the Passion of Christ in Spirituals
BRC Productions; [19--]; LP
Piano

3146

My Lord What a Morning
Composer not identified
Verdejo, Awilda (Soprano)
Awilda Verdejo Sings Spirituals
Angeluz Performances; 1999; CD
Piano

3147

My Lord, What a Mornin'
Burleigh, Harry T.
Warfield, William (Bass-baritone)
*Spirituals: 200 Years of African-American
    Spirituals*
ProArte CDD 3443; 1993; CD
Piano
Heavy dialect

3148

My Lord What a Mornin'
Composer not identified
Williams, Wayne (Tenor)
Music from My Life
Movideo Productions 02-1993; 1993; CD
Piano

3149

My Lord What a Morning
Schweizer, Rolf
Wolf, Lars (Vocalist)
Die Schwarze Stimme Europas
Cantate 666000; 1971; LP
Chorus, organ, percussion

3150

My Lord, What a Morning
Hayes, Mark
Yovanovich, Amy (Mezzo-soprano)
Great Day!
Prince Productions 9808P; 2007; CD

Piano
Light dialect

3151

My Lord, What a Mornin'
Burleigh, Harry T.
Alexander, Roberta (Soprano)
Roberta Alexander.... A Retrospective
Etcetera KTC1222; 2013; CD
Piano
Moderate dialect

3152

Мой бог, что за утро (Moy bog, chto za
    utro)
Composer not identified
Filatova, Ludmila (Mezzo-soprano)
*Негритянские Спиричузлс (Negrityanskiye
    Spirichuzls—Negro Spirituals)*
Melodiâ S10 21833 009; 1985; LP
Organ
No dialect discerned

· · · · · · ·

My Lord's a-Writin'
All de Time

3153

My Lord's a-Writin' All de Time [from
    Green Pastures]
Johnson, Hall
Toppin, Louise (Soprano)
The Hall Johnson Collection
Carl Fischer VF5 CD1–VF5 CD2; 2003; Score
    w/CD
Piano
Moderate dialect

· · · · · · ·

My Soul Is Going
to Glory

3154

My Soul Is Going to Glory
Boardman, Reginald
Jenkins, Isaiah (Tenor)
Lyric Tenor
Trans Radio TR 1010A; [195-]; LP
Piano

My Soul Wants Something New

3155

My Soul Wants Something New
Dett, Robert Nathaniel
Oglesby, Isador (Tenor)
Life of Jesus in Negro Spirituals
Oglesby Recordings Album 2; 1980; LP
Piano

My Soul's Been Anchored in the Lord

[Hebrews 6:19, Psalm 62:5-6, Acts 27:29]

"In the Lord, in the Lord, my soul's been anchored in the Lord; ... Before I'd stay in Hell one day, I'd sing and pray myself away, ..."

[Available in ASSA, FP44, JJBA]

3156

My Soul's Been Anchored in de Lord
Price, Florence
Alexander, Roberta (Soprano)
Songs My Mother Taught Me
Etcetera KTC 1208; 1999; CD
Piano
Heavy dialect

3157

My Soul's Been Anchored in the Lord
Johnson, Hall
Anderson, Alfonse (Tenor)
The Lily of the Valley
American Spiritual Ensemble; [2003]; CD
Piano

3158

My Soul's Been Anchored in de Lord
Burleigh, Harry T.
Anderson, Marian (Contralto)
Let Freedom Ring!
JSP Records 683; 2016; CD
Piano
Light dialect

3159

My Soul's Been Anchored in the Lord
Price, Florence
Anderson, Marian (Contralto)
Go Down Moses (Let My People Go)/My Soul's Been Anchored in the Lord
Victor 1799; 1937; 78 RPM
Piano
Moderate dialect

3160

My Soul's Been Anchored in the Lord
Price, Florence
Anderson, Marian (Contralto)
Go Down Moses/My Soul's Been Anchored in the Lord
His Master's Voice D.A. 1560; 1939; 78 RPM
Piano
Light dialect

3161

My Soul's Been Anchored in the Lord
Price, Florence
Anderson, Marian (Contralto)
Songs and Spirituals by Marian Anderson
RCA Victor 10-1122--10-1125; 1944; 78 RPM
Piano
Heavy dialect

3162

My Soul's Been Anchored
Price, Florence
Anderson, Marian (Contralto)
The Lady from Philadelphia
Pearl GEMM CD 9069; 1993; CD
Piano

3163

My Soul's Been Anchored in de Lord
Price, Florence
Anderson, Marian (Contralto)
He's Got the Whole World in His Hands: Spirituals
RCA Victor 09026-61960-2; 1994; CD
Piano
Light dialect

3164

My Soul's Been Anchored in the Lord
Price, Florence
Anderson, Marian (Contralto)
Prima Voce
Nimbus NI 7882; 1996; CD
Piano
Light dialect

3165

My Soul's Been Anchored in de Lord
Price, Florence
Anderson, Marian (Contralto)
Marian Anderson: Rare and Unpublished Recordings, [1936]1954
VAI Audio VAIA 1168; 1998; CD
Piano
Moderate dialect

3166

My Soul's Been Anchored in the Lord
Price, Florence
Anderson, Marian (Contralto)
Spirituals
RCA Victor Red Seal 09026-63306-2; 1999; CD
Piano
Moderate dialect

3167

My Soul's Been Anchored in the Lord
Price, Florence
Anderson, Marian (Contralto)
Softly Awakes My Heart: Arias, Songs and Spirituals, Original Recordings [1924] 1947
Naxos Nostalgia 8.120566; 2001; CD
Piano
Light dialect

3168

My Soul's Been Anchored in the Lord
Price, Florence
Anderson, Marian (Contralto)
Negro Spirituals: 1924–1949
Frémeaux & Associés FA 184; 2004; CD
Orchestra

3169

My Soul's Been Anchored in the Lord
Price, Florence

Anderson, Marian (Contralto)
Softly Awakes My Heart: Very Best of Marian Anderson
Alto ALN1955; 2016; CD
Piano
Moderate dialect

3170

My Soul's Been Anchored in the Lord
Price, Florence
Anderson, Marian (Contralto)
Marian Anderson: Beyond the Music; Her Complete RCA Victor Recordings
Sony Classical 19439836492; 2021; CD
Piano
Moderate dialect

3171

My Soul's Been Anchored in the Lord
Price, Florence
Anderson, Marian (Contralto)
Marian Anderson: Beyond the Music; Her Complete RCA Victor Recordings
Sony Classical 19439836492; 2021; CD
Piano
Light dialect

3172

My Soul's Been Anchored in the Lord
Price, Florence
Anderson, Marian (Contralto)
Marian Anderson: Beyond the Music; Her Complete RCA Victor Recordings
Sony Classical 19439836492; 2021; CD
Piano
Light dialect

3173

My Soul's Been Anchored in the Lord
Price, Florence
Anderson, Marian (Contralto)
Anderson Sings Negro Spirituals
Victor Golden Series EK-1007; [19--]; 45 RPM
Piano

3174

My Soul's Been Anchored in the Lord
Price, Florence
Anderson, Marian (Contralto)

Songs and Spirituals
RCA Victor M 986; [1945]; 78 RPM
Piano

3175

My Soul's Been Anchored
[Price, Florence]
Anderson, Marian (Contralto)
Marian Anderson Sings Spirituals
Flapper Past CD 7073; 1995; CD
Piano

3176

My Soul's Been Anchored in the Lord
[Price, Florence]
Anderson, Marian (Contralto)
The Very Best of Marian Anderson
Master Classics Records; 2009; CD
Piano
No dialect discerned

3177

My Soul's Been Anchored in the Lord
[Price, Florence]
Anderson, Marian (Contralto)
The Rich Voice of Marian Anderson
Editions Audiovisuel Beulah; 2019;
    Streaming audio
Piano

3178

My Soul's Been Anchored in de Lord
Jones, G. L.
Bazile, Bridget (Soprano)
Negro Spirituals
Virgin Classics 0946 363305 2 5; 2006; CD
Chorus
Light dialect

3179

My Soul's Been Anchored
Price, Florence; Brown, Angela; Cooper,
    Tyron
Brown, Angela (Soprano)
*Mosiac: A Collection of African-American
    Spirituals with Piano, guitar*
Albany Records TROY721; 2004; CD
Guitar
Light dialect

3180

My Soul's Been Anchored in the Lord
Composer not identified
Brown, Anthony (Baritone)
Spirituals
Brown/Smith Productions; 1995; CD
Piano
Heavy dialect

3181

My Soul Is Anchored in the Lord [from *Two
    Spirituals*]
Nelson, Robert
Brown, Débria (Mezzo-soprano)
An American Voice: Music of Robert Nelson
Albany Records TROY381; 2000; CD
Orchestra
Moderate dialect

3182

My Soul's Been Anchored in the Lord
Price, Florence
Bumbry, Grace (Mezzo-soprano)
Portrait, A
Gala GL 100.539; 1999; CD
Piano
Heavy dialect

3183

My Souls Been Anchored in duh Lord
Price, Florence
Clemmons, François (Tenor)
Negro Spirituals Live! In Concert
American Negro Spiritual Research
    Foundation 8177 2048 3779; 1998; CD
Piano
Light dialect

3184

My Soul's Been Anchored in the Lord
Price, Florence
Davis, Ellabelle (Soprano)
Ellabelle Davis Sings Negro Spirituals
London LPS 182; [1950]; LP
Piano

3185

My Soul's Been Anchored in the Lord
Price, Florence

Davis, Ellabelle (Soprano)
Recital of Negro Spirituals by Ellabelle Davis
Decca LM.4504; [1950]; LP
Piano

3186

My Soul's Been Anchored in the Lord
[Price, Florence]
Davis, Ellabelle (Soprano)
Were You There?
Decca DFE 8618; 1965; 45 RPM
Orchestra

3187

My Soul's Been Anchored in the Lord
[Price, Florence]
Davis, Ellabelle (Soprano)
Great Negro Spirituals
Replay Record; 2013; Streaming audio
Piano

3188

My Soul's Been Anchored in the Lord
Price, Florence
Dillard, Pamela (Mezzo-soprano)
Watch and Pray: Spirituals and Art Songs by African-American Women Composers
Koch International Classics 3-7247-2H1; 1994; CD
Piano
Heavy dialect

3189

My Soul's Been Anchored in de Lord
Price, Florence
English-Robinson, Laura (Soprano)
Let It Shine!
ACA Digital Recording CM20020; 1994; CD
Piano
Light dialect

3190

My Soul's Been Anchored in de Lord
Price, Florence
Gibson, Caroline (Soprano)
On Ma Journey Now: Negro Spirituals in Concert
Twin Productions; 2016; CD

Piano
Heavy dialect

3191

My Soul's Been Anchored in the Lord
Composer not identified
Green, Elnora E. (Contralto)
This Is My Task
Private Label NR 18650; 1991; LP

3192

My Soul's Been Anchored in the Lord
Wheatley, Andres
Haniotis, Mario (Bass)
Negro Spirituals
Pastorale et Musique PM 17.047; [196-]; 45 RPM
Piano
No dialect discerned

3193

My Soul's Been Anchored in the Lord
Price, Florence
Harris, Inetta (Soprano)
My Heritage Sings: A Selection of Spirituals & Hymns
Private Label; [199-]; CD
Piano

3194

My Soul's Been Anchored in the Lord
Composer not identified
Humphrey Flynn, Edwina (Soprano)
The Lord Will Make a Way
Private Label; 2000; CD
Chorus

3195

My Soul's Been Anchored in the Lord
Clinton, Irving
Irving, Clinton (Bass-baritone)
Clinton Irving Sings Spirituals: A Tribute
Rogers; 2001; CD

3196

My Soul's Been Anchored in de Lord
Price, Florence
Little, Vera (Mezzo-soprano)
My Good Lord Done Been Here

Decca 123737; 1957; LP
Piano

3197

My Soul Been Anchored
Raphael, Michael
Maynor, Kevin (Bass)
The Spiritual: An Underground Railroad
Southeastern Virginia Arts Assoc.; [2000];
    CD
Piano

3198

My Souls' Been Anchored in de' Lord
Price, Florence
Oby, Jason (Tenor)
The Life of Christ: Collected Spirituals
Private Label TSU4749; [200-]; CD
Piano
Light dialect

3199

My Soul's Been Anchored in the Lord
Composer not identified
Price, Eudora (Vocalist)
My Favorite Songs & Spirituals
Private Label; 2006; CD
Organ
Moderate dialect

3200

My Soul's Been Anchored in the Lord
Composer not identified
Price, Leontyne (Soprano)
Great Moments at Carnegie Hall
RCA Red Seal 88985304202; 2016; CD
Piano
Heavy dialect

3201

My Soul's Been Anchored in de Lord
Price, Florence; de Paur, Leonard
Price, Leontyne (Soprano)
*Swing Low, Sweet Chariot: Fourteen
    Spirituals*
RCA Victor LSC 2600; 1962; LP
Orchestra
Heavy dialect

3202

My Soul's Been Anchored in de Lord
Price, Florence
Price, Leontyne (Soprano)
*The Lord's Prayer and 24 Other Great Songs
    of Faith and Inspiration*
RCA Red Seal VCS-7083; 1971; LP
Orchestra

3203

My Soul's Been Anchored in the Lord
Price, Florence
Price, Leontyne (Soprano)
*Leontyne Price Live! At the Historic Opening
    of the Ordway Music Theatre*
Pro Arte CDD 231; 1985; CD
Piano
Moderate dialect

3204

My Soul's Been Anchored in de Lord
Price, Florence; de Paur, Leonard
Price, Leontyne (Soprano)
*The Essential Leontyne Price: Spirituals,
    Hymns & Sacred Songs*
BMG Classics 09026-68157-2; 1996; CD
Orchestra
Heavy dialect

3205

My Soul's Been Anchored in de Lord
Price, Florence
Price, Leontyne (Soprano)
The Essential Leontyne Price
BMG Classics 09026-68153-2; 1996; CD
Orchestra
Heavy dialect

3206

My Soul's Been Anchored in the Lord
Price, Florence; de Paur, Leonard
Price, Leontyne (Soprano)
*Complete Collection of Songs and Spiritual
    Albums*
RCA Red Seal 88697940502; 2011; CD
Orchestra

3207
My Soul's Been Anchored in the Lord
Price, Florence; de Paur, Leonard
Price, Leontyne (Soprano)
Leontyne Price Sings Spirituals
RCA Red Seal 88691928242; 2012; CD
Orchestra
Heavy dialect

3208
My Soul's Been Anchored in de Lord
Price, Florence; de Paur, Leonard
Price, Leontyne (Soprano)
Singers of the Century: Leontyne Price:
Spiritual and Religious Songs
Jube Classic; 2016; Streaming audio
Orchestra
Heavy dialect

3209
My Soul's Been Anchored in the Lord
[Price, Florence]
Price, Leontyne (Soprano)
Leontyne Price reDiscovered
RCA Victor Red Seal 09026-63908-2; 2002; CD
Piano
Heavy dialect

3210
My Soul's Been Anchored in de Lord
Scharnberg, Kim
Robinson, Faye (Soprano)
Remembering Marian Anderson
d'Note Classics DND 1014; 1997; CD
Orchestra
Heavy dialect

3211
My Soul's Been Anchored in the Lord
Composer not identified
Robinson, Marie Hadley (Soprano)
Come Down Angels
Meyer Media; 2011; Streaming audio
Piano
Moderate dialect

3212
My Soul's Been Anchored in the Lord
Price, Florence

Yovanovich, Amy (Mezzo-soprano)
Great Day!
Prince Productions 9808P; 2007; CD
Piano
Light dialect

3213
My Soul's Been Anchored in the Lord
Price, Florence
Alexander, Roberta (Soprano)
Roberta Alexander.... A Retrospective
Etcetera KTC1222; 2013; CD
Piano
Heavy dialect

· · · · · · ·

My Way's Cloudy

3214
My Way's Cloudy
Burleigh, Harry T.
Anderson, Marian (Contralto)
My Way's Cloudy
Victor 19227-B; 1923; 78 RPM
Orchestra
No dialect discerned

3215
My Way's Cloudy
Burleigh, Harry T.
Anderson, Marian (Contralto)
Softly Awakes My Heart: Arias, Songs and
Spirituals, Original Recordings [1924] 1948
Naxos Nostalgia 8.120566; 2001; CD
Orchestra
Light dialect

3216
My Way's Cloudy
Burleigh, Harry T.
Anderson, Marian (Contralto)
Rare Live Broadcast Performances
VAI VAIA 1275; 2013; CD
Orchestra
Light dialect

3217
My Way's Cloudy
Burleigh, Harry T.

Anderson, Marian (Contralto)
*Marian Anderson: Beyond the Music; Her
    Complete RCA Victor Recordings*
Sony Classical 19439836492; 2021; CD
Orchestra
Light dialect

3218

My Way Is Cloudy
[Burleigh, Harry T.]
Anderson, Marian (Contralto)
Marian Anderson & Dorothy Maynor
Parnassus Recordings PAR 1004; [19--]; LP

3219

My Way's Cloudy
Composer not identified
Green, Elnora E. (Contralto)
This Is My Task
Private Label NR 18650; 1991; LP

3220

My Way Is Cloudy
Burleigh, Harry T.
Payne, John C. (Baritone)
*My Lord What a Morning/My Way Is
    Cloudy*
Columbia 3644; 1925; 78 RPM
Piano

3221

My Way Is Cloudy
[Burleigh, Harry T.]
Payne, John C. (Baritonc)
*Black Europe: Sounds & Images of Black
    People in Europe pre–1927*
Bear Family Productions BCD 16095; 2013;
    CD
Piano
Moderate dialect

3222

My Way Is Cloudy
Burleigh, Harry T.
Price, Leontyne (Soprano)
The Essential Leontyne Price
BMG Classics 09026-68153-2; 1996; CD
Chorus
Moderate dialect

3223

My Way Is Cloudy
Hall, Fred
Price, Leontyne (Soprano)
*The Essential Leontyne Price: Spirituals,
    Hymns & Sacred Songs*
BMG Classics 09026-68157-2; 1996; CD
Chorus
Moderate dialect

3224

My Way Is Cloudy
Hall, Fred
Price, Leontyne (Soprano)
*Complete Collection of Songs and Spiritual
    Albums*
RCA Red Seal 88697940502; 2011; CD
Chorus

3225

My Way Is Cloudy
Hall, Fred
Price, Leontyne (Soprano)
I Wish I Knew How It Would Feel to Be Free
RCA Red Seal LSC 3183; 2011; CD
Chorus

3226

My Way Is Cloudy
Hall, Fred
Price, Leontyne (Soprano)
Leontyne Price Sings Spirituals
RCA Red Seal 88691928242; 2012; CD
Chorus
Moderate dialect

· · · · · · ·

New Born Again

3227

New Born Again
[Hellman, William Clifford]
Duncan, Todd (Baritone)
Spirituals
Royale 1810; [1950]; LP

    Also released with *Negro Spirituals*
(Allegro ALG3022; [1952]; LP) and *African
American Spirituals* ([Apple Music]; 2008;
Streaming audio)

3228

New-Born Again
Heilman, W. C.
Holland, Charles (Tenor)
Negro Spirituals
Pathé 45 ED. 29; 1954; 45 RPM
Piano

3229

New-Born Again
Heilman, William
Matthews, Inez (Mezzo-soprano)
Inez Matthews Sings Spirituals (Great New Voices of Today, v. 6)
Period SPL-580; [1950]; LP
Piano
Heavy dialect

Also released with *Inez Matthews Sings Spirituals* (Essential Media Group; 2011; CD)

3230

New Born Again
Hellman, William Clifford
Oglesby, Isador (Tenor)
Negro Spirituals: The Musical Roots of American Folk Songs
Praise PR 658; 1978; LP
Piano

3231

New Born Again
Composer not identified
Stuart, Avon (Baritone)
Avon Stuart Recital
Edition Rhodos ERS 1218; 1975; LP
Piano

3232

New-Born Again
Composer not identified
Verdejo, Awilda (Soprano)
Awilda Verdejo Sings Spirituals
Angeluz Performances; 1999; CD
Piano

. . . .

Nobody Knows the Trouble I've Seen

[Job 13:15; Thessalonians 5:25; Revelation 2:2, 9:1]

Oh, nobody knows the trouble I've seen, Nobody knows but Jesus, Nobody knows the trouble I've seen, Glory Hallelujah! Sometimes I'm up, sometimes I'm down, ...

[Available in CW40, EM34, FHFN, HCTN, HLBS, HT25, HTBA, HTBS, HTC1, JARS, JAS1, JBTS, JHSS, JJAN, JJBA, JSSp, LB5N, RS12, RWSC, SBFD, SOTS, WF10, WF70]

As is generally the case for folk spirituals, the creator of this spiritual is unknown. However, the song appeared in *Slave Songs of the United States*, a compilation of songs gathered by William Francis Allen (1830-89), Charles Pickard Ware (1840–1921), and Lucy McKim Garrison (1842–1877) and originally published in 1867. Several verses typically have not appeared in published concert spirituals as well as a text entitled "Nobody Knows the Trouble I Feel" that came from St. Helena Island, South Carolina. No recording of this text seems to be available.

Burleigh used dialect extensively in his setting of this concert spiritual. Singers should heed this since the dialect serves a powerful interpretive function in the singing of this sorrow song. While there are opportunities for melodic improvisation of the vocal line, a small amount goes a long way. Lower-voiced singers should explore the Lawrence Brown concert spiritual setting, which is out of print as of the publication of this guide. However, it is possible to acquire it via vendors of reprints and through interlibrary loans.

3233

Nobody Knows de Trouble I've Seen
Brown, Lawrence
Anderson, Marian (Contralto)
Nobody Knows de Trouble I've Seen
Victor [1956]-A; 1924; 78 RPM
Orchestra
Moderate dialect

3234

Nobody Knows the Trouble I See
Brown, Lawrence
Anderson, Marian (Contralto)
Marian Anderson Sings Spirituals
RCA Victor Red Seal MO 1238; 1948; 78
    RPM
Piano

3235

Nobody Knows the Trouble I See
Brown, Lawrence
Anderson, Marian (Contralto)
Negro Spirituals
La Voix de Son Maître FBLP1039; 1953; LP
Piano

3236

Nobody Knows the Trouble I've Seen
Brown, Lawrence
Anderson, Marian (Contralto)
Marian Anderson in Concert 1943–1952
Eklipse Records EKR CD19; 1993; CD
Orchestra

3237

Nobody Knows the Trouble I've Seen
Brown, Lawrence
Anderson, Marian (Contralto)
Rarities: Broadcast Performances 1943–1952
Video Artists International VAIA 1200;
    1998; CD
Orchestra

3238

Nobody Knows the Trouble I See
Brown, Lawrence
Anderson, Marian (Contralto)
Spirituals
RCA Victor Red Seal 09026-63306-2; 1999; CD
Piano
No dialect discerned

3239

Nobody Knows de Trouble I've Seen
Brown, Lawrence
Anderson, Marian (Contralto)
*Sacred Roots of the Blues (When the Sun
    Goes Down Series)*

Bluebird 82876 60084 2; 2004; CD
Orchestra
Light dialect

3240

Nobody Knows de Trouble I've see
Brown, Lawrence
Anderson, Marian (Contralto)
Negro Spirituals: 1924–1949
Frémeaux & Associés FA 184; 2004; CD
Orchestra

3241

Nobody Knows the Trouble I've Seen
Brown, Lawrence
Anderson, Marian (Contralto)
*Softly Awakes My Heart: Very Best of Marian
    Anderson*
Alto ALN1955; 2016; CD
Piano
Moderate dialect

3242

Nobody Knows the Trouble I've Seen
Brown, Lawrence
Anderson, Marian (Contralto)
*Marian Anderson: Beyond the Music; Her
    Complete RCA Victor Recordings*
Sony Classical 19439836492; 2021; CD
Orchestra
No dialect discerned

3243

Nobody Knows the Trouble I See
Brown, Lawrence
Anderson, Marian (Contralto)
Marian Anderson Sings Negro Spirituals
His Master's Voice BLP 1060; [19--]; LP
Piano

    Also released with *Marian Anderson:
Beyond the Music; Her Complete RCA Victor
Recordings* Sony Classical 19439836492; 2021;
CD

3244

Nobody Knows the Trouble I See
Brown, Lawrence
Anderson, Marian (Contralto)
Negro Spirituals

RCA Victor LM 2032; [1956]; LP
Piano

3245
Nobody Knows the Trouble I See
[Brown, Lawrence]
Anderson, Marian (Contralto)
Marian Anderson Sings Spirituals
RCA Victor LM 110; 1949; LP
Piano

3246
Nobody Knows the Trouble I've Seen
[Brown, Lawrence]
Anderson, Marian (Contralto)
R-E-S-P-E-C-T: A Century of Woman in Music
Rhino R2 75815; 1999; CD

3247
Nobody Knows the Trouble I See
[Brown, Lawrence]
Anderson, Marian (Contralto)
Alto Rhapsody; Selected Spirituals
Urania URN 22.328; 2007; CD
Piano

3248
Nobody Knows the Trouble I See
[Brown, Lawrence]
Anderson, Marian (Contralto)
The Very Best of Marian Anderson
Master Classics Records; 2009; CD
Piano
No dialect discerned

3249
Nobody Knows the Trouble I See
[Brown, Lawrence]
Anderson, Marian (Contralto)
Great Spirituals
Kipepeo Publishing; 2017; CD
Piano

3250
Nobody Knows the Trouble I've Seen
[Brown, Lawrence]
Anderson, Marian (Contralto)
*Grandes Contraltos de la Musique Classique,
    Les: Marian Anderson, Vol. 12*

Mon Patrimoine Musical Collection; 2017;
    Streaming audio
Piano

3251
Nobody Knows the Trouble I See
[Brown, Lawrence]
Anderson, Marian (Contralto)
Negro Spirituals
RCA Gold Seal RVC-1570; [19--]; LP
Piano

3252
Nobody Knows the Trouble I See
[Brown, Lawrence]
Anderson, Marian (Contralto)
Negro Spirituals
RCA Victor 630.396 A; [19--]; LP
Piano

3253
Nobody Knows the Trouble I See
[Brown, Lawrence]
Anderson, Marian (Contralto)
Great Spirituals
RCA Victor ERA 62; [195-]; 7" Vinyl
Piano

3254
Nobody Known de Trouble I've Seen
Burleigh, Harry T.
Arroyo, Martina (Soprano)
Spirituals
Centaur CRC 2060; 1991; CD
Piano
Moderate dialect

3255
Ingen Har Sett Min Oro Och Sorg (Nobody
    Knows the Trouble I've Seen)
Sköld, Yngve
Björker, Leon (Bass)
I Djupa Kallarvalvet
Artist AEP 1001; 1953; 7-in EP
Piano

3256
Nobody Knows de Trouble I see
Boatwright, McHenry

Boatwright, McHenry (Bass-baritone)
Art of McHenry Boatwright: Spirituals
Golden Crest Records RE 7024; 1968; LP
Piano
Light dialect

3257

Nobody Knows de Trouble I've Seen
Burleigh, Harry T.
Brown, Anthony (Baritone)
Toil and Triumph
Spirituals Project; 2002; CD
Piano
Moderate dialect

3258

Nobody Knows de Trouble I've Seen
Burleigh, Harry T.
Burton, Dashon (Bass-baritone)
*Songs of Struggle & Redemption: We Shall
    Overcome*
Acis Productions APL08685; 2015; CD
Piano
Heavy dialect

3259

Nobody Knows the Trouble I've Seen
Composer not identified
Carey, Thomas (Baritone)
*Sechs Amerikanische Volkslieder/Sechs
    Negro Spirituals*
Colosseum SM 3003; 1970; LP
Orchestra

3260

Nobody Knows de Trouble I've Seen
Burleigh, Harry T.
Carlsen, Svein (Bass)
Negro Spirituals
EuroMaster AS ECD19005; 1996; CD
Piano

3261

Nobody Knows de Trouble I've Seen
Burleigh, Harry T.
Carnette, Count (Vocalist)
*Count Carnette Sings Favorite Negro
    Spirituals*
Carnette Archive Recordings; 1983; LP

Piano
Moderate dialect

3262

Nobody Knows the Trouble I've Seen
[Burleigh, Harry T.]
Chaiter, Yoram (Bass)
Spirituals & Other Songs
Romeo Records 7311; 2014; CD
Piano
No dialect discerned

3263

Nobody Knows
Composer not identified
Charles, Lee (Tenor)
*Swing Low Sweet Chariot: And Other
    Spirituals*
Riverside RLP 12-651; 1957; LP
Piano, guitar

3264

Nobody Know de Trouble I've Seen
Composer not identified
Clark, Clarence Carroll (Baritone)
*Nobody Knows de Trouble I've Seen/By the
    Waters of Minnetonka*
Black Swan 2006; 1921; 78 RPM
Piano
No dialect discerned

3265

Nobody Knows the Trouble I've Seen
White, Clarence Cameron
Cole-Talbert, Florence (Soprano)
Black Swans
Parnassus Recordings PACD 96067; 2019;
    CD
Piano
No dialect discerned

3266

Nobody Knows de Trouble I've Seen
White, Clarence Cameron
Cole-Talbert, Florence (Soprano)
Nobody Knows de Trouble I've Seen
Broome Special Phonograph 55; [19--];
    78 RPM

3267
Nobody Knows the Trouble I seen
Johnson, John Rosamond
Dalhart, Vernon (Tenor)
Nobody Knows de Trouble I've Seen
Edison Blue Amberol 3480; 1918; Cylinder
Orchestra
Heavy dialect

3268
Nobody Knows de Trouble I've Seen
Burleigh, Harry T.
D'Alvarez, Marguerite (Contralto)
Nobody Knows de Trouble I've Seen/My Lord,
What a Mornin'
Gramophone DA-796; [1927]; 78 RPM
Piano

3269
Nobody Knows de Trouble I've Seen
Burleigh, Harry T.
Davis, Ellabelle (Soprano)
Ellabelle Davis Sings Negro Spirituals
London LPS 182; [1950]; LP
Piano

3270
Nobody Knows de Trouble I've Seen
Burleigh, Harry T.
Davis, Ellabelle (Soprano)
Recital of Negro Spirituals by Ellabelle Davis
Decca LM.4504; [1950]; LP
Piano

3271
Nobody Knows de Trouble I've Seen
[Price, Florence]
Davis, Ellabelle (Soprano)
Great Negro Spirituals
Replay Record; 2013; Streaming audio
Piano

3272
Nobody Knows de Trouble I've Seen
Burleigh, Harry T.
Dove, Evelyn (Contralto)
Water Boy/Nobody Knows de Trouble I've
Seen

ACO G-15548; [1924]; 78 RPM
Piano

3273
Nobody Knows de Trouble I've Seen
Brown, Lawrence
Duncan, Todd (Baritone)
African American Spirituals
[Apple Music]; 2008; Streaming audio
Piano
Light dialect

3274
Nobody Knows de Trouble I've Seen
Brown, Lawrence
Duncan, Todd (Baritone)
Negro Spirituals
Allegro ALG3022; [1952]; LP
Piano

3275
Nobody Knows de Trouble I've Seen
[Brown, Lawrence]
Duncan, Todd (Baritone)
Spirituals
Royale 1810; [1950]; LP

3276
Nobody Knows the Trouble I've Seen
Althouse, Jay
Ellis, Rochelle (Soprano)
Introducing Rochelle Ellis
Janice Mayer & Assoc.; [200-]; CD

3277
Nobody Knows the Trouble I've Seen
Johnson, John Rosamond
Elzy, Ruby (Soprano)
Ruby Elzy in Song: Rare Recordings
Cambria Records CD-1154; 2006; CD
Piano
Moderate dialect

3278
Nobody Knows the Trouble I've Seen
[Johnson, John Rosamond]
Elzy, Ruby (Soprano)
The 78 RPM Collection

Master Classics Records; 2010; CD
Piano

3279

Nobody Knows the Trouble I've Seen
Roberts, Howard
Estes, Simon (Bass-baritone)
Spirituals
Philips 412 631-2; 1985; CD
Orchestra
No dialect discerned

     Also released with *Famous Spirituals*
(Philips 462 062-2; 1997; CD)

3280

Nobody Knows the Trouble I've Seen
Ryan, Donald
Estes, Simon (Bass-baritone)
Steal Away: My Favorite Negro Spirituals
Deutsche Schallplatten DS 1041-2; 1994; CD
Piano
No dialect discerned

     Also released with *Save the Children,
Save Their Lives* (CD Baby; 2010; CD)

3281

Nobody Knows the Trouble I've Seen
Kaelin, Pierre
Evans, Allan (Bass-baritone)
Negro Spirituals
Electromusic Records EMCD 6885; 1985; CD
Chorus, other instrument(s)

3282

Nobody Knows the Trouble I've Seen
Althouse, Jay
Evans, Charlie (Vocalist)
Sing God's Plan
Private Label; 2005; CD
Piano, saxophone
Moderate dialect

3283

Nobody Knows the Trouble I've Seen
Composer not identified
Farrell, Eileen (Soprano)
Golden Voices Sing Golden Favorites
Reader's Digest WCD4-5781–WCD4-5784;
   1990; CD

3284

Nobody Knows de Trouble I've Seen
Sharples, Robert
Farrell, Eileen (Soprano)
Songs America Loves
London OS 25920; 1965; LP
Chorus, organ
No dialect discerned

     Also released with *Magnificent Voice of
Eileen Farrell* (Jasnet Records; 2015; Streaming audio)

3285

Никто не знает моих страданий (Nikto ne
   znayet moikh stradaniy)
Composer not identified
Filatova, Ludmila (Mezzo-soprano)
Negro Spirituals, Negritânskie Spiricuels
Melodiâ S10 21833 009; 1985; LP
Organ
No dialect discerned

3286

Nobody Knows
Robbiani, Mario
Fisher, Dorothy (Contralto)
Negro Spirituals
Edizione D'Arte Del Lions Club Milano Al
   Cenacolo; [19--]; LP
Instrumental ensemble
Moderate dialect

3287

Nobody Knows de Trouble I've Seen
[Burleigh, Harry T.]
Hagen-William, Louis (Bass-baritone)
Negro Spirituals
Quantum QM 6909; 1993; CD
Piano
Light dialect

3288

Nobody Knows de Trouble I've Seen
[Burleigh, Harry T.]
Hall, Adelaide (Mezzo-soprano)
Spirituals
London LA 52; 1948; 78 RPM
Organ, piano

3289

Nobody Knows de Trouble I've Seen
Composer not identified
Hall, Nell (Soprano)
Nell Hall in a Recital of Arias, Ballads,
   Spirituals, Folk Songs
Colonial COL LP-211; [19--]; LP
Piano

3290

Nobody Knows de Trouble I've Seen
Composer not identified
Hendricks, Barbara (Soprano)
Espirituales Negros
EMI Classics/Altaya 01636; 1983; CD
Piano

3291

Nobody Knows de Trouble I've Seen
Composer not identified
Hendricks, Barbara (Soprano)
Schubert, Debussy, Fauré, Negro Spirituals
EMI Electrola CDZ 2523322; 1990; CD
Piano

3292

Nobody Knows de Trouble I've Seen
Composer not identified
Hendricks, Barbara (Soprano)
Spirituals
EMI Classics 0946 346641 2 7; 2005; CD
Piano

3293

Nobody Knows
Composer not identified
Hendricks, Barbara (Soprano)
No Borders
Altara ALT 1010; 2005; CD
Chorus
No dialect discerned

3294

Nobody Knows de Trouble I've Seen
Hendricks, Barbara; Alexeev, Dmitri
Hendricks, Barbara (Soprano)
Negro Spirituals
EMI CDC7470262; 1983; CD

Piano
Light dialect

3295

Nobody Knows de Trouble I've Seen
Burleigh, Harry T.
Holmes, Eugene (Baritone)
Eugene Holmes Sings Spirituals
Avant Garde AV-115; [1968]; LP
Piano
Light dialect

3296

Nobody Knows de Trouble I've Seen
Johnson, Hall
Hopkins, Gregory (Tenor)
Best of the Hall Johnson Centennial Festival
   Celebrating the 100th Anniversary of Hall
   Johnson's Birth
Hall Johnson Collection O33D2; 2002; CD
Piano

3297

Nobody Knows de Trouble I've Seen
Composer not identified
Hunt, Arthur Billings (Baritone)
Hymns and Spirituals
Cook Laboratories 1090; [195-]; LP
Organ

3298

Nobody Knows de Trouble
Burleigh, Harry T.
Hynninen, Jorma (Bass-baritone)
Negro Spirituals
Ondine ODE 715-2; 1988; CD
Piano

3299

Nobody Knows the Trouble I've Seen
Clinton, Irving
Irving, Clinton (Bass-baritone)
Clinton Irving Sings Spirituals: A Tribute
Rogers; 2001; CD

3300

Nobody Knows the Trouble I've Seen
Brown, Lawrence
Jackson, Zaidee (Vocalist)

Nobody Knows de Trouble I've Seen/
Scandalize My Name
Duophone D. 534; [19--]; 78 RPM
Orchestra
Light dialect

3301

Nobody Knows the Trouble I've Seen
Composer not identified
Johnson, John (Baritone)
Spirituals
Royale EP 180; [19--]; 45 RPM

3302

Nobody Knows the Trouble I've Seen
Composer not identified
Johnson, Yolanda F (Soprano)
Feel the Spirit!
Jublianti Artists; 2011; Streaming audio
Piano
No dialect discerned

3303

Nobody Knows
Composer not identified
Jones, Fanni (Mezzo-soprano)
Negro Spirituals
Phonotec 815; 1977; LP
Organ

3304

Nobody Knows the Trouble I seen
Composer not identified
Judkins, Edith (Soprano)
Sacred Recital, A
United Sound USR 3845; [19--]; LP

3305

Nobody Knows de Trouble I've Seen
Burleigh, Harry T.
Karle, Theo (Tenor)
Hard Trials/Nobody Knows de Trouble I've
Seen
Brunswick 13071; 1921; 78 RPM
Orchestra

3306

Nobody Knows de' Trouble I've Seen
Composer not identified

Loiselle, Henri (Bass-baritone)
One Day at a Time
Hum Recordings HRHLCD001; 1996; CD
Piano

3307

Nobody Knows the Trouble I've Seen
Meyer, Fredrich
London, George (Bass-baritone)
Spirituals
Deutsche Grammophon 00289 477 6193;
    2006; CD
Chorus
Heavy dialect

3308

Nobody Knows the Trouble I've Seen
Britton, John Charles
Lynch, Lester (Baritone)
On My Journey Now: Spirituals & Hymns
Pentatone Music PTC 5186 57'; 2017; CD
Guitar, harmonica

3309

Nobody Knows de Trouble I see [from
    Journey Beyond Time]
Crumb, George
Martin, Barbara Ann (Soprano)
American Songbooks II & IV
BRIDGE 9275A/B; 2008; CD
Piano, percussion

3310

Nobody Knows de Trouble I've Seen
Composer not identified
Maynor, Dorothy (Soprano)
Negro Spirituals
RCA Victor M879; 1942; 78 RPM
Men's voices

3311

Nobody Knows the Trouble I've Seen
Composer not identified
Maynor, Dorothy (Soprano)
Dorothy Maynor Sings Spirituals and Sacred
    Songs
RCA Camden CAL-344; 1957; LP
Chorus

Also released with *Spirituals, Arias, Songs (1940–1943)* (Claremont CD GSE 78-50-59; 1994; CD)

3312

Nobody Knows the Trouble I've Seen
Composer not identified
Maynor, Dorothy (Soprano)
The Art of Dorothy Maynor
RCA Red Seal LM 3086; 1969; LP
Men's voices

3313

Nobody Knows the Trouble I've Seen
Composer not identified
Maynor, Dorothy (Soprano)
*First Time Buyer's Guide to American Negro
    Spirituals*
Moderate dialect

3314

Nobody Knows the Trouble I've Seen
Composer not identified
Maynor, Dorothy (Soprano)
Spirituals
Past Classics; 2013; Streaming audio
Men's voices
No dialect discerned

3315

Nobody Knows de Trouble I've Seen
Composer not identified
Maynor, Dorothy (Soprano)
Negro Spirituals
Kipepeo Publishing; 2018; CD
Men's voices

3316

Nobody Knows the Trouble I've Seen
Composer not identified
Maynor, Dorothy (Soprano)
The Concerto: African American Spirituals
Orange Amaro; 2019; Streaming audio
Men's voices

3317

Nobody Knows the Trouble I've Seen
Composer not identified
Maynor, Dorothy (Soprano)

*Negro Spirituals: The Concert Tradition
    1909–1948*
Frémeaux & Associés FA 168; 1999; CD
Men's voices
No dialect discerned

3318

Nobody Knows the Trouble I've Seen
Raphael, Michael
Maynor, Kevin (Bass)
The Spiritual: An Underground Railroad
Southeastern Virginia Arts Assoc.; [2000]; CD
Piano

3319

Nobody Knows the Trouble I've Seen
Welsh, Nicky
McCue, Bill (Bass-baritone)
Bill McCue Sings the Great Spirituals
Beltona SBE 173; 1974; LP
Orchestra

3320

Nobody Knows de Trouble I see (rare
    version)
Composer not identified
McDaniel, Yvette (Soprano)
Simply Spiritual
YM01 DIDX 046103; 1997; CD
Piano

3321

Nobody Knows the Trouble I See
Burleigh, Harry T.
Merrill, Robert (Baritone)
Nobody Knows the Trouble I See/Shadrach
RCA Victor 10-1427; 1948; 78 RPM
Orchestra

3322

Nobody Knows
Composer not identified
Monzo, Oscar (Baritone)
Negro Spirituals
Dial Discos 50-2020; 1983; LP

3323

Nobody Knows the Trouble I See
Composer not identified

Moses, Oral (Bass-baritone)
Extreme Spirituals
Cuneiform Record Rune 241; 2006; CD
Instrumental ensemble

3324

Nobody Knows de Trouble I see
Traditional
Moses, Oral (Bass-baritone)
Spirituals in Zion: A Spiritual Heritage for the Soul
Albany Records TROY587; 2003; CD
A cappella

3325

Nobody Knows de Trouble I've Seen
Brown, Lawrence
Pankey, Aubrey (Baritone)
Negro Spirituals
Eterna 830010; 1983; LP
Piano
Light dialect

3326

Nobody Knows de Trouble I've Seen
[Brown, Lawrence]
Pankey, Aubrey (Baritone)
Aubrey Pankey Singt Negro-Spirituals
Eterna 7 30 005; 1959; LP
Piano
Light dialect

3327

Nobody Knows the Trouble I've Seen
[Brown, Lawrence]
Pankey, Aubrey (Baritone)
Negro-Spirituals
Eterna 5 30 022; [19--]; 45 RPM
Piano
Light dialect

3328

Nobody Knows de Trouble I've Seen
Burleigh, Harry T.
Parks, Karen (Soprano)
Nobody Knows
Ottimavoce 52736; 2007; CD
Instrumental ensemble
Light dialect

3329

Nobody Knows the Trouble I've Seen
Brown, Lawrence
Payne, John C. (Baritone)
It's Me, O Lord/Nobody Knows the Trouble I've Seen; Every Time I Feel de Spirit
Columbia 3662; 1925; 78 RPM
Piano

3330

Nobody Knows de Trouble I've Seen
Burleigh, Harry T.
Philogene, Ruby (Soprano)
Steal Away
EMI Classics 7243 5 69707 2 4; 1997; CD
Piano

3331

Nobody Knows the Trouble I've Seen
Composer not identified
Porter, John (Bass)
No More Crying: Negro Spirituals
Pan Verlag OV-84; [1978]; LP

3332

Nobody Knows the Trouble I Seen
Hall, Fred
Price, Leontyne (Soprano)
The Essential Leontyne Price: Spirituals, Hymns & Sacred Songs
BMG Classics 09026-68157-2; 1996; CD
Chorus
Moderate dialect

3333

Nobody Knows the Trouble I've Seen
Hall, Fred
Price, Leontyne (Soprano)
The Essential Leontyne Price
BMG Classics 09026-68153-2; 1996; CD
Chorus
Moderate dialect

3334

Nobody Knows the Trouble I've Seen
Hall, Fred
Price, Leontyne (Soprano)
Complete Collection of Songs and Spiritual Albums

RCA Red Seal 88697940502; 2011; CD
Chorus

3335
Nobody Knows the Trouble I've Seen
Hall, Fred
Price, Leontyne (Soprano)
I Wish I Knew How It Would Feel to Be Free
RCA Red Seal LSC 3183; 2011; CD
Chorus

3336
Nobody Knows the Trouble I've Seen
Hall, Fred
Price, Leontyne (Soprano)
Leontyne Price Sings Spirituals
RCA Red Seal 88691928242; 2012; CD
Chorus
Moderate dialect

3337
Kukaan Ei Tiedä (Nobody Knows)
Composer not identified
Putkonen, Marko (Bass)
Deep River: Negro Spirituals
Lilium LILP 101; 1991; LP

3338
Nobody Knows the Trouble I've Seen
Burleigh, Harry T.
Ragin, Derek Lee (Countertenor)
Ev'ry Time I Feel the Spirit: Spirituals
Channel Classics CCS 2991; 1991; CD
Piano
Moderate dialect

3339
Nobody Knows de Trouble I seen
Giesen, Hubert
Ray, William (Baritone)
Negro Spirituals
Intercord; [19--]; LP
Piano

3340
Nobody Knows de Trouble I seen
Giesen, Hubert
Ray, William (Baritone)

Sings Arias, Duets, Musical Selections and Negro Spirituals
Intercord; [19--]; CD
Piano

3341
Nobody Knows the Trouble I See
Jackson King, Betty
Rhodes, Yolanda (Soprano)
The Angels Bowed Down
Cambria Master Recordings CD-1237; 2019; CD

3342
Nobody Knows de Trouble I've Seen
Brown, Lawrence
Robeson, Paul (Bass-baritone)
Nobody Knows de Trouble I've Seen/Swing Low, Sweet Chariot
Victor 20068; 1926; 78 RPM
Piano

3343
Nobody Knows de Trouble I've Seen
Brown, Lawrence
Robeson, Paul (Bass-baritone)
Spirituals
Columbia Masterworks 17379-D; 1945; 78 RPM
Piano
Light dialect

3344
Nobody Knows de Trouble I've Seen
Brown, Lawrence
Robeson, Paul (Bass-baritone)
Joshua Fit de Battle of Jericho/Nobody Knows de Trouble I've Seen
Columbia Masterworks 17470-D; 1946; 78 RPM
Piano
Light dialect

3345
Nobody Knows de Trouble I've Seen
Brown, Lawrence
Robeson, Paul (Bass-baritone)
Sometimes I Feel Like a Motherless Child/ Nobody Knows de Trouble I've Seen

Columbia D.B. 2491; 1949; 78 RPM
Piano
No dialect discerned

3346

Nobody Knows de Trouble I've Seen
Brown, Lawrence
Robeson, Paul (Bass-baritone)
Spirituals
Philips 409.115 AE; 1959; 45 RPM
Piano

3347

Nobody Knows de Trouble I've Seen
Brown, Lawrence
Robeson, Paul (Bass-baritone)
Songs of My People
RCA Red Seal LM-3292; 1972; LP
Piano

3348

Nobody Knows the Trouble I've Seen
Brown, Lawrence
Robeson, Paul (Bass-baritone)
The Power and the Glory
Columbia/Legacy CK 47337; 1991; CD
Piano
No dialect discerned

3349

Nobody Knows de Trouble I've Seen
Brown, Lawrence
Robeson, Paul (Bass-baritone)
Songs for Free Men, 1940-45
Pearl GEMM CD 9264; 1997; CD
Piano

3350

Nobody Knows de Trouble I've Seen
Brown, Lawrence
Robeson, Paul (Bass-baritone)
Paul Robeson Collection
Hallmark Recordings 390692; 1998; CD

3351

Nobody Knows de Trouble I've Seen
Brown, Lawrence
Robeson, Paul (Bass-baritone)
Spirituals: Original Recordings 1925–1936

Naxos Gospel Legends 8.120638; 2003; CD
Piano

3352

Nobody Knows de Trouble I've Seen
Brown, Lawrence
Robeson, Paul (Bass-baritone)
*Nobody Knows de Trouble I've Seen/
    Sometimes I Feel Like a Motherless Child*
Columbia CD 35557; [19--]; 78 RPM
Piano

3353

Nobody Knows de Trouble I've Seen
Brown, Lawrence
Robeson, Paul (Bass-baritone)
*Sometimes I Feel Like a Motherless Child/
    Nobody Knows de Trouble I've Seen*
Columbia DS 1783; [19--]; 78 RPM
Piano
Light dialect

3354

Nobody Knows de Trouble I've Seen
Brown, Lawrence
Robeson, Paul (Bass-baritone)
Spirituals
Columbia Masterworks ML 4105; CBS
    62483; [1948]; LP

3355

Nobody Knows de Trouble I've Seen
Brown, Lawrence
Robeson, Paul (Bass-baritone)
Spirituals
Philips 429 395 BE; [195-]; 45 RPM

3356

Nobody Knows de Trouble I've Seen
[Brown, Lawrence]
Robeson, Paul (Bass-baritone)
Spirituals
Columbia Masterworks M-610; 1946; 78
    RPM
Piano

3357

Nobody Knows the Trouble I've Seen
[Brown, Lawrence]

Robeson, Paul (Bass-baritone); Brown,
　Lawrence (Vocalist)
Scandalize My Name
Classics Record Library 30-5647; 1976; LP
Piano
Light dialect

3358

Nobody Knows the Trouble I've Seen
[Brown, Lawrence]
Robeson, Paul (Bass-baritone)
Deep River
Great Voices of the Century GVC 2004;
　1999; CD

3359

Nobody Knows the Trouble I've Seen
[Brown, Lawrence]
Robeson, Paul (Bass-baritone)
The Essential Paul Robeson
ASV CD AJS 244; 2000; CD

3360

Nobody Knows the Trouble I've Seen
[Brown, Lawrence]
Robeson, Paul (Bass-baritone)
Good News: Vintage Negro Spirituals
Living Era AJA 5622; 2006; CD
Piano
Light dialect

3361

Nobody Knows the Troubles I've Seen
[Brown, Lawrence]
Robeson, Paul (Bass-baritone)
The Originals: "Spirituals"
Yoyo USA; 2006; Streaming audio

3362

Nobody Knows the Trouble I've Seen
[Brown, Lawrence]
Robeson, Paul (Bass-baritone)
Ol' Man River: His 56 Finest 1925–1945
Retrospective RTS 4116; 2008; CD

3363

Nobody Knows de Trouble I've Seen
[Brown, Lawrence]
Robeson, Paul (Bass-baritone)

Paul Robeson's Treasure Chest
Leverage; 2008; Streaming audio
Piano

3364

Nobody Knows the Trouble I've Seen
[Brown, Lawrence]
Robeson, Paul (Bass-baritone)
Negro Spirituals (And More)
Discmedi DM-4674-02; 2009; CD

3365

Nobody Knows the Trouble I've Seen
[Brown, Lawrence]
Robeson, Paul (Bass-baritone)
Drink to Me Only with Thine Eyes
MD Music; 2010; Streaming audio
Piano
No dialect discerned

3366

Nobody Knows de Trouble I've Seen
[Brown, Lawrence]
Robeson, Paul (Bass-baritone)
Ol' Man River: The Ultimate Collection
Roslin Records; 2011; Streaming audio
Piano
Light dialect

3367

Nobody Knows the Trouble I've Seen
[Brown, Lawrence]
Robeson, Paul (Bass-baritone)
*Ol' Man River: The Very Best of Paul
　Robeson*
Memory Lane; 2012; CD

3368

Nobody Knows the Trouble I've Seen
[Brown, Lawrence]
Robeson, Paul (Bass-baritone)
Classic Gospel Songs
Emerald/K-Tel; 2013; Streaming audio
Piano

3369

Nobody Knows the Trouble I've Seen
[Brown, Lawrence]
Robeson, Paul (Bass-baritone)

Five Classic Albums Plus Bonus Tracks
Real Gone Music RGMCD287; 2017; CD

3370

Nobody Knows the Trouble I've Seen
[Brown, Lawrence]
Robeson, Paul (Bass-baritone)
The Essential Collection
Primo PRMCD6233; 2018; CD

3371

Nobody Knows the Trouble I've Seen
[Brown, Lawrence]
Robeson, Paul (Bass-baritone)
Complete Recordings
Universal Digital Enterprises; 2018;
    Streaming audio

3372

Nobody Knows the Trouble I've Seen
Composer not identified
Rustin, Bayard (Tenor)
Bayard Rustin Sings Spirituals, Work &
    Freedom Songs
Bayard Rustin Fund; 1988; Cassette
Piano
Moderate dialect

3373

Nobody Knows the Trouble I've Seen
Composer not identified
Rustin, Bayard (Tenor)
Bayard Rustin, the Singer
Bayard Rustin Fund; 1992; CD
Piano

3374

Nobody Knows the Trouble I've Seen
Composer not identified
Rustin, Bayard (Tenor)
Bayard Rustin Sings Spirituals, Work &
    Freedom Songs
Bayard Rustin Fund; 2003; CD
Piano
Moderate dialect

3375

Nobody Knows the Trouble I've Seen
Composer not identified

Rustin, Bayard (Tenor)
Elizabethan Songs & Negro Spirituals
Fellowship Records 102; [1952]; 10" LP
Piano

    Also released with: *Bayard Rustin-The
Singer: Negro Spirituals, Lute Songs & More*;
Black Swan Series; Parnassus Records PACD
96083; 2022; CD

3376

Nobody Knows de Trouble I've Seen
Burleigh, Harry T.
Seagle, Oscar (Baritone)
*Nobody Knows de Trouble I've Seen/I Don't
    Feel No Ways Tired*
Columbia Record A2469; 1917; 78 RPM
Orchestra

3377

Nobody Knows de Trouble I've Seen
Burleigh, Harry T.
Seagle, Oscar (Baritone)
*Nobody Knows de Trouble I've Seen/I Don't
    Feel No Ways Tired*
Columbia 71-M; 1917; 78 RPM
Orchestra

3378

Nobody Knows the Trouble I've Seen [from
    Motherless Child Songs]
Dunner, Leslie B.
Sebron, Carolyn (Mezzo-soprano)
Open Boundaries
Innova Recordings MN 108; 1989; CD
Piano, clarinet
No dialect discerned

3379

Nobody Knows the Trouble I've Seen
Composer not identified
Lee, Seung Hyun (Soprano)
*Sweet Blessing: Spirituals & Hymns by
    Seung-Hyun Lee*
Seoul Records; [20--]; CD

3380

Nobody Knows the Trouble I've Seen
Burleigh, Harry T.
Smith, Muriel (Mezzo-soprano)

Negro Spirituals
Philips NBE11007; [195-]; 45 RPM
Piano

3381

Nobody Knows de Trouble I've Seen
Brown, Lawrence
Spencer, Kenneth (Bass-baritone)
Nobody Knows de Trouble I've Seen/I Stood on the Ribber ob Jerdon
Supraphon G 23272; [19--]; 78 RPM
Piano, organ

3382

Nobody Knows the Trouble I've Seen
Dumont, C.
Spencer, Kenneth (Bass-baritone)
Deep River/Nobody Knows the Trouble I've Seen
Elite Special 45-A-441; [1963]; 45 RPM
Orchestra

3383

Nobody Knows the Trouble I've Seen
Composer not identified
St. Hill, Krister (Baritone)
Svenska Folkvisor/Negro Spirituals
Polar POLS 398; 1985; LP

3384

Nobody Knows the Trouble I've Seen
Meyer, Friedrich
Streich, Rita (Soprano)
Volkslieder Der Welt / Folksongs of the World / Chansons Populaires du Monde
Deutsche Grammophon Gesellschaft 19 376; 1963; LP
Chorus
Light dialect

3385

Nobody Knows de Trouble I see
Price, Deon Nielson
Taylor, Darryl (Countertenor)
How Sweet the Sound: A Charm of Spirituals
Albany TROY1244; 2011; CD
Piano

3386

Nobody Knows de Trouble I See [from Spiritual Songs]
Price, Deon Nielson
Taylor, Darryl (Countertenor)
Radiance in Motion
Cambria CD-1236; 2016; CD
Piano
Light dialect

3387

Nobody Knows the Trouble I've Seen
Browne, George
Taylor, Geoffrey (Baritone)
Negro Spirituals
P&R; 2011; Streaming audio
Chorus, orchestra
Moderate dialect

3388

Nobody Knows the Trouble I've Seen
Browne, George
Taylor, Geoffrey (Baritone)
Negro Spirituals
World Record Club MW-2005; [196-]; LP
Chorus, orchestra
Moderate dialect

Also released with *Negro Spirituals* (Marathon Media International; 2013; Streaming audio)

3389

Nobody Knows de Trouble I sees
Guion, David
Thomas, Edna (Soprano)
I Got Shoes/Nobody Knows de Trouble I Sees
Columbia 1863-D; 1928; 78 RPM
Piano

3390

Nobody Knows
Karreman, A.; Thompson, Jeanette
Thompson, Jeanette (Soprano)
Negro Spirituals
Pavane Records ADW 7267; 1992; CD
Chorus
No dialect discerned

3391

Nobody Knows the Trouble I've Seen
Bohmler, Craig
Thomson, Jeannette (Soprano)
Christmas Around the World
ARTS Music ARTS49008-2; 2000; CD
Orchestra
No dialect discerned

3392

Nobody Knows de Trouble I've Seen
Composer not identified
Traubel, Helen (Soprano)
*Negro Spirituals: Helen Traubel in Popular
  Ballads*
Columbia ML 4221; 1949; LP
Piano

3393

Nobody Knows the Trouble I've Seen
Hattey, Philip
Tucker, Eric Hoy (Bass-baritone)
*Southern Salute: Southern Songs &
  Spirituals*
White Pine Music WPM218; 2012; CD
Piano
Light dialect

3394

Nobody Knows de Trouble I've Seen
[Burleigh, Harry T.]
Ventriglia, Franco (Baritone)
Franco Ventriglia Sings Negro Spirituals
Vedette Records VRMS 316; [19--]; LP
Piano, organ
Light dialect

    Also released with *Franco Ventriglia
Sings Negro Spirituals* (Vedette Records; 2007;
Streaming audio)

3395

Nobody Knows de Trouble I've Seen
Burleigh, Harry T.
Warfield, William (Bass-baritone)
*Spirituals: 200 Years of African-American
  Spirituals*
ProArte CDD 3443; 1993; CD
Piano
Light dialect

3396

Nobody Knows de Trouble I've Seen
Burleigh, Harry T.
West, Lucretia (Mezzo-soprano)
Negro Spirituals III
Club français du disque 176; 1959; LP
Piano
Moderate dialect

3397

Nobody Knows
Burleigh, Harry T.
West, Lucretia (Mezzo-soprano)
Negro Spirituals mit Lukretia West
Opera 3408; [195-]; LP
Piano

3398

Nobody Knows
Burleigh, Harry T.
West, Lucretia (Mezzo-soprano)
Negro Spirituals
Club français du disque 215; [196-]; 7-in
  EP
Piano

3399

Nobody Knows the Trouble I've Seen
Composer not identified
West, Lucretia (Mezzo-soprano)
Lucretia West Sings Spirituals
Westminster WP 6063; [1957]; LP

3400

Nobody Knows de Trouble I've Seen
Morgenstern, Sam
West, Lucretia (Mezzo-soprano)
Spirituals
Westminster WL 5338; 1954; LP
Men's voices

3401

Nobody Knows the Trouble/Steal Away
Coil, Pat; Kimbrough, Steven
Wilson-Felder, Cynthia (Soprano);
  Kimbrough, Steven (Baritone)
*Spirituals: Songs from the American
  Experience*

GBGMusik CD 1-005; 1996; CD
Instrumental ensemble

3402

Nobody Knows de Trouble I've Seen
Burleigh, Harry T.
Winter, Georg (Vocalist)
Eine Kleine Hausmusik
Teldec 66.22670; 1981; LP
Piano

3403

Nobody Knows the Trouble I Have Seen
[Burleigh, Harry T.]
Winters, Lawrence (Bass-baritone)
Lawrence Winters: Recital
Hamburger Archiv fur Gesangskunst 10397;
    2007; CD
Orchestra
No dialect discerned

3404

Nobody Knows the Trouble I Have
    Seen
[Burleigh, Harry T.]
Winters, Lawrence (Bass-baritone)
Singer Portrait: Lawrence Winters
Apple Music; 2012; Streaming audio
Orchestra
No dialect discerned

3405

Oh, Nobody Knows de Troubles I've seen
Schweizer, Rolf
Wolf, Lars (Vocalist)
Die Schwarze Stimme Europas
Cantate 666000; 1971; LP
Chorus, organ, percussion

· · · · · · ·

Not a Word

3406

Not a Word
Baker, Bradley
Baker, Bradley (Baritone)
Not a Word: Spirituals, Hymns, Songs
AYA Worldwide Records 6-09682-2; 2001;
    CD

· · · · · · ·

Now Let Me Fly

3407

Now Let Me Fly
Johnson, John Rosamond
Glover, Andre Solomon (Baritone)
Opera Ebony Sings Spirituals
Ebony Classic Recordings; 2002; CD

· · · · · · ·

Now We Take
This Feeble Body

3408

Now We Take This Feeble Body
Dett, Robert Nathaniel
Glover, Andre Solomon (Baritone)
Opera Ebony Sings Spirituals
Ebony Classic Recordings; 2002; CD

· · · · · · ·

O de Angels Done
Bowed Down

3409

O de Angels Done Bowed Down
Perry, Zenobia Powell
Peri, Janis-Rozena (Soprano)
*Music of Zenobia Powell Perry: Art Songs
    and Piano Music*
Cambria CD-1138; 2010; CD
Piano
Moderate dialect

· · · · · · ·

O Gimme Your Han'

3410

O Gimme Your Han'
Brown, Lawrence
Robeson, Paul (Bass-baritone)
Swing Low, Sweet Chariot
Columbia Masterworks MM-819; 1949; 78
    RPM
Piano

3411
O Gimme Your Han'
Brown, Lawrence
Robeson, Paul (Bass-baritone); Brown,
   Lawrence (Vocalist)
Paul Robeson Chante ... 16 Spirituals
Philips G 05.639 R; 1959; LP
Piano

3412
O Gimme Your Han'
Brown, Lawrence
Robeson, Paul (Bass-baritone)
Paul Robeson Sings Negro Spirituals
Philips GBL 5584; [19--]; LP
Piano

3413
O Give Me Your Han'
[Brown, Lawrence]
Robeson, Paul (Bass-baritone)
Negro Spirituals, v. 2
Philips NBE11102; 1956; 7" Vinyl

3414
O Gimme Your Han'
[Brown, Lawrence]
Robeson, Paul (Bass-baritone)
Swing Low, Sweet Chariot
Columbia Masterworks ML 2038; [195-]; LP
Piano

· · · · · · ·

O Mary

3415
O Mary
Dorsey, ?
Oglesby, Isador (Tenor)
Life of Jesus in Negro Spirituals
Oglesby Recordings Album 2; 1980; LP
Piano

· · · · · · ·

O Mary What You Gonna Call Your Pretty Little Baby

3416
O Mary What You Gonna Call Your Pretty
   Little Baby

Brown, Uzee, Jr.
English-Robinson, Laura (Soprano)
Great Day!
Allgood; 2005; CD
Piano
Light dialect

3417
Oh, Mary, What You Gonna Call Your
   Pretty Little Baby?
Brown, Uzee, Jr.
Moses, Oral (Bass-baritone)
*Amen! African-American Composers of the
   20th Century*
Albany Records TROY459; 2001; CD
Piano
Moderate dialect

· · · · · · ·

O Poor Little Jesus

3418
O Poor Little Jesus
Composer not identified
Norman, Jessye (Soprano)
*Jessye Norman at Notre Dame: A Christmas
   Concert*
Philips 432 731-2; 1992; CD

   Also released with *Festkonzert aus
Notre-Dame* (Philips 438 079-2; 1992; CD)
and *Jessye Norman à Notre-Dame: Récital de
Noël* (Philips 438 078-2; 1992; CD)

· · · · · · ·

Oh de Lan' I Am Boun' for

3419
Oh de Lan' I Am Boun' for
Composer not identified
Delmore, Harry A. (Tenor)
*Oh de Lan' I Am Boun' for/Ride Up in de
   Chariot*
Radiex 4166; [19--]; 78 RPM

· · · · · · ·

Oh Freedom

3420
Oh, Freedom
Composer not identified

Carey, Thomas (Baritone)
Go Down Moses
Da Camera Song SM 95028; 1970; LP
Piano

3421

Oh, Freedom
Composer not identified
Charles, Lee (Tenor)
*Swing Low Sweet Chariot: And Other
    Spirituals*
Riverside RLP 12-651; 1957; LP
Piano, guitar

3422

Oh Freedom
Traditional
Hendricks, Barbara (Soprano)
Blues Everywhere I Go
Arte Verum ARV-013; 2015; CD
A cappella
Light dialect

3423

Oh Freedom
Johnson, Hall
Hopkins, Gregory (Tenor)
*Best of the Hall Johnson Centennial Festival
    Celebrating the 100th Anniversary of Hall
    Johnson's Birth*
Hall Johnson Collection O33D2; 2002; CD
Piano

3424

O Freedom
Okpebholo, Shawn
Jefferson, Othello (Tenor)
*Good News: African American Spirituals
    and Art Songs*
Cambria Records CD 1270; 2021; CD
Piano

3425

Oh, Freedom
Okpebholo, Shawn
Liverman, Will (Baritone)
Steal Away
Yellow Einstein; 2014; CD
Piano, flute
No dialect discerned

3426

Oh, Freedom
Weisner, Nancy
Miller, Jeanette (Soprano)
No Man Canna Hinder Me
MiJon Record Productions MJ240; 1979; CD
Piano

3427

Oh Freedom
Composer not identified
Moses, Oral (Bass-baritone)
Extreme Spirituals
Cuneiform Record Rune 241; 2006; CD
Instrumental ensemble

3428

Oh Freedom
Traditional
Moses, Oral (Bass-baritone)
*Spirituals in Zion: A Spiritual Heritage for
    the Soul*
Albany Records TROY587; 2003; CD
A cappella
Heavy dialect

3429

Oh Freedom!
Traditional
Nobles, NaGuanda (Soprano)
Homage to the Journey
Selbon Records; 2014; Streaming audio
A cappella
Moderate dialect

3430

O Freedom
Composer not identified
Porter, John (Bass)
No More Crying: Negro Spirituals
Pan Verlag OV-84; [1978]; LP

3431

Oh, Freedom
Carter, Roland
Robinson-Oturo, Gail (Soprano)
*Sweetest Sound I Ever Heard: Spirituals for
    Solo Voice and Piano, Vol. 1*
CD Baby; 2020; Streaming audio

Piano
Moderate dialect

3432

Oh Freedom
Composer not identified
Rustin, Bayard (Tenor)
*Bayard Rustin Sings Spirituals, Work &
    Freedom Songs*
Bayard Rustin Fund; 1988; Cassette
Piano
Moderate dialect

3433

Oh Freedom
Composer not identified
Rustin, Bayard (Tenor)
*Bayard Rustin Sings Spirituals, Work &
    Freedom Songs*
Bayard Rustin Fund; 2003; CD
Piano
Moderate dialect

3434

Oh Freedom
Traditional
Sebron, Carolyn (Mezzo-soprano)
Resurrection, Pt. 1
Private Label; 2006; CD
A cappella
Light dialect

3435

O Freedom
Perkinson, Coleridge-Taylor
Shirley, George (Tenor)
The New Negro Spiritual
W. C. Patterson; 2002; Score w/CD
Piano
Heavy dialect

3436

O Freedom
Perkinson, Coleridge-Taylor
Shirley, George (Tenor)
George Shirley at 80: My Time Has Come!
Videmus Records; 2014; CD
Piano

3437

Oh, Freedom
Johnson, Hall
Straughter, Maralyn (Soprano)
Negro Spirituals of Hall Johnson
Variety Recording Service Var 0753; [196-];
    LP
Piano

3438

Oh Freedom /I Want to Be Ready
Thompson, Jeanette
Thompson, Jeanette (Soprano)
Negro Spirituals
Pavane Records ADW 7267; 1992; CD
Percussion
No dialect discerned

3439

Oh, Freedom
Composer not identified
Verrett, Shirley (Mezzo-soprano)
Shirley Verrett: Edition
Newton Classics 8802167; 2013; CD
Guitar

3440

Oh, Freedom
de Paur, Leonard
Verrett, Shirley (Mezzo-soprano)
Singin' in the Storm
Sony 82318; 2011; CD
Orchestra

· · · · · · ·

Oh, Give Me Your Hand

3441

Oh, Give Me Your Hand
Composer not identified
Robeson, Paul (Bass-baritone)
Songs for Free Men, 1940–45
Pearl GEMM CD 9264; 1997; CD
Piano

Oh, Glory

3442
Oh, Glory!
Johnson, Hall
Anderson, Marian (Contralto)
Jus' Keep on Singin'
RCA Victor LSC 2796; 1965; LP
Piano

3443
Oh, Glory!
Johnson, Hall
Anderson, Marian (Contralto)
Marian Anderson: Beyond the Music; Her Complete RCA Victor Recordings
Sony Classical 19439836492; 2021; CD
Piano
Light dialect

3444
Oh, Glory
Simpson-Curenton, Evelyn
Battle, Kathleen (Soprano)
Spirituals in Concert
Deutsche Grammophon 429 790-2; 1991; CD
Chorus, orchestra, flute
Heavy dialect

3445
Oh, Glory
Okpebholo, Shawn
Bridges, J'nai (Mezzo-soprano)
Lord How Come Me Here?
Navona Records NV6408; 2022; CD
Piano
No dialect discerned

3446
O Glory
Simpson-Curenton, Evelyn; Brown, Angela
Brown, Angela (Soprano)
Mosiac: A Collection of African-American Spirituals with Piano, guitar
Albany Records TROY721; 2004; CD
A cappella
Moderate dialect

3447
O Glory!
Simpson-Currenton, Evelyn
Chandler-Eteme, Janice (Soprano)
Devotions
Sligo Records; 2007; CD
Piano

3448
Oh Glory
Johnson, Hall
Foreman, Blanche (Contralto)
Best of the Hall Johnson Centennial Festival Celebrating the 100th Anniversary of Hall Johnson's Birth
Hall Johnson Collection O33D2; 2002; CD
Piano

3449
Oh, Glory
Johnson, Hall
Graves, Denyce (Mezzo-soprano)
Angels Watching Over Me
NPR Classics CD 0006; 1997; CD
Chorus, piano
No dialect discerned

3450
Oh Glory!
Johnson, Hall
Holmes, Eugene (Baritone)
Spirituals
Schubert Records SCH-102; [1988]; LP
Piano
Light dialect

3451
Oh Glory
Bonds, Margaret
Maynor, Kevin (Bass)
The Spiritual: An Underground Railroad
Southeastern Virginia Arts Assoc.; [2000]; CD
Piano

3452
Oh Glory
Composer not identified
McFerrin, Robert (Baritone)

Negro Spirituals
Jacques Canetti 27 193; 1965; 45 RPM

3453

Oh, Glory
Johnson, Hall
McFerrin, Robert (Baritone)
Deep River and Other Classic Negro Spirituals
Riverside Records RLP 12-812; 1959; LP
Piano
No dialect discerned

  Also released with *Classic Negro Spirituals* (Washington Records WLP 466; 1959; LP)

3454

Oh, Glory!
Johnson, Hall
Moses, Oral (Bass-baritone)
Songs of America
Albany Records TROY1011; 2008; CD
Piano
Light dialect

3455

Oh Glory
Johnson, Hall
Pierson, Edward (Bass-baritone)
Edward Pierson Sings Hymns and Spirituals
Kemco 98-44; [19--]; LP

3456

Oh, Glory
Johnson, Hall
Simpson, Eugene Thamon (Bass)
Hear Me, Ye Winds and Waves
Black Heritage Publications; 2005; CD
Piano
Light dialect

3457

Oh Glory
Johnson, Hall
Simpson, Eugene Thamon (Bass)
Hall Johnson Spirituals and Other Folk Songs
Private Label; 2016; CD
Piano

3458

Oh, Glory!
Johnson, Hall
Toppin, Louise (Soprano)
The Hall Johnson Collection
Carl Fischer VF5 CD1–VF5 CD2; 2003; Score w/CD
Piano
Light dialect

3459

Oh, Glory
Johnson, Hall
Toppin, Louise (Soprano)
He'll Bring It to Pass: The Spirituals of Hall Johnson for Voice and Piano
Albany Records TROY846; 2006; CD
Piano
Light dialect

3460

O Glory
Composer not identified
Verrett, Shirley (Soprano)
The Very Best of Gospel
Disconforme CDX7720; 2007; CD

3461

Oh, Glory!
Composer not identified
Verrett, Shirley (Mezzo-soprano)
Great Moments at Carnegie Hall
RCA Red Seal 88985304202; 2016; CD
Piano
No dialect discerned

3462

O Glory!
Johnson, Hall
Verrett, Shirley (Mezzo-soprano)
Shirley Verrett Recital
Suiza OSCD 223; 1991; CD
Piano

3463

Oh, Glory!
Johnson, Hall
Verrett, Shirley (Soprano)

Met Stars in the New World
MET 216CD; 1992; CD

3464
Oh, Glory!
Johnson, Hall
Verrett, Shirley (Mezzo-soprano)
Carnegie Hall Recital
Sony Music 82319; 2011; CD
Piano
No dialect discerned

3465
Oh, Glory!
Johnson, Hall
Verrett, Shirley (Mezzo-soprano)
Shirley Verrett: Edition
Newton Classics 8802167; 2013; CD
Piano

3466
Oh Glory
[Johnson, Hall]
Verrett, Shirley (Mezzo-soprano)
Gospels & Spirituals Gold Collection
Retro R2CD 40-26; 1995; CD
Piano
Light dialect

. . . .

Oh, Graveyard

3467
Oh, Graveyard
Johnson, Hall
Moses, Oral (Bass-baritone)
*Come Down Angels and Trouble the Water:
    Negro Spirituals, an American National
    Treasure!*
Albany Records TROY 1489; 2014; CD
Piano
Light dialect

. . . .

Oh, Heaven
Is One Beautiful Place

3468
Oh, Heaven Is One Beautiful Place, I Know
Johnson, Hall

Anderson, Marian (Contralto)
Jus' Keep on Singin'
RCA Victor LSC 2796; 1965; LP
Piano

     Also released with *Marian Anderson:
Beyond the Music; Her Complete RCA Victor
Recordings* Sony Classical 19439836492; 2021;
CD

3469
Oh, Heaven Is One Beautiful Place, I Know
Johnson, Hall
Anderson, Marian (Contralto)
*He's Got the Whole World in His Hands:
    Spirituals*
RCA Victor 09026-61960-2; 1994; CD
Piano
Light dialect

3470
Oh, Heaven Is One Beautiful Place, I Know
Johnson, Hall
Anderson, Marian (Contralto)
The Best of Negro Spirituals
BMG BVCM-37416; 2003; CD
Piano
Light dialect

3471
Heaven Is One Beautiful Place
Johnson, Hall
Toppin, Louise (Soprano)
*He'll Bring It to Pass: The Spirituals of Hall
    Johnson for Voice and Piano*
Albany Records TROY846; 2006; CD
Piano
Moderate dialect

3472
Heaven Is One Beautiful Place
Johnson, Hall
Warfield, William (Bass-baritone)
*Spirituals: 200 Years of African-American
    Spirituals*
ProArte CDD 3443; 1993; CD
Piano
Heavy dialect

3473

Heaven Is One Beautiful Place
Johnson, Hall
Warfield, William (Bass-baritone)
A Tribute to William Warfield
Mark Records MCD-1409; 1994; CD
Piano

. . . .

Oh Lord, I Done, Done

3474

Oh Lord, I Done, Done
Boatner, Edward
Miller, Jeanette (Soprano)
No Man Canna Hinder Me
MiJon Record Productions MJ240; 1979; CD
Piano

. . . .

O Mary Don't You Weep

3475

O Mary, Don't You Weep, Don't You Mourn
Composer not identified
Corbett, Patricia (Soprano)
Patricia Corbett Sings.... Best Loved Songs
RCA Victor Custom GO8P-0267; [1956]; LP

3476

O' Mary Don't You Weep
Composer not identified
Davis, Frank (Bass-baritone)
16 Spirituals My Father Taught Me
DeWitt Records 601; 1960; LP

3477

O, Mary, Don't You Weep
Composer not identified
Franklin, Lavinia A. (Vocalist)
*Historical Interpretation of Negro Spirituals
    and Lift Every Voice and Sing*
Recorded Publications JZB-02591; 1970; LP
Organ

3478

O Mary Don't You Weep
Composer not identified

Hayes, Roland (Tenor)
*Roland Hayes Sings: Negro Spirituals,
    Aframerican Folk Songs*
Amadeo Records AVRS 6033; [19--]; LP
Piano

3479

O Mary Don't You Weep
Hayes, Roland
Hayes, Roland (Tenor)
*The Art of Roland Hayes: Six Centuries of
    Song*
Preiser Records; 2010; CD
A cappella
Heavy dialect

3480

Oh, Mary Don't You Weep
Composer not identified
Rustin, Bayard (Tenor)
*Bayard Rustin Sings Spirituals, Work &
    Freedom Songs*
Bayard Rustin Fund; 2003; CD

3481

Oh, Mary, Doncher Weep [from *Green
    Pastures*]
Johnson, Hall
Toppin, Louise (Soprano)
The Hall Johnson Collection
Carl Fischer VF5 CD1–VF5 CD2; 2003; Score
    w/CD
Piano
Heavy dialect

. . . .

Oh, Redeemed

3482

O, Redeemed!
Brown, Uzee, Jr.
Harris, Crystal (Mezzo-soprano)
Great Day!
Allgood; 2005; CD
Piano
Light dialect

3483

O Redeemed
Brown, Uzee, Jr.

English-Robinson, Laura (Soprano)
Let It Shine!
ACA Digital Recording CM20020; 1994; CD
Piano
No dialect discerned

3484

O Redeemed!
Brown, Uzee, Jr.
Tucker, Eric Hoy (Bass-baritone)
Southern Salute: Southern Songs & Spirituals
White Pine Music WPM218; 2012; CD
Piano
Moderate dialect

· · · · · · ·

Oh, Rise an' Shine

3485

Oh, Rise an' Shine [from *Green Pastures*]
Johnson, Hall
Toppin, Louise (Soprano)
The Hall Johnson Collection
Carl Fischer VF5 CD1–VF5 CD2; 2003; Score
    w/CD
Piano
Moderate dialect

· · · · · · ·

Oh, Rock-a My Soul

3486

Oh, a-Rock-a My Soul [from *Journey Beyond Time*]
Crumb, George
Martin, Barbara Ann (Soprano)
American Songbooks II & IV
BRIDGE 9275A/B; 2008; CD
Piano, percussion

· · · · · · ·

Oh, the Angels Done Bowed Down

3487

Oh, the Angels Done Bowed Down
McLin, Lena
Rucker, Mark (Baritone)

Mark Rucker Sings Lena McLin: Songs for Voice & Piano
Kjos Music Press KCD8; 2002; CD
Piano
Light dialect

· · · · · · ·

Oh, What a Beautiful City

[Revelation 21:12, 21; I Thessalonians 4:17]

"Oh, what a beautiful city, ... Twelve gates-a to the city, Hallelujah! Three gates in-a the east, three gates in-a the west, three gates in-a the north, three gates in-a the south; Making it twelve gates-a in the city, Hallelujah! My Lord built-a that city, And He said it was just-a four square; And He said He wanted you sinners, To meet Him in-a the air. 'Cause He built twelve gates-a to the city. Hallelujah!"

[Available in ESAA, FRMA]

3488

Oh, What a Beautiful City!
Boatner, Edward
Alexander, Roberta (Soprano)
Songs My Mother Taught Me
Etcetera KTC 1208; 1999; CD
Piano
Moderate dialect

3489

Oh, What a Beautiful City
Boatner, Edward
Alexander, Roberta (Soprano)
Roberta Alexander.... A Retrospective
Etcetera KTC1222; 2013; CD
Piano
Moderate dialect

3490

Oh! What a Beautiful City
Boatner, Edward
Anderson, Marian (Contralto)
Farewell Recital
RCA Victor LSC 2781; 1964; LP
Piano

3491

Oh! What a Beautiful City
Boatner, Edward
Anderson, Marian (Contralto)
Tribute
Pro Arte CDD 3447; 1993; CD
Piano

3492

Oh. What a Beautiful City
Boatner, Edward
Anderson, Marian (Contralto)
The Lady
Magnum Music MCCD 017; 1996; CD
Piano

3493

Oh What a Beautiful City
Boatner, Edward
Anderson, Marian (Contralto)
Prima Voce
Nimbus NI 7882; 1996; CD
Piano
Light dialect

3494

Oh! What a Beautiful City
Boatner, Edward
Anderson, Marian (Contralto)
Great Voices of the Century
Memoir Classics CDMOIR 432; 1996; CD
Piano

3495

O What a Beautiful City!
Boatner, Edward
Anderson, Marian (Contralto)
Spirituals
RCA Victor Red Seal 09026-63306-2; 1999;
  CD
Piano
Heavy dialect

3496

Oh! What a Beautiful City
Boatner, Edward
Anderson, Marian (Contralto)
Ev'Ry Time I Feel the Spirit (1930–1947)

Naxos Nostalgia 8.120779; 2004; CD
Piano

3497

Oh, What a Beautiful City
Boatner, Edward
Anderson, Marian (Contralto)
Negro Spirituals: 1924–1949
Frémeaux & Associés FA 184; 2004; CD
Orchestra

3498

Oh! What a Beautiful City
Boatner, Edward
Anderson, Marian (Contralto)
Softly Awakes My Heart: Very Best of Marian
    Anderson
Alto ALN1955; 2016; CD
Piano
Moderate dialect

3499

O What a Beautiful City!
Boatner, Edward
Anderson, Marian (Contralto)
Let Freedom Ring!
JSP Records 683; 2016; CD
Piano
Light dialect

3500

Oh, What a Beautiful City!
Boatner, Edward
Anderson, Marian (Contralto)
Marian Anderson: Beyond the Music; Her
    Complete RCA Victor Recordings
Sony Classical 19439836492; 2021; CD
Piano
Moderate dialect

3501

O What a Beautiful City
Boatner, Edward
Anderson, Marian (Contralto)
Marian Anderson: Beyond the Music; Her
    Complete RCA Victor Recordings
Sony Classical 19439836492; 2021; CD
Piano
Moderate dialect

3502

O What a Beautiful City
Boatner, Edward
Anderson, Marian (Contralto)
*Marian Anderson: Beyond the Music; Her
    Complete RCA Victor Recordings*
Sony Classical 19439836492; 2021; CD
Piano
Moderate dialect

3503

Oh! What a Beautiful City
Boatner, Edward
Anderson, Marian (Contralto)
*Let Us Break Bread Together/Oh! What a
    Beautiful City*
Victor 10-1040; [19--]; 78 RPM
Piano
Moderate dialect

3504

O What a Beautiful City!
Boatner, Edward
Anderson, Marian (Contralto)
Negro Spirituals
RCA Victor LM 2032; [1956]; LP
Piano

3505

O What a Beautiful City!
[Boatner, Edward]
Anderson, Marian (Contralto)
*Marian Anderson Sings Eleven Great
    Spirituals*
RCA Victor LRM 7006; 1955; LP
Piano

3506

Oh! What a Beautiful City
[Boatner, Edward]
Anderson, Marian (Contralto)
Marian Anderson Sings Spirituals
Flapper Past CD 7073; 1995; CD
Piano

3507

Oh! What a Beautiful City!
[Boatner, Edward]
Anderson, Marian (Contralto)

Softly Awakes My Heart
ASV CD AJA 5262; 1999; CD
Piano

3508

O What a Beautiful City!
[Boatner, Edward]
Anderson, Marian (Contralto)
Alto Rhapsody; Selected Spirituals
Urania URN 22.328; 2007; CD
Piano

3509

O What a Beautiful City!
[Boatner, Edward]
Anderson, Marian (Contralto)
The Very Best of Marian Anderson
Master Classics Records; 2009; CD
Piano
Moderate dialect

3510

Oh, What a Beautiful City!
[Boatner, Edward]
Anderson, Marian (Contralto)
Inspirations
Emerald Echoes; 2015; Streaming audio
Piano
Heavy dialect

3511

O What a Beautiful City!
[Boatner, Edward]
Anderson, Marian (Contralto)
*Marian Anderson Sings Eleven Great
    Spirituals*
Kipepeo Publishing; 2017; CD
Piano

3512

O What a Beautiful City
[Boatner, Edward]
Anderson, Marian (Contralto)
*Grandes Contraltos de la Musique Classique,
    Les: Marian Anderson, Vol. 11*
Mon Patrimoine Musical Collection; 2017;
    Streaming audio
Piano

3513

Oh What a Beautiful City
[Boatner, Edward]
Anderson, Marian (Contralto)
Ave Maria: And Other Schubert Songs
43 North Broadway, LLC; 2019; Streaming
    audio
Piano
Moderate dialect

3514

O, What a Beautiful City
[Boatner, Edward]
Anderson, Marian (Contralto)
Negro Spirituals
RCA Gold Seal RVC-1570; [19--]; LP
Piano

3515

O What a Beautiful City!
[Boatner, Edward]
Anderson, Marian (Contralto)
Negro Spirituals
RCA Victor 630.396 A; [19--]; LP
Piano

3516

Oh! What a Beautiful City
[Boatner, Edward]
Anderson, Marian (Contralto)
Deep River
Audio Book & Music; [20--]; CD

3517

Oh, What a Beautiful City
Kerr, Thomas H., Jr.; Brown, Charles B.
    Gianono, Joseph
Battle, Kathleen (Soprano); Norman, Jessye
    (Soprano)
Spirituals in Concert
Deutsche Grammophon 429 790-2; 1991;
    CD
Orchestra
Moderate dialect

3518

O What a Beautiful City
Boatner, Edward
Bryant, Peter (Vocalist)

I Will Pass This Way but Once
Facts of Faith Records WR 5161; 1977; LP
Organ

3519

Oh, What a Beautiful City
Blair Lindsay, Tedrin
Burnett, Janinah (Soprano); Cunningham-
    Fleming, Jeryl (Soprano)
Swing Low, Sweet Chariot
American Spiritual Ensemble; 2011; CD

3520

Oh, What a Beautiful City
Clark, Joe
Cabell, Nicole (Soprano); Cambridge,
    Alyson (Soprano)
Sisters in Song
Cedille Records CDR 90000 181; 2018; CD
Orchestra
No dialect discerned

3521

Oh, What a Beautiful City
Composer not identified
Carey, Thomas (Baritone)
Go Down Moses
Da Camera Song SM 95028; 1970; LP
Piano

3522

Oh, What a Beautiful City!
Boatner, Edward
Carnette, Count (Vocalist)
*Count Carnette Sings Favorite Negro
    Spirituals*
Carnette Archive Recordings; 1983; LP
Piano
No dialect discerned

3523

Oh What a Beautiful City [from *Songs for
    Joy (A Suite of Spirituals)*]
Simpson-Currenton, Evelyn
Chandler-Eteme, Janice (Soprano)
Devotions
Sligo Records; 2007; CD
Piano

3524

Oh, What a Beautiful City!
[Boatner, Edward]
Cole, Vinson (Tenor)
Strauss, Duparc, Puccini, Nin
Connoisseur Society CD4184; 1991; CD
Piano
Heavy dialect

3525

Oh What a Beautiful City
Composer not identified
Cunningham-Fleming, Jeryl (Soprano)
*Stand the Storm: Anthems, Hymns, and
    Spirituals of Faith and Hope*
Private Label; 2016; CD
Piano

3526

Oh, What a Beautiful City
Boatner, Edward
Davis, Ellabelle (Soprano)
Ellabelle Davis Sings Negro Spirituals
London LPS 182; [1950]; LP
Orchestra
Light dialect

    Also released with *Recital of Negro Spir-
ituals by Ellabelle Davis* (Decca LM.4504;
[1950]; LP)

3527

Oh What a Beautiful City
[Boatner, Edward]
Davis, Ellabelle (Soprano)
Were You There?
Decca DFE 8618; 1965; 45 RPM
Orchestra

3528

Oh, What a Beautiful City
[Boatner, Edward]
Davis, Ellabelle (Soprano)
Great Negro Spirituals
Replay Record; 2013; Streaming audio
Orchestra

3529

Oh, What a Beautiful City
[Boatner, Edward]

Dobbs, Mattiwilda (Soprano)
M. Dobbs Sings (U.S.A.)
Soviet Gramophone Records (Melodiya)
    GOST 5289-56; 1960; LP
Piano

    Also released with *Rarities* (House of
Opera CD96547; [20--]; CD)

3530

Oh, What a Beautiful City
[Boatner, Edward]
Dobbs, Mattiwilda (Soprano)
*Mattiwilda Dobbs Sings Franz Schubert/
    American Negro Spirituals*
Aprelevsky 5846; [1961]; LP
Piano

3531

O What a Beautiful City
Composer not identified
Duckworth, Zorita (Mezzo-soprano)
Forget Me Not…. Negro Spirituals
Private Label; [20--]; CD

3532

Oh What a Beautiful City (Twelve Gates to
    the City)
Boatner, Edward
Duncan, Todd (Baritone)
African American Spirituals
[Apple Music]; 2008; Streaming audio
Piano
Moderate dialect

3533

Oh What a Beautiful City
Boatner, Edward
Duncan, Todd (Baritone)
Negro Spirituals
Allegro ALG3022; [1952]; LP
Piano

3534

Oh What a Beautiful City
Boatner, Edward
Fernandez, Wilhelmenia (Soprano)
Spirituals
Tioch Digital Records TD 1009; 1982; LP
Piano

Also released with *Negro Spirituals* (Milan A 192; 1982; LP), *Sings Favorite Spirituals* (Phoenix PHCD 134; 1997; CD) and *Negro Spirituals* (Transart 131; 2005; CD)

3535

О, как прекрасен град (O, kak prekrasen grad)
Composer not identified
Filatova, Ludmila (Mezzo-soprano)
Негритянские Спиричузлс (Negrityanskiye Spirichuzls—Negro Spirituals)
Melodiâ S10 21833 009; 1985; LP
Organ
No dialect discerned

3536

Oh! What a Beautiful City
Boatner, Edward
Forest, Michael (Tenor)
The Spirit Sings: American Spirituals
Shenandoah Conservatory SU003; [199-]; CD

3537

Oh, What a Beautiful City
Composer not identified
Green, Elnora E. (Contralto)
15 Spirituals
Private Label J3RS 2286; 1979; LP
Piano

3538

Oh What a Beautiful City!
Composer not identified
Hendricks, Barbara (Soprano)
Espirituales Negros
EMI Classics/Altaya 01636; 1983; CD
Piano
Light dialect

3539

Oh, What a Beautiful City
Composer not identified
Hendricks, Barbara (Soprano)
Met Stars in the New World
MET 216CD; 1992; CD

3540

Oh What a Beautiful City
Composer not identified

Hendricks, Barbara (Soprano)
Spirituals
EMI Classics 0946 346641 2 7; 2005; CD
Piano
Light dialect

3541

Oh What a Beautiful City
Hendricks, Barbara; Alexeev, Dmitri
Hendricks, Barbara (Soprano)
Negro Spirituals
EMI CDC7470262; 1983; CD
Piano
Light dialect

Also released with *Great American Spirituals* (Angel CDM 7 64669 2; 1992; CD) and *Great American Spirituals* (Musical Heritage Society 513725Z; 1994; CD)

3542

Oh, What a Beautiful City!
Boatner, Edward
Holland, Charles (Tenor)
Negro Spirituals
Pathé 45 ED. 29; 1954; 45 RPM
Piano

3543

O, What a Beautiful City
Composer not identified
Humphrey Flynn, Edwina (Soprano)
The Lord Will Make a Way
Private Label; 2000; CD
Piano

3544

Oh! What a Beautiful City
Boatner, Edward
Jones, Fanni (Mezzo-soprano)
Fanni Jones et Oswald Russell
Audio-Visual Enterprises AVE 30701; [19--]; LP

3545

Oh! What a Beautiful City
Burleigh, Harry T.
Little, Vera (Mezzo-soprano)
My Good Lord Done Been Here

Decca 123737; 1957; LP
Piano

3546

Oh, What a Beautiful City
Meyer, Fredrich
London, George (Bass-baritone)
Spirituals
Deutsche Grammophon 00289 477 6193;
    2006; CD
Organ
Moderate dialect

3547

Twelve Gates to the City [from *The Winds of
    Destiny*]
Crumb, George
Martin, Barbara Ann (Soprano)
American Songbooks II & IV
BRIDGE 9275A/B; 2008; CD
Piano, percussion

3548

Oh What a Beautiful City
Boatner, Edward
Mayes, Doris (Mezzo-soprano)
Deep River
La voix de son maître FDLP 1080; 1959; LP
Piano

3549

Oh What a Beautiful City
[Boatner, Edward]
Norman, Jessye (Soprano)
An Evening with Jessye Norman
Opera D'Oro Recitals OPD-2011; 1999; CD
Piano
Moderate dialect

3550

Oh What a Beautiful City
Composer not identified
Norman, Jessye (Soprano)
*Oh, Happy Day! Gospels & Spirituals: The
    Ultimate CD*
Ultimate; 2010; CD

3551

What a Beautiful City
[Boatner, Edward]

Norman, Jessye (Soprano)
Gospels & Spirituals Gold Collection
Retro R2CD 40-26; 1995; CD
Piano
Moderate dialect

3552

Oh, What a Beautiful City
Dawson, William L.
Oglesby, Isador (Tenor)
*Negro Spirituals: The Musical Roots of
    American Folk Songs*
Praise PR 658; 1978; LP
Piano

3553

Oh, What a Beautiful City
Boatner, Edward
Patton. John (Tenor)
Black Spirituals and Art Songs
Narthex Recording 827N-4581; 1970; LP
Piano
Moderate dialect

3554

Oh What a Beautiful City
Boatner, Edward
Philogene, Ruby (Soprano)
Steal Away
EMI Classics 7243 5 69707 2 4; 1997; CD
Piano

3555

O What a Beautiful City
Boatner, Edward
Powell, Angela (Soprano)
City Called Heaven
Private Label AP6957; 2003; CD
Piano

3556

Oh, What a Beautiful City!
[Boatner, Edward]
Price, Eudora (Vocalist)
My Favorite Songs & Spirituals
Private Label; 2006; CD
Organ
No dialect discerned

3557

Oh, What a Beautiful City!
Boatner, Edward
Ragin, Derek Lee (Countertenor)
Ev'ry Time I Feel the Spirit: Spirituals
Channel Classics CCS 2991; 1991; CD
Piano
Heavy dialect

3558

Oh, What a Beautiful City
Brown, Lawrence
Reese, Ruth (Contralto)
Motherless Child
OPS 1006/79; 1979; LP

3559

Oh, What a Beautiful City
Boatner, Edward
West, Lucretia (Mezzo-soprano)
Negro Spirituals III
Club français du disque 176; 1959; LP
Piano
Moderate dialect

3560

Oh! What a Beautiful City
Boatner, Edward
West, Lucretia (Mezzo-soprano)
Negro Spirituals
Club français du disque 215; [196-]; 7-in EP
Piano

3561

O' What a Beautiful City
Boatner, Edward
Williams, Camilla (Soprano)
O' What a Beautiful City/City Called Heaven
RCA Victor 10-1425; [19--]; 78 RPM
Piano
Light dialect

3562

Oh, What a Beautiful City
[Boatner, Edward]
Williams, Camilla (Soprano)
A Camilla Williams Recital
MGM Records E-140; [1952]; LP

Piano
Light dialect

3563

Oh, What a Beautiful City
[Boatner, Edward]
Williams, Camilla (Soprano)
Camilla Williams Sings Spirituals
MGM Records M-G-M E-156; [195-]; LP
Piano
Light dialect

· · · · · · ·

Old Ark's a-Moverin'

3564

De Ol' Ark's a Moverin' [from *Green Pastures*]
Johnson, Hall
Brown, William (Tenor)
The Hall Johnson Collection
Carl Fischer VF5 CD1–VF5 CD2; 2003; Score w/CD
Piano
Heavy dialect

3565

O, de Ol' Ark's Amoverin'
Dørumsgaard, Arne
Carlsen, Svein (Bass)
Negro Spirituals
EuroMaster AS ECD19005; 1996; CD
Piano

3566

De Ol' Ark's a Moverin'
Johnson, [John Rosamond]
Robeson, Paul (Bass-baritone)
Paul Robeson: Great Voices of the Century, v. 2
Memoir Classics CDMOIR 426; 1994; CD

3567

De Ole Ark's a-Movering
Johnson, [John Rosamond]
Robeson, Paul (Bass-baritone)
Spirituals: Original Recordings 1925–1936
Naxos Gospel Legends 8.120638; 2003; CD
Piano

3568
De Old Ark's a Movering
Johnson, John Rosamond
Robeson, Paul (Bass-baritone)
The Complete EMI Sessions (1928–1939)
EMI Classics 50999 2 15586 2 7; 2008; CD
Piano
Heavy dialect

3569
De Ole Ark's a-Movering
[Johnson, John Rosamond]
Robeson, Paul (Bass-baritone)
Spirituals/Folksongs/Hymns
Pearl GEMM CD 9382; 1989; CD

3570
De Ole Ark's a-Movering
[Johnson, John Rosamond]
Robeson, Paul (Bass-baritone)
The Ultimate Collection
Burning Fire; 2009; Streaming audio
Piano
Heavy dialect

3571
Ol' Arks a Moverin
Composer not identified
Watts, Leonardo (Baritone)
*On Ma Journey: A Memorable Collection of
   Negro Spirituals*
Onyx Recording Associates ORA-101; 1961; LP
Chorus

. . . .

Old Ship of Zion

3572
Tis the old Ship of Zion
Traditional
Moses, Oral (Bass-baritone)
*Spirituals in Zion: A Spiritual Heritage for
   the Soul*
Albany Records TROY587; 2003; CD
A cappella

3573
Old Ship of Zion
Composer not identified

Spencer, Kenneth (Bass-baritone)
*The Negro Spirituals Concert Tradition,
   1909–1948*
Frémeaux & Associés FA 168; 1999; CD
Chorus
Light dialect

3574
Old Ship of Zion
Composer not identified
Spencer, Kenneth (Bass-baritone)
The Very Best of Gospel
Disconforme CDX7720; 2007; CD

. . . .

Old Time Religion

3575
Give Me That Old Time Religion
Boatwright, McHenry
Boatwright, McHenry (Bass-baritone)
Art of McHenry Boatwright: Spirituals
Golden Crest Records RE 7024; 1968; LP
Piano
Light dialect

3576
Gimme Dat Ol' Time Religion
Composer not identified
Chaiter, Yoram (Bass)
Spirituals & Other Songs
Romeo Records 7311; 2014; CD
Piano
Moderate dialect

3577
Gimme That Ol-Time Religion
Composer not identified
Corbett, Patricia (Soprano)
Patricia Corbett Sings…. Best Loved Songs
RCA Victor Custom GO8P-0267; [1956]; LP

3578
Ol' Time Religion Medley
Credit, Roosevelt André
Credit, Roosevelt André (Bass-baritone)
Ol' Time Religion
CD Baby; 2007; CD, Streaming audio

Piano
Moderate dialect

3579

Old Time Religion
Composer not identified
Hendricks, Barbara (Soprano)
100 Plus Beaux Airs de Barbara Hendricks,
Les
EMI Classics 50999 085683 2 8; 2012; CD
Chorus

3580

Old Time Religion
Hogan, Moses; Harlan, Benjamin
Hendricks, Barbara (Soprano)
Give Me Jesus
EMI Classics 7243 5 56788 2 9; 1998; CD
Chorus
Moderate dialect

3581

Gimme Dat Old Time Religion
Clinton, Irving
Irving, Clinton (Bass-baritone)
Clinton Irving Sings Spirituals: A Tribute
Rogers; 2001; CD

3582

Ole-Time Religion
Composer not identified
Maynor, Dorothy (Soprano)
Negro Spirituals
RCA Victor M879; 1942; 78 RPM
Men's voices

3583

Ole Time Religion
Composer not identified
Maynor, Dorothy (Soprano)
Dorothy Maynor Sings Spirituals and Sacred
Songs
RCA Camden CAL-344; 1957; LP
Chorus

3584

Ole Time Religion
Composer not identified
Maynor, Dorothy (Soprano)

Spirituals, Arias, Songs ([1940]1943)
Claremont CD GSE 78-50-59; 1994; CD
Chorus

3585

Old Time Religion
Raphael, Michael
Maynor, Kevin (Bass)
The Spiritual: An Underground Railroad
Southeastern Virginia Arts Assoc.; [2000];
   CD
Piano

3586

Old-Time Religion
Composer not identified
Porter, John (Bass)
No More Crying: Negro Spirituals
Pan Verlag OV-84; [1978]; LP
Piano

3587

Ole Time Religion
Hogan, Moses
Ragin, Derek Lee (Countertenor)
Ev'ry Time I Feel the Spirit: Spirituals
Channel Classics CCS 2991; 1991; CD
Chorus
Moderate dialect

3588

Old-Time Religion
Composer not identified
West, Lucretia (Mezzo-soprano)
Lucretia West Sings Spirituals
Westminster WP 6063; [1957]; LP
Men's voices

. . . .

On Ma Journey

[Psalm 125:1; Mark 1:10; John 1:51; Acts
7:56]

   "On ma journey now, Mount Zion, Well
I wouldn't take nothing, Mount Zion, For ma
journey now, Mount Zion. One day, one day I
was talking along, Well the elements opened
and the love come down, Mount Zion…."
   [No version found in listed collections]

3589
On Ma Journey
Boatner, Edward
Anderson, Marian (Contralto)
Marian Anderson Sings Spirituals
RCA Victor Red Seal MO 1238; 1948; 78
    RPM
Piano

3590
On Ma Journey
Boatner, Edward
Anderson, Marian (Contralto)
Negro Spirituals
La Voix de Son Maître FBLP1039; 1953; LP
Piano

3591
On Ma Journey
Boatner, Edward
Anderson, Marian (Contralto)
Spirituals
RCA Victor Red Seal 09026-63306-2; 1999;
    CD
Piano
Light dialect

3592
On Ma Journey
Boatner, Edward
Anderson, Marian (Contralto)
Ev'Ry Time I Feel the Spirit (1930–1947)
Naxos Nostalgia 8.120779; 2004; CD
Piano

3593
On Ma Journey
Boatner, Edward
Anderson, Marian (Contralto)
*Marian Anderson: Beyond the Music; Her
    Complete RCA Victor Recordings*
Sony Classical 19439836492; 2021; CD
Piano
Heavy dialect

3594
On Ma Journey
Boatner, Edward
Anderson, Marian (Contralto)

Marian Anderson Sings Negro Spirituals
His Master's Voice BLP 1060; [19--]; LP
Piano

3595
On Ma Journey
Boatner, Edward
Anderson, Marian (Contralto)
Negro Spirituals
RCA Victor LM 2032; [1956]; LP
Piano

3596
On Ma Journey
[Boatner, Edward]
Anderson, Marian (Contralto)
Marian Anderson Sings Spirituals
RCA Victor LM 110; 1949; LP
Piano

3597
On Ma Journey
[Boatner, Edward]
Anderson, Marian (Contralto)
Alto Rhapsody; Selected Spirituals
Urania URN 22.328; 2007; CD
Piano

3598
On Ma Journey
[Boatner, Edward]
Anderson, Marian (Contralto)
The Very Best of Marian Anderson
Master Classics Records; 2009; CD
Piano
Light dialect

3599
On My Journey
[Boatner, Edward]
Anderson, Marian (Contralto)
*Grandes Contraltos de la Musique Classique,
    Les: Marian Anderson, Vol. 0*
Mon Patrimoine Musical Collection; 2017;
    Streaming audio
Piano

3600
On Ma Journey
[Boatner, Edward]

Anderson, Marian (Contralto)
Negro Spirituals
RCA Victor 630.396 A; [19--]; LP
Piano

3601

On Ma Journey
de Paur, Leonard
Arroyo, Martina (Soprano)
There's a Meeting Here Tonight
Angel S-36072; 1974; LP
Chorus

3602

On Ma Journey
de Paur, Leonard
Arroyo, Martina (Soprano)
Negro Spirituals
EMI 7243 5 72790 2 4; 1998; CD
Chorus
Moderate dialect

3603

On Ma Journey
Boatner, Edward
Brice, Carol (Contralto)
A Carol Brice Recital
Columbia ML 2108; 1950; LP
Piano
Moderate dialect

3604

On Ma Journey
Boatncr, Edward
Brice, Carol (Contralto)
On Ma Journey/My Good Lord Done Been Here
Columbia Masterworks 17524-D; [1948]; 78
    RPM
Piano
Moderate dialect

3605

On Mah Journey Now, Mount Zion
Boatner, Edward; Joubert, Joseph
Conrad, Barbara (Mezzo-soprano)
Spirituals
Naxos 8.553036; 1995; CD
Orchestra
Heavy dialect

3606

Mount Zion
Composer not identified
Cook, Dixon & Young (Tenor)
Triptych: A Celebration of the Negro Spiritual
CDY Records 649241879206; 2009; CD
Piano
Light dialect

3607

On Ma Journey
Boatner, Edward
Davis, Ellabelle (Soprano)
Ellabelle Davis Sings Negro Spirituals
London LPS 182; [1950]; LP
Piano

        Also released with *Recital of Negro Spir-
    ituals by Ellabelle Davis* (Decca LM.4504;
    [1950]; LP) and *Great Negro Spirituals* (Replay
    Record; 2013; Streaming audio)

3608

On My Journey
Boatner, Edward
Davy, Gloria (Soprano)
Spirituals
Decca LW 5215; 1959; LP

3609

On My Journey
Boatner, Edward
Dobbs, Mattiwilda (Soprano)
*Tva Sidor Av Mattiwilda Dobbs Och
    Gotthard Arner*
Proprius 25 04-02-0004; [19--]; LP
Organ

3610

Oh My Journey Now
Boatner, Edward
Duncan, Todd (Baritone)
African American Spirituals
[Apple Music]; 2008; Streaming audio
Piano
Moderate dialect

3611

On Ma Journey
Boatner, Edward

Duncan, Todd (Baritone)
Negro Spirituals
Allegro ALG3022; [1952]; LP
Piano

3612

On Ma Journey Now
[Boatner, Edward]
Duncan, Todd (Baritone)
Spirituals
Royale 1810; [1950]; LP

3613

On My Journey Now
Boatner, Edward
Elzy, Ruby (Soprano)
Ruby Elzy in Song: Rare Recordings
Cambria Records CD-1154; 2006; CD
Piano
Heavy dialect

    Also released with *The 78 RPM Collection* (Master Classics Records; 2010; CD)

3614

On My Journey
Robbiani, Mario
Fisher, Dorothy (Contralto)
Negro Spirituals
Edizione D'Arte Del Lions Club Milano Al
    Cenacolo; [19--]; LP
Piano

3615

On Ma Journey
Boatner, Edward
Forest, Michael (Tenor)
The Spirit Sings: American Spirituals
Shenandoah Conservatory SU003; [199-];
    CD

3616

On Ma Journey
Boatner, Edward
Gibson, Caroline (Soprano)
*On Ma Journey Now: Negro Spirituals in
    Concert*
Twin Productions; 2016; CD
Piano
Light dialect

3617

On Ma Journey
Composer not identified
Green, Elnora E. (Contralto)
15 Spirituals
Private Label J3RS 2286; 1979; LP
Piano

3618

Mount Zion
Hicks, Lori
Hicks, Lori (Soprano)
Music of My Voice
CelestialSong Productions; 2015; CD
Piano

3619

On Ma Journey
Boatner, Edward
Lewis, Cheryse McLeod (Mezzo-soprano)
Spirituals
CheryseMusic; 2012; CD
Piano

3620

On My Journey Now
Britton, John Charles
Lynch, Lester (Baritone)
On My Journey Now: Spirituals & Hymns
Pentatone Music PTC 5186 57'; 2017; CD
Guitar

3621

On My Journey
Boatner, Edward
Matthews, Benjamin (Baritone)
A Balm in Gilead
Ebony Classic Recordings ECR 0001; 2000;
    CD
Piano

3622

On Ma Journey
Boatner, Edward
Maynor, Kevin (Bass)
Paul Robeson Remembered
Fleur de Son Classics FDS 57929; 1998; CD
Piano
Moderate dialect

3623
On Ma Journey Now
Boatner, Edward
Miller, Jeanette (Soprano)
No Man Canna Hinder Me
MiJon Record Productions MJ240; 1979; CD
Piano

3624
On Ma' Journey Now
Boatner, Edward
Oglesby, Isador (Tenor)
*Negro Spirituals: The Musical Roots of
    American Folk Songs*
Praise PR 658; 1978; LP
Piano

3625
On Ma Journey
Boatner, Edward; de Paur, Leonard
Price, Leontyne (Soprano)
*Swing Low, Sweet Chariot: Fourteen
    Spirituals*
RCA Victor LSC 2600; 1962; LP
Chorus
Heavy dialect

3626
On Ma Journey
Boatner, Edward; de Paur, Leonard
Price, Leontyne (Soprano)
Songs Our Mothers Taught Us
Met MET 210CD; 1990; CD
Chorus

3627
On Ma Journey
Boatner, Edward; de Paur, Leonard
Price, Leontyne (Soprano)
*The Essential Leontyne Price: Spirituals,
    Hymns & Sacred Songs*
BMG Classics 09026-68157-2; 1996; CD
Chorus
Moderate dialect

Also released with *The Essential Leontyne Price* (BMG Classics 09026-68153-2; 1996; CD); *Complete Collection of Songs and Spiritual Albums* (RCA Red Seal 8869794 0502; 2011; CD) and *Leontyne Price Sings Spirituals* (RCA Red Seal 88691928242; 2012; CD)

3628
On Ma Journey
Boatner, Edward; de Paur, Leonard
Price, Leontyne (Soprano)
*Singers of the Century: Leontyne Price:
    Spiritual and Religious Songs*
Jube Classic; 2016; Streaming audio
Chorus
Moderate dialect

3629
On Ma Journey
Boatner, Edward
Quivar, Florence (Mezzo-soprano)
Great American Spirituals
Angel CDM 7 64669 2; 1992; CD
Piano
Heavy dialect

3630
On Ma Journey
Boatner, Edward
Quivar, Florence (Mezzo-soprano)
Great American Spirituals
Musical Heritage Society 513725Z; 1994; CD
Piano
Heavy dialect

Also released with *Negro Spirituals* (EMI 7243 5 72790 2 4; 1998; CD) and *Ride On, King Jesus! Florence Quivar Sings Black Music of America* (EMI Classics 9 67138 2; 2010; CD)

3631
On Ma Journey
Boatner, Edward
Robeson, Paul (Bass-baritone)
*Sometimes I Feel Like a Motherless Child/On
    Ma Journey*
Victor 20013; 1926; 78 RPM
Piano
Light dialect

3632
On Ma Journey
Boatner, Edward

Robeson, Paul (Bass-baritone)
Sometimes I Feel Like a Motherless Child/On Ma Journey
His Master's Voice B 2326; 1926; 78 RPM
Piano
Moderate dialect

3633

On Ma Journey
Boatner, Edward
Robeson, Paul (Bass-baritone)
Swing Low, Sweet Chariot/On Ma Journey
Victor 25547; 1933; 78 RPM
Piano
Light dialect

3634

On Ma Journey
Boatner, Edward
Robeson, Paul (Bass-baritone)
On Ma Journey/Swing Low, Swing Chariot
His Master's Voice B.8372; 1935; 78 RPM
Piano
Light dialect

3635

On Ma Journey
Boatner, Edward
Robeson, Paul (Bass-baritone)
Songs of My People
RCA Red Seal LM-3292; 1972; LP
Piano

3636

On My Journey
Boatner, Edward
Robeson, Paul (Bass-baritone)
The Odyssey of Paul Robeson
Omega Classics OCD 3007; 1992; CD
Piano

3637

On My Journey
Boatner, Edward
Robeson, Paul (Bass-baritone)
The Complete EMI Sessions (1928–1939)
EMI Classics 50999 2 15586 2 7; 2008; CD
Piano
Heavy dialect

3638

Mount Zion (On My Journey)
Composer not identified
Robeson, Paul (Bass-baritone)
Encore, Robeson!
Monitor MP 581; 1960; LP

3639

Mount Zion (On My Journey)
Composer not identified
Robeson, Paul (Bass-baritone)
The Collector's Paul Robeson
Monitor MCD-61580; 1989; CD
Piano
Moderate dialect

3640

Mount Zion
Composer not identified
Robeson, Paul (Bass-baritone)
Paul Robeson Singt Negro Spirituals
Musical Masterpiece Society MMS-2162;
    [19--]; LP
Piano

3641

Mount Zion
Composer not identified
Robeson, Paul (Bass-baritone)
Negro Spirituals
Concert Hall SVS 2611; [19--]; LP

3642

Mount Zion: "On My Journey"
Composer not identified
Robeson, Paul (Bass-baritone)
Negro Spirituals
Chant du Monde LDX 74376; 1982; LP
Piano

3643

On My Journey
[Boatner, Edward]
Robeson, Paul (Bass-baritone)
Ballad for Americans and Great Songs of Faith, Love and Patriotism
Vanguard VCD-117/18; 1989; CD
Piano

3644

On Mah Journey
[Boatner, Edward]
Robeson, Paul (Bass-baritone)
Paul Robeson
Flapper; 1993; CD

3645

On Mah Journey
[Boatner, Edward]
Robeson, Paul (Bass-baritone)
Paul Robeson Collection
Hallmark Recordings 390692; 1998; CD

3646

On Mah Journey
[Boatner, Edward]
Robeson, Paul (Bass-baritone)
Deep River
Great Voices of the Century GVC 2004;
    1999; CD
Piano

3647

On My Journey, Mount Zion
[Boatner, Edward]
Robeson, Paul (Bass-baritone)
*On My Journey: Paul Robeson's Independent
    Recordings*
Smithsonian Folkways Recordings SFW CD
    40178; 2007; CD
Piano

3648

On My Journey
[Boatner, Edward]
Robeson, Paul (Bass-baritone)
*The Golden Voice of Paul Robeson: Great
    Voices of the 20th Century*
Acrobat Music AC-5160-2; 2008; CD

3649

On My Journey
[Boatner, Edward]
Robeson, Paul (Bass-baritone)
Negro Spirituals (And More)
Discmedi DM-4674-02; 2009; CD

3650

On My Journey
[Boatner, Edward]
Robeson, Paul (Bass-baritone)
The Very Best of Paul Robeson
Future Noise Music FVDD033; 2009; CD
Piano

3651

On Ma Journey
[Boatner, Edward]
Robeson, Paul (Bass-baritone)
The Ultimate Collection
Burning Fire; 2009; Streaming audio
Piano
Light dialect

3652

On Mah Journey
[Boatner, Edward]
Robeson, Paul (Bass-baritone)
Ol' Man River: The Ultimate Collection
Roslin Records; 2011; Streaming audio
Piano
Light dialect

3653

O Ma Journey Now
Boatner, Edward
Shirley, George (Tenor)
George Shirley at 80: My Time Has Come!
Videmus Records; 2014; CD
Piano

3654

On Ma Journey
Composer not identified
Watts, Leonardo (Baritone)
*On Ma Journey: A Memorable Collection of
    Negro Spirituals*
Onyx Recording Associates ORA-101; 1961;
    LP
Chorus

3655

On My Journey
Boatner, Edward
West, Lucretia (Mezzo-soprano)

Negro Spirituals III
Club français du disque 176; 1959; LP
Piano
Heavy dialect

3656
On Ma Journey
Boatner, Edward
West, Lucretia (Mezzo-soprano)
Negro Spirituals mit Lukretia West
Opera 3408; [195-]; LP
Piano

3657
On My Journey Now
Composer not identified
White, Willard (Bass-baritone)
The Paul Robeson Legacy
Linn AKD 190; 2015; CD
Instrumental ensemble

3658
On Ma Journey
[Boatner, Edward]
Williams, Camilla (Soprano)
A Camilla Williams Recital
MGM Records E-140; [1952]; LP
Piano
Light dialect

3659
On ma' journey
[Boatner, Edward]
Williams, Camilla (Soprano)
Camilla Williams Sings Spirituals
MGM Records M-G-M E-156; [195-]; LP
Piano
Light dialect

• • • • • • •

On Our Knees

3660
On Our Knees
Composer not identified
Robeson, Paul (Bass-baritone)
Paul Robeson Singt Negro Spirituals
Musical Masterpiece Society MMS-2162;
    [19--]; LP
Piano

3661
On Our Knees
Composer not identified
Robeson, Paul (Bass-baritone)
Negro Spirituals
Concert Hall SVS 2611; [19--]; LP

• • • • • • •

One of You Shall Betray Me

3662
One of You Shall Betray Me [from *The Life of
    Christ*]
Hayes, Roland
Hayes, Roland (Tenor)
*Roland Hayes Sings the Life of Christ: As Told
    Through Aframerican Folksong*
Vanguard VRS-462; 1954; LP
Piano

    Also released with *Aframerican Folk-
song: Telling the Story of The Life of Christ*
(Top Rank 39 620; [1961]; LP); *Roland Hayes
Sings the Life of Christ: As Told Through
Aframerican Folksong* (Vanguard SRV 352;
1976; LP) and *Charlton Heston Reads from
The Life and Passion of Jesus Christ* (Van-
guard Classics ATM-CD-1259; 2003; CD)

3663
One of You Shall Betray Me [from *The Life of
    Christ*]
Hayes, Roland
Hayes, Roland (Tenor)
Favorite Spirituals
Vanguard Classics OVC 6022; 1995; CD
Piano
Light dialect

3664
One of You Shall Betray Me [from *The Life of
    Christ*]
[Hayes, Roland]
Hayes, Roland (Tenor)
Big Psalms, Hymns and Spirituals Box
eOne Music/Vanguard Classics; 2015;
    Streaming audio
Piano

. . . .

Over My Head I Hear Music

3665

Over My Head I Hear Music
Traditional
Battle, Kathleen (Soprano)
Kathleen Battle at Carnegie Hall
Deutsche Grammophon 435 440-2; 1992; CD
A cappella
Light dialect

3666

Over My Head I Hear Music in the air
Brown, Uzee, Jr.
English-Robinson, Laura (Soprano)
Great Day!
Allgood; 2005; CD
Piano
No dialect discerned

3667

Over My Head
Traditional
Jones, Arthur (Tenor)
Wade in the Water
Orbis Books; 1993; Book w/cass
A cappella
Heavy dialect

. . . .

Over Yonder

3668

Over Yonder
Johnson, Hall
Holland, Charles (Tenor)
My Lord What a Mornin'
Musical Heritage Society MHS 912250X;
    1982; LP
Piano
Moderate dialect

3669

Over Yonder
Johnson, Hall
Holland, Charles (Tenor)
My Lord What a Mornin'
Musical Heritage Society MHS 512250K;
    1988; CD
Piano
Moderate dialect

. . . .

Peter, Go Ring Dem Bells

3670

Oh, Peter, Go Ring Dem Bells
Burleigh, Harry T.
Anderson, Marian (Contralto)
He's Got the Whole World in His Hands:
    Spirituals
RCA Victor 09026-61960-2; 1994; CD
Piano
Moderate dialect

　　Also released with *Marian Anderson:*
Beyond the Music; Her Complete RCA Victor
Recordings Sony Classical 19439836492; 2021;
CD

3671

Peter Go Ring Dem Bells (Prelude/Rondo)
    [from *Cantata*]
Carter, John D.
Brewer, Christine (Soprano)
Saint Louis Woman
Opera Theatre of Saint Louis OTSL CD93;
    1993; CD
Piano
Moderate dialect

3672

Peter Go Ring Dem Bells (Prelude/Rondo)
    [from *Cantata*]
Carter, John
Brewer, Christine (Soprano)
Songs by Wagner, Wolf, Britten and John
    Carter
Wigmorc Hall Live WHLive0022; 2008; CD
Piano
Moderate dialect

3673

Oh, Peter, Go Ring Them Bells
Dørumsgaard, Arne

Carlsen, Svein (Bass)
Negro Spirituals
EuroMaster AS ECD19005; 1996; CD
Piano

3674

Prelude/Rondo [from *Cantata*]
Carter, John D.; Link, Peter
Davis, Osceola (Soprano)
Climbing High Mountains
Watchfire Music; 2008; CD
Piano, orchestra
Light dialect

3675

Peter Go Ring Dem Bells (Prelude/Rondo)
    [from *Cantata*]
Carter, John D.
English-Robinson, Laura (Soprano)
Let It Shine!
ACA Digital Recording CM20020; 1994; CD
Piano
Light dialect

3676

Peter, Go Ring Them Bells
Kaelin, Pierre
Evans, Allan (Bass-baritone)
Negro Spirituals
Electromusic Records EMCD 6885; 1985; CD
Chorus, other instrument(s)

3677

Peter Go Ring Dem Bells (Prelude/Rondo)
    [from *Cantata*]
Carter, John D.
Givens, Melissa (Soprano)
Let the Rain Kiss You
Divameg Productions 141434; 2001; CD
Piano

3678

Prelude/Rondo [from *Cantata*]
Carter, John D.
Gormley, Clare (Soprano)
Where Morning Lies: Spiritual Songs
ABC Classics 461 766-2; 2002; CD
Piano
Light dialect

3679

Oh, Peter, Go Ring-a Dem Bells
Composer not identified
Hall, Nell (Soprano)
*Nell Hall in a Recital of Arias, Ballads,
    Spirituals, Folk Songs*
Colonial COL LP-211; [19--]; LP
Piano

3680

Peter, Go Ring-a Them Bells
Johnson, John Rosamond
Jones, Arthur (Tenor)
Wade in the Water
Orbis Books; 1993; Book w/cass
Piano
Light dialect

3681

O Peter, Go Ring-a Dem Bells
Burleigh, Harry T.
Jones, Fanni (Mezzo-soprano)
Negro Spirituals en Concert
Suisa; 1987; LP
Organ
Moderate dialect

3682

Prelude/Rondo (Peter Go Ring Dem Bells)
    [from *Cantata*]
Carter, John D.
Jones, Randye (Soprano)
Come Down Angels
Ahhjay Records AHHJ-0001; 2003; CD
Piano
Light dialect

3683

O Peter Go Ring-a-Dem Bells
Composer not identified
Monzo, Oscar (Baritone)
Negro Spirituals
Dial Discos 50-2020; 1983; LP

3684

Peter Go Ring-a Dem Bells
Pankey, Aubrey
Pankey, Aubrey (Baritone)
Negro Spirituals

Eterna 830010; 1983; LP
Piano
Light dialect

3685

Peter, Go Ring-a Dem Bells
[Pankey, Aubrey]
Pankey, Aubrey (Baritone)
Aubrey Pankey Singt Negro-Spirituals
Eterna 7 30 005; 1959; LP
Piano
Light dialect

3686

Peter Go Ring-a Dem Bells
[Pankey, Aubrey]
Pankey, Aubrey (Baritone)
Negro-Spirituals
Eterna 5 30 022; [19--]; 45 RPM
Piano
Light dialect

3687

Peter Go Ring Dem Bells (Prelude/Rondo)
    [from *Cantata*]
Carter, John D.
Pickens, Jo Ann (Soprano)
*My Heritage: American Melodies/Negro
    Spirituals*
Koch Schwann 3-1447-2; 1993; CD

3688

Peter Go Ring Dem Bells (Prelude/Rondo)
    [from *Cantata*]
[Carter, John D.]
Pleas III, Henry H. (Tenor)
Cantata
Private Label; 2003; CD
Piano

3689

Peter, Go Ring a Dem Bells
Composer not identified
Robeson, Paul (Bass-baritone)
Paul Robeson
Music Video Dist. MDGC23420.2; 2007; CD

3690

Peter, Go Ring Dem Bells
Bonds, Margaret

Taylor, Darryl (Countertenor)
*How Sweet the Sound: A Charm of
    Spirituals*
Albany TROY1244; 2011; CD
Piano

3691

Prelude/Rondo: Peter Go Ring Them Bells
    [from *Cantata*]
[Carter, John D.]
Thoms, Treva (Soprano)
Come Sunday: Sacred American Songs
Private Label; 2007; CD
Piano

3692

Peter, Go Ring a Dem Bells
Thomas, André J.
Tucker, Eric Hoy (Bass-baritone)
*Southern Salute: Southern Songs &
    Spirituals*
White Pine Music WPM218; 2012; CD
Piano
Light dialect

3693

Peter Go Ring Dem Bells (Prelude/Rondo)
    [from *Cantata*]
[Carter, John D.]
Verdejo, Awilda (Soprano)
Awilda Verdejo Sings Spirituals
Angeluz Performances; 1999; CD
Piano

3694

Peter Go Ring Dem Bells (Prelude/Rondo)
    [from *Cantata*]
Carter, John D.
Wade, Jr., Ray (Tenor)
Sence You Went Away
Albany Records TROY 387; 1998; CD
Piano
Moderate dialect

3695

Peter, Go Ring Dem Bells
Composer not identified
West, Lucretia (Mezzo-soprano)
Spirituals

Westminster WL 5338; 1954; LP
Piano

3696

Peter Go Ring the Bells
Composer not identified
West, Lucretia (Mezzo-soprano)
Lucretia West Sings Spirituals
Westminster WP 6063; [1957]; LP

3697

Peter Go Ring Dem Bells (Prelude/Rondo)
    [from *Cantata*]
Carter, John D.
Williams, Wayne (Tenor)
Music from My Life
Movideo Productions 02-1993; 1993; CD
Piano

3698

O Peter Go Ring-a-Dem Bells
Burleigh, Harry T.
Winter, Georg (Vocalist)
Eine Kleine Hausmusik
Teldec 66.22670; 1981; LP
Piano

. . . .
Pity a Po' Boy

3699

Pity a Po' Boy
Traditional
Matthews, Benjamin (Baritone)
Three Generations Live
Canti Records; 2000; CD
A cappella
Heavy dialect

3700

Pity a Po' Boy
Hayes, Roland
Sims, Robert (Baritone)
*Robert Sims Sings the Spirituals of Roland
    Hayes*
Canti Classics 2014-01; 2015; CD
A cappella
Heavy dialect

. . . .
Plenty Good Room

3701

Plenty Good Room
Boatner, Edward
Anderson, Marian (Contralto)
Spirituals
RCA Victor Red Seal 09026-63306-2; 1999;
    CD
Piano
No dialect discerned

3702

Plenty Good Room
Boatner, Edward
Anderson, Marian (Contralto)
Negro Spirituals
RCA Victor LM 2032; [1956]; LP
Piano

    Also released with *Marian Anderson:
Beyond the Music; Her Complete RCA Victor
Recordings* Sony Classical 19439836492; 2021;
CD

3703

Plenty Good Room
[Boatner, Edward]
Anderson, Marian (Contralto)
*Marian Anderson Sings Eleven Great
    Spirituals*
RCA Victor LRM 7006; 1955; LP
Piano

3704

Plenty Good Room
[Boatner, Edward]
Anderson, Marian (Contralto)
Alto Rhapsody; Selected Spirituals
Urania URN 22.328; 2007; CD
Piano

3705

Plenty Good Room
[Boatner, Edward]
Anderson, Marian (Contralto)
The Very Best of Marian Anderson
Master Classics Records; 2009; CD

Piano
No dialect discerned

3706

Plenty Good Room
[Boatner, Edward]
Anderson, Marian (Contralto)
*Marian Anderson Sings Eleven Great
    Spirituals*
Kipepeo Publishing; 2017; CD
Piano

3707

Plenty Good Room
[Boatner, Edward]
Anderson, Marian (Contralto)
*Grandes Contraltos de la Musique Classique,
    Les: Marian Anderson, Vol. 5*
Mon Patrimoine Musical Collection; 2017;
    Streaming audio
Piano

3708

Plenty Good Room
[Boatner, Edward]
Anderson, Marian (Contralto)
Negro Spirituals
RCA Victor 630.396 A; [19--]; LP
Piano

3709

Plenty Good Room
Hayes, Roland
Caesar, Jackson (Tenor)
*Spirituals: Celebrating the Music, Life,
    Legacy of Roland Hayes*
CD Baby 7048606059; 2021; CD
Piano
Moderate dialect

3710

Plenty Good Room
Corley, Maria Thompson
Clark, Maria (Soprano)
Soul Sanctuary: Spirituals & Hymns
Navona Records NV6406; 2022; CD
Piano
Moderate dialect

3711

Plenty Good Room
Boatner, Edward
Davis, Ellabelle (Soprano)
*I Stood on de Ribber ob Jordan/Plenty Good
    Room*
Decca 14624; [19--]; 78 RPM
Orchestra

3712

Plenty Good Room
Boatner, Edward
Davis, Ellabelle (Soprano)
Ellabelle Davis Sings Negro Spirituals
London LPS 182; [1950]; LP
Orchestra

3713

Plenty Good Room
Boatner, Edward
Davis, Ellabelle (Soprano)
*Recital of Negro Spirituals by Ellabelle
    Davis*
Decca LM.4504; [1950]; LP
Orchestra

3714

Plenty Good Room
[Boatner, Edward]
Davis, Ellabelle (Soprano)
Were You There?
Decca DFE 8618; 1965; 45 RPM
Orchestra

3715

Plenty Good Room
[Boatner, Edward]
Davis, Ellabelle (Soprano)
Great Negro Spirituals
Replay Record; 2013; Streaming audio
Orchestra
No dialect discerned

3716

Plenty Good Room
Roberts, Howard
Estes, Simon (Bass-baritone)
Spirituals
Philips 412 631-2; 1985; CD

Orchestra
No dialect discerned

    Also released with *Famous Spirituals* (Philips 462 062-2; 1997; CD)

3717

Plenty Good Room
Composer not identified
Hayes, Roland (Tenor)
Classic Gospel Songs
Emerald/K-Tel; 2013; Streaming audio
Piano

3718

Plenty Good Room
Composer not identified
Hayes, Roland (Tenor)
Roland Hayes Sings: Negro Spirituals, Aframerican Folk Songs
Amadeo Records AVRS 6033; [19--]; LP
Piano

3719

Plenty Good Room
Hayes, Roland
Hayes, Roland (Tenor)
Were You There/Hear de Lambs a Cryin'/ Plenty Good Room
Columbia Masterworks 69812-D; 1940; 78 RPM
Piano

3720

Plenty Good Room [from *The Life of Christ*]
Hayes, Roland
Hayes, Roland (Tenor)
Roland Hayes Sings the Life of Christ: As Told Through Aframerican Folksong
Vanguard VRS-462; 1954; LP
Piano

    Also released with *Aframerican Folksong: Telling the Story of The Life of Christ* (Top Rank 39 620; [1961]; LP); *Roland Hayes Sings the Life of Christ: As Told Through Aframerican Folksong* (Vanguard SRV 352; 1976; LP); *The Art of Roland Hayes* (Smithsonian Collection RD 041; 1990; CD); *Favorite Spirituals* (Vanguard Classics OVC 6022;

1995; CD) and *Charlton Heston Reads from The Life and Passion of Jesus Christ* (Vanguard Classics ATM-CD-1259; 2003; CD)

3721

Plenty Good Room
Hayes, Roland
Hayes, Roland (Tenor)
Good News: Vintage Negro Spirituals
Living Era AJA 5622; 2006; CD
Piano
Light dialect

3722

Plenty Good Room
Hayes, Roland
Hayes, Roland (Tenor)
The Art of Roland Hayes: Six Centuries of Song
Preiser Records; 2010; CD
Piano
Light dialect

3723

Plenty Good Room
[Hayes, Roland]
Hayes, Roland (Tenor)
Art Songs and Spirituals
Veritas VM 112; 1967; LP
Piano
Heavy dialect

3724

Plenty Good Room [from *The Life of Christ*]
[Hayes, Roland]
Hayes, Roland (Tenor)
Big Psalms, Hymns and Spirituals Box
eOne Music/Vanguard Classics; 2015; Streaming audio
Piano

3725

Plenty Good Room [from *The Conversion (Invitation III)*]
Cornelius, II, John
Heaston, Nicole (Soprano)
Marilyn Horne Foundation Presents on Wings of Song. Recital No. 9

Marilyn Horne Foundation DCD 5028;
2001; CD
Piano

3726

Plenty Good Room
Composer not identified
Hendricks, Barbara (Soprano)
Espirituales Negros
EMI Classics/Altaya 01636; 1983; CD
Piano

3727

Plenty Good Room
Composer not identified
Hendricks, Barbara (Soprano)
Spirituals
EMI Classics 0946 346641 2 7; 2005; CD
Piano

3728

Plenty Good Room
Hendricks, Barbara; Alexeev, Dmitri
Hendricks, Barbara (Soprano)
Negro Spirituals
EMI CDC7470262; 1983; CD
Piano
Light dialect

Also released with *Negro Spirituals* (EMI CDC7470262; 1983; CD)

3729

Plenty Good Room
Hayes, Roland
Jenkins, Isaiah (Tenor)
Lyric Tenor
Trans Radio TR 1010A; [195-]; LP
Piano

3730

Plenty Good Room
Hayes, Roland
Matthews, Inez (Mezzo-soprano)
Inez Matthews Sings Spirituals (*Great New Voices of Today, v. 6*)
Period SPL-580; [1950]; LP
Piano
Light dialect

Also released with *Inez Matthews Sings Spirituals* (Essential Media Group; 2011; CD)

3731

Plenty Good Room
Composer not identified
Pickens, Jo Ann (Soprano)
My Heritage: American Melodies/Negro Spirituals
Koch Schwann 3-1447-2; 1993; CD

3732

Plenty Good Room
Composer not identified
Pleas III, Henry H. (Tenor)
Deep River: A Spiritual Journey
Rowe House Productions; 1999; CD

3733

Plenty Good Room
Hayes, Roland
Quivar, Florence (Mezzo-soprano)
Great American Spirituals
Angel CDM 7 64669 2; 1992; CD
Piano
Heavy dialect

Also released with *Great American Spirituals* (Musical Heritage Society 513725Z; 1994; CD)

3734

Plenty Good Room
Hayes, Roland
Quivar, Florence (Mezzo-soprano)
Negro Spirituals
EMI 7243 5 72790 2 4; 1998; CD
Piano
Heavy dialect

3735

Plenty Good Room
Hayes, Roland
Quivar, Florence (Mezzo-soprano)
Ride On, King Jesus! Florence Quivar Sings Black Music of America
EMI Classics 9 67138 2; 2010; CD
Piano

3736

Plenty Good Room [from *The Life of Christ*]
Hayes, Roland
Sims, Robert (Baritone)
*Robert Sims Sings the Spirituals of Roland
　Hayes*
Canti Classics 2014-01; 2015; CD
Piano
Heavy dialect

3737

Plenty Good Room [from *The Life of Christ*]
Hayes, Roland
Warfield, William (Bass-baritone)
*Spirituals: 200 Years of African-American
　Spirituals*
ProArte CDD 3443; 1993; CD
Piano
Heavy dialect

3738

Plenty Good Room
Hayes, Roland
Warfield, William (Bass-baritone)
Three Generations Live
Canti Records; 2000; CD
Piano
Heavy dialect

3739

Plenty Good Room [from *The Life of
　Christ*]
Hayes, Roland
Williams, Willie (Vocalist)
My Tribute
Discovery V42227; 1974; LP
Piano

· · · · · · ·

Po' Mo' ner Got
a Home at Las'

3740

Po' Mo'ner Got a Home at Las'
Composer not identified
Ayers, Vanessa (Mezzo-soprano)
Done Crossed Every River: Freedom's Journey
Arcadia ARC 2004-2; 1995; CD

3741

Po' Mo'ner Got a Home at Las'
Johnson, Hall
Blackmon, Henry (Baritone)
Geestelijke Liederen En Negro Spirituals
Mirasound Records SGLP 6047; 1974; LP
Piano

3742

Po' Mo'ner Got a Home at Last
Johnson, Hall
Brown, William (Tenor)
Fi-Yer!: a century of African American song
Albany Records TROY 329; 1999; CD
Piano
Heavy dialect

3743

Po' Moner Got a Home at Las'
Johnson, Hall
Conrad, Barbara (Mezzo-soprano)
Spirituals
Naxos 8.553036; 1995; CD
Piano
Heavy dialect

3744

Po' Mo'ner Got a Home at Las'
Johnson, Hall
Fernandez, Wilhelmenia (Soprano)
Negro Spirituals
Transart 131; 2005; CD
Piano

3745

Po' Mo'ner Got a Home at Las'
Johnson, Hall
Gibson, Caroline (Soprano)
*On Ma Journey Now: Negro Spirituals in
　Concert*
Twin Productions; 2016; CD
Piano
Moderate dialect

3746

Po' Mo'ner Got a Home
Lloyd, Charles, Jr.
Johnson, Karen (Soprano)
The New Negro Spiritual

W. C. Patterson; 2002; Score w/CD
Piano
Heavy dialect

3747

Po' Mourner [from Cycle of Six Spirituals]
Owens, Robert
Moses, Oral (Bass-baritone)
Come Down Angels and Trouble the Water: Negro Spirituals, an American National Treasure!
Albany Records TROY 1489; 2014; CD
Piano
Heavy dialect

3748

Po' Mo'ner Got a Home at Las' [from *Settings for Spirituals*]
Chadabe, Joel
Oliver, Irene (Soprano)
Settings for Spirituals; Solo
Lovely Music VR-3804; 1984; LP
Electronics

3749

Po' Mon'ner Got a Home at Las'
Giesen, Hubert
Ray, William (Baritone)
Negro Spirituals
Intercord; [19--]; LP
Piano

3750

Po' Mon'ner Got a Home at Las'
Giesen, Hubert
Ray, William (Baritone)
Sings Arias, Duets, Musical Selections and Negro Spirituals
Intercord; [19--]; CD
Piano

3751

Po' Mo' ner Got a Home at Las'
Johnson, Hall
Straughter, Maralyn (Soprano)
Negro Spirituals of Hall Johnson
Variety Recording Service Var 0753; [196-]; LP
Piano

3752

Po Mo'ner Got a Home at Las
Johnson, Hall
Toppin, Louise (Soprano)
He'll Bring It to Pass: The Spirituals of Hall Johnson for Voice and Piano
Albany Records TROY846; 2006; CD
Piano
Heavy dialect

. . . .

Po' Pilgrim

3753

Po' Pilgrim
Hayes, Roland
Hamilton, Ruth (Contralto)
Good News
Videmus Records VIS735; 2007; CD
Piano
Heavy dialect

3754

Po' Pilgrim
Hayes, Roland
Matthews, Inez (Mezzo-soprano)
Inez Matthews Sings Spirituals
Essential Media Group; 2011; CD
Piano
Heavy dialect

3755

Po' Pilgrim
Hayes, Roland
Matthews, Inez (Mezzo-soprano)
Inez Matthews Sings Spirituals (Great New Voices of Today, v. 6)
Period SPL-580; [1950]; LP
Piano
Heavy dialect

. . . .

Poor Me

3756

Poor Me
Dett, Robert Nathaniel
Anderson, Marian (Contralto)

Spirituals
RCA Victor Red Seal 09026-63306-2; 1999; CD
Piano
No dialect discerned

3757

Poor Me
Dett, Robert Nathaniel
Anderson, Marian (Contralto)
Ev'Ry Time I Feel the Spirit (1930–1947)
Naxos Nostalgia 8.120779; 2004; CD
Piano

3758

Poor Me
Dett, Robert Nathaniel
Anderson, Marian (Contralto)
Negro Spirituals: 1924–1949
Frémeaux & Associés FA 184; 2004; CD
Orchestra

3759

Poor Me
Dett, Robert Nathaniel
Anderson, Marian (Contralto)
*Marian Anderson: Beyond the Music; Her
    Complete RCA Victor Recordings*
Sony Classical 19439836492; 2021; CD
Piano
No dialect discerned

3760

Poor Me
Dett, Robert Nathaniel
Anderson, Marian (Contralto)
*Marian Anderson: Beyond the Music; Her
    Complete RCA Victor Recordings*
Sony Classical 19439836492; 2021; CD
Piano
No dialect discerned

3761

Poor Me
Dett, Robert Nathaniel
Anderson, Marian (Contralto)
Poor Me/Hold On!
RCA Victor 10-1278; [1948]; 78 RPM
Piano
No dialect discerned

3762

Poor Me
[Dett, Robert Nathaniel]
Anderson, Marian (Contralto)
The Very Best of Marian Anderson
Master Classics Records; 2009; CD
Piano
No dialect discerned

3763

Po' Me! [from *Five Negro Worksongs*]
Composer not identified
Hayes, Roland (Tenor)
Evening with Roland Hayes, Tenor
Heritage LP-SS-1204; 1953; LP
Piano

3764

Po' Me! [from *Five Negro Worksongs*]
Johnson, Hall
Hayes, Roland (Tenor)
Roland Hayes Recital, A
A 440 Records AC1203; [19--]; LP
Piano

3765

Poor Me
Composer not identified
Rustin, Bayard (Tenor)
*Bayard Rustin Sings Spirituals, Work &
    Freedom Songs*
Bayard Rustin Fund; 1988; Cassette
Piano
Heavy dialect

3766

Poor Me
Composer not identified
Rustin, Bayard (Tenor)
*Bayard Rustin Sings Spirituals, Work &
    Freedom Songs*
Bayard Rustin Fund; 2003; CD
Piano
Heavy dialect

3767

Poor Me (Trouble Will Bury Me Down)
[Dett, Robert Nathaniel]
Williams, Camilla (Soprano)

Camilla Williams Sings Spirituals
MGM Records M-G-M E-156; [195-]; LP
Piano
No dialect discerned

3768

Poor Me (Trouble Will Bury Me Down)
[Dett, Robert Nathaniel]
Williams, Camilla (Soprano)
A Camilla Williams Recital
MGM Records E-140; [1952]; LP
Piano
No dialect discerned

· · · · · · ·

Poor Monah

3769

Poor Monah
Bledsoe, Jules
Bledsoe, Jules (Baritone)
Wake Up Jacob/He Rose/Poor Monah
Ultraphone AP 393; 1931; 78 RPM
Orchestra
Heavy dialect

3770

Poor Monah
Composer not identified
Bledsoe, Jules (Baritone)
Wake Up, Jacob/Poor Monah
Royale 1701; 1939; 78 RPM
Orchestra
Heavy dialect

3771

Poor Monah
Composer not identified
Bledsoe, Jules (Baritone)
Poor Monah/Go Down Moses
Joe Davis 8001; [19--]; 78 RPM
Orchestra
Heavy dialect

· · · · · · ·

Poor Pilgrim

3772

Poor Pilgrim
Composer not identified

Charles, Lee (Tenor)
*Swing Low Sweet Chariot: And Other
    Spirituals*
Riverside RLP 12-651; 1957; LP
Piano, guitar

· · · · · · ·

Poor Wayfarin' Stranger

3773

Poor Wayfaring Stranger
Morgan, Haydn
Blackmon, Henry (Baritone)
Negro Spirituals
Vega 19179; [19--]; LP
Chorus, piano

3774

Poor Wayfaring Stranger
Evans, Allan
Evans, Allan (Bass-baritone)
Negro Spirituals
Electromusic Records EMCD 6885; 1985;
    CD
Chorus, other instrument(s)

3775

Poor Wayfaring Stranger
Composer not identified
Humphrey Flynn, Edwina (Soprano)
The Lord Will Make a Way
Private Label; 2000; CD
Piano

3776

Poor Wayfarin' Stranger
Lloyd, Charles, Jr.
Jefferson, Othello (Tenor)
*Good News: African American Spirituals and
    Art Songs*
Cambria Records CD 1270; 2021; CD
Piano
Light dialect

3777

Poor Wayfarin' Stranger
Meyer, Fredrich
London, George (Bass-baritone)
Spirituals

Deutsche Grammophon 00289 477 6193;
2006; CD
Chorus
Heavy dialect

3778

Poor Wayfarin' Stranger
Lloyd, Charles, Jr.
Paige-Green, Jacqueline (Soprano)
The Spiritual Art Song Collection
Warner Bros. SVBM00004; 2000; Score w/
CD
Piano

3779

Poor Wayfarin' Stranger
Brown, Lawrence
Robeson, Paul (Bass-baritone)
Swing Low, Sweet Chariot
Columbia Masterworks MM-819; 1949; 78
RPM
Piano

3780

Poor Wayfarin' Stranger
Brown, Lawrence
Robeson, Paul (Bass-baritone)
Paul Robeson Chante … 16 Spirituals
Philips G 05.639 R; 1959; LP
Piano

3781

Poor Wayfarin' Stranger
[Brown, Lawrence]
Robeson, Paul (Bass-baritone)
Swing Low, Sweet Chariot
Columbia Masterworks ML 2038; [195-]; LP
Piano

. . . .

Prayer Is de Key

3782

Prayer Is de Key
Johnson, Hall
Anderson, Marian (Contralto)
Jus' Keep on Singin'
RCA Victor LSC 2796; 1965; LP
Piano

3783

Prayer Is de Key
Johnson, Hall
Anderson, Marian (Contralto)
*He's Got the Whole World in His Hands:
Spirituals*
RCA Victor 09026-61960-2; 1994; CD
Piano
Moderate dialect

3784

Prayer Is de Key
Johnson, Hall
Anderson, Marian (Contralto)
*Marian Anderson: Beyond the Music; Her
Complete RCA Victor Recordings*
Sony Classical 19439836492; 2021; CD
Piano
Heavy dialect

. . . .

Prepare Me One Body

3785

Prepare Me One Body [from *The Life of
Christ*]
Hayes, Roland
Caesar, Jackson (Tenor)
*Spirituals: Celebrating the Music, Life,
Legacy of Roland Hayes*
CD Baby 7048606059; 2021; CD
Piano

3786

Prepare Me One Body [from *The Life of
Christ*]
Hayes, Roland
Clemmons, François (Tenor)
Negro Spirituals Live! In Concert
American Negro Spiritual Research
Foundation 8177 2048 3779; 1998; CD
Piano
Light dialect

3787

Prepare Me One Body [from *The Life of
Christ*]
Hayes, Roland
George, Roderick L. (Tenor)

The Spirit of the Holidays
American Spiritual Ensemble; 2009; CD

3788

Prologue: Prepare Me One Body [from *The Life of Christ*]
Hayes, Roland
Hayes, Roland (Tenor)
Roland Hayes Sings the Life of Christ: As Told Through Aframerican Folksong
Vanguard VRS-462; 1954; LP
Piano

3789

Prologue: Prepare Me One Body [from *The Life of Christ*]
Hayes, Roland
Hayes, Roland (Tenor)
Roland Hayes Sings the Life of Christ: As Told Through Aframerican Folksong
Vanguard SRV 352; 1976; LP
Piano

3790

Prepare Me One Body [from *The Life of Christ*]
Hayes, Roland
Hayes, Roland (Tenor)
Favorite Spirituals
Vanguard Classics OVC 6022; 1995; CD
Piano
No dialect discerned

3791

Prologue: Prepare Me One Body [from *The Life of Christ*]
Hayes, Roland
Hayes, Roland (Tenor)
Charlton Heston Reads from The Life and Passion of Jesus Christ
Vanguard Classics ATM-CD-1259; 2003; CD
Piano

3792

Prologue: Prepare Me One Body [from *The Life of Christ*]
Hayes, Roland
Hayes, Roland (Tenor)

Aframerican Folksong: Telling the Story of The Life of Christ
Top Rank 39 620; [1961]; LP
Piano

3793

Prepare Me One Body
[Hayes, Roland]
Hayes, Roland (Tenor)
Big Psalms, Hymns and Spirituals Box
eOne Music/Vanguard Classics; 2015; Streaming audio
Piano

3794

Prepare Me One Body [from *The Life of Christ*]
Hayes, Roland
Holland, Charles (Tenor)
Cinq Negro Spirituals
Pathé 45 ED. 28; 1954; 45 RPM
Piano

3795

Prepare Me One Body [from *The Life of Christ*]
Hayes, Roland
Holland, Charles (Tenor)
My Lord What a Mornin'
Musical Heritage Society MHS 912250X; 1982; LP
Piano
No dialect discerned

3796

Prepare Me One Body [from *The Life of Christ*]
Hayes, Roland
Holland, Charles (Tenor)
My Lord What a Mornin'
Musical Heritage Society MHS 512250K; 1988; CD
Piano
No dialect discerned

3797

Prepare Me One Body [from *The Life of Christ*]
[Hayes, Roland]

Jenkins, Isaiah (Tenor)
Lyric Tenor
Trans Radio TR 1010A; [195-]; LP
Piano

3798

Prepare Me One Body [from *The Life of Christ*]
Hayes, Roland
Oby, Jason (Tenor)
The Life of Christ: Collected Spirituals
Private Label TSU4749; [200-]; CD
Piano
No dialect discerned

3799

Prepare Me One Body [from *The Life of Christ*]
Hayes, Roland
Shirley, George (Tenor)
George Shirley at 80: My Time Has Come!
Videmus Records; 2014; CD
Piano

3800

Prepare Me One Body [from *The Life of Christ*]
Hayes, Roland
Sims, Robert (Baritone)
Robert Sims Sings the Spirituals of Roland Hayes
Canti Classics 2014-01; 2015; CD
Piano
Moderate dialect

3801

Prepare Me One Body [from *The Life of Christ*]
Hayes, Roland
Williams, Willie (Vocalist)
My Tribute
Discovery V42227; 1974; LP
Piano

. . . .

Reign, King Jesus

3802

Reign, King Jesus
James, Willis Laurence

Ayers, Vanessa (Mezzo-soprano)
Black Christmas: Spirituals in the African-American Tradition
Essay Recordings CD1011; 1990; CD
Chorus
No dialect discerned

. . . .

Religion Is a Fortune

3803

Religion Is a Fortune
Composer not identified
Jones, Fanni (Mezzo-soprano)
Negro Spirituals
Phonotec 815; 1977; LP
Organ

. . . .

Ride On, Jesus

3804

Ride On, Jesus
Dett, Robert Nathaniel
Alexander, Roberta (Soprano)
Songs My Mother Taught Me
Etcetera KTC 1208; 1999; CD
Piano
Heavy dialect

Also released with *Roberta Alexander.... A Retrospective* (Etcetera KTC1222; 2013; CD)

3805

Ride On, Jesus
Composer not identified
Ayers, Vanessa (Mezzo-soprano)
Done Crossed Every River: Freedom's Journey
Arcadia ARC 2004-2; 1995; CD

3806

Ride On, Jesus
Hairston, Jacqueline
Glover, Andre Solomon (Baritone)
Opera Ebony Sings Spirituals
Ebony Classic Recordings; 2002; CD

3807

Ride On, Jesus
Dett, Robert Nathaniel

Harris, Inetta (Soprano)
My Heritage Sings: A Selection of Spirituals & Hymns
Private Label; [199-]; CD
Piano

3808

Ride On, Jesus
Johnson, Hall
Hopkins, Gregory (Tenor)
Best of the Hall Johnson Centennial Festival Celebrating the 100th Anniversary of Hall Johnson's Birth
Hall Johnson Collection O33D2; 2002; CD
Piano

3809

Ride On, Jesus
Dett, Robert Nathaniel
Jones, Randye (Soprano)
Come Down Angels
Ahhjay Records AHHJ-0001; 2003; CD
Piano
Light dialect

3810

Ride On, Jesus
Dett, Robert Nathaniel
Maynor, Dorothy (Soprano)
Dorothy Maynor in Concert at Library of Congress
Library of Congress, Music Division LCM 2141; 2007; CD
Piano
Heavy dialect

3811

Ride On, Jesus
Dett, Robert Nathaniel
Maynor, Dorothy (Soprano)
Dorothy Maynor, Soprano
Bridge Records 9233; 2007; CD
Piano
Heavy dialect

3812

Ride On, Jesus
Dett, Robert Nathaniel
Overton, Kenneth (Baritone)

Been in de Storm So Long (Songs My Fathers Taught Me)
American Spiritual Ensemble; 2012; CD
Piano
Heavy dialect

3813

Ride On, Jesus
Dett, Robert Nathaniel
Quivar, Florence (Mezzo-soprano)
Negro Spirituals
EMI 7243 5 72790 2 4; 1998; CD
Piano
Heavy dialect

Also released with *Ride On, King Jesus!* *Florence Quivar Sings Black Music of America* (EMI Classics 9 67138 2; 2010; CD)

3814

Ride On, Jesus!
Giesen, Hubert
Ray, William (Baritone)
Negro Spirituals
Intercord; [19--]; LP
Piano

3815

Ride On, Jesus!
Giesen, Hubert
Ray, William (Baritone)
Sings Arias, Duets, Musical Selections and Negro Spirituals
Intercord; [19--]; CD
Piano

3816

Ride On, Jesus!
Scharnberg, Kim
Robinson, Faye (Soprano)
Remembering Marian Anderson
d'Note Classics DND 1014; 1997; CD
Orchestra
Light dialect

3817

Ride On, Jesus
Composer not identified
Tyler, Veronica (Soprano)
Sings ... the Passion of Christ in Spirituals

BRC Productions; [19--]; LP
Piano

· · · · · · ·

Ride On, King Jesus

[1 Chronicles 29:11; Job 9:12; 1 Corinthians 9:24; Galatians 5:7; Philippians 2:5-11; Hebrews 12:1-2]

"Ride on, King Jesus, No man can hinder me. For He Is King of Kings, He is Lord of Lords; Jesus Christ, first and last, No man works like Him. King Jesus rides a milk-white horse, No man works like Him; The river of Jordan He did cross, No man works like Him...."

[Available in HCTN, HJCO, HTBS, JCCA, RS12, SBFD, SOTS, WF10, WF70]

3818

He Is King of Kings
Traditional
Rustin, Bayard (Tenor)
Bayard Rustin Sings Twelve Spirituals on the Life of Christ
Fellowship Records E2-KL 1771; [195-]; LP
A cappella
Moderate dialect

    Also released with *Bayard Rustin—The Singer* (Black Swan Series; Parnassus Records PACD 96083; 2022; CD)

3819

Ride On, King Jesus
Burleigh, Harry T.
Anderson, Marian (Contralto)
Marian Anderson Sings Spirituals
RCA Victor Red Seal MO 1238; 1948; 78 RPM
Piano

3820

Ride On, King Jesus
Burleigh, Harry T.
Anderson, Marian (Contralto)
Negro Spirituals
La Voix de Son Maître FBLP1039; 1953; LP
Piano

3821

Ride On, King Jesus
Burleigh, Harry T.
Anderson, Marian (Contralto)
Farewell Recital
RCA Victor LSC 2781; 1964; LP
Piano

3822

Ride On, King Jesus
Burleigh, Harry T.
Anderson, Marian (Contralto)
Spirituals
RCA Victor Red Seal 09026-63306-2; 1999; CD
Piano
Heavy dialect

3823

Ride On, King Jesus
Burleigh, Harry T.
Anderson, Marian (Contralto)
Marian Anderson Sings Negro Spirituals
His Master's Voice BLP 1060; [19--]; LP
Piano
Light dialect

    Also released with *Marian Anderson: Beyond the Music; Her Complete RCA Victor Recordings* Sony Classical 19439836492; 2021; CD

3824

Ride On, King Jesus
Burleigh, Harry T.
Anderson, Marian (Contralto)
Negro Spirituals
RCA Victor LM 2032; [1956]; LP
Piano

    Also released with *Marian Anderson: Beyond the Music; Her Complete RCA Victor Recordings* Sony Classical 19439836492; 2021; CD

3825

Ride On, King Jesus
Johnson, Hall
Anderson, Marian (Contralto)
Jus' Keep on Singin'

RCA Victor LSC 2796; 1965; LP
Piano

Also released with *Marian Anderson: Beyond the Music; Her Complete RCA Victor Recordings* Sony Classical 19439836492; 2021; CD

3826

Ride On, King Jesus
[Burleigh, Harry T.]
Anderson, Marian (Contralto)
Marian Anderson Sings Spirituals
RCA Victor LM 110; 1949; LP
Piano

3827

Ride On, King Jesus
[Burleigh, Harry T.]
Anderson, Marian (Contralto)
Alto Rhapsody; Selected Spirituals
Urania URN 22.328; 2007; CD
Piano

3828

Ride On, King Jesus
[Burleigh, Harry T.]
Anderson, Marian (Contralto)
The Very Best of Marian Anderson
Master Classics Records; 2009; CD
Piano
No dialect discerned

3829

Ride On, King Jesus
[Burleigh, Harry T.]
Anderson, Marian (Contralto)
Negro Spirituals
RCA Gold Seal RVC-1570; [19--]; LP
Piano

3830

Ride On, King Jesus
[Burleigh, Harry T.]
Anderson, Marian (Contralto)
Negro Spirituals
RCA Victor 630.396 A; [19--]; LP
Piano

3831

He Is King of Kings
Composer not identified
Arroyo, Martina (Soprano); Anonymous
 ([Tenor])
Negro Spirituals
EMI 7243 5 72790 2 4; 1998; CD
Chorus
Light dialect

3832

Ride On, King Jesus!
Venanzi, Henri
Arroyo, Martina (Soprano)
Spirituals
Centaur CRC 2060; 1991; CD
Piano
Light dialect

3833

Ride On, King Jesus!
Johnson, Hall; Russ, Patrick
Battle, Kathleen (Soprano)
Pleasures of Their Company
EMI/Angel CDC-7 47196 2; 1986; CD
Guitar
Light dialect

3834

Ride On, King Jesus
[Johnson, Hall]
Battle, Kathleen (Soprano)
Golden Voices Sing Golden Favorites
Reader's Digest WCD4-5781-WCD4-5784;
 1990; CD

3835

Ride On, King Jesus
[Johnson, Hall]
Battle, Kathleen (Soprano)
Great American Spirituals
Angel CDM 7 64669 2; 1992; CD
Guitar
Light dialect

Also released with *Great American Spirituals* (Musical Heritage Society 513725Z; 1994; CD)

3836

Ride On, King Jesus
Johnson, Hall
Benham, Dorothy (Soprano)
The Lord Is My Light
In His Light Productions; 2000; CD
Piano, violin

3837

Ride On, King Jesus
[Johnson, Hall]
Blue, Angel (Soprano)
Joy Alone
Opus Arte OA CD9020 D; 2014; CD
Piano
Light dialect

3838

Ride On, King Jesus (Toccata) [from *Cantata*]
Carter, John D.
Brewer, Christine (Soprano)
Saint Louis Woman
Opera Theatre of Saint Louis OTSL CD93;
    1993; CD
Piano
No dialect discerned

3839

Ride On, King Jesus (Toccata) [from *Cantata*]
Carter, John D.
Brewer, Christine (Soprano)
*Songs by Wagner, Wolf, Britten and John
    Carter*
Wigmore Hall Live WHLive0022; 2008; CD
Piano
No dialect discerned

3840

Ride On, King Jesus
Okpebholo, Shawn
Bridges, J'nai (Mezzo-soprano)
Lord How Come Me Here?
Navona Records NV6408; 2022; CD
Piano
Light dialect

3841

Ride On, King Jesus!
Johnson, Hall

Brown, Anthony (Baritone)
Spirituals
Brown/Smith Productions; 1995; CD
Piano
Light dialect

3842

Ride On, King Jesus
Johnson, Hall
Brown, Peggy Lee (Soprano)
Simply Peggy
Independent Records; 2003; CD
Piano
Light dialect

3843

Ride on, King [sic] Jesus
Dett, Robert Nathaniel
Brown, William (Tenor)
*Fi-Yer!: a century of African American
    song*
Albany Records TROY 329; 1999; CD
Piano
Light dialect

3844

Ride On, King Jesus
Johnson, Hall
Bryant, Peter (Vocalist)
I Will Pass This Way but Once
Facts of Faith Records WR 5161; 1977; LP
Organ

3845

Ride On, King Jesus
Johnson, Hall
Bumbry, Grace (Mezzo-soprano)
Portrait, A
Gala GL 100.539; 1999; CD
Piano
Light dialect

3846

Ride On, King Jesus!
Burleigh, Harry T.
Burton, Dashon (Bass-baritone)
*Songs of Struggle & Redemption: We Shall
    Overcome*
Acis Productions APL08685; 2015; CD

Piano
Moderate dialect

3847

Ride On, King Jesus
Burleigh, Harry T.
Carnette, Count (Vocalist)
Count Carnette Sings Favorite Negro Spirituals
Carnette Archive Recordings; 1983; LP
Piano
No dialect discerned

3848

Ride On, King Jesus
[Johnson, Hall]
Clifford, Rochelle Small (Soprano)
Sacred Spaces
Private Label; 2008; CD
Piano
No dialect discerned

3849

Ride On, King Jesus!
Johnson, Hall; Wilson. Robert
Conrad, Barbara (Mezzo-soprano)
Spirituals
Naxos 8.553036; 1995; CD
Orchestra
Heavy dialect

3850

Ride On, King Jesus
Johnson, Hall
Curtis, Nancy (Soprano)
Nancy Curtis
Nancy Curtis Productions; 2003; CD

3851

Ride On, King Jesus
Johnson, Hall
Davis, Ollie Watts (Soprano)
Here's One: Spiritual Songs
KJAC Publishing KJAC0123; 2003; CD
Piano
Heavy dialect

3852

Tocatta [sic] [from *Cantata*]
Carter, John D.; Link, Peter

Davis, Osceola (Soprano)
Climbing High Mountains
Watchfire Music; 2008; CD
Piano
No dialect discerned

3853

Ride On, King Jesus (Toccata) [from *Cantata*]
Carter, John D.
English-Robinson, Laura (Soprano)
Let It Shine!
ACA Digital Recording CM20020; 1994; CD
Piano
Light dialect

3854

Ride On, King Jesus!
Johnson, Hall
English-Robinson, Laura (Soprano)
Let It Shine!
ACA Digital Recording CM20020; 1994; CD
Piano
No dialect discerned

3855

Ride On, King Jesus
Roberts, Howard
Estes, Simon (Bass-baritone)
Spirituals
Philips 412 631-2; 1985; CD
Chorus, orchestra
Light dialect

　　　Also released with *Famous Spirituals* (Philips 462 062-2; 1997; CD)

3856

Ride On, King Jesus
Ryan, Donald
Estes, Simon (Bass-baritone)
Steal Away: My Favorite Negro Spirituals
Deutsche Schallplatten DS 1041-2; 1994;
　　CD
Piano
Light dialect

　　　Also released with *Simon Sings His Favorite Gospels & Spirituals* (Praise Productions SMG-SE; 1999; CD) and *Save the Children, Save Their Lives* (CD Baby; 2010; CD)

3857

Ride On, King Jesus
[Johnson, Hall]
Ferguson, Margaret (Soprano)
Margaret Ferguson
Private Label; [20--]; CD
Piano

3858

Ride On, King Jesus
Johnson, Hall
Fernandez, Wilhelmenia (Soprano)
Spirituals
Tioch Digital Records TD 1009; 1982; LP
Piano
Moderate dialect

    Also released with *Negro Spirituals* (Milan A 192; 1982; LP); *Sings Favorite Spirituals* (Phoenix PHCD 134; 1997; CD) and *Negro Spirituals* (Transart 131; 2005; CD)

3859

Ride On, King Jesus
Johnson, Paul [Hall]
Foye, Hope (Soprano)
The Best of Hope Foye: 20th and 21st Century Legendary Song Collection
Permanent Productions PP00115; 2010; CD

3860

Ride On, King Jesus
[Johnson, Hall]
Foye, Hope (Soprano)
Singing Her Song: The Story of Hope Foye
Union Bank of California; 2008; CD
Piano
No dialect discerned

3861

Ride On, King Jesus
Johnson, Hall
Gibson, Caroline (Soprano)
On Ma Journey Now: Negro Spirituals in Concert
Twin Productions; 2016; CD
Piano
Moderate dialect

3862

Ride On, King Jesus (Toccata) [from *Cantata*]
Carter, John D.
Givens, Melissa (Soprano)
Let the Rain Kiss You
Divameg Productions 141434; 2001; CD
Piano

3863

Toccata [from *Cantata*]
Carter, John D.
Gormley, Clare (Soprano)
Where Morning Lies: Spiritual Songs
ABC Classics 461 766-2; 2002; CD
Piano
Light dialect

3864

Ride On, King Jesus
Composer not identified
Green, Elnora E. (Contralto)
15 Spirituals
Private Label J3RS 2286; 1979; LP
Piano

3865

Ride On, King Jesus
[Johnson, Hall]
Hagen-William, Louis (Bass-baritone)
Negro Spirituals
Quantum QM 6909; 1993; CD
Piano
Moderate dialect

3866

Ride On, King Jesus
Boatner, Edward
Heard, Richard (Tenor)
Ain't a That Good News: African-American Art Songs and Spirituals
HM Classics HMC9602; 1998; CD
Piano
Moderate dialect

3867

Ride On, King Jesus
Composer not identified
Hines, Jerome (Bass)

Black & White Spirituals
Supreme S 3005; 1974; LP

3868
Ride On, King Jesus
Johnson, Hall
Holland, Charles (Tenor)
My Lord What a Mornin'
Musical Heritage Society MHS 912250X;
    1982; LP
Piano
Light dialect

Also released with *My Lord What a Mornin'* (Musical Heritage Society MHS 512250K; 1988; CD)

3869
Ride On, King Jesus
Johnson, Hall
Holmes, Eugene (Baritone)
Eugene Holmes Sings Spirituals
Avant Garde AV-115; [1968]; LP
Piano
Light dialect

Also released with *Spirituals* (Schubert Records SCH-102; [1988]; LP)

3870
Ride On, King Jesus
Johnson, Hall
Honeysucker, Robert (Baritone)
Good News
Videmus Records VIS735; 2007; CD
Piano
Light dialect

3871
Ride On, King Jesus
Johnson, Hall
Hynninen, Jorma (Bass-baritone)
Negro Spirituals
Ondine ODE 715-2; 1988; CD
Piano

3872
Ride On, King Jesus
Johnson, Hall
Ingram, Paula Dione (Soprano)

Art. Legacy. Celebration: A Salute to Black-American Composers of Art Songs and Spirituals, v. 1
Private Label; 2014; CD
Piano

3873
Toccata (Ride On, King Jesus) [from *Cantata*]
Carter, John D.
Jones, Randye (Soprano)
Come Down Angels
Ahhjay Records AHHJ-0001; 2003; CD
Piano
Light dialect

3874
Ride On, King Jesus [from *Five Spirituals for Baritone and Cello*]
Balentine, James Scott
Jones, Timothy (Baritone)
Love Comes in at the Eye
Albany TROY1734; 2018; CD
Cello
Moderate dialect

3875
Ride On, King Jesus
Johnson, Hall
Knight, Sadie (Soprano)
Town Hall Concerts
LF Artists LP-SRS-012; [1970]; LP
Piano

3876
Ride On, King Jesus
Johnson, Hall
Lewis, Cheryse McLeod (Mezzo-soprano)
Spirituals
CheryseMusic; 2012; CD
Piano

3877
Ride On, King Jesus
Johnson, Hall
Little, Ricky (Baritone)
The Lily of the Valley
American Spiritual Ensemble; [2003]; CD
Piano

3878

Ride On, King Jesus
Burleigh, Harry T.
Little, Vera (Mezzo-soprano)
My Good Lord Done Been Here
Decca 123737; 1957; LP
Piano

3879

Ride On, King Jesus
Meyer, Fredrich
London, George (Bass-baritone)
Spirituals
Deutsche Grammophon 00289 477 6193;
    2006; CD
Chorus
Moderate dialect

3880

Ride On, King Jesus!
Johnson, Hall
Lynch, Lester (Baritone)
On My Journey Now: Spirituals & Hymns
Pentatone Music PTC 5186 57'; 2017; CD
Piano

3881

Ride On, King Jesus
Johnson, Hall
Mayes, Doris (Mezzo-soprano)
Deep River
La voix de son maître FDLP 1080; 1959; LP
Piano

3882

Ride On, King Jesus
Raphael, Michael
Maynor, Kevin (Bass)
The Spiritual: An Underground Railroad
Southeastern Virginia Arts Assoc.; [2000];
    CD
Piano

3883

Ride On, King Jesus
Composer not identified
McFerrin, Robert (Baritone)
Negro Spirituals
Jacques Canetti 27 193; 1965; 45 RPM

Piano
Moderate dialect

    Also released with *Deep River and Other Classic Negro Spirituals* (Riverside Records RLP 12-812; 1959; LP) and *Classic Negro Spirituals* (Washington Records WLP 466; 1959; LP)

3884

Ride On, King Jesus
Johnson, Hall
Miles, John (Tenor)
The Classic Spirituals
Epiphany 83-1027; 1983; LP
Instrumental ensemble

3885

Ride On, King Jesus
Johnson, Hall
Miller, Jeanette (Soprano)
No Man Canna Hinder Me
MiJon Record Productions MJ240; 1979;
    CD
Piano

3886

Toccata (Ride On, King Jesus) [from *Cantata*]
Carter, John D.
Miller, Timothy (Tenor)
*Bound for the Promised Land: Songs and
    Words of Equality and Freedom*
Albany Records TROY1798; 2019; CD
Piano

3887

Ride On, King Jesus
Johnson, Hall
Mims, A. Grace Lee (Soprano)
Spirituals
H & GM Records HGM 8101; 1981; LP
Piano
Moderate dialect

3888

Ride On, King Jesus
Johnson, Hall; Fax, Mark
Norman, Jessye (Soprano)
Spirituals in Concert
Deutsche Grammophon 429 790-2; 1991; CD

Orchestra
Moderate dialect

3889

Ride On, King Jesus
Johnson, Hall
Oby, Jason (Tenor)
The Life of Christ: Collected Spirituals
Private Label TSU4749; [200-]; CD
Piano
Moderate dialect

3890

Ride On, King Jesus!
Burleigh, Harry T.
Philogene, Ruby (Soprano)
Steal Away
EMI Classics 7243 5 69707 2 4; 1997; CD
Piano

3891

Ride On, King Jesus (Toccata) [from
    Cantata]
Carter, John D.
Pickens, Jo Ann (Soprano)
*My Heritage: American Melodies/Negro
    Spirituals*
Koch Schwann 3-1447-2; 1993; CD

3892

Ride On, King Jesus
Johnson, Hall
Pierson, Edward (Bass-baritone)
*Edward Pierson Sings Hymns and
    Spirituals*
Kemco 98-44; [19--]; LP

3893

Ride On, King Jesus
Composer not identified
Pleas III, Henry H. (Tenor)
Deep River: A Spiritual Journey
Rowe House Productions; 1999; CD

3894

Ride On, King Jesus (Toccata) [from
    Cantata]
[Carter, John D.]
Pleas III, Henry H. (Tenor)

Cantata
Private Label; 2003; CD
Piano

3895

Ride On, King Jesus
Composer not identified
Price, Eudora (Vocalist)
My Favorite Songs & Spirituals
Private Label; 2006; CD
Organ
Light dialect

3896

Ride On, King Jesus
Composer not identified
Price, Eudora (Vocalist)
*Classic Duo Serbia Meets New York:
    From Handel to Spirituals*
Private Label; 2007; CD
Piano

3897

Ride On, King Jesus
Composer not identified
Price, Leontyne (Soprano)
Great Moments at Carnegie Hall
RCA Red Seal 88985304202; 2016; CD
Piano
Heavy dialect

3898

Ride On, King Jesus
Johnson, Hall; de Paur, Leonard
Price, Leontyne (Soprano)
Swing Low, Sweet Chariot: Fourteen Spirituals
RCA Victor LSC 2600; 1962; LP
Chorus, orchestra
Heavy dialect

3899

Ride On, King Jesus!
Johnson, Hall
Price, Leontyne (Soprano)
*Leontyne Price Live! At the Historic
    Opening of the Ordway Music Theatre*
Pro Arte CDD 231; 1985; CD
Piano
Heavy dialect

3900

Ride On, King Jesus: Spiritual
Johnson, Hall
Price, Leontyne (Soprano)
Return to Carnegie Hall
RCA Victor Red Seal 09026-68435-2; 1996;
    CD
Piano
Heavy dialect

3901

Ride On, King Jesus
Johnson, Hall; de Paur, Leonard
Price, Leontyne (Soprano)
The Essential Leontyne Price
BMG Classics 09026-68153-2; 1996; CD
Chorus, orchestra
Heavy dialect

Also released with *The Essential Leontyne Price: Spirituals, Hymns & Sacred Songs* (BMG Classics 09026-68157-2; 1996; CD); *Complete Collection of Songs and Spiritual Albums* (RCA Red Seal 88697940502; 2011; CD) and *Leontyne Price Sings Spirituals* (RCA Red Seal 88691928242; 2012; CD)

3902

Ride On, King Jesus
Johnson, Hall; de Paur, Leonard
Price, Leontyne (Soprano)
Singers of the Century: Leontyne Price: Spiritual and Religious Songs
Jube Classic; 2016; Streaming audio
Chorus, orchestra
Heavy dialect

3903

Ride On, King Jesus
Johnson, John Rosamond
Price, Leontyne (Soprano)
Christmas' Greatest Voices
RCA Victor 09026682652; 1995; CD
Chorus, orchestra
Heavy dialect

3904

Ride On, King Jesus!
Johnson, Hall
Quivar, Florence (Mezzo-soprano)
Negro Spirituals
EMI 7243 5 72790 2 4; 1998; CD
Piano
Heavy dialect

Also released with *Ride On, King Jesus! Florence Quivar Sings Black Music of America* (EMI Classics 9 67138 2; 2010; CD)

3905

Ride On, King Jesus
Burleigh, Harry T.
Ray, Carline (Contralto)
Music for Contralto & Piano
Music Minus One MMO 9021; 1995; Score w/CD
Piano

3906

Ride On, King Jesus
Burleigh, Harry T.
Salters, Stephen (Baritone)
Spirit: Are You There, You Are There
HarmonizedDisharmony 0001; 2015; CD

3907

Ride On, King Jesus
Johnson, Hall
Simpson, Icy (Soprano)
I, Too
Longhorn Music; 2012; CD
Piano

3908

Ride On, King Jesus
Johnson, Hall
Slack, Karen (Soprano)
Swing Low, Sweet Chariot
American Spiritual Ensemble; 2011; CD

3909

Ride On, King Jesus
Johnson, Hall
Straughter, Maralyn (Soprano)
Negro Spirituals of Hall Johnson
Variety Recording Service Var 0753; [196-];
    LP
Piano

3910

Ride On, King Jesus
Composer not identified
Stuart, Avon (Baritone)
Avon Stuart Recital
Edition Rhodos ERS 1218; 1975; LP
Piano

3911

Ride On, King Jesus
Rice, Mark
Sykes, Jubilant (Baritone)
Jubilant Sykes Sings Copland and Spirituals
Arioso Classics AC 00011; 2008; CD
Orchestra

3912

Ride On, King Jesus
Johnson, Hall
Thomas, Indra (Soprano)
Great Day: Indra Thomas Sings Spirituals
Delos DE 3427; 2012; CD
Piano
Light dialect

3913

Ride On, King Jesus
[Johnson, Hall]
Thompson, Derrick (Baritone)
Spirituals
Private Label; 2014; CD
Piano
No dialect discerned

3914

Toccata: Ride On, King Jesus
[Carter, John D.]
Thoms, Treva (Soprano)
Come Sunday: Sacred American Songs
Private Label; 2007; CD
Piano

3915

Ride On, King Jesus! [from *Son of Man*]
Johnson, Hall
Toppin, Louise (Soprano)
The Hall Johnson Collection
Carl Fischer VF5 CD1–VF5 CD2; 2003; Score
  w/CD

Piano
Moderate dialect

3916

Ride On, King Jesus [from *Cantata*]
[Carter, John D.]
Verdejo, Awilda (Soprano)
Awilda Verdejo Sings Spirituals
Angeluz Performances; 1999; CD
Piano

3917

Ride On, King Jesus (Toccata) [from
  Cantata]
Carter, John D.
Wade, Ray, Jr. (Tenor)
Sence You Went Away
Albany Records TROY 387; 1998; CD
Piano
Moderate dialect

3918

Ride On, King Jesus
Composer not identified
West, Lucretia (Mezzo-soprano)
Lucretia West Sings Spirituals
Westminster WP 6063; [1957]; LP

3919

Ride On, King Jesus
Morgenstern, Sam
West, Lucretia (Mezzo-soprano)
Spirituals
Westminster WL 5338; 1954; LP
Orchestra

3920

Ride On, King Jesus
Composer not identified
White, Portia (Contralto)
Think on Me
White House Records WH-6901; 1968; LP
Piano

3921

Ride On, King Jesus
Composer not identified
White, Portia (Contralto)
First You Dream

C. White PW 001-2; 1990s; CD
Piano

3922

Ride On, King Jesus (Toccata) [from
   Cantata]
Carter, John D.
Williams, Wayne (Tenor)
Music from My Life
Movideo Productions 02-1993; 1993; CD
Piano

3923

Ride On, King Jesus
Johnson, Hall
Wilson, Robin (Soprano)
*Best of the Hall Johnson Centennial Festival
   Celebrating the 100th Anniversary of Hall
   Johnson's Birth*
Hall Johnson Collection O33D2; 2002; CD
Piano

3924

Ride On, King Jesus
Johnson, Hall
Yovanovich, Amy (Mezzo-soprano)
Great Day!
Prince Productions 9808P; 2007; CD
Piano
Light dialect

. . . .

Ride Up in the Chariot

3925

Ride in the Chariot
Simpson, Elmur
Matthews, Benjamin (Baritone)
Bon Voyage Recital @ McCormick Place
S.P.S. SS-8993-018; 1966; LP
Piano

3926

Ride the Chariot
Smith, William
Forest, Michael (Tenor)
The Spirit Sings: American Spirituals
Shenandoah Conservatory SU003; [199-]; CD
Chorus

3927

Ride the Chariot
Smith, Hale
Ragin, Derek Lee (Countertenor); Clansy,
   Cheryl (Soprano)
Negro Spirituals
Virgin Classics 0946 363305 2 5; 2006; CD
Chorus
Light dialect

3928

Ride Up in the Chariot
Jackson King, Betty; Joubert, Joseph;
   Cooper, Tyron
Brown, Angela (Soprano)
*Mosiac: A Collection of African-American
   Spirituals with Piano, guitar*
Albany Records TROY721; 2004; CD
Piano, guitar
Moderate dialect

3929

Goin' to Ride Up in de Chariot
Composer not identified
Carey, Thomas (Baritone)
*Sechs Amerikanische Volkslieder/Sechs
   Negro Spirituals*
Colosseum SM 3003; 1970; LP
Orchestra

3930

Ride Up in the Chariot
Composer not identified
Charles, Lee (Tenor)
Swing Low Sweet Chariot: And Other Spirituals
Riverside RLP 12-651; 1957; LP
Piano, guitar

3931

Ride Up in the Chariot
Jackson King, Betty
Cunningham-Fleming, Jeryl (Soprano)
The Lily of the Valley
American Spiritual Ensemble; [2003]; CD
Piano

3932

Ride Up in the Chariot
Joubert, Joseph

Cunningham-Fleming, Jeryl (Soprano);
   Brown, Angela (Soprano)
The Lily of the Valley
American Spiritual Ensemble; [2003]; CD

3933
Ride Up in the Chariot
Jackson King, Betty
Davis, Ollie Watts (Soprano)
Here's One: Spiritual Songs
KJAC Publishing KJAC0123; 2003; CD
Piano
Heavy dialect

3934
Ride Up in the Chariot (after B.J. King)
   [from *Four Spirituals for Soprano and
   String Quartet*]
Taylor, Stephen Andrew
Davis, Ollie Watts (Soprano)
Rootsongs
Azica AZI 71311; 2016; CD
Instrumental ensemble
Moderate dialect

3935
Ride Up in the Chariot
Jackson King, Betty; Link, Peter
Davis, Osceola (Soprano)
Climbing High Mountains
Watchfire Music; 2008; CD
Piano
Moderate dialect

3936
Ride Up in de Chariot
Composer not identified
Delmore, Harry A. (Tenor)
*Oh de Lan' I Am Boun' for/Ride Up in de
   Chariot*
Radiex 4166; [19--]; 78 RPM

3937
Ride Up in the Chariot
Jackson King, Betty
Dixon, Janice (Soprano)
The Beauty of Two Worlds
Finetone; 2015; CD
Piano
Moderate dialect

3938
Going to Rise Up in de Chariot
Brown, Lawrence
Duncan, Todd (Baritone)
African American Spirituals
[Apple Music]; 2008; Streaming audio
Piano
Heavy dialect

3939
Goin' to Ride Up in de Chariot
Brown, Lawrence
Duncan, Todd (Baritone)
Negro Spirituals
Allegro ALG3022; [1952]; LP
Piano

3940
Ride Up in the Chariot
Jackson King, Betty
English-Robinson, Laura (Soprano)
Let It Shine!
ACA Digital Recording CM20020; 1994; CD
Piano
Light dialect

3941
Ride Up in the Chariot
Jackson King, Betty
Harris, Inetta (Soprano)
*My Heritage Sings: A Selection of Spirituals
   & Hymns*
Private Label; [199-]; CD
Piano

3942
Ride Up in the Chariot
Jackson King, Betty
Hill, Heather (Soprano)
Swing Low, Sweet Chariot
American Spiritual Ensemble; 2011; CD

3943
Ride Up in the Chariot
Composer not identified
Humphrey Flynn, Edwina (Soprano)
The Lord Will Make a Way
Private Label; 2000; CD
Piano

3944

Goin' to Ride Up in the Chariot
Composer not identified
Jones, Fanni (Mezzo-soprano)
Negro Spirituals
Phonotec 815; 1977; LP
Organ

3945

Gonna Ride Up in de Chariot
Withers, Byron
Matthews, Inez (Mezzo-soprano)
Inez Matthews Sings Spirituals
Essential Media Group; 2011; CD
Piano
Heavy dialect

3946

Gonna Ride Up in de Chariot
Withers, Byron
Matthews, Inez (Mezzo-soprano)
Inez Matthews Sings Spirituals (Great New Voices of Today, v. 6)
Period SPL-580; [1950]; LP
Piano
Heavy dialect

3947

Gwinter Ride Up in de Chariot soon-a in de mornin'
Johnson, John Rosamond
Mims, A. Grace Lee (Soprano)
Spirituals
H & GM Records HGM 8101; 1981; LP
Piano
Heavy dialect

3948

Ride Up in the Chariot
Composer not identified
Parks, Karen (Soprano)
Done Crossed Every River: Freedom's Journey
Arcadia ARC 2004-2; 1995; CD

3949

Ride Up in the Chariot
Jackson King, Betty
Parks, Karen (Soprano)

Opera Ebony Sings Spirituals
Ebony Classic Recordings; 2002; CD

3950

Gonna Ride Up in the Chariot
Swanson, Howard
Peterson, Elwood (Baritone)
Negro Spirituals
Boîte à Musique LD 073; 1961; LP
Piano

3951

Goin' to Ride Up in de Chariot
Brown, Lawrence
Robeson, Paul (Bass-baritone)
Swing Low, Sweet Chariot
Columbia Masterworks MM-819; 1949; 78 RPM
Piano

3952

Goin' to Ride Up in de Chariot
Brown, Lawrence
Robeson, Paul (Bass-baritone); Brown, Lawrence (Vocalist)
Paul Robeson Chante ... 16 Spirituals
Philips G 05.639 R; 1959; LP
Piano

3953

Goin' to Ride Up in de Chariot
Brown, Lawrence
Robeson, Paul (Bass-baritone); Brown, Lawrence (Vocalist)
The Complete EMI Sessions (1928–1939)
EMI Classics 50999 2 15586 2 7; 2008; CD
Piano
Heavy dialect

3954

Goin' to Ride Up in de Chariot
Brown, Lawrence
Robeson, Paul (Bass-baritone)
Paul Robeson Sings Negro Spirituals
Philips GBL 5584; [19--]; LP
Piano

3955

Goin' to Ride Up in de Chariot
[Brown, Lawrence]

Robeson, Paul (Bass-baritone)
Negro Spirituals, v. 2
Philips NBE11102; 1956; 7" Vinyl

3956

Goin' to Ride Up in de Chariot
[Brown, Lawrence]
Robeson, Paul (Bass-baritone); Brown,
　Lawrence (Vocalist)
The Ultimate Collection
Burning Fire; 2009; Streaming audio
Piano
Heavy dialect

3957

Goin' to Ride Up in de Chariot
[Brown, Lawrence]
Robeson, Paul (Bass-baritone)
Swing Low, Sweet Chariot
Columbia Masterworks ML 2038; [195-]; LP
Piano

3958

Ride Up in the Chariot
Composer not identified
Robinson, Marie Hadley (Soprano)
Come Down Angels
Meyer Media; 2011; Streaming audio
Piano
Moderate dialect

3959

Ride Up in the Chariot
Jackson King, Betty
Salters, Stephen (Baritone)
Stephen Salters/Shiela Kibbe
Musica Numeris CYP 9602; 2005; CD

3960

Ride Up in the Chariot
Jackson King, Betty
Salters, Stephen (Baritone)
Spirit: Are You There, You Are There
HarmonizedDisharmony 0001; 2015; CD

3961

Goin' to Ride Up in de Chariot
[Brown, Lawrence]
Spencer, Kenneth (Bass-baritone)

American Spirituals
Sonora MS-478; [1945]; 78 RPM
Piano
Heavy dialect

3962

Ride Up in the Chariot
Jackson King, Betty
Toppin, Louise (Soprano)
Ah! Love, But a Day
Albany Records/ Videmus TROY 385; 2000;
　CD
Piano
Heavy dialect

3963

Ride Up in de Chariot
Jackson King, Betty
Wimberly, Brenda (Soprano)
The New Negro Spiritual
W. C. Patterson; 2002; Score w/CD
Piano
Heavy dialect

· · · · · · ·

Rise Up, Shepherd

3964

Rise Up, Shepherd
Composer not identified
Battle, Kathleen (Soprano)
A Christmas Celebration
EMI CDC-7 47587 2; 1986; CD
Chorus, orchestra
No dialect discerned

3965

Rise Up, Shepherd
Sadin, Robert
Battle, Kathleen (Soprano)
Negro Spirituals
EMI 7243 5 72790 2 4; 1998; CD
Chorus, orchestra
No dialect discerned

3966

Rise Up Shepherd and Follow
Hayes, Mark
Black, Randall (Tenor)

All Is Calm, All Is Bright: A Collection of Christmas Carols and Spirituals
Private label; 2006; CD
Piano

3967

Rise Up, Shepherd, and Follow
Mills, Marvin
Graves, Denyce (Mezzo-soprano)
Angels Watching Over Me
NPR Classics CD 0006; 1997; CD
Piano
Light dialect

3968

Rise Up, Shepherd, and Follow
Composer not identified
Hendricks, Barbara (Soprano)
Shout for Joy: Spiritual Christmas (Noël sacré)
Arte Verum ARV-009; 2010; CD
Instrumental ensemble
Moderate dialect

3969

Rise Up, Shepherd, an' Foller
Dett, Robert Nathaniel
Maynor, Dorothy (Soprano)
Negro Spirituals
RCA Victor M879; 1942; 78 RPM
Men's voices

3970

Rise Up Shepherd and Foller
Dett, Robert Nathaniel
Maynor, Dorothy (Soprano)
Dorothy Maynor Sings Spirituals and Sacred Songs
RCA Camden CAL-344; 1957; LP
Chorus

3971

Rise Up Shepherd and Foller
Dett, Robert Nathaniel
Maynor, Dorothy (Soprano)
Spirituals, Arias, Songs ([1940]1943)
Claremont CD GSE 78-50-59; 1994; CD
Chorus

3972

Rise Up, Shepherd, an' Foller
Dett, Robert Nathaniel
Maynor, Dorothy (Soprano)
Negro Spirituals
Kipepeo Publishing; 2018; CD
Men's voices

3973

Rise Up Shepherd and Foller
Dorsey, ?
Oglesby, Isador (Tenor)
Life of Jesus in Negro Spirituals
Oglesby Recordings Album 2; 1980; LP
Piano

3974

Rise Up Shepherd
Composer not identified
White, Portia (Contralto)
Great Voices of Canada, v. 5: Sing Christmas
Analekta AN 2 7806; 1994; CD
Piano
Light dialect

3975

Rise Up, Shepherd
Young, Thomas J.
Young, Thomas (Tenor)
Black Christmas: Spirituals in the African-American Tradition
Essay Recordings CD1011; 1990; CD
Piano
No dialect discerned

3976

Rise Up, Shepherd
Young, Thomas J.
Young, Thomas (Tenor)
A Spiritual Christmas
Musical Heritage Society 5167448; 2002; CD
Piano
No dialect discerned

. . . .

Rise, Shine, Give God the Glory

3977

Rise, Shine, Give God the Glory
Lloyd, Charles, Jr.
Paige-Green, Jacqueline (Soprano)
The Spiritual Art Song Collection
Warner Bros. SVBM00004; 2000; Score w/
    CD
Piano

. . . .

Rock My Soul in the Bosom of Abraham

3978

Rock My Soul in the Bosom of Abraham
Composer not identified
Spencer, Kenneth (Bass-baritone)
Negro Spirituals
Life Records C 1108; [19--]; LP

3979

Rock o' My Soul
Composer not identified
Thomas, Edna (Soprano)
*Somebody's Knockin' at Your Door/Rock o'
    My Soul*
Columbia 3473; 1924; 78 RPM
Orchestra

. . . .

Rockin' Jerusalem

3980

Rockin' Jerusalem
Composer not identified
Humphrey Flynn, Edwina (Soprano)
The Lord Will Make a Way
Private Label; 2000; CD
Percussion

3981

Rockin' Jerusalem
Work, John Wesley
Koehler, Hope (Soprano)

The Spirit of the Holidays
American Spiritual Ensemble; 2009; CD

3982

Rockin' Jerusalem! (Dramatic Declaration)
    [from *Lyric Suite*]
Morris, Robert L.
Toppin, Louise (Soprano)
*Heart on the Wall: African American Art
    Songs for Orchestra*
Albany Records TROY1314; 2011; CD
Orchestra
Heavy dialect

. . . .

Roll de Ole Chariot Along

3983

Roll de Ole Chariot Along
Clapham, Ruthland
Robeson, Paul (Bass-baritone)
The Complete EMI Sessions (1928–1939)
EMI Classics 50999 2 15586 2 7; 2008; CD
Piano
Heavy dialect

3984

Roll de Ole Chariot Along
Clapham, Ruthland; Robeson, Paul
Robeson, Paul (Bass-baritone)
Paul Robeson
World Record Club W9648/EMI SM 431;
    [19--]; LP
Piano

. . . .

Roll, Jordan, Roll

3985

Roll, Jerd'n, Roll!
Johnson, Hall
Anderson, Marian (Contralto)
Spirituals
RCA Victor Red Seal 09026-63306-2; 1999;
    CD
Piano
Heavy dialect

3986

Roll, Jerd'n, Roll!
Johnson, Hall
Anderson, Marian (Contralto)
*Marian Anderson: Beyond the Music; Her
　Complete RCA Victor Recordings*
Sony Classical 19439836492; 2021; CD
Piano
Heavy dialect

3987

Roll, Jerd'n, Roll!
Johnson, Hall
Anderson, Marian (Contralto)
Negro Spirituals
RCA Victor LM 2032; [1956]; LP
Piano
Heavy dialect

3988

Roll, Jerd'n, Roll!
[Johnson, Hall]
Anderson, Marian (Contralto)
*Marian Anderson Sings Eleven Great
　Spirituals*
RCA Victor LRM 7006; 1955; LP
Piano

3989

Roll, Jordan, Roll
[Johnson, Hall]
Anderson, Marian (Contralto)
Inspiration in Song
Demand Performance DPC-521; 1987;
　Cassette

3990

Roll, Jerd'n, Roll!
[Johnson, Hall]
Anderson, Marian (Contralto)
Alto Rhapsody; Selected Spirituals
Urania URN 22.328; 2007; CD
Piano

3991

Roll, Jerd'n, Roll!
[Johnson, Hall]
Anderson, Marian (Contralto)

The Very Best of Marian Anderson
Master Classics Records; 2009; CD
Piano
Moderate dialect

3992

Roll, Jerd'n, Roll!
[Johnson, Hall]
Anderson, Marian (Contralto)
*Marian Anderson Sings Eleven Great
　Spirituals*
Kipepeo Publishing; 2017; CD
Piano

3993

Roll and Roll
[Johnson, Hall]
Anderson, Marian (Contralto)
*Grandes Contraltos de la Musique Classique,
　Les: Marian Anderson, Vol. 10*
Mon Patrimoine Musical Collection; 2017;
　Streaming audio
Piano

3994

Roll, Jord'n, Roll
[Johnson, Hall]
Anderson, Marian (Contralto)
Negro Spirituals
RCA Gold Seal RVC-1570; [19--]; LP
Piano

3995

Roll, Jerd'n, Roll!
[Johnson, Hall]
Anderson, Marian (Contralto)
Negro Spirituals
RCA Victor 630.396 A; [19--]; LP
Piano

3996

Roll, Jordan, Roll (Container: Roll, Jerd'n,
　Roll)
Johnson, Hall
Blackmon, Henry (Baritone)
Negro Spirituals
Stichting St. Josefkerk Discofonds
　Leidschendam JK 1006; [1964]; 45 RPM
Organ

3997
Roll, Jordan, Roll
Johnson, Hall
Duncan, Todd (Baritone)
African American Spirituals
[Apple Music]; 2008; Streaming audio
Piano
Heavy dialect

3998
Roll, Jerd'n, Roll!
Johnson, Hall
Duncan, Todd (Baritone)
Negro Spirituals
Allegro ALG3022; [1952]; LP
Piano

3999
Roll, Jerdin, Roll!
[Johnson, Hall]
Duncan, Todd (Baritone)
American Negro Spirituals
Allegro LEG 9026; [19--]; LP

4000
Roll, Jerd'n Roll
[Johnson, Hall]
Duncan, Todd (Baritone)
America's Great Baritone: Sings Folk Songs
Royale EP181; [195-]; 45 RPM

4001
Roll, Jord'n Roll
[Johnson, Hall]
Duncan, Todd (Baritone)
Spirituals
Royale 1810; [1950]; LP

4002
Roll, Jordan, Roll
Ryan, Donald
Estes, Simon (Bass-baritone)
Steal Away: My Favorite Negro Spirituals
Deutsche Schallplatten DS 1041-2; 1994;
    CD
Piano
Moderate dialect

4003
Roll, Jerd'n Roll
Johnson, Hall
Foreman, Blanche (Contralto)
*Best of the Hall Johnson Centennial Festival
    Celebrating the 100th Anniversary of Hall
    Johnson's Birth*
Hall Johnson Collection O33D2; 2002;
    CD
Piano

4004
Roll, Jordan, Roll
Mills, Marvin
Graves, Denyce (Mezzo-soprano)
Angels Watching Over Me
NPR Classics CD 0006; 1997; CD
Piano
Moderate dialect

4005
Roll, Jerd'n, Roll
Composer not identified
Green, Elnora E. (Contralto)
15 Spirituals
Private Label J3RS 2286; 1979; LP
Piano

4006
Roll, Jerd'n Roll
Johnson, Hall
Holland, Charles (Tenor)
My Lord What a Mornin'
Musical Heritage Society MHS 912250X;
    1982; LP
Piano
Heavy dialect

4007
Roll, Jerd'n Roll
Johnson, Hall
Holland, Charles (Tenor)
My Lord What a Mornin'
Musical Heritage Society MHS 512250K;
    1988; CD
Piano
Heavy dialect

4008

Roll Jordon Roll
Composer not identified
Humphrey Flynn, Edwina (Soprano)
The Lord Will Make a Way
Private Label; 2000; CD
Piano

4009

Roll Jordan Roll
Composer not identified
Hunt, Arthur Billings (Baritone)
Hymns and Spirituals
Cook Laboratories 1090; [195-]; LP
Organ

4010

Roll, Jerd'n, Roll
Johnson, Hall
Jones, Randye (Soprano)
Come Down Angels
Ahhjay Records AHHJ-0001; 2003; CD
Piano
Heavy dialect

4011

Roll Jordan, Roll
Lloyd, Charles, Jr.; Norman, Jessye
Norman, Jessye (Soprano)
Great Day in the Morning
Philips 6769 104; 1982; LP
Chorus
Heavy dialect

4012

Roll, Jordan, Roll
Johnson, Hall
Oglesby, Isador (Tenor)
Isador Sings Negro Spirituals
Oglesby Recordings Album 3; 1983; LP
Piano

4013

Roll, Jerd'n, Roll
Johnson, Hall
Simpson, Eugene Thamon (Bass)
Honors and Arms
Black Heritage Publications; 2005; CD
Piano

4014

Roll Jerd'n, Roll
Johnson, Hall
Simpson, Eugene Thamon (Bass)
*Hall Johnson Spirituals and Other Folk
    Songs*
Private Label; 2016; CD
Piano

4015

Roll, Jord'n, Roll
Composer not identified
Spencer, Kenneth (Bass-baritone)
Alte Lied von Alabama, Das
Vollstaedt CDRV2337; 2010; CD
Orchestra

4016

Roll, Jord'n, Roll
Composer not identified
Spencer, Kenneth (Bass-baritone)
Heimweh Nach Virginia
Music Tales 2087269; 2015; CD

4017

Roll, Jord'n, Roll!
Kuhn,
Spencer, Kenneth (Bass-baritone)
Spirituals Sung by Kenneth Spencer
E.M.I. Records Ltd. SEG 7813; [19--]; 45
    RPM

4018

Roll Jord'n Roll
Johnson, Hall
Toppin, Louise (Soprano)
*He'll Bring It to Pass: The Spirituals of Hall
    Johnson for Voice and Piano*
Albany Records TROY846; 2006; CD
Piano
Heavy dialect

4019

Roll Jord'n Roll
Johnson, Hall
Verrett, Shirley (Mezzo-soprano)
Shirley Verrett Recital
Suiza OSCD 223; 1991; CD
Piano

4020
Roll Jord'n Roll
[Johnson, Hall]
Verrett, Shirley (Mezzo-soprano)
Gospels & Spirituals Gold Collection
Retro R2CD 40-26; 1995; CD
Piano
Heavy dialect

4021
Roll Jordan Roll
Composer not identified
West, Lucretia (Mezzo-soprano)
Lucretia West Sings Spirituals
Westminster WP 6063; [1957]; LP

4022
Roll, Jordan, Roll
Morgenstern, Sam
West, Lucretia (Mezzo-soprano)
Spirituals
Westminster WL 5338; 1954; LP
Men's voices

· · · · · · ·

Round About
the Mountain

4023
Roun' About de Mountain
Hayes, Roland; Brown, Angela; Cooper,
   Tyron
Brown, Angela (Soprano)
*Mosiac: A Collection of African-American
   Spirituals with Piano, guitar*
Albany Records TROY721; 2004; CD
Guitar
Light dialect

4024
Round About the Mountain
Hayes, Roland
Bryant, Peter (Vocalist)
I Will Pass This Way but Once
Facts of Faith Records WR 5161; 1977; LP
Organ

4025
Roun' About de Mountain
Hayes, Roland
Caesar, Jackson (Tenor)
*Spirituals: Celebrating the Music, Life,
   Legacy of Roland Hayes*
CD Baby 7048606059; 2021; CD
Piano, percussion
Moderate dialect

4026
Roun' About de Mountain
Hayes, Roland
Caesar, Jackson (Tenor)
*Spirituals: Celebrating the Music, Life,
   Legacy of Roland Hayes*
CD Baby 7048606059; 2021; CD
Piano
Moderate dialect

4027
Round About the Mountain
Composer not identified
Charles, Lee (Tenor)
*Swing Low Sweet Chariot: And Other
   Spirituals*
Riverside RLP 12-651; 1957; LP
Piano, guitar

4028
Round About the Mountain
[Hayes, Roland]
Cook, Dixon & Young (Tenor)
*Triptych: A Celebration of the Negro
   Spiritual*
CDY Records 649241879206; 2009; CD
Piano
Moderate dialect

4029
Round About de Mountain
Hayes, Roland; Link, Peter
Davis, Osceola (Soprano)
Climbing High Mountains
Watchfire Music; 2008; CD
Piano, orchestra
Light dialect

4030
Roun' About de Mountain
Hayes, Roland
Forest, Michael (Tenor)
The Spirit Sings: American Spirituals
Shenandoah Conservatory SU003; [199-];
    CD

4031
Round About the Mountain
Hayes, Roland
Graves, Denyce (Mezzo-soprano)
Angels Watching Over Me
NPR Classics CD 0006; 1997; CD
Chorus, piano
Heavy dialect

4032
Recessional ('Roun 'Bout de Mountain)
Composer not identified
Hayes, Roland (Tenor)
Classic Gospel Songs
Emerald/K-Tel; 2013; Streaming audio
Piano

4033
Roun' About the Mountain
Composer not identified
Hayes, Roland (Tenor)
*Roland Hayes Sings: Negro Spirituals,
    Aframerican Folk Songs*
Amadeo Records AVRS 6033; [19--]; LP
Piano

4034
Roun' About de Mountain
Hayes, Roland
Hayes, Roland (Tenor)
*The Art of Roland Hayes: Six Centuries of
    Song*
Preiser Records; 2010; CD
Piano
Heavy dialect

4035
Roun' 'Bout de Mountain
Parham, R. P.
Hayes, Roland (Tenor)
Song Recital, A

Columbia Masterworks M 393; 1939; 78 RPM
Piano

4036
Roun' 'Bout de Mountain
Parham, R. P.
Hayes, Roland (Tenor)
*Negro Spirituals: The Concert Tradition
    1909–1948*
Frémeaux & Associés FA 168; 1999; CD
Piano
Heavy dialect

4037
Round' 'Bout de Mountain
[Hayes, Roland]
Hayes, Roland (Tenor)
Art Songs and Spirituals
Veritas VM 112; 1967; LP
Piano
Heavy dialect

4038
Roun' bout de Mountain
[Hayes, Roland]
Hayes, Roland (Tenor)
*Brother, Can You Spare a Dime?: The Roots of
    American Song*
Pearl Gemm CD 9484; 1991; CD
Piano
Heavy dialect

4039
Roun' 'Bout de Mountain
[Hayes, Roland]
Hayes, Roland (Tenor)
Good News: Vintage Negro Spirituals
Living Era AJA 5622; 2006; CD
Piano
Heavy dialect

4040
Round bout the Mountain
[Hayes, Roland]
Hayes, Roland (Tenor)
Big Psalms, Hymns and Spirituals Box
eOne Music/Vanguard Classics; 2015;
    Streaming audio
Piano

4041

Roun' 'Bout the Mountain
[Hayes, Roland]
Hayes, Roland (Tenor)
The Concerto: African American Spirituals
Orange Amaro; 2019; Streaming audio
Piano

4042

Roun' About de Mountain
Hayes, Roland
Helm, Alicia (Soprano)
The Lily of the Valley
American Spiritual Ensemble; [2003]; CD
Piano

4043

Roun' About de Mountain
Composer not identified
Hendricks, Barbara (Soprano)
Espirituales Negros
EMI Classics/Altaya 01636; 1983; CD
Piano

4044

Roun' About de Mountain
Composer not identified
Hendricks, Barbara (Soprano)
Spirituals
EMI Classics 0946 346641 2 7; 2005; CD
Piano

4045

Roun' About de Mountain
Hendricks, Barbara; Alexeev, Dmitri
Hendricks, Barbara (Soprano)
Negro Spirituals
EMI CDC7470262; 1983; CD
Piano
Heavy dialect

4046

Round About the Mountain
Hicks, Lori
Hicks, Lori (Soprano)
Music of My Voice
CelestialSong Productions; 2015; CD
Piano

4047

Roun' About de Mountain
Hayes, Roland
Jones, Randye (Soprano)
Come Down Angels
Ahhjay Records AHHJ-0001; 2003; CD
Piano
Heavy dialect

4048

Round About de Mountain
Hayes, Roland
Matthews, Inez (Mezzo-soprano)
Inez Matthews Sings Spirituals
Period SPL-580; [1950]; LP
Piano
Moderate dialect

> Also released with *Inez Matthews Sings Spirituals* (Essential Media Group; 2011; CD)

4049

Round About the Mountain
Raphael, Michael
Maynor, Kevin (Bass)
The Spiritual: An Underground Railroad
Southeastern Virginia Arts Assoc.; [2000]; CD
Piano

4050

Roun about the Mountain
Hayes, Roland
Oglesby, Isador (Tenor)
Isador Sings Negro Spirituals
Oglesby Recordings Album 3; 1983; LP
Piano

4051

Roun' About de Mountain
de Paur, Leonard
Price, Leontyne (Soprano)
Leontyne Price Sings Spirituals
RCA Red Seal 88691928242; 2012; CD
Chorus, orchestra
Heavy dialect

4052

Roun' About de Mountain
Hayes, Roland; de Paur, Leonard

Price, Leontyne (Soprano)
*Swing Low, Sweet Chariot: Fourteen
    Spirituals*
RCA Victor LSC 2600; 1962; LP
Chorus, orchestra
Heavy dialect

4053

Roun' About de Mountain
Hayes, Roland; de Paur, Leonard
Price, Leontyne (Soprano)
*The Essential Leontyne Price: Spirituals,
    Hymns & Sacred Songs*
BMG Classics 09026-68157-2; 1996; CD
Chorus, orchestra
Heavy dialect

4054

Roun about de Mountain
Hayes, Roland
Price, Leontyne (Soprano)
The Essential Leontyne Price
BMG Classics 09026-68153-2; 1996; CD
Chorus, orchestra
Heavy dialect

4055

Roun' About the Mountain
Hayes, Roland; de Paur, Leonard
Price, Leontyne (Soprano)
*Complete Collection of Songs and Spiritual
    Albums*
RCA Red Seal 88697940502; 2011; CD
Orchestra

4056

Roun' About de Mountain
Hayes, Roland; de Paur, Leonard
Price, Leontyne (Soprano)
*Singers of the Century: Leontyne Price:
    Spiritual and Religious Songs*
Jube Classic; 2016; Streaming audio
Chorus, orchestra
Heavy dialect

4057

Roun' About de Mountain
Hayes, Roland
Quivar, Florence (Mezzo-soprano)

Great American Spirituals
Angel CDM 7 64669 2; 1992; CD
Piano
Heavy dialect

4058

Roun' About de Mountain
Hayes, Roland
Quivar, Florence (Mezzo-soprano)
Great American Spirituals
Musical Heritage Society 513725Z; 1994; CD
Piano
Heavy dialect

4059

Roun' About de Mountain
Hayes, Roland
Quivar, Florence (Mezzo-soprano)
Negro Spirituals
EMI 7243 5 72790 2 4; 1998; CD
Piano
Heavy dialect

4060

Roun' About de Mountain
Hayes, Roland
Quivar, Florence (Mezzo-soprano)
*Ride On, King Jesus! Florence Quivar Sings
    Black Music of America*
EMI Classics 9 67138 2; 2010; CD
Piano
Heavy dialect

4061

Round About de Mountain
Composer not identified
Robinson, Marie Hadley (Soprano)
Come Down Angels
Meyer Media; 2011; Streaming audio
Piano
Light dialect

4062

Round About de Mountain
McLin, Lena
Rucker, Mark (Baritone)
*Mark Rucker Sings Lena McLin: Songs for
    Voice & Piano*
Kjos Music Press KCD8; 2002; CD

Piano
Light dialect

. . . .

Round the Glory Manger

4063

Round the Glory Manger
Hairston, Jacqueline
Wright, John Wesley (Tenor)
The Spirit of the Holidays
American Spiritual Ensemble; 2009; CD

. . . .

Run, Mary, Run

4064

Run, Mary, Run
Composer not identified
Galloway, Dee (Vocalist)
They Slice the Air
Spirituals Project; 2007; CD
Chorus
Moderate dialect

4065

Run, Mary, Run
Guion, David
Thomas, Edna (Soprano)
Run, Mary, Run/Nobody Knows de Trouble I Sees
Columbia 1606-D; 1928; 78 RPM
Piano

4066

Run, Mary, Run
Guion, David
Thomas, Edna (Soprano)
Run, Mary, Run/Samson and Dulilie
Columbia 4197; [19--]; 78 RPM
Piano

. . . .

Run, Sinner, Run

4067

Run Sinner, Run
Edwards, Leo

Matthews, Benjamin (Baritone)
Three Generations Live
Canti Records; 2000; CD
Piano
Heavy dialect

4068

Run Sinner Run
Edwards, Leo
Matthews, Benjamin (Baritone)
A Balm in Gilead
Ebony Classic Recordings ECR 0001; 2000; CD
Piano

4069

Run, Sinner, Run! [from *Green Pastures*]
Johnson, Hall
Toppin, Louise (Soprano)
The Hall Johnson Collection
Carl Fischer VF5 CD1–VF5 CD2; 2003; Score w/CD
Piano
Moderate dialect

. . . .

Same Train

4070

Same Train
Carter, Roland
Robinson-Oturo, Gail (Soprano)
Sweetest Sound I Ever Heard: Spirituals for Solo Voice and Piano, Vol. 1
CD Baby; 2020; Streaming audio
Piano
Light dialect

. . . .

Scandalize My Name

4071

Scandalize My Name
Composer not identified
Adams, Robert (Vocalist)
All God's Children Got Wings/Scandalize My Name Scandalize My Name/It's Me O Lord/Joshua Fit de Battle of Jericho
Ultraphon C 18121; [19--]; 78 RPM

4072

Scandalize My Name
Burleigh, Harry T.
Aluko, Tayo (Baritone)
Recalling Robeson: Songs from Call Mr. Robeson
Tayo Aluko and Friends TAAF CD 001; 2007; CD
Piano

4073

Scandalize My Name
Burleigh, Harry T.
Anderson, Marian (Contralto)
He's Got the Whole World in His Hands: Spirituals
RCA Victor 09026-61960-2; 1994; CD
Piano
Light dialect

4074

Scandalize My Name
Burleigh, Harry T.
Anderson, Marian (Contralto)
Marian Anderson: Beyond the Music; Her Complete RCA Victor Recordings
Sony Classical 19439836492; 2021; CD
Piano
Heavy dialect

4075

Scandalize My Name
Olden Lee, Sylvia; Simpson-Curenton, Evelyn
Battle, Kathleen (Soprano); Norman, Jessye (Soprano)
Spirituals in Concert
Deutsche Grammophon 429 790-2; 1991; CD
Piano
Heavy dialect

4076

Scandalize My Name
Hayes, Roland
Broughton, Gregory (Tenor)
The Lily of the Valley
American Spiritual Ensemble; [2003]; CD
Piano

4077

Scandalize My Name
Johnson, Hall
Brown, Anthony (Baritone); Jones, Arthur (Tenor)
Toil and Triumph
Spirituals Project; 2002; CD
Piano
Heavy dialect

4078

Scandalize Ma Name
Clemmons, François; Marder, Jeffrey
Clemmons, François (Tenor)
Negro Spirituals Live! In Concert
American Negro Spiritual Research Foundation 8177 2048 3779; 1998; CD
Piano
Heavy dialect

4079

Scandalize My Name
Robbiani, Mario
Fisher, Dorothy (Contralto)
Negro Spirituals
Edizione D'Arte Del Lions Club Milano Al Cenacolo; [19--]; LP
Piano
Light dialect

4080

Scandalize My Name
Composer not identified
Foye, Hope (Soprano)
Scandalize My Name/Merry-Go-Round/Let Us Break Bread Together
CCCP Lighthouse B 20667/20668; 1951; 78 RPM
Piano

4081

Scandalize My Name
Hayes, Roland; Boardman. Reginald
Hayes, Roland (Tenor)
The Art of Roland Hayes
Smithsonian Collection RD 041; 1990; CD
Piano
Moderate dialect

4082

Scandalize My Name
Burleigh, Harry T.
Jackson, Zaidee (Vocalist)
Nobody Knows de Trouble I've Seen/
  Scandalize My Name
Duophone D. 534; [19--]; 78 RPM
Orchestra

4083

Scandalize My Name
Johnson, Hall
Jones, Arthur (Tenor)
Wade in the Water
Orbis Books; 1993; Book w/cass
Piano
Heavy dialect

4084

Scandalize My Name
Simpson, Elmur
Matthews, Benjamin (Baritone)
Bon Voyage Recital @ McCormick Place
S.P.S. SS-8993-018; 1966; LP
Piano

4085

Scandalize My Name
Warfield, William; Maynor, Kevin
Maynor, Kevin (Bass)
Paul Robeson Remembered
Fleur de Son Classics FDS 57929; 1998; CD
A cappella
Light dialect

4086

Scandalize My Name
Burleigh, Harry T.
Mims, A. Grace Lee (Soprano)
Spirituals
H & GM Records HGM 8101; 1981; LP
Piano
Heavy dialect

4087

Scandalize My Name
Giesen, Hubert
Ray, William (Baritone)
Negro Spirituals

Intercord; [19--]; LP
Piano

    Also released with *Sings Arias, Duets, Musical Selections and Negro Spirituals* (Intercord; [19--]; CD)

4088

Scandalize My Name
Burleigh, Harry T.
Robeson, Paul (Bass-baritone)
Favorite Songs
Monitor Recordings MPS 580; 1959; LP
Piano
Heavy dialect

4089

Scandalize My Name
Burleigh, Harry T.
Robeson, Paul (Bass-baritone)
A Lonesome Road: Paul Robeson Sings
  Spirituals and Songs
ASV Living Era CD AJA 5027; 1984; CD
Piano
Moderate dialect

4090

Scandalize My Name
Burleigh, Harry T.
Robeson, Paul (Bass-baritone)
The Collector's Paul Robeson
Monitor MCD-61580; 1989; CD
Piano
No dialect discerned

4091

Scandalise My Name
Burleigh, Harry T.
Robeson, Paul (Bass-baritone)
Spirituals/Folksongs/Hymns
Pearl GEMM CD 9382; 1989; CD

4092

Scandalize My Name
Burleigh, Harry T.
Robeson, Paul (Bass-baritone)
Legendary Moscow Concert: Live Concert
  from Tchaikovsky Hall, Moscow
Revelation Records RV70004; 1997; CD
Piano

4093

Scandalize My Name
Burleigh, Harry T.
Robeson, Paul (Bass-baritone)
Spirituals: Original Recordings 1925–1936
Naxos Gospel Legends 8.120638; 2003; CD
Piano

4094

Scandalize My Name
Burleigh, Harry T.
Robeson, Paul (Bass-baritone)
The Complete EMI Sessions (1928–1939)
EMI Classics 50999 2 15586 2 7; 2008; CD
Piano
Heavy dialect

4095

Scandalize My Name
Burleigh, Harry T.
Robeson, Paul (Bass-baritone)
Paul Robeson
World Record Club W9648/EMI SM 431;
　　[19--]; LP
Piano

4096

Scandalize My Name
[Burleigh, Harry T.]
Robeson, Paul (Bass-baritone)
Scandalize My Name
Classics Record Library 30-5647; 1976; LP
Piano
Moderate dialect

4097

Scandalize My Name
[Burleigh, Harry T.]
Robeson, Paul (Bass-baritone)
*Ballad for Americans and Great Songs of
　　Faith, Love and Patriotism*
Vanguard VCD-117/18; 1989; CD
Piano

4098

Scandalize My Name
[Burleigh, Harry T.]
Robeson, Paul (Bass-baritone)
American Balladeer

Collectables Records COL-CD-6502; 1990;
　　CD
Piano
Light dialect

4099

Scandaliz' My Name
[Burleigh, Harry T.]
Robeson, Paul (Bass-baritone)
The Peace Arch Concerts
Folk Era Records FE1442CD; 1998; CD
Piano
Heavy dialect

4100

Scandalize My Name
[Burleigh, Harry T.]
Robeson, Paul (Bass-baritone)
*On My Journey: Paul Robeson's Independent
　　Recordings*
Smithsonian Folkways Recordings SFW CD
　　40178; 2007; CD
Piano

4101

Scandalize My Name
[Burleigh, Harry T.]
Robeson, Paul (Bass-baritone)
Negro Spirituals (And More)
Discmedi DM-4674-02; 2009; CD

4102

Scandalize My Name
[Burleigh, Harry T.]
Robeson, Paul (Bass-baritone)
Ol' Man River: The Very Best of Paul Robeson
Memory Lane; 2012; CD

4103

Scandalize My Name
[Burleigh, Harry T.]
Robeson, Paul (Bass-baritone)
Black Historian and His Music
Entertainment Group International; 2012; CD
Piano

4104

Scandalize My Name
[bUrleigh, Harry T.]

Robeson, Paul (Bass-baritone)
Paul Robeson: Black Historian and His Music
Entertainment Group International; 2016;
   CD
Piano
Light dialect

4105

Scandalize My Name
[Burleigh, Harry T.]
Robeson, Paul (Bass-baritone)
Paul Robeson Singt Negro Spirituals
Musical Masterpiece Society MMS-2162;
   [19--]; LP
Piano

4106

Scandalize My Name
[Burleigh, Harry T.]
Robeson, Paul (Bass-baritone)
Negro Spirituals
Concert Hall SVS 2611; [19--]; LP

4107

Scandalize My Name
[Burleigh, Harry T.]
Robeson, Paul (Bass-baritone)
The Historic Paul Robeson
Murray Hill Records 959062; [19--]; LP

4108

Scandalize My Name
[Burleigh, Harry T.]
Robeson, Paul (Bass-baritone)
Negro Spirituals and Blues
Concert Hall M-2340; [19--]; LP
Piano

4109

Scandalize My Name
[Burleigh, Harry T.]
Robeson, Paul (Bass-baritone)
Negro Spirituals
Chant du Monde LDX 74376; 1982; LP
Piano

4110

The Deceivers
Hayes, Roland

Salters, Stephen (Baritone)
Stephen Salters/Shiela Kibbe
Musica Numeris CYP 9602; 2005; CD
Piano
Moderate dialect

4111

Scandalized My Name
Composer not identified
Rustin, Bayard (Tenor)
*Bayard Rustin Sings Spirituals, Work &
   Freedom Songs*
Bayard Rustin Fund; 1988; Cassette
Piano
Heavy dialect

      Also released with *Bayard Rustin Sings
Spirituals, Work & Freedom Songs* (Bayard
Rustin Fund; 2003; CD)

4112

Scandaliz' My Name! (Humoresque) [from
   Lyric Suite]
Morris, Robert L.
Toppin, Louise (Soprano)
*Heart on the Wall: African American Art
   Songs for Orchestra*
Albany Records TROY1314; 2011; CD
Orchestra
Moderate dialect

4113

Scandalizing My Name
Composer not identified
Warfield, William (Bass-baritone)
Something Within Me
Delmark Records DE-772; 2000; CD
Instrumental ensemble

4114

Scandalise My Name
Composer not identified
White, Willard (Bass-baritone)
The Paul Robeson Legacy
Linn AKD 190; 2015; CD
Instrumental ensemble

4115

Scandalize My Name
Schweizer, Rolf

Wolf, Lars (Vocalist)
Die Schwarze Stimme Europas
Cantate 666000; 1971; LP
Chorus, organ, percussion

. . . .

See How They Done My Lord

4116

See How They Done My Lord
Composer not identified
Matthews, Benjamin (Baritone)
Bon Voyage Recital @ McCormick Place
S.P.S. SS-8993-018; 1966; LP
Piano

. . . .

Seekin' for a City

4117

Seekin' for a City
Miller, James
Jones, Fanni (Mezzo-soprano)
Negro Spirituals en Concert
Suisa; 1987; LP
Organ
Moderate dialect

. . . .

Shepherd, Where'd You Lose Your Sheep

4118

Shepherd, Where'd You Lose Your Sheep?
Composer not identified
Rustin, Bayard (Tenor)
Bayard Rustin, the Singer
Bayard Rustin Fund; 1992; CD
Piano

4119

Shepherd, Where'd You Lose Your Sheep?
Traditional
Rustin, Bayard (Tenor)
*Bayard Rustin Sings Twelve Spirituals on the
    Life of Christ*
Fellowship Records E2-KL 1771; [195-]; LP

A cappella
Heavy dialect
        Also released with *Bayard Rustin-The
Singer* (Black Swan Series; Parnassus Records
PACD 96083; 2022; CD)

. . . .

Singing with a Sword

4120

Singing with a Sword
Composer not identified
Porter, John (Bass)
No More Crying: Negro Spirituals
Pan Verlag OV-84; [1978]; LP

. . . .

Sinner Man So Hard, Believe

4121

Sinner Man So Hard, Believe!
Perry, Zenobia Powell
Jefferson, Othello (Tenor)
*Good News: African American Spirituals and
    Art Songs*
Cambria Records CD 1270; 2021; CD
Piano

4122

Sinner Man So Hard, Believe!
Perry, Zenobia Powell
Taylor, Darryl (Tenor)
*Music of Zenobia Powell Perry: Art Songs
    and Piano Music*
Cambria CD-1138; 2010; CD
Piano
Moderate dialect

. . . .

Sinner, Please Don't Let This Harvest Pass

4123

Sinner, Please Don't Let Dis Harves' Pass
Composer not identified
Blackmon, Henry (Baritone)

Negro-Spirituals
ARC AG 1006; [19--]; 45 RPM
Piano

4124

Sinner, Please
Burleigh, Harry T.
Anderson, Marian (Contralto)
Marian Anderson Sings Spirituals
RCA Victor Red Seal MO 1238; 1948; 78
    RPM
Piano

4125

Sinner, Please
Burleigh, Harry T.
Anderson, Marian (Contralto)
Negro Spirituals
La Voix de Son Maître FBLP1039; 1953; LP
Piano

4126

Sinner, Please Doan Let Dis Harves' Pass
Burleigh, Harry T.
Anderson, Marian (Contralto)
*Marian Anderson: Rare and Unpublished
    Recordings, 1936–1955*
VAI Audio VAIA 1168; 1998; CD
Piano
Moderate dialect

4127

Sinner, Please
Burleigh, Harry T.
Anderson, Marian (Contralto)
Spirituals
RCA Victor Red Seal 09026-63306-2; 1999;
    CD
Piano
Light dialect

4128

Sinner, Please
Burleigh, Harry T.
Anderson, Marian (Contralto)
Marian Anderson Sings Negro Spirituals
His Master's Voice BLP 1060; [19--]; LP
Piano

Also released with *Marian Anderson:
Beyond the Music; Her Complete RCA Victor
Recordings* Sony Classical 19439836492; 2021;
CD

4129

Sinner, Please
Burleigh, Harry T.
Anderson, Marian (Contralto)
Negro Spirituals
RCA Victor LM 2032; [1956]; LP
Piano

Also released with *Marian Anderson:
Beyond the Music; Her Complete RCA Victor
Recordings* Sony Classical 19439836492; 2021;
CD

4130

Sinner, Please
[Burleigh, Harry T.]
Anderson, Marian (Contralto)
Marian Anderson Sings Spirituals
RCA Victor LM 110; 1949; LP
Piano

Also released with *Marian Anderson:
Beyond the Music; Her Complete RCA Victor
Recordings* Sony Classical 19439836492; 2021;
CD

4131

Sinner, Please
[Burleigh, Harry T.]
Anderson, Marian (Contralto)
Alto Rhapsody; Selected Spirituals
Urania URN 22.328; 2007; CD
Piano

4132

Sinner, Please
[Burleigh, Harry T.]
Anderson, Marian (Contralto)
The Very Best of Marian Anderson
Master Classics Records; 2009; CD
Piano
No dialect discerned

4133

Sinner, Please
[Burleigh, Harry T.]

Anderson, Marian (Contralto)
Negro Spirituals
RCA Victor 630.396 A; [19--]; LP
Piano

4134

Sinner Please Don't Let This Harvest Pass
Sneed, Damien
Brownlee, Lawrence (Tenor)
Spiritual Sketches
LeChateau Earl Records 888174029597; 2013;
    CD
Piano
No dialect discerned

4135

Sinnuh Please Don't Let This Harvest Pass
Simpson-Currenton, Evelyn
Chandler-Eteme, Janice (Soprano)
Devotions
Sligo Records; 2007; CD
Piano

4136

Sinner Please Don't Let This Harvest Pass
Traditional
Cheatham, Kitty (Soprano)
Swing Low, Sweet Chariot/I Don't Feel No-
    ways Tired or "I Am Seeking for a City"/
    Walk in Jerusalem Just Like John/Sinner
    Please Don't Let This Harvest Pass
Victor 45086; 1916; 78 RPM
A cappella
Heavy dialect

4137

Sinner, Please Doan Let Dis Harves' Pass
Burleigh, Harry T.
Davis, Ollie Watts (Soprano)
Here's One: Spiritual Songs
KJAC Publishing KJAC0123; 2003; CD
Piano
Moderate dialect

4138

Sinner Please Doan' Let Dis Harves' Pass
Burleigh, Harry T.
Little, Vera (Mezzo-soprano)
My Good Lord Done Been Here

Decca 123737; 1957; LP
Piano

4139

Sinner Please Don't Let This Harvest Pass
Simpson-Curenton, Evelyn
Moses, Oral (Bass-baritone)
Come Down Angels and Trouble the Water:
    Negro Spirituals, an American National
    Treasure!
Albany Records TROY 1489; 2014; CD
Piano
Heavy dialect

4140

Sinner, Please Don't Let This Harvest Pass
Simpson-Curenton, Evelyn
Norman, Jessye (Soprano)
Spirituals in Concert
Deutsche Grammophon 429 790-2; 1991;
    CD
Orchestra
Heavy dialect

4141

Sinner Please Don't Let This Harvest Pass
Bonds, Margaret
Price, Leontyne (Soprano)
The Essential Leontyne Price
BMG Classics 09026-68153-2; 1996; CD
Chorus
Heavy dialect

Also released with *The Essential Leon-*
tyne Price: Spirituals, Hymns & Sacred Songs
(BMG Classics 09026-68157-2; 1996; CD);
Complete Collection of Songs and Spiritual
Albums (RCA Red Seal 88697940502; 2011;
CD) and *Leontyne Price Sings Spirituals* (RCA
Red Seal 88691928242; 2012; CD)

4142

Sinner, Please Don't Let This Harvest Pass
Bonds, Margaret
Price, Leontyne (Soprano)
I Wish I Knew How It Would Feel to Be
    Free
RCA Red Seal LSC 3183; 2011; CD
Chorus

4143

Sinner, Please Don't Let This Harvest Pass
Brown, Lawrence
Robeson, Paul (Bass-baritone)
*A Lonesome Road: Paul Robeson Sings
    Spirituals and Songs*
ASV Living Era CD AJA 5027; 1984; CD
Piano
Light dialect

4144

Sinner Please Doan' Let This Harves' Pass
Burleigh, Harry T.
Robeson, Paul (Bass-baritone)
Spirituals: Original Recordings 1925–1936
Naxos Gospel Legends 8.120638; 2003; CD
Piano

4145

Sinner, Please Doan' Let Dis Harves' Pass
Burleigh, Harry T.
Robeson, Paul (Bass-baritone)
The Complete EMI Sessions (1928–1939)
EMI Classics 50999 2 15586 2 7; 2008; CD
Piano
Heavy dialect

4146

Sinner Please Doan' Let This Harves' Pass
Composer not identified
Robeson, Paul (Bass-baritone)
Spirituals/Folksongs/Hymns
Pearl GEMM CD 9382; 1989; CD

4147

Sinner, Please Don't Let This Harvest Pass
Composer not identified
Thompson, Derrick (Baritone)
Spirituals
Private Label; 2014; CD
Piano
No dialect discerned

4148

Sinner Please Don't Let This Harvest Pass
Composer not identified
West, Lucretia (Mezzo-soprano)
Lucretia West Sings Spirituals
Westminster WP 6063; [1957]; LP

4149

Sinner, Please Don't Let Dis Harves' Pass
Morgenstern, Sam
West, Lucretia (Mezzo-soprano)
Spirituals
Westminster WL 5338; 1954; LP
Men's voices

4150

Sinner Please Doan Let Dis Harves' Pass
Composer not identified
Williams, Wayne (Tenor)
Music from My Life
Movideo Productions 02-1993; 1993; CD
Piano

. . . .

Sister Mary
Had-a But One Child

4151

Sister Mary Had-a But One Child [from *The
    Life of Christ*]
Hayes, Roland
Brown, William (Tenor)
Fi-Yer!: a century of African American song
Albany Records TROY 329; 1999; CD
Piano
Moderate dialect

4152

Sister Mary
Composer not identified
Carey, Thomas (Baritone)
*Sechs Amerikanische Volkslieder/Sechs
    Negro Spirituals*
Colosseum SM 3003; 1970; LP
Orchestra
Light dialect

4153

Sister Mary
Hayes, Roland
Carey, Thomas (Baritone)
Black Swans: At Mid-Century
Parnassus PACD 96078/9; 2021; CD
Piano
Heavy dialect

4154

Sister Mary Had a But One Child
Hayes, Roland
Clemmons, François (Tenor)
Negro Spirituals Live! In Concert
American Negro Spiritual Research
    Foundation 8177 2048 3779; 1998;
    CD
Piano
No dialect discerned

4155

Sister Mary Had but One Child [from
    The Life of Christ]
[Hayes, Roland]
Cook, Dixon & Young (Tenor)
*Triptych: A Celebration of the Negro
    Spiritual*
CDY Records 649241879206; 2009; CD
Piano
Heavy dialect

4156

Sister Mary Had-a But One Child [from
    The Life of Christ]
Hayes, Roland
Davis, Osceola (Soprano)
Negro Spirituals
Ondine ODE 715-2; 1988; CD
Piano
Light dialect

4157

Sister Mary Had-a But One Child [from
    The Life of Christ]
Hayes, Roland
Davy, Gloria (Soprano)
Spirituals
Decca LW 5215; 1959; LP

4158

Sister Mary [from *The Life of Christ*]
Hayes, Roland
Forrester, Maureen (Contralto)
*An Evening with Maureen Forrester and
    Andrew Davis*
Fanfare DFCD-9024; 1987; CD
Piano

4159

Three Wise Men to Jerusalem Came [from
    The Life of Christ]
Hayes, Roland
Hayes, Roland (Tenor)
*Roland Hayes Sings the Life of Christ: As Told
    Through Aframerican Folksong*
Vanguard VRS-462; 1954; LP
Piano
Light dialect

Also released with *Aframerican Folksong: Telling the Story of the Life of Christ*
(Top Rank 39 620; [1961]; LP); *Roland Hayes
Sings the Life of Christ: As Told Through
Aframerican Folksong* (Vanguard SRV 352;
1976; LP); *Favorite Spirituals* (Vanguard
Classics OVC 6022; 1995; CD); *Charlton Heston Reads from The Life and Passion of Jesus
Christ* (Vanguard Classics ATM-CD-1259;
2003; CD) and (*Big Psalms, Hymns and Spirituals Box* [eOne Music/Vanguard Classics];
2015; Streaming audio)

4160

Sister Mary Had-a But One Child [from *The
    Life of Christ*]
Hayes, Roland
Holland, Charles (Tenor)
Cinq Negro Spirituals
Pathé 45 ED. 28; 1954; 45 RPM
Piano

4161

Sister Mary Had-a But One Child [from *The
    Life of Christ*]
Hayes, Roland
Holland, Charles (Tenor)
My Lord What a Mornin'
Musical Heritage Society MHS 912250X;
    1982; LP
Piano
No dialect discerned

Also released as *My Lord What a Mornin'*
(Musical Heritage Society MHS 512250K;
1988; CD)

4162

Sister Mary Had a But One Chile
Composer not identified

Matthews, Benjamin (Baritone)
Bon Voyage Recital @ McCormick Place
S.P.S. SS-8993-018; 1966; LP
Piano

4163

Sister Mary Had-a But One Child [from *The Life of Christ*]
Hayes, Roland
Oby, Jason (Tenor)
The Life of Christ: Collected Spirituals
Private Label TSU4749; [200-]; CD
Piano
Light dialect

4164

Sister Mary Had-a But One Chile [from *The Life of Christ*]
Hayes, Roland
Overton, Kenneth (Baritone)
Been in de Storm So Long (Songs My Fathers Taught Me)
American Spiritual Ensemble; 2012; CD
Piano
Light dialect

4165

Sister Mary Had-a But One Child [from *The Life of Christ*]
Hayes, Roland
Overton, Kenneth (Baritone)
The Spirit of the Holidays
American Spiritual Ensemble; 2009; CD

4166

Sister Mary Had-a But One Child
[Hayes, Roland]
Peterson, Elwood (Baritone)
Negro Spirituals
Boîte à Musique LD 073; 1961; LP
Piano

4167

Sister Mary [from *The Life of Christ*]
Hayes, Roland; Sadin, Robert
Robinson, Morris (Bass)
Going Home
Decca B0008277-02; 2007; CD

Instrumental ensemble
Light dialect

4168

Sister Mary Had'a But One Child [from *The Life of Christ*]
Hayes, Roland
Shirley, George (Tenor)
George Shirley at 80: My Time Has Come!
Videmus Records; 2014; CD
Piano

4169

Sister Mary Had-a But One Child [from *The Life of Christ*]
Hayes, Roland
Sims, Robert (Baritone)
Robert Sims Sings the Spirituals of Roland Hayes
Canti Classics 2014-01; 2015; CD
Piano
Heavy dialect

4170

Sister Mary Had-a But One Child [from *The Life of Christ*]
Hayes, Roland
Sims, Robert (Baritone)
Soul of a Singer: Robert Sims Sings African-American Folk Songs
Canti Classics 9801; 2013; CD
Piano
Heavy dialect

4171

Sister Mary Had'a But One Child
Composer not identified
Smith, Muriel (Mezzo-soprano)
The Glory of Christmas
Philips BL 7586; [196-]; LP
Chorus, orchestra

4172

Sister Mary Had-a But One Child [from *The Life of Christ*]
Hayes, Roland
Warfield, William (Bass-baritone)
Spirituals: 200 Years of African-American Spirituals

ProArte CDD 3443; 1993; CD
Piano
Heavy dialect

4173

Sister Mary Had-a But One Child [from *The
    Life of Christ*]
Hayes, Roland
Williams, Willie (Vocalist)
My Tribute
Discovery V42227; 1974; LP
Piano

4174

Sister Mary Had-a But One Child [from *The
    Life of Christ*]
Hayes, Roland
Young, Thomas (Tenor)
*Black Christmas: Spirituals in the African-
    American Tradition*
Essay Recordings CD1011; 1990; CD
Piano
Light dialect

4175

Sister Mary Had-a But One Child [from *The
    Life of Christ*]
Hayes, Roland
Young, Thomas (Tenor)
A Spiritual Christmas
Musical Heritage Society 5167448; 2002; CD
Piano
Heavy dialect

· · · · · · ·

Sit Down

4176

Sit Down
Composer not identified
Hayes, Roland (Tenor)
Classic Gospel Songs
Emerald/K-Tel; 2013; Streaming audio
Piano

4177

Sit Down
Hayes, Roland
Hayes, Roland (Tenor)

Good News: Vintage Negro Spirituals
Living Era AJA 5622; 2006; CD
Piano
Moderate dialect

4178

Sit Down
[Hayes, Roland]
Hayes, Roland (Tenor)
*Black Europe: Sounds & Images of Black
    People in Europe Pre–1927*
Bear Family Productions BCD 16095; 2013;
    CD
Piano
Light dialect

· · · · · · ·

Sit Down, Servant

4179

Sit Down, Servant
Blair Lindsay, Tedrin
Anderson, Alfonse (Tenor); Little, Ricky
    (Baritone); Wright, John Wesley (Tenor)
Swing Low, Sweet Chariot
American Spiritual Ensemble; 2011; CD

4180

Sit Down Servant [from *Five Creek-
    Freedmen Spirituals*]
Bonds, Margaret
Forest, Michael (Tenor)
The Spirit Sings: American Spirituals
Shenandoah Conservatory SU003; [199-];
    CD

4181

Sit Down Servant [from *Five Creek-
    Freedmen Spirituals*]
Bonds, Margaret
Hamilton, Ruth (Contralto)
Good News
Videmus Records VIS735; 2007; CD
Piano
Heavy dialect

4182

Sit Down Servant, Sit Down
Composer not identified

Pleas III, Henry H. (Tenor)
Deep River: A Spiritual Journey
Rowe House Productions; 1999; CD

4183

Sit Down, Servant [from *Five Creek-
    Freedmen Spirituals*]
Bonds, Margaret
Price, Leontyne (Soprano)
*Swing Low, Sweet Chariot: Fourteen
    Spirituals*
RCA Victor LSC 2600; 1962; LP
Chorus, orchestra
Heavy dialect

Also released with *The Essential Leontyne Price* (BMG Classics 09026-68153-2;
1996; CD); *The Essential Leontyne Price: Spirituals, Hymns & Sacred Songs* (BMG Classics
09026-68157-2; 1996; CD) and *Leontyne Price
Sings Spirituals* (RCA Red Seal 88691928242;
2012; CD)

4184

Sit Down, Servant [from *Five Creek-
    Freedmen Spirituals*]
Bonds, Margaret
Price, Leontyne (Soprano)
*Complete Collection of Songs and Spiritual
    Albums*
RCA Red Seal 88697940502; 2011; CD
Orchestra

4185

Sit Down, Servant [from *Five Creek-
    Freedmen Spirituals*]
Bonds, Margaret
Price, Leontyne (Soprano)
*Singers of the Century: Leontyne Price:
    Spiritual and Religious Songs*
Jube Classic; 2016; Streaming audio
Chorus, orchestra
Heavy dialect

4186

Sit Down, Servant
Roberts, Howard
Quivar, Florence (Mezzo-soprano)
Negro Spirituals
EMI 7243 5 72790 2 4; 1998; CD

Chorus, piano
Heavy dialect

Also released with *Ride On, King Jesus!
Florence Quivar Sings Black Music of America* (EMI Classics 9 67138 2; 2010; CD)

4187

Sit Down, Servant
Roberts, Howard
Salters, Stephen (Baritone)
Spirit: Are You There, You Are There
HarmonizedDisharmony 0001; 2015; CD

4188

Set Down
Smith Moore, Undine
Toppin, Louise (Soprano)
Ah! Love but a Day
Albany Records/ Videmus TROY 385; 2000;
    CD
Piano
Heavy dialect

4189

Set Down
Smith Moore, Undine
Toppin, Louise (Soprano)
The New Negro Spiritual
W. C. Patterson; 2002; Score w/CD
Piano
Heavy dialect

4190

Sit Down Servant
Composer not identified
Verdejo, Awilda (Soprano)
Awilda Verdejo Sings Spirituals
Angeluz Performances; 1999; CD
Piano

4191

Sit Down, Sister [from *Journey Beyond
    Time*]
Crumb, George
Martin, Barbara Ann (Soprano)
American Songbooks II & IV
BRIDGE 9275A/B; 2008; CD
Piano, percussion

· · · · · · ·

Sit Down, Sit Down

4192

Sit Down, Sit Down
Composer not identified
Rustin, Bayard (Tenor)
Bayard Rustin Sings Spirituals, Work &
    Freedom Songs
Bayard Rustin Fund; 1988; Cassette
Piano
Heavy dialect

Also released with *Bayard Rustin Sings Spirituals, Work & Freedom Songs* (Bayard Rustin Fund; 2003; CD)

· · · · · · ·

So Glad

4193

So Glad
Carter, Roland
Robinson-Oturo, Gail (Soprano)
Sweetest Sound I Ever Heard: Spirituals for
    Solo Voice and Piano, Vol. 1
CD Baby; 2020; Streaming audio
Piano
Light dialect

· · · · · · ·

Some Day He'll Make It Plain to Me

4194

Some Day He'll Make It Plain to Me
Composer not identified
Robeson, Paul (Bass-baritone)
Encore, Robeson!
Monitor MP 581; 1960; LP

4195

Some Day He'll Make It Plain to Me
Composer not identified
Robeson, Paul (Bass-baritone)
Negro Spirituals
Chant du Monde LDX 74376; 1982; LP
Piano

· · · · · · ·

Some o' Dese Days

4196

Some o' Dese Days [from *Green Pastures*]
Johnson, Hall
Brown, William (Tenor)
The Hall Johnson Collection
Carl Fischer VF5 CD1–VF5 CD2; 2003; Score
    w/CD
Piano
Heavy dialect

· · · · · · ·

Somebody's Knocking at Your Door

4197

Somebody's Knocking at Your Door
Composer not identified
Davis, Frank (Bass-baritone)
16 Spirituals My Father Taught Me
DeWitt Records 601; 1960; LP

4198

Somebody's Knockin' at Yo' Door
Composer not identified
Hayes, Roland (Tenor)
Evening with Roland Hayes, Tenor
Heritage LP-SS-1204; 1953; LP
Piano

4199

Somebody's Knockin' at Yo' Door
Composer not identified
Hayes, Roland (Tenor)
The Art of Roland Hayes: Six Centuries of
    Song
Preiser Records; 2010; CD
Piano
Heavy dialect

4200

Somebody's Knockin' at Yo' Door [from
    Three Aframerican Religious Folksongs]
Hayes, Roland
Hayes, Roland (Tenor)
Roland Hayes Recital, A

A 440 Records AC1203; [19--]; LP
Piano

4201

Somebody's Knocking
Composer not identified
Hendricks, Barbara (Soprano)
No Borders
Altara ALT 1010; 2005; CD
Chorus
No dialect discerned

4202

Somebody's knocking at yo' do'
Johnson, John Rosamond
Jones, Fanni (Mezzo-soprano)
Negro Spirituals en Concert
Suisa; 1987; LP
Organ
Heavy dialect

4203

Somebody's Knockin' at Your Door
Dett, Robert Nathaniel
Oglesby, Isador (Tenor)
Life of Jesus in Negro Spirituals
Oglesby Recordings Album 2; 1980; LP
Piano

4204

Somebody's Knockin' at Your Door
Composer not identified
Thomas, Edna (Soprano)
*Somebody's Knockin' at Your Door/Rock o'
My Soul*
Columbia 3473; 1924; 78 RPM
Orchestra

4205

Somebody's Knockin' at Your Door
Thomas, Edna
Thomas, Edna (Soprano)
*I Been Buked and I Been Scorned; Gwine-a
Lay Down Mah Life for Mah Lawd/
Somebody's Knockin' at Your Door!*
Columbia 1404-D; 1928; 78 RPM
Piano

4206

Somebody's Knocking at Your Door
Hogan, Moses
Tucker, Eric Hoy (Bass-baritone)
*Southern Salute: Southern Songs &
Spirituals*
White Pine Music WPM218; 2012; CD
Piano
Light dialect

4207

Somebody's Knockin' at Yo' Door
Hogan, Moses
Walker, Alfred (Bass)
*Deep River: Featuring 10 Spirituals
Arranged for Solo Voice....*
MGH Records 5000; 2000; CD
Piano
Light dialect

4208

Somebody's Knockin' at Your Door
Hogan, Moses
Walker, Alfred (Bass)
Songs of Reflection
MGH Records 0800CD; 2020; CD

·······

Sometimes I Feel Like a Motherless Child

[Mark 14:33, 35-36]

"Sometimes I feel like a motherless child (3x), A long way from home. Sometimes I feel like I'm almost gone (3x), A long way from home. True believer,...."

[Available in AASP, CW40, EM34, ESAA, FHFN, HLBS, HT25, HTBA, HTBN, HTBS, JBES, JCCA, JJAN, JJBA, JSSp, LB5N, MHDR, PLSY, RWBC, RWSC, RWSS, RW15, SBFD, VLCH, WF10, WF70, WR5N]

Because the enslaved were considered to be the property of their masters, they never knew when the master would decide to sell or otherwise separate the families of the enslaved, usually permanently. This spiritual is the outcry of one tormented by their separation from family and all they knew.

Yet, as powerful and deeply felt the

sorrow, there is the sense of hope that is a staple of the sorrow song. The enslaved used spirituals like this as a way to channel or release that sorrow.

4209

Sometimes I Feel Like a Motherless Child
Traditional
Addison, Adele (Soprano)
Little David Play on Your Harp
Kapp Records KL 1109; 1959; LP
A cappella
Moderate dialect

4210

Motherless Chile
McCoy, Tom
Adkins, Paul Spencer (Tenor)
How Can I Keep from Singing?
PSA PSA-2002; 2002; CD
Piano
Moderate dialect

4211

Sometimes I Feel Like a Motherless Chile
Burleigh, Harry T.
Alexander, Roberta (Soprano)
Songs My Mother Taught Me
Etcetera KTC 1208; 1999; CD
Piano
Light dialect

  Also released with *Roberta Alexander.... A Retrospective* (Etcetera KTC1222; 2013; CD)

4212

Sometimes I Feel Like a Motherless Child
Brown, Lawrence
Anderson, Marian (Contralto)
Negro Spirituals
La Voix de Son Maître 7EJF2; 1955; 45 RPM
Orchestra

4213

Sometimes I Feel Like a Motherless Child
Brown, Lawrence
Anderson, Marian (Contralto)

Negro Spirituals, vol. II
La Voix de Son Maître 7 ERF 17025; 1962; EP 45 RPM
Orchestra

4214

Sometimes I Feel Like a Motherless Child
Brown, Lawrence
Anderson, Marian (Contralto)
Songs Our Mothers Taught Us
Met MET 210CD; 1990; CD
Piano

4215

Sometimes I Feel Like a Motherless Child
Brown, Lawrence
Anderson, Marian (Contralto)
V-Disc: The Songs That Went to War (World War II 50th Anniversary Collector's Edition)
Time-Life Music R139-39/OPCD-4537; 1992; CD
Piano
Moderate dialect

4216

Sometimes I Feel Like a Motherless Child
Brown, Lawrence
Anderson, Marian (Contralto)
Tribute
Pro Arte CDD 3447; 1993; CD

4217

Sometimes I Feel Like a Motherless Child
Brown, Lawrence
Anderson, Marian (Contralto)
He's Got the Whole World in His Hands: Spirituals
RCA Victor 09026-61960-2; 1994; CD
Piano
Light dialect

4218

Sometimes I Feel Like a Motherless Child
Brown, Lawrence
Anderson, Marian (Contralto)
The Lady
Magnum Music MCCD 017; 1996; CD
Piano

4219

Sometimes I Feel Like a Motherless Child
Brown, Lawrence
Anderson, Marian (Contralto)
Prima Voce
Nimbus NI 7882; 1996; CD
Piano
Light dialect

4220

Sometime I Feel Like a Motherless Child
Brown, Lawrence
Anderson, Marian (Contralto)
Spirituals
RCA Victor Red Seal 09026-63306-2; 1999;
    CD
Piano
Moderate dialect

4221

Sometimes I Feel Like a Motherless Chil'
Brown, Lawrence
Anderson, Marian (Contralto)
The Best of Negro Spirituals
BMG BVCM-37416; 2003; CD
Piano
Heavy dialect

4222

Sometimes I Feel Like a Motherless Child
Brown, Lawrence
Anderson, Marian (Contralto)
Ev'Ry Time I Feel the Spirit (1930–1947)
Naxos Nostalgia 8.120779; 2004; CD
Piano

4223

Sometimes I Feel Like a Motherless Child
Brown, Lawrence
Anderson, Marian (Contralto)
Negro Spirituals: 1924–1949
Frémeaux & Associés FA 184; 2004; CD
Orchestra

4224

Sometimes I Feel Like a Motherless Child
Brown, Lawrence
Anderson, Marian (Contralto)

Good News: Vintage Negro Spirituals
Living Era AJA 5622; 2006; CD

4225

Sometimes I Feel Like a Motherless Child
Brown, Lawrence
Anderson, Marian (Contralto)
*Softly Awakes My Heart: Very Best of Marian
    Anderson*
Alto ALN1955; 2016; CD
Piano
Heavy dialect

4226

Sometimes I Feel Like a Motherless Child
Brown, Lawrence
Anderson, Marian (Contralto)
*Sometimes I Feel Like a Motherless Child/I
    Don't Feel No-ways Tired*
Victor Red Seal; [19--]; 78 RPM
Piano
No dialect discerned

4227

Sometime I Feel Like a Motherless Child
Brown, Lawrence
Anderson, Marian (Contralto)
Negro Spirituals
RCA Victor LM 2032; [1956]; LP
Piano

    Also released with *Marian Anderson:
Beyond the Music; Her Complete RCA Victor
Recordings* Sony Classical 19439836492; 2021;
CD

4228

Sometimes I Feel Like a Motherless Child
Burleigh, Harry T.
Anderson, Marian (Contralto)
Recital: Opera, Lieder, Oratorio
SYM1270.2; Symposium; 2005; CD
Piano

4229

Sometimes I Feel Like a Motherless Child
[Brown, Lawrence]
Anderson, Marian (Contralto)
*Marian Anderson Sings Eleven Great
    Spirituals*

RCA Victor LRM 7006; 1955; LP
Piano

Also released with *Marian Anderson Sings Eleven Great Spirituals* (Kipepeo Publishing; 2017; CD) and *Marian Anderson: Beyond the Music; Her Complete RCA Victor Recordings* Sony Classical 19439836492; 2021; CD

4230

Sometimes I Feel Like a Motherless Child
[Brown, Lawrence]
Anderson, Marian (Contralto)
Marian Anderson in Concert 1943–1952
Eklipse Records EKR CD19; 1993; CD
Orchestra

4231

Sometimes I Feel Like a Motherless Child
[Brown, Lawrence]
Anderson, Marian (Contralto)
Marian Anderson and Dorothy Maynor in Concert
Eklipse Records EKR 49; 1995; CD
Piano

4232

Sometimes I Feel
[Brown, Lawrence]
Anderson, Marian (Contralto)
Marian Anderson Sings Spirituals
Flapper Past CD 7073; 1995; CD
Piano

4233

Sometimes I Feel Like a Motherless Child
[Brown, Lawrence]
Anderson, Marian (Contralto)
Rarities: Broadcast Performances 1943–1952
Video Artists International VAIA 1200; 1998; CD
Orchestra

4234

Sometimes I Feel Like a Motherless Child
[Brown, Lawrence]
Anderson, Marian (Contralto)
Softly Awakes My Heart

ASV CD AJA 5262; 1999; CD
Piano

4235

Sometimes I Feel Like a Motherless Child
[Brown, Lawrence]
Anderson, Marian (Contralto)
When Marian Sang: Selected Songs from Marian Anderson's Repertoire
BMG Special Products DPC13280; 2002; CD

4236

Sometimes I Feel Like a Motherless Child
[Brown, Lawrence]
Anderson, Marian (Contralto)
Alto Rhapsody; Selected Spirituals
Urania URN 22.328; 2007; CD
Piano

4237

Sometime I Feel Like a Motherless Child
[Brown, Lawrence]
Anderson, Marian (Contralto)
The Very Best of Marian Anderson
Master Classics Records; 2009; CD
Piano
No dialect discerned

4238

Sometimes I Feel Like a Motherless Child
[Brown, Lawrence]
Anderson, Marian (Contralto)
Living Stereo 60 CD Collection
Sony Music Entertainment 88765414972; 2012; CD

4239

Motherless Child
[Brown, Lawrence]
Anderson, Marian (Contralto)
Classic Gospel Songs
Emerald/K-Tel; 2013; Streaming audio
Piano

4240

Sometimes I Feel Like a Motherless Child
[Brown, Lawrence]
Anderson, Marian (Contralto)
Inspirations

Emerald Echoes; 2015; Streaming audio
Piano
No dialect discerned

4241

Sometimes I Feel Like a Motherless Child
[Brown, Lawrence]
Anderson, Marian (Contralto)
Grandes Contraltos de la Musique Classique,
   Les: Marian Anderson, Vol. 7
Mon Patrimoine Musical Collection; 2017;
   Streaming audio
Piano

4242

Sometimes I Feel Like a Motherless Child
[Brown, Lawrence]
Anderson, Marian (Contralto)
The Rich Voice of Marian Anderson
Editions Audiovisuel Beulah; 2019;
   Streaming audio
Piano

4243

Sometimes I Feel Like a Motherless Child
[Brown, Lawrence]
Anderson, Marian (Contralto)
Ave Maria: And Other Schubert Songs
43 North Broadway, LLC; 2019; Streaming
   audio
Piano
Heavy dialect

4244

Sometimes I Feel Like a Motherless Child
[Brown, Lawrence]
Anderson, Marian (Contralto)
Negro Spirituals
RCA Gold Seal RVC-1570; [19--]; LP
Piano

4245

Sometimes I Feel Like a Motherless Child
[Brown, Lawrence]
Anderson, Marian (Contralto)
Marian Anderson
Davis Records 11749; [19--]; 78 RPM
Piano
Moderate dialect

4246

Sometimes I Feel Like a Motherless Child
[Brown, Lawrence]
Anderson, Marian (Contralto)
Negro Spirituals
RCA Victor 630.396 A; [19--]; LP
Piano

4247

Sometimes I Feel Like a Motherless Child
[Brown, Lawrence]
Anderson, Marian (Contralto)
Sometimes I Feel Like a Motherless Child/
   Heav'n, Heav'n
Ultraphone AP 1504; [193-]; 78 RPM
Piano

4248

Sometimes I Feel Like a Motherless Child
[Brown, Lawrence]
Anderson, Marian (Contralto)
Sometimes I Feel Like a Motherless Child/
   Heav'n, Heav'n
Royale 1765; 1936-; 78 RPM
Piano

4249

Sometimes I Feel Like a Motherless Child
[Brown, Lawrence]
Anderson, Marian (Contralto)
Marian Anderson Sings an International
   Concert
Royale 1764; [194-]; 78 RPM
Piano

4250

Sometimes I Feel Like a Motherless Child
[Brown, Lawrence]
Anderson, Marian (Contralto)
Heav'n, Heav'n/Sometimes I Feel Like a
   Motherless Child
Masterpiece 8532; [1940]; 78 RPM
Piano
Moderate dialect

4251

Sometimes I Feel Like a Motherless Child
[Brown, Lawrence]
Anderson, Marian (Contralto)

Deep River
Audio Book & Music; [20--]; CD

4252
Sometimes I Feel Like a Motherless Child
Composer not identified
Anonymous (Contralto)
Heav'n, Heav'n/Sometimes I Feel Like a Motherless Child
Concertone 318; [193-]; 78 RPM
Piano

4253
Sometimes I Feel Like a Motherless Child
Burleigh, Harry T.
Arroyo, Martina (Soprano)
Spirituals
Centaur CRC 2060; 1991; CD
Piano
Heavy dialect

4254
Sometimes I Feel Like a Motherless Child
Brown, Lawrence
Blackmon, Henry (Baritone)
Geestelijke Liederen En Negro Spirituals
Mirasound Records SGLP 6047; 1974; LP
Piano

4255
Sometimes I Feel Like a Motherless Child
Composer not identified
Blackmon, Henry (Baritone)
Negro-Spirituals
ARC AG 1006; [19--]; 45 RPM
Piano

4256
Sometimes I Feel Like a Motherless Child
Burleigh, Harry T.
Boatner, Edward (Baritone)
Lost Sounds: Blacks and the Birth of the Recording Industry 1891–1923
Archeophone Records ARCH 1005; 2005; CD
Piano
No dialect discerned

4257
Sometimes I Feel Like a Motherless Child
Burleigh, Harry T.

Boatner, Edward H.S. (Bass-baritone)
Black Swans
Parnassus Recordings PACD 96067; 2019; CD
Piano
No dialect discerned

4258
Sometimes I Feel Like a Motherless Child
Burleigh, Harry T.
Boston, Gretha (Contralto)
Swing Low, Sweet Chariot
American Spiritual Ensemble; 2011; CD

4259
Sometimes I Feel Like a Motherless Child (Recitative) [from *Cantata*]
Carter, John D.
Brewer, Christine (Soprano)
Saint Louis Woman
Opera Theatre of Saint Louis OTSL CD93; 1993; CD
Piano
Heavy dialect

   Also released with *Songs by Wagner, Wolf, Britten and John Carter* (Wigmore Hall Live WHLive0022; 2008; CD)

4260
Sometimes I Feel Like a Motherless Child
Burleigh, Harry T.
Brown, Anne (Soprano)
Sometimes I Feel Like a Motherless Child
Sonora SE-23511; 1950; 78 RPM
Piano
Heavy dialect

   Also released with *Anne Brown Sings Spirituals* (Mercury EP-1-5038; [195-]; LP) and *Black Swans: At Mid-Century* (Parnassus PACD 96078/9; 2021; CD)

4261
Sometimes I Feel Like a Motherless Child
Burleigh, Harry T.
Brown, Anne (Soprano)
Sometimes I Feel Like a Motherless Child/ Hold On!
Tono L 28021; [19--]; 78 RPM

Piano
Heavy dialect

4262

Sometimes I Feel Like a Motherless Child
Burleigh, Harry T.
Brown, Anthony (Baritone)
Toil and Triumph
Spirituals Project; 2002; CD
Piano
Heavy dialect

4263

Sometimes I Feel Like a Motherless Child
[from *Through This Vale of Tears*]
Baker, David
Brown, William (Tenor)
Works by T.J. Anderson, David Baker, Donal Fox, Olly Wilson
New World Records 80423-2; 2007; CD
Instrumental ensemble
No dialect discerned

4264

Sometimes
Wilson, Olly
Brown, William (Tenor)
Works by T.J. Anderson, David Baker, Donal Fox, Olly Wilson
New World Records 80423-2; 2007; CD
Tape
No dialect discerned

4265

Sometimes I Feel Like a Motherless Child
Burleigh, Harry T.
Browning, Marcus (Vocalist)
By an' By/Sometimes I Feel Like a Motherless Child
Edison Bell Radio 1384; 1930; 78 RPM
Piano

4266

Sometimes I Feel Like a Motherless Child
Burleigh, Harry T.
Brownlee, Lawrence (Tenor)
The Heart That Flutters
Opus Arte OA CD9015 D; 2013; CD

Piano
Heavy dialect

4267

Sometimes I Feel Like a Motherless Child
Sneed, Damien
Brownlee, Lawrence (Tenor)
Spiritual Sketches
LeChateau Earl Records 888174029597; 2013; CD
Piano
No dialect discerned

4268

Sometimes I Feel Like a Motherless Child
Burleigh, Harry T.
Burton, Dashon (Bass-baritone)
Songs of Struggle & Redemption: We Shall Overcome
Acis Productions APL08685; 2015; CD
Piano
Moderate dialect

4269

Sometimes I Feel Like a Motherless Child
Clark, Joe
Cabell, Nicole (Soprano); Cambridge, Alyson (Soprano)
Sisters in Song
Cedille Records CDR 90000 181; 2018; CD
Orchestra
Moderate dialect

4270

Sometimes I Feel
Dørumsgaard, Arne
Carlsen, Svein (Bass)
Negro Spirituals
EuroMaster AS ECD19005; 1996; CD
Piano

4271

Sometimes I Feel Like a Motherless Child
Burleigh, Harry T.
Carnette, Count (Vocalist)
Count Carnette Sings Favorite Negro Spirituals
Carnette Archive Recordings; 1983; LP

Piano
Light dialect

4272

Sometimes I Feel Like a Motherless Child
[Burleigh, Harry T.]
Chaiter, Yoram (Bass)
Spirituals & Other Songs
Romeo Records 7311; 2014; CD
Piano
No dialect discerned

4273

Motherless Child [from *Songs for Joy* (A
    Suite of Spirituals)]
Simpson-Currenton, Evelyn
Chandler-Eteme, Janice (Soprano)
Devotions
Sligo Records; 2007; CD
Piano

4274

Motherless Child
Composer not identified
Charles, Lee (Tenor)
*Swing Low Sweet Chariot: And Other
    Spirituals*
Riverside RLP 12-651; 1957; LP
Piano, guitar

4275

Sometimes I Feel Like a Motherless Child
Cooke, Barbara Logan
Cooke, Barbara (Vocalist)
*Sometimes I Feel: A Collection of Negro
    Spirituals for Voice and Instruments*
Private Label KDISC420; 2002; CD
Piano

4276

Sometimes I Feel Like a Motherless Child
    [from *Cantata*]
Carter, John D.
Davis, Ollie Watts (Soprano)
Here's One: Spiritual Songs
KJAC Publishing KJAC0123; 2003; CD
Piano
Moderate dialect

4277

Recitative [from *Cantata*]
Carter, John D.; Link, Peter
Davis, Osceola (Soprano)
Climbing High Mountains
Watchfire Music; 2008; CD
Piano, orchestra
Light dialect

4278

Sometimes I Feel Like a Motherless Child
Composer not identified
Elzy, Ruby (Soprano)
Ruby Elzy in Song: Rare Recordings
Cambria Records CD-1154; 2006; CD
Piano
Heavy dialect
      Also released with *The 78 RPM Collec-
tion* (Master Classics Records; 2010; CD)

4279

Sometimes I Feel Like a Motherless Child
    (Recitative) [from *Cantata*]
Carter, John D.
English-Robinson, Laura (Soprano)
Let It Shine!
ACA Digital Recording CM20020; 1994;
    CD
Piano
Light dialect

4280

Sometimes I Feel Like a Motherless Child
[Burleigh, Harry T.]
Essin, Sonia (Contralto)
The Art of Sonia Essin
Orion ORS 77271; 1977; LP
Piano
Heavy dialect

4281

Sometimes I Feel Like a Motherless Child
Composer not identified
Estes, Simon (Bass-baritone)
Save the Children, Save Their Lives
CD Baby; 2010; CD
Piano
No dialect discerned

4282

Sometimes I Feel Like a Motherless Child
Roberts, Howard
Estes, Simon (Bass-baritone)
Spirituals
Philips 412 631-2; 1985; CD
Chorus
No dialect discerned

   Also released with *Famous Spirituals* (Philips 462 062-2; 1997; CD)

4283

Sometimes I Feel Like a Motherless Child
Ryan, Donald
Estes, Simon (Bass-baritone)
Steal Away: My Favorite Negro Spirituals
Deutsche Schallplatten DS 1041-2; 1994; CD
Piano
No dialect discerned

4284

Sometimes I Feel Like a Motherless Child
Burleigh, Harry T.
Evans, Allan (Bass-baritone)
Negro Spirituals
Electromusic Records EMCD 6885; 1985; CD
Chorus, other instrument(s)

4285

Sometimes I Feel Like a Motherless Child
Darden, George
Fernandez, Wilhelmenia (Soprano)
Spirituals
Tioch Digital Records TD 1009; 1982; LP
Piano
Heavy dialect

   Also released with *Negro Spirituals* (Milan A 192; 1982; LP) and *Sings Favorite Spirituals* (Phoenix PHCD 134; 1997; CD)

4286

Сирота (Sirota)
Composer not identified
Filatova, Ludmila (Mezzo-soprano)
Негритянские Спиричузлс (Negrityanskiye Spirichuzls—Negro Spirituals)
Melodiâ S10 21833 009; 1985; LP
Organ
Light dialect

4287

Sometimes I Feel Like a Motherless Child
Robbiani, Mario
Fisher, Dorothy (Contralto)
Negro Spirituals
Edizione D'Arte Del Lions Club Milano Al Cenacolo; [19--]; LP
Instrumental ensemble

4288

Sometimes I Feel Like a Motherless Child
Composer not identified
Foye, Hope (Soprano)
Alle hübschen Pferdchen = All the Pretty Horses / Schlafe, Kleines Baby! = Hush, Little Baby! / Manchmal Fühle Ich Mich Wie ein Waisenkind Volkslied = Sometimes I feel like am Motherless Child
Eterna ET 2390–ET 2391; 1950; 78 RPM
Piano

4289

Sometimes I Feel Like a Motherless Child
Composer not identified
Foye, Hope (Soprano)
Singing Her Song: The Story of Hope Foye
Union Bank of California; 2008; CD
Piano
No dialect discerned

4290

Sometimes I Feel Like a Motherless Child
Composer not identified
Foye, Hope (Soprano)
The Best of Hope Foye: 20th and 21st Century Legendary Song Collection
Permanent Productions PP00115; 2010; CD

4291

Sometimes I Feel Like a Motherless Child (Recitative) [from *Cantata*]
Carter, John D.
Givens, Melissa (Soprano)
Let the Rain Kiss You
Divameg Productions 141434; 2001; CD
Piano

4292

Recitative [from *Cantata*]
Carter, John D.
Gormley, Clare (Soprano)
Where Morning Lies: Spiritual Songs
ABC Classics 461 766-2; 2002; CD
Piano
Light dialect

4293

Sometimes I Feel Like a Motherless Child
Simpson-Curenton, Evelyn
Graves, Denyce (Mezzo-soprano)
Angels Watching Over Me
NPR Classics CD 0006; 1997; CD
Piano
Heavy dialect

4294

Sometimes I Feel Like a Motherless Child
[Burleigh, Harry T.]
Hagen-William, Louis (Bass-baritone)
Negro Spirituals
Quantum QM 6909; 1993; CD
Piano
Light dialect

4295

Sometimes I Feel Like a Motherless Child
[Burleigh, Harry T.]
Hall, Adelaide (Mezzo-soprano)
Spirituals
London LA 52; 1948; 78 RPM
Organ, piano

4296

Sometimes I Feel Like a Motherless Child
Composer not identified
Hampton, Jonathon (Vocalist)
Negro Spirituals: Songs of Trial and Triumph
Private Label; 2017; Streaming audio
Piano
Light dialect

4297

Sometimes I Feel Like a Motherless Child
Burleigh, Harry T.
Harness, William (Vocalist)
New Song, A

William Harness Sacred Concerts 102;
    [197-]; LP
Piano

4298

Sometimes I Feel Like a Motherless
    Child
Burleigh, Harry T.
Harness, William (Vocalist)
The Early Years
Private Label #1234; [20--]; CD
Piano

4299

Sometimes I Feel Like a Motherless
    Child
Composer not identified
Harris, Lloyd (Bass)
Negro Spirituals
Pléïade P45301; 1960; 45 RPM
Piano

4300

Sometimes I Feel Like a Motherless Child
Composer not identified
Hayes, Roland (Tenor)
Evening with Roland Hayes, Tenor
Heritage LP-SS-1204; 1953; LP
Piano

4301

Sometimes I Feel Like a Motherless Child
Composer not identified
Hayes, Roland (Tenor)
*The Art of Roland Hayes: Six Centuries of
    Song*
Preiser Records; 2010; CD
A cappella
Moderate dialect

4302

Sometimes I Feel Like a Motherless Child
    [from *Three Aframerican Religious
    Folksongs*]
Hayes, Roland
Hayes, Roland (Tenor)
Roland Hayes Recital, A
A 440 Records AC1203; [19--]; LP
Piano

4303

Sometimes I Feel Like a Motherless Child
Burleigh, Harry T.
Heard, Richard (Tenor)
*Ain't a That Good News: African-American
    Art Songs and Spirituals*
HM Classics HMC9602; 1998; CD
Piano
Moderate dialect

4304

Sometimes I Feel Like a Motherless Child
Composer not identified
Hendricks, Barbara (Soprano)
Espirituales Negros
EMI Classics/Altaya 01636; 1983; CD
Piano

4305

Sometime I Feel Like a Motherless Child
Composer not identified
Hendricks, Barbara (Soprano)
Schubert, Debussy, Fauré, Negro Spirituals
EMI Electrola CDZ 2523322; 1990; CD
Piano

4306

Sometimes I Feel Like a Motherless Child
Composer not identified
Hendricks, Barbara (Soprano)
La Voix du Ciel
EMI Classics 077775491227; 1991; CD

4307

Sometimes I Feel Like a Motherless Child
Composer not identified
Hendricks, Barbara (Soprano)
Spirituals
EMI Classics 0946 346641 2 7; 2005; CD
Piano

4308

Sometimes I Feel Like a Motherless Child
Hendricks, Barbara; Alexeev, Dmitri
Hendricks, Barbara (Soprano)
Negro Spirituals
EMI CDC7470262; 1983; CD
Piano
No dialect discerned

Also released with *Great American
Spirituals* (Angel CDM 7 64669 2; 1992; CD);
Great American Spirituals (Musical Heritage
Society 513725Z; 1994; CD); *Negro Spirituals*
(EMI 7243 5 72790 2 4; 1998; CD) and *The
Very Best of Barbara Hendricks* (EMI Classics 7243 5 86323 2 3; 2005; CD)

4309

Sometimes I Feel Like a Motherless Child
Traditional
Hendricks, Barbara (Soprano)
Chants sacrés = Sacred songs
EMI France CDC 7 54098 2; 1990; CD
A cappella
Light dialect

    Also released with *Spirituals* (EMI Classics 0946 346641 2 7; 2005; CD)

4310

Sometimes I Feel Like a Motherless Child
Traditional
Hendricks, Barbara (Soprano)
*100 Plus Beaux Airs de Barbara Hendricks,
    Les*
EMI Classics 50999 085683 2 8; 2012; CD
A cappella

4311

Sometimes I Feel
[Burleigh, Harry T.]
Henriksson, Deborah (Soprano)
Simple Gifts
Nosag NOSAGCD143; 2007; CD
Piano, dulcimer
Light dialect

4312

Sometimes I Feel Like a Motherless Child
Burleigh, Harry T.
Holland, Charles (Tenor)
Negro Spirituals
Pathé 45 ED. 29; 1954; 45 RPM
Piano

4313

Sometimes I Feel Like a Motherless Child
Burleigh, Harry T.
Holmes, Eugene (Baritone)

Spirituals
Schubert Records SCH-102; [1988]; LP
Piano
Light dialect

4314
Sometimes I Feel Like a Motherless Child
Davis, Carl
Horne, Marilyn (Mezzo-soprano)
The Complete Decca Recitals
Decca 478 0165; 2008; CD
Chorus
Heavy dialect

4315
Sometimes I Feel Like a Motherless Child
Burleigh, Harry T.
Hynninen, Jorma (Bass-baritone)
Negro Spirituals
Ondine ODE 715-2; 1988; CD
Piano

4316
Sometimes I Feel Like a Motherless Child
Clinton, Irving
Irving, Clinton (Bass-baritone)
Clinton Irving Sings Spirituals: A Tribute
Rogers; 2001; CD

4317
Sometimes I Feel Like a Motherless Child
Composer not identified
Jo, Sumi (Soprano)
Prayers
Erato 8573-85772-2; 2000; CD
Piano

4318
Sometimes I Feel Like a Motherless Child
Burleigh, Harry T.
Jones, Arthur (Tenor)
Wade in the Water
Orbis Books; 1993; Book w/cass
Piano
Heavy dialect

4319
Sometimes I Feel Like a Motherless Child
Composer not identified

Jones, Fanni (Mezzo-soprano)
Negro Spirituals
Phonotec 815; 1977; LP
Organ

4320
Recitative (Sometimes I Feel Like a
    Motherless Child) [from *Cantata*]
Carter, John D.
Jones, Randye (Soprano)
Come Down Angels
Ahhjay Records AHHJ-0001; 2003; CD
Piano
Light dialect

4321
Sometimes I Feel Like a Motherless Child
Composer not identified
Judkins, Edith (Soprano)
Sacred Recital, A
United Sound USR 3845; [19--]; LP

4322
Sometimes I Feel Like a Motherless Child
Hogan, Moses
Lewis, Cheryse McLeod (Mezzo-soprano)
Spirituals
CheryseMusic; 2012; CD
Piano

4323
Sometimes I Feel Like a Motherless Child
[Burleigh, Harry T.]
Loiselle, Henri (Bass-baritone)
Encore
Hum Recordings HRHLCD004; 2008;
    CD
Piano
Heavy dialect

4324
Sometimes I Feel Like a Motherless Child
Meyer, Fredrich
London, George (Bass-baritone)
Spirituals
Deutsche Grammophon 00289 477 6193;
    2006; CD
Chorus
Moderate dialect

4325

Sometimes I Feel Like a Motherless Child
Browne, George
Lucas, Isabelle (Soprano)
Negro Spirituals
P&R; 2011; Streaming audio
Orchestra
Heavy dialect

4326

Sometimes I Feel Like a Motherless Child
Browne, George
Lucas, Isabelle (Soprano)
Negro Spirituals
Marathon Media International; 2013;
    Streaming audio
Orchestra
Heavy dialect

4327

Sometimes I Feel Like a Motherless Child
Browne, George
Lucas, Isabelle (Soprano)
Negro Spirituals
World Record Club MW-2005; [196-]; LP
Orchestra
Heavy dialect

4328

Sometimes I Feel Like a Motherless Child
Hogan, Moses
Lynch, Lester (Baritone)
On My Journey Now: Spirituals & Hymns
Pentatone Music PTC 5186 57'; 2017; CD
Piano

4329

Sometimes I Feel Like a Motherless Child
    [from *Feel the Spirit*]
Rutter, John
Marshall, Melanie (Mezzo-soprano)
Feel the Spirit
Collegium Records COLCD 128; 2001; CD
Chorus, orchestra

4330

Sometimes I Feel Like a Motherless Child
    [from *Journey Beyond Time*]
Crumb, George

Martin, Barbara Ann (Soprano)
American Songbooks II & IV
BRIDGE 9275A/B; 2008; CD
Piano, percussion

4331

Sometimes I Feel Like a Motherless Child
Burleigh, Harry T.
Maynor, Kevin (Bass)
The Spiritual: An Underground Railroad
Southeastern Virginia Arts Assoc.; [2000]; CD
Piano

4332

Sometimes I Feel Like a Motherless Child
Burleigh, Harry T.
McKinney, Jason (Bass-baritone)
Songs Inspired by Paul Robeson
United in Music; 2014; CD
Piano
Light dialect

4333

Sometimes I Feel Like a Motherless Child
Burleigh, Harry T.
Moses, Oral (Bass-baritone)
*Amen! African-American Composers of the
    20th Century*
Albany Records TROY459; 2001; CD
Piano
Heavy dialect

4334

Sometimes I Feel Like a Motherless Child
Burleigh, Harry T.; Lindgren, E.
Moses, Oral (Bass-baritone)
*Come Down Angels and Trouble the Water:
    Negro Spirituals, an American National
    Treasure!*
Albany Records TROY 1489; 2014; CD
Piano, flute
Heavy dialect

    Also released with *Sankofa: A Spiritual
Reflection* (Albany Records TROY1802; 2019;
CD)

4335

Sometimes I Feel Like a Motherless Child
Composer not identified

Moses, Oral (Bass-baritone)
Extreme Spirituals
Cuneiform Record Rune 241; 2006; CD
Instrumental ensemble

4336

Sometimes I Feel Like a Motherless Child
Composer not identified
Newby, Marion Crowley (Contralto)
A Motherless Child
Compassion; [19--]; LP

4337

Sometimes I Feel Like a Motherless Child
Composer not identified
Norman, Jessye (Soprano)
*Oh, Happy Day! Gospels & Spirituals: The
     Ultimate CD*
Ultimate; 2010; CD

4338

Motherless Child
[Burleigh, Harry T.]
Norman, Jessye (Soprano)
Gospels & Spirituals Gold Collection
Retro R2CD 40-26; 1995; CD
Piano
Heavy dialect

4339

Sometimes I Feel Like a Motherless Child
[Burleigh, Harry T.]
Norman, Jessye (Soprano)
An Evening with Jessye Norman
Opera D'Oro Recitals OPD-2011; 1999; CD
Piano
Heavy dialect

4340

Sometimes I Feel Like a Motherless Child
[Burleigh, Harry T.]
Norman, Jessye (Soprano)
Roots: My Life, My Song
Sony Classical 88697642632; 2010; CD
Piano

4341

Sometimes I Feel Like a Motherless Child
[Burleigh, Harry T.]

Norman, Jessye (Soprano)
Une Vie Pour le Chant
Sony Classical 88883704512; 2013; CD
Piano

4342

Sometimes I Feel Like a Motherless
     Chile'
Traditional
Oby, Jason (Tenor)
The Life of Christ: Collected Spirituals
Private Label TSU4749; [200-]; CD
A cappella
Heavy dialect

4343

Sometimes I Feel Like a Motherless Child
Brown, Lawrence
Pankey, Aubrey (Baritone)
Negro Spirituals
Eterna 830010; 1983; LP
Piano
Light dialect

4344

Sometimes I Feel Like a Motherless Child
[Brown, Lawrence]
Pankey, Aubrey (Baritone)
Aubrey Pankey Singt Negro-Spirituals
Eterna 7 30 005; 1959; LP
Piano
Light dialect

4345

Sometimes I Feel Like a Motherless Child
Flynn, William
Paris, Virginia (Contralto)
Spirituals
Spotlight Classic SC 1008; 1957; LP
Orchestra

4346

Sometimes I Feel Like a Motherless
     Child
Flynn, William
Paris, Virginia (Contralto)
Virginia Paris in Australia
Lyric Records CD 178; [2005]; CD
Orchestra

4347

Sometimes I Feel Like a Motherless Chile
Burleigh, Harry T.
Philogene, Ruby (Soprano)
Steal Away
EMI Classics 7243 5 69707 2 4; 1997; CD
Piano

4348

Sometimes I Feel Like a Motherless Child
  (Recitative) [from *Cantata*]
Carter, John D.
Pickens, Jo Ann (Soprano)
*My Heritage: American Melodies/Negro
  Spirituals*
Koch Schwann 3-1447-2; 1993; CD

4349

Sometimes I Feel Like a Motherless Child
  (Recitative) [from *Cantata*]
[Carter, John D.]
Pleas III, Henry H. (Tenor)
Cantata
Private Label; 2003; CD
Piano

4350

Like a Motherless Child
Composer not identified
Porter, John (Bass)
No More Crying: Negro Spirituals
Pan Verlag OV-84; [1978]; LP

4351

Sometimes I Feel Like a Motherless Child
Holmes, Charles
Price, Leontyne (Soprano)
*Complete Collection of Songs and Spiritual
  Albums*
RCA Red Seal 88697940502; 2011; CD
Chorus

4352

Sometimes I Feel Like a Motherless Child
Holmes, Charles
Price, Leontyne (Soprano)
I Wish I Knew How It Would Feel to Be Free
RCA Red Seal LSC 3183; 2011; CD
Chorus

4353

Sometimes I Feel Like a Motherless Child
Johnson, Hall
Ragin, Derek Lee (Countertenor)
Ev'ry Time I Feel the Spirit: Spirituals
Channel Classics CCS 2991; 1991; CD
Piano
Moderate dialect

4354

Sometimes I Feel Like a Motherless Child
Giesen, Hubert
Ray, William (Baritone)
Negro Spirituals
Intercord; [19--]; LP
Piano

4355

Sometimes I Feel Like a Motherless Child
Giesen, Hubert
Ray, William (Baritone)
*Sings Arias, Duets, Musical Selections and
  Negro Spirituals*
Intercord; [19--]; CD
Piano

4356

Sometimes I Feel Like a Motherless Child
Brown, Lawrence
Reese, Ruth (Contralto)
Motherless Child
OPS 1006/79; 1979; LP

4357

Sometimes I Feel Like a Motherless Child
Brown, Lawrence
Robeson, Paul (Bass-baritone)
*Sometimes I Feel Like a Motherless Child/On
  Ma Journey*
Victor 20013; 1926; 78 RPM
Piano
No dialect discerned

4358

Sometimes I Feel Like a Motherless Child
Brown, Lawrence
Robeson, Paul (Bass-baritone)
*Sometimes I Feel Like a Motherless Child/On
  Ma Journey*

His Master's Voice B 2326; 1926; 78 RPM
Piano
No dialect discerned

4359

Sometimes I Feel Like a Motherless Child
Brown, Lawrence
Robeson, Paul (Bass-baritone)
Sometimes I Feel Like a Motherless Child;
   Poem (Minstrel Man)/The Wanderer
His Master's Voice B.8604; 1937; 78 RPM
Piano
Light dialect

4360

Sometimes I Feel Like a Motherless Child
Brown, Lawrence
Robeson, Paul (Bass-baritone)
Spirituals
Columbia Masterworks 17379-D; 1945; 78
   RPM
Piano
No dialect discerned

4361

Sometimes I Feel Like a Motherless Child
Brown, Lawrence
Robeson, Paul (Bass-baritone)
Sometimes I Feel Like a Motherless Child/
   Nobody Knows de Trouble I've Seen
Columbia D.B. 2491; 1949; 78 RPM
Piano
Light dialect

4362

Sometimes I Feel Like a Motherless Child
Brown, Lawrence
Robeson, Paul (Bass-baritone)
Paul Robeson with Chorus, orchestra
Fontana BIG.417-1Y; 1958; LP

4363

Sometimes I Feel Like a Motherless Child
Brown, Lawrence
Robeson, Paul (Bass-baritone)
Spirituals
Philips 409.115 AE; 1959; 45 RPM
Piano

4364

Sometimes I Feel Like a Motherless Child
Brown, Lawrence
Robeson, Paul (Bass-baritone)
Paul Robeson in Live Performance
Columbia M 30424; 1971; LP
Piano
Light dialect

4365

Sometimes I Feel Like a Motherless Child
Brown, Lawrence
Robeson, Paul (Bass-baritone)
Songs of My People
RCA Red Seal LM-3292; 1972; LP
Piano

4366

Sometimes I Feel Like a Motherless Child
Brown, Lawrence
Robeson, Paul (Bass-baritone)
Golden Voice of Paul Robeson
EMI Music PLAY-1020; 1983; CD

4367

Sometimes I Feel Like a Motherless Child
Brown, Lawrence
Robeson, Paul (Bass-baritone)
The Power and the Glory
Columbia/Legacy CK 47337; 1991; CD
Piano
Light dialect

4368

Sometimes I Feel Like a Motherless Child
Brown, Lawrence
Robeson, Paul (Bass-baritone)
The Odyssey of Paul Robeson
Omega Classics OCD 3007; 1992; CD
Piano

4369

Sometimes I Feel Like a Motherless Child
Brown, Lawrence
Robeson, Paul (Bass-baritone)
Songs of Free Men: a Paul Robeson Recital
Sony Classical MHK 63223; 1997; CD
Piano
Light dialect

4370

Sometimes I Feel Like a Motherless Child
Brown, Lawrence
Robeson, Paul (Bass-baritone)
Songs for Free Men, 1940-45
Pearl GEMM CD 9264; 1997; CD
Piano

4371

Sometimes I Feel Like a Motherless
    Child
Brown, Lawrence
Robeson, Paul (Bass-baritone)
Paul Robeson Collection
Hallmark Recordings 390692; 1998; CD

4372

Sometimes I Feel Like a Motherless Child
Brown, Lawrence
Robeson, Paul (Bass-baritone)
*Negro Spirituals: The Concert Tradition
    1909–1948*
Frémeaux & Associés FA 168; 1999; CD
Piano
Light dialect

4373

Sometimes I Feel Like a Motherless
    Child
Brown, Lawrence
Robeson, Paul (Bass-baritone)
Legends of the 20th Century: Paul Robeson
EMI Records 7243 520140; 1999; CD
Piano

4374

Sometimes I Feel Like a Motherless
    Child
Brown, Lawrence
Robeson, Paul (Bass-baritone)
The Essential Paul Robeson
ASV CD AJS 244; 2000; CD

4375

Sometimes I Feel Like a Motherless Child
Brown, Lawrence
Robeson, Paul (Bass-baritone)
The Great Paul Robeson
Pegasus PGN CD 811; 2000; CD

4376

Sometimes I Feel Like a Motherless Child
Brown, Lawrence
Robeson, Paul (Bass-baritone)
Spirituals: Original Recordings 1925–1936
Naxos Gospel Legends 8.120638; 2003; CD
Piano

4377

Sometimes I Feel Like a Motherless Child
Brown, Lawrence
Robeson, Paul (Bass-baritone)
*First Time Buyer's Guide to American Negro
    Spirituals*
Primo Collection PRMCD6038; 2006; CD
Piano
No dialect discerned

4378

Sometimes I Feel Like a Motherless Child
Brown, Lawrence
Robeson, Paul (Bass-baritone)
The Complete EMI Sessions (1928–1939)
EMI Classics 50999 2 15586 2 7; 2008; CD
Piano
Moderate dialect

4379

Sometimes I Feel Like a Motherless Child
Brown, Lawrence
Robeson, Paul (Bass-baritone)
*Nobody Knows de Trouble I've Seen/
    Sometimes I Feel Like a Motherless Child*
Columbia CD 35557; [19--]; 78 RPM
Piano

4380

Sometimes I Feel Like a Motherless Child
Brown, Lawrence
Robeson, Paul (Bass-baritone)
Paul Robeson
World Record Club W9648/EMI SM 431;
    [19--]; LP
Piano

4381

Sometimes I Feel Like a Motherless Child
Brown, Lawrence
Robeson, Paul (Bass-baritone)

*Sometimes I Feel Like a Motherless Child/
Nobody Knows de Trouble I've Seen*
Columbia DS 1783; [19--]; 78 RPM
Piano
No dialect discerned

4382
Sometimes I Feel Like a Motherless Child
Brown, Lawrence
Robeson, Paul (Bass-baritone)
Spirituals
Columbia Masterworks ML 4105 ; CBS
    62483; [1948]; LP

4383
Sometimes I Feel Like a Motherless Child
Brown, Lawrence
Robeson, Paul (Bass-baritone)
Spirituals
Philips 429 395 BE; [195-]; 45 RPM

4384
Sometimes I Feel Like a Motherless Child
Burleigh, Harry T.
Robeson, Paul (Bass-baritone)
*By an' By/Sometimes I Feel Like a Motherless
    Child*
Columbia Masterworks 17468-D; 1946; 78
    RPM
Piano
Light dialect

4385
Sometimes I Feel Like a Motherless Child
DeCormier, Robert
Robeson, Paul (Bass-baritone)
The Essential Paul Robeson
Vanguard VSD 57/58; 1974; LP
Chorus
Light dialect

4386
Sometimes I Feel Like a Motherless Child
[Brown, Lawrence]
Robeson, Paul (Bass-baritone)
Spirituals
Columbia Masterworks M-610; 1946; 78
    RPM
Piano

4387
Sometimes I Feel Like a Motherless Child
[Brown, Lawrence]
Robeson, Paul (Bass-baritone)
Recital
Supraphon SUA 10062; 1961; LP
Piano

4388
Sometimes I Feel Like a Motherless Child
[Brown, Lawrence]
Robeson, Paul (Bass-baritone)
Andere Amerika, Das
Eterna 8 10 021; 1966; LP
Piano

4389
Sometimes I Feel Like a Motherless Child
[Brown, Lawrence]
Robeson, Paul (Bass-baritone)
Scandalize My Name
Classics Record Library 30-5647; 1976; LP
Chorus
Light dialect

4390
Sometimes I Feel Like a Motherless Child
[Brown, Lawrence]
Robeson, Paul (Bass-baritone)
*Ballad for Americans and Great Songs of
    Faith, Love and Patriotism*
Vanguard VCD-117/18; 1989; CD
Chorus

4391
Sometimes I Feel Like a Motherless Child
[Brown, Lawrence]
Robeson, Paul (Bass-baritone)
The Essential Spirituals
Columbia 473788 2; 1993; CD

4392
Sometimes I Feel Like a Motherless Child
[Brown, Lawrence]
Robeson, Paul (Bass-baritone)
Deep River
Great Voices of the Century GVC 2004;
    1999; CD

4393

Sometimes I Feel Like a Motherless Child
[Brown, Lawrence]
Robeson, Paul (Bass-baritone)
Paul Robeson
Forever Gold FG019; 2001; CD
Chorus

4394

Sometimes I Feel Like a Motherless Child
[Brown, Lawrence]
Robeson, Paul (Bass-baritone)
Walk Right In (When the Sun Goes Down Series)
Bluebird/BMG/RCA Records 09026-63986-2; 2002; CD
Piano
No dialect discerned

4395

Sometimes I Feel Like a Motherless Child
[Brown, Lawrence]
Robeson, Paul (Bass-baritone)
Ol Man River
Leverage; 2005; Streaming audio
Piano
Moderate dialect

4396

Sometimes I Feel Like a Motherless Child
[Brown, Lawrence]
Robeson, Paul (Bass-baritone)
The Originals: "Spirituals"
Yoyo USA; 2006; Streaming audio

4397

Sometimes I Feel Like a Motherless Child
[Brown, Lawrence]
Robeson, Paul (Bass-baritone)
Collection
RGS Music 1404-2; 2007; CD

4398

Sometimes I Feel Like a Motherless Child
[Brown, Lawrence]
Robeson, Paul (Bass-baritone)
The Best of Paul Robeson
Delta Music Group CD6252; 2008; CD

4399

Sometimes I Feel Like a Motherless Child
[Brown, Lawrence]
Robeson, Paul (Bass-baritone)
Ol' Man River: His 56 Finest 1925–1945
Retrospective RTS 4116; 2008; CD

4400

Sometimes I Feel Like a Motherless Child
[Brown, Lawrence]
Robeson, Paul (Bass-baritone)
Paul Robeson's Treasure Chest
Leverage; 2008; Streaming audio
Piano

4401

Sometimes I Feel Like a Motherless Child
[Brown, Lawrence]
Robeson, Paul (Bass-baritone)
Negro Spirituals (And More)
Discmedi DM-4674-02; 2009; CD

4402

Sometimes I Feel Like a Motherless Child
[Brown, Lawrence]
Robeson, Paul (Bass-baritone)
The Very Best of Paul Robeson
Future Noise Music FVDD033; 2009; CD
Piano

4403

Sometimes I Feel Like a Motherless Child
[Brown, Lawrence]
Robeson, Paul (Bass-baritone)
The Ultimate Collection
Burning Fire; 2009; Streaming audio

4404

Sometimes I Feel Like a Motherless Child
[Brown, Lawrence]
Robeson, Paul (Bass-baritone)
Drink to Me Only with Thine Eyes
MD Music; 2010; Streaming audio
Piano
No dialect discerned

4405

Sometimes I Feel Like a Motherless Child
[Brown, Lawrence]

Robeson, Paul (Bass-baritone)
Ol' Man River: The Ultimate Collection
Roslin Records; 2011; Streaming audio
Piano
Light dialect

4406

Sometimes I Feel Like a Motherless Child
[Brown, Lawrence]
Robeson, Paul (Bass-baritone)
*Ol' Man River: The Very Best of Paul
    Robeson*
Memory Lane; 2012; CD

4407

Sometimes I Feel Like a Motherless Child
[Brown, Lawrence]
Robeson, Paul (Bass-baritone)
Sometimes I Feel Like a Motherless Child
JazzAge; 2012; Streaming audio
Piano

4408

Sometimes I Feel Like a Motherless Child
[Brown, Lawrence]
Robeson, Paul (Bass-baritone)
Five Classic Albums Plus Bonus Tracks
Real Gone Music RGMCD287; 2017; CD

4409

Sometimes I Feel Like a Motherless Child
[Brown, Lawrence]
Robeson, Paul (Bass-baritone)
The Essential Collection
Primo PRMCD6233; 2018; CD

4410

Sometimes I Feel Like a Motherless Child
[Brown, Lawrence]
Robeson, Paul (Bass-baritone)
Complete Recordings
Universal Digital Enterprises; 2018;
    Streaming audio

4411

Sometimes I Feel Like a Motherless Child
[Brown, Lawrence]
Robeson, Paul (Bass-baritone)
The Concerto: African American Spirituals

Orange Amaro; 2019; Streaming audio
Piano

4412

Sometimes I Feel Like a Motherless Child
[Brown, Lawrence]
Robeson, Paul (Bass-baritone)
The Historic Paul Robeson
Murray Hill Records 959062; [19--]; LP
Piano

4413

Sometimes I Feel Like a Motherless Child
[Brown, Lawrence]
Robeson, Paul (Bass-baritone)
Robeson
Vanguard VSD-2015; 1958?; LP
Chorus, orchestra

4414

Sometimes I Feel Like a Motherless Child
Sadin, Robert
Robinson, Morris (Bass)
Going Home
Decca B0008277-02; 2007; CD
Instrumental ensemble
Heavy dialect

4415

Sometimes I Feel Like a Motherless Child
Composer not identified
Rustin, Bayard (Tenor)
*Bayard Rustin Sings Spirituals, Work &
    Freedom Songs*
Bayard Rustin Fund; 1988; Cassette
Piano
Heavy dialect

　　　Also released with *Bayard Rustin, the
Singer* (Bayard Rustin Fund; 1992; CD) and
*Bayard Rustin Sings Spirituals, Work & Free-
dom Songs* (Bayard Rustin Fund; 2003; CD)

4416

Sometimes I Feel Like a Motherless Child
Traditional
Rustin, Bayard (Tenor)
*Bayard Rustin Sings Twelve Spirituals on the
    Life of Christ*
Fellowship Records E2-KL 1771; [195-]; LP

A cappella
Moderate dialect

   Also released with *Bayard Rustin-The Singer* (Black Swan Series; Parnassus Records PACD 96083; 2022; CD)

4417

Sometimes I Feel Like a Motherless Child
Burleigh, Harry T.
Salters, Stephen (Baritone)
Spirit: Are You There, You Are There
HarmonizedDisharmony 0001; 2015; CD

4418

Motherless Child [from *Motherless Child Songs*]
Dunner, Leslie B.
Sebron, Carolyn (Mezzo-soprano)
Open Boundaries
Innova Recordings MN 108; 1989; CD
Piano, clarinet
No dialect discerned

4419

Sometimes I Feel Like a Motherless Child
Traditional
Sebron, Carolyn (Mezzo-soprano)
Resurrection, Pt. 1
Private Label; 2006; CD
A cappella
No dialect discerned

4420

Sometimes I Feel Like a Motherless Child
Composer not identified
Lee, Seung Hyun (Soprano)
Sweet Blessing: Spirituals & Hymns by Seung-Hyun Lee
Seoul Records; [20--]; CD

4421

Sometimes I Feel Like a Motherless Child (Recitative) [from *Cantata*]
Carter, John D.
Smith, Derrick (Baritone)
A Tribute to William Warfield
Mark Records MCD-1409; 1994; CD
Piano

4422

Sometimes I Feel Like a Motherless Child
Composer not identified
St. Hill, Krister (Baritone)
Svenska Folkvisor/Negro Spirituals
Polar POLS 398; 1985; LP

4423

Sometimes I Feel Like a Motherless Child
Walters, Richard (ed.)
Stolen, Steven (Tenor)
15 Easy Spiritual Arrangements for the Progressing Singer
Hal Leonard HL00000391 (high) ; HL00000392 (low); 2005; Score w/CD
Piano
Moderate dialect

4424

Sometimes I Feel Like a Motherless Child
Composer not identified
Sykes, Jubilant (Baritone)
Jubilation
EMI Classics/Angel 7243 5 57591 2 2; 2007; CD
Guitar

4425

Sometimes I Feel Like a Motherless Child
Hogan, Moses
Taylor, Darryl (Countertenor)
How Sweet the Sound: A Charm of Spirituals
Albany TROY1244; 2011; CD
Piano

4426

Sometimes I Feel Like a Motherless Child
Traditional
Tenet (female solo voices) (Vocalist)
A Feast for the Senses
Private Label; 2011; CD
A cappella

4427

Sometimes I Feel Like a Motherless Child
Carter, John D.
Thomas, Indra (Soprano)
Great Day: Indra Thomas Sings Spirituals
Delos DE 3427; 2012; CD

Piano
No dialect discerned

4428

Recitative: Sometimes I Feel Like a
    Motherless Child [from *Cantata*]
[Carter, John D.]
Thoms, Treva (Soprano)
Come Sunday: Sacred American Songs
Private Label; 2007; CD
Piano

4429

Sometimes I Feel Like a Motherless Child
Composer not identified
Treigle, Norman (Bass-baritone)
I Believe
New York City Opera Guild COG 1001;
    [197-]; LP
Keyboard

4430

Sometimes I Feel Like a Motherless
    Child
Composer not identified
Tyler, Veronica (Soprano)
*Sings ... the Passion of Christ in
    Spirituals*
BRC Productions; [19--]; LP
Piano

4431

Sometimes I Feel Like a Motherless Child
Burleigh, Harry T.
Vaughan, Sarah (Vocalist)
*The Lord's Prayer/Sometimes I Feel Like a
    Motherless Child*
Musicraft 525; 1947; 78 RPM
Orchestra
Heavy dialect

4432

Sometimes I Feel Like a Motherless Child
[Burleigh, Harry T.]
Ventriglia, Franco (Baritone)
Franco Ventriglia Sings Negro Spirituals
Vedette Records; 2007; Streaming audio
Piano, organ
Heavy dialect

4433

Sometimes I Feel Like a Motherless Child
[Burleigh, Harry T.]
Ventriglia, Franco (Baritone)
Franco Ventriglia Sings Negro Spirituals
Vedette Records VRMS 316; [19--]; LP
Piano, organ
Heavy dialect

4434

Sometimes I Feel Like a Motherless Child
    (Recitative) [from *Cantata*]
[Carter, John D.]
Verdejo, Awilda (Soprano)
Awilda Verdejo Sings Spirituals
Angeluz Performances; 1999; CD
Piano

4435

Sometimes I Feel Like a Motherless Child
    (Recitative) [from *Cantata*]
Carter, John D.
Wade, Ray, Jr. (Tenor)
Sence You Went Away
Albany Records TROY 387; 1998; CD
Piano
Heavy dialect

4436

Sometimes I Feel Like a Motherless Child
Hogan, Moses
Walker, Alfred (Bass)
*Deep River: Featuring 10 Spirituals Arranged
    for Solo Voice....*
MGH Records 5000; 2000; CD
Piano
No dialect discerned

4437

Sometimes I Feel Like a Motherless Child
Hogan, Moses
Walker, Alfred (Bass)
Songs of Reflection
MGH Records 0800CD; 1997; CD

4438

Sometimes I Feel Like a Motherless Child
Composer not identified
Webb, George (Tenor)

Famous Negro Spirituals and Songs of Elizabethan England, Ireland & the Caribbean
[Unknown] WLP7804; 1978; LP

4439
Sometimes I Feel Like a Motherless Chil'
Brown, Lawrence
West, Lucretia (Mezzo-soprano)
Negro Spirituals III
Club français du disque 176; 1959; LP
Piano
Moderate dialect

4440
Sometimes I Feel
Brown, Lawrence
West, Lucretia (Mezzo-soprano)
Negro Spirituals mit Lukretia West
Opera 3408; [195-]; LP
Piano

4441
Sometimes I Feel Like a Motherless Child
Composer not identified
West, Lucretia (Mezzo-soprano)
Lucretia West Sings Spirituals
Westminster WP 6063; [1957]; LP

4442
Sometimes I Feel Like a Motherless Child
Morgenstern, Sam
West, Lucretia (Mezzo-soprano)
Spirituals
Westminster WL 5338; 1954; LP
Orchestra

4443
Sometimes I Feel Like a Motherless Child
[Burleigh, Harry T.]
White, Cassandra (Soprano)
Remembering the Spirituals
CBW Entertainment 837101334068; 2007; CD
Piano
Light dialect

4444
Sometimes I Feel Like a Motherless Child
(Recitative) [from *Cantata*]

Carter, John D.
Williams, Wayne (Tenor)
Music from My Life
Movideo Productions 02-1993; 1993; CD
Piano

4445
Sometimes I Feel Like a Motherless Child
Schweizer, Rolf
Wolf, Lars (Vocalist)
Die Schwarze Stimme Europas
Cantate 666000; 1971; LP
Chorus, organ, percussion

. . . .

Somewhere Around a Throne

4446
Somewhere Around a Throne
Clinton, Irving
Irving, Clinton (Bass-baritone)
Clinton Irving Sings Spirituals: A Tribute
Rogers; 2001; CD

4447
Somewhere Around a Throne
White, Clarence Cameron
Mims, A. Grace Lee (Soprano)
Spirituals
H & GM Records HGM 8101; 1981; LP
Piano
Heavy dialect

. . . .

Soon I Will Be Done

4448
Soon-a Will Be Done
Boatner, Edward
Anderson, Marian (Contralto)
Marian Anderson Sings Spirituals
RCA Victor Red Seal MO 1238; 1948; 78 RPM
Piano

4449
Soon-a Will Be Done
Boatner, Edward

Anderson, Marian (Contralto)
Negro Spirituals
La Voix de Son Maître FBLP1039; 1953; LP
Piano

4450

Soon-a Will Be Done
Boatner, Edward
Anderson, Marian (Contralto)
Spirituals
RCA Victor Red Seal 09026-63306-2; 1999;
    CD
Piano
Heavy dialect

4451

Soon-a Will Be Done
Boatner, Edward
Anderson, Marian (Contralto)
Great Spirituals
Kipepeo Publishing; 2017; CD
Piano

4452

Soon-a Will Be Done
Boatner, Edward
Anderson, Marian (Contralto)
Marian Anderson Sings Negro Spirituals
His Master's Voice BLP 1060; [19--]; LP
Piano

Also released with *Marian Anderson: Beyond the Music; Her Complete RCA Victor Recordings* (Sony Classical 19439836492; 2021; CD)

4453

Soon-a Will Be Done
Boatner, Edward
Anderson, Marian (Contralto)
Great Spirituals
RCA Victor ERA 62; [195-]; 7" Vinyl
Piano

4454

Soon-a Will Be Done
Boatner, Edward
Anderson, Marian (Contralto)
Negro Spirituals

RCA Victor LM 2032; [1956]; LP
Piano

4455

Soon-a Will Be Done
[Boatner, Edward]
Anderson, Marian (Contralto)
Marian Anderson Sings Spirituals
RCA Victor LM 110; 1949; LP
Piano

4456

Soon-a Will Be Done
[Boatner, Edward]
Anderson, Marian (Contralto)
Alto Rhapsody; Selected Spirituals
Urania URN 22.328; 2007; CD
Piano

4457

Soon-a Will Be Done
[Boatner, Edward]
Anderson, Marian (Contralto)
The Very Best of Marian Anderson
Master Classics Records; 2009; CD
Piano
Light dialect

4458

Soon-a Will Be Done
[Boatner, Edward]
Anderson, Marian (Contralto)
Negro Spirituals
RCA Victor 630.396 A; [19--]; LP
Piano

4459

Soon I Will Be Done
Sneed, Damien
Brownlee, Lawrence (Tenor)
Spiritual Sketches
LeChateau Earl Records 888174029597;
    2013; CD
Piano
No dialect discerned

4460

Soon I Will Be Done
Boatner, Edward

Davis, Ellabelle (Soprano)
Soon I Will Be Done/I'm Goin' to March Down to Jordan
Philips A 56002 H; 1952; 78 RPM
Piano

4461

Soon a Will Be Done
Composer not identified
Franklin, Lavinia A. (Vocalist)
Historical Interpretation of Negro Spirituals and Lift Every Voice and Sing
Recorded Publications JZB-02591; 1970; LP
Organ

4462

Soon Ah Will Be Done
Raphael, Michael
Maynor, Kevin (Bass)
The Spiritual: An Underground Railroad
Southeastern Virginia Arts Assoc.; [2000]; CD
Piano

4463

Soon I Will Be Done
Boatner, Edward
Miller, Jeanette (Soprano)
No Man Canna Hinder Me
MiJon Record Productions MJ240; 1979; CD
Piano

4464

Soon Ah Will Be Done
Patterson. Willis
Norman, Jessye (Soprano)
Negro Spirituals
Philips 9500 580; 1979; LP
Chorus

4465

Soon Ah Will Be Done
Patterson. Willis
Norman, Jessye (Soprano)
Spirituals
Philips 416 462-2; 1990; CD
Chorus
Moderate dialect

4466

Soon Ah Will Be Done
[Patterson. Willis]
Norman, Jessye (Soprano)
The Jessye Norman Collection: Sacred Songs & Spirituals
Philips B0004506-02; 2005; CD
Chorus
Heavy dialect

. . . .

Soon One Morn

4467

Soon One Morn'
Dent, Cedric
Taylor, Richard (Baritone)
The New Negro Spiritual
W. C. Patterson; 2002; Score w/CD
Piano
Heavy dialect

. . . .

Stan' Still Jordan

4468

Stan' Still Jordan
[Burleigh, Harry T.]
Chaiter, Yoram (Bass)
Spirituals & Other Songs
Romeo Records 7311; 2014; CD
Piano
Light dialect

4469

Stand Still Jordan
Ryan, Donald
Estes, Simon (Bass-baritone)
Steal Away: My Favorite Negro Spirituals
Deutsche Schallplatten DS 1041-2; 1994; CD
Piano
Light dialect

4470

Stand Still, Jordan
Robbiani, Mario
Fisher, Dorothy (Contralto)
Negro Spirituals

Edizione D'Arte Del Lions Club Milano Al
    Cenacolo; [19--]; LP
Orchestra
Moderate dialect

4471

Stand Still Jordan
Composer not identified
Green, Elnora E. (Contralto)
15 Spirituals
Private Label J3RS 2286; 1979; LP
Piano

4472

Stan' Still Jordan
Clinton, Irving
Irving, Clinton (Bass-baritone)
Clinton Irving Sings Spirituals: A Tribute
Rogers; 2001; CD

4473

Stand Still, Jordan
Burleigh, Harry T.
Lynch, Lester (Baritone)
On My Journey Now: Spirituals & Hymns
Pentatone Music PTC 5186 57'; 2017; CD
Piano

4474

Stan Still Jordan
Burleigh, Harry T.
Maynor, Kevin (Bass)
Paul Robeson Remembered
Fleur de Son Classics FDS 57929; 1998; CD
Piano
Light dialect

4475

Stan' Still, Jordan
Burleigh, Harry T.
Mims, A. Grace Lee (Soprano)
Spirituals
H & GM Records HGM 8101; 1981; LP
Piano
Light dialect

4476

Stan' Still, Jordan
Burleigh, Harry T.

Moses, Oral (Bass-baritone)
*Deep River: Songs and Spirituals of Harry T.
    Burleigh*
Northeastern NR 252-CD; 1995; CD
Piano

4477

Stan Still Jordan
Burleigh, Harry T.
Oby, Jason (Tenor)
The Life of Christ: Collected Spirituals
Private Label TSU4749; [200-]; CD
Piano
Moderate dialect

4478

Stan' Still Jer'dn
Burleigh, Harry T.
Oglesby, Isador (Tenor)
*Negro Spirituals: The Musical Roots of
    American Folk Songs*
Praise PR 658; 1978; LP
Piano

4479

Stan' Still Jordan
Burleigh, Harry T.
Parks, Karen (Soprano)
Nobody Knows
Ottimavoce 52736; 2007; CD
Instrumental ensemble
Light dialect

4480

Stan's Still Jordan
Composer not identified
Peterson, Elwood (Baritone)
Negro Spirituals
Vergara 55.1.004 C; [1963]; 45 RPM
Piano

4481

Stan' Still, Jordan
Johnson, John Rosamond
Peterson, Elwood (Baritone)
Negro Spirituals
Boîte à Musique LD 073; 1961; LP
Piano

4482

Stand Still Jordan
Composer not identified
Porter, John (Bass)
No More Crying: Negro Spirituals
Pan Verlag OV-84; [1978]; LP

4483

Stand Still, Jordan
[Burleigh, Harry T.]
Robeson, Paul (Bass-baritone)
Favorite Songs
Monitor Recordings MPS 580; 1959; LP
Piano
Light dialect

4484

Stand Still, Jordan
[Burleigh, Harry T.]
Robeson, Paul (Bass-baritone)
The Collector's Paul Robeson
Monitor MCD-61580; 1989; CD
Piano
Light dialect

4485

Stand Still, Jordan
[Burleigh, Harry T.]
Robeson, Paul (Bass-baritone)
*On My Journey: Paul Robeson's Independent
    Recordings*
Smithsonian Folkways Recordings SFW CD
    40178; 2007; CD
Piano

4486

Stand Still Jordan
[Burleigh, Harry T.]
Robeson, Paul (Bass-baritone)
Negro Spirituals (And More)
Discmedi DM-4674-02; 2009; CD

4487

Stand Still Jordan
[Burleigh, Harry T.]
Robeson, Paul (Bass-baritone)
Paul Robeson Singt Negro Spirituals
Musical Masterpiece Society MMS-2162;
    [19--]; LP
Piano

4488

Stand Still, Jordan
[Burleigh, Harry T.]
Robeson, Paul (Bass-baritone)
Negro Spirituals
Concert Hall SVS 2611; [19--]; LP

4489

Stand Still, Jordan
[Burleigh, Harry T.]
Robeson, Paul (Bass-baritone)
Negro Spirituals
Chant du Monde LDX 74376; 1982; LP
Piano

4490

Stan' Still Jordan
Burleigh, Harry T.
Wright, John Wesley (Tenor)
*Wade in the Water: Songs of the River, the
    Lake, and the Sea*
Donald L. Robinson & Associates DLR-001;
    2004; CD
Piano

. . . .

Stand Steady

4491

Stand Steady
Hayes, Roland
Sims, Robert (Baritone)
*Robert Sims Sings the Spirituals of Roland
    Hayes*
Canti Classics 2014-01; 2015; CD
Piano
Moderate dialect

. . . .

Stand the Storm

4492

Stand the Storm
Jackson King, Betty; Sanders, Wayne
Anonymous (Vocalist)
Opera Ebony Sings Spirituals
Ebony Classic Recordings; 2002; CD

4493

Stand the Storm
Composer not identified
Cunningham-Fleming, Jeryl (Soprano)
Stand the Storm: Anthems, Hymns, and Spirituals of Faith and Hope
Private Label; 2016; CD
Piano

4494

Stand the Storm
Composer not identified
Parks, Karen (Soprano)
Done Crossed Every River: Freedom's Journey
Arcadia ARC 2004-2; 1995; CD

· · · · · · ·

Standing in the Need of Prayer

4495

It's Me O Lord
Composer not identified
Adams, Robert (Vocalist)
All God's Children Got Wings/Scandalize My Name Scandalize My Name/It's Me O Lord/Joshua Fit de Battle of Jericho
Ultraphon C 18121; [19--]; 78 RPM
Piano

4496

It's Me O Lord
Boatwright, McHenry
Boatwright, McHenry (Bass-baritone)
Art of McHenry Boatwright: Spirituals
Golden Crest Records RE 7024; 1968; LP
Piano
Light dialect

4497

Standing in the Need of Prayer
Composer not identified
Davis, Frank (Bass-baritone)
16 Spirituals My Father Taught Me
DeWitt Records 601; 1960; LP

4498

It's Me, Oh Lord
Jackson King, Betty

Dry, Marion (Contralto)
Let's Have a Union
Brave Records BRAV-0923; 2009; CD
Piano
Light dialect

4499

It's Me O Lord
Composer not identified
Duckworth, Zorita (Mezzo-soprano)
Forget Me Not.... Negro Spirituals
Private Label; [20--]; CD

4500

Standin' in the Need of Prayer
Roberts, Howard
Estes, Simon (Bass-baritone)
Spirituals
Philips 412 631-2; 1985; CD
Chorus
Light dialect

     Also released with *Famous Spirituals* (Philips 462 062-2; 1997; CD)

4501

It's Me Oh Lord
Kaelin, Pierre
Evans, Allan (Bass-baritone)
Negro Spirituals
Electromusic Records EMCD 6885; 1985; CD
Chorus, other instrument(s)

4502

Standin' in de Need o'Prayer
Reddick, William J.
Hindermyer, Harvey (Tenor)
Standin' in de Need o'Prayer/Wait 'till Ah Put on My Crown
Edison 80539-L; [1919]; 78 RPM
Orchestra

4503

It's Me O Lord
Henderson, Skitch
Hines, Jerome (Bass)
Standin' in the Need of Prayer
RCA Victor LPM-2047; [1960]; LP

4504

It's Me, O Lord
Jackson King, Betty
Honeysucker, Robert (Baritone)
*Watch and Pray: Spirituals and Art Songs by
   African-American Women Composers*
Koch International Classics 3-7247-2H1;
   1994; CD
Piano
Light dialect

4505

Tis Me, Oh Lord
Burleigh, Harry T.
Jones, Fanni (Mezzo-soprano)
Fanni Jones et Oswald Russell
Audio-Visual Enterprises AVE 30701; [19--];
   LP

4506

Tis Me
Composer not identified
Jones, Fanni (Mezzo-soprano)
Negro Spirituals
Evasion Disques LP613; 1974; LP

4507

Tis Me, O Lord
Composer not identified
Jones, Fanni (Mezzo-soprano)
Negro Spirituals
Phonotec 815; 1977; LP
Organ

4508

It's Me, O Lord
Jackson King, Betty
Lightfoot, Peter (Baritone)
An American Tapestry
Blue Griffin Recording BGR315; 2014; CD
Piano

4509

Tis Me, O Lord
Composer not identified
Monzo, Oscar (Baritone)
Negro Spirituals
Dial Discos 50-2020; 1983; LP

4510

It's Me, O Lord
Jackson King, Betty
Moses, Oral (Bass-baritone)
*Amen! African-American Composers of the
   20th Century*
Albany Records TROY459; 2001; CD
Piano
Light dialect

4511

It's Me, O Lord
Brown, Lawrence
Payne, John C. (Baritone); Brown, Lawrence
   (Vocalist)
*It's Me, O Lord/Nobody Knows the Trouble
   I've Seen; Every Time I Feel de Spirit*
Columbia 3662; 1925; 78 RPM
Piano

4512

It's Me O Lord
Composer not identified
Payne, John C. (Baritone)
Classic Gospel Songs
Emerald/K-Tel; 2013; Streaming audio
Piano

4513

I[t]'s Me, O Lord, Standin' in the Need of
   Prayer
Payne, John C.
Payne, John C. (Baritone); Brown, Lawrence
   (Vocalist)
Good News: Vintage Negro Spirituals
Living Era AJA 5622; 2006; CD
Piano
Light dialect

4514

Standin' in de Need o' Prayer
[Payne, John C.]
Payne, John C. (Baritone); Brown, Lawrence
   (Vocalist)
*Brother, Can You Spare a Dime?: The Roots of
   American Song*
Pearl Gemm CD 9484; 1991; CD
Piano
Light dialect

4515

Standin' in de Need o' Prayer
[Payne, John C.]
Payne, John C. (Baritone); Additional singer
(Vocalist)
*Black Europe: Sounds & Images of Black
People in Europe Pre–1927*
Bear Family Productions BCD 16095; 2013;
CD
Piano
Light dialect

4516

Tis Me, O Lord
Burleigh, Harry T.
Philogene, Ruby (Soprano)
Steal Away
EMI Classics 7243 5 69707 2 4; 1997; CD
Piano

4517

Standing in the Need of Prayer
Composer not identified
Porter, John (Bass)
No More Crying: Negro Spirituals
Pan Verlag OV-84; [1978]; LP

4518

Standin' in the Need of Prayer
Bonds, Margaret
Price, Leontyne (Soprano)
*Complete Collection of Songs and Spiritual
Albums*
RCA Red Seal 88697940502; 2011; CD
Chorus

4519

Standin' in the Need of Prayer
Bonds, Margaret
Price, Leontyne (Soprano)
I Wish I Knew How It Would Feel to Be Free
RCA Red Seal LSC 3183; 2011; CD
Chorus

4520

It's Me, O Lord
Jackson King, Betty
Rhodes, Yolanda (Soprano)

The Angels Bowed Down
Cambria Master Recordings CD-1237; 2019;
CD

4521

Standin in the Need o' Prayer
Reddick, William J.
Seagle, Oscar (Baritone)
*Standin' in the Need o' Prayer/Golden
Crown*
Columbia Record A2889; 1920; 78 RPM
Orchestra

4522

Standin' in de Need of Prayer
[Payne, John C.]
Watts, Leonardo (Baritone)
*On Ma Journey: A Memorable Collection of
Negro Spirituals*
Onyx Recording Associates ORA-101; 1961;
LP
Chorus

• • • • • • •

Steal Away

[Jeremiah 17:8; Matthew 6:6, 24:27-31; 2
Timothy 1:9]

"Steal away, steal away, steal away to
Jesus. Steal away, steal away home; I ain't got
long to stay here. My Lord, He calls me, He
calls me by the thunder. The trumpet sounds
within my soul; I ain't got long to stay here....
Green trees a-bending; poor sinner stands
a-trembling...."

[Available in AB10, CW40, DRSA,
DSSS, EM34, FHFN, HCTN, HJCO, HLBS,
HT25, HTBS, HTC1, JJAN, JJBA, JSSp, LLS2,
RCSS, RHMF, RS12, RWSC, RW15, SBFD,
SONS, SOTS, WF10, WF70]

While several spirituals are known to
contain messages or "secret signals" that
the enslaved used to communicate to one
another without the awareness of their
masters, "Steal Away" has been specifically
connected to Nat Turner, leader of the 1831
Southampton, Virginia, slave rebellion.
Turner is believed to have authored the song
about six years previously and have used it

to notify his followers of impending secret meetings.

The text itself is a call to action, to hear the Lord's call, expressed through the thunder and the lightning. Yet, while the words are sacred, there are clear political connotations.

4523

Steal Away
Traditional
Addison, Adele (Soprano)
Little David Play on Your Harp
Kapp Records KL 1109; 1959; LP
A cappella
Light dialect

4524

Steal Away
Composer not identified
Allen, Betty (Mezzo-soprano)
On Wings of Song
RCA Custom Reader's Digest RDA43-A;
    [1960]; LP
Chorus
Light dialect

4525

Steal Away
Burleigh, Harry T.
Arroyo, Martina (Soprano)
Spirituals
Centaur CRC 2060; 1991; CD
Piano
Moderate dialect

4526

Steal Away to Jesus
Composer not identified
Arroyo, Martina (Soprano); Lane, Betty
    (Vocalist)
There's a Meeting Here Tonight
Angel S-36072; 1974; LP
Chorus

4527

Steal Away to Jesus
Composer not identified
Arroyo, Martina (Soprano)

Negro Spirituals
EMI 7243 5 72790 2 4; 1998; CD
Chorus
Light dialect

4528

Improvisation on a Spiritual (Steal Away)
Walker, Neil; Baker, Bradley
Baker, Bradley (Baritone)
Not a Word: Spirituals, Hymns, Songs
AYA Worldwide Records 6-09682-2; 2001; CD
Piano

4529

Steal Away
Battle, Kathleen; Sadin, Robert
Battle, Kathleen (Soprano)
So Many Stars
Sony Classical SK 68473; 1995; CD
Instrumental ensemble
Heavy dialect

Also released with *The Complete Sony Recordings* (Sony Classical 88985381362; 2016; CD)

4530

Steal Away
Blackmon, Henry (Baritone)
Negro Spirituals
Stichting St. Josefkerk Discofonds
    Leidschendam JK 1006; [1964]; 45 RPM

4531

Steal Away
Boatwright, McHenry
Boatwright, McHenry (Bass-baritone)
Art of McHenry Boatwright: Spirituals
Golden Crest Records RE 7024; 1968; LP
Piano
Heavy dialect

4532

Steal Away
Burleigh, Harry T.
Brown, Anthony (Baritone)
Spirituals
Brown/Smith Productions; 1995; CD
Piano
Moderate dialect

4533

Steal Away
Hayes, Roland
Burton, Dashon (Bass-baritone)
Songs of Struggle & Redemption: We Shall Overcome
Acis Productions APL08685; 2015; CD
Piano
Moderate dialect

4534

Steal Away
Hayes, Roland
Caesar, Jackson (Tenor)
Spirituals: Celebrating the Music, Life, Legacy of Roland Hayes
CD Baby 7048606059; 2021; CD
Piano
Light dialect

4535

Steal Away
Dørumsgaard, Arne
Carlsen, Svein (Bass)
Negro Spirituals
EuroMaster AS ECD19005; 1996; CD
Piano

4536

Steal Away
Corley, Maria Thompson
Clark, Maria (Soprano)
Soul Sanctuary: Spirituals & Hymns
Navona Records NV6406; 2022; CD
Piano
Heavy dialect

4537

Steal Away to Jesus!
Hopkins, Gregory
Conrad, Barbara (Mezzo-soprano)
Spirituals
Naxos 8.553036; 1995; CD
Chorus, instrumental ensemble
Light dialect

4538

Steal Away
Composer not identified

Deguil, Arlette (Vocalist)
Negro Spirituals
Pathé 45 ED 1; 1953; 45 RPM
Men's voices
No dialect discerned

    Also released with *Negro Spirituals* (Pathé 45-ED 1; 1953; LP)

4539

Steal Away
Composer not identified
Dosher, George (Bass)
Steal Away
Suncoast Music; 2015; Streaming audio
Piano
Moderate dialect

4540

Steal Away
Composer not identified
Dosher, George (Bass)
Religious Music, vol. 2
Document Records; [1999]; CD
Piano
Moderate dialect

4541

Steal Away to Jesus
Roberts, Howard
Estes, Simon (Bass-baritone)
Spirituals
Philips 412 631-2; 1985; CD
Chorus
Light dialect

    Also released with *Famous Spirituals* (Philips 462 062-2; 1997; CD)

4542

Steal Away
Ryan, Donald
Estes, Simon (Bass-baritone)
Steal Away: My Favorite Negro Spirituals
Deutsche Schallplatten DS 1041-2; 1994; CD
Piano
Light dialect

    Also released with *Simon Sings His Favorite Gospels & Spirituals* (Praise Productions SMG-SE; 1999; CD) and *Save the*

Children, Save Their Lives (CD Baby; 2020; Streaming audio)

4543

Steal Away
Composer not identified
Ferguson, Margaret (Soprano)
Unfailing Love
Private Label; [20--]; CD

4544

Steal Away
Burleigh, Harry T.
Forest, Michael (Tenor)
The Spirit Sings: American Spirituals
Shenandoah Conservatory SU003; [199-];
    CD

4545

Steal Away
Composer not identified
Franklin, Lavinia A. (Vocalist)
*Historical Interpretation of Negro Spirituals
    and Lift Every Voice and Sing*
Recorded Publications JZB-02591; 1970; LP
Organ

4546

Steal Away
Burleigh, Harry T.
Gibson, Caroline (Soprano)
*On Ma Journey Now: Negro Spirituals in
    Concert*
Twin Productions; 2016; CD
Piano
Moderate dialect

4547

Steal Away
Composer not identified
Hampton, Jonathon (Vocalist)
Negro Spirituals: Songs of Trial and Triumph
Private Label; 2017; Streaming audio
Piano
Light dialect

4548

Steal Away
Brown, Lawrence

Hayes, Roland (Tenor)
Swing Low Sweet Chariot/Steal Away
Vocalion 21003; 1922; 78 RPM
Piano

4549

Steal Away
Brown, Lawrence
Hayes, Roland (Tenor)
Steal Away
Vocalion B-3033; 1923; 78 RPM
Piano

4550

Steal Away
Brown, Lawrence
Hayes, Roland (Tenor)
*Brother, Can You Spare a Dime?: The Roots of
    American Song*
Pearl Gemm CD 9484; 1991; CD
Piano
Light dialect

4551

Steal Away
Burleigh, Harry T.
Hayes, Roland (Tenor)
Good News: Vintage Negro Spirituals
Living Era AJA 5622; 2006; CD
Piano
Light dialect

4552

Steal Away to Jesus
Composer not identified
Hayes, Roland (Tenor)
*Black Europe: Sounds & Images of Black
    People in Europe pre–1927*
Bear Family Productions BCD 16095; 2013;
    CD
Piano

4553

Steal Away
Composer not identified
Hayes, Roland (Tenor)
Classic Gospel Songs
Emerald/K-Tel; 2013; Streaming audio
Piano

4554

Steal Away to Jesus
Composer not identified
Hayes, Roland (Tenor)
Black Swans
Parnassus Recordings PACD 96067; 2019; CD
Orchestra
Light dialect

4555

Steal Away
Hayes, Roland
Hayes, Roland (Tenor)
Roland Hayes: My Songs
Vanguard VRS-494; 1956; LP
Piano

4556

Steal Away [from *My Songs: Dream of Heaven*]
Hayes, Roland
Hayes, Roland (Tenor)
Favorite Spirituals
Vanguard Classics OVC 6022; 1995; CD
Piano
Moderate dialect

4557

Steal Away [from *My Songs: Dream of Heaven*]
[Hayes, Roland]
Hayes, Roland (Tenor)
Big Psalms, Hymns and Spirituals Box
eOne Music/Vanguard Classics; 2015; Streaming audio
Piano

4558

Steal Away
Composer not identified
Heard, William N. (Vocalist)
Songs from the Sanctuary: Hymns, Spirituals & Classic Gospels, Volume III
Heardsong Productions; 2012; CD
Piano
Moderate dialect

4559

Steal Away
Hogan, Moses

Hendricks, Barbara (Soprano)
Give Me Jesus
EMI Classics 7243 5 56788 2 9; 1998; CD
Chorus
Light dialect

4560

Steal Away to Jesus
Henderson, Skitch
Hines, Jerome (Bass)
Standin' in the Need of Prayer
RCA Victor LPM-2047; [1960]; LP

4561

Steal Away
Burleigh, Harry T.
Hynninen, Jorma (Bass-baritone)
Negro Spirituals
Ondine ODE 715-2; 1988; CD
Piano

4562

Steal Away
Boatner, Edward
Ingram, Paula Dione (Soprano)
Art. Legacy. Celebration: A Salute to Black-American Composers of Art Songs and Spirituals, v. 1
Private Label; 2014; CD
Piano

4563

Steal Away
Clinton, Irving
Irving, Clinton (Bass-baritone)
Clinton Irving Sings Spirituals: A Tribute
Rogers; 2001; CD

4564

Steal Away
Composer not identified
Johnson, Yolanda F (Soprano)
Feel the Spirit!
Jublianti Artists; 2011; Streaming audio
Piano
No dialect discerned

4565

Steal Away
Composer not identified

Jones, Fanni (Mezzo-soprano)
Negro Spirituals
Evasion Disques LP613; 1974; LP

4566
Steal Away
Composer not identified
Jones, Fanni (Mezzo-soprano)
Negro Spirituals
Phonotec 815; 1977; LP
Organ

4567
Steal Away
Corley, Maria Thompson
Jones, Randye (Soprano)
Come Down Angels
Ahhjay Records AHHJ-0001; 2003; CD
Piano
Moderate dialect

4568
Steal Away
Walters, Richard (ed.)
Kruse, Tanya (Soprano)
*15 Easy Spiritual Arrangements for the
    Progressing Singer*
Hal Leonard HL00000391 (high);
    HL00000392 (low); 2005; Score w/CD
Piano
Light dialect

4569
Steal Away
Jennings, Joseph
Little, Ricky (Baritone); Wright, John
    Wesley (Tenor)
*The Spirituals: Featuring the American
    Spiritual Ensemble*
LexArts; [20--]; CD
Chorus

4570
Steal Away
Okpebholo, Shawn
Liverman, Will (Baritone)
Steal Away
Yellow Einstein; 2014; CD
Piano
Light dialect

4571
Steal Away [from *Feel the Spirit*]
Rutter, John
Marshall, Melanie (Mezzo-soprano)
Feel the Spirit
Collegium Records COLCD 128; 2001; CD
Chorus, orchestra

4572
Steal Away [from *Journey Beyond Time*]
Crumb, George
Martin, Barbara Ann (Soprano)
American Songbooks II & IV
BRIDGE 9275A/B; 2008; CD
Piano, percussion

4573
Steal Away to Jesus
Dett, Robert Nathaniel
Maynor, Dorothy (Soprano)
Negro Spirituals
RCA Victor M879; 1942; 78 RPM
Men's voices

4574
Steal Away to Jesus
Dett, Robert Nathaniel
Maynor, Dorothy (Soprano)
*First Time Buyer's Guide to American Negro
    Spirituals*
Primo Collection PRMCD6038; 2006; CD
Men's voices
Light dialect

4575
Steal Away to Jesus
Dett, Robert Nathaniel
Maynor, Dorothy (Soprano)
Negro Spirituals
Kipepeo Publishing; 2018; CD
Men's voices

4576
Steal Away to Jesus
[Dett, Robert Nathaniel]
Maynor, Dorothy (Soprano)
*Negro Spirituals: The Concert Tradition
    1909–1948*

Frémeaux & Associés FA 168; 1999; CD
Men's voices
Light dialect

4577

Steal Away to Jesus
[Dett, Robert Nathaniel]
Maynor, Dorothy (Soprano)
Spirituals
Past Classics; 2013; Streaming audio
Men's voices
Light dialect

4578

Steal Away to Jesus
[Dett, Robert Nathaniel]
Maynor, Dorothy (Soprano)
The Concerto: African American Spirituals
Orange Amaro; 2019; Streaming audio
Men's voices
Light dialect

4579

Steal Away
Welsh, Nicky
McCue, Bill (Bass-baritone)
Bill McCue Sings the Great Spirituals
Beltona SBE 173; 1974; LP
Orchestra

4580

Steal Away
Fisher, William Arms
Miller, Jeanette (Soprano)
No Man Canna Hinder Me
MiJon Record Productions MJ240; 1979; CD
Piano

4581

Steal Away
Composer not identified
Monzo, Oscar (Baritone)
Negro Spirituals
Dial Discos 50-2020; 1983; LP

4582

Steal Away
Traditional
Moses, Oral (Bass-baritone)

Spirituals in Zion: A Spiritual Heritage for the Soul
Albany Records TROY587; 2003; CD
A cappella

4583

Steal Away
Composer not identified
Norman, Jessye (Soprano)
Spirituals: Great Day in the Morning
Philips 412 240-1; 1982; LP
Chorus, other instrument(s)

4584

Steal Away
Composer not identified
Norman, Jessye (Soprano)
Honor! A Celebration of the African American Cultural Legacy
Decca B0012660-02; 2009; CD

4585

Steal Away
Traditional
Norman, Jessye (Soprano)
Great Day in the Morning
Philips 6769 104; 1982; LP
A cappella
Light dialect

4586

Steal Away
Traditional
Norman, Jessye (Soprano)
Amazing Grace
Philips 432 546-2; 1990; CD
A cappella
Heavy dialect

4587

Steal Away
Flynn, William
Paris, Virginia (Contralto)
Spirituals
Spotlight Classic SC 1008; 1957; LP
Orchestra

4588

Steal Away
Flynn, William

Paris, Virginia (Contralto)
Virginia Paris in Australia
Lyric Records CD 178; [2005]; CD
Orchestra

4589

Steal Away
Burleigh, Harry T.
Philogene, Ruby (Soprano)
Steal Away
EMI Classics 7243 5 69707 2 4; 1997; CD
Piano

4590

Steal Away
Johnson, Hall
Ragin, Derek Lee (Countertenor)
Ev'ry Time I Feel the Spirit: Spirituals
Channel Classics CCS 2991; 1991; CD
Piano
Heavy dialect

4591

Steal Away
Brown, Lawrence
Robeson, Paul (Bass-baritone)
Steal Away/Water Boy
His Master's Voice B 2187; 1926; 78 RPM
Piano
Heavy dialect

4592

Steal Away
Brown, Lawrence
Robeson, Paul (Bass-baritone)
Steal Away/Water Boy
His Master's Voice B.8103; 1934; 78 RPM
Piano
Moderate dialect

4593

Steal Away
Brown, Lawrence
Robeson, Paul (Bass-baritone)
Songs of My People
RCA Red Seal LM-3292; 1972; LP
Piano

4594

Steal Away
Brown, Lawrence
Robeson, Paul (Bass-baritone)
The Best of Paul Robeson
EMI NTS 181; 1979; LP

4595

Steal Away
Brown, Lawrence
Robeson, Paul (Bass-baritone)
*A Lonesome Road: Paul Robeson Sings
    Spirituals and Songs*
ASV Living Era CD AJA 5027; 1984; CD
Piano
Light dialect

4596

Steal Away
Brown, Lawrence
Robeson, Paul (Bass-baritone)
The Complete EMI Sessions (1928–1939)
EMI Classics 50999 2 15586 2 7; 2008; CD
Piano
Moderate dialect

4597

Steal Away
Brown, Lawrence
Robeson, Paul (Bass-baritone)
Negro Spirituals
His Master's Voice 7EG 8422; [19--]; 45
    RPM
Piano

4598

Steal Away
Brown, Lawrence
Robeson, Paul (Bass-baritone)
Paul Robeson
World Record Club W9648/EMI SM 431;
    [19--]; LP
Piano

4599

Steal Away
[Brown, Lawrence]
Robeson, Paul (Bass-baritone)

Were You There?/Steal Away
Victor 19742; 1925; 78 RPM
Piano
Moderate dialect

4600

Steal Away
[Brown, Lawrence]
Robeson, Paul (Bass-baritone)
Ol' Man River: His 25 Greatest 1925–1938
ASV Ltd. CD AJA 5276; 1998; CD

4601

Steal Away
[Brown, Lawrence]
Robeson, Paul (Bass-baritone)
The Essential Paul Robeson
ASV CD AJS 244; 2000; CD

4602

Steal Away
[Brown, Lawrence]
Robeson, Paul (Bass-baritone)
Spirituals: Original Recordings 1925–1936
Naxos Gospel Legends 8.120638; 2003; CD
Piano

4603

Steal Away
[Brown, Lawrence]
Robeson, Paul (Bass-baritone)
Ol' Man River: His 56 Finest 1925–1945
Retrospective RTS 4116; 2008; CD

4604

Steal Away
[Brown, Lawrence]
Robeson, Paul (Bass-baritone)
Ol' Man River: The Very Best of Paul Robeson
Memory Lane; 2012; CD

4605

Steal Away
[Brown, Lawrence]
Robeson, Paul (Bass-baritone)
Ol' Man River: The Best of Paul Robeson
Emerald Echoes; 2015; Streaming audio
Piano

4606

Steal Away
[Brown, Lawrence]
Robeson, Paul (Bass-baritone)
Five Classic Albums Plus Bonus Tracks
Real Gone Music RGMCD287; 2017; CD

4607

Steal Away
[Brown, Lawrence]
Robeson, Paul (Bass-baritone)
The Essential Collection
Primo PRMCD6233; 2018; CD

4608

Steal Away
[Brown, Lawrence]
Robeson, Paul (Bass-baritone)
Complete Recordings
Universal Digital Enterprises; 2018;
    Streaming audio

4609

Steal Away to Jesus
Robeson, Paul (Bass-baritone)
Songs of Struggle & Love
Alto ALC 1416; 2020; CD
Piano
Light dialect

4610

Steal Away
[Brown, Lawrence]
Robeson, Paul (Bass-baritone)
The Paul Robeson Story
Columbia 5C 052-04830; [19--]; LP

4611

Steal Away
Carter, Roland
Robinson-Oturo, Gail (Soprano)
*Sweetest Sound I Ever Heard: Spirituals for
    Solo Voice and Piano, Vol. 1*
CD Baby; 2020; Streaming audio
Piano
Moderate dialect

4612

Steal Away
Composer not identified
Rustin, Bayard (Tenor)
Bayard Rustin Sings Spirituals, Work &
Freedom Songs
Bayard Rustin Fund; 1988; Cassette
Piano
Light dialect

4613

Steal Away
Composer not identified
Rustin, Bayard (Tenor)
Bayard Rustin Sings Spirituals, Work &
Freedom Songs
Bayard Rustin Fund; 2003; CD
Piano
Light dialect

4614

Steal Away
Traditional
Sebron, Carolyn (Mezzo-soprano)
Resurrection, Pt. 1
Private Label; 2006; CD
A cappella
Light dialect

4615

Steal Away
Cloud, Lee
Sims, Robert (Baritone)
Soul of a Singer: Robert Sims Sings African-
American Folk Songs
Canti Classics 9801; 2013; CD
Piano
Heavy dialect

4616

Steal Away
Traditional
Swan, Walter (Baritone)
He's Got the Whole World in His Hands
Walter Swan; 2004; CD
A cappella
Moderate dialect

4617

Steal Away
Corley, Maria Thompson
Taylor, Darryl (Countertenor)
How Sweet the Sound: A Charm of
Spirituals
Albany TROY1244; 2011; CD
Piano

4618

Steal Away
Burleigh, Harry T.
Thomas, Indra (Soprano)
Great Day: Indra Thomas Sings Spirituals
Delos DE 3427; 2012; CD
Piano
Light dialect

4619

Steal Away
Johnson, Hall
Thomas, John Charles (Baritone)
Down to de Rivah/Steal Away
Victor 1687; 1934; 78 RPM
Piano

4620

Steal Away
Composer not identified
Thompson, Derrick (Baritone)
Spirituals
Private Label; 2014; CD
Piano
No dialect discerned

4621

Steal Away [from *Run Li'l Chillun*]
Johnson, Hall
Toppin, Louise (Soprano)
The Hall Johnson Collection
Carl Fischer VF5 CD1–VF5 CD2; 2003; Score
w/CD
Piano
Moderate dialect

4622

Steal Away
Johnson, Hall

Traubel, Helen (Soprano)
*Negro Spirituals: Helen Traubel in Popular
    Ballads*
Columbia ML 4221; 1949; LP
Piano

4623
Steal Away
Composer not identified
Ventriglia, Franco (Baritone)
Franco Ventriglia Sings Negro Spirituals
Vedette Records; 2007; Streaming audio
Piano, organ
Light dialect

4624
Steal Away
Composer not identified
Ventriglia, Franco (Baritone)
Franco Ventriglia Sings Negro Spirituals
Vedette Records VRMS 316; [19--]; LP
Piano, organ
Light dialect

4625
Steal Away
Traditional
White, Cassandra (Soprano)
Remembering the Spirituals
CBW Entertainment 837101334068; 2007;
    CD
A cappella
Light dialect

4626
Steal Away
Composer not identified
White, Portia (Contralto)
First You Dream
C. White PW 001-2; 1990s; CD
Piano, organ
Light dialect

4627
Steal Away to Jesus
Marshall, Melanie
White, Willard (Bass-baritone)
*Willard White Sings: Copland; American
    Spirituals; Folk-Songs*

Chandos Records CHAN 8960; 1991; CD
Piano
Heavy dialect

4628
Steal Away
Composer not identified
Williams, Wayne (Tenor)
Music from My Life
Movideo Productions 02-1993; 1993; CD
Piano, organ
Light dialect

4629
Steal Away
Johnson, Hall
Wilson, Robin (Soprano)
*Best of the Hall Johnson Centennial Festival
    Celebrating the 100th Anniversary of Hall
    Johnson's Birth*
Hall Johnson Collection O33D2; 2002;
    CD
Piano

4630
Still Away
[Burleigh, Harry T.]
Winters, Lawrence (Bass-baritone)
Lawrence Winters: Recital
Hamburger Archiv fur Gesangskunst 10397;
    2007; CD
Orchestra
Light dialect

4631
Still Away
[Burleigh, Harry T.]
Winters, Lawrence (Bass-baritone)
Singer Portrait: Lawrence Winters
Apple Music; 2012; Streaming audio
Orchestra
Light dialect

4632
Steal Away to Jesus
Helvey, Howard
Yovanovich, Amy (Mezzo-soprano)
Great Day!
Prince Productions 9808P; 2007; CD

Piano
No dialect discerned

4633

Steal Away to Jesus
Burleigh, Harry T.
Zeppenfeld, Georg (Bass)
Dvořák und Seine Zeit
Orfeo International Music C 656 052 I; 2005;
    CD

4634

Steal Away Jesus
Composer not identified
Maynor, Dorothy (Soprano)
Dorothy Maynor Sings Spirituals and Sacred Songs
RCA Camden CAL-344; 1957; LP
Chorus

Also released with *Spirituals, Arias, Songs (1940–1943)* (Claremont CD GSE 78-50-59; 1994; CD)

. . . .

The Storm Is Passing Over

4635

The Storm Is Passing Over
Composer not identified
Matthews, Benjamin (Baritone)
Opera Ebony Sings Spirituals
Ebony Classic Recordings; 2002; CD

. . . .

Sweet Jesus

4636

Sweet Jesus
Wendell Whalum
English-Robinson, Laura (Soprano)
Let It Shine!
ACA Digital Recording CM20020; 1994; CD
Piano
No dialect discerned

4637

Sweet Jesus
Whalum, Wendell

McKelton, Sam (Tenor)
Sence You Went Away
Albany Records TROY 387; 1998; CD
Piano
Heavy dialect

. . . .

Sweet Little Jesus Boy

[Isaiah 9:6, 11:1; Jeremiah 29:11; Matthew 1:18-25, 2:1-12; Mark 15:25; Luke 2:7; John 3:16; 1 Corinthians 10:13]

"Sweet Little Jesus Boy, They made You be born in a manger, sweet little Holy Child; Didn't know who You was. Didn't know You'd come to save us, Lord, To take our sins away; Our eyes was blind, we couldn't see; Didn't know who you was...."

[Not found in song collection]

Robert MacGimsey (1898–1979) composed "Sweet Little Jesus Boy" in the style of the Negro spirituals and work songs he heard on his parents' plantation. Published in 1934, the song text was printed in Standard English with some dialect printed below that text. Despite the perception that the dialect is optional, the composer intended for the dialect to be performed.

Although most of the text is like a lullaby, sung slowly and softly as if to a child, the third verse grows intense as the text shifts to the Crucifixion of Christ and the struggles of His children before settling back into a reprise of the lullaby.

Recordings of this song range from orchestrated accompaniments that require the singer to maintain a fairly strict tempo to *a cappella* performances that gave the singer complete freedom to improvise the tempo of the vocal line.

4638

Sweet Little Jesus Boy
[MacGimsey, Robert]; Young, Thomas J.
Mosely, Robert (Baritone)
A Spiritual Christmas
Musical Heritage Society 5167448; 2002; CD
Piano
Light dialect

4639

Sweet Little Jesus Boy
[MacGimsey, Robert]
Andrews, Julie (Soprano)
Hallmark Presents Julie Andrews: The Sounds of Christmas from around the World
Hallmark Cards 620XPR9707; 1990; CD

4640

Sweet Little Jesus Boy
MacGimsey, Robert
Balthrop, Carmen (Soprano)
The Art of Christmas, Volume 1
Private label cb5893; 2004; CD
Piano
Light dialect

4641

Sweet Little Jesus Boy
MacGimsey, Robert; Kaiser, Kurt
Battle, Kathleen (Soprano)
Pleasures of Their Company
EMI/Angel CDC-7 47196 2; 1986; CD
Guitar
Moderate dialect

4642

Sweet Little Jesus Boy
MacGimsey, Robert; Hairston, Jacqueline
Battle, Kathleen (Soprano)
Angels' Glory
Sony Classical SK 62723; 1996; CD
Guitar
Heavy dialect

Also released with *The Complete Sony Recordings* (Sony Classical 88985381362; 2016; CD)

4643

Sweet Little Jesus Boy
[MacGimsey, Robert]
Battle, Kathleen (Soprano)
Great American Spirituals
Angel CDM 7 64669 2; 1992; CD
Guitar
Moderate dialect

Also released with *Great American Spirituals* (Musical Heritage Society 513725Z; 1994; CD)

4644

Sweet Little Jesus Boy
MacGimsey, Robert
Berry, Avis (Soprano)
True Light: The Berlin Christmas Concert
Coviello Classics COV 50508; 2005; CD
Piano

4645

Sweet Little Jesus Boy
MacGimsey, Robert
Black, Randall (Tenor)
All Is Calm, All Is Bright: A Collection of Christmas Carols and Spirituals
Private label; 2006; CD
Piano

4646

Sweet Little Jesus Boy
MacGimsey, Robert
Brice, Carol (Contralto)
The Christmas Album
Sony Classical MHK 63309; 1997; CD
Piano
Light dialect

4647

Sweet Little Jesus Boy
MacGimsey, Robert
Brice, Carol (Contralto)
To the Queen of Heaven: Old English Poem/ Sweet Little Jesus Boy
Columbia Masterworks 17559-D; [1948]; 78 RPM
Piano
Light dialect

4648

Sweet Little Jesus Boy
MacGimsey, Robert
Brown, Anthony (Baritone)
Spirituals
Brown/Smith Productions; 1995; CD
Piano
Heavy dialect

4649

Sweet Little Jesus Boy
MacGimsey, Robert

Bumbry, Grace (Mezzo-soprano)
Portrait, A
Gala GL 100.539; 1999; CD
Piano
Moderate dialect

4650

Sweet Little Jesus Boy
[MacGimsey, Robert]
Clifford, Rochelle Small (Soprano)
Sacred Spaces
Private Label; 2008; CD
Piano
Light dialect

4651

Sweet Little Jesus Boy
[MacGimsey, Robert]
Cunningham Fleming, Jeryl (Soprano)
The Spirit of the Holidays
American Spiritual Ensemble; 2009; CD

4652

Sweet Little Jesus Boy
MacGimsey, Robert
Dry, Marion (Contralto)
Let's Have a Union
Brave Records BRAV-0923; 2009; CD
Piano
No dialect discerned

4653

Sweet Little Jesus Boy
[MacGimsey, Robert]
English-Robinson, Laura (Soprano)
Christmas Chestnuts: A Message and a Gift
Alewa ENT; 2014; CD
Organ
Light dialect

4654

Sweet Little Jesus Boy
MacGimsey, Robert
Graves, Denyce (Mezzo-soprano)
Angels Watching Over Me
NPR Classics CD 0006; 1997; CD
Chorus
Heavy dialect

4655

Sweet Little Jesus Boy
MacGimsey, Robert
Hendricks, Barbara (Soprano)
Barbara Hendricks Sings Christmas
EMI Classics D 113675; 1995; CD
A cappella
Moderate dialect

4656

Sweet Little Jesus Boy
MacGimsey, Robert
Hendricks, Barbara (Soprano)
Noël!: Voices of Christmas
Angel Records 50999 2 42605 2 7; 2008; CD

4657

Sweet Little Jesus
Traditional
Henriksson, Deborah (Soprano)
Simple Gifts
Nosag NOSAGCD143; 2007; CD
A cappella
Light dialect

4658

Sweet Little Jesus Boy
MacGimsey, Robert
Hines, Jerome (Bass)
Black & White Spirituals
Supreme S 3005; 1974; LP

4659

Sweet Little Jesus Boy
MacGimsey, Robert
Jones, Randye (Soprano)
Come Down Angels
Ahhjay Records AHHJ-0001; 2003; CD
Piano
Heavy dialect

4660

Sweet Little Jesus Boy
MacGimsey, Robert
Knight, Sadie (Soprano)
Town Hall Concerts
LF Artists LP-SRS-012; [1970]; LP
Piano

4661

Sweet Little Jesus Boy
MacGimsey, Robert
Little, Vera (Mezzo-soprano)
My Good Lord Done Been Here
Decca 123737; 1957; LP
Piano

4662

Sweet Little Jesus Boy
Browne, George
Lucas, Isabelle (Soprano)
Negro Spirituals
P&R; 2011; Streaming audio
Orchestra
Heavy dialect

4663

Sweet Little Jesus Boy
Browne, George
Lucas, Isabelle (Soprano)
Negro Spirituals
World Record Club MW-2005; [196-]; LP
Orchestra
Heavy dialect

      Also released with *Negro Spirituals* (Marathon Media International; 2013; Streaming audio)

4664

Sweet Little Jesus Boy
Welsh, Nicky
McCue, Bill (Bass-baritone)
Bill McCue Sings the Great Spirituals
Beltona SBE 173; 1974; LP
Orchestra

4665

Sweet Little Jesus Boy
MacGimsey, Robert
Merrill, Robert (Baritone)
To My Mother/Sweet Little Jesus Boy
RCA Victor 10-1303; 1947; 78 RPM
Orchestra
Moderate dialect

4666

Sweet Little Jesus Boy
Young, Thomas J.

Mosley, Robert (Bass-baritone)
Black Christmas: Spirituals in the African-American Tradition
Essay Recordings CD1011; 1990; CD
Piano

4667

Sweet Little Jesus Boy
[MacGimsey, Robert]
Nobles, NaGuanda (Soprano)
Sweet Little Jesus Boy
Private Label; 2019; Streaming audio
A cappella
Light dialect

4668

Sweet Little Jesus Boy
MacGimsey, Robert
Norman, Jessye (Soprano)
Sacred Songs
Philips 400 019-2; 1983; CD
A cappella
Light dialect

4669

Sweet Little Jesus Boy
MacGimsey, Robert
Norman, Jessye (Soprano)
Amazing Grace
Philips 432 546-2; 1990; CD
A cappella
Light dialect

4670

Sweet Little Jesus Boy
MacGimsey, Robert
Norman, Jessye (Soprano)
The Jessye Norman Collection: Sacred Songs & Spirituals
Philips B0004506-02; 2005; CD
A cappella
Heavy dialect

4671

Sweet Little Jesus Boy
MacGimsey, Robert
Price, Leontyne (Soprano)
Grandi voce: Mozart, Verdi, Puccini, Strauss
London 440 402-2; 1993; CD

A cappella
Light dialect

4672

Sweet Little Jesus Boy
MacGimsey, Robert
Price, Leontyne (Soprano)
The Essential Leontyne Price
BMG Classics 09026-68153-2; 1996; CD
A cappella
Heavy dialect

Also released with *The Essential Leontyne Price: Spirituals, Hymns & Sacred Songs* (BMG Classics 09026-68157-2; 1996; CD); *I Wish I Knew How It Would Feel to Be Free* (RCA Red Seal LSC 3183; 2011; CD) and *Leontyne Price Sings Spirituals* (RCA Red Seal 88691928242; 2012; CD)

4673

Sweet Little Jesus Boy
MacGimsey, Robert
Price, Leontyne (Soprano)
Complete Collection of Songs and Spiritual Albums
RCA Red Seal 88697940502; 2011; CD
Chorus

4674

Sweet Little Jesus Boy
MacGimsey, Robert
Price, Leontyne (Soprano)
The Voice of Leontyne Price
Regis RRC1409; 2013; CD

4675

Sweet Li'l Jesus
Traditional [MacGimsey, Robert]
Price, Leontyne (Soprano)
A Christmas Offering
London OS 25280; [1961]; LP
A cappella
Heavy dialect

4676

Sweet Little Jesus Boy
[MacGimsey, Robert]
Price, Leontyne (Soprano)
Christmas Songs

London 421 103-2; 1987; CD
A cappella
Heavy dialect

4677

Sweet Little Jesus Boy
[MacGimsey, Robert]
Price, Leontyne (Soprano)
Christmas Stars: Joy to the World
London 433010-2; 1991; CD

4678

Sweet Little Jesus Boy
[MacGimsey, Robert]
Price, Leontyne (Soprano)
The Voice of Christmas
Decca 289 472 569-2; 2002; CD
A cappella
Heavy dialect

4679

Sweet Li'l Jesus Boy
[MacGimsey, Robert]
Price, Leontyne (Soprano)
Singers of the Century: Leontyne Price: Spiritual and Religious Songs
Jube Classic; 2016; Streaming audio
A cappella
Heavy dialect

4680

Sweet Li'l Jesus
[MacGimsey, Robert]
Price, Leontyne (Soprano)
A Christmas Offering
Millennium Digital Remaster; 2017; Streaming audio
A cappella
Heavy dialect

4681

Sweet Little Jesus Boy
MacGimsey, Robert
Quivar, Florence (Mezzo-soprano)
Victoria Christmas in Song, A
Angel CDM 7 64896 2 9; 1993; CD
Piano
Heavy dialect

4682

Sweet Little Jesus Boy
MacGimsey, Robert
Quivar, Florence (Mezzo-soprano)
Negro Spirituals
EMI 7243 5 72790 2 4; 1998; CD
Piano
Heavy dialect

4683

Sweet Little Jesus Boy
MacGimsey, Robert
Quivar, Florence (Mezzo-soprano)
*Ride On, King Jesus! Florence Quivar Sings
    Black Music of America*
EMI Classics 9 67138 2; 2010; CD
Piano
Heavy dialect

4684

Sweet Little Jesus Boy
MacGimsey, Robert
Ray, Carline (Contralto)
Music for Contralto & Piano
Music Minus One MMO 9021; 1995; Score
    w/CD
Piano

4685

Sweet Little Jesus Boy
MacGimsey, Robert
Salters, Stephen (Baritone)
Stephen Salters/Shiela Kibbe
Musica Numeris CYP 9602; 2005; CD

4686

Sweet Little Jesus Boy
MacGimsey, Robert
Sebron, Carolyn (Mezzo-soprano)
*Carolyn Sebron, Mezzo-soprano, Marie-
    Claude Arbaretaz, Piano*
Fondation Crédit Lyonnais; 1993; CD
A cappella

4687

Sweet Little Jesus Boy
[MacGimsey, Robert]; Bach, Jan
Sims, Robert (Baritone)
Three Generations Live

Canti Records; 2000; CD
Cello, harp
Heavy dialect

    Also released with *In the Spirit: Spiritu-
als and American Songs with Orchestra and
Chorus* (Canti Classics; 2009; CD)

4688

Sweet Little Jesus Boy
[MacGimsey, Robert]
Smith, Muriel (Mezzo-soprano)
The Glory of Christmas
Philips BL 7586; [196-]; LP
Guitar
Moderate dialect

4689

Sweet Little Jesus Boy
MacGimsey, Robert
Tenet (male soloist) (Vocalist)
A Feast for the Senses
Private Label; 2011; CD
A cappella

4690

Sweet Little Jesus Boy
MacGimsey, Robert
Thompson, Jeanette (Soprano)
Negro Spirituals
Pavane Records ADW 7267; 1992; CD
Piano
No dialect discerned

4691

Sweet Little Jesus Boy
Traditional [MacGimsey, Robert]
Vaughn, Tichina (Mezzo-soprano)
Christmas at My Home
Bauer-Studios ACD 6085; 2005; CD
A cappella

4692

Sweet Little Jesus Boy
MacGimsey, Robert
West, Lucretia (Mezzo-soprano)
Negro Spirituals III
Club français du disque 176; 1959; LP
Piano
Moderate dialect

4693
Sweet Little Jesus Boy
MacGimsey, Robert
West, Lucretia (Mezzo-soprano)
Negro Spirituals
Club français du disque 215; [196-]; 7-in EP
Piano

· · · · · · ·

Sweetest Sound I Ever Heard

4694
Sweetest Sound I Ever Heard
Carter, Roland
Robinson-Oturo, Gail (Soprano)
Sweetest Sound I Ever Heard: Spirituals for Solo Voice and Piano, Vol. 1
CD Baby; 2020; Streaming audio
Piano
Moderate dialect

· · · · · · ·

Swing Low Sweet Chariot

[2 Kings 2:11; Isaiah 16:1-14]

"Swing low, sweet chariot, Coming forth to carry me home; Swing low, sweet chariot, Coming forth to carry me home. I looked over Jordan and what did I see? A band of angels coming after me...."

[Available in AAGS, CW40, ERCN, FHFN, HCTN, HJTS, HLBS, HT25, HTBN, HTBS, JBES, JJAN, JJBA, JSSp, LB5N, LLS2, MM4S, PLSY, RWSC, RW15, SOTS, WF10, WF70]

"Swing Low" is classified as call-and-response despite its slower tempo than other spirituals that normally fall into this category. The reference to the River Jordan suggests a secret signal referring to the Ohio River, which was often a crossing point on The Underground Railroad, and the "band of angels" certainly suggests those assisting in the escape attempt. Of course, the text of the refrain contains references rife with hidden meanings.

4695
Swing Low, Sweet Chariot
Composer not identified
Battle, Kathleen (Soprano)
The Art of Kathleen Battle
Deutsche Grammophon 474 184-2; 2002?; CD
Moderate dialect

4696
Swing Low, Sweet Chariot
Traditional
Battle, Kathleen (Soprano)
Kathleen Battle at Carnegie Hall
Deutsche Grammophon 435 440-2; 1992; CD
A cappella
Moderate dialect

4697
Swing Low, Sweet Chariot
Composer not identified
Bledsoe, Jules (Baritone)
Brother, Can You Spare a Dime?: The Roots of American Song
Pearl Gemm CD 9484; 1991; CD
Piano
Moderate dialect

4698
Swing Low, Sweet Chariot
Composer not identified
Bledsoe, Jules (Baritone)
The Negro Spirituals Concert Tradition, 1909–1948
Frémeaux & Associés FA 168; 1999; CD
Piano
Light dialect

4699
Swing Low, Sweet Chariot
Composer not identified
Bledsoe, Jules (Baritone)
First Time Buyer's Guide to American Negro Spirituals
Primo Collection PRMCD6038; 2006; CD
Piano
Moderate dialect

4700

Swing Low, Sweet Chariot
Composer not identified
Bledsoe, Jules (Baritone)
Spirituals
Past Classics; 2013; Streaming audio
Piano
Light dialect

4701

Swing Low, Sweet Chariot
White, Clarence Cameron
Bledsoe, Jules (Baritone)
*Swing Low, Sweet Chariot/Goin' to Shout All
    Over God's Heaven*
Decca F.3486; 1935; 78 RPM
Piano
Light dialect

4702

Swing Low, Sweet Chariot
[White, Clarence Cameron]
Bledsoe, Jules (Baritone)
The Concerto: African American Spirituals
Orange Amaro; 2019; Streaming audio
Piano
Light dialect

4703

Swing Low, Sweet Chariot
Boatwright, McHenry
Boatwright, McHenry (Bass-baritone)
Art of McHenry Boatwright: Spirituals
Golden Crest Records RE 7024; 1968; LP
Piano
Light dialect

4704

Swing Low, Sweet Chariot
Composer not identified
Boston, Gretha (Contralto)
Swing Low, Sweet Chariot
American Spiritual Ensemble; 2011; CD

4705

Swing Low, Sweet Chariot
Burleigh, Harry T.
Brown, Anthony (Baritone)
Spirituals
Brown/Smith Productions; 1995; CD
Piano
Moderate dialect

4706

Swing Low, Sweet Chariot
Tillis, Frederick
Brown, William (Tenor)
Symphonic Spirituals
Columbia JC 36267; 1979; LP
Orchestra
Moderate dialect

4707

Swing Low, Sweet Chariot
Tillis, Frederick
Brown, William (Tenor)
Symphonic Spirituals
Spotify; [2019]; Streaming audio
Orchestra
Moderate dialect

4708

Swing Low, Sweet Chariot
Burleigh, Harry T.
Cantril, Kenneth (Baritone)
Swing Low, Sweet Chariot/Unknown
London 289; [19--]; 78 RPM
Piano

4709

Swing Low, Sweet Chariot
[Burleigh, Harry T.]
Cantril, Kenneth (Baritone)
Spirituals
London LA 52; 1948; 78 RPM
Piano

4710

Swing Low Sweet Chariot
Composer not identified
Carey, Thomas (Baritone)
Go Down Moses
Da Camera Song SM 95028; 1970; LP
Piano

4711

Swing Low Sweet Chariot
Dørumsgaard, Arne

Carlsen, Svein (Bass)
Negro Spirituals
EuroMaster AS ECD19005; 1996; CD
Piano

4712
Swing Low, Sweet Chariot
[Burleigh, Harry T.]
Chaiter, Yoram (Bass)
Spirituals & Other Songs
Romeo Records 7311; 2014; CD
Piano
No dialect discerned

4713
Swing Low, Sweet Chariot
Composer not identified
Charles, Lee (Tenor)
*Swing Low Sweet Chariot: And Other
    Spirituals*
Riverside RLP 12-651; 1957; LP
Piano, guitar

4714
Swing Low, Sweet Chariot
Traditional
Cheatham, Kitty (Soprano)
*Swing Low, Sweet Chariot/I Don't Feel No-
    ways Tired or "I Am Seeking for a City"/
    Walk in Jerusalem Just Like John/Sinner
    Please Don't Let This Harvest Pass*
Victor 45086; 1916; 78 RPM
A cappella
Heavy dialect

4715
Swing Low, Sweet Chariot
Still, William Grant
Clark, Clarence Carroll (Baritone)
*Swing Low, Sweet Chariot/One Sweetly
    Solemn Thought*
Black Swan 2024; [1921]; 78 RPM

4716
Swing Low, Sweet Chariot
[Still, William Grant]
Clark, Clarence Carroll (Baritone)
*Swing Low, Sweet Chariot/I Stood on de
    Ribber ob Jordan*

Paramount 12038; 1924; 78 RPM
Piano

4717
Swing Low Sweet Chariot
Traditional
Cook, Dixon & Young (Tenor)
Triptych: A Celebration of the Negro Spiritual
CDY Records 649241879206; 2009; CD
A cappella
No dialect discerned

4718
Swing Low, Sweet Chariot
[Burleigh, Harry T.]
Delmore, Harry A. (Tenor)
Were You There/Swing Low Sweet Chariot
Grey Gull 4154; [1927]; 78 RPM

4719
Swing Low, Sweet Chariot
Burleigh, Harry T.
Delmore, Harry A. (Tenor)
*Swing Low, Sweet Chariot/I'm So Glad
    Trouble Don't Last Alway*
Grey Gull 9001; [1924]; 78 RPM
Piano
No dialect discerned

4720
Swing Low, Sweet Chariot
Brown, Lawrence
Duncan, Todd (Baritone)
African American Spirituals
[Apple Music]; 2008; Streaming audio
Piano
Heavy dialect

4721
Swing Low, Sweet Chariot
Brown, Lawrence
Duncan, Todd (Baritone)
Negro Spirituals
Allegro ALG3022; [1952]; LP
Piano

4722
Swing Low, Sweet Chariot
[Brown, Lawrence]

Duncan, Todd (Baritone)
Spirituals
Royale 1810; [1950]; LP

4723

Swing Low, Sweet Chariot
Dawson, William L.
Entriken, Ellen Goff (Soprano)
Ain't Got Time to Die: Songs of the American
　Spirit
First Presbyterian Church in the City of
　New York FPC 1002; 1997; CD
Chorus

4724

Swing Low, Sweet Chariot
Roberts, Howard
Estes, Simon (Bass-baritone)
Spirituals
Philips 412 631-2; 1985; CD
Chorus
Light dialect

　　　Also released with *Famous Spirituals*
(Philips 462 062-2; 1997; CD)

4725

Swing Low Sweet Chariot
Kaelin, Pierre
Evans, Allan (Bass-baritone)
Negro Spirituals
Electromusic Records EMCD 6885; 1985; CD
Chorus, other instrument(s)

4726

Swing Low
Laster, James
Forest, Michael (Tenor)
The Spirit Sings: American Spirituals
Shenandoah Conservatory SU003; [199-];
　CD

4727

Swing Low Sweet Chariot
Composer not identified
Franklin, Lavinia A. (Vocalist)
Historical Interpretation of Negro Spirituals
　and Lift Every Voice and Sing
Recorded Publications JZB-02591; 1970; LP
Organ

4728

Swing Low, Sweet Chariot
Burleigh, Harry T.
Garrison, Mabel (Soprano)
Swing Low, Sweet Chariot
Victrola 64969; 1921; 78 RPM
Orchestra
Moderate dialect

4729

Swing Low, Sweet Chariot
Mills, Marvin
Graves, Denyce (Mezzo-soprano)
Angels Watching Over Me
NPR Classics CD 0006; 1997; CD
Piano
Light dialect

4730

Swing Low, Sweet Chariot
Composer not identified
Hagen-William, Louis (Bass-baritone)
Negro Spiritual
Quantum QM 6909; 1993; CD
Piano
Moderate dialect

4731

Swing Low, Sweet Chariot
[Burleigh, Harry T.]
Hampton, Jonathon (Vocalist)
Negro Spirituals: Songs of Trial and Triumph
Private Label; 2017; Streaming audio
Piano
Moderate dialect

4732

Swing Low, Sweet Chariot
Burleigh, Harry T.
Harris, Hilda (Mezzo-soprano)
From the Southland: Songs, Piano Sketches
　and Spirituals of Harry T. Burleigh
Premier Recordings PRCD 1041; 1995; CD
Piano
Heavy dialect

4733

Swing Low, Sweet Chariot
Burleigh, Harry T.

Hayes, Roland (Tenor)
Swing Low Sweet Chariot/Steal Away
Vocalion 21003; 1922; 78 RPM
Piano

4734
Swing Low, Sweet Chariot
Burleigh, Harry T.
Hayes, Roland (Tenor)
Swing Low, Sweet Chariot
Columbia Graphophone 62050; [1917]; 78
   RPM
Piano

4735
Swing Low, Sweet Chariot
Composer not identified
Hayes, Roland (Tenor)
Afro-American Folksongs
Pelican Records LP 2028; 1983; LP
Piano

4736
Swing Low, Sweet Chariot
Composer not identified
Hayes, Roland (Tenor)
Roland Hayes Sings: Negro Spirituals,
   Aframerican Folk Songs
Amadeo Records AVRS 6033; [19--]; LP
Piano

4737
Swing Low, Sweet Chariot
Hayes, Roland
Hayes, Roland (Tenor)
The Art of Roland Hayes
Smithsonian Collection RD 041; 1990; CD
A cappella
Moderate dialect

4738
Swing Low, Sweet Chariot
Hayes, Roland
Hayes, Roland (Tenor)
The Art of Roland Hayes: Six Centuries of
   Song
Preiser Records; 2010; CD
Piano
Moderate dialect

4739
Swing Low, Sweet Chariot
[Burleigh, Harry T.]
Hayes, Roland (Tenor)
Black Europe: Sounds & Images of Black
   People in Europe pre–1927
Bear Family Productions BCD 16095; 2013;
   CD
Piano
No dialect discerned

4740
Swing Low, Sweet Chariot
Composer not identified
Hayes, Roland (Tenor)
Black Swans
Parnassus Recordings PACD 96067; 2019; CD
Piano
No dialect discerned

4741
Swing Low, Sweet Chariot
[Hendricks, Barbara]
Hendricks, Barbara (Soprano)
Spirituals
EMI Classics 0946 346641 2 7; 2005; CD
Piano

4742
Swing Low, Sweet Chariot
Hendricks, Barbara; Alexeev, Dmitri
Hendricks, Barbara (Soprano)
Negro Spirituals
EMI CDC7470262; 1983; CD
Piano
Moderate dialect

    Also released with *Great American
Spirituals* (Angel CDM 7 64669 2; 1992; CD)
and *Great American Spirituals* (Musical Heritage Society 513725Z; 1994; CD)

4743
Swing Low, Sweet Chariot
Hendricks, Barbara; Alexeev, Dmitri
Hendricks, Barbara (Soprano)
The Very Best of Barbara Hendricks
EMI Classics 7243 5 86323 2 3; 2005; CD
Piano
Heavy dialect

4744

Swing Low, Sweet Chariot!
[Hendricks, Barbara]
Hendricks, Barbara (Soprano)
Espirituales Negros
EMI Classics/Altaya 01636; 1983; CD
Piano

4745

Swing Low, Sweet Chariot
Henderson, Skitch
Hines, Jerome (Bass)
Standin' in the Need of Prayer
RCA Victor LPM-2047; [1960]; LP

4746

Swing Low, Sweet Chariot
Johnson, Hall
Holmes, Eugene (Baritone)
Eugene Holmes Sings Spirituals
Avant Garde AV-115; [1968]; LP
Piano
Heavy dialect

    Also released with *Spirituals* (Schubert
Records SCH-102; [1988]; LP)

4747

Swing Low, Sweet Chariot
Composer not identified
Humphrey Flynn, Edwina (Soprano)
The Lord Will Make a Way
Private Label; 2000; CD
Chorus

4748

Swing Low, Sweet Chariot
Clinton, Irving
Irving, Clinton (Bass-baritone)
Clinton Irving Sings Spirituals: A Tribute
Rogers; 2001; CD

4749

Swing Low, Sweet Chariot
Burleigh, Harry T.
Jimerson, Douglas (Tenor)
Stephen Foster's America
Amerimusic AM1003; 1998; CD
Piano
Light dialect

4750

Swing Low Sweet Chariot
Composer not identified
Johnson, John (Baritone)
Spirituals
Royale EP 180; [19--]; 45 RPM

4751

Swing Low, Sweet Chariot
Composer not identified
Johnson, Yolanda F (Soprano)
Feel the Spirit!
Jublianti Artists; 2011; Streaming audio
Piano
Light dialect

4752

Swing Low, Sweet Chariot
Okpebholo, Shawn
Liverman, Will (Baritone)
Lord How Come Me Here?
Navona Records NV6408; 2022; CD
Piano, flute
Light dialect

4753

Swing Low, Sweet Chariot
Meyer, Fredrich
London, George (Bass-baritone)
Spirituals
Deutsche Grammophon 00289 477 6193;
    2006; CD
Orchestra
Moderate dialect

4754

Swing Low, Sweet Chariot [from *Journey
    Beyond Time*]
Crumb, George
Martin, Barbara Ann (Soprano)
American Songbooks II & IV
BRIDGE 9275A/B; 2008; CD
Piano, percussion

4755

Swing Low, Sweet Chariot
Dawson, William L.
Martin, Marvis (Soprano)
The Spirituals of William L. Dawson

St. Olaf Records E-2159; 1997; CD
Chorus

4756

Swing Low, Sweet Chariot
Composer not identified
Maynor, Kevin (Bass)
The Spiritual: An Underground Railroad
Southeastern Virginia Arts Assoc.; [2000];
    CD
Piano

4757

Swing Low Sweet Chariot
Traditional
Maynor, Kevin (Bass)
Paul Robeson Remembered
Fleur de Son Classics FDS 57929; 1998; CD
A cappella
Moderate dialect

4758

Swing Low, Sweet Chariot
Welsh, Nicky
McCue, Bill (Bass-baritone)
Bill McCue Sings the Great Spirituals
Beltona SBE 173; 1974; LP
Orchestra

4759

Swing Low, Sweet Chariot
Johnson, Hall
McFerrin, Robert (Baritone)
*Deep River and Other Classic Negro
    Spirituals*
Riverside Records RLP 12-812; 1959; LP
Piano
Heavy dialect

> Also released with *Classic Negro Spirituals* (Washington Records WLP 466; 1959; LP)

4760

Swing Low Sweet Chariot
Burleigh, Harry T.
McKinney, Jason (Bass-baritone)
Songs Inspired by Paul Robeson
United in Music; 2014; CD
Piano
Moderate dialect

4761

Swing Low, Sweet Chariot
Burleigh, Harry T.
Melba, Nellie (Soprano)
The First Recordings
Australian Broadcasting Corporation ABC
    476 3556; 2008; CD
Piano

4762

Swing Low, Sweet Chariot
Burleigh, Harry T.
Melba, Nellie (Soprano)
*Melba's Farewell: Dame Nellie Melba's
    Famous Farewell from Covert Garden
    and Other Recordings*
Decca Eloquence 482 8093; 2017; CD
Piano

4763

Swing Low, Sweet Chariot
Johnson, Hall
Miller, Jeanette (Soprano)
No Man Canna Hinder Me
MiJon Record Productions MJ240; 1979;
    CD
Piano

4764

Swing Low, Sweet Chariot
Composer not identified
Monzo, Oscar (Baritone)
Negro Spirituals
Dial Discos 50-2020; 1983; LP

4765

Swing Low Sweet Chariot
Composer not identified
Moses, Oral (Bass-baritone)
Extreme Spirituals
Cuneiform Record Rune 241; 2006; CD
Instrumental ensemble

4766

Swing Low, Sweet Chariot
Traditional
Moses, Oral (Bass-baritone)
*Spirituals in Zion: A Spiritual Heritage for
    the Soul*

Albany Records TROY587; 2003; CD
A cappella

4767

Swing Low
Burleigh, Harry T.
Nash, Lorna (Contralto)
Lorna Nash, Contralto in Concert
Mark Custom Records UMC 2160; [197-];
    LP
Piano

4768

Swing Low, Sweet Chariot
Composer not identified
Nobles, NaGuanda (Soprano)
Homage to the Journey
Selbon Records; 2014; Streaming audio
Chorus, piano
Light dialect

4769

Swing Low, Sweet Chariot
Burleigh, Harry T.
Oglesby, Isador (Tenor)
*Negro Spirituals: The Musical Roots of
    American Folk Songs*
Praise PR 658; 1978; LP
Piano

4770

Swing Low, Sweet Chariot
Brown, Lawrence
Pankey, Aubrey (Baritone)
Negro Spirituals
Eterna 830010; 1983; LP
Piano
Light dialect

4771

Swing Low, Sweet Chariot
[Brown, Lawrence]
Pankey, Aubrey (Baritone)
Aubrey Pankey Singt Negro-Spirituals
Eterna 7 30 005; 1959; LP
Piano
Light dialect

4772

Swing Low, Sweet Chariot
[Brown, Lawrence]
Pankey, Aubrey (Baritone)
Negro-Spirituals
Eterna 5 30 022; [19--]; 45 RPM
Piano
Light dialect

4773

Swing Low Sweet Chariot
Flynn, William
Paris, Virginia (Contralto)
Spirituals
Spotlight Classic SC 1008; 1957; LP
Orchestra

4774

Swing Low Sweet Chariot
Flynn, William
Paris, Virginia (Contralto)
Virginia Paris in Australia
Lyric Records CD 178; [2005]; CD
Orchestra

4775

Swing Low, Sweet Chariot
Burleigh, Harry T.
Parks, Karen (Soprano)
Nobody Knows
Ottimavoce 52736; 2007; CD
Piano
Moderate dialect

4776

Swing Low, Sweet Chariot
Burleigh, Harry T.
Pierson, Edward (Bass-baritone)
Edward Pierson Sings Hymns and Spirituals
Kemco 98-44; [19--]; LP

4777

Swing Low, Sweet Chariot
Burleigh, Harry T.; de Paur, Leonard
Price, Leontyne (Soprano)
*Complete Collection of Songs and Spiritual
    Albums*
RCA Red Seal 88697940502; 2011; CD
Orchestra

4778

Swing Low, Sweet Chariot
de Paur, Leonard
Price, Leontyne (Soprano)
Swing Low, Sweet Chariot: Fourteen Spirituals
RCA Victor LSC 2600; 1962; LP
Chorus
Heavy dialect

Also released with *The Essential Leontyne Price: Spirituals, Hymns & Sacred Songs* (BMG Classics 09026-68157-2; 1996; CD); *The Essential Leontyne Price* (BMG Classics 09026-68153-2; 1996; CD) and *Leontyne Price Sings Spirituals* (RCA Red Seal 88691928242; 2012; CD)

4779

Swing Low, Sweet Chariot
de Paur, Leonard
Price, Leontyne (Soprano)
Complete Collection of Songs and Spiritual Albums
RCA Red Seal 88697940502; 2011; CD
Orchestra

4780

Swing Low, Sweet Chariot
de Paur, Leonard
Price, Leontyne (Soprano)
Singers of the Century: Leontyne Price: Spiritual and Religious Songs
Jube Classic; 2016; Streaming audio
Chorus
Heavy dialect

4781

Hiljaa Vie Vaunut (Swing Low, Sweet Chariot)
Composer not identified
Putkonen, Marko (Bass)
Deep River: Negro Spirituals
Lilium LILP 101; 1991; LP

4782

Swing Low, Sweet Chariot
Meyer, Fredrich
Quasthoff, Thomas (Bass-baritone)
Consider My Soul: Sacred Arias

Deutsche Grammophon B0007103-02; 2006; CD
Orchestra
No dialect discerned

4783

Swing Low, Sweet Chariot
Hogan, Moses
Ragin, Derek Lee (Countertenor)
Negro Spirituals
Virgin Classics 0946 363305 2 5; 2006; CD
Piano
Moderate dialect

4784

Swing Low, Sweet Chariot
Giesen, Hubert
Ray, William (Baritone)
Negro Spirituals
Intercord; [19--]; LP
Piano

Also released with *Sings Arias, Duets, Musical Selections and Negro Spirituals* (Intercord; [19--]; CD)

4785

Swing Low, Sweet Chariot
Brown, Lawrence
Reese, Ruth (Contralto)
Motherless Child
OPS 1006/79; 1979; LP

4786

Swing Low, Sweet Chariot
Burleigh, Harry T.
Ripley, Gladys (Contralto)
Deep River/Swing Low Sweet Chariot
HMV B.9689; [1948]; 78 RPM
Piano

4787

Swing Low, Sweet Chariot
Brown, [Lawrence]
Robeson, Paul (Bass-baritone)
The Best of Paul Robeson
EMI NTS 181; 1979; LP

4788

Swing Low, Sweet Chariot
Brown, Lawrence
Robeson, Paul (Bass-baritone)
Nobody Knows de Trouble I've Seen/Swing Low, Sweet Chariot
Victor 20068; 1926; 78 RPM
Piano
Light dialect

4789

Swing Low, Sweet Chariot
Brown, Lawrence
Robeson, Paul (Bass-baritone)
Swing Low, Sweet Chariot/Joshua Fit de Battle ob Jericho
His Master's Voice B 2339; 1926; 78 RPM
Piano
Light dialect

4790

Swing Low, Sweet Chariot
Brown, Lawrence
Robeson, Paul (Bass-baritone)
Swing Low, Sweet Chariot/On Ma Journey
Victor 25547; 1933; 78 RPM
Piano
Light dialect

4791

Swing Low, Sweet Chariot
Brown, Lawrence
Robeson, Paul (Bass-baritone)
On Ma Journey/Swing Low, Swing Chariot
His Master's Voice B.8372; 1935; 78 RPM
Piano
Moderate dialect

4792

Swing Low, Sweet Chariot
Brown, Lawrence
Robeson, Paul (Bass-baritone)
Swing Low, Sweet Chariot
Columbia Masterworks MM-819; 1949; 78 RPM
Piano
Heavy dialect

4793

Swing Low, Sweet Chariot
Brown, Lawrence
Robeson, Paul (Bass-baritone)
Paul Robeson Chante … 16 Spirituals
Philips G 05.639 R; 1959; LP
Piano
Moderate dialect

4794

Swing Low, Sweet Chariot
Brown, Lawrence
Robeson, Paul (Bass-baritone)
Paul Robeson in Live Performance
Columbia M 30424; 1971; LP
Piano
Moderate dialect

4795

Swing Low, Sweet Chariot
Brown, Lawrence
Robeson, Paul (Bass-baritone)
Songs of My People
RCA Red Seal LM-3292; 1972; LP
Piano

4796

Swing Low, Sweet Chariot
Brown, Lawrence
Robeson, Paul (Bass-baritone)
Paul Robeson
Pearl GEMM CD 9356; 1989; CD

4797

Swing Low, Sweet Chariot
Brown, Lawrence
Robeson, Paul (Bass-baritone)
Legendary Moscow Concert: Live Concert from Tchaikovsky Hall, Moscow
Revelation Records RV70004; 1997; CD
Piano

4798

Swing Low, Sweet Chariot
Brown, Lawrence
Robeson, Paul (Bass-baritone)
Ol' Man River: His 25 Greatest 1925–1940
ASV Ltd. CD AJA 5276; 1998; CD

4799

Swing Low, Sweet Chariot
Brown, Lawrence
Robeson, Paul (Bass-baritone)
Paul Robeson Collection
Hallmark Recordings 390692; 1998; CD

4800

Swing Low, Sweet Chariot
Brown, Lawrence
Robeson, Paul (Bass-baritone)
Legends of the 20th Century: Paul Robeson
EMI Records 7243 520140; 1999; CD
Piano

4801

Swing Low, Sweet Chariot
Brown, Lawrence
Robeson, Paul (Bass-baritone)
The Essential Paul Robeson
ASV CD AJS 244; 2000; CD

4802

Swing Low, Sweet Chariot
Brown, Lawrence
Robeson, Paul (Bass-baritone)
The Great Paul Robeson
Pegasus PGN CD 811; 2000; CD

4803

Swing Low, Sweet Chariot
Brown, Lawrence
Robeson, Paul (Bass-baritone)
Good News: Vintage Negro Spirituals
Living Era AJA 5622; 2006; CD
Piano
Light dialect

4804

Swing Low, Sweet Chariot
Brown, Lawrence
Robeson, Paul (Bass-baritone)
*On My Journey: Paul Robeson's Independent
    Recordings*
Smithsonian Folkways Recordings SFW CD
    40178; 2007; CD
Piano

4805

Swing Low, Sweet Chariot
Brown, Lawrence
Robeson, Paul (Bass-baritone)
The Complete EMI Sessions (1928–1939)
EMI Classics 50999 2 15586 2 7; 2008; CD
Piano
Moderate dialect

4806

Swing Low Sweet Chariot
Brown, Lawrence
Robeson, Paul (Bass-baritone)
Sacred Songs and Ballads of Yesteryear
Griffin; 2011; CD
Piano

4807

Swing Low, Sweet Chariot
Brown, Lawrence
Robeson, Paul (Bass-baritone)
Classic Gospel Songs
Emerald/K-Tel; 2013; Streaming audio
Piano

4808

Swing Low, Sweet Chariot
Burleigh, Harry T.
Robeson, Paul (Bass-baritone)
Golden Voice of Paul Robeson
EMI Music PLAY-1020; 1983; CD

4809

Swing Low, Sweet Chariot
Burleigh, Harry T.
Robeson, Paul (Bass-baritone)
The Voice of Mississippi: 20 Great Tracks
Prism Leisure PLATCD 119; 1996; CD

4810

Swing Low, Sweet Chariot
Burleigh, Harry T.
Robeson, Paul (Bass-baritone)
Paul Robeson
World Record Club W9648/EMI SM 431;
    [19--]; LP
Piano

4811

Swing Low, Sweet Chariot
[Brown, Lawrence]
Robeson, Paul (Bass-baritone)
Negro Spirituals, v. 2
Philips NBE11102; 1956; 7" Vinyl

4812

Swing Low, Sweet Chariot
[Brown, Lawrence]
Robeson, Paul (Bass-baritone)
Favorite Songs
Monitor Recordings MPS 580; 1959; LP
Piano

4813

Swing Low, Sweet Chariot
[Brown, Lawrence]
Robeson, Paul (Bass-baritone)
Andere Amerika, Das
Eterna 8 10 021; 1966; LP
Piano

4814

Swing Low, Sweet Chariot
[Brown, Lawrence]
Robeson, Paul (Bass-baritone)
Scandalize My Name
Classics Record Library 30-5647; 1976; LP
Piano
Heavy dialect

4815

Swing Low, Sweet Chariot
[Brown, Lawrence]
Robeson, Paul (Bass-baritone)
The Collector's Paul Robeson
Monitor MCD-61580; 1989; CD
Piano
Heavy dialect

4816

Swing Low, Sweet Chariot
[Brown, Lawrence]
Robeson, Paul (Bass-baritone)
*Paul Robeson: Great Voices of the Century,
v. 1*

Memoir Classics CDMOIR 415; 1992; CD
Piano

4817

Swing Low, Sweet Chariot
[Brown, Lawrence]
Robeson, Paul (Bass-baritone)
Paul Robeson
Flapper; 1993; CD

4818

Swing Low Sweet Chariot
[Brown, Lawrence]
Robeson, Paul (Bass-baritone)
Gospels & Spirituals Gold Collection
Retro R2CD 40-26; 1995; CD
Piano
Moderate dialect

4819

Swing Low, Sweet Chariot
[Brown, Lawrence]
Robeson, Paul (Bass-baritone)
Deep River
Great Voices of the Century GVC 2004;
1999; CD
Piano

4820

Swing Low Sweet Chariot
[Brown, Lawrence]
Robeson, Paul (Bass-baritone)
Paul Robeson
Forever Gold FG019; 2001; CD
Piano

4821

Swing Low, Sweet Chariot
[Brown, Lawrence]
Robeson, Paul (Bass-baritone)
The Great Paul Robeson
Velvet CDVELV 101; 2001; CD
Piano

4822

Swing Low, Sweet Chariot
[Brown, Lawrence]
Robeson, Paul (Bass-baritone)

Great Voices of the Twentieth Century
Pulse PLSCD 754; 2005; CD

4823
Swing Low, Sweet Chariot
[Brown, Lawrence]
Robeson, Paul (Bass-baritone)
Paul Robeson
Music Video Dist. MDGC23420.2; 2007; CD

4824
Swing Low, Sweet Chariot
[Brown, Lawrence]
Robeson, Paul (Bass-baritone)
Collection
RGS Music 1404-2; 2007; CD

4825
Swing Low, Sweet Chariot
[Brown, Lawrence]
Robeson, Paul (Bass-baritone)
The Very Best of Gospel
Disconforme CDX7720; 2007; CD

4826
Swing Low Sweet Chariot
[Brown, Lawrence]
Robeson, Paul (Bass-baritone)
The Best of Paul Robeson
Delta Music Group CD6252; 2008; CD

4827
Swing Low, Sweet Chariot
[Brown, Lawrence]
Robeson, Paul (Bass-baritone)
*The Golden Voice of Paul Robeson: Great
    Voices of the 20th Century*
Acrobat Music AC-5160-2; 2008; CD

4828
Swing Low Sweet Chariot
[Brown, Lawrence]
Robeson, Paul (Bass-baritone)
Ol' Man River: His 56 Finest 1925–1945
Retrospective RTS 4116; 2008; CD

4829
Swing Low, Sweet Chariot
[Brown, Lawrence]

Robeson, Paul (Bass-baritone)
Paul Robeson's Treasure Chest
Leverage; 2008; Streaming audio
Piano

4830
Swing Low, Sweet Chariot
[Brown, Lawrence]
Robeson, Paul (Bass-baritone)
Negro Spirituals (And More)
Discmedi DM-4674-02; 2009; CD

4831
Swing Low, Sweet Chariot
[Brown, Lawrence]
Robeson, Paul (Bass-baritone)
The Very Best of Paul Robeson
Future Noise Music FVDD033; 2009; CD
Piano

4832
Swing Low Sweet Chariot
[Brown, Lawrence]
Robeson, Paul (Bass-baritone)
*Oh, Happy Day! Gospels & Spirituals: The
    Ultimate CD*
Ultimate; 2010; CD

4833
Swing Low, Sweet Chariot
[Brown, Lawrence]
Robeson, Paul (Bass-baritone)
Voice of the People
Regis RRC 1056; 2011; CD
Piano
Light dialect

4834
Swing Low Sweet Chariot
[Brown, Lawrence]
Robeson, Paul (Bass-baritone)
Ol' Man River: The Ultimate Collection
Roslin Records; 2011; Streaming audio
Piano
Moderate dialect

4835
Swing Low, Sweet Chariot
[Brown, Lawrence]

Robeson, Paul (Bass-baritone)
Ol' Man River: The Very Best of Paul Robeson
Memory Lane; 2012; CD

4836

Swing Low, Sweet Chariot
[Brown, Lawrence]
Robeson, Paul (Bass-baritone)
Ol' Man River: The Best of Paul Robeson
Emerald Echoes; 2015; Streaming audio
Piano

4837

Swing Low, Sweet Chariot
[Brown, Lawrence]
Robeson, Paul (Bass-baritone)
Five Classic Albums Plus Bonus Tracks
Real Gone Music RGMCD287; 2017; CD

4838

Swing Low, Sweet Chariot
[Brown, Lawrence]
Robeson, Paul (Bass-baritone)
The Essential Collection
Primo PRMCD6233; 2018; CD

4839

Swing Low Sweet Chariot
[Brown, Lawrence]
Robeson, Paul (Bass-baritone)
Complete Recordings
Universal Digital Enterprises; 2018;
    Streaming audio

4840

Swing Low, Sweet Chariot
[Brown, Lawrence]
Robeson, Paul (Bass-baritone)
Paul Robeson Singt Negro Spirituals
Musical Masterpiece Society MMS-2162;
    [19--]; LP
Piano

4841

Swing Low Sweet Chariot
[Brown, Lawrence]
Robeson, Paul (Bass-baritone)
Negro Spirituals
Concert Hall SVS 2611; [19--]; LP

4842

Swing Low, Sweet Chariot
[Brown, Lawrence]
Robeson, Paul (Bass-baritone)
Negro Spirituals and Blues
Concert Hall M-2340; [19--]; LP
Piano

4843

Swing Low, Sweet Chariot
[Brown, Lawrence]
Robeson, Paul (Bass-baritone)
Swing Low, Sweet Chariot
Columbia Masterworks ML 2038; [195-]; LP
Piano

4844

Swing Low, Sweet Chariot
[Brown, Lawrence]
Robeson, Paul (Bass-baritone)
Ol' Man River
Golden Options GO 3820; [2000]; CD

4845

Swing Low, Sweet Chariot
[Brown, Lawrence]
Robeson, Paul (Bass-baritone)
Negro Spirituals
Chant du Monde LDX 74376; 1982; LP
Piano

4846

Swing Low, Sweet Chariot
Traditional
Rucker, Jennie (Vocalist); Pettis, Jordan
    (Vocalist)
They Slice the Air
Spirituals Project; 2007; CD
A cappella
Light dialect

4847

Swing Low Sweet Chariot
Composer not identified
Rustin, Bayard (Tenor)
*Bayard Rustin Sings Spirituals, Work &
    Freedom Songs*
Bayard Rustin Fund; 1988; Cassette

Piano
Heavy dialect

    Also released with *Bayard Rustin, the Singer* (Bayard Rustin Fund; 1992; CD)

4848

Swing Low Sweet Chariot
Composer not identified
Rustin, Bayard (Tenor)
Bayard Rustin Sings Spirituals, Work & Freedom Songs
Bayard Rustin Fund; 2003; CD
Piano
Heavy dialect

4849

Swing Low, Sweet Chariot
Traditional
Rustin, Bayard (Tenor)
Elizabethan Songs & Negro Spirituals
Fellowship Records 102; [1952]; 10" LP
A cappella

    Also released with: *Bayard Rustin-The Singer* (Black Swan Series; Parnassus Records PACD 96083; 2022; CD)

4850

Swing Low, Sweet Chariot
Composer not identified
Lee, Seung Hyun (Soprano)
Sweet Blessing: Spirituals & Hymns by Seung-Hyun Lee
Seoul Records; [20--]; CD

4851

Swing Low Sweet Chariot
Brown, Lawrence
Smith, Muriel (Mezzo-soprano)
Negro Spirituals
Philips NBE11007; [195-]; 45 RPM
Piano

4852

Swing Low Sweet Chariot
Composer not identified
St. Hill, Krister (Baritone)
Svenska Folkvisor/Negro Spirituals
Polar POLS 398; 1985; LP

4853

Swing Low, Sweet Chariot
Walters, Richard (ed.)
Stolen, Steven (Tenor)
15 Easy Spiritual Arrangements for the Progressing Singer
Hal Leonard HL00000391 (high); HL00000392 (low); 2005; Score w/CD
Piano
Heavy dialect

4854

Swing Low Sweet Chariot
Turn Me Loose White Man
Bledsoe, Jules (Baritone)
[United States]: Constant Sorrow Press; 2020; CD

4855

Swing Low, Sweet Chariot
Traditional
Swan, Walter (Baritone)
He's Got the Whole World in His Hands
Walter Swan; 2004; CD
A cappella
Heavy dialect

4856

Swing Low Sweet Chariot
Burleigh, Harry T.
Te Wiata, Inia (Bass)
A Popular Recital
Kiwi Pacific CD SLC-248; 1997; CD
Piano

4857

Swing Low, Sweet Chariot
Composer not identified
Terfel, Bryn (Baritone)
Bryn Terfel Sings Favorites
Deutsche Grammophon B0001305-02; 2003; CD
Chorus
Light dialect

4858

Swing Low, Sweet Chariot
Composer not identified

Thomas, Edna (Soprano)
Swing Low, Sweet Chariot/Mamzelle Zizi
Columbia 3487; 1924; 78 RPM
Harp

4859

Swing Low Sweet Chariot
Thomas, Edna
Thomas, Edna (Soprano)
Were You Dere/Swing Low, Sweet Chariot
Columbia 1476-D; 1928; 78 RPM
Piano

4860

Swing Low, Sweet Chariot
Composer not identified
Thomas, John Charles (Baritone)
*Swing Low, Sweet Chariot/Ev'ry Time I Feel
    de Spirit*
Victor His Master's Voice 2168; 1941; 78
    RPM
Orchestra

4861

Swing Low, Sweet Chariot
Composer not identified
Thomas, John Charles (Baritone)
*John Charles Thomas: an American
    Classic*
Nimbus Records NI 7838; 1992; CD
Orchestra

4862

Swing Low, Sweet Chariot
Dawson, William L.
Thompson, Jeanette (Soprano)
Negro Spirituals
Pavane Records ADW 7267; 1992; CD
Chorus
No dialect discerned

4863

Swing Low Sweet Chariot
Bohmler, Craig
Thomson, Jeannette (Soprano)
Christmas Around the World
ARTS Music ARTS49008-2; 2000; CD
Orchestra
No dialect discerned

4864

Swing Low, Sweet Chariot
Burleigh, Harry T.
Traubel, Helen (Soprano)
*Negro Spirituals: Helen Traubel in Popular
    Ballads*
Columbia ML 4221; 1949; LP
Piano

4865

Swing Low, Sweet Chariot
Composer not identified
Tynes, Margaret (Mezzo-soprano)
Margaret E. Tynes Sings Negro Spirituals
Qualiton EP 1578; 1962; 45 RPM
Orchestra

4866

Swing Low, Sweet Chariot
Composer not identified
Ventriglia, Franco (Baritone)
Franco Ventriglia Sings Negro Spirituals
Vedette Records; 2007; Streaming audio
Piano, organ
Moderate dialect

4867

Swing Low, Sweet Chariot
Composer not identified
Ventriglia, Franco (Baritone)
Franco Ventriglia Sings Negro Spirituals
Vedette Records VRMS 316; [19--]; LP
Piano, organ
Moderate dialect

4868

Swing Low, Sweet Chariot
Brown, Lawrence
West, Lucretia (Mezzo-soprano)
Negro Spirituals III
Club français du disque 176; 1959; LP
Piano
Heavy dialect

4869

Swing Low, Sweet Chariot
Brown, Lawrence
West, Lucretia (Mezzo-soprano)
Negro Spirituals mit Lukretia West

Opera 3408; [195-]; LP
Piano

4870

Swing Low, Sweet Chariot
Traditional
White, Willard (Bass-baritone)
*Willard White Sings: Copland; American
    Spirituals; Folk-Songs*
Chandos Records CHAN 8960; 1991; CD
A cappella
Light dialect

4871

Swing Low
[Burleigh, Harry T.]
Winters, Lawrence (Bass-baritone)
Lawrence Winters: Recital
Hamburger Archiv fur Gesangskunst 10397;
    2007; CD
Chorus, orchestra
Light dialect

4872

Swing Low
[Burleigh, Harry T.]
Winters, Lawrence (Bass-baritone)
Singer Portrait: Lawrence Winters
Apple Music; 2012; Streaming audio
Chorus, orchestra
Light dialect

4873

Swing Low, Sweet Chariot
Schweizer, Rolf
Wolf, Lars (Vocalist)
Die Schwarze Stimme Europas
Cantate 666000; 1971; LP
Chorus, organ, percussion

4874

Swing Low, Sweet Chariot
Burleigh, Harry T.
Wright, John Wesley (Tenor)
*Wade in the Water: Songs of the River, the
    Lake, and the Sea*
Donald L. Robinson & Associates DLR-001;
    2004; CD
Piano

· · · · · · ·

Take My Mother Home

4875

Take My Mother Home [from *Son of Man*]
Johnson, Hall
Conrad, Barbara (Mezzo-soprano)
Spirituals
Naxos 8.553036; 1995; CD
Piano
Moderate dialect

4876

Take My Mother Home
Robbiani, Mario
Fisher, Dorothy (Contralto)
Negro Spirituals
Edizione D'Arte Del Lions Club Milano Al
    Cenacolo; [19--]; LP
Orchestra
Light dialect

4877

Take My Mother Home [from *Son of Man*]
Johnson, Hall
Hopkins, Gregory (Tenor)
*Best of the Hall Johnson Centennial Festival
    Celebrating the 100th Anniversary of Hall
    Johnson's Birth*
Hall Johnson Collection O33D2; 2002; CD
Piano

4878

Take My Mother Home [from *Son of Man*]
Johnson, Hall
Mims, A. Grace Lee (Soprano)
Spirituals
H & GM Records HGM 8101; 1981; LP
Piano
Moderate dialect

4879

Take My Mother Home [from *Son of Man*]
Johnson, Hall; Sadin, Robert
Robinson, Morris (Bass)
Going Home
Decca B0008277-02; 2007; CD
Instrumental ensemble
Heavy dialect

4880
Take My Mother Home [from *Son of Man*]
Johnson, Hall
Simpson, Eugene Thamon (Bass)
Hall Johnson Spirituals and Other Folk Songs
Private Label; 2016; CD
Piano

4881
Take My Mother Home [from *Son of Man*]
Johnson, Hall
Toppin, Louise (Soprano)
The Hall Johnson Collection
Carl Fischer VF5 CD1–VF5 CD2; 2003; Score
  w/CD
Piano
Moderate dialect

4882
Take My Mother Home [from *The Life of
  Christ*]
Johnson, Hall
Warfield, William (Bass-baritone)
*Spirituals: 200 Years of African-American
  Spirituals*
ProArte CDD 3443; 1993; CD
Piano
Heavy dialect

. . . .

Takin' Names

4883
Takin' Names
[Brown, Lawrence]
Robeson, Paul (Bass-baritone)
The Collector's Paul Robeson
Monitor MCD-61580; 1989; CD
Piano
Moderate dialect

. . . .

Talk About a Child

4884
Talk About a Child
Dawson, William L.; Smith, Hale
Battle, Kathleen (Soprano)

Spirituals in Concert
Deutsche Grammophon 429 790-2; 1991; CD
Orchestra
Moderate dialect

4885
Talk About a Child
Dawson, William L.
Battle, Kathleen (Soprano)
The Best of Kathleen Battle
Deutsche Grammophon 000349502; 2004;
  CD
Orchestra
Heavy dialect

4886
Talk About a Child That Do Love Jesus
Dawson, William L.
Blackmon, Henry (Baritone)
Geestelijke Liederen En Negro Spirituals
Mirasound Records SGLP 6047; 1974; LP
Piano

4887
Talk About a Child That Do Love Jesus
Dawson, William L.
Forest, Michael (Tenor)
The Spirit Sings: American Spirituals
Shenandoah Conservatory SU003; [199-];
  CD

4888
Talk About a Child That Do Love Jesus
Hendricks, Barbara; Alexeev, Dmitri
Hendricks, Barbara (Soprano)
Negro Spirituals
EMI CDC7470262; 1983; CD
Piano
Light dialect

4889
Talk About a Child That Do Love Jesus
[Hendricks, Barbara]
Hendricks, Barbara (Soprano)
Espirituales Negros
EMI Classics/Altaya 01636; 1983; CD
Piano
Light dialect

4890

Talk About a Child That Do Love Jesus
[Hendricks, Barbara]
Hendricks, Barbara (Soprano)
Great American Spirituals
Angel CDM 7 64669 2; 1992; CD
Piano
Light dialect

Also released with *Great American Spirituals* (Musical Heritage Society 513725Z; 1994; CD)

4891

Talk About a Child That Do Love Jesus
[Hendricks, Barbara]
Hendricks, Barbara (Soprano)
Spirituals
EMI Classics 0946 346641 2 7; 2005; CD
Piano
Light dialect

4892

Talk About a Child That Do Love Jesus
Dawson, William L.
Holland, Charles (Tenor)
Black Swans: At Mid-Century
Parnassus PACD 96078/9; 2021; CD
Piano
Moderate dialect

4893

Talk About a Child That Do Love Jesus
Dawson, William L.
Holland, Charles (Tenor)
Honor! Honor!/Talk About a Child That Do Love Jesus
Victor Red Seal 4556; [19--]; 78 RPM
Piano

4894

Talk About a Child That Do Love Jesus
Dawson, William L.
Little, Vera (Mezzo-soprano)
My Good Lord Done Been Here
Decca 123737; 1957; LP
Piano

4895

Talk about a Chile
Dawson, William L.
Matthews, Inez (Mezzo-soprano)
Inez Matthews Sings Spirituals
Essential Media Group; 2011; CD
Piano
Moderate dialect

4896

Talk about a Chile
Dawson, William L.
Matthews, Inez (Mezzo-soprano)
Inez Matthews Sings Spirituals (Great New Voices of Today, v. 6)
Period SPL-580; [1950]; LP
Piano
Moderate dialect

4897

Talk About a Child That Do Love Jesus
Composer not identified
Parks, Karen (Soprano)
Done Crossed Every River: Freedom's Journey
Arcadia ARC 2004-2; 1995; CD

4898

Talk About a Child
Composer not identified
Parks, Karen (Soprano)
Opera Ebony Sings Spirituals
Ebony Classic Recordings; 2002; CD

4899

Talk About a Child
[Dawson, William L.]
Williams, Camilla (Soprano)
A Camilla Williams Recital
MGM Records E-140; [1952]; LP
Piano
Light dialect

4900

Talk About a Child
[Dawson, William L.]
Williams, Camilla (Soprano)
Camilla Williams Sings Spirituals
MGM Records M-G-M E-156; [195-]; LP

Piano
Light dialect

．．．．．．．

There Are Angels Hovering Roun'

4901

There Are Angels Hov'rin' Roun'
Composer not identified
English-Robinson, Laura (Soprano)
Christmas Chestnuts: A Message and a Gift
Alewa ENT; 2014; CD
Piano
Light dialect

4902

There Are Angels Hov'rin' Roun'
Brown, Uzee, Jr.
Harris, Crystal (Mezzo-soprano)
Great Day!
Allgood; 2005; CD
Piano
Light dialect

4903

There Are Angels Hoverin' Round
Brown, Uzee, Jr.
Moses, Oral (Bass-baritone)
*Amen! African-American Composers
   of the 20th Century*
Albany Records TROY459; 2001; CD
Piano
Light dialect

4904

There Are Angels Hoverin' Round
Brown, Uzee, Jr.
Moses, Oral (Bass-baritone)
Sankofa: A Spiritual Reflection
Albany Records TROY1802; 2019; CD
Piano
Moderate dialect

．．．．．．．

There's a Little Wheel

4905

There's a Little Wheel
Hayes, Roland; Boardman, Reginald

Hayes, Roland (Tenor)
The Art of Roland Hayes
Smithsonian Collection RD 041; 1990;
   CD
Piano
Heavy dialect

4906

There's a Little Wheel
[Hayes, Roland]
Hayes, Roland (Tenor)
Afro-American Folksongs
Pelican Records LP 2028; 1983; LP
Piano
Heavy dialect

．．．．．．．

There's a Man Going Round

4907

There's a Man Goin' 'Roun'
Baker, Bradley
Baker, Bradley (Baritone)
Not a Word: Spirituals, Hymns, Songs
AYA Worldwide Records 6-09682-2; 2001;
   CD

4908

Dere's a Man Goin' Roun' Takin' Names
Brown, Lawrence
Blackmon, Henry (Baritone)
Negro Spirituals
Jubilate JB 1716; 1961; 45 RPM
Organ

4909

Dere's a Man Goin' Roun' Takin' Names
Brown, Lawrence
Blackmon, Henry (Baritone)
Negro Spirituals
Vega 19179; [19--]; LP
Chorus, piano

4910

There's a Man Going Round Taking Names
Composer not identified
Carlsen, Svein (Bass)

Negro Spirituals
EuroMaster AS ECD19005; 1996; CD
Piano

4911

Takin' Names
Robbiani, Mario
Fisher, Dorothy (Contralto)
Negro Spirituals
Edizione D'Arte Del Lions Club Milano Al
    Cenacolo; [19--]; LP
Orchestra
Moderate dialect

4912

There's a Man Goin' Round
Hogan, Moses
Hendricks, Barbara (Soprano)
Give Me Jesus
EMI Classics 7243 5 56788 2 9; 1998; CD
Chorus
Light dialect

4913

There's a Man Goin' Round
Hogan, Moses
Hendricks, Barbara (Soprano)
Spirituals
EMI Classics 0946 346641 2 7; 2005; CD
Chorus
Light dialect

4914

Dere's a Man Goin' 'Round Takin' Names
Lloyd, Charles, Jr.
Hobson, Richard (Baritone)
The Spiritual Art Song Collection
Warner Bros. SVBM00004; 2000; Score w/
    CD
Piano

4915

Dere's a Man Goin' 'Round Takin' Names
Composer not identified
Jones, Fanni (Mezzo-soprano)
Negro Spirituals
Phonotec 815; 1977; LP
Organ

4916

Dere's a Man Goin' Round Takin' Names
Brown, Lawrence
Maynor, Kevin (Bass)
Paul Robeson Remembered
Fleur de Son Classics FDS 57929; 1998; CD
Piano
Light dialect

4917

There's a Man Going Round
Traditional
Norman, Jessye (Soprano)
Negro Spirituals
Philips 9500 580; 1979; LP
A cappella
Heavy dialect

    Also released with *Amazing Grace*
(Philips 432 546-2; 1990; CD) and *The Jessye
Norman Collection: Sacred Songs & Spiritu-
als* (Philips B0004506-02; 2005; CD)

4918

There's a Man Going Round
Traditional
Norman, Jessye (Soprano)
Spirituals
Philips 416 462-2; 1990; CD
A cappella
Light dialect

4919

There's a Man Going Round
Traditional
Norman, Jessye (Soprano)
*Honor! A Celebration of the African
    American Cultural Legacy*
Decca B0012660-02; 2009; CD
A cappella

4920

There Is a Man Going Round
Traditional
Norman, Jessye (Soprano)
The Jessye Norman Collection
Philips Classics 422 893-2; [1988]; CD
A cappella
Moderate dialect

4921
There's a Man Goin' Roun' Takin' Names
Hogan, Moses
Overton, Kenneth (Baritone)
My God Is a Rock
Winston-Salem State University; [20--];
  CD
Chorus

4922
There's a Man Goin' Round
Composer not identified
Pickens, Jo Ann (Soprano)
*My Heritage: American Melodies/Negro
  Spirituals*
Koch Schwann 3-1447-2; 1993; CD

4923
Nimet Kirjaan Kerran Kirjoitetaan (There Is
  a Man Going Round Taking Names)
Composer not identified
Putkonen, Marko (Bass)
Deep River: Negro Spirituals
Lilium LILP 101; 1991; LP

4924
There's a Man Goin Round
Hogan, Moses
Ragin, Derek Lee (Countertenor)
Ev'ry Time I Feel the Spirit: Spirituals
Channel Classics CCS 2991; 1991; CD
A cappella
Heavy dialect

4925
Dere's a Man Goin' 'Round
Brown, Lawrence
Robeson, Paul (Bass-baritone)
Swing Low, Sweet Chariot
Columbia Masterworks MM-819; 1949; 78
  RPM
Piano

4926
Dere's a Man Goin' Round
Brown, Lawrence
Robeson, Paul (Bass-baritone)
Paul Robeson Chante ... 16 Spirituals

Philips G 05.639 R; 1959; LP
Piano

4927
Dere's a Man Goin' Roun' Takin' Names
Brown, Lawrence
Robeson, Paul (Bass-baritone)
Spirituals/Folksongs/Hymns
Pearl GEMM CD 9382; 1989; CD

4928
Dere's a Man Goin' Round/I Know de
  Lord
Brown, Lawrence
Robeson, Paul (Bass-baritone); Brown,
  Lawrence (Vocalist)
The Power and the Glory
Columbia/Legacy CK 47337; 1991; CD
Piano
Heavy dialect

4929
Takin' Names
Brown, Lawrence
Robeson, Paul (Bass-baritone); Brown,
  Lawrence (Vocalist)
*On My Journey: Paul Robeson's Independent
  Recordings*
Smithsonian Folkways Recordings SFW CD
  40178; 2007; CD
Piano

4930
Dere's a Man Goin' Round Takin' Names
Brown, Lawrence
Robeson, Paul (Bass-baritone)
The Complete EMI Sessions (1928–1939)
EMI Classics 50999 2 15586 2 7; 2008; CD
Piano
Heavy dialect

4931
Dere's a Man Goin' Round
Brown, Lawrence
Robeson, Paul (Bass-baritone)
Paul Robeson Sings Negro Spirituals
Philips GBL 5584; [19--]; LP
Piano
Moderate dialect

4932

Dere's a Man Goin' Roun' Takin' Names
Brown, Lawrence
Robeson, Paul (Bass-baritone)
Paul Robeson
World Record Club W9648/EMI SM 431;
　[19--]; LP
Piano

4933

There's a Man Going 'Round Taking
　Names
[Brown, Lawrence]
Robeson, Paul (Bass-baritone)
Récital Paul Robeson
Chant du Monde, Le LD-M-8132; 1955; LP
Piano

4934

There's a Man Going 'Round Taking
　Names
[Brown, Lawrence]
Robeson, Paul (Bass-baritone)
Negro Spirituals par Paul Robeson
Chant du Monde LD-45 3008; 1958; 45
　RPM

4935

Takin' Names
[Brown, Lawrence]
Robeson, Paul (Bass-baritone)
Favorite Songs
Monitor Recordings MPS 580; 1959; LP
Piano
Heavy dialect

4936

Dere's a Man Goin' Round Takin' Names
[Brown, Lawrence]
Robeson, Paul (Bass-baritone)
The Ultimate Collection
Burning Fire; 2009; Streaming audio

4937

There's a Man Goin' Round Takin' Names
[Brown, Lawrence]
Robeson, Paul (Bass-baritone)
Paul Robeson Singt Negro Spirituals

Musical Masterpiece Society MMS-2162;
　[19--]; LP
Piano

4938

Dere's a Man Goin' 'Round
[Brown, Lawrence]
Robeson, Paul (Bass-baritone)
Swing Low, Sweet Chariot
Columbia Masterworks ML 2038; [195-]; LP
Piano

4939

Dere's a Man Goin' Roun' Takin' Names
[Brown, Lawrence]
Robeson, Paul (Bass-baritone)
Ol' Man River
Golden Options GO 3820; [2000]; CD

4940

Takin' Names
[Brown, Lawrence]
Robeson, Paul (Bass-baritone)
Negro Spirituals
Chant du Monde LDX 74376; 1982; LP
Piano

4941

There's a Man Goin' Roun' Takin' Names
[Brown, Lawrence]
Spencer, Kenneth (Bass-baritone)
American Spirituals
Sonora MS-478; [1945]; 78 RPM
Piano
Moderate dialect

· · · · · · ·

There's a Meeting
Here Tonight

4942

There's a Meeting Here Tonight
Dett, Robert Nathaniel
Arroyo, Martina (Soprano); Lawrence, T.
　Ray (Vocalist)
There's a Meeting Here Tonight
Angel S-36072; 1974; LP
Chorus

4943

There's a Meeting Here Tonight
Dett, Robert Nathaniel
Arroyo, Martina (Soprano); Anonymous
    ({Baritone})
Negro Spirituals
EMI 7243 5 72790 2 4; 1998; CD
Chorus
Moderate dialect

4944

There's a Meeting Here Tonight
Burleigh, Harry T.
Spencer, Kenneth (Bass-baritone)
Volkslieder & Spirituals
Discoton 75546; [197-]; LP
Piano
Moderate dialect

· · · · · · ·

There's No Hiding Place Down There

4945

Dere's No Hidin' Place Down Dere
Brown, Lawrence
Anderson, Marian (Contralto)
Negro Spirituals
La Voix de Son Maître 7EJF2; 1955; 45 RPM
Orchestra

4946

Dere's No Hidin' Place Down Dere
Brown, Lawrence
Anderson, Marian (Contralto)
Negro Spirituals, vol. II
La Voix de Son Maître 7 ERF 17025; 1962;
    EP 45 RPM
Orchestra

4947

Dere's No Hiding Place Down Dere
Brown, Lawrence
Anderson, Marian (Contralto)
*The Art of Marian Anderson: Arias, Songs
    and Spirituals*
His Master's Voice EG 29001614; 1986; LP
Piano

4948

Dere's No Hiding Place Down Dere
Brown, Lawrence
Anderson, Marian (Contralto)
Marian Anderson: Portraits in Memory
Metropolitan Opera Guild MET 220; 1993;
    CD
Piano
Heavy dialect

4948

Dere's No Hidin' Place Down Here
Brown, Lawrence
Anderson, Marian (Contralto)
Tribute
Pro Arte CDD 3447; 1993; CD
Piano

4950

Dere's No Hidin' Place
Brown, Lawrence
Anderson, Marian (Contralto)
*He's Got the Whole World in His Hands:
    Spirituals*
RCA Victor 09026-61960-2; 1994; CD
Piano
Heavy dialect

    Also released with *Marian Anderson:
Beyond the Music; Her Complete RCA Victor Recordings* (Sony Classical 19439836492;
2021; CD)

4951

Dere's No Hiding Place Down Dere
Brown, Lawrence
Anderson, Marian (Contralto)
Negro Spirituals
EMI 7243 5 72790 2 4; 1998; CD
Piano
Heavy dialect

    Also released with *Marian Anderson:
Beyond the Music; Her Complete RCA Victor Recordings* (Sony Classical 19439836492;
2021; CD)

4952

Dere's No Hidin' Place Down Dere
Brown, Lawrence

Anderson, Marian (Contralto)
Spirituals
RCA Victor Red Seal 09026-63306-2; 1999; CD
Piano
Moderate dialect

4953

Dere's No Hidin' Place
Brown, Lawrence
Anderson, Marian (Contralto)
Ev'Ry Time I Feel the Spirit (1930–1947)
Naxos Nostalgia 8.120779; 2004; CD
Piano

4954

Dere's No Hidin' Place Down Dere
Brown, Lawrence
Anderson, Marian (Contralto)
Lebendige Vergangenheit
Austro Mechana Historic Recordings
    MONO 89604; 2004; CD
Piano

4955

Dere's No Hidin' Place Down Dere/Ev'ry
    Time I Feel the Spirit
Brown, Lawrence
Anderson, Marian (Contralto)
Negro Spirituals: 1924–1949
Frémeaux & Associés FA 184; 2004; CD
Orchestra

4956

Dere's No Hiding Place Down Dere
Brown, Lawrence
Anderson, Marian (Contralto)
Good News: Vintage Negro Spirituals
Living Era AJA 5622; 2006; CD
Piano
Heavy dialect

4957

Dere's No Hidin' Place Down Dere
Brown, Lawrence
Anderson, Marian (Contralto)
*Marian Anderson: Beyond the Music; Her
    Complete RCA Victor Recordings*
Sony Classical 19439836492; 2021; CD

Piano
Heavy dialect

4958

Dere's No Hidin' Place Down Dere
Brown, Lawrence
Anderson, Marian (Contralto)
Deep River
RCA Victor 2032; [194-]; 78 RPM
Piano
Moderate dialect

4959

Dere's No Hidin' Place Down Dere
Brown, Lawrence
Anderson, Marian (Contralto)
Songs and Spirituals
RCA Victor M 986; [1945]; 78 RPM
Piano

4960

No Hidin' Place
[Brown, Lawrence]
Anderson, Marian (Contralto)
The Lady from Philadelphia
Pearl GEMM CD 9069; 1993; CD
Piano

4961

Dere's No Hiding Place Down Dere
[Brown, Lawrence]
Anderson, Marian (Contralto)
Softly Awakes My Heart
ASV CD AJA 5262; 1999; CD
Piano

4962

Dere's No Hidin' Place Down Dere
[Brown, Lawrence]
Anderson, Marian (Contralto)
The Very Best of Marian Anderson
Master Classics Records; 2009; CD
Piano
Heavy dialect

4963

There's No Hiding Place Down There
[Brown, Lawrence]

Anderson, Marian (Contralto)
Classic Gospel Songs
Emerald/K-Tel; 2013; Streaming audio
Piano

4964

There's No Hiding Place Down There
[Brown, Lawrence]
Anderson, Marian (Contralto)
Inspirations
Emerald Echoes; 2015; Streaming audio
Piano
Heavy dialect

4965

Dere's No Hidin' Place Down Dere
Boatwright, McHenry
Boatwright, McHenry (Bass-baritone)
Art of McHenry Boatwright: Spirituals
Golden Crest Records RE 7024; 1968; LP
Piano
Moderate dialect

4966

Dere's No Hidin' Place Down Dere
Johnson, Hall
Carnette, Count (Vocalist)
*Count Carnette Sings Favorite Negro
    Spirituals*
Carnette Archive Recordings; 1983; LP
Piano
Light dialect

4967

No Hiding Place
Corley, Maria Thompson
Clark, Maria (Soprano)
Soul Sanctuary: Spirituals & Hymns
Navona Records NV6406; 2022; CD
Piano
Moderate dialect

4968

No Hidin' Place
Clemmons, François; Marder, Jeffrey
Clemmons, François (Tenor)
Negro Spirituals Live! In Concert

American Negro Spiritual Research
    Foundation 8177 2048 3779; 1998; CD
Piano
Heavy dialect

4969

Dere's No Hidin' Place
Cooke, Barbara Logan
Cooke, Barbara (Vocalist); Deloatch, Lois
    (Vocalist)
*Sometimes I Feel: A Collection of Negro
    Spirituals for Voice and Instruments*
Private Label KDISC420; 2002; CD
Piano

4970

No Hidin' Place
Roberts, Howard
Estes, Simon (Bass-baritone)
Spirituals
Philips 412 631-2; 1985; CD
Chorus
Light dialect

4971

No Hiding Place
Roberts, Howard
Estes, Simon (Bass-baritone)
Famous Spirituals
Philips 462 062-2; 1997; CD
Chorus
Moderate dialect

4972

There's No Hidin' Place down there
Henderson, Skitch
Hines, Jerome (Bass)
Standin' in the Need of Prayer
RCA Victor LPM-2047; [1960]; LP

4973

Dere's No Hidin' Place Down Dere
Composer not identified
Osborne, Bill (Baritone)
Songs of Faith
SESAC YTNY 6088-YTNY 6089; [19--]; LP
    16 in.

4974

There's No Hiding Place Down Here
Southall, Mitchell
Price, Leontyne (Soprano)
Complete Collection of Songs and Spiritual Albums
RCA Red Seal 88697940502; 2011; CD
Chorus

4975

There's No Hiding Place Down Here
Southall, Mitchell
Price, Leontyne (Soprano)
I Wish I Knew How It Would Feel to Be Free
RCA Red Seal LSC 3183; 2011; CD
Chorus

4976

No Hiding Place
Giesen, Hubert
Ray, William (Baritone)
Negro Spirituals
Intercord; [19--]; LP
Piano

4977

No Hiding Place
Giesen, Hubert
Ray, William (Baritone)
Sings Arias, Duets, Musical Selections and Negro Spirituals
Intercord; [19--]; CD
Piano

4978

Dere's No Hidin' Place
Brown, Lawrence
Robeson, Paul (Bass-baritone)
Weepin' Mary/I Want to Be Ready/Git on Board, Lil' Chillun/Dere's No Hidin' Place
Victor 22225; 1928; 78 RPM
Piano
Heavy dialect

4979

There's No Hiding Place
Brown, Lawrence
Robeson, Paul (Bass-baritone)

A Lonesome Road: Paul Robeson Sings Spirituals and Songs
ASV Living Era CD AJA 5027; 1984; CD
Piano
Heavy dialect

4980

There's No Hiding Place
Brown, Lawrence
Robeson, Paul (Bass-baritone)
Paul Robeson Collection
Hallmark Recordings 390692; 1998; CD

4981

Dere's No Hidin' Place
Brown, Lawrence
Robeson, Paul (Bass-baritone)
The Complete EMI Sessions (1928–1939)
EMI Classics 50999 2 15586 2 7; 2008; CD
Piano
Heavy dialect

4982

Dere's No Hidin' Place
[Brown, Lawrence]
Robeson, Paul (Bass-baritone)
Songs of My People
RCA Red Seal LM-3292; 1972; LP
Piano

4983

Dere's No Hidin' Place Down Dere
[Brown, Lawrence]
Robeson, Paul (Bass-baritone)
Ol' Man River: His 56 Finest 1925–1945
Retrospective RTS 4116; 2008; CD

4984

Dere's No Hidin' Place
[Brown, Lawrence]
Robeson, Paul (Bass-baritone)
The Ultimate Collection
Burning Fire; 2009; Streaming audio
Piano
Heavy dialect

4985

There's No Hiding Place
[Brown, Lawrence]

Robeson, Paul (Bass-baritone)
Ol' Man River: The Ultimate Collection
Roslin Records; 2011; Streaming audio
Piano
Moderate dialect

4986

Dere's No Hidin' Place Down Dere [from
     Green Pastures]
Johnson, Hall
Toppin, Louise (Soprano)
The Hall Johnson Collection
Carl Fischer VF5 CD1–VF5 CD2; 2003; Score
     w/CD
Piano
Moderate dialect

4987

Dere's No Hidin' Place Down Dere
Composer not identified
Ventriglia, Franco (Baritone)
Franco Ventriglia Sings Negro Spirituals
Vedette Records; 2007; Streaming audio
Piano, organ
Heavy dialect

4988

Dere's No Hidin' Place Down Dere
Composer not identified
Ventriglia, Franco (Baritone)
Franco Ventriglia Sings Negro Spirituals
Vedette Records VRMS 316; [19--]; LP
Piano, organ
Heavy dialect

4989

No Hidin' Place Down Dere
Composer not identified
Watts, Leonardo (Baritone)
*On Ma Journey: A Memorable Collection of
     Negro Spirituals*
Onyx Recording Associates ORA-101; 1961;
     LP
Chorus

· · · · · · ·

They Crucified My Lord

4990

They Crucified My Lord [from *Cycle of Six
     Spirituals*]
Owens, Robert
Moses, Oral (Bass-baritone)
*Come Down Angels and Trouble the Water:
     Negro Spirituals, an American National
     Treasure!*
Albany Records TROY 1489; 2014; CD
Piano
Light dialect

4991

They Crucified My Lord
Schweizer, Rolf
Wolf, Lars (Vocalist)
Die Schwarze Stimme Europas
Cantate 666000; 1971; LP
Chorus, organ, percussion

· · · · · · ·

They Led My Lord Away

4992

They Led My Lord Away [from *The Life of
     Christ*]
Hayes, Roland
Brown, Anthony (Baritone)
Spirituals
Brown/Smith Productions; 1995; CD
Piano
Light dialect

4993

They Led My Lord Away [from *The Life of
     Christ*]
Hayes, Roland
Caesar, Jackson (Tenor)
*Spirituals: Celebrating the Music, Life,
     Legacy of Roland Hayes*
CD Baby 7048606059; 2021; CD
Piano
Light dialect

4994

They Led My Lord Away [from *The Life of Christ*]
Hayes, Roland
Hayes, Roland (Tenor)
Roland Hayes Sings the Life of Christ: As Told Through Aframerican Folksong
Vanguard VRS-462; 1954; LP
Piano
Light dialect

    Also released with *Roland Hayes Sings the Life of Christ: As Told Through Aframerican Folksong* (Vanguard SRV 352; 1976; LP); *Charlton Heston Reads from The Life and Passion of Jesus Christ* (Vanguard Classics ATM-CD-1259; 2003; CD) and *Big Psalms, Hymns and Spirituals Box* (eOne Music/Vanguard Classics; 2015; Streaming audio)

4995

They Led My Lord Away [from *The Life of Christ*]
Hayes, Roland
Hayes, Roland (Tenor)
Favorite Spirituals
Vanguard Classics OVC 6022; 1995; CD
Piano

4996

They Led My Lord Away [from *The Life of Christ*]
Hayes, Roland
Hayes, Roland (Tenor)
Aframerican Folksong: Telling the Story of the Life of Christ
Top Rank 39 620; [1961]; LP
Piano

4997

They Led My Lord Away [from *The Life of Christ*]
Hayes, Roland
Holland, Charles (Tenor)
My Lord What a Mornin'
Musical Heritage Society MHS 912250X; 1982; LP
Piano
No dialect discerned

4998

They Led My Lord Away [from *The Life of Christ*]
Hayes, Roland
Holland, Charles (Tenor)
My Lord What a Mornin'
Musical Heritage Society MHS 512250K; 1988; CD
Piano
No dialect discerned

4999

They Led My Lord Away [from *The Life of Christ*]
Hayes, Roland
Matthews, Benjamin (Baritone)
A Balm in Gilead
Ebony Classic Recordings ECR 0001; 2000; CD
Piano

5000

They Led My Lord Away [from *The Life of Christ*]
Johnson, Hall
Matthews, Inez (Mezzo-soprano)
Inez Matthews Sings Spirituals
Essential Media Group; 2011; CD
Piano
Moderate dialect

5001

They Led My Lord Away [from *The Life of Christ*]
Johnson, Hall
Matthews, Inez (Mezzo-soprano)
Inez Matthews Sings Spirituals (Great New Voices of Today, v. 6)
Period SPL-580; [1950]; LP
Piano
Moderate dialect

5002

They Led My Lord Away [from *The Life of Christ*]
Hayes, Roland
Oby, Jason (Tenor)
The Life of Christ: Collected Spirituals
Private Label TSU4749; [200-]; CD

Piano
Light dialect

5003

They Lead My Lord Away
Ringwald, Roy
Oglesby, Isador (Tenor)
Life of Jesus in Negro Spirituals
Oglesby Recordings Album 2; 1980; LP
Piano

5004

They Led My Lord Away [from *The Life of Christ*]
Hayes, Roland
Rolle, Gilbert-Michel (Tenor)
Musical Voyage
Centaurus Classics; 2007; CD
Instrumental ensemble
No dialect discerned

5005

They Led My Lord Away [from *The Life of Christ*]
Hayes, Roland
Shirley, George (Tenor)
George Shirley at 80: My Time Has Come!
Videmus Records; 2014; CD
Piano

5006

They Led My Lord Away [from *The Life of Christ*]
Hayes, Roland
Sims, Robert (Baritone)
Robert Sims Sings the Spirituals of Roland Hayes
Canti Classics 2014-01; 2015; CD
Piano
Heavy dialect

5007

They Led My Lord Away
Blanchard, Terence
Sykes, Jubilant (Baritone)
Jubilant Sykes
Sony Classical SK 63294; 1998; CD
Instrumental ensemble

5008

They Led My Lord Away
Composer not identified
Tyler, Veronica (Soprano)
Sings ... the Passion of Christ in Spirituals
BRC Productions; [19--]; LP
Piano

5009

They Led My Lord Away [from *The Life of Christ*]
Hayes, Roland
Warfield, William (Bass-baritone)
Spirituals: 200 Years of African-American Spirituals
ProArte CDD 3443; 1993; CD
Piano
Moderate dialect

5010

They Led My Lord Away [from *The Life of Christ*]
Hayes, Roland
Williams, Willie (Vocalist)
My Tribute
Discovery V42227; 1974; LP
Piano

· · · · · · ·

This Is de Healin' Water

5011

This Is de Healin' Water
Johnson, Hall
Blackmon, Henry (Baritone)
Geestelijke Liederen En Negro Spirituals
Mirasound Records SGLP 6047; 1974; LP
Piano

· · · · · · ·

This Little Light of Mine

[Matthew 5:15-16; Luke 11:33]

"This little light of mine, I'm going to let it shine (3x); Let it shine, let it shine, let it shine.

Everywhere I go, I'm going to let it shine, ... All through the night, ..."

[JB3b, JHSS, MBRM, PLSY, RWBC, RWSS, WPNN (2)]

5012

This Littl' Light o' Mine
McCoy, Tom
Adkins, Paul Spencer (Tenor)
How Can I Keep from Singing?
PSA PSA-2002; 2002; CD
Piano
Heavy dialect

5013

This Little Light of Mine
Traditional
Battle, Kathleen (Soprano)
Pleasures of Their Company
EMI/Angel CDC-7 47196 2; 1986; CD
A cappella
Heavy dialect

5014

This Little Light of Mine
Traditional
Battle, Kathleen (Soprano)
Great American Spirituals
Angel CDM 7 64669 2; 1992; CD
A cappella
Light dialect

5015

This Little Light of Mine
Traditional
Battle, Kathleen (Soprano)
Great American Spirituals
Musical Heritage Society 513725Z; 1994;
    CD
A cappella
Light dialect

5016

This Little Light of Mine
Work, John Wesley
Blackmon, Henry (Baritone)
Negro Spirituals
Mirasound Records SGLP 6047; [19--]; LP
Organ

5017

This Little Light o'Mine
Work, John Wesley
Blackmon, Henry (Baritone)
Negro Spirituals
Vega 19179; [19--]; LP
Chorus, piano

5018

This Little Light of Mine
Joubert, Joseph
Brown, Angela (Soprano)
*Mosiac: A Collection of African-American
    Spirituals with Piano, guitar*
Albany Records TROY721; 2004; CD
Piano
Moderate dialect

5019

This Little Light of Mine
Hairston, Jacqueline
Brown, Anthony (Baritone)
How Can I Keep from Singing?
Private label; 2013; CD
Piano
Light dialect

5020

This Little Light of Mine
Smith, Hale
Brown, William (Tenor)
Symphonic Spirituals
Columbia JC 36267; 1979; LP
Orchestra
Heavy dialect

5021

This Little Light of Mine
Smith, Hale
Brown, William (Tenor)
Symphonic Spirituals
Spotify; [2019]; Streaming audio
Orchestra
Heavy dialect

5022

This Little Light o'Mine
MacGimsey, Robert
Bumbry, Grace (Mezzo-soprano)

Portrait, A
Gala GL 100.539; 1999; CD
A cappella
Light dialect

5023
This Little Light of Mine
[Work, John Wesley]
Cole, Vinson (Tenor)
Strauss, Duparc, Puccini, Nin
Connoisseur Society CD4184; 1991; CD
Piano
Heavy dialect

5024
This Little Light of Mine
Composer not identified
Cook, Dixon & Young (Tenor)
*Triptych: A Celebration of the Negro
    Spiritual*
CDY Records 649241879206; 2009; CD
Piano
Heavy dialect

5025
This Little Light of Mine
Cooke, Barbara Logan
Cooke, Barbara (Vocalist)
*Sometimes I Feel: A Collection of Negro
    Spirituals for Voice and Instruments*
Private Label KDISC420; 2002; CD
Instrumental ensemble

5026
This Little Light of Mine
Cooke, Barbara Logan
Cooke, Barbara (Vocalist); Deloatch, Lois
    (Vocalist)
*Sometimes I Feel: A Collection of Negro
    Spirituals for Voice and Instruments*
Private Label KDISC420; 2002; CD
Piano

5027
This Little Light of Mine
Composer not identified
Credit, Roosevelt André (Bass-baritone)
Get on Board
Private label; 2016; Streaming audio

Piano
Light dialect

5028
This Little Light of Mine
Work, J[ohn Wesley]
Davis, Osceola (Soprano)
Negro Spirituals
Ondine ODE 715-2; 1988; CD
Piano
No dialect discerned

5029
This Little Light of Mine
Smith, Hale
Dixon, Janice (Soprano)
The Beauty of Two Worlds
Finetone; 2015; CD
Piano
Moderate dialect

5030
This Little Light of Mine
Work, John Wesley
English-Robinson, Laura (Soprano)
Let It Shine!
ACA Digital Recording CM20020; 1994;
    CD
Piano
No dialect discerned

5031
This Little Light of Mine
Robbiani, Mario
Fisher, Dorothy (Contralto)
Negro Spirituals
Edizione D'Arte Del Lions Club Milano Al
    Cenacolo; [19--]; LP
Orchestra
Moderate dialect

5032
This Little Light o' Mine
Work, John Wesley
Forest, Michael (Tenor)
The Spirit Sings: American Spirituals
Shenandoah Conservatory SU003; [199-];
    CD

5033
This Little Light o' Mine
Work, John Wesley
Gibson, Caroline (Soprano)
On Ma Journey Now: Negro Spirituals in Concert
Twin Productions; 2016; CD
Piano
Moderate dialect

5034
This Little Light of Mine
Traditional
Graves, Denyce (Mezzo-soprano)
Angels Watching Over Me
NPR Classics CD 0006; 1997; CD
A cappella
Moderate dialect

5035
This Little Light of Mine
Composer not identified
Green, Elnora E. (Contralto)
15 Spirituals
Private Label J3RS 2286; 1979; LP
Piano

5036
This Lil' Light of Mine
Smith, Hale
Heard, Richard (Tenor)
Ain't a That Good News: African-American Art Songs and Spirituals
HM Classics HMC9602; 1998; CD
Piano
Light dialect

5037
This Little Light of Mine
Smith, Hale
Heaston, Nicole (Soprano)
Marilyn Horne Foundation Presents on Wings of Song. Recital No. 9
Marilyn Horne Foundation DCD 5028; 2001; CD
Piano

5038
This Lil' Light of Mine
Traditional

Humphrey Flynn, Edwina (Soprano)
The Lord Will Make a Way
Private Label; 2000; CD
A cappella

5039
This Little Light of Mine
Hairston, Jacqueline
Johnson, Karen (Soprano)
The New Negro Spiritual
W. C. Patterson; 2002; Score w/CD
Piano
Heavy dialect

5040
This Little Light of Mine
Smith, Hale
Jones, Randye (Soprano)
Come Down Angels
Ahhjay Records AHHJ-0001; 2003; CD
Piano
Moderate dialect

5041
This Little Light of Mine
Walters, Richard (ed.)
Kruse, Tanya (Soprano)
15 Easy Spiritual Arrangements for the Progressing Singer
Hal Leonard HL00000391 (high); HL00000392 (low); 2005; Score w/CD
Piano
No dialect discerned

5042
This Little Light o' Mine
Work, John Wesley
Maynor, Kevin (Bass)
Songs of America from Another American
Guild GMCD 7247; 2002; CD
Piano

5043
This Little Light of Mine
Composer not identified
McDaniel, Yvette (Soprano)
Simply Spiritual
YM01 DIDX 046103; 1997; CD
Piano

5044
Little Light of Mine
Composer not identified
Miles, John (Tenor)
The Classic Spirituals
Epiphany 83-1027; 1983; LP
Instrumental ensemble

5045
This Little Light of Mine
Traditional
Mims, A. Grace Lee (Soprano)
Spirituals
H & GM Records HGM 8101; 1981; LP
A cappella
Heavy dialect

5046
This Little Light of Mine
Work, III, John W.
Moses, Oral (Bass-baritone)
Sankofa: A Spiritual Reflection
Albany Records TROY1802; 2019; CD
Piano
Light dialect

5047
This Little Light o' Mine
Work, John Wesley
Moses, Oral (Bass-baritone)
Amen! African-American Composers of the 20th Century
Albany Records TROY459; 2001; CD
Piano
No dialect discerned

5048
This Little Light of Mine
Work, John Wesley
Oglesby, Isador (Tenor)
Isador Sings Negro Spirituals
Oglesby Recordings Album 3; 1983; LP
Piano

5049
This Little Light o' Mine
Composer not identified
Pickens, Jo Ann (Soprano)
My Heritage: American Melodies/Negro Spirituals
Koch Schwann 3-1447-2; 1993; CD

5050
This Little Light o' Mine
Bonds, Margaret
Price, Leontyne (Soprano)
Return to Carnegie Hall
RCA Victor Red Seal 09026-68435-2; 1996; CD
Piano
Heavy dialect

5051
This Little Light o'Mine
Bonds, Margaret
Price, Leontyne (Soprano)
The Essential Leontyne Price
BMG Classics 09026-68153-2; 1996; CD
Piano
Heavy dialect

5052
This Little Light of Mine
Bonds, Margaret
Price, Leontyne (Soprano)
Complete Collection of Songs and Spiritual Albums
RCA Red Seal 88697940502; 2011; CD
Piano

5053
This Little Light o' Mine
Composer not identified
Price, Leontyne (Soprano)
Great Moments at Carnegie Hall
RCA Red Seal 88985304202; 2016; CD
Piano
Heavy dialect

5054
This Little Light of Mine
Work, John Wesley
Price, Leontyne (Soprano)
Complete Collection of Songs and Spiritual Albums
RCA Red Seal 88697940502; 2011; CD
Chorus

5055

This Little Light of Mine
Work, John Wesley
Price, Leontyne (Soprano)
*I Wish I Knew How It Would Feel to Be
    Free*
RCA Red Seal LSC 3183; 2011; CD
Chorus

5056

This Little Light of Mine
Traditional
Ragin, Derek Lee (Countertenor)
Ev'ry Time I Feel the Spirit: Spirituals
Channel Classics CCS 2991; 1991; CD
A cappella
Moderate dialect

5057

This Little Light of Mine
Hairston, Jacqueline
Rhodes, Yolanda (Soprano)
The Angels Bowed Down
Cambria Master Recordings CD-1237; 2019;
    CD

5058

This Little Light of Mine
Composer not identified
Robeson, Paul (Bass-baritone)
American Balladeer
Collectables Records COL-CD-6502; 1990;
    CD
Piano
Light dialect

5059

This Little Light of Mine
Composer not identified
Robeson, Paul (Bass-baritone)
The Historic Paul Robeson
Murray Hill Records 959062; [19--]; LP

5060

I'm Gonna Let It Shine
[Work, John Wesley]
Robeson, Paul (Bass-baritone)
Encore, Robeson!
Monitor MP 581; 1960; LP

5061

I'm Gonna Let It Shine
[Work, John Wesley]
Robeson, Paul (Bass-baritone)
*On My Journey: Paul Robeson's Independent
    Recordings*
Smithsonian Folkways Recordings SFW CD
    40178; 2007; CD
Piano

5062

I'm Gonna Let It Shine
[Work, John Wesley]
Robeson, Paul (Bass-baritone)
Paul Robeson Sings Negro Spirituals
Musical Masterpiece Society MMS-2162;
    [19--]; LP
Piano

5063

I'm Gonna Let It Shine
[Work, John Wesley]
Robeson, Paul (Bass-baritone)
Negro Spirituals
Concert Hall SVS 2611; [19--]; LP

5064

I'm Gonna Let It Shine
[Work, John Wesley]
Robeson, Paul (Bass-baritone)
Negro Spirituals
Chant du Monde LDX 74376; 1982; LP
Piano

5065

This 'Lil Light of Mine
Scharnberg, Kim
Robinson, Faye (Soprano)
Remembering Marian Anderson
d'Note Classics DND 1014; 1997; CD
Orchestra
Light dialect

5066

This Little Light of Mine
Carter, Roland
Robinson-Oturo, Gail (Soprano)
*Sweetest Sound I Ever Heard: Spirituals for
    Solo Voice and Piano, Vol. 1*

CD Baby; 2020; Streaming audio
Piano
Heavy dialect

5067

This Little Light of Mine
Smith, Hale
Simpson, Icy (Soprano)
I, Too
Longhorn Music; 2012; CD
Piano

5068

This Little Light of Mine
Sims, Robert
Sims, Robert (Baritone)
*Soul of a Singer: Robert Sims Sings African-
    American Folk Songs*
Canti Classics 9801; 2013; CD
A cappella
Heavy dialect

5069

This Little Light o Mine
Composer not identified
Stuart, Avon (Baritone)
Avon Stuart Recital
Edition Rhodos ERS 1218; 1975; LP
Piano

5070

This Little Light of Mine
Work, John Wesley
Suderman, Ingrid (Soprano)
Sacred Arias, Songs & Spirituals
World Records WRC1-4390; 1986; LP

5071

This Little Light
Lutters, Sandra
Thomas, Indra (Soprano)
Great Day: Indra Thomas Sings Spirituals
Delos DE 3427; 2012; CD
Piano
Light dialect

5072

This Little Light of Mine
Work, John Wesley; Thompson, Jeanette
Thompson, Jeanette (Soprano)
Negro Spirituals
Pavane Records ADW 7267; 1992; CD
Chorus
No dialect discerned

5073

This Little Light of Mine
Lee, III, James
Tillman, Alice (Soprano)
The New Negro Spiritual
W. C. Patterson; 2002; Score w/CD
Piano
Moderate dialect

5074

This Little Light of Mine [from *Four Negro
    Spirituals*]
Smith, Hale
Toppin, Louise (Soprano)
Witness
Albany Records TROY868; 2006; CD
Orchestra
Light dialect

5075

This Little Light o' Mine
Composer not identified
Verdejo, Awilda (Soprano)
Awilda Verdejo Sings Spirituals
Angeluz Performances; 1999; CD
Piano

· · · · · · ·

This May Be
the Last Time

5076

This May Be the Last Time
Composer not identified
Cook, Dixon & Young (Tenor)
*Triptych: A Celebration of the Negro
    Spiritual*
CDY Records 649241879206; 2009; CD

Piano
Light dialect

5077
Lament [from *Lyric Suite*]
Morris, Robert L.
Taylor, Darryl (Countertenor)
How Sweet the Sound: A Charm of Spirituals
Albany TROY1244; 2011; CD
Piano

5078
This May Be My Las' Time (Lament) [from
    Lyric Suite]
Morris, Robert L.
Toppin, Louise (Soprano)
*Heart on the Wall: African American Art
    Songs for Orchestra*
Albany Records TROY1314; 2011; CD
Orchestra
Light dialect

· · · · · · ·

This River

5079
This River
Brown, Uzee, Jr.
Harris, Crystal (Mezzo-soprano)
Great Day!
Allgood; 2005; CD
Piano
Light dialect

· · · · · · ·

Thunderin', Wonderin'

5080
Thunderin,' Wonderin'
MacGimsey, Robert
Pierson, Edward (Bass-baritone)
Edward Pierson Sings Hymns and Spirituals
Kemco 98-44; [19--]; LP

5081
Thunderin,' Wonderin'
MacGimsey, Robert

Pinza, Ezio (Bass)
Deep River/Thunderin,' Wonderin'
Columbia Masterworks 17383-D; 1945;
    10-in LP
Piano

5082
To See God's Bleeding Lamb
Composer not identified
Porter, John (Bass)
No More Crying: Negro Spirituals
Pan Verlag OV-84; [1978]; LP

· · · · · · ·

To Be Baptized

5083
To Be Baptized
Smith Moore, Undine
Rhodes, Yolanda (Soprano)
The Angels Bowed Down
Cambria Master Recordings CD-1237; 2019;
    CD

5084
To Be Baptized
Smith Moore, Undine
Toppin, Louise (Soprano)
Ah! Love but a Day
Albany Records/ Videmus TROY 385; 2000;
    CD
Piano
Light dialect

5085
To Be Baptized
Smith Moore, Undine
Toppin, Louise (Soprano)
The New Negro Spiritual
W. C. Patterson; 2002; Score w/CD
Piano
Heavy dialect

· · · · · · ·

Tone de Bell

5086
Tone de Bell
Campbell, Colin M.

Thomas, Edna (Soprano)
Classic Gospel Songs
Emerald/K-Tel; 2013; Streaming audio
Piano

5087

Tone de Bell
[Campbell, Colin M.]
Thomas, Edna (Soprano)
Good News: Vintage Negro Spirituals
Living Era AJA 5622; 2006; CD
Piano
Moderate dialect

· · · · · · ·

Tramping

5088

Tramping
Boatner, Edward
Anderson, Marian (Contralto)
Negro Spirituals
La Voix de Son Maître 7EJF2; 1955; 45 RPM
Orchestra

5089

Tramping
Boatner, Edward
Anderson, Marian (Contralto)
Negro Spirituals, vol. II
La Voix de Son Maître 7 ERF 17025; 1962;
    EP 45 RPM
Orchestra

5090

Trampin'
Boatner, Edward
Anderson, Marian (Contralto)
He's Got the Whole World in His Hands:
    Spirituals
RCA Victor 09026-61960-2; 1994; CD
Piano
Heavy dialect

    Also released with *Marian Anderson:*
Beyond the Music; Her Complete RCA Victor
Recordings Sony Classical 19439836492; 2021;
CD

5091

Trampin
Boatner, Edward
Anderson, Marian (Contralto)
Prima Voce
Nimbus NI 7882; 1996; CD
Piano
Light dialect

5092

Trampin'
Boatner, Edward
Anderson, Marian (Contralto)
Marian Anderson: Rare and Unpublished
    Recordings, 1936–1956
VAI Audio VAIA 1168; 1998; CD
Piano
Heavy dialect

5093

Trampin'
Boatner, Edward
Anderson, Marian (Contralto)
Spirituals
RCA Victor Red Seal 09026-63306-2; 1999;
    CD
Piano
Moderate dialect

    Also released with *Marian Anderson:*
Beyond the Music; Her Complete RCA Victor
Recordings Sony Classical 19439836492; 2021;
CD

5094

Trampin'
Boatner, Edward
Anderson, Marian (Contralto)
Softly Awakes My Heart: Arias, Songs and
    Spirituals, Original Recordings 1924–1950
Naxos Nostalgia 8.120566; 2001; CD
Piano
Heavy dialect

5095

Trampin'
Boatner, Edward
Anderson, Marian (Contralto)
Negro Spirituals: 1924–1949

Frémeaux & Associés FA 184; 2004; CD
Orchestra

5096

Trampin'
Boatner, Edward
Anderson, Marian (Contralto)
Let Freedom Ring!
JSP Records 683; 2016; CD
Piano
Moderate dialect

5097

Trampin'
Boatner, Edward
Anderson, Marian (Contralto)
*Marian Anderson: Beyond the Music; Her
Complete RCA Victor Recordings*
Sony Classical 19439836492; 2021; CD
Piano
Heavy dialect

5098

Trampin'
Boatner, Edward
Anderson, Marian (Contralto)
*Trampin'/I Know Lord Laid His Hands on
Me*
Victor 1896; [19--]; 78 RPM
Piano
Light dialect

5099

Tramping
Boatner, Edward
Anderson, Marian (Contralto)
*Tramping/I Know de Lord's Laid His Hands
on Me*
His Master's Voice D.A. 1669; [19--]; 78 RPM
Piano
Light dialect

5100

Trampin'
[Boatner, Edward]
Anderson, Marian (Contralto)
Marian Anderson, Volume 1
Pearl GEMM CD 9318; 1988; CD

5101

Tryin' to Make Heaven My Home
[Boatner, Edward]
Anderson, Marian (Contralto)
The Legendary Marian Anderson "Live"
Legendary Recordings LRCD 1031; 1990;
    CD
Piano

5102

Tramping
[Boatner, Edward]
Anderson, Marian (Contralto)
Marian Anderson Sings Spirituals
Flapper Past CD 7073; 1995; CD
Piano

5103

Trampin'
[Boatner, Edward]
Anderson, Marian (Contralto)
Softly Awakes My Heart
ASV CD AJA 5262; 1999; CD
Piano

5104

Trampin'
[Boatner, Edward]
Anderson, Marian (Contralto)
The Very Best of Marian Anderson
Master Classics Records; 2009; CD
Piano
Heavy dialect

5105

Trampin'
[Boatner, Edward]
Anderson, Marian (Contralto)
Inspirations
Emerald Echoes; 2015; Streaming audio
Piano
Moderate dialect

5106

I'm Trampin'
Brown, Uzee, Jr.
Brown, Uzee, Jr. (Baritone)
Great Day!
Allgood; 2005; CD

Piano
Heavy dialect

5107

Trampin'
Composer not identified
Carey, Thomas (Baritone)
Go Down Moses
Da Camera Song SM 95028; 1970; LP
Piano

5108

Trampin'
Composer not identified
Franklin, Lavinia A. (Vocalist)
Historical Interpretation of Negro Spirituals and Lift Every Voice and Sing
Recorded Publications JZB-02591; 1970; LP
Organ

5109

Trampin'
Boatner, Edward
Matthews, Benjamin (Baritone)
A Spiritual Journey
Ebony Classic Recordings ECR 0001; 2000; CD
Piano

5110

Trampin
Boatner, Edward
Matthews, Benjamin (Baritone)
A Balm in Gilead
Ebony Classic Recordings ECR 0001; 2000; CD
Piano

5111

Trampin'
Brown, Uzee, Jr.
Moses, Oral (Bass-baritone)
Come Down Angels and Trouble the Water: Negro Spirituals, an American National Treasure!
Albany Records TROY 1489; 2014; CD
Piano
Light dialect

5112

Trampin'
[Boatner, Edward]
Moyer, Del-Louise (Mezzo-soprano)
He'll Bring to Pass: Spirituals & Americanegro Suite
Alyssum ALY-9001; 1997; CD
Piano
Light dialect

5113

Trampin'
Boatner, Edward
Oglesby, Isador (Tenor)
Isador Sings Negro Spirituals
Oglesby Recordings Album 3; 1983; LP
Piano

5114

Trampin'
Composer not identified
Watts, Leonardo (Baritone)
On Ma Journey: A Memorable Collection of Negro Spirituals
Onyx Recording Associates ORA-101; 1961; LP
Chorus

5115

Trampin'
Boatner, Edward
West, Lucretia (Mezzo-soprano)
Negro Spirituals III
Club français du disque 176; 1959; LP
Piano
Moderate dialect

5116

Trampin'
Boatner, Edward
West, Lucretia (Mezzo-soprano)
Negro Spirituals mit Lukretia West
Opera 3408; [195-]; LP
Piano

5117

Trampin'
Boatner, Edward

West, Lucretia (Mezzo-soprano)
Negro Spirituals
Club français du disque 215; [196-]; 7-in EP
Piano

. . . .

True Religion

5118

True Religion
Simpson, Eugene Thamon
Philogene, Ruby (Soprano)
Steal Away
EMI Classics 7243 5 69707 2 4; 1997; CD
Chorus

. . . .

Tryin' to Get Home

5119

Tryin' to Get Home
Carter, Roland
Robinson-Oturo, Gail (Soprano)
Sweetest Sound I Ever Heard: Spirituals for Solo Voice and Piano, Vol. 1
CD Baby; 2020; Streaming audio
Piano
Light dialect

. . . .

Tryin' to Get Ready

5120

Tryin' to Get Ready
Traditional
Moses, Oral (Bass-baritone)
Spirituals in Zion: A Spiritual Heritage for the Soul
Albany Records TROY587; 2003; CD
A cappella
Light dialect

. . . .

Two Wings

5121

Two Wings [from *My Songs*]
Hayes, Roland
Caesar, Jackson (Tenor)

Spirituals: Celebrating the Music, Life, Legacy of Roland Hayes
CD Baby 7048606059; 2021; CD
Piano
Moderate dialect

5122

I Want Two Wings [from *My Songs*]
Composer not identified
Hayes, Roland (Tenor)
Afro-American Folksongs
Pelican Records LP 2028; 1983; LP
Piano

5123

Two Wings [from *My Songs*]
Hayes, Roland
Hayes, Roland (Tenor)
Roland Hayes: My Songs
Vanguard VRS-494; 1956; LP
Piano

5124

Two Wings [from *My Songs*]
Hayes, Roland
Hayes, Roland (Tenor)
Favorite Spirituals
Vanguard Classics OVC 6022; 1995; CD
Piano
Heavy dialect

5125

Two Wings [from *My Songs: Dream of Heaven*]
[Hayes, Roland]
Hayes, Roland (Tenor)
Big Psalms, Hymns and Spirituals Box
eOne Music/Vanguard Classics; 2015; Streaming audio
Piano

5126

Two Wings [from *My Songs*]
Composer not identified
McKelton, Samuel (Tenor)
Done Crossed Every River: Freedom's Journey
Arcadia ARC 2004-2; 1995; CD

5127

Two Wings [from *My Songs*]
Hayes, Roland
McKelton, Samuel (Tenor)
Opera Ebony Sings Spirituals
Ebony Classic Recordings; 2002; CD

5128

Two Wings [from *My Songs*]
Hayes, Roland
Sims, Robert (Baritone)
*Robert Sims Sings the Spirituals of Roland
    Hayes*
Canti Classics 2014-01; 2015; CD
Piano
Heavy dialect

5129

Two Wings [from *My Songs*]
McLin, Lena
Sims, Robert (Baritone)
*Soul of a Singer: Robert Sims Sings African-
    American Folk Songs*
Canti Classics 9801; 2013; CD
Piano
Heavy dialect

· · · · · · ·

Upon the Mountain

5130

Upon the Mountain
Robbiani, Mario
Fisher, Dorothy (Contralto)
Negro Spirituals
Edizione D'Arte Del Lions Club Milano
    Al Cenacolo; [19--]; LP
Orchestra
Heavy dialect

· · · · · · ·

Virgin Mary Had
a Baby Boy

5131

The Virgin Mary Had a Baby Boy
Hairston, Jacqueline
Battle, Kathleen (Soprano)
Angels' Glory

Sony Classical SK 62723; 1996; CD
Guitar
Light dialect

5132

The Virgin Mary Had a Baby Boy
Hairston, Jacqueline
Battle, Kathleen (Soprano)
The Complete Sony Recordings
Sony Classical 88985381362; 2016; CD
Guitar
Light dialect

5133

Virgin Mary Had a Baby Boy
Welsh, Nicky
McCue, Bill (Bass-baritone)
Bill McCue Sings the Great Spirituals
Beltona SBE 173; 1974; LP
Orchestra

· · · · · · ·

Wade in the Water

5134

Wade in the Water
Boatner, Edward
Brown, Anthony (Baritone)
Spirituals
Brown/Smith Productions; 1995; CD
Piano
Heavy dialect

5135

Wade in de Water
Burleigh, Harry T.
Burton, Dashon (Bass-baritone)
*Songs of Struggle & Redemption: We Shall
    Overcome*
Acis Productions APL08685; 2015; CD
Piano
Heavy dialect

5136

Wade in the Water [from *Crossing Jordan*]
Corley, Maria Thompson
Clark, Maria (Soprano)
Soul Sanctuary: Spirituals & Hymns

Navona Records NV6406; 2022; CD
Piano, cello
Heavy dialect

5137

Wade in the Water
Johnson, Hall; Joubert, Joseph
Conrad, Barbara (Mezzo-soprano)
Spirituals
Naxos 8.553036; 1995; CD
Piano
Heavy dialect

5138

Wade in de Water
Cooke, Barbara Logan
Cooke, Barbara (Vocalist)
*Sometimes I Feel: A Collection of Negro
    Spirituals for Voice and Instruments*
Private Label KDISC420; 2002; CD
Instrumental ensemble

5139

Wade in the Water
Ryan, Donald
Estes, Simon (Bass-baritone)
Steal Away: My Favorite Negro Spirituals
Deutsche Schallplatten DS 1041-2; 1994; CD
Piano
Light dialect

   Also released with *Simon Sings His
Favorite Gospels & Spirituals* (Praise Pro-
ductions SMG-SE; 1999; CD) and *Save the
Children, Save Their Lives* (CD Baby; 2020;
Streaming audio)

5140

Wade in de Water
Johnson, Hall
Foreman, Blanche (Contralto)
*Best of the Hall Johnson Centennial Festival
    Celebrating the 100th Anniversary of Hall
    Johnson's Birth*
Hall Johnson Collection O33D2; 2002; CD
Piano

5141

Wade in the Water
Composer not identified

Franklin, Lavinia A. (Vocalist)
*Historical Interpretation of Negro Spirituals
    and Lift Every Voice and Sing*
Recorded Publications JZB-02591; 1970; LP
Organ

5142

Wade in the Water
[Johnson, Hall]
Hagen-William, Louis (Bass-baritone)
Negro Spirituals
Quantum QM 6909; 1993; CD
Piano
Moderate dialect

5143

Wade in the Water
Wheatley, Andres
Haniotis, Mario (Bass)
Negro Spirituals
Pastorale et Musique PM 17.047; [196-];
    45 RPM
Piano
Light dialect

5144

Wade in the Water
Composer not identified
Hendricks, Barbara (Soprano)
*100 Plus Beaux Airs de Barbara Hendricks,
    Les*
EMI Classics 50999 085683 2 8; 2012; CD
Chorus
Moderate dialect

5145

Wade in the Water
Hogan, Moses
Hendricks, Barbara (Soprano)
Give Me Jesus
EMI Classics 7243 5 56788 2 9; 1998; CD
Chorus
Moderate dialect

   Also released with *Spirituals* (EMI Classics 0946 346641 2 7; 2005; CD)

5146

Wade in the Water
Clinton, Irving

Irving, Clinton (Bass-baritone)
Clinton Irving Sings Spirituals: A Tribute
Rogers; 2001; CD

5147

Wade in the Water
Boatner, Edward
Jones, Arthur (Tenor)
Wade in the Water
Orbis Books; 1993; Book w/cass
Piano
Moderate dialect

5148

Wade in the Water
Burleigh, Harry T.
Kennedy, Charles (Vocalist)
Heart & Soul: Songs of Harry T. Burleigh
Publisher not known; 1994; Cassette

5149

Wade in the Water
Okpebholo, Shawn
Liverman, Will (Baritone)
Steal Away
Yellow Einstein; 2014; CD
Piano
Light dialect

5150

Wade in de Water
Composer not identified
Loiselle, Henri (Bass-baritone)
One Day at a Time
Hum Recordings HRHLCD001; 1996; CD
Piano

5151

Wade in the Water
Lynch, Lester; Simonson, Victor & Brian
    Farrell
Lynch, Lester (Baritone)
On My Journey Now: Spirituals & Hymns
Pentatone Music PTC 5186 57'; 2017; CD
Chorus, piano, organ

5152

Wade in the Water
Burleigh, Harry T.

McKinney, Jason (Bass-baritone)
Songs Inspired by Paul Robeson
United in Music; 2014; CD
Piano
Heavy dialect

5153

Wade in the Water
Composer not identified
Monzo, Oscar (Baritone)
Negro Spirituals
Dial Discos 50-2020; 1983; LP

5154

Wade in de Water
Burleigh, Harry T.
Moses, Oral (Bass-baritone)
*Deep River: Songs and Spirituals of Harry T.
    Burleigh*
Northeastern NR 252-CD; 1995; CD
Piano

5155

Wade in the Water
Composer not identified
Newby, Marion Crowley (Contralto)
*Hymns and Spirituals for Canada's
    Centennial*
A.T.C.M.; 1967; LP

5156

Wade in the Water
Pankey, Aubrey
Pankey, Aubrey (Baritone)
Negro Spirituals
Eterna 830010; 1983; LP
Piano

5157

Wade in the Water
Roberts, Howard
Parks, Kenneth (?) (Vocalist)
They Slice the Air
Spirituals Project; 2007; CD
Chorus, instrumental ensemble
Heavy dialect

5158

Wade in the Water
Composer not identified

Pickens, Jo Ann (Soprano)
My Heritage: American Melodies/Negro Spirituals
Koch Schwann 3-1447-2; 1993; CD

5159

Wade in the Water
Hogan, Moses
Ragin, Derek Lee (Countertenor)
Negro Spirituals
Virgin Classics 0946 363305 2 5; 2006; CD
Chorus
Heavy dialect

5160

Wade in the Water
Sadin, Robert
Robinson, Morris (Bass)
Going Home
Decca B0008277-02; 2007; CD
Chorus, instrumental ensemble
Heavy dialect

5161

Wade in the Water
Johnson, Hall
Simpson, Eugene Thamon (Bass)
Hear Me, Ye Winds and Waves
Black Heritage Publications; 2005; CD
Piano
Heavy dialect

Also released with *Hall Johnson Spirituals and Other Folk Songs* (Private Label; 2016; CD)

5162

Wade in the Water
Hayes, Mark
Simpson, Icy (Soprano)
I, Too
Longhorn Music; 2012; CD
Piano

5163

Wade in the Water
Hogan, Moses
Simpson, Marietta (Mezzo-soprano)

Songs of Reflection
MGH Records 0800CD; 1997; CD

5164

Wade in the Water
Composer not identified
St. Hill, Krister (Baritone)
Svenska Folkvisor/Negro Spirituals
Polar POLS 398; 1985; LP

5165

Wade in de Water
Johnson, Hall
Toppin, Louise (Soprano)
He'll Bring It to Pass: The Spirituals of Hall Johnson for Voice and Piano
Albany Records TROY846; 2006; CD
Piano
Heavy dialect

5166

Wade in de Water
Morgenstern, Sam
West, Lucretia (Mezzo-soprano)
Spirituals
Westminster WL 5338; 1954; LP
Men's voices

5167

Wade in the Water
Coil, Pat; Wilson-Felder, Cynthia
Wilson-Felder, Cynthia (Soprano)
Spirituals: Songs from the American Experience
GBGMusik CD 1-005; 1996; CD
Instrumental ensemble

5168

Wade in de Water
Burleigh, Harry T.
Woodley, Arthur (Bass)
From the Southland: Songs, Piano Sketches and Spirituals of Harry T. Burleigh
Premier Recordings PRCD 1041; 1995; CD
Piano
Heavy dialect

· · · · · · ·
Wait Till I Put on My Crown

5169
Wait Till I Put on My Crown
McLin, Lena
Barnes, Sebronette (Soprano)
You Can Tell the World: Songs by African-American Women Composers
Senrab Record SRR7988; 2000; CD
Piano
Light dialect

5170
Wait Till I Put on My Crown
McLin, Lena
English-Robinson, Laura (Soprano)
Let It Shine!
ACA Digital Recording CM20020; 1994; CD
Piano
No dialect discerned

5171
Wait 'Till Ah Put on My Crown
Reddick, William J.
Hindermyer, Harvey (Tenor)
Standin' in de Need o'Prayer/Wait 'till Ah Put on My Crown
Edison 80539-L; [1919]; 78 RPM
Orchestra

5172
Wait Till I Put on My Crown
McLin, Lena
Rhodes, Yolanda (Soprano)
The Angels Bowed Down
Cambria Master Recordings CD-1237; 2019; CD

5173
Wait Till I Put on My Crown
McLin, Lena
Rucker, Mark (Baritone)
Mark Rucker Sings Lena McLin: Songs for Voice & Piano
Kjos Music Press KCD8; 2002; CD

Piano
Light dialect

5174
Wait 'Til I Put on My Crown
McLin, Lena
Sims, Robert (Baritone)
Soul of a Singer: Robert Sims Sings African-American Folk Songs
Canti Classics 9801; 2013; CD
Piano
Heavy dialect

· · · · · · ·
Waitin' on You

5175
Waitin' on You
Traditional
Brown, Anthony (Baritone)
Each Other's Light: Songs of Peace, Hope & Justice
Private label AB0906; [2017]; CD
Chorus
Moderate dialect

· · · · · · ·
Wake Up Jacob

5176
Wake Up Jacob
White, Clarence Cameron
Bledsoe, Jules (Baritone)
Wake Up Jacob/He Rose/Poor Monah
Ultraphone AP 393; 1931; 78 RPM
Orchestra
Light dialect

5177
Wake Up, Jacob
White, Clarence Cameron
Bledsoe, Jules (Baritone)
He Rose/Wake Up, Jacob
Royale 1701; [19--]; 78 RPM
Orchestra
Light dialect

5178

Wake Up Jacob
[White, Clarence Cameron]
Bledsoe, Jules (Baritone)
Wake Up, Jacob/Poor Monah
Royale 1701; 1939; 78 RPM
Orchestra
Light dialect

5179

Wake Up Jacob
[White, Clarence Cameron]
Bledsoe, Jules (Baritone)
Wake Up Jacob/Deep River
Joe Davis 8002; 1945; 78 RPM
Orchestra
Light dialect

· · · · · · ·

Walk Together Children

5180

Walk Together Children
Hogan, Moses
Bazile, Bridget (Soprano)
Songs of Reflection
MGH Records 0800CD; 1997; CD

5181

Walk Together Children
Hogan, Moses
Blanchard, Gerald (Baritone)
With a Song in My Heart
Blue Griffin Recording BGR117; 2004; CD
Piano
Moderate dialect

5182

Walk Together Children
Hogan, Moses
Brown, Angela (Soprano)
*Mosiac: A Collection of African-American
    Spirituals with Piano, guitar*
Albany Records TROY721; 2004; CD
Piano
Moderate dialect

5183

Walk Together Children
Hogan, Moses

Davis, Henrietta (Soprano)
*Deep River: Featuring 10 Spirituals Arranged
    for Solo Voice....*
MGH Records 5000; 2000; CD
Piano
Light dialect

5184

Walk Together Children
[Hogan, Moses]
Fernandez, Wilhelmenia (Soprano)
The Diva Live
Transart Records TAP110; 2003; CD
Piano
Light dialect

5185

Walk Together Children
Hogan, Moses
Fernandez, Wilhelmenia (Soprano)
Negro Spirituals
Transart 131; 2005; CD
Piano

5186

Walk Together Children
Hogan, Moses
Moses, Oral (Bass-baritone)
Songs of America
Albany Records TROY1011; 2008; CD
Piano
Heavy dialect

5187

Walk Together Children
[Patterson, Willis]
Norman, Jessye (Soprano)
*The Jessye Norman Collection: Sacred Songs
    & Spirituals*
Philips B0004506-02; 2005; CD
Chorus
Heavy dialect

5188

Walk Together Children
Patterson. Willis
Norman, Jessye (Soprano)
Negro Spirituals
Philips 9500 580; 1979; LP

Chorus
No dialect discerned

    Also released with *Spirituals* (Philips
416 462-2; 1990; CD)

5189

Walk Together Children
Smith, Hale; Hogan, Moses
Ragin, Derek Lee (Countertenor)
Negro Spirituals
Virgin Classics 0946 363305 2 5; 2006; CD
Piano
Moderate dialect

5190

Walk Together Children
Hogan, Moses
Salters, Stephen (Baritone)
Spirit: Are You There, You Are There
HarmonizedDisharmony 0001; 2015; CD

5191

Walk Together Children
Hogan, Moses
White, Cassandra (Soprano)
Remembering the Spirituals
CBW Entertainment 837101334068; 2007; CD
Piano
No dialect discerned

• • • • • • •

Walk with Me

5192

Walk with Me
Burton, Ken
Philogene, Ruby (Soprano)
Steal Away
EMI Classics 7243 5 69707 2 4; 1997; CD
Piano

5193

Walk with Me
Composer not identified
White, Cassandra (Soprano)
Remembering the Spirituals
CBW Entertainment 837101334068; 2007; CD
Piano
No dialect discerned

• • • • • • •

Wasn't Dat a Wide Ribber

5194

Oh, Wasn't Dat a Wide Ribber
Burleigh, Harry T.
Anderson, Marian (Contralto)
*He's Got the Whole World in His Hands:
    Spirituals*
RCA Victor 09026-61960-2; 1994; CD
Piano
Moderate dialect

5195

Oh Wasn't Dat a Wide Ribber
Burleigh, Harry T.
Anderson, Marian (Contralto)
*Softly Awakes My Heart: Arias, Songs and
    Spirituals, Original Recordings 1924–1949*
Naxos Nostalgia 8.120566; 2001; CD
Piano
Heavy dialect

5196

Oh, Wasn't Dat a Wide, Wide Ribber
[Burleigh, Harry T.]
Anderson, Marian (Contralto)
Marian Anderson, Volume 1
Pearl GEMM CD 9318; 1988; CD

5197

O Wasn't Dat a Wide, Wide Ribber
[Burleigh, Harry T.]
Anderson, Marian (Contralto)
Marian Anderson Sings Spirituals
Flapper Past CD 7073; 1995; CD
Piano

    Also released with *Marian Anderson:
Beyond the Music; Her Complete RCA Victor
Recordings* Sony Classical 19439836492; 2021;
CD

5198

Oh, Wasn't Dat a Wide Ribber
[Burleigh, Harry T.]
Anderson, Marian (Contralto)
The Rich Voice of Marian Anderson

Editions Audiovisuel Beulah; 2019;
    Streaming audio
Piano

5199

Oh, Wasn't Dat a Wide River
Johnson, John Rosamond
Anonymous (Vocalist)
Opera Ebony Sings Spirituals
Ebony Classic Recordings; 2002; CD

5200

Oh Wasn't Dat a Wide River
Composer not identified
Ayers, Vanessa (Mezzo-soprano)
Done Crossed Every River: Freedom's Journey
Arcadia ARC 2004-2; 1995; CD

5201

Oh Wasn't Dat a Wide Ribber
Clinton, Irving
Irving, Clinton (Bass-baritone)
Clinton Irving Sings Spirituals: A Tribute
Rogers; 2001; CD

5202

Oh, Wasn't Dat a Wide Ribber?
Composer not identified
Verdejo, Awilda (Soprano)
Awilda Verdejo Sings Spirituals
Angeluz Performances; 1999; CD
Piano

5203

O Wasn't That a Wide River?
Composer not identified
White, Portia (Contralto)
Think on Me
White House Records WH-6901; 1968; LP
Piano

5204

O Wasn't That a Wide River?
Composer not identified
White, Portia (Contralto)
First You Dream
C. White PW 001-2; 1990s; CD
Piano

. . . .

Wasn't That a Mighty Day

5205

Wasn't That a Mighty Day
Young, Thomas J.
Ayers, Vanessa (Mezzo-soprano)
A Spiritual Christmas
Musical Heritage Society 5167448; 2002; CD
Piano
Light dialect

5206

Wasn't That a Mighty Day?
Young, Thomas J.
Ayers, Vanessa (Mezzo-soprano)
*Black Christmas: Spirituals in the African-
    American Tradition*
Essay Recordings CD1011; 1990; CD
Piano
No dialect discerned

5207

Wasn't That a Mighty Day
Hairston, Jacqueline
Battle, Kathleen (Soprano)
Angels' Glory
Sony Classical SK 62723; 1996; CD
A cappella
No dialect discerned

5208

Wasn't That a Mighty Day
Hairston, Jacqueline
Battle, Kathleen (Soprano)
The Complete Sony Recordings
Sony Classical 88985381362; 2016; CD
Guitar
No dialect discerned

5209

Wasn't That a Mighty Day?
Composer not identified
Rustin, Bayard (Tenor)
Bayard Rustin, the Singer
Bayard Rustin Fund; 1992; CD
Piano

5210

Wasn't That a Mighty Day?
Traditional
Rustin, Bayard (Tenor)
*Bayard Rustin Sings Twelve Spirituals on the
    Life of Christ*
Fellowship Records E2-KL 1771; [195-]; LP
A cappella
Light dialect

Also released with *Bayard Rustin-The
Singer* (Black Swan Series; Parnassus Records
PACD 96083; 2022; CD)

. . . .

Watch and Pray

5211

Watch and Pray
Smith Moore, Undine
Brown, Angela (Soprano)
*Mosiac: A Collection of African-American
    Spirituals with Piano, guitar*
Albany Records TROY721; 2004; CD
Piano
Moderate dialect

5212

Watch and Pray
Smith Moore, Undine
Brown, Angela (Soprano)
The Lily of the Valley
American Spiritual Ensemble; [2003]; CD
Piano

5213

Watch and Pray
Smith Moore, Undine
Dillard, Pamela (Mezzo-soprano)
*Watch and Pray: Spirituals and Art Songs
    by African-American Women Composers*
Koch International Classics 3-7247-2H1;
    1994; CD
Piano
Heavy dialect

5214

Watch and Pray
Smith Moore, Undine

Rhodes, Yolanda (Soprano)
The Angels Bowed Down
Cambria Master Recordings CD-1237; 2019;
    CD

5215

Watch and Pray
Smith Moore, Undine
Salters, Stephen (Baritone)
Spirit: Are You There, You Are There
HarmonizedDisharmony 0001; 2015; CD

5216

Watch and Pray
Smith Moore, Undine
Simpson, Icy (Soprano)
I, Too
Longhorn Music; 2012; CD
Piano

. . . .

Way By an' By

5217

Way By an' By
Jackson King, Betty
Matthews, Benjamin (Baritone)
A Balm in Gilead
Ebony Classic Recordings ECR 0001; 2000;
    CD
Piano

5218

Way by an' By
Jackson King, Betty
Rhodes, Yolanda (Soprano)
The Angels Bowed Down
Cambria Master Recordings CD-1237; 2019;
    CD

. . . .

Way in the Middle
of the Air

5219

Way in the Middle of the Air
[Hayes, Roland]

Hayes, Roland (Tenor)
Big Psalms, Hymns and Spirituals Box
eOne Music/Vanguard Classics; 2015;
    Streaming audio
Piano

. . . .

Way Up in Heaven

5220

Way Up in Heaven
Johnson, Hall
Toppin, Louise (Soprano)
Good News
Videmus Records VIS735; 2007; CD
A cappella
Moderate dialect

5221

Way Up in Heaven
Johnson, Hall
Wilson, Robin (Soprano)
*Best of the Hall Johnson Centennial Festival
    Celebrating the 100th Anniversary of Hall
    Johnson's Birth*
Hall Johnson Collection O33D2; 2002; CD
Piano

. . . .

We Are Climbing Jacob's Ladder

5222

We Are Climbin' Jacob's Ladder
Boatwright, McHenry
Boatwright, McHenry (Bass-baritone)
Art of McHenry Boatwright: Spirituals
Golden Crest Records RE 7024; 1968; LP
Piano
No dialect discerned

5223

We Are Climbing Jacob's Ladder
Composer not identified
Duckworth, Zorita (Mezzo-soprano)
Forget Me Not.... Negro Spirituals
Private Label; [20--]; CD

5224

We Are Clim'in' Jacob's Ladder
[Johnson, John Rosamond]
Duncan, Todd (Baritone)
American Negro Spirituals
Allegro LEG 9026; [19--]; LP

5225

We Are Climbing Jacob's Ladder
Johnson, John Rosamond
Duncan, Todd (Baritone)
African American Spirituals
[Apple Music]; 2008; Streaming audio
Piano
Light dialect

5226

Clim'in Jacob's Ladder
Johnson, John Rosamond
Duncan, Todd (Baritone)
Negro Spirituals
Allegro ALG3022; [1952]; LP
Piano

5227

We Are Clim'in Jacob's Ladder
[Johnson, John Rosamond]
Duncan, Todd (Baritone)
Spirituals
Royale 1810; [1950]; LP

5228

A Paraphrase (Jacob's Ladder)
Simpson, Ralph
English-Robinson, Laura (Soprano)
Let It Shine!
ACA Digital Recording CM20020; 1994; CD
Piano
No dialect discerned

5229

Climbin' Jacob's Ladder
Bledsoe, Jules
Hinds, Esther (Soprano)
The Art of Esther Hinds
Quattro Corde 5003; 1998; CD

5230

Jacob's Ladder
Walters, Richard (ed.)

Kruse, Tanya (Soprano)
15 Easy Spiritual Arrangements for the Progressing Singer
Hal Leonard HL00000391 (high); HL00000392 (low); 2005; Score w/CD
Piano
No dialect discerned

5231

Jacob's Ladder
Composer not identified
Maynor, Kevin (Bass)
Paul Robeson Remembered
Fleur de Son Classics FDS 57929; 1998; CD
Piano
Light dialect

5232

We Are Climbing Jacob's Ladder
Raphael, Michael
Maynor, Kevin (Bass)
Jazz Hymns
Guild GMCD 7224; 2001; CD
Piano

5233

Jacob's Ladder
Bagley, Christopher
McKinney, Jason (Bass-baritone)
Songs Inspired by Paul Robeson
United in Music; 2014; CD
Piano
Moderate dialect

5234

Jacob's Ladder
[Johnson, John Rosamond]
Robeson, Paul (Bass-baritone)
Favorite Songs
Monitor Recordings MPS 580; 1959; LP
Piano
Moderate dialect

5235

We Are Climbing Jacob's Ladder
[Johnson, John Rosamond]
Robeson, Paul (Bass-baritone)
Recital
Supraphon SUA 10062; 1961; LP
Piano

5236

We Are Climbing Jacob's Ladder
[Johnson, John Rosamond]
Robeson, Paul (Bass-baritone)
Paul Robeson in Live Performance
Columbia M 30424; 1971; LP
Piano
Light dialect

5237

Jacob's Ladder
[Johnson, John Rosamond]
Robeson, Paul (Bass-baritone)
The Essential Paul Robeson
Vanguard VSD 57/58; 1974; LP
Piano
Light dialect

5238

We Are Climbing Jacob's Ladder
[Johnson, John Rosamond]
Robeson, Paul (Bass-baritone)
Scandalize My Name
Classics Record Library 30-5647; 1976; LP
Piano
Moderate dialect

5239

Jacob's Ladder
[Johnson, John Rosamond]
Robeson, Paul (Bass-baritone)
Paul Robeson Live at Carnegie Hall
Vanguard VCD-72020; 1987; CD
Piano
Moderate dialect

5240

Jacob's Ladder
[Johnson, John Rosamond]
Robeson, Paul (Bass-baritone)
The Collector's Paul Robeson
Monitor MCD-61580; 1989; CD
Piano
Light dialect

5241

Jacob's Ladder
[Johnson, John Rosamond]
Robeson, Paul (Bass-baritone)

Gospels & Spirituals Gold Collection
Retro R2CD 40-26; 1995; CD
Piano
Light dialect

5242

Jacob's Ladder
[Johnson, John Rosamond]
Robeson, Paul (Bass-baritone)
The Peace Arch Concerts
Folk Era Records FE1442CD; 1998; CD
Piano
Light dialect

5243

We Are Climbing Jacob's Ladder
[Johnson, John Rosamond]
Robeson, Paul (Bass-baritone)
*On My Journey: Paul Robeson's Independent
    Recordings*
Smithsonian Folkways Recordings SFW CD
    40178; 2007; CD
Piano

5244

Jacob's Ladder
[Johnson, John Rosamond]
Robeson, Paul (Bass-baritone)
Negro Spirituals (And More)
Discmedi DM-4674-02; 2009; CD

5245

We Are Climbing Jacob's Ladder
[Johnson, John Rosamond]
Robeson, Paul (Bass-baritone)
The Very Best of Paul Robeson
Future Noise Music FVDD033; 2009; CD
Piano

5246

We Are Climbing Jacob's Ladder
[Johnson, John Rosamond]
Robeson, Paul (Bass-baritone)
Sometimes I Feel Like a Motherless Child
JazzAge; 2012; Streaming audio
Piano

5247

Jacob's Ladder
[Johnson, John Rosamond]

Robeson, Paul (Bass-baritone)
Five Classic Albums Plus Bonus Tracks
Real Gone Music RGMCD287; 2017; CD

5248

Jacob's Ladder
[Johnson, John Rosamond]
Robeson, Paul (Bass-baritone)
Complete Recordings
Universal Digital Enterprises; 2018;
    Streaming audio

5249

We Are Climbing Jacob's Ladder
[Johnson, John Rosamond]
Robeson, Paul (Bass-baritone)
Paul Robeson Singt Negro Spirituals
Musical Masterpiece Society MMS-2162;
    [19--]; LP
Piano

5250

We Are Climbing Jacob's Ladder
[Johnson, John Rosamond]
Robeson, Paul (Bass-baritone)
Negro Spirituals
Concert Hall SVS 2611; [19--]; LP

5251

We Are Climbing Jacob's Ladder
[Johnson, John Rosamond]
Robeson, Paul (Bass-baritone)
The Historic Paul Robeson
Murray Hill Records 959062; [19--]; LP
Piano

5252

Jacob's Ladder
[Johnson, John Rosamond]
Robeson, Paul (Bass-baritone)
Negro Spirituals
Chant du Monde LDX 74376; 1982; LP
Piano

5253

We Are Clim'in' Jacob's Ladder
Composer not identified
West, Lucretia (Mezzo-soprano)
Spirituals

Westminster WL 5338; 1954; LP
Piano

5254

We Are Climbing Jacob's Ladder
Composer not identified
West, Lucretia (Mezzo-soprano)
Lucretia West Sings Spirituals
Westminster WP 6063; [1957]; LP

· · · · · · ·

We Has a Hard Time

5255

We Has a Hard Time [from *Witness:
    Original Compositions in Spiritual Style*]
Baker, David
Toppin, Louise (Soprano)
Witness
Albany Records TROY868; 2006; CD
Orchestra
Heavy dialect

· · · · · · ·

We Will All Bow
Together

5256

We Will All Bow Together
Bledsoe, Jules
Hinds, Esther (Soprano)
The Art of Esther Hinds
Quattro Corde 5003; 1998; CD

5257

We Will All Bow
Bledsoe, Jules
Oglesby, Isador (Tenor)
Isador Sings Negro Spirituals
Oglesby Recordings Album 3; 1983; LP
Piano

· · · · · · ·

Weepin' Mary

5258

Weepin' Mary
Burleigh, Harry T.

Arroyo, Martina (Soprano)
Spirituals
Centaur CRC 2060; 1991; CD
Piano
Light dialect

5259

Weeping Mary
Ryan, Donald
Estes, Simon (Bass-baritone)
Steal Away: My Favorite Negro Spirituals
Deutsche Schallplatten DS 1041-2; 1994;
    CD
Piano
Light dialect

5260

Weepin' Mary
Burleigh, Harry T.
Hayes, Roland (Tenor)
The Art of Roland Hayes
Smithsonian Collection RD 041; 1990; CD
Piano
Light dialect

5261

Weepin' Mary
[Burleigh, Harry T.]
Henriksson, Deborah (Soprano)
Simple Gifts
Nosag NOSAGCD143; 2007; CD
Piano, dulcimer
Light dialect

5262

Weepin' Mary
Burleigh, Harry T.
Holmes, Eugene (Baritone)
Spirituals
Schubert Records SCH-102; [1988]; LP
Piano
Light dialect

5263

Weepin' Mary
Burleigh, Harry T.
Kennedy, Charles (Vocalist)
Heart & Soul: Songs of Harry T. Burleigh
Publisher not known; 1994; Cassette

5264

Weepin' Mary
Burleigh, Harry T.
Oby, Jason (Tenor)
The Life of Christ: Collected Spirituals
Private Label TSU4749; [200-]; CD
Piano
Light dialect

5265

Weepin' Mary
Burleigh, Harry T.
Parks, Karen (Soprano)
Nobody Knows
Ottimavoce 52736; 2007; CD
Instrumental ensemble
Light dialect

5266

Weepin' Mary
Burleigh, Harry T.
Robeson, Paul (Bass-baritone)
*Weepin' Mary/I Want to Be Ready/Git on
    Board, Lil' Chillun/Dere's No Hidin' Place*
Victor 22225; 1928; 78 RPM
Piano
Light dialect

5267

Weepin' Mary
Burleigh, Harry T.
Robeson, Paul (Bass-baritone)
The Complete EMI Sessions (1928–1939)
EMI Classics 50999 2 15586 2 7; 2008; CD
Piano
Heavy dialect

5268

Weepin' Mary
[Burleigh, Harry T.]
Robeson, Paul (Bass-baritone)
Songs of My People
RCA Red Seal LM-3292; 1972; LP
Piano

5269

Weepin' Mary
[Burleigh, Harry T.]
Robeson, Paul (Bass-baritone)

Paul Robeson Collection
Hallmark Recordings 390692; 1998; CD

5270

Weepin' Mary
[Burleigh, Harry T.]
Robeson, Paul (Bass-baritone)
Ol Man River
Leverage; 2005; Streaming audio
Piano
Light dialect

5271

Weepin' Mary
[Burleigh, Harry T.]
Robeson, Paul (Bass-baritone)
Ol' Man River: The Ultimate Collection
Roslin Records; 2011; Streaming audio
Piano
No dialect discerned

5272

Weepin' Mary
Burleigh, Harry T.
Smith, Muriel (Mezzo-soprano)
Negro Spirituals
Philips NBE11007; [195-]; 45 RPM
Piano

5273

Weepin' Mary
Composer not identified
St. Hill, Krister (Baritone)
Svenska Folkvisor/Negro Spirituals
Polar POLS 398; 1985; LP
Piano

5274

Weepin' Mary
Burleigh, Harry T.; Russ, Patrick
Sykes, Jubilant (Baritone)
Jubilant Sykes Sings Copland and Spirituals
Arioso Classics AC 00011; 2008; CD
Orchestra

5275

Weepin Mary
Composer not identified
West, Lucretia (Mezzo-soprano)

Lucretia West Sings Spirituals
Westminster WP 6063; [1957]; LP
Instrumental ensemble

5276

Weepin' Mary
Morgenstern, Sam
West, Lucretia (Mezzo-soprano)
Spirituals
Westminster WL 5338; 1954; LP
Orchestra
Welcome to the Dyin' Lamb

5277

Welcome to the "Dyin Lamb"
Brown, Uzee, Jr.
Brown, Uzee, Jr. (Baritone)
Great Day!
Allgood; 2005; CD
Piano
Light dialect

· · · · · · ·

We'll Understand It Better By and By

5278

We'll Understand It Better By and By
Composer not identified
Hunt, Arthur Billings (Baritone)
Hymns and Spirituals
Cook Laboratories 1090; [195-]; LP
Organ

· · · · · · ·

Were You There

[Matthew 27:27-61; Mark 15:6-47; Luke 23:18-56; John 19:1-42]

"Were you there when they crucified my Lord? Were you there when they crucified my Lord? Oh, sometimes it causes me to tremble, tremble, tremble. Were you there when they crucified my Lord?

Were you there when they nailed Him to the tree?…

Were you there when the sun refused to shine?…"

[Available in CLSA, CW40, DRSA, DSSS, ESAA, FH25, HCTN, HJTS, HTBA, HTBN, HTBS, JHSS, JJAN, JJBA, JW10, MHDR, RHMF, RW15, SONS, VLCH, WF70]

This spiritual focused on the leader asking the congregants whether they had witnessed the crucifixion of Christ, an event so powerful and distressing that it caused the leader to tremble in retelling the story. The line of each verse is repeated three times as was often done as a means to emphasize the words.

Part of the power of this spiritual is, indeed, in its simplicity. Singers from Roland Hayes, Adele Addison, to Jessye Norman opted to perform "Were You There" a cappella, which allowed them freedom of interpretative expression.

5279

Were You There
Traditional
Addison, Adele (Soprano)
Little David Play on Your Harp
Kapp Records KL 1109; 1959; LP
A cappella
No dialect discerned

5280

Were You There?
Composer not identified
Allen, Betty (Mezzo-soprano)
On Wings of Song
RCA Custom Reader's Digest RDA43-A; [1960]; LP
Chorus
No dialect discerned

5281

Were You There
Burleigh, Harry T.
Amaize, Odekhiren (Bass-baritone)
For Darfur! Irin Ajo and Other Sacred Songs and Spirituals
MSR Classics MS 1296; 2008; CD
Piano
No dialect discerned

5282

Were You There
Burleigh, Harry T.

Anderson, Marian (Contralto)
I Can't Stay Away/Were You There
Victor Red Seal 1966; 1939; 78 RPM
Piano
No dialect discerned

5283

Were You There?
Burleigh, Harry T.
Anderson, Marian (Contralto)
Marian Anderson Sings Spirituals
RCA Victor Red Seal MO 1238; 1948; 78
    RPM
Piano

5284

Where You There
Burleigh, Harry T.
Anderson, Marian (Contralto)
Negro Spirituals
La Voix de Son Maître FBLP1039; 1953; LP
Piano

5285

Were You There
Burleigh, Harry T.
Anderson, Marian (Contralto)
Negro Spirituals
La Voix de Son Maître 7 EJF 3; 1955; 45 RPM
Piano

5286

Were You There
Burleigh, Harry T.
Anderson, Marian (Contralto)
Negro Spirituals, Vol. I
La Voix de Son Maître 7 ERF 17026; 1960;
    45 RPM

5287

Were You There?
Burleigh, Harry T.
Anderson, Marian (Contralto)
*The Art of Marian Anderson: Arias, Songs
    and Spirituals*
His Master's Voice EG 29001614; 1986; LP
Piano

5288

Were You There?
Burleigh, Harry T.
Anderson, Marian (Contralto)
Marian Anderson: Portraits in Memory
Metropolitan Opera Guild MET 220; 1993;
    CD
Piano
Light dialect

5289

Were You There?
Burleigh, Harry T.
Anderson, Marian (Contralto)
Prima Voce
Nimbus NI 7882; 1996; CD
Piano
Light dialect

5290

Were You There?
Burleigh, Harry T.
Anderson, Marian (Contralto)
Negro Spirituals
EMI 7243 5 72790 2 4; 1998; CD
Piano
No dialect discerned

5291

Were You There?
Burleigh, Harry T.
Anderson, Marian (Contralto)
Spirituals
RCA Victor Red Seal 09026-63306-2; 1999;
    CD
Piano
No dialect discerned

5292

Were You There
Burleigh, Harry T.
Anderson, Marian (Contralto)
Ev'Ry Time I Feel the Spirit (1930–1947)
Naxos Nostalgia 8.120779; 2004; CD
Piano

5293

Were You There?
Burleigh, Harry T.

Anderson, Marian (Contralto)
Lebendige Vergangenheit
Austro Mechana Historic Recordings
    MONO 89604; 2004; CD
Piano

5294

Were You There?
Burleigh, Harry T.
Anderson, Marian (Contralto)
Negro Spirituals: 1924–1949
Frémeaux & Associés FA 184; 2004; CD
Orchestra

5295

Were You There?
Burleigh, Harry T.
Anderson, Marian (Contralto)
Good News: Vintage Negro Spirituals
Living Era AJA 5622; 2006; CD
Piano
Light dialect

5296

Were You There When They Crucified My
    Lord?
Burleigh, Harry T.
Anderson, Marian (Contralto)
*Softly Awakes My Heart: Very Best of Marian
    Anderson*
Alto ALN1955; 2016; CD
Piano
Light dialect

5297

Were You There?
Burleigh, Harry T.
Anderson, Marian (Contralto)
Great Spirituals
Kipepeo Publishing; 2017; CD
Piano

5298

Were You There
Burleigh, Harry T.
Anderson, Marian (Contralto)
Negro Spirituals
La Voix de Son Maître 7 ERF 157; [19--];
    45 RPM

5299

Were You There?
Burleigh, Harry T.
Anderson, Marian (Contralto)
Marian Anderson Sings Negro Spirituals
His Master's Voice BLP 1060; [19--]; LP
Piano

5300

Were You There?
Burleigh, Harry T.
Anderson, Marian (Contralto)
Great Spirituals
RCA Victor ERA 62; [195-]; 7" Vinyl
Piano

5301

Were You There?
Burleigh, Harry T.
Anderson, Marian (Contralto)
Negro Spirituals
RCA Victor LM 2032; [1956]; LP
Piano

Also released with *Marian Anderson:
Beyond the Music; Her Complete RCA Victor
Recordings* Sony Classical 19439836492; 2021;
CD

5302

Were You There?
[Burleigh, Harry T.]
Anderson, Marian (Contralto)
Marian Anderson Sings Spirituals
RCA Victor LM 110; 1949; LP
Piano

5303

Were You There?
[Burleigh, Harry T.]
Anderson, Marian (Contralto)
Marian Anderson Sings Spirituals
Flapper Past CD 7073; 1995; CD
Piano

5304

Were You There?
[Burleigh, Harry T.]
Anderson, Marian (Contralto)

Softly Awakes My Heart
ASV CD AJA 5262; 1999; CD
Piano

5305

Were You There?
[Burleigh, Harry T.]
Anderson, Marian (Contralto)
*When Marian Sang: Selected Songs from
   Marian Anderson's Repertoire*
BMG Special Products DPC13280; 2002; CD

5306

Were You There
[Burleigh, Harry T.]
Anderson, Marian (Contralto)
Alto Rhapsody; Selected Spirituals
Urania URN 22.328; 2007; CD
Piano

5307

Were You There?
[Burleigh, Harry T.]
Anderson, Marian (Contralto)
The Very Best of Marian Anderson
Master Classics Records; 2009; CD
Piano
No dialect discerned

5308

Were You There
Anderson, Marian (Contralto)
Classic Gospel Songs
Emerald/K-Tel; 2013; Streaming audio
Piano

5309

Were You There?
[Burleigh, Harry T.]
Anderson, Marian (Contralto)
Inspirations
Emerald Echoes; 2015; Streaming audio
Piano
Light dialect

5310

Were You There?
[Burleigh, Harry T.]
Anderson, Marian (Contralto)

Negro Spirituals
RCA Gold Seal RVC-1570; [19--]; LP
Piano

5311

Were You There
[Burleigh, Harry T.]
Anderson, Marian (Contralto)
Negro Spirituals
RCA Victor 630.396 A; [19--]; LP
Piano

5312

Were You There
Burleigh, Harry T.
Arroyo, Martina (Soprano)
Spirituals
Centaur CRC 2060; 1991; CD
Piano
No dialect discerned

5313

Were You There?
Composer not identified
Arroyo, Martina (Soprano)
There's a Meeting Here Tonight
Angel S-36072; 1974; LP
Chorus

5314

Were You There?
Composer not identified
Arroyo, Martina (Soprano)
Negro Spirituals
EMI 7243 5 72790 2 4; 1998; CD
Chorus
Light dialect

5315

Were You There
Ledger, Philip
Baker, Janet (Mezzo-soprano)
Songs for Sunday
EMI ASD 3981; 1981; LP
Organ

5316

Were You There When They Crucified My
   Lord?

Sadin, Robert
Battle, Kathleen (Soprano)
Grace
Sony Classical SK 62035; 1997; CD
A cappella
No dialect discerned

     Also released with *The Complete Sony Recordings* (Sony Classical 88985381362; 2016; CD)

5317

Were You There
Brown, Angela; Webb, Charles
Brown, Angela (Soprano)
Soprano
Caboose Productions; 1995; CD
Piano
No dialect discerned

5318

Were You There
Burleigh, Harry T.
Burton, Dashon (Bass-baritone)
Songs of Struggle & Redemption: We Shall Overcome
Acis Productions APL08685; 2015; CD
Piano
Light dialect

5319

Were You There?
Hayes, Roland
Caesar, Jackson (Tenor)
Spirituals: Celebrating the Music, Life, Legacy of Roland Hayes
CD Baby 7048606059; 2021; CD
A cappella
Light dialect

5320

Were You There
Dørumsgaard, Arne
Carlsen, Svein (Bass)
Negro Spirituals
EuroMaster AS ECD19005; 1996; CD
Piano

5321

Were You There
Traditional

Carnette, Count (Vocalist)
Count Carnette Sings Favorite Negro Spirituals
Carnette Archive Recordings; 1983; LP
A cappella
No dialect discerned

5322

Were You There
Composer not identified
Clark, Clarence Carroll (Baritone)
Ain't That Good News/Were You There
Okeh 8044; 1922; 78 RPM
Orchestra

5323

Were You There
McElroy, Michael
Cook, Victor Trent (Tenor)
Three Mo' Tenors
RCA Victor 09026-63827-2; 2001; CD
Chorus
No dialect discerned

5324

Were You There?
Burleigh, Harry T.
Davis, Ellabelle (Soprano)
Ellabelle Davis Sings Negro Spirituals
London LPS 182; [1950]; LP
Orchestra
No dialect discerned

5325

Were You There?
Burleigh, Harry T.
Davis, Ellabelle (Soprano)
Recital of Negro Spirituals by Ellabelle Davis
Decca LM.4504; [1950]; LP
Orchestra

5326

Were You There?
[Burleigh, Harry T.]
Davis, Ellabelle (Soprano)
Were You There?
Decca DFE 8618; 1965; 45 RPM
Orchestra

5327

Were You There
[Burleigh, Harry T.]
Davis, Ellabelle (Soprano)
Great Negro Spirituals
Replay Record; 2013; Streaming audio
Orchestra

5328

Were You There
Burleigh, Harry T.
Davis, Ollie Watts (Soprano)
Here's One: Spiritual Songs
KJAC Publishing KJAC0123; 2003; CD
Piano
Light dialect

5329

Where You There
Composer not identified
Deguil, Arlette (Vocalist)
Negro Spirituals
Pathé 45 ED 1; 1953; 45 RPM
Men's voices
No dialect discerned

    Also released with *Negro Spirituals* (Pathé 45-ED 1; 1953; LP)

5330

Were You There
Composer not identified
Delmore, Harry A. (Tenor)
Were You There/Swing Low Sweet Chariot
Grey Gull 4154; [1927]; 78 RPM

5331

Were You There?
Lloyd, Charles, Jr.
English-Robinson, Laura (Soprano)
Let It Shine!
ACA Digital Recording CM20020; 1994; CD
Piano
No dialect discerned

5332

Were You There
Kaelin, Pierre
Evans, Allan (Bass-baritone)

Negro Spirituals
Electromusic Records EMCD 6885; 1985; CD
Chorus, other instrument(s)

5333

Were You There
Burleigh, Harry T.
Evans, Charlie (Vocalist)
Sing God's Plan
Private Label; 2005; CD
Piano
No dialect discerned

5334

Were You There?
Composer not identified
Ferguson, Margaret (Soprano)
Unfailing Love
Private Label; [20--]; CD

5335

Were You There
Darden, George
Fernandez, Wilhelmenia (Soprano)
Spirituals
Tioch Digital Records TD 1009; 1982; LP
Piano

    Also released with *Negro Spirituals* (Milan A 192; 1982; LP)

5336

Were You There
Darden, George
Fernandez, Wilhelmenia (Soprano)
Sings Favorite Spirituals
Phoenix PHCD 134; 1997; CD
Piano
Moderate dialect

5337

Знал ли ты (Znal li ty)
Composer not identified
Filatova, Ludmila (Mezzo-soprano)
Негритянские Спиричуэлс (Negrityanskiye Spirichuzls—Negro Spirituals)
Melodiâ S10 21833 009; 1985; LP
Organ
Light dialect

5338

Were You There When They Crucified My
  Lord
Burleigh, Harry T.
Gustafson, Edra (Soprano)
Favorite Sacred Songs
Echos of Faith CAM 33-64140; [1950]; LP
Organ

5339

Were You There
[Burleigh, Harry T.]
Hagen-William, Louis (Bass-baritone)
Negro Spirituals
Quantum QM 6909; 1993; CD
Piano
No dialect discerned

5340

Were You There?
Composer not identified
Hall, Nell (Soprano)
*Nell Hall in a Recital of Arias, Ballads,
  Spirituals, Folk Songs*
Colonial COL LP-211; [19--]; LP
Piano

5341

Were You There?
Burleigh, Harry T.
Halstead, Michael (Baritone)
The Lord's Prayer/Were You There
Victory Records A-102; [19--]; 78 RPM
Piano
Light dialect

5342

Were You There?
[Burleigh, Harry T.]
Hampton, Jonathon (Vocalist)
Negro Spirituals: Songs of Trial and Triumph
Private Label; 2017; Streaming audio
Piano
No dialect discerned

5343

Were You There?
Composer not identified
Harris, Lloyd (Bass)

Negro Spirituals
Pléïade P45301; 1960; 45 RPM
Piano

5344

Were You There? [from *The Life of Christ*]
Hayes, Roland
Hayes, Roland (Tenor)
*Roland Hayes Sings the Life of Christ: As Told
  Through Aframerican Folksong*
Vanguard VRS-462; 1954; LP
Piano

5345

Were You There? [from *The Life of Christ*]
Hayes, Roland
Hayes, Roland (Tenor)
*Roland Hayes Sings the Life of Christ: As Told
  Through Aframerican Folksong*
Vanguard SRV 352; 1976; LP
Piano

5346

Were You There? [from *The Life of Christ*]
Hayes, Roland
Hayes, Roland (Tenor)
Favorite Spirituals
Vanguard Classics OVC 6022; 1995; CD
Piano
Light dialect

5347

Were You There? [from *The Life of Christ*]
Hayes, Roland
Hayes, Roland (Tenor)
*Charlton Heston Reads from The Life and
  Passion of Jesus Christ*
Vanguard Classics ATM-CD-1259; 2003; CD
Piano

5348

Were You There?
Hayes, Roland
Hayes, Roland (Tenor)
*The Art of Roland Hayes: Six Centuries of
  Song*
Preiser Records; 2010; CD
A cappella
No dialect discerned

5349

Were You There?
Hayes, Roland
Hayes, Roland (Tenor)
Lit'l Boy/Were You There
Angel-Mo' AN 3122 E; [1941]; 78 RPM
A cappella

5350

Were You There? [from The Life of Christ]
Hayes, Roland
Hayes, Roland (Tenor)
*Aframerican Folksong: Telling the Story of
    the Life of Christ*
Top Rank 39 620; [1961]; LP
Piano

5351

Were You There
Traditional
Hayes, Roland (Tenor)
*Were You There/Hear de Lambs a Cryin'/
    Plenty Good Room*
Columbia Masterworks 69812-D; 1940; 78
    RPM
A cappella

5352

Were You There
Traditional
Hayes, Roland (Tenor)
*Brother, Can You Spare a Dime?: The Roots of
    American Song*
Pearl Gemm CD 9484; 1991; CD
A cappella
Light dialect

5353

Were You There?
[Hayes, Roland]
Hayes, Roland (Tenor)
Art Songs and Spirituals
Veritas VM 112; 1967; LP
A cappella
Moderate dialect

5354

Were You There? [from The Life of Christ]
[Hayes, Roland]

Hayes, Roland (Tenor)
Big Psalms, Hymns and Spirituals Box
eOne Music/Vanguard Classics; 2015;
    Streaming audio
Piano

5355

Were You There?
[Hayes, Roland]
Hayes, Roland (Tenor)
*Roland Hayes Sings: Negro Spirituals,
    Aframerican Folk Songs*
Amadeo Records AVRS 6033; [19--]; LP
Piano

5356

Were You There
Hendricks, Barbara; Alexeev, Dmitri
Hendricks, Barbara (Soprano)
Negro Spirituals
EMI CDC7470262; 1983; CD
Piano
Light dialect

5357

Were You There?
[Hendricks, Barbara]
Hendricks, Barbara (Soprano)
Espirituales Negros
EMI Classics/Altaya 01636; 1983; CD
Piano

5358

Were You There
[Hendricks, Barbara]
Hendricks, Barbara (Soprano)
Spirituals
EMI Classics 0946 346641 2 7; 2005; CD
Piano

5359

Were You There
[Hendricks, Barbara]
Hendricks, Barbara (Soprano)
No Borders
Altara ALT 1010; 2005; CD
Chorus
No dialect discerned

5360

Were You There? [from The Life of Christ]
Hayes, Roland
Holland, Charles (Tenor)
My Lord What a Mornin'
Musical Heritage Society MHS 912250X;
   1982; LP
Piano
No dialect discerned

5361

Were You There? [from The Life of Christ]
Hayes, Roland
Holland, Charles (Tenor)
My Lord What a Mornin'
Musical Heritage Society MHS 512250K;
   1988; CD
Piano
No dialect discerned

5362

Were You There?
[Burleigh, Harry T.]
Holmes, Eugene (Baritone)
Eugene Holmes Sings Spirituals
Avant Garde AV-115; [1968]; LP
Piano

5363

Where You There When They Crucified My
   Lord?
Composer not identified
Hunt, Arthur Billings (Baritone)
Hymns and Spirituals
Cook Laboratories 1090; [195-]; LP
Organ

5364

Were You There?
Burleigh, Harry T.
Hynninen, Jorma (Bass-baritone)
Negro Spirituals
Ondine ODE 715-2; 1988; CD
Piano

5365

Were You There When They Crucified My
   Lord
Clinton, Irving

Irving, Clinton (Bass-baritone)
Clinton Irving Sings Spirituals: A Tribute
Rogers; 2001; CD

5366

Were You There? [from The Life of Christ]
[Hayes, Roland]
Jenkins, Isaiah (Tenor)
Lyric Tenor
Trans Radio TR 1010A; [195-]; LP
Piano

5367

Were You There?
Composer not identified
Jones, Fanni (Mezzo-soprano)
Negro Spirituals
Evasion Disques LP613; 1974; LP

5368

Were You There?
Burleigh, Harry T.
Kimbrough, Steven (Baritone)
The Life of Christ in Song
Ebony Classic Recordings; 2011; CD

5369

Were You There?
Okpebholo, Shawn
Liverman, Will (Baritone)
Steal Away
Yellow Einstein; 2014; CD
Piano
No dialect discerned

5370

Were You There
Burleigh, Harry T.
Lynch, Lester (Baritone)
On My Journey Now: Spirituals & Hymns
Pentatone Music PTC 5186 57'; 2017; CD
Piano

5371

Were You There?
Composer not identified
Martin, Vivian (Soprano)
Sings Spirituals and Songs
Halo 50277; 1957; LP

5372

Where You There
Burleigh, Harry T.
Mayes, Doris (Mezzo-soprano)
Deep River
La voix de son maître FDLP 1080; 1959;
   LP
Piano

5373

Were You There?
Composer not identified
Maynor, Dorothy (Soprano)
*Rare Concert Recital Gospel Music
   (1966–1980)*
Pewburner Records 742; 2007; CD

5374

Where You There
Composer not identified
Maynor, Dorothy (Soprano)
Marian Anderson & Dorothy Maynor
Parnassus Recordings PAR 1004; [19--];
   LP

5375

Were You There?
Dett, Robert Nathaniel
Maynor, Dorothy (Soprano)
Negro Spirituals
RCA Victor M879; 1942; 78 RPM
Men's voices

5376

Were You There?
Dett, Robert Nathaniel
Maynor, Dorothy (Soprano)
*Dorothy Maynor Sings Spirituals and Sacred
   Songs*
RCA Camden CAL-344; 1957; LP
Chorus

5377

Were You There?
Dett, Robert Nathaniel
Maynor, Dorothy (Soprano)
Spirituals, Arias, Songs ([1940]1943)
Claremont CD GSE 78-50-59; 1994; CD
Chorus

5378

Were You There?
Dett, Robert Nathaniel
Maynor, Dorothy (Soprano)
Negro Spirituals
Kipepeo Publishing; 2018; CD
Men's voices

5379

Were You There
Traditional
Maynor, Dorothy (Soprano)
*Marian Anderson and Dorothy Maynor
   in Concert*
Eklipse Records EKR 50; 1995; CD
A cappella
Light dialect

5380

Were You There
Traditional
Maynor, Dorothy (Soprano)
*Dorothy Maynor in Concert at Library of
   Congress*
Library of Congress, Music Division LCM
   2141; 2007; CD
A cappella
Light dialect

5381

Were You There
Traditional
Maynor, Dorothy (Soprano)
Dorothy Maynor, Soprano
Bridge Records 9233; 2007; CD
A cappella
Light dialect

5382

Were You There When They Crucified the
   Lord?
Welsh, Nicky
McCue, Bill (Bass-baritone)
Bill McCue Sings the Great Spirituals
Beltona SBE 173; 1974; LP
Orchestra

5383

Were You There? [from Spiritual Songs for
    Tenor and Cello]
Banfield, William C.
Melvin, Lee (Tenor)
Extensions of the Tradition
Innova 510; 1996; CD
Cello

5384

Were You There?
Burleigh, Harry T.
Miller, Jeanette (Soprano)
No Man Canna Hinder Me
MiJon Record Productions MJ240; 1979;
    CD
Piano

5385

Were You There?
[Burleigh, Harry T.]
Milnes, Sherrill (Baritone)
Abide with Me
RCA Red Seal ARL1-1403; 1976; LP
Organ
No dialect discerned

5386

Where You There?
Composer not identified
Monzo, Oscar (Baritone)
Negro Spirituals
Dial Discos 50-2020; 1983; LP

5387

Were You There?
Burleigh, Harry T.
Nash, Lorna (Contralto)
Lorna Nash, Contralto in Concert
Mark Custom Records UMC 2160; [197-]; LP
Piano

5388

Were You There
Patterson. Willis
Norman, Jessye (Soprano)
Negro Spirituals
Philips 9500 580; 1979; LP
A cappella

5389

Were You There
Traditional
Norman, Jessye (Soprano)
Spirituals
Philips 416 462-2; 1990; CD
A cappella
No dialect discerned

5390

Were You There
Traditional
Norman, Jessye (Soprano)
*The Jessye Norman Collection: Sacred Songs
    & Spirituals*
Philips B0004506-02; 2005; CD
A cappella
Moderate dialect

5391

Were You There
[Burleigh, Harry T.]
Norman, Jessye (Soprano)
Amazing Grace
Philips 432 546-2; 1990; CD
A cappella
No dialect discerned

5392

Were You There? [from *The Life of Christ*]
Hayes, Roland
Oby, Jason (Tenor)
The Life of Christ: Collected Spirituals
Private Label TSU4749; [200-]; CD
Piano
Light dialect

5393

Were You There
Manney, Charles
Oglesby, Isador (Tenor)
Life of Jesus in Negro Spirituals
Oglesby Recordings Album 2; 1980; LP
Piano

5394

Were You There?
Lloyd, Charles, Jr.
Paige-Green, Jacqueline (Soprano)

The Spiritual Art Song Collection
Warner Bros. SVBM00004; 2000; Score w/CD
Piano

5395

Were You There?
Flynn, William
Paris, Virginia (Contralto)
Spirituals
Spotlight Classic SC 1008; 1957; LP
Orchestra

5396

Were You There?
Flynn, William
Paris, Virginia (Contralto)
Virginia Paris in Australia
Lyric Records CD 178; [2005]; CD
Orchestra

5397

Were You There?
Composer not identified
Porter, John (Bass)
No More Crying: Negro Spirituals
Pan Verlag OV-84; [1978]; LP

5398

Were You There
Bonds, Margaret
Price, Leontyne (Soprano)
Complete Collection of Songs and Spiritual Albums
RCA Red Seal 88697940502; 2011; CD
Orchestra

5399

Were You There
Traditional
Price, Leontyne (Soprano)
Swing Low, Sweet Chariot: Fourteen Spirituals
RCA Victor LSC 2600; 1962; LP
A cappella
No dialect discerned

5400

Were You There
Traditional

Price, Leontyne (Soprano)
The Essential Leontyne Price: Spirituals, Hymns & Sacred Songs
BMG Classics 09026-68157-2; 1996; CD
A cappella
Light dialect

5401

Were You There When They Crucified My Lord?
Traditional
Price, Leontyne (Soprano)
The Essential Leontyne Price
BMG Classics 09026-68153-2; 1996; CD
A cappella
Light dialect

5402

Were You There?
Traditional
Price, Leontyne (Soprano)
The Best of Negro Spirituals
BMG BVCM-37416; 2003; CD
A cappella
No dialect discerned

5403

Were You There
Traditional
Price, Leontyne (Soprano)
Leontyne Price Sings Spirituals
RCA Red Seal 88691928242; 2012; CD
A cappella
Light dialect

5404

Were You There
Traditional
Price, Leontyne (Soprano)
Singers of the Century: Leontyne Price: Spiritual and Religious Songs
Jube Classic; 2016; Streaming audio
A cappella
No dialect discerned

5405

Where You There
Composer not identified
Putkonen, Marko (Bass)

Deep River: Negro Spirituals
Lilium LILP 101; 1991; LP

5406
Were You There
Traditional
Ragin, Derek Lee (Countertenor)
Ev'ry Time I Feel the Spirit: Spirituals
Channel Classics CCS 2991; 1991; CD
A cappella
Moderate dialect

5407
Were You There
Composer not identified
Ray, William (Baritone)
Negro Spirituals
Intercord; [19--]; LP

Also released with *Sings Arias, Duets, Musical Selections and Negro Spirituals* (Intercord; [19--]; CD)

5408
Were You There? (When They Crucified My Lord)
Burleigh, Harry T.
Robeson, Paul (Bass-baritone)
Bye and Bye/Were You There?
His Master's Voice B 2126; 1925; 78 RPM
Piano

5409
Were You There?
Burleigh, Harry T.
Robeson, Paul (Bass-baritone)
Songs of My People
RCA Red Seal LM-3292; 1972; LP
Piano

5410
Were You There (When They Crucified My Lord)
Burleigh, Harry T.
Robeson, Paul (Bass-baritone)
Paul Robeson: Great Voices of the Century, v. 2
Memoir Classics CDMOIR 426; 1994; CD

5411
Were You There When They Crucified My Lord
Burleigh, Harry T.
Robeson, Paul (Bass-baritone)
The Voice of Mississippi: 20 Great Tracks
Prism Leisure PLATCD 119; 1996; CD

5412
Were You There When They Crucified My Lord?
Burleigh, Harry T.
Robeson, Paul (Bass-baritone)
Paul Robeson Collection
Hallmark Recordings 390692; 1998; CD

5413
Were You There?
Burleigh, Harry T.
Robeson, Paul (Bass-baritone)
Negro Spirituals: The Concert Tradition 1909–1948
Frémeaux & Associés FA 168; 1999; CD
Piano
Light dialect

5414
Were You There When They Crucified My Lord?
Burleigh, Harry T.
Robeson, Paul (Bass-baritone)
First Time Buyer's Guide to American Negro Spirituals
Primo Collection PRMCD6038; 2006; CD
Piano
No dialect discerned

5415
Were You There?
Burleigh, Harry T.
Robeson, Paul (Bass-baritone)
The Complete EMI Sessions (1928–1939)
EMI Classics 50999 2 15586 2 7; 2008; CD
Piano
Heavy dialect

5416
Were You There?
Burleigh, Harry T.

Robeson, Paul (Bass-baritone)
The Very Best of Paul Robeson
Future Noise Music FVDD033; 2009; CD
Piano

5417

Were You There?
Burleigh, Harry T.
Robeson, Paul (Bass-baritone)
Negro Spirituals
His Master's Voice 7EG 8422; [19--]; 45 RPM
Piano

5418

Were You There When They Crucified My
   Lord
Burleigh, Harry T.
Robeson, Paul (Bass-baritone)
Paul Robeson
World Record Club W9648/EMI SM 431;
   [19--]; LP
Piano

5419

Were You There?
Burleigh, Harry T.
Robeson, Paul (Bass-baritone)
Were You There?/By an' By
His Master's Voice B.4480; [19--]; 78 RPM
Piano
Light dialect

5420

Were You There? (When They Crucified My
   Lord)
[Burleigh, Harry T.]
Robeson, Paul (Bass-baritone)
Were You There?/Steal Away
Victor 19742; 1925; 78 RPM
Piano
Light dialect

5421

Were You There
[Burleigh, Harry T.]
Robeson, Paul (Bass-baritone)
The Great Paul Robeson
Velvet CDVELV 101; 2001; CD
Piano

5422

Were You There When They Crucified My
   Lord?
[Burleigh, Harry T.]
Robeson, Paul (Bass-baritone)
Ol' Man River: His 56 Finest 1925–1945
Retrospective RTS 4116; 2008; CD

5423

Were You There
[Burleigh, Harry T.]
Robeson, Paul (Bass-baritone)
Negro Spirituals (And More)
Discmedi DM-4674-02; 2009; CD

5424

Were You There When They Crucified My
   Lord
[Burleigh, Harry T.]
Robeson, Paul (Bass-baritone)
Ol' Man River: The Ultimate Collection
Roslin Records; 2011; Streaming audio
Piano
No dialect discerned

5425

Were You There When They Crucified My
   Lord
[Burleigh, Harry T.]
Robeson, Paul (Bass-baritone)
Spirituals
Past Classics; 2013; Streaming audio
Piano
No dialect discerned

5426

Were You There When They Crucified My
   Lord?
[Burleigh, Harry T.]
Robeson, Paul (Bass-baritone)
The Essential Collection
Primo PRMCD6233; 2018; CD

5427

Were You There?
[Burleigh, Harry T.]
Robeson, Paul (Bass-baritone)
*The Concerto: African American
   Spirituals*

Orange Amaro; 2019; Streaming audio
Piano

5428
Were You There
Robeson, Paul (Bass-baritone)
Songs of Struggle & Love
Alto ALC 1416; 2020; CD
Piano
Moderate dialect

5429
Were You There
[Burleigh, Harry T.]
Robeson, Paul (Bass-baritone)
The Paul Robeson Story
Columbia 5C 052-04830; [19--]; LP

5430
Were You There
Sadin, Robert
Robinson, Morris (Bass)
Going Home
Decca B0008277-02; 2007; CD
Instrumental ensemble
No dialect discerned

5431
Were You There When They Crucified My
    Lord?
Traditional
Rustin, Bayard (Tenor)
*Bayard Rustin Sings Twelve Spirituals on the
    Life of Christ*
Fellowship Records E2-KL 1771; [195-]; LP
A cappella
Moderate dialect
        Also released with *Bayard Rustin, the
Singer* (Bayard Rustin Fund; 1992; CD) and
Bayard Rustin-The Singer (Black Swan Series;
Parnassus Records PACD 96083; 2022; CD)

5432
Were You There?
Burleigh, Harry T.
Shanks, Donald (Bass)
Songs of Inspiration
ABC Classics Eloquence 426 803-2; 1989; CD
A cappella
No dialect discerned

5433
Were You There?
Hayes, Roland
Shirley, George (Tenor)
George Shirley at 80: My Time Has Come!
Videmus Records; 2014; CD
Piano

5434
Were You There [from The Life of Christ]
Hayes, Roland
Sims, Robert (Baritone)
*Robert Sims Sings the Spirituals of Roland
    Hayes*
Canti Classics 2014-01; 2015; CD
Piano
Heavy dialect

5435
Were You There
Burleigh, Harry T.
Smith, Muriel (Mezzo-soprano)
Negro Spirituals
Philips NBE11007; [195-]; 45 RPM
A cappella

5436
Were You There?
Walters, Richard (ed.)
Stolen, Steven (Tenor)
*15 Easy Spiritual Arrangements for the
    Progressing Singer*
Hal Leonard HL00000391 (high);
    HL00000392 (low); 2005; Score w/CD
Piano
Moderate dialect

5437
Were You There
Hogan, Moses
Stratton, Brian (Tenor)
Songs of Reflection
MGH Records 0800CD; 1997; CD

5438
Were You There?
Blanchard, Terence
Sykes, Jubilant (Baritone)
Jubilant Sykes

Sony Classical SK 63294; 1998; CD
Instrumental ensemble

5439

Were You There?
Erb, Clayton; Sykes, Jubilant; Rice, Rice
Sykes, Jubilant (Baritone)
Jubilant Sykes Sings Copland and Spirituals
Arioso Classics AC 00011; 2008; CD
Orchestra

5440

Were You There?
Golde, Walter
Thomas, Edna (Soprano)
Were You There?/Little Wheel A-Turnin' in my Heart/Keep A-Inching Along
Columbia 3398; 1924; 78 RPM
Piano

5441

Were You Dere?
Thomas, Edna
Thomas, Edna (Soprano)
Were You Dere/Swing Low, Sweet Chariot
Columbia 1476-D; 1928; 78 RPM

5442

Were You There
Hayes, Mark
Thomas, Indra (Soprano)
Great Day: Indra Thomas Sings Spirituals
Delos DE 3427; 2012; CD
Piano
No dialect discerned

5443

Were You There When They Crucified My Lord
Composer not identified
Thomas, John Charles (Baritone)
Were You There When They Crucified My Lord/Flee as a Bird
International Sacred Recordings 1501-45; [19--]; 45 RPM
Chorus, organ

5444

Were You There?
Composer not identified

Thompson, Derrick (Baritone)
Spirituals
Private Label; 2014; CD
Piano
No dialect discerned

5445

Were You There
Thompson, Jeanette
Thompson, Jeanette (Soprano)
Negro Spirituals
Pavane Records ADW 7267; 1992; CD
Chorus
No dialect discerned

5446

Were You There?
Composer not identified
Traubel, Helen (Soprano)
Negro Spirituals: Helen Traubel in Popular Ballads
Columbia ML 4221; 1949; LP
Piano

5447

Were You There
Composer not identified
Tyler, Veronica (Soprano)
Sings ... the Passion of Christ in Spirituals
BRC Productions; [19--]; LP
Piano

5448

Were You There When They Crucified My Lord?
Composer not identified
Ventriglia, Franco (Baritone)
Franco Ventriglia Sings Negro Spirituals
Vedette Records; 2007; Streaming audio
Piano, organ
Light dialect

5449

Were You There When They Crucified My Lord?
Composer not identified
Ventriglia, Franco (Baritone)
Franco Ventriglia Sings Negro Spirituals
Vedette Records VRMS 316; [19--]; LP

Piano, organ
Light dialect

5450
Were You There?
Hogan, Moses
Walker, Alfred (Bass)
Deep River: Featuring 10 Spirituals Arranged for Solo Voice....
MGH Records 5000; 2000; CD
Piano
No dialect discerned

5451
Were You There
Composer not identified
Webb, George (Tenor)
Famous Negro Spirituals and Songs of Elizabethan England, Ireland & the Caribbean
[Unknown] WLP7804; 1978; LP

5452
Were You There
Burleigh, Harry T.
West, Lucretia (Mezzo-soprano)
Negro Spirituals III
Club français du disque 176; 1959; LP
Piano
Moderate dialect

5453
Were You There
Burleigh, Harry T.
West, Lucretia (Mezzo-soprano)
Negro Spirituals mit Lukretia West
Opera 3408; [195-]; LP
Piano

5454
Were You There
Burleigh, Harry T.
West, Lucretia (Mezzo-soprano)
Negro Spirituals
Club français du disque 215; [196-]; 7-in EP
Piano

5455
Were You There
Composer not identified

White, Cassandra (Soprano)
Remembering the Spirituals
CBW Entertainment 837101334068; 2007; CD
Piano
Light dialect

5456
Were You There When They Crucified My Lord?
Marshall, Melanie
White, Willard (Bass-baritone)
Willard White Sings: Copland; American Spirituals; Folk-Songs
Chandos Records CHAN 8960; 1991; CD
Piano
Light dialect

5457
Were You There? [from *The Life of Christ*]
Hayes, Roland
Williams, Willie (Vocalist)
My Tribute
Discovery V42227; 1974; LP
Piano

• • • • • • •

What Kinda' Shoes You Gonna Wear

5458
What Kinda' Shoes You Gonna Wear
Dett, Robert Nathaniel
Oglesby, Isador (Tenor)
Isador Sings Negro Spirituals
Oglesby Recordings Album 3; 1983; LP
Piano

• • • • • • •

What Shall I Do

5459
Gospel Blues [from *Lyric Suite*]
Morris, Robert L.
Day, Calesta (Soprano)
Swing Low, Sweet Chariot
American Spiritual Ensemble; 2011; CD

5460

What Shall I Do? (Gospel Blues) [from *Lyric Suite*]
Morris, Robert L.
Toppin, Louise (Soprano)
Heart on the Wall: African American Art Songs for Orchestra
Albany Records TROY1314; 2011; CD
Orchestra
Moderate dialect

· · · · · · ·

What She Gonna Do When de River Runs Dry

5461

What She Gonna Do, When de River Runs Dry
Schweizer, Rolf
Wolf, Lars (Vocalist)
Die Schwarze Stimme Europas
Cantate 666000; 1971; LP
Chorus, organ, percussion

· · · · · · ·

When de Saints Come Marchin' In

5462

When de Saints Come Marchin' In [from *Green Pastures*]
Johnson, Hall
Brown, William (Tenor)
The Hall Johnson Collection
Carl Fischer VF5 CD1–VF5 CD2; 2003; Score w/CD
Piano
Light dialect

· · · · · · ·

When I Lay My Burden Down

5463

When I Lay My Burden Down
Ching, [Michael]

Gormley, Clare (Soprano)
Where Morning Lies: Spiritual Songs
ABC Classics 461 766-2; 2002; CD
Piano
Moderate dialect

5464

When I Lay My Burden Down
Hendricks, Barbara; Alexeev, Dmitri
Hendricks, Barbara (Soprano)
Great American Spirituals
Angel CDM 7 64669 2; 1992; CD
Piano
Heavy dialect

   Also released with *Great American Spirituals* (Musical Heritage Society 513725Z; 1994; CD)

5465

When I Lay My Burden Down
[Hendricks, Barbara]
Hendricks, Barbara (Soprano)
Espirituales Negros
EMI Classics/Altaya 01636; 1983; CD
Piano

5466

When I Lay My Burden Down
[Hendricks, Barbara]
Hendricks, Barbara (Soprano)
Spirituals
EMI Classics 0946 346641 2 7; 2005; CD
Piano

5467

When I Lay My Burden Down
Johnson, Hall
White, Willard (Bass-baritone)
Willard White Sings: Copland; American Spirituals; Folk-Songs
Chandos Records CHAN 8960; 1991; CD
Piano
Moderate dialect

· · · · · · ·

When They Ring the Golden Bells

5468

When They Ring the Golden Bells
Welsh, Nicky
McCue, Bill (Bass-baritone)
Bill McCue Sings the Great Spirituals
Beltona SBE 173; 1974; LP
Orchestra

· · · · · · ·

Who Betrayed My Lord

5469

Who Betrayed My Lord? [from *The Life of Christ*]
Hayes, Roland
Hayes, Roland (Tenor)
Roland Hayes Sings the Life of Christ: As Told Through Aframerican Folksong
Vanguard VRS-462; 1954; LP
Piano

    Also released with *Roland Hayes Sings the Life of Christ: As Told Through Aframerican Folksong* (Vanguard SRV 352; 1976; LP); *Charlton Heston Reads from The Life and Passion of Jesus Christ* (Vanguard Classics ATM-CD-1259; 2003; CD) and *Big Psalms, Hymns and Spirituals Box* (eOne Music/Vanguard Classics; 2015; Streaming audio)

5470

Who Betrayed My Lord? [from *The Life of Christ*]
Hayes, Roland
Hayes, Roland (Tenor)
Favorite Spirituals
Vanguard Classics OVC 6022; 1995; CD
Piano
Light dialect

5471

Who Betrayed My Lord? [from *The Life of Christ*]
Hayes, Roland
Hayes, Roland (Tenor)

Aframerican Folksong: Telling the Story of the Life of Christ
Top Rank 39 620; [1961]; LP
Piano

· · · · · · ·

Who's Been Here

5472

Who's Been Here?
Brown, Lawrence
Pankey, Aubrey (Baritone)
Negro Spirituals
Eterna 830010; 1983; LP
Piano

· · · · · · ·

Who's Gonna Mourn for Me

5473

Who's Gonna Mourn for Me?
Composer not identified
Melton, James (Tenor)
James Melton
Rococo 5310; [1970]; LP

· · · · · · ·

Witness

[Genesis 5:27, 6:1-22; Judges 16:17-19, 21-31; Proverbs 14:25; Matthew 5:16, 18:16; John 3:1-36; Acts 1:8]

"My soul is a witness for my Lord, My soul is a witness for my Lord, ... You read in the Bible and you understand, Methusalah was the oldest man; ... You read about Samson, from his birth, strongest man that ever lived on earth; Way back yonder in ancient times, he killed ten thousand of the Philistines; ... There's another witness for my Lord, My soul is a witness for my Lord."

[Found in: CW40, HCTN, HJCO, JAS2, JJBA, RHMF]

Musicologist Natalie Curtis Burlin (1875–1921) listed this spiritual as "God's a-Gwine ter Move All de Troubles Away" in her 1918 publication, *Negro Folk-Songs* (New

York: G. Schirmer). While her collection was written for quartet, composer John Rosamond Johnson (1873–1954) published his setting, "Who'll Be a Witness for My Lord," for solo voice and piano in the *Book of American Negro Spirituals* (New York: Viking, 1925) with his brother, poet James Weldon Johnson (1871–1938).

By far, the most recorded setting of this spiritual is the 1940 version by Hall Johnson (1888–1970). Johnson authority Eugene Thamon Simpson (1932–2021) concluded his *Hall Johnson Concert Spirituals* (West Conshohocken, PA: Infinity Publishing, 2015) with a comprehensive description of the composer's setting, including suggesting the singer interpret in the manner of an old-time preacher. While Johnson was known for wishing his settings to be performed as written in the score, there are recordings, particularly Robert McFerrin's performance, where the baritone opted to swing the melody. Singers interpreting this concert spiritual are advised to carefully consider the effects of this deviation from the score.

Dialect can be used very effectively in the performance of this spiritual; however, care must be used to make certain that the enunciation of the text is clean. The tempo should not be so fast that the audience cannot understand the stories told in the song.

5474
Witness
Johnson, Hall
Arroyo, Martina (Soprano)
Spirituals
Centaur CRC 2060; 1991; CD
Piano
Heavy dialect

5475
Witness
[Johnson, Hall]
Arroyo, Martina (Soprano)
Liederabend 1968
Hänssler Classic 93.719; 2012; CD
Piano
Light dialect

5476
Witness
Johnson, Hall
Battle, Kathleen (Soprano)
Salzburg Recital
Deutsche Grammophon 415 361-2; 1986; CD
Piano
Heavy dialect

5477
Witness
Johnson, Hall
Battle, Kathleen (Soprano)
Kathleen Battle in Concert
Deutsche Grammophon 445 524-2; 1994; CD
Piano
Heavy dialect

5478
Oh Lord, What Manner of Man Is Dis? (Witness)
Johnson, Hall
Battle, Kathleen (Soprano)
The Best of Kathleen Battle
Deutsche Grammophon 000349502; 2004; CD
Piano
Heavy dialect

5479
Witness
[Johnson, Hall]
Battle, Kathleen (Soprano)
The Art of Kathleen Battle
Deutsche Grammophon 474 184-2; [2002]; CD
Heavy dialect

5480
Witness for Ma Lord
Blanchard, Gerald
Blanchard, Gerald (Baritone)
With a Song in My Heart
Blue Griffin Recording BGR117; 2004; CD
A cappella
Heavy dialect

5481

Witness
Johnson, Hall
Brice, Carol (Contralto)
A Carol Brice Recital
Columbia ML 2108; 1950; LP
Piano
Heavy dialect

5482

Witness
Johnson, Hall
Brown, Angela (Soprano)
Soprano
Caboose Productions; 1995; CD
Piano
Heavy dialect

5483

Witness
Johnson, Hall
Brown, Anthony (Baritone)
Spirituals
Brown/Smith Productions; 1995; CD
Piano
Moderate dialect

5484

Witness
Johnson, Hall
Brown, Anthony (Baritone)
Toil and Triumph
Spirituals Project; 2002; CD
Piano
Light dialect

5485

Witness
Smith, Hale
Brown, William (Tenor)
Symphonic Spirituals
Columbia JC 36267; 1979; LP
Orchestra
Moderate dialect

5486

Witness
Smith, Hale
Brown, William (Tenor)
Symphonic Spirituals
Spotify; [2019]; Streaming audio
Orchestra
Moderate dialect

5487

A Witness
Hayes, Roland
Caesar, Jackson (Tenor)
*Spirituals: Celebrating the Music, Life,
    Legacy of Roland Hayes*
CD Baby 7048606059; 2021; CD
Piano
Light dialect

5488

Witness
Johnson, Hall
Davis, Ollie Watts (Soprano)
Here's One: Spiritual Songs
KJAC Publishing KJAC0123; 2003; CD
Piano
Moderate dialect

5489

Witness
Johnson, Hall
Duncan, Todd (Baritone)
African American Spirituals
[Apple Music]; 2008; Streaming audio
Piano
Light dialect

5490

Witness
Johnson, Hall
Duncan, Todd (Baritone)
Negro Spirituals
Allegro ALG3022; [1952]; LP
Piano

5491

Witness for My Lord
[Johnson, Hall]
Duncan, Todd (Baritone)
*Rare Concert Recital Gospel Music
    (1966–1980)*
Pewburner Records 742; 2007; CD

5492

Witness
Roberts, Howard
Estes, Simon (Bass-baritone)
Spirituals
Philips 412 631-2; 1985; CD
Chorus, orchestra
Light dialect

5493

Witness
Roberts, Howard
Estes, Simon (Bass-baritone)
Famous Spirituals
Philips 462 062-2; 1997; CD
Chorus, orchestra
Heavy dialect

5494

Witness
Johnson, Hall
Fernandez, Wilhelmenia (Soprano)
Spirituals
Tioch Digital Records TD 1009; 1982; LP
Piano

5495

Witness
Johnson, Hall
Fernandez, Wilhelmenia (Soprano)
Negro Spirituals
Milan A 192; 1982; LP
Piano

5496

Witness
Johnson, Hall
Fernandez, Wilhelmenia (Soprano)
Sings Favorite Spirituals
Phoenix PHCD 134; 1997; CD
Piano
Heavy dialect

5497

Witness
Johnson, Hall
Forest, Michael (Tenor)
The Spirit Sings: American Spirituals
Shenandoah Conservatory SU003; [199-]; CD

5498

Witness
Johnson, Hall
Gibson, Caroline (Soprano)
On Ma Journey Now: Negro Spirituals in Concert
Twin Productions; 2016; CD
Piano
Moderate dialect

5499

Witness
Johnson, Hall
Graves, Denyce (Mezzo-soprano)
Angels Watching Over Me
NPR Classics CD 0006; 1997; CD
Piano
Heavy dialect

5500

Witness
Hayes, Roland
Hayes, Roland (Tenor)
Roland Hayes: My Songs
Vanguard VRS-494; 1956; LP
Piano

5501

A Witness [from *My Songs*]
Hayes, Roland
Hayes, Roland (Tenor)
Favorite Spirituals
Vanguard Classics OVC 6022; 1995; CD
Piano
Moderate dialect

5502

A Witness [from *My Songs: Dream of Heaven*]
[Hayes, Roland]
Hayes, Roland (Tenor)
Big Psalms, Hymns and Spirituals Box
eOne Music/Vanguard Classics; 2015; Streaming audio
Piano

5503

Witness
Johnson, Hall

Holmes, Eugene (Baritone)
Eugene Holmes Sings Spirituals
Avant Garde AV-115; [1968]; LP
Piano

5504

Witness
Johnson, Hall
Hopkins, Gregory (Tenor)
Best of the Hall Johnson Centennial Festival Celebrating the 100th Anniversary of Hall Johnson's Birth
Hall Johnson Collection O33D2; 2002; CD
Piano

5505

Witness
Composer not identified
Jones, Fanni (Mezzo-soprano)
Negro Spirituals
Evasion Disques LP613; 1974; LP

5506

Witness
Johnson, Hall
Jones, Fanni (Mezzo-soprano)
Negro Spirituals en Concert
Suisa; 1987; LP
Organ
Moderate dialect

5507

Witness
Johnson, Hall
Lewis, Cheryse McLeod (Mezzo-soprano)
Spirituals
CheryseMusic; 2012; CD
Piano

5508

Witness
Johnson, Hall
Martin, Marvis (Soprano)
Live from the Spoleto Festival, 1988
Musical Heritage Society 5169615; 2003; CD
Piano
Light dialect

5509

Witness
Johnson, Hall
Matthews, Inez (Mezzo-soprano)
Inez Matthews Sings Spirituals (Great New Voices of Today, v. 6)
Period SPL-580; [1950]; LP
Piano
Moderate dialect

    Also released with *Inez Matthews Sings Spirituals* (Essential Media Group; 2011; CD)

5510

Witness
Brown, Lawrence
Maynor, Kevin (Bass); Vocalist not identified (Baritone)
Paul Robeson Remembered
Fleur de Son Classics FDS 57929; 1998; CD
Piano
Moderate dialect

5511

Witness
Johnson, Hall
McFerrin, Robert (Baritone)
Deep River and Other Classic Negro Spirituals
Riverside Records RLP 12-812; 1959; LP
Piano
Heavy dialect

    Also released with *Classic Negro Spirituals* (Washington Records WLP 466; 1959; LP)

5512

Witness
Johnson, Hall
Melton, James (Tenor)
Song Program by James Melton, A
RCA Victor M 947; [194-]; 78 RPM
Piano

5513

Witness
Composer not identified
Moen, Judith (Soprano)
I Had a Dream About You
JAM Concerts JAM1001; 1996; CD

5514

Witness
Johnson, Hall
Moses, Oral (Bass-baritone)
Amen! African-American Composers of the 20th Century
Albany Records TROY459; 2001; CD
Piano
Light dialect

        Also released with *Sankofa: A Spiritual Reflection* (Albany Records TROY1802; 2019; CD)

5515

Witness
[Johnson, Hall]
Moyer, Del-Louise (Mezzo-soprano)
He'll Bring to Pass: Spirituals & Americanegro Suite
Alyssum ALY-9001; 1997; CD
Piano
Light dialect

5516

Witness
Lloyd, Charles, Jr.; Norman, Jessye
Norman, Jessye (Soprano)
Great Day in the Morning
Philips 6769 104; 1982; LP
Chorus, other instrument(s)

5517

Witness [from *Settings for Spirituals*]
Chadabe, Joel
Oliver, Irene (Soprano)
Settings for Spirituals ; Solo
Lovely Music VR-3804; 1984; LP
Electronics

5518

Witness
Johnson, Hall
Peterson, Elwood (Baritone)
Negro Spirituals
Boîte à Musique LD 073; 1961; LP
Piano

5519

Witness
Composer not identified

Pleas III, Henry H. (Tenor)
Deep River: A Spiritual Journey
Rowe House Productions; 1999; CD

5520

Witness
Composer not identified
Price, Leontyne (Soprano)
Great Moments at Carnegie Hall
RCA Red Seal 88985304202; 2016; CD
Piano
Heavy dialect

5521

Witness
Johnson, Hall
Price, Leontyne (Soprano)
Return to Carnegie Hall
RCA Victor Red Seal 09026-68435-2; 1996; CD
Piano
Heavy dialect

5522

Witness
Johnson, Hall
Price, Leontyne (Soprano)
Complete Collection of Songs and Spiritual Albums
RCA Red Seal 88697940502; 2011; CD
Piano

5523

Witness
Johnson, Hall
Quivar, Florence (Mezzo-soprano)
Negro Spirituals
EMI 7243 5 72790 2 4; 1998; CD
Piano
Heavy dialect

5524

Witness
Johnson, Hall
Quivar, Florence (Mezzo-soprano)
Ride On, King Jesus! Florence Quivar Sings Black Music of America
EMI Classics 9 67138 2; 2010; CD
Piano
Heavy dialect

5525

Witness
Johnson, Hall
Ragin, Derek Lee (Countertenor)
Ev'ry Time I Feel the Spirit: Spirituals
Channel Classics CCS 2991; 1991; CD
Piano
Light dialect

5526

Witness
[Brown, Lawrence]
Robeson, Paul (Bass-baritone)
Negro Spirituals (And More)
Discmedi DM-4674-02; 2009; CD

5527

Witness
Brown, Lawrence
Robeson, Paul (Bass-baritone); Brown,
   Lawrence (Vocalist)
I Got a Home in-a Dat Rock / Witness
Victor 21109; 1927; 78 RPM
Piano
Moderate dialect

5528

Witness
Brown, Lawrence
Robeson, Paul (Bass-baritone); Brown,
   Lawrence (Vocalist)
I Got a Home in Dat Rock / Witness
His Master's Voice B 2727; 1928; 78 RPM
Piano

5529

Witness
Brown, Lawrence
Robeson, Paul (Bass-baritone); Brown,
   Lawrence (Vocalist)
Favorite Songs
Monitor Recordings MPS 580; 1959; LP
Piano
Light dialect

5530

Witness
Brown, Lawrence

Robeson, Paul (Bass-baritone); Brown,
   Lawrence (Vocalist)
Songs of My People
RCA Red Seal LM-3292; 1972; LP
Piano

5531

Witness
Brown, Lawrence
Robeson, Paul (Bass-baritone); Brown,
   Lawrence (Vocalist)
*A Lonesome Road: Paul Robeson Sings
   Spirituals and Songs*
ASV Living Era CD AJA 5027; 1984; CD
Piano
Light dialect

5532

Witness
Brown, Lawrence
Robeson, Paul (Bass-baritone); Brown,
   Lawrence (Vocalist)
The Collector's Paul Robeson
Monitor MCD-61580; 1989; CD
Piano
Heavy dialect

5533

Witness
Brown, Lawrence
Robeson, Paul (Bass-baritone)
Paul Robeson Collection
Hallmark Recordings 390692; 1998; CD

5534

Witness
Brown, Lawrence
Robeson, Paul (Bass-baritone); Brown,
   Lawrence (Vocalist)
*The Negro Spirituals Concert Tradition,
   1909–1948*
Frémeaux & Associés FA 168; 1999; CD
Piano
Moderate dialect

5535

Witness
Brown, Lawrence
Robeson, Paul (Bass-baritone)

Spirituals: Original Recordings 1925–1936
Naxos Gospel Legends 8.120638; 2003;
    CD
Piano

5536

Witness
Brown, Lawrence
Robeson, Paul (Bass-baritone); Brown,
    Lawrence (Vocalist)
*First Time Buyer's Guide to American Negro
    Spirituals*
Primo Collection PRMCD6038; 2006; CD
Piano
Light dialect

5537

Witness
Brown, Lawrence
Robeson, Paul (Bass-baritone); Brown,
    Lawrence (Vocalist)
*On My Journey: Paul Robeson's Independent
    Recordings*
Smithsonian Folkways Recordings SFW CD
    40178; 2007; CD
Piano

5538

Witness
[Brown, Lawrence]
Robeson, Paul (Bass-baritone); Brown,
    Lawrence (Vocalist)
Spirituals/Folksongs/Hymns
Pearl GEMM CD 9382; 1989; CD

5539

Witness
[Brown, Lawrence]
Robeson, Paul (Bass-baritone); Brown,
    Lawrence (Vocalist)
American Balladeer
Collectables Records COL-CD-6502; 1990;
    CD
Piano
Moderate dialect

5540

Witness
[Brown, Lawrence]

Robeson, Paul (Bass-baritone); Brown,
    Lawrence (Vocalist)
Ol Man River
Leverage; 2005; Streaming audio
Piano
Light dialect

5541

Witness
[Brown, Lawrence]
Robeson, Paul (Bass-baritone); Brown,
    Lawrence (Vocalist)
Ol' Man River: The Ultimate Collection
Roslin Records; 2011; Streaming audio
Piano
Light dialect

5542

Witness
[Brown, Lawrence]
Robeson, Paul (Bass-baritone); Brown,
    Lawrence (Vocalist)
Spirituals
Past Classics; 2013; Streaming audio
Piano
No dialect discerned

5543

Witness
[Brown, Lawrence]
Robeson, Paul (Bass-baritone); Brown,
    Lawrence (Vocalist)
The Concerto: African American Spirituals
Orange Amaro; 2019; Streaming audio
Piano

5544

Who'll Be a Witness for My Lord
[Brown, Lawrence]
Robeson, Paul (Bass-baritone)
Paul Robeson Singt Negro Spirituals
Musical Masterpiece Society MMS-2162;
    [19--]; LP
Piano

5545

Witness
[Brown, Lawrence]
Robeson, Paul (Bass-baritone)

The Historic Paul Robeson
Murray Hill Records 959062; [19--]; LP
Piano

5546
Who'll Be a Witness for My Lord
[Brown, Lawrence]
Robeson, Paul (Bass-baritone)
Negro Spirituals and Blues
Concert Hall M-2340; [19--]; LP
Piano

5547
Witness
[Brown, Lawrence]
Robeson, Paul (Bass-baritone); Brown,
   Lawrence (Vocalist)
Negro Spirituals
Chant du Monde LDX 74376; 1982; LP
Piano

5548
Witness
Johnson, Hall
Sebron, Carolyn (Mezzo-soprano)
*Carolyn Sebron, Mezzo-soprano, Marie-
   Claude Arbaretaz, Piano*
Fondation Crédit Lyonnais; 1993; CD
Piano

5549
Witness
Johnson, Hall
Shirley, George (Tenor)
George Shirley at 80: My Time Has Come!
Videmus Records; 2014; CD
Piano

5550
Witness
Johnson, Hall
Simpson, Eugene Thamon (Bass)
Hear Me, Ye Winds and Waves
Black Heritage Publications; 2005; CD
Piano
Heavy dialect

5551
Witness
Johnson, Hall

Simpson, Eugene Thamon (Bass)
Hall Johnson Spirituals and Other Folk Songs
Private Label; 2016; CD
Piano

5552
Who'll Be a Witness for My Lord
Johnson, John Rosamond
Spencer, Kenneth (Bass-baritone)
Volkslieder & Spirituals
Discoton 75546; [197-]; LP
Piano
Moderate dialect

5553
Witness
Johnson, Hall
Straughter, Maralyn (Soprano)
Negro Spirituals of Hall Johnson
Variety Recording Service Var 0753; [196–];
   LP
Piano

5554
Witness
Sykes, Jubilant
Sykes, Jubilant (Baritone)
Jubilant Sykes Sings Copland and Spirituals
Arioso Classics AC 00011; 2008; CD
Orchestra

5555
Witness
Johnson, Hall
Thomas, Indra (Soprano)
Great Day: Indra Thomas Sings Spirituals
Delos DE 3427; 2012; CD
Piano
Heavy dialect

5556
Witness
Johnson, Hall
Toppin, Louise (Soprano)
The Hall Johnson Collection
Carl Fischer VF5 CD1–VF5 CD2; 2003; Score
   w/CD
Piano
Heavy dialect

5557

Witness [from *Four Negro Spirituals*]
Smith, Hale
Toppin, Louise (Soprano)
Witness
Albany Records TROY868; 2006; CD
Orchestra
Heavy dialect

5558

Witness
Johnson, Hall
Verrett, Shirley (Mezzo-soprano)
Carnegie Hall Recital
Sony Music 82319; 2011; CD
Piano
No dialect discerned

5559

Witness
Johnson, Hall
Verrett, Shirley (Mezzo-soprano)
Shirley Verrett: Edition
Newton Classics 8802167; 2013; CD
Piano
No dialect discerned

5560

Witness
[Johnson, Hall]
Verrett, Shirley (Mezzo-soprano)
Great Moments at Carnegie Hall
RCA Red Seal 88985304202; 2016; CD
Piano
No dialect discerned

5561

Witness
[Johnson, Hall]
White, Cassandra (Soprano)
Remembering the Spirituals
CBW Entertainment 837101334068; 2007;
    CD
Piano
No dialect discerned

5562

Witness
Composer not identified

White, Willard (Bass-baritone)
The Paul Robeson Legacy
Linn AKD 190; 2015; CD
Instrumental ensemble

· · · · · · ·

You Better Mind

5563

You Better Min'! [from *Green Pastures*]
Johnson, Hall
Brown, William (Tenor)
The Hall Johnson Collection
Carl Fischer VF5 CD1–VF5 CD2; 2003; Score
    w/CD
Piano
Heavy dialect

5564

You Better Mind
McIntyre, Philip
Forest, Michael (Tenor)
The Spirit Sings: American Spirituals
Shenandoah Conservatory SU003; [199-];
    CD

· · · · · · ·

You Can Tell the World

5565

You Can Tell the World [from *Five Creek-
    Freedmen Spirituals*]
Bonds, Margaret
Barnes, Sebronette (Soprano)
*You Can Tell the World: Songs by African-
    American Women Composers*
Senrab Record SRR7988; 2000; CD
Piano
Moderate dialect

5566

You Can Tell the World
[Bonds, Margaret]
Cunningham-Fleming, Jeryl (Soprano)
*Stand the Storm: Anthems, Hymns, and
    Spirituals of Faith and Hope*
Private Label; 2016; CD
Piano

5567

You Can Tell the World [from *Five Creek-Freedmen Spirituals*]
Bonds, Margaret; Link, Peter
Davis, Osceola (Soprano)
Climbing High Mountains
Watchfire Music; 2008; CD
Piano
Light dialect

5568

You Can Tell the World [from *Five Creek-Freedmen Spirituals*]
Bonds, Margaret
Eaton, Patrice (Soprano)
Ol' Time Religion
American Spiritual Ensemble ASE012; 2001; CD

5569

You Can Tell the World [from *Five Creek-Freedmen Spirituals*]
Bonds, Margaret
English-Robinson, Laura (Soprano)
Let It Shine!
ACA Digital Recording CM20020; 1994; CD
Piano
No dialect discerned

5570

You Can Tell the World [from *Five Creek-Freedmen Spirituals*]
Bonds, Margaret
Fernandez, Wilhelmenia (Soprano)
Spirituals
Tioch Digital Records TD 1009; 1982; LP
Piano

   Also released with *Negro Spirituals* (Milan A 192; 1982; LP)

5571

You Can Tell the World [from *Five Creek-Freedmen Spirituals*]
Bonds, Margaret
Fernandez, Wilhelmenia (Soprano)
Sings Favorite Spirituals
Phoenix PHCD 134; 1997; CD
Piano
Moderate dialect

5572

You Can Tell the World [from *Five Creek-Freedmen Spirituals*]
Bonds, Margaret
Forest, Michael (Tenor)
The Spirit Sings: American Spirituals
Shenandoah Conservatory SU003; [199-]; CD

5573

You Can Tell the World About This
Composer not identified
Miles, John (Tenor)
The Classic Spirituals
Epiphany 83-1027; 1983; LP
Instrumental ensemble

5574

You Can Tell the World [from *Five Creek-Freedmen Spirituals*]
Bonds, Margaret; Fax, Mark
Norman, Jessye (Soprano)
Spirituals in Concert
Deutsche Grammophon 429 790-2; 1991; CD
Orchestra
Heavy dialect

5575

You Can Tell the World [from *Five Creek-Freedmen Spirituals*]
Bonds, Margaret
Rhodes, Yolanda (Soprano)
The Angels Bowed Down
Cambria Master Recordings CD-1237; 2019; CD

5576

You Can Tell the World
Composer not identified
Tyler, Veronica (Soprano)
Sings … the Passion of Christ in Spirituals
BRC Productions; [19--]; LP
Piano

· · · · · · ·

You Go

5577

You Go!
Johnson, Hall

Anderson, Marian (Contralto)
Jus' Keep on Singin'
RCA Victor LSC 2796; 1965; LP
Piano

5578
You Go!
Johnson, Hall
Anderson, Marian (Contralto)
Marian Anderson: Beyond the Music; Her Complete RCA Victor Recordings
Sony Classical 19439836492; 2021; CD
Piano
Light dialect

5579
You Go!
Johnson, Hall
Anderson, Marian (Contralto)
He's Got the Whole World in His Hands: Spirituals
RCA Victor 09026-61960-2; 1994; CD
Piano
Light dialect

5580
You Go I'll Go with You
Traditional
Sebron, Carolyn (Mezzo-soprano)
Resurrection, Pt. 1
Private Label; 2006; CD
A cappella
Light dialect

· · · · · · ·

You May Bury Me in de East

5581
You May Bury Me in de East [from *Cycle of Six Spirituals*]
Owens, Robert
Moses, Oral (Bass-baritone)
Come Down Angels and Trouble the Water: Negro Spirituals, an American National Treasure!
Albany Records TROY 1489; 2014; CD
Piano
Heavy dialect

5582
You May Bury Me in the East
Lloyd, Charles, Jr.
Sebron, Carolyn (Mezzo-soprano)
Carolyn Sebron, Mezzo-soprano, Marie-Claude Arbaretaz, Piano
Fondation Crédit Lyonnais; 1993; CD
Piano

5583
You May Bury Me in de East
Brown, Lawrence
Sims, Robert (Baritone)
Soul of a Singer: Robert Sims Sings African-American Folk Songs
Canti Classics 9801; 2013; CD
Piano
Heavy dialect

· · · · · · ·

You May Run On

5584
You May Run On
Sims, Robert
Sims, Robert (Baritone)
Soul of a Singer: Robert Sims Sings African-American Folk Songs
Canti Classics 9801; 2013; CD
A cappella
Heavy dialect

· · · · · · ·

You Must Have That True Religion

5585
You Must Have That True Religion
Carter, Roland
Brown, Angela (Soprano); Hocker Young, Amira (Soprano)
The Lily of the Valley
American Spiritual Ensemble; [2003]; CD

5586
You Must Have That True Religion
Composer not identified
Davy, Gloria (Soprano)

Spirituals
Decca LW 5215; 1959; LP

. . . .

You Won't Find a Friend

5587
You Won't Find a Friend
Carter, Roland
Robinson-Oturo, Gail (Soprano)
Sweetest Sound I Ever Heard: Spirituals for Solo Voice and Piano, Vol. 1
CD Baby; 2020; Streaming audio
Piano
No dialect discerned

. . . .

You Won't Find a Man Like Jesus

5588
You Won't Find a Man Like Jesus
Price, Florence
Heard, Richard (Tenor)
My Dream: Art Songs and Spirituals
Percentage Records/Sound of Art Recordings CD147597; 2012; CD
Piano
No dialect discerned

. . . .

You're Tired Chile

5589
You're Tired, Chile
Hayes, Roland
Caesar, Jackson (Tenor)
Spirituals: Celebrating the Music, Life, Legacy of Roland Hayes
CD Baby 7048606059; 2021; CD
Piano, percussion
Light dialect

5590
You're Tired, Chile [from *My Songs: Dream of Heaven*]
Hayes, Roland
Caesar, Jackson (Tenor)

Spirituals: Celebrating the Music, Life, Legacy of Roland Hayes
CD Baby 7048606059; 2021; CD
Piano
Light dialect

5591
You're Tired, Child [from *My Songs: Dream of Heaven*]
Hayes, Roland
Hayes, Roland (Tenor)
Favorite Spirituals
Vanguard Classics OVC 6022; 1995; CD
Piano
Light dialect

5592
You're Tired, Chile! [from *My Songs: Dream of Heaven*]
Hayes, Roland
Hayes, Roland (Tenor)
Lit'l Boy/I Want to Go Home/You're Tired, Chile!
Columbia 17275-D; [1941]; 78 RPM
Piano

5593
You're Tired, Chile! [from *My Songs: Dream of Heaven*]
[Hayes, Roland]
Hayes, Roland (Tenor)
Art Songs and Spirituals
Veritas VM 112; 1967; LP
Piano
Moderate dialect

5594
You're Tired, Child [from *My Song*]
[Hayes, Roland]
Hayes, Roland (Tenor)
Big Psalms, Hymns and Spirituals Box
eOne Music/Vanguard Classics; 2015; Streaming audio
Piano

5595
You're Tired, Chile [from *My Songs: Dream of Heaven*]
Hayes, Roland

Jenkins, Isaiah (Tenor)
Lyric Tenor
Trans Radio TR 1010A; [195-]; LP
Piano

5596

You're Tired, Chile [from *My Songs: Dream of Heaven*]
Hayes, Roland
Matthews, Inez (Mezzo-soprano)
Inez Matthews Sings Spirituals
Essential Media Group; 2011; CD
Piano
Heavy dialect

5597

You're Tired, Chile [from *My Songs: Dream of Heaven*]
Hayes, Roland
Matthews, Inez (Mezzo-soprano)
Inez Matthews Sings Spirituals (Great New Voices of Today, v. 6)
Period SPL-580; [1950]; LP
Piano
Heavy dialect

5598

You're Tired, Chile [from *My Songs: Dream of Heaven*]
Hayes, Roland
Mims, A. Grace Lee (Soprano)
Spirituals
H & GM Records HGM 8101; 1981; LP
Piano
Moderate dialect

5599

You're Tired Chile
Composer not identified
Peterson, Elwood (Baritone)
Negro Spirituals
Vergara 55.1.004 C; [1963]; 45 RPM
Piano

5600

You're Tired, Chile [from *My Songs: Dream of Heaven*]
Hayes, Roland
Peterson, Elwood (Baritone)
Negro Spirituals
Boîte à Musique LD 073; 1961; LP
Piano

. . . .

Zion Hallelujah

5601

Zion Hallelujah
Dett, Robert Nathaniel
Moses, Oral (Bass-baritone)
Amen! African-American Composers of the 20th Century
Albany Records TROY459; 2001; CD
Piano
No dialect discerned

5602

Zion Hallelujah
Dett, Robert Nathaniel
Pankey, Aubrey (Baritone)
Negro Spirituals
Eterna 830010; 1983; LP
Piano

Bibliography

Dictionaries and Encyclopedias

Black Biographical Dictionaries, 1790–1950. Microform. Alexandria, VA: Chadwyck-Healey, 1987.

Burkett, Randall K., Nancy Hall Burkett, and Henry Louis Gates, Jr. *Black Biography, 1790–1950: A Cumulative Index.* Alexandria, VA: Chadwyck-Healey, 1991.

Hitchcock, H. Wiley, and Stanley Sadie, eds. *The New Grove Dictionary of American Music.* 4 v. London: Macmillan, 1986.

Peters, Erskine, ed. *Lyrics of the Afro-American Spiritual: A Documentary Collection. The Greenwood Encyclopedia of Black Music.* Westport, CT: Greenwood, 1993.

Sadie, Stanley, and John Tyrrell, eds. *The New Grove Dictionary of Music and Musicians,* 2nd ed. 29 v. New York: Grove, 2001.

Salzman, Jack, David Lionel Smith, and Cornel West, eds. *Encyclopedia of African-American Culture and History.* New York: Macmillan Library Reference, 1996.

Biographies and Biographical Sources

Abdul, Raoul. *Blacks in Classical Music: A Personal History.* New York: Dodd, Mead, 1978.

Arsenault, Raymond. *Marian Anderson: Beyond the Music.* Gëtersloh, Germany: Sony Classical, 2021.

Arvey, Verna. *In One Lifetime.* Fayetteville: University of Arkansas Press, 1984.

Berry, Lemuel. *Biographical Dictionary of Black Musicians and Music Educators.* Educational Book Publishers, 1978.

Carter, Madison H. *An Annotated Catalog of Composers of African Ancestry.* New York: Vantage, 1986.

Cuney-Hare, Maud. *Negro Musicians and Their Music.* New York: Da Capo Press, 1974.

Green, Mildred Denby. *Black Women Composers: A Genesis.* Boston: Twayne, 1983.

Holly, Ellistine Perkins. *Biographies of Black Composers and Songwriters: A Supplementary Textbook.* Dubuque: Wm. C. Brown, 1990.

Perry, Frank, Jr. *Afro-American Vocal Music: A Select Guide to Fifteen Composers.* Berrien Spring, MI: Vande Vere, 1991.

Reis, Claire. *Composers in America: Biographical Sketches of Living Composers with a Record of Their Works, 1912–1937.* New York: Macmillan, 1938.

Robinson, Wilhelmena S. *International Library of Negro Life and History: Historical Negro Biographies.* International Library of Afro-American Life and History, v. 5. New York: Publishers Co., 1967.

Southern, Eileen. *Biographical Dictionary of Afro-American and African Musicians.* Westport, CT: Greenwood, 1982.

Still, Judith Anne, Michael J. Dabrishus, and Carolyn L. Quin. *William Grant Still: A Bio-Bibliography.* Westport, CT: Greenwood, 1996.

Story, Rosalyn M. *And So I Sing: African-American Divas of Opera and Concert.* New York: Warner, 1990.

Thompson, Allan L. *Paul Robeson: Artist and Activist On Records, Radio and Television,* 2nd ed. Wellingborough, England: Allan L. Thompson, 2000.

Woodward, Sidney. *Out of Bondage to a Place of Esteem and Trust: The Story of a Career Unique in Musical History.* New York: Mercantile Press, 1918.

Histories and Chronologies

Ammer, Christine. *Unsung: A History of Women in American Music.* Century ed. Portland, OR: Amadeus Press, 2001.

Caldwell, Hansonia LaVerne. *African American Music: A Chronology 1619–1995.* Los Angeles: Ikoro Communications, 1996.

Floyd, Samuel A., Jr. *The Power of Black Music: Interpreting Its History from Africa to the United States.* New York: Oxford University Press, 1995.

Green, Mildred Denby. "A Study of the Lives and Works of Five Black Women Composers in America." D.Mus.E. thesis, University of Oklahoma, 1975.

Haskins, James. *Black Music in America: A History through Its People.* New York: T.Y. Crowell, 1987.

Holland, Ted. *This Day in African-American Music.* San Francisco: Pomegranate Artbooks, 1993.

Locke, Alain. *The Negro and His Music: Negro Art Past and Present.* New York: Arno Press and New York Times, 1969.

Patterson, Lindsay, ed. *The Afro-American in Music and Art*. International Library of Afro-American Life and History, v. 6. Cornwells Heights, PA: Publishers Agency, 1978.

Roach, Hildred. *Black American Music: Past and Present*, 2nd ed. Malabar, FL: Krieger, 1992.

Southern, Eileen. *The Music of Black Americans: A History*, 3rd ed. New York: W.W. Norton, 1997.

Spencer, Jon Michael. *Protest & Praise: Sacred Music of Black Religion*. Minneapolis: Fortress Press, 1990.

_____. *Re-Searching Black Music*. Knoxville: University of Tennessee Press, 1996.

Stewart, Earl E. *African-American Music: An Introduction*. New York: Schirmer Books; London: Prentice-Hall International, 1998.

Bibliographies, Discographies, Catalogs, Congresses and Iconographies

Abromeit, Kathleen A. *Spirituals: A Multidisciplinary Bibliography for Research and Performance*. Middleton, WI: A-R Editions, Music Library Association, 2015.

Brown, Rae Linda. *Music, Printed and Manuscript, in the James Weldon Johnson Memorial Collection of Negro Arts and Letters: An Annotated Catalog*. New York: Garland, 1982.

Clough, Francis F., and G.J. Cuming. *The World's Encyclopedia of Recorded Music*. London: Sidgwick & Jackson Limited, 1952.

de Lerma, Dominique-René. *Bibliography of Black Music*. 4 v. Westport, CT: Greenwood, 1981–84.

_____. *Concert Music and Spirituals: A Selective Discography*. Nashville: Fisk University, Institute for Research in Black American Music, 1981.

Floyd, Samuel A., Jr., ed. *Black Music in the United States: An Annotated Bibliography of Selected Reference and Research Materials*. Millwood, NY: Scarecrow Press, 1987.

George, Zelma W. *A Guide to Negro Music: An Annotated Bibliography of Negro Folk Music, and Art Music by Negro Composers or Based on Negro Thematic Material*. Ann Arbor: University Microfilms, 1953.

Gray, John, comp. *Blacks in Classical Music: A Bibliographical Guide to Composers, Performers and Ensembles*. New York: Greenwood, 1988.

Greene, Richard. *Black Classical Music Composers: a Comprehensive Discography of Recordings Available on Compact Disc*. Ardmore, PA, 1998.

Johnson, James Peter. *Bibliographic Guide to the Study of Afro-American Music*. Washington, D.C.: Howard University Libraries, 1973.

Miller, Philip C. *Vocal Music*. New York: Alfred A. Knopf, 1955.

Oja, Carol J. *American Music Recordings: Discography of 20th Century U.S. Composers*. Brooklyn: Institute for Studies in American Music, Conservatory of Music, Brooklyn College of the City University of New York, 1982.

Skowronski, JoAnn. *Black Music in America: A Bibliography*. Metuchen, NJ: Scarecrow Press, 1981.

Southern, Eileen, and Josephine Wright, comps. *African-American Traditions in Song, Sermon, Tale, and Dance, 1600–1920: An Annotated Bibliography of Literature, Collections, and Artworks*. New York: Greenwood, 1990.

_____. *Images: Iconography of Music in African-American Culture, 1770s–1920s*. New York: Garland, 2000.

Stewart-Green, Miriam. *Women Composers: A Checklist of Works for the Solo Voice*. Boston: G.K. Hall, 1980.

Tischler, Alice. *Fifteen Black American Composers: A Bibliography of Their Works*. Detroit: Information Coordinators, 1981.

Turner, Patricia K. *Afro-American Singers: An Index and Preliminary Discography of Long-Playing Recordings of Opera, Choral Music, and Song*. Minneapolis: Challenge Productions, 1977.

_____. *Dictionary of Afro-American Performers: 78 RPM and Cylinder Recordings of Opera, Choral Music and Songs, c. 1900–1949*. New York: Garland, 1990.

Walker-Hill, Helen. *Music by Black Women Composers: A Bibliography of Available Scores*. CBMR Monograph, no. 5. Chicago: Center for Black Music Research, 1995.

White, Evelyn Davidson. *Choral Music by African American Composers: A Selected, Annotated Bibliography*, 2nd ed. Lanham, MD: Scarecrow Press, 1999.

Indexes and Atlases

De Charms, Desiree, and Paul F. Breed. *Songs in Collections: An Index*. Detroit: Information Coordinators, 1966.

de Lerma, Dominique-René, and Marsha J. Reisser. *Black Music and Musicians in the New Grove Dictionary of American Music and the New Harvard Dictionary of Music*. CBMR Monographs, no. 1. Chicago: Center for Black Music Research, Columbia College, 1989.

Sears, Minnie E. *Song Index*. Reprint. Hamden, CT: Shoe String Press, 1966.

Vann, Kimberly R. *Black Music in Ebony: An Annotated Guide to the Articles on Music in Ebony Magazine, 1945–1985*. CBMR Monographs, no. 2. Chicago: Center for Black Music Research, Columbia College, 1990.

Music Criticism—Spirituals

Clark, Roy Lester. "A Fantasy Theme Analysis of Negro Spirituals." Ph.D. diss., Southern Illinois University at Carbondale, 1979.

Cruz, Jon. *Culture on the Margins: The Black Spiritual and the Rise of American Cultural Interpretation*. Princeton: Princeton University Press, 1999.

Dunn-Powell, Rosephanye. "The Solo Vocal Writing

Style of William Grant Still." Mus.D. thesis, Florida State University, 1993.

Epstein, Dena J. *Sinful Tunes and Spirituals: Black Folk Music to the Civil War.* Urbana: University of Illinois Press, 1977.

_____. "Slave Music in the United States before 1860: a Survey of Sources." *Notes* 20 (Spring 1963): 195–212.

_____. "A White Origin for the Black Spiritual? An Invalid Theory and How It Grew." *American Music* 1 (Summer 1983): 53–59.

Fenner, Thomas P. *Religious Folk Songs of the Negro: As Sung on the Plantations*, new ed. Hampton, VA: The Institute Press, 1909.

Garrett, Romeo B. "African Survivals in American Culture." *Journal of Negro History* 51 (October 1966): 239–245.

Garst, John F. "Mutual Reinforcement and the Origins of Spirituals." *American Music* 4 (Winter 1986): 390–406.

Grant, Eric Bernard. "'Message in Our Music': Spirituals and the Cultural Politics of Race and Nation, 1871 to 1945." Thesis Ph.D. diss., Yale University, 2005.

Guenther, Eileen. *In Their Own Words: Slave Life and the Power of Spirituals.* St. Louis: MorningStar Music Publishers, 2016.

Hawkins, Kimberly. "Heard an Angel Singing: African-American Spirituals in the Harlem Renaissance." Ph.D. diss., University of California, Santa Barbara, 1997.

Hurston, Zora Neale. "Spirituals and Neo-Spirituals." 1969. *Negro Anthology*, 359–362.

Jones, Randye. *So You Want to Sing Spirituals: A Guide for Performers.* Lanham, MD: Rowman & Littlefield, 2019.

Katz, Bernard, ed. *The Social Implications of Early Negro Music in the United States.* New York: Arno Press, 1969.

Keck, George R., and Sherrill V. Martin, ed. *Feel the Spirit: Studies in Nineteenth-Century Afro-American Music.* Contributions in Afro-American and African Studies, no. 119. New York: Greenwood Press, 1988.

Kerby, Marion. "A Warning Against Over-Refinement of the Negro Spiritual." *The Musician* 32 (July 1928): 9, 29–30.

Krehbiel, Henry Edward. *Afro-American Folk Songs: A Study in Racial and National Music.* New York: G. Schirmer, 1914.

Lawrence-McIntyre, Charshee Charlotte. "The Double Meanings of the Spirituals." *Journal of Black Studies* 17 (June 1987): 397–401.

Lee, Henry. "Swing Low, Sweet Charity." *The Black Perspective in Music* 2 (Summer 1984): 84–86. (Reprinted from *Coronet*, July 1947.)

Lovell, John, Jr. *Black Song: The Forge and the Flame.* New York: Paragon House, 1972.

McCorvey, Everett David. "The Art Songs of Black American Composers." Ph.D. diss., University of Alabama, 1989.

McGee, Daniel Bennett. "Religious Beliefs and Ethical Motifs of the Negro Spirituals." Ph.D. diss., Southeastern Baptist Theological Seminary, 1960.

Perry, James A. "African Roots of African-American Culture." *Black Collegian* 29 (October 1998): 145–146.

Plant, Lourin. "Singing African-American Spirituals: a Reflection on Racial Barriers in Classical Vocal Music." *Journal of Singing* 61 (January 2005): 451–468.

Reed-Walker, Rosalynd Patricia. "Preserving the Negro Spiritual: An Examination of Contemporary Practices." Ed.D thesis, Wilmington University, 2007.

Simpson, Eugene Thamon. *The Hall Johnson Concert Spirituals: An Annotated Guide to Interpretation and Performance.* West Conshohocken, PA: Infinity, 2015.

Steinhaus-Jordan, Barbara. "An Analysis of Marian Anderson's Interpretation of Black Spiritual Art Songs in Selected Recordings." *The Southeastern Journal of Music Education* 11 (1999): 99–105.

Still, William Grant, and Jon Michael Spencer. *The William Grant Still Reader: Essays on American Music.* Black Sacred Music, v. 6, no. 2. Durham: Duke University Press, 1992.

Stinson, Sonya. "The Fisk Jubilee Singers." *Cobblestone* 19 (February 1998): 34–35.

Thomas, André J. *Way Over in Beulah Lan': Understanding and Performing the Negro Spiritual.* Dayton, OH: Heritage Music Press, 2007.

Thurman, Howard. *Deep River; and the Negro Spiritual Speaks of Life and Death.* Richmond, IN: Friends United Press, 1999.

Tyler, Tyrico Z. *Listen to the Voices: Slaves Speak Through Their Music.* Ann Arbor: Robbie Dean Press, 2005.

Music Criticism—Vocal Music

Ames, Russell. "Art of Negro Folk Song." *Journal of American Folklore* 56 (October 1943): 241–255.

Baker, Sony G., and Eileen Strempel. "Jubilee: An Overview of the Song Literature of African American Women Composers." *Journal of Singing* 67 (January 2011).

Boyer, Horace Clarence. "The Afro-American Vocal Tradition: An Introduction." *Massachusetts Music News* 25 (April 1977): 34, 36–38.

Dawson, William L. "Interpretation of the Religious Folk-Songs of the American Negro." *Etude* 73 (March 1955): 11, 58, 61.

Heape, Mary Willis. "Sacred Songs and Arias by Women Composers: A Survey of the Literature and Performer's Analysis of Selected Works by Isabella Leonarda, Luise Reichardt, Ethel Smyth, Violet Archer, Margaret Bonds and Edith Borroff." D.Mus.A diss., Southwestern Baptist Theological Seminary, 1995.

Lawhon, Sharon Leding. "A Performer's Guide to Selected Twentieth-Century Sacred Solo Art Songs Composed by Women from the United States of America." D.Mus.A. diss, Southern Baptist Theological Seminary, 1993.

McCorvey, Everett David. "The Art Songs of Black

American Composers." Ph.D. diss., University of Alabama, 1989.

Nash, Elizabeth. *Autobiographical Reminiscences of African-American Classical Singers, 1853-Present: Introducing Their Spiritual Heritage into the Concert Repertoire*. Lewiston: Edwin Mellen Press, c2007.

Reagon, Bernice Johnson. *If You Don't Go, Don't Hinder Me: The African American Sacred Song Tradition*. Lincoln: University of Nebraska Press, 2001.

Seigrist, Mark Andrew. "Diction and Dialect Performance Practice in the American Negro Spiritual and Slave Songs." D.Mus.A thesis, University of Texas at Austin, 1996.

Shirley, Wayne D. "The Coming of 'Deep River.'" *American Music* 15 (Winter 1997): 493–534.

Thompson-Cornwall, Lonieta Aurora. "The African American Art Song: A Continuum in the Art of Song." Ed.D thesis, Teachers College, Columbia University, 2006.

Upton, William Treat. *Art-Song in America: A Study in the Development of American Music*. Boston: Oliver Ditson, 1930.

Wilson, Olly. "Black Music As an Art Form." *Black Music Research Journal* 12 (1984): 1–22.

Vocal Pedagogy/Music Education

Allison, Roland Lewis. "Classification of the Vocal Works of Harry T. Burleigh (1866–1949) and Some Suggestions for Their Use in Teaching Diction in Singing." Ph.D. diss., Indiana University, 1969.

Barber, Felicia Raphael Marie. *A New Perspective for the Use of Dialect in African American Spirituals: History, Context, and Linguistics*. Lanham: Lexington Books, 2021.

Dunn-Powell, Rosephanye. "The African-American Spiritual: Preparation and Performance Considerations." *Journal of Singing* 61 (January 2005): 469–475.

Steinhaus-Jordan, Barbara. "Black Spiritual Art Song: Interpretative Guidelines for Studio Teachers." *Journal of Singing* 61 (January 2005): 477–485.

Stephens, Emery, and Caroline Helton. "Diversifying the Playing Field: Solo Performance of African American Spirituals and Art Songs by Voice Students from All Racial Backgrounds." *Journal of Singing* 70 (November/December 2013): 165–172.

Miscellaneous Subjects

Barr, Steven C. *The Almost Complete 78 RPM Record Dating Guide (II)*. Huntington Beach, CA: Yesterday Once Again, 1992.

Donovan, Richard X. *Black Musicians of America*. Portland, OR: National Book, 1991.

James, Shaylor L. "Contributions of Four Selected Twentieth-Century Afro-American Classical Composers: William Grant Still, Howard Swanson, Ulysses Kay, and Olly Wilson." Ph.D. thesis, Florida State University, 1988.

Songs of Zion. Nashville: Abingdon Press, 1981.

Spencer, Jon Michael. *The Rhythms of Black Folk: Race, Religion, and Pan-Africanism*. Trenton: Africa World Press, 1995.

Standifer, James A. and Barbara Reeder. *Source Book of African and Afro-American Materials for Music Educators*. [Washington]: Contemporary Music Project, [1972].

Still, Judith Ann, and Celeste Anne Headlee. *William Grant Still and the Fusion of Cultures in American Music*, 2nd ed. Flagstaff: Master-Player Library, 1995.

Trotter, James Monroe. *Music and Some Highly Musical People*. New York: Lee & Shepard, 1878.

Walker, Wyatt Tee. *"Somebody's Calling My Name": Black Sacred Music and Social Change*. Valley Forge: Judson Press, 1990.

Walker-Hill, Helen. *From Spirituals to Symphonies: African-American Women Composers and Their Music*. Westport, CT: Greenwood Press, 2002.

Journals and Journal Guides

Black Music Research Bulletin. Chicago: Columbia College Center for Black Music Research, 1988.

Black Music Research Journal. Nashville: Institute for Research in Black American Music, Fisk University, 1981.

The Black Perspective in Music. Cambria Heights, NY: Foundation for the Research in the Afro-American Creative Arts, 1973–1990.

The Negro Spiritual. Oakland: Friends of Negro Spirituals, 1999.

Articles from Periodicals/Serials/ Newspapers

Ames, Russell. "Art of Negro Folk Song." *Journal of American Folklore* 56 (October 1943): 241–255.

Boyer, Horace Clarence. "The Afro-American Vocal Tradition: An Introduction." *Massachusetts Music News* 25 (April 1977): 34, 36–38.

Dawson, William L. "Interpretation of the Religious Folk-Songs of the American Negro." *Etude* 73 (March 1955): 11, 58, 61.

Dvorak, Antonin. "Music in America." *Harper's* 90 (1895): 428–434.

Epstein, Dena J. "A White Origin for the Black Spiritual? An Invalid Theory and How It Grew." *American Music* 1 (Summer 1983): 53–59.

Garst, John F. "Mutual Reinforcement and the Origins of Spirituals." *American Music* 4 (Winter 1986): 390–406.

Kerby, Marion. "A Warning Against Over-Refinement of the Negro Spiritual." *The Musician* 32 (July 1928): 9, 29–30.

Lee, Henry. "Swing Low, Sweet Charity." *The Black Perspective in Music* 2 (Summer 1984): 84–86. (Reprinted from *Coronet*, July 1947.)

Walker-Hill, Helen. "Music by Black Women Composers at the American Music Research Center." *American Music Research Center Journal* 2 (1992): 23–51.

Wilson, Olly. "Black Music as an Art Form." *Black Music Research Journal* 3 (1983). https://jazzstudies online.org/files/jso/resources/pdf/3%20Black %20Music%20as%20an%20Art%20Form.pdf.

Online Resources

All Music—https://www.allmusic.com.

Art of the Negro Spiritual—http://www.artofthe nengrspiritual.com.

Art Song Central—http://artsongcentral.com/.

Classical Vocal Reprints, Spirituals—http://www. classicalvocalreprints.com/search.php?search_ terms=spiritual&search_type=text.

Discography of American Historical Recordings (DAHR)—http://adp.library.ucsb.edu.

Discogs—https://www.discogs.com/.

The Durbeck Archive, Black Classically Trained Singers album covers—http://www.durbeck archive.com/blacksingers.htm.

Facebook Discussion Group—https://www.face book.com/groups/artofthespiritual/.

IMSLP Spirituals Category—http://imslp.org/wiki/ Category:Spirituals.

Internet Archive—https://archive.org/.

JW Pepper, Spirituals selections—http://www.jw pepper.com/sheet-music/search.jsp?keywords= spirituals&pageview=list-view&departments= Vocal.

LiederNet Archive—https://www.lieder.net.

MusicBrainz—https://musicbrainz.org/.

The Negro Spiritual Scholarship Foundation— http://www.negrospiritual.org/.

Negro Spirituals, by Thomas Wentworth Higginson—http://xroads.virginia.edu/~hyper/TWH/ Higg.html.

Negro Spirituals Songs (Lyrics)—http://www. negrospirituals.com/songs/index.htm.

Recorded Sound Archives, Florida Atlantic University—https://rsa.fau.edu/.

Sheet Music Plus, Spirituals selection—http://www. sheetmusicplus.com/search/instruments/vocal/9 00120?Ntt=negro+spirituals.

The Spirituals Database—http://spiritualsdatabase. com.

Sweet Chariot: The Story of the Spirituals—http:// www.spiritualsproject.org/sweetchariot/.

Topical Bible—https://www.openbible.info/topics/.

WPA Federal Writers' Project, Spirituals results

General Index

Entries are either based on track number (1001) or page number (p1).
Song titles with introductory notes are bolded.
Contents based on the compiler's assessments are bracketed.

Index of Songs

Titles are listed as they appear on the recording or the source
from which that title information was derived.

Index of Musicians

Numbers in brackets reflect unidentified musicians accessed by compiler;
p before number is page number. Remainder are track numbers.